P9-DYE-037

MANAGING COMPUTER RESOURCES

The Irwin Series in Information and Decision Sciences

Consulting Editors   Robert B. Fetter   Claude McMillan
Yale University   *University of Colorado*

MANAGING COMPUTER RESOURCES

Donna Hussain

K. M. Hussain

New Mexico State University

Second Edition

1988

Homewood, Illinois 60430

We recognize that certain terms in this book are trademarks, and we have made every effort to print these throughout the text with the capitalization and punctuation used by the holder of the trademark.

The previous edition of this book was published under the title *Information Resource Management*.

© RICHARD D. IRWIN, INC., 1984 and 1988

All rights reserved. No part of this publication may be reproduced, stored in a retrieval system, or transmitted, in any form or by any means, electronic, mechanical, photocopying, recording, or otherwise, without the prior written permission of the publisher.

This book was set in Melior by J. M. Post Graphics, Corp.
The editors were Lawrence E. Alexander, Jani M. Diedrick, Joan A. Hopkins.
The production manager was Carma W. Fazio.
The designer was Keith J. McPherson.
The drawings were done by John Foote.
R. R. Donnelley & Sons Company was the printer and binder.

ISBN 0-256-03627-6

Library of Congress Catalog Card No. 87–81576

Printed in the United States of America

3 4 5 6 7 8 9 0 DO 5 4 3 2 1 0 9

To Arthur L. Samuel

PREFACE

Computers today are used for operations, control, and planning and to improve office efficiency. Indeed, few organization have been left untouched by the computer revolution. Although computers facilitate decision making and management of operations, they do add to the work of managers, because computing resources require supervision. This book explains how to acquire, organize, monitor, and control information resources and discusses management problems unique to computer environments. While many of the references in the text are business oriented, most of the issues discussed refer to computer use in government and nonprofit organizations as well. The chapters are addressed primarily to managers (or students of management) but should also be of interest to data processing professionals.

This book began as a new edition of the textbook *Information Resource Management*, which we published in 1984. However, so many changes have occurred in the field of computing since that time that a new book evolved during the rewrite. Today, managers are concerned not only with mainframe computing by EDP professionals but with end-user computing (use of computers by persons who lack a data processing background). They want to know how to control use of desktop micros, how to initiate micro to mainframe links, how to utilize computer networks, and how to employ information as a strategic weapon. We have addressed these topics by adding new sections to almost every chapter of the original text, by updating those remaining, and by including a totally new chapter on information centers. Another topic not covered in the original text but added to this book is how to design a computer center.

We made some deletions from the contents of *Information Resource Management* as well. To make the reworked text manageable in size,

ix

we eliminated the four chapters that reviewed basic computer concepts and terminology. According to reviewers and our publisher, most professors who have adopted the textbook do not assign those chapters, assuming that students have already mastered that material in other courses. The elimination of the chapters means that this book is no longer a stand-alone text; it requires at least a basic course on computing as a prerequisite. The text might be used as a capstone course for majors in management information systems, since it pulls together topics covered in other classes in the MIS curriculum.

This textbook is written for the upper division undergraduate or the master's student as a companion volume to *Information Processing Systems for Management*, a book that focuses on how computers assist managers in their jobs. Between the two books, the DPMA model curriculum recommendation CIS15 is covered, as are most of the curricula suggestions provided by the Association for Computing Machinery in courses UD8 and UD9. Neither text discusses the internal workings of a computer, how to program, or the history of computing.

Each chapter includes a list of study keys, questions for review or discussion, and at least one case that requires the reader to apply the principles introduced in the chapter to a real-life situation. To assist students who desire supplementary reading, current references appear in the bibliographies at the end of each chapter.

An instructor's manual has been prepared to accompany the text. Included in the manual are answers to selected chapter questions, more than 1,000 multiple-choice questions for reviews or exams, plus supplementary diagrams and summary lists in the form of transparency masters that can be used in the classroom.

The authors wish to thank colleagues and reviewers for their helpful comments and corrections to the manuscript. These include Robert Brennan, Don Cartlidge, Dan Costley, Joseph Denk, William Daugherty, John Eoff, Keith Hennigh, James Mensching, Dick Waugh, and Emery Peterson. We would also like to acknowledge that parts of Chapter 2, 3, 4, and 15 have been drawn from our manuscript *Systems Development*, which is being readied for publication.

Donna Hussain

K. M. Hussain

CONTENTS

PART TWO

ACQUISITION OF HARDWARE   110

PART THREE

CONTROL OF RESOURCES   160

PART FIVE

ORGANIZATION OF RESOURCES 356

MANAGING COMPUTER RESOURCES

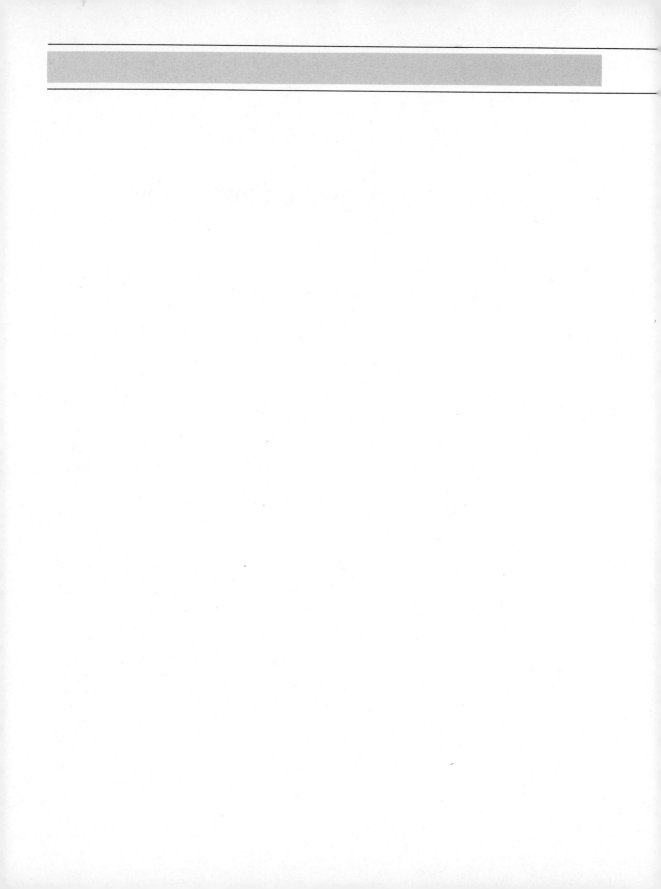

CHAPTER 1

Introduction

The old world was characterized by a need to manage things. The new world is characterized by a need to manage complexity.

Stafford Beer

Worldwide, computers are a billion-dollar industry. Every year, the number of installed computers is on the rise, as is the number of employees who need a working knowledge of computers to carry out their jobs. We are an information-based society with more than half of our work force engaged in the production of information or employed by organizations that manufacture or sell information products. No wonder the development of computers with the ability to process and manipulate information on a large scale has had a revolutionary effect on the way Americans do business.

Modern information machines emerged during World War II. The emphasis at that time was on data processing, the use of machines to reduce both clerical costs and the volume of paperwork. Early computers processed business transactions primarily for financial applications. The use was economically justified since the computers performed some of the functions of clerks and helped to increase their productivity.

As performance improved with advances in technology and as equipment became cheaper, more robust, and portable, computer applications expanded. Companies began to use computers to process information related to production, marketing, inventory control, and other business functions. With this expansion, focus shifted away from systems that would simply save money and toward computers that would improve methods of operation as well. By the mid-1960s, when computers with miniaturized solid logic technology and integrated circuits reached the market, the computer revolution was launched.

The economics of information technology is one force contributing to the growth of modern computing. Year after year, there has been a 30–40 percent improvement in the cost performance of circuitry and mass storage. Computers today deliver nearly 1,700 times the performance of computers in the early 1950s. A modern computer logic chip that fits in the eye of a needle contains the processing power of about 4,000 2-inch vacuum tubes of 30 years ago. A personal computer priced at $5,000 today is almost equivalent in capability to a million-dollar mainframe of the 1960s. IBM's cost for one character of memory has been reduced from about 95 cents in 1970 to about 1.5 cents today. Compare the hundreds of hours and tens of thousands of dollars that were required to program financial performance analysis a decade ago with the ease and low cost of acquiring an off-the-shelf spreadsheet program today. Further miniaturization, faster speeds, greater reliability, and lower costs are predicted for the future.

Another force driving information technology is the intense global competition that faces modern business. Organizations that do not take advantage of information technology are likely to lose customers and market share. In industry, for example, computer-aided design, robotics, process and numerical control, decision support systems, and electronic offices are technologies that are helping revitalize many American manufacturing concerns. The challenge for business managers is to utilize information technology to improve the strategic position of their companies.

MANAGEMENT OF INFORMATION RESOURCES

So much information is being produced by computers in modern businesses that the term *information glut* has been coined. In order to utilize this information effectively, it has been necessary to change the way information resources are managed. No longer can responsibility for these resources be delegated to data processing managers and technicians, as in the past. Their expertise is systems design, programming, and the operation of hardware. Managerial skill in the areas of computer personnel management, planning, data resource acquisition and allocation, applications, and networks is needed in order to ensure that the information generated by computers meets organizational needs. This explains why responsibility for information resources, particularly in the areas of systems development, operations, and control, is shifting to corporate management and to managers of functional departments that use information.

In many organizations, responsibility for information resource management is shifting also to end-users at operational levels. A number of technological advances have led to this development. For example, advances in telecommunications facilitate distributed data processing and the independence of processing nodes. The establishment of computer networks, improved user interface, the marketing of data base management systems, and the widespread use of microcomputers have contributed to the ability of users to manage information resources. Today, end-users frequently choose equipment, design and develop new systems, and handle their own computer operations. End-users, as well as managers, are faced with the problems of how to:

- Select and acquire hardware and software.
- Provide enough computer power to satisfy demand.
- Make technology as accessible and easy to use as possible.
- Reduce applications backlogs.
- Plan, budget, and monitor information systems.
- Improve investment payoffs.
- Minimize systems maintenance effort.
- Ensure the privacy and security of data.
- Mitigate "people problems" associated with computerization, such as resistance to change.
- Speed development of new systems.

INFORMATION AS A CORPORATE ASSET

Today, most corporations recognize that information is an asset and can be a weapon to enhance the corporation's competitive posture. As illustrated in Figure 1–1, information can improve a firm's product and its relationship with clients. Consider the following ways in which information technology has helped suppliers of goods and services to become low-cost producers, to stake out a market niche, or to differentiate their product from the products of competitors.[1]

- Owens Corning Fiberglass uses information technology to help customers estimate future needs for Owens' products. For example, data on energy efficiency is provided free to builders to help them evaluate insulation requirements for new building designs, if the insulation will be purchased from Owens.
- American Hospital Supply has enhanced customer service through an automated round-the-clock order-entry system.

---

[1]The discussion that follows is based on an article by Blake Ives and Gerard P. Learmouth, "The Information System as a Competitive Weapon," *Communications of the ACM*, vol. 27, no. 12 (December 1984), pp. 1193–1201.

- Exxon is developing a debit-card network to give customers the convenience of a credit card but the same discount given cash receipts. The cost of a purchase is immediately debited from the customer's bank account through this network.
- Western Union uses information technology to match freight shippers with motor-freight carriers as a service.
- Bergen Brunswin monitors drug sales for pharmacists and then uses the data collected to help druggists stock their pharmacies and arrange their shelves.
- The Washington Hotel in Tokyo has automated its registration procedures. A robot checks in guests without manual assistance.

Throughout this book, similar examples will be cited of ways information technology can assist firms in the acquisition of corporate resources, in stewardship of these resources, and in their retirement or disposition. We will show how information itself has become an in-

Figure 1–1   **The information system as a weapon**

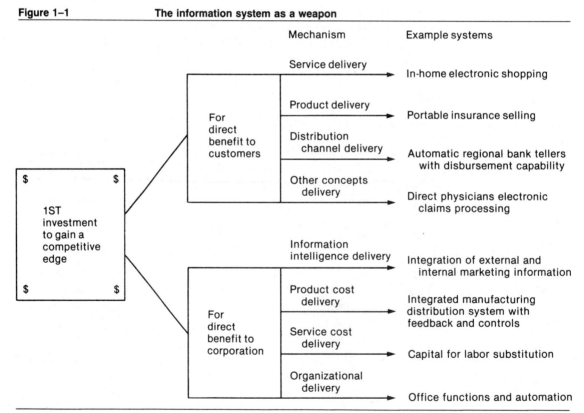

Source: Blake Ives and Gerald P. Learmouth, *Communications of the ACM*, vol. 27, no. 12 (December 1984), p. 1197.

valuable resource that needs to be managed with as much care as raw materials, personnel, and monetary resources.

NEED FOR TRAINING TO MANAGE INFORMATION

Managers at top levels of organizations have traditionally been trained in the management of physical materials (natural and man-made), not in the management of information. And many information users at operational levels have no management training at all. Both corporate managers and information users, therefore, are unprepared for their new responsibilities with regard to the management of information technology.

They are discovering that concepts applicable to the management of things (such as property, depletion, monopoly, and depreciation) do not apply to information. For example, information when used, is not depleted as are raw materials such as coal and iron. Information, when exchanged, does not become the exclusive property of one individual but is shared. Information has a tendency to leak. To hoard or monopolize information is only possible in specialized fields and then only for short periods of time. Traditional hierarchies of power have been based on ownership, access, or control of physical resources. These hierarchies crumble when the resource is information. Clearly, many of the basic assumptions in the management of materials and manufactured goods do not apply to information.

This helps explain why a course in information resource management—one that teaches how to manage an enterprise's information requirements, using contemporary technology in a profitable way—has been added to the curriculum of most business schools. This explains why so many corporate managers and information users in the field are studying textbooks such as this one.

PURPOSE OF BOOK

It is assumed that students using this textbook have a background in the basic concepts of computing, such as a functional knowledge of hardware, peripherals, telecommunications, and software. The book discusses how to develop information systems, acquire information resources, and organize and manage an information processing environment. In addition, the text addresses many of the problems that plague corporations today, such as information systems with inflexible design, obsolete applications, lack of systems integration, applications backlogs, shortage of computing professionals, and ineffective information processing steering committees. The purpose of the book is to prepare readers for a role in the management of information resources in the computerized society of today and tomorrow.

BOOK OUTLINE

This textbook is divided into six parts, as shown in Figure 1–2.

Part One describes how to mobilize information resources so that business needs are met. First, planning for a computerized information system is described. Stages of systems development and different development methodologies are explained next. Finally, control of information resources during development (project management) is examined.

To implement new information systems, hardware and software must be acquired. Part Two describes how to solicit bids for computer equipment and software, select a vendor, arrange financing, and negotiate vendor contracts.

Once a new system is operational, the information resources of that system must be controlled. Part Three describes how to evaluate systems to ensure that resources are being fully utilized, how to monitor processing to minimize machine and human error, how to protect the privacy of data, and how to secure resources from misuse or abuse. The role of auditing in a computer environment is also discussed. All of the mechanisms of control described in this part must be incorporated in the system's design.

Part Four on the management of processing discusses day-to-day concerns of managers responsible for information resources. Scheduling, budgeting, standards, and management of resistance to change are subjects of the chapters in this part.

The organization of information resources is the focus of Part Five. The design of a computer room and the structure of computer departments are described, as is the organization of distributed processing. Also presented is the concept of an information center to assist endusers in learning how best to utilize the information function. Computing services, oversight mechanisms, and staffing are examined as well.

Finally, Part Six discusses issues that concern managers of information resources regarding the computer environment. The part opens with an overview of the computer industry. Chapters follow that deal with the impact of information systems on management and with computers and the law. The book closes with a review of why some information systems succeed and others fail, why some systems grow in an orderly way and others do not.

At least one case, a list of key words, and a set of discussion questions

Figure 1–2 **Organization of book**

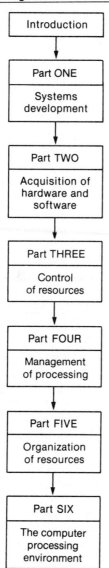

follow each chapter in addition to a selected annotated bibliography recommending supplementary reading.

Two glossaries appear in the appendixes. The "Contextual Glossary" (Appendix A) introduces basic computer terminology and provides an overview of the contents of the book. Readers may find it helpful to peruse this glossary before beginning to read this text or when studying for exams. (A more detailed outline of the contents of this book can be obtained by reading in a series the part introductions or by reading the summaries that appear at the end of each chapter.)

Appendix B contains an alphabetical index with the page number on which each term is located in the contextual glossary. A standard glossary, with operational definitions of computer terms, is located in Appendix C, with a list of the abbreviations and acronyms found in the text provided in Appendix D.

CASE: "FACTORY OF THE FUTURE" PROVES TO BE A HEADACHE

Automobile manufacturers have designed their new plants to be showcases for industrial high technology. Unfortunately, many of these plants are building fewer cars per hour than originally expected. So many problems have resulted from the use of robots on the assembly line, from use of automated guided vehicles to deliver parts, and from use of laser beams and computers to inspect and control the manufacturing process, that management of these plants has become a monumental headache.

To give an example, cars starting down the assembly line at GM's Hamtramck plant are equipped with a programmable "box" that specifies the car's make, model, color, and equipment. Along the line, electronic scanners read the box. This information, fed to a computer, is used to program robots and other machines to build that particular car. In addition, codes are displayed on a monitor telling workers who add parts by hand what fixtures to install. The problem is that the computer sometimes flashes the wrong codes. This leads to errors like the bolting of Cadillac bumpers onto Oldsmobiles.

In other factories, robots assigned the task of applying sealants to a car's joints sometimes miss the right places and drip the glue-like sealant on the floor. Lack of proper depth perception in vision-equipped robots that set windshields in place has resulted in breakage because the robots push too hard. The hoses on robots that twist and turn to spray-paint car bodies have burst because of constant bending. Robots have spray-painted each other and painted cars so unevenly that they have had to be repainted with old-fashioned handheld spray guns. In

Source: Amal Nag, "Auto Makers Discover Factory of the Future Is Headache Just Now," *The Wall Street Journal*, vol. 124, no. 93 (May 13, 1986), p. 1.

one factory, a robotic system designed to make 100 welds in 27 seconds smashed into a car body and stopped the assembly line altogether.

Because of problems such as these, some car manufacturers are scaling back their automation plans. For example, GM has canceled several robot orders for plants that will build its new generation of midsized cars. According to a spokesman, the company is going to phase in automation more slowly than originally planned.

Questions

1. Why is the automobile industry interested in the implementation of information technology in car manufacture?
2. Why are car manufacturers having problems with their automated systems? How can they resolve these problems? What is the role of corporate management and computer center management in this regard?
3. Do you believe that the problem has been one of absorbing new technology? According to one automobile executive, it may be necessary to slow the process of automation and the use of computer technology until the work force has been carefully trained and the goodwill of unions has been gained. Comment.
4. "High technology, like strong medicine, must be taken in carefully measured doses." How does this statement apply to automobile construction? To all growth industries that use computer technology?
5. The Japanese are emphasizing new technology more in cars themselves than in car plants, according to one reporter. Who in a car manufacturing plant makes such a decision? How will such a strategy affect the organization and management of computer resources?

SELECTED ANNOTATED BIBLIOGRAPHY

Appleton, Daniel S. "Information Asset Management." *Datamation*, vol. 32, no. 3 (February 1, 1986), pp. 71–76.

The author examines organizations with large management information systems (MIS) projects and large information assets and discusses their management. He suggests that information resource management is today where business management was 20 years ago—just beginning to feel the need for asset management.

"Developing Strategic Information Systems." *EDP Analyzer*, vol. 22, no. 5 (May 1984), pp. 1–16.

The coverage of this article is broader than the title suggests. The management of information systems is discussed, as well as their development.

Iterative development, external orientation, resistance, rejuvenating old systems, and tying MIS to company goals are topics covered. Two cases are presented: American Express and TRW.

Guimaraes, Tor. "IRM Revisited." *Datamation*, vol. 31, no. 5 (March 1, 1985), pp. 130–34.
This article surveys how 35 companies interpret the role of information resource management (IRM) and to what extent the companies have implemented such management. Factors leading to successful implementation of IRM are identified, and the role of a chief information officer is discussed.

Gunn, Thomas. "The CIM Connection." *Datamation*, vol. 32, no. 3 (February 1986), pp. 50–58.
Computer-integrated manufacturing has been demonstrated as a viable method of producing better information, greater sales, and lower costs. But it has only been implemented in a few U.S. factories. Factory automation is not a subject covered in this textbook but is an extremely important subject for information resource managers in firms with production facilities.

Ives, Blake, and Gerard P. Learmouth. "The Information Systems as a Competitive Weapon." *Communications of the ACM*, vol. 27, no. 12 (December 1984), pp. 1193–1201.
Information systems technology can help a company become competitive in all phases of its customer relationships. A 13-stage customer resource life cycle model is presented.

Klein, Mark. "Information Politics." *Datamation*, vol. 31, no. 15 (August 1, 1985), pp. 87–92.
An excellent overview of how the relationship between MIS and a host enterprise has changed and is changing. For example, organizational changes have taken place. These are not necessarily a result of rational economic behavior but take place because of political realities.

Lucas, Henry C. *Coping with Computers*. New York: Free Press, 1982, 162 pp.
This is a senior manager's handbook on how to control information processing. The author answers questions such as: How much should we spend on computing? How do I know if things are going well? Can we trust the vendor? How do we design a system?

Nolan, Richard L., ed. *Managing the Data Resource Function*. St. Paul, Minn.: West Publishing, 1982, 417 pp.
An excellent set of readings relating to information resource management. The style is choppy, as might be expected in a set of readings, but the material is well integrated.

Porter, M. E., and V. E. Millar. "How Information Gives You Competitive Advantage." *Harvard Business Review*, vol. 63, no. 4 (July–August 1985), pp. 149–60.
The authors argue that information is transforming the nature of competition. It is changing the way companies operate internally as well as altering the relationship among firms and their suppliers, customers, and

rivals. Five steps are suggested for assessing the unique impact of information on one's own company.

Sassone, Peter G., and A. Perry Schwartz. "Cost-Justifying OA." *Datamation*,
vol. 32, no. 4 (February 15, 1986), pp. 83–88.
An office automation discussion is beyond the scope of this textbook, but
cost savings are too important to be ignored or even slighted by any manager. Office work is a labor-intensive activity and the next logical stage for
automation after factory automation. Furthermore, savings are possible in
all enterprises—manufacturing, wholesale, and distribution; business or
government; urban or rural; large or small.

Strassmann, Paul A. *Information Payoff*. New York: Free Press, 1985, 298 pp.
Payoff in this information age comes not from information technology itself
but from people, according to the author. Everything depends on how
managers and employees are organized, educated, and trained. Strassmann
looks at information technology from three perspectives: individual, organizational, and societal.

PART ONE

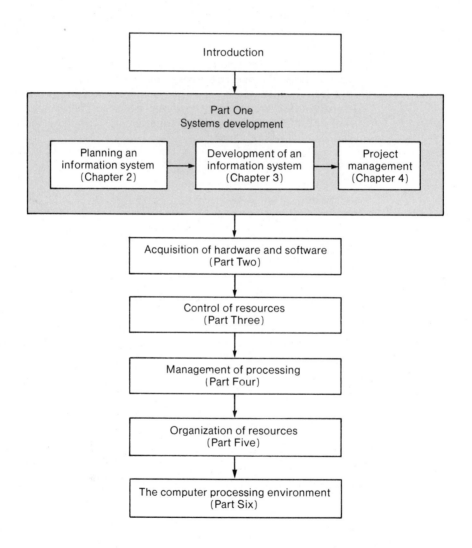

SYSTEMS DEVELOPMENT

Introduction to Part One

Part One of this text tells how to mobilize computer resources to meet the information needs of a business. The three chapters describe how to plan for information systems, develop them, and control resources during development.

Chapter 2 is the planning chapter. It discusses the necessity of establishing planning goals, outlines approaches to planning, and lists common planning errors.

Systems development is the subject of Chapter 3. The system life cycle methodology begins with ascertaining the output needed in decision making. Then a feasibility study is conducted to determine whether or not a system can be designed to produce the desired output, given the firm's objectives and constraints. Specifications for the system are next defined in operational terms. Computer programs are written, forms for collecting data are designed, and operational procedures are formulated. Once the system is tested and results are satisfactory, conversion takes place. All of these steps are discussed in the chapter. In addition, the chapter discusses prototyping and software tools that contribute to the development process.

The final chapter in this part, Chapter 4, concerns management of systems development. The chapter outlines the responsibilities of a project manager for systems development, examines project organization, and reviews project control techniques, such as Program Evaluation Review Technique (PERT) and Graphic Evaluation Review Technique (GERT).

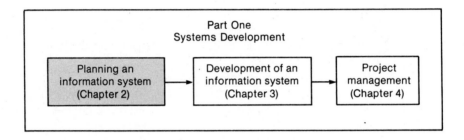

Part One
Systems Development

Planning an information system (Chapter 2) → Development of an information system (Chapter 3) → Project management (Chapter 4)

CHAPTER 2

Planning information systems

When you fail to plan, you are planning to fail.
Dr. Robert Schuller

No business can introduce a new product line or penetrate a competitor's market without careful **planning**. Sometimes, a firm's very survival depends on it. Without question, planning the distribution of a firm's resources is a prime responsibility of top management. In today's computerized world, information is a business resource of considerable value. Only through planning can information be managed effectively for use in daily operations and for charting a firm's future.

Another important reason for information planning is that information systems are costly. Indeed, total expenditures for computer processing are on the rise.[1] As the demand for information multiplies, firms allocate larger and larger slices of their budgets to information systems. By organizing information resources through planning, corporate management can help ensure a return on this investment. That the development of information systems is a time-consuming activity and that a long lead time is often needed for resource acquisition are additional reasons for planning.

Furthermore, planning is technologically important. In building construction, a second story cannot be added to a house unless the foundation, when poured, allows for this addition. Information systems likewise require careful planning for future use. At the start, a firm may be able to implement only a subsystem in a functional area because of

---

[1]According to *Datamation* magazine, which conducts an annual data processing budget survey, the growth in data processing (DP) spending continues to rise in spite of the fact that the economy has been relatively stagnant in the mid-1980s. According to the magazine's 1986 figures, the average DP budget increase was 4.2 percent over 1985, compared to the average corporate revenue rise of 3.1 percent. For smaller companies not included in the Fortune 1,000, the data processing spending rise was expected to be 13 percent. *Datamation*'s annual DP budget survey appears in March or April issues each spring.

financial constraints. But a future integrated system should be envisioned from the beginning, and planners should design a system to permit growth and flexibility. Failure to lay the groundwork (such as failure to establish linking elements, key words, and a plan for integration) may result in costly reconstruction and considerable dislocation when the information needs of a company grow.

In other words, planning is a framework for orderly development of information systems. The nature of planning will be examined in this chapter. A four-tier planning structure will be recommended, planning tools will be introduced, and common planning errors will be listed. In addition, you will learn how project priorities are set and what type of planning is necessary to implement new information systems.

PLANNING SET IN MOTION

Where does the impetus for new or expanded information systems begin? Management may initiate planning in response to altered market conditions, technological advances, or any number of circumstances that signal the need for change. Sometimes, the necessity for new directions is first perceived by personnel at operational levels. For example, computer technicians or information users may become dissatisfied with existing information processing and request the development of new (or redeveloped) information systems. This request will be passed to the person or committee assigned responsibility for planning tasks within the organization.

Until recently, most corporations delegated decisions regarding new information systems to the department involved or to an **ad hoc planning committee**. The problem with these modes of operation was that each computer processing application was planned independently. Too often, little attention was paid to sharing information across application boundaries. Functional autonomy was the rule. The result was data redundancy, excessive use of data processing resources, and insufficient return on data processing investment. Most importantly, little (if any) effort was spent to coordinate information systems planning with corporate goals and corporate strategic planning.

Organizations today recognize that information, like funds, facilities, materials, and personnel, is a resource that should serve the entire organization. To make certain that use of the information resource is not limited to an individual function or department, a standing planning committee—commonly called the **MIS** (management information systems) **planning committee**, the information systems planning committee, or some similar title—is formed with responsibility for information resource planning. The size of the corporation and the complexity of the firm's information resources are factors that determine the composition of the committee. Generally, the information systems director is part of it; so are top management and user representatives. In addition, data processing personnel with technical expertise in systems development should be members or have an advisory role. Some organizations hire consultants to work with the committee as well.

The MIS planning committee makes certain that information technology serves the organization as a whole. In most organizations today, the committee follows a **top-down planning** strategy. This strategy ensures that all planning supports corporate objectives, that key data files are consolidated, and that the information produced can be used by management to make multifunctional decisions.

CORPORATE STRATEGIC PLAN

Top-down planning begins with a **corporate strategic plan**, which states the goals and objectives of the company and charts the direction

Figure 2–1   **Top-down approach to planning**

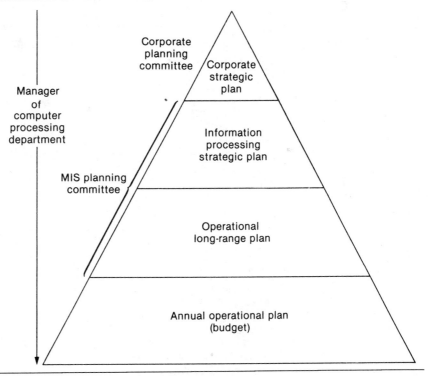

of the firm for the next four to five years.[2] (In this text, a goal is defined as a broad, general direction or intent; an objective is a measurable element of a goal.[3]) For example, the plan will address issues such as company expansion, product diversification, marketing strategies, and the possible injection of new technology. The formulation of this strategic plan is the responsibility of corporate management or a corporate planning committee. Planning issues for the company as a whole are addressed at this level. The MIS planning committee is one step lower in the planning hierarchy, as illustrated in Figure 2–1.

STRATEGIC PLAN FOR INFORMATION PROCESSING

The role of the MIS planning committee begins with the formulation of a **strategic plan for information processing**. This plan states information processing goals and objectives—for example, the design of information systems to reduce business operating costs. Other processing goals might be:

- To avoid overlapping development of major systems elements.
- To help ensure a uniform basis for determining sequence of development in terms of payoff potential, natural precedence, and probability of success.
- To minimize the cost of integrating related systems with each other.
- To reduce the total number of small, isolated systems to be developed, maintained, and operated.
- To provide adaptability of systems to business change and growth without periodic major overhaul.
- To provide a foundation for coordinated development of consistent, comprehensive, corporatewide, and interorganizational information systems.
- To provide guidelines for and direction to continuing systems development studies and projects.
- To develop systems that are user oriented and user friendly, incorporating ergonomic and human factor principles.[4]

The goals in this list are fairly typical, but the list is by no means complete.

---

[2]For more on this subject, see Robert E. Lief, Robert D. Dodge, and Ralph L. Ogden, "Adapting DP Strategy to Management Style," *Computerworld*, vol. 18, no. 49 (December 5, 1983), pp. ID/25–32.

[3]Some writers reverse these definitions. They use the term *goal* to measure elements and *objectives* for broad general directions.

[4]Many of the goals in this list were first proposed by the late Sherman C. Blumenthal in *Managerial Information Systems: A Framework for Planning and Development* (Englewood Cliffs, N.J.: Prentice-Hall, 1969), p. 13.

All goals and objectives for information processing should be consistent with the corporate strategic plan. The purpose of information processing goals and objectives is to provide guidelines for the development of both a long-range operational plan and specific information systems. Computer systems performance should be periodically measured against these goals and objectives.

The strategic plan should also address strategies for:

- The organization of computer processing.
- The enhancement of hardware capacity.
- New applications development and reduced backlogs.
- Improved productivity and competence of technical staff.
- The injection of new technology.
- Better financial return on investments.

LONG–RANGE OPERATIONAL PLAN FOR COMPUTER PROCESSING

The framing of a **long-range operational plan** for computer processing, also the responsibility of the MIS planning committee, is the next planning phase. (Figure 2–1 helps to clarify the different roles of the MIS planning committee.) At this planning stage, the operational plans for the information function are formulated. Users have considerable input at this planning level. Perhaps they want to upgrade hardware, improve security, or develop new systems or subsystems. Their requests will be considered by the committee if they are consistent with goals and objectives of the strategic plan for information processing.

The first step in developing a long-range operational plan is to list current and future information processing needs and objectives. Then, processing capabilities (staff and systems) and status are evaluated, such as staff professionalism, the quality and reliability of installed systems, financial performance, and user satisfaction. Finally, external factors (for example, the business climate and tax laws) that will have a bearing on information resource utilization are assessed.

This background information provides a starting point for planning specific information processing projects for the coming two to four years. In other words, the committee responsible for the long-range plan decides at this stage what will be done and when. Of course, the operational plan is expected to fulfill the objectives set forth in the information processing strategic plan and in the corporate strategic plan.

A major problem in making a long-range operational plan is that basic assumptions in computer processing quickly become obsolete. In addition, the proliferation of technology and the existence of technology gaps complicate the planning effort. In the 1980s, for example, planners have been uncertain about future micro–mainframe links and local area networks (LANs).

ANNUAL OPERATIONAL PLAN

The lowest level of planning for the information function in the top-down planning structure is preparation of a short-range, one-year **operating budget**: that is, the **annual operational plan**. On the basis of the budget, funds are allocated to implement the long-range operational plan on a daily and annual basis. Although responsibility for this budget will be delegated to the manager of the computer processing department (or someone with a similar title), the budget will require the approval of the MIS planning committee and corporate management.

An important advantage of the top-down planning structure is that corporate management can easily trace the relationship between corporate strategic goals and spending for information processing. When spending on information resources is perceived as an extension of corporate strategy, management is less reluctant to open the purse strings to fund information projects. (In the past, computer processing was frequently viewed by management as a "black hole" into which enormous sums of money disappeared with little tangible return on investment.) The top-down planning strategy gives management confidence that corporate financial resources are being spent in a beneficial way consistent with corporate goals.

Although planning is top-down, the implementation of systems or subsystems may be bottom-up. A given information system may be a composite of modular subsystems that have been designed, implemented, and integrated over time. The top-down planning strategy ensures that the growth of this modular system is controlled and consistent with corporate goals and objectives.

TOOLS FOR PLANNING

One of the more comprehensive methodologies for planning information systems is IBM's **Business Systems Planning (BSP)**. This methodology is defined by IBM as a "structured approach to assist a corporation in establishing an information systems plan to satisfy its near- and long-term information requirements." The methodology provides guidelines for the following planning activities:

- Gaining the commitment.
- Preparing for the study.
- Conducting the kickoff meeting.

- Defining business processes.
- Defining data classes.
- Analyzing business systems relationships.
- Determining the executive perspective.
- Assessing business problems.
- Defining information architecture.
- Determining architectural priorities.
- Reviewing information system management.
- Developing recommendations and action plans.
- Reporting results.

During the six to eight weeks it takes to conduct a BSP study, the organization identifies the data and systems it needs to support business goals and objectives. At the end of the study, planners have an action plan for applications development, data base development, and continued·information systems planning.

BSP was developed in 1970. Its widespread use reflects the value of this planning methodology. Although not the only strategic planning methodology in existence today, the roots of many others can be traced back to BSP.

Information specialists who participate in information systems planning encourage use of information technology to speed and improve the planning process. In addition to planning methodologies like BSP, a number of software tools are on the market to assist planners. For example, SCERT, CASE, and SAM are computer software packages that simulate workload processing on different equipment configurations and generate performance and other measures for each set of alternatives. Planners can use these results in deciding what computer resource configurations to acquire.

Information Quality Analysis (IQA), an automated version of the BSP methodology, has recently become available. IQA, assisted by IBM simulation software, diagnoses problem areas in the flow of data and information within an organization. Reports are produced on the quality of data in each functional area of the company, and recommendations are made for improvements. The objective of IQA is to provide critical information for the formulation of a strategic plan for information systems. In addition, the data collected can provide information for the development of applications and data architectures. IQA also ensures that the goals and plans of the business are accurately reflected in the strategic plan for information systems.

Another software tool for planning is the **Information System Model and Architecture Generator (ISMOD)**. Like IQA, this tool was developed to assist planners in the analysis of the information needs of an enterprise. The primary job of the software is to identify enterprise processes (functions) and data required to manage corporate resources. When planners group various processes into subsystems (process clusters), a simulation capability of ISMOD makes it possible to project the impact of these subsystems in terms of user satisfaction.

Both IQA and ISMOD are automated tools that support the top-down planning strategy. They are valuable for organizations that have shifted their emphasis from stand-alone operational systems to integrated, shared-data systems. Since many organizations today recognize that a development methodology that creates stand-alone applications is no longer appropriate, use of planning tools such as these will undoubtedly become increasingly popular.

ASSESSING THE CORPORATE CULTURE

Every company has a distinct **corporate culture**, which can be defined as an accepted way of doing things, unwritten rules of interaction, shared values, or expected conduct in adapting to the organization's environment. Understanding this culture helps employees function effectively in their jobs. Likewise, an understanding of this culture helps planners formulate strategic and operational information processing plans that have a likelihood of successful implementation.[5]

For example, some firms are entrepreneurial, while others are conservative. An entrepreneurial culture is one in which management is willing to take risks. Planning for the development of information systems using still unproven technologies would be appropriate in such an environment. A conservative culture, on the other hand, is averse to risk. Projects are favored that use proven technologies so that management can be assured of tangible savings and return on investment. Other differences in these two cultures are listed in Table 2–1. Although this table is an oversimplification of complex behavior and many firms have attributes of both cultures, planners should be aware that such differences exist. A planner who perceives his or her role as that of a proactive change agent will be more effective in planning for an entrepreneurial company than for a conservative one.

Information systems should also be responsive to the way in which a company is organized. Many companies have clear lines of authority, and responsibility for decision making is delegated to functional department heads. In such firms, distributed data processing systems with local control of information resources are appropriate. Other firms have ambiguous lines of authority. In such companies, "unowned" shared information systems fit well.

Some firms have a cooperative environment that emphasizes teamwork. An information system that builds a common data base, with one

---

[5]For more on this subject, see Jane Linder, "Harnessing Corporate Culture," *Computerworld*, vol. 19, no. 38 (September 23, 1985), pp. ID/1–11.

Table 2–1   **Entrepreneurial versus conservative corporate culture**

	Entrepreneurial	Conservative
Types of systems	Ad hoc. Easy to change. State of the art.	Proceduralized. Hard to change. Proven and burned in.
Project methodology and tools	Prototyping. Loose project definition. Fourth-generation tools. Heavy use of simulation.	Traditional life cycle methodology. Strong project control. Traditional language tools—COBOL.
Planning and control	Top-down systems architecture. Bottom-up systems definition.	Return-on-investment and risk assessment for all projects. Strong chargeback system. Steering committees for resource allocation.
Organization	Resources dedicated to specific user areas. Strong data administration and information systems training functions. Staff of business analysts and technical wizards.	Pooled resources for development. Maintenance people dedicated to particular systems. Superb data center operations network control. Staff of solid technicians.
Key issues for information systems	Prudent resource management. Maintaining information systems as a professional unit. Providing sufficient access to certified data.	Enforcing technology followership. Maintaining high-quality development staff. Selling "soft"-benefit projects.

Source: Jane Linder, "Harnessing Corporate Culture," *Computerworld*, vol. 19, no. 38 (September 23, 1985), p. ID/3.

group entering data that others use, is appropriate in this environment. Others use competition between departments as a spur to productivity. A separate data center for each business function may be optimal in such firms. Some companies place an emphasis on ethical practices, stressing privacy and security of data, audits, and supervisory reviews. Management expects a different type of systems control in these companies than management in amoral organizations that value success regardless of how it is achieved.

Of course, not all managers within a given organization have the same managerial style, and not all employees are homogeneous. Indi-

vidual divisions or departments may have their own subculture. Nevertheless, an effort should be made to assess the overall climate of the
organization so that strategic information processing plans and annual
operational plans are appropriate.

PRIORITY SETTING

An important planning decision is choosing the order of development for approved information projects. The exact role of the MIS
planning committee with regard to **priority setting** varies from one
organization to another. Alternative roles include:

- The MIS planning committee sets project priorities.
- The committee classifies projects into high-, medium-, and low-prior-
  ity groups based on corporate objectives and financial criteria, but
  the systems development manager responsible for all projects sets
  priorities within each group on the basis of technological criteria.
- Priority guidelines are set by the committee, but actual project priorities are left to the systems manager. For example, the committee may
  establish goals, such as the implementation of the distributed computing concept or faster response speed in a specific functional area.
  The systems manager decides the order of projects to meet these goals.
- A mix of the above. That is, the MIS planning committee may propose
  priorities, which are passed to project personnel for comment. Corporate management reviews the recommendations, then makes a final
  determination of priorities.

Priority criteria

Regardless of who makes priority decisions, criteria such as those
listed in Table 2–2 should be the basis for priority setting. The problem
is that a given project may deserve high priority according to certain
criteria and low according to others. Suppose that one project contributes to profitability but has little impact on growth rate, while a competing project has the reverse effect. Assuming that the projects are
matched in other economic respects, which should be given higher
priority when resources are limited?

In such cases, the choice may be based on noneconomic and non-
financial considerations. For example, a competitor may offer a service
that the company wishes to match, or a lawsuit to which the firm is a
party may require that resources be delegated to projects related to the
suit. Sometimes federal, state, or local regulations favor the implementation of one project over another. A delayed delivery date of needed
equipment or the unavailability of programmers and analysts can also
affect priority scheduling. In many organizations, highly visible projects
are given priority because they enhance public relations.

Table 2–2   **Criteria for setting priorities among EDP projects**

Type of Criteria	*Considerations*
Economic and financial	Benefit-cost ratio. Rate of return. Contribution to profitability. Growth rate. Payback period. Risk factors.
Organizational/ institutional	Contribution to organizational goals/objectives. Internal political decisions (e.g., personal preference of decision maker). Public relations effect (e.g., improve corporate image).
Environmental	Required by regulations. Federal. State. Impact on competition (e.g., response time must equal or better competitors'). Lawsuit requires information.
Technical	Isolated, simple, and modular project. High visibility of project. User understanding, cooperation, and commitment to project. Management support and commitment. Basic subsystem to system. Basic module for operations (e.g., data base system). Availability of skilled personnel. User/operator. Technical personnel for development and maintenance. Availability of needed technology. Current. Future.
Managerial	Contribution to quality of decision making. Better information. Faster availability. Information easy to assimilate. Human factors (e.g., employee resistance).

When computer professionals evaluate priorities, they prefer projects where user cooperation, support, and enthusiasm are assured. Analysts like projects that are simple and modular, especially when the development team has been newly constituted and is yet untried. They also prefer projects with quick and conspicuous results and projects that are basic to systems integration. These priorities often conflict with the priorities of end-users.

Risk

Another major factor that will affect priority setting is **risk**—risk in schedule slippage, risk of degraded quality of product, risk of cost overruns, and risk of failure.

What causes some projects to be more risky than others? F. Warren

Table 2–3   **Risk assessment factors in priority setting**

Project	Size	Structure	Technology	Priority assignment
A	Small	Stable	Old	1
B	Small	Stable	New	2
C	Small	Unstable	Old	3
D	Small	Unstable	New	4
E	Large	Stable	Old	5
F	Large	Stable	New	6
G	Large	Unstable	Old	7
H	Large	Unstable	New	8

McFarlan suggests three factors: size, stability of structure, and technology.[6] Size risk includes the number of work hours required for the project, the estimated project time, and the number of user projects involved. Structural risk includes factors such as the attitude of the user, the degree of commitment of top-level users, and the degree and number of changes required. Technical risk involves the degree of user unfamiliarity with hardware, the degree of project team unfamiliarity with software, and both user's and team's degree of knowledge of the proposed new application.

McFarlan gives no quantitative or cardinal rules for measuring these variables. But one might prepare a table like the one in Table 2–3 for use in priority setting. This table considers eight projects with different risk assessments. For simplicity, only two states of each variable have been allowed. Projects have been ranked in the right-hand column by the authors, but the exercise is highly subjective. No formulas exist for establishing numerical weights to risk factors. A planning committee might choose a different order of priority.

Business Systems Planning (BSP) evaluates risk in another manner. Potential benefits matrixes for a given project are prepared based on probability predictions. (See Table 2–4 for a sample blank matrix.) Suppose that an automated production planning subsystem is being proposed[7] and that benefits of the subsystem are estimated by the planning team as:

$1,000,000—materials reduction.

$3,000,000—labor reductions.

$6,000,000—increased production.

$5,000,000—sales increase.

---

[6] F. Warren McFarlan, "Portfolio Approach to Information Systems," *Harvard Business Review*, vol. 59, no. 3 (September–October 1981), pp. 142–50.

[7] The following discussion is based on IBM, *Business Systems Planning/Information Systems Planning Guide*, GE20–0527–4 (White Plains, N.Y.: IBM Technical Publications, 1984), pp. 120–21.

Table 2–4 **Benefits matrix**

	High probability	Medium probability	Low probability
Displaced costs			
Increased productivity			
Increased income			

Using the estimated maximum potential savings, the team would then estimate total possible return for which there is high probability, medium probability, and low probability of realization. For example, in the materials reduction category, the estimated $1,000,000 reduction might be distributed as follows:

1. High probability that raw material can be reduced by $5,000.
2. Moderate probability of an additional saving of $200,000 in finished goods inventory.
3. Low probability of an additional $300,000 in other savings.

These figures and estimates on probability for labor reductions, increased production, and sales increase would then be added to the potential-benefits matrix, as shown in Table 2–5. Note that a number has been assigned to each cell in the matrix (see lower left-hand corner of each cell). This number represents the planners' assessment of the

Table 2–5 **Potential benefits**

	High probability	Medium probability	Low probability	
Displaced costs	$ 500,000 100,000 1	$ 200,000 100,000 3	$ 300,000 100,000 6	Materials reduction Labor reduction
Increased productivity	$ 300,000 2	$ 200,000 5	$ 100,000 8	Increased production
Increased income	$ 200,000 4	$ 200,000 7	$ 100,000 9	Profit increase
Total	$ 1,100,000	$ 700,000	$ 600,000	

Table 2–6   **Benefit level/risk level table**

Subsystem	Potential benefit level *									Total
	1	2	3	4	5	6	7	8	9	
Production planning [†]	600	300	300	200	200	400	200	100	100	2,400
Production scheduling										
Plant status										
Order entry										
Order status										
Sales control										
Cost										
Bills of material										
Product data control										
Purchasing										
Raw materials inventory										
Finished goods inventory										
Sales analysis										
Forecasting										
Financial modeling										
Territory analysis										
Engineering design										
Skills inventory										
Compensation administration										
Financial planning										

*The numbers correspond to the numbers assigned to
the cells in the matrix in Table 2-5.

[†] The figures in this row are derived from adding
the values in each cell in Table 2-5.

relative risk in realizing the potential benefit of each cell. (There is a
higher probability of realizing the benefits in Cell 1, and hence less
risk, than in realizing the benefits in Cell 9.) Next, the data in the matrix
would be listed in a potential benefit level risk level table, as shown
in Table 2–6.

When a matrix has been prepared for each potential benefit of a
project and the data from these matrixes have been added to Table 2–
6 the planning team has a useful tool for summarizing in dollar terms
the potential benefits of a given system. Subsystems can also be compared (and/or ranked) on the basis of total risk (right-hand column,
Table 2–6) or any combination of risk levels (from right to left).

Other priority
factors

The overall position of the firm is an additional factor that should be taken into consideration when establishing priorities. No firms should become encumbered with too many high-risk projects at one time. A balance between short-term and long-term projects should be sought. In addition, a balance is advisable between service-oriented projects and those that improve the infrastructure of the firm.

The many variables to be considered when ranking projects and the highly subjective nature of many of these variables means that priority setting is a difficult task. The problem facing planners is that large sums of money may be involved and that the success of information systems development may well depend on astute priority decision making.

PLANNING SYSTEMS DEVELOPMENT PROJECTS

Let us now turn to the way in which the MIS planning committee plans for the development of new information systems. Figure 2–2 shows inputs taken into consideration by the committee during the planning process. Users' needs are studied. The competitive environ-

Figure 2–2   **Inputs to the planning process**

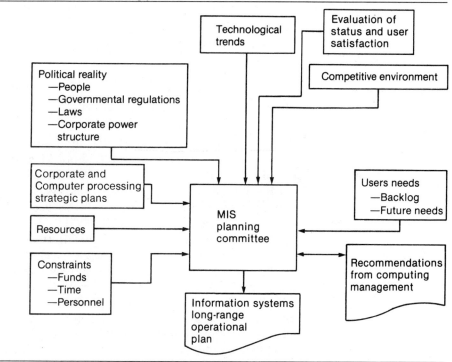

Figure 2–3   **Data flow for planning information systems**

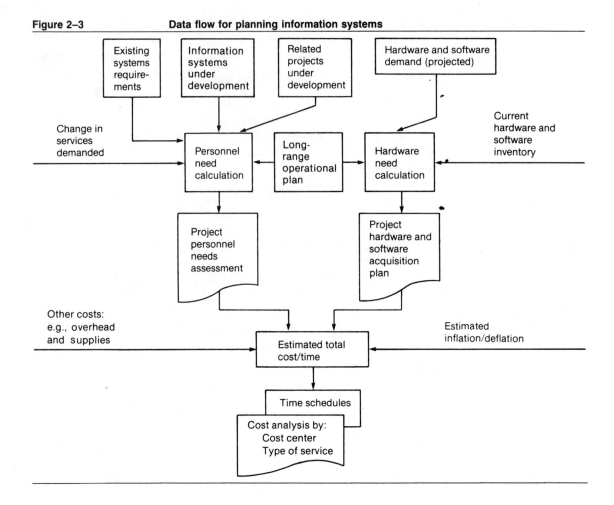

ment of the firm is analyzed. (What information and facilities would be competitively advantageous?) Technological trends are evaluated, and political realities are assessed. (Are there legal and regulatory restraints? What will people accept? What is feasible, given the corporate power structure?) In addition, the firm's goals, resources, and constraints are reviewed.

Figure 2–3 shows the data flow in information systems planning. The chart traces how, given the constraints and long-range operational plan, planners determine hardware, software, and personnel needs for a proposed information system and how these needs add to existing corporate requirements. For example, a change in services will make it necessary to recalculate resource needs. So will the development of a new information system. Because time and cost are interrelated, their projections should be made simultaneously. For example, the amount of time programmers will spend developing software and the time needed to train technicians to operate a new information system will affect costs.

In planning systems development projects, the committee may call upon information users and computer personnel for assistance. In many organizations, such participation is encouraged because it leads to job enlargement (in this case, experience in planning) for the individuals involved. In addition, their participation should contribute to acceptance of new systems in the future, since involvement in planning usually stimulates interest and interest usually dissipates resistance to change.

Planning is a cyclical process, as shown in Figure 2–4. Since the implementation of plans (2) made by the MIS planning committee (1) is the responsibility of the manager of the computer processing de-

Figure 2–4   **Planning: A cyclical process**

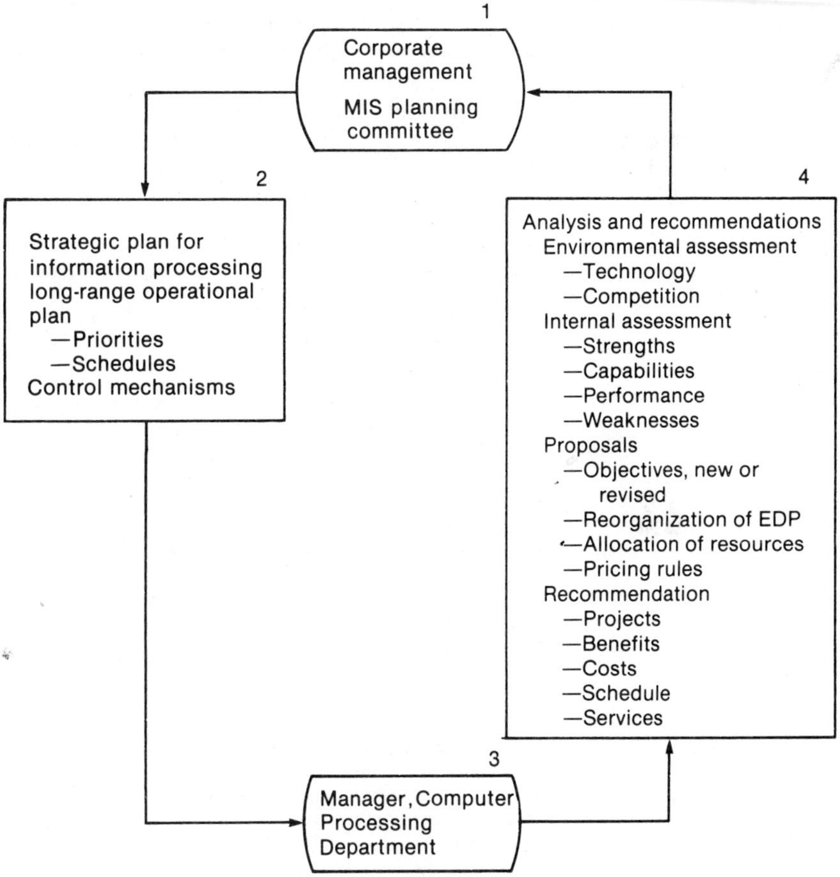

partment (3), plans are sent to this manager for consideration.[8] The plans are reviewed by the manager and EDP staff on the criteria listed in Box 4. Their evaluation and recommendations are then submitted to the MIS planning committee for consideration in plan revision and updating. Of course, all plans must receive the approval of corporate management before implementation.

There is no formula to ensure good planning. But flexibility, a responsiveness on the part of planners and management to changing technology and business conditions, is a must. Periodic revision and updating of plans should be an integral phase of planning.

SYSTEMS DEVELOPMENT IMPLEMENTATION

Once corporate management approves plans for the development of new information systems, tactical plans are formulated for implementation. Figure 2–5 shows implementation steps. The manager of the computer processing department (2) plans for operations (4) based on the information systems plan (1) and supports systems development (3).

Systems development is organized into projects, each consisting of a discrete set of activities targeted for completion on given dates. If the long-range operation plan has not set the priorities for systems projects, the manager of the computer processing department will determine project priorities.

Implementation of new systems and operations (5) is also the responsibility of the manager of the computer processing department. The output and services produced (6) will be periodically evaluated (7). Corrective action may be necessary to remedy problems identified. This may mean modification of the long-range operational plan or new strategies and schedules for implementation.

PROBLEMS IN PLANNING

Firms that adopt top-down planning and follow the planning procedures described in this chapter are more likely to develop successful systems than those that do not. However, even they experience systems

---

[8]Today, computers process words, images, and speech, as well as data. For this reason, the term *EDP* (electronic data processing) *management* is outdated. Nevertheless, it continues in use. Possible substitutes are computer center head, computing management, information system director, MIS management, or head of IRM (information resource management).

Figure 2–5   **Implementation of plans**

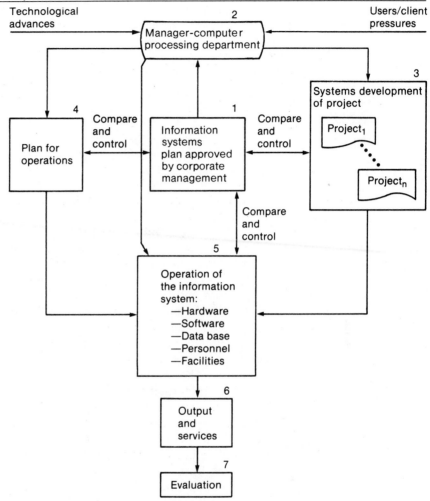

failures from time to time. Some common reasons for systems failure are:

- Lack of top management involvement in the planning process.
- Lack of free communication and commitment to change.
- Failure to establish planning objectives and strategies in line with the corporate strategic plan.
- Lack of formal planning procedures.
- Planner overoptimism.
- Top-down analysis not performed.

- Shortage of time.
- Ignorance of corporate politics.
- Alternative MIS strategies not defined and/or evaluated.
- Long-range plan draft not reviewed by user management.
- Failure to plan implementation step-by-step.

SUMMING UP

Planning is of prime importance in managing a firm's assets, such as equipment, personnel, and goodwill. Computer processing has added information to this list of valued resources, and planning the development of information systems has become an important responsibility of management.

These days, information systems are commonly planned within the framework of a four-tier planning structure. First, a corporate strategic plan that establishes the business direction of the company is developed. Next, an information processing strategic plan is formulated that specifies information resources to be available for stated information processing goals and objectives. This is followed by a long-range operational plan. The lowest level of planning is preparation of a one-year operating budget for computer processing.

Planning goals and objectives differ from one organization to the next and may change over time even within a single corporation. For example, few planning committees spoke 10 years ago of the need for user-oriented, user-friendly systems. But today, the creation of user-friendly systems is an objective near the top of the list in most organizations. Users are demanding such systems, and both corporate management and planners recognize the importance of incorporating ergonomic and human factor principles in systems design.

A number of planning tools such as IBM's Business Systems Planning and software like SCERT, IQA, and ISMOD can contribute to the planning process. The computer processing department should review all plans and make recommendations for improvements, revisions, or updating, since that division will be responsible for implementation of the plans.

When formulating the long-range operational plan for computer processing, new systems development projects are planned. Inputs in new systems planning have been described in this chapter, as well as the data flow in information systems planning. Common errors in planning include lack of management and user involvement in the planning process, lack of formal planning procedures, failure to develop top-down planning strategies, and failure to consider the corporate culture in planning.

CASE: PLANNING FAILURE AT A HOSPITAL SUPPLY COMPANY

ABC, a company with a large market share in the manufacture of hospital supplies, is a conservative company with a long-standing ethical and cooperative culture. The company lacks strong leadership and has no long-range plan. Instead, one-year financial goals placed on the organization by its parent company determine the direction of the firm.

When ABC began to lose business to a rival firm, a planning committee was organized to outline a computer processing system that would make ABC more competitive. The committee recommended a marketing system with distributed architecture, a turnkey system with communications links and a programming language new to ABC. Although a feasibility study showed that the project would cost $9 million with a payback period of eight years, the project was approved.

When a pilot system was delivered, there were so many technical and political problems that funding for the project was withdrawn after a trial run. The reason for failure can be attributed, in part, to the fact that the planning committee committed two fatal cultural errors. First, a short-term-oriented company that is managed, not led, is not a good candidate for a long-range information system plan. This environment calls for projects that can be funded within a single budget cycle. Secondly, the planning committee should have recognized that firms managed by conservatives are hesitant to undertake projects with long paybacks and intangible benefits.

Questions

1. Should failure of this project have been anticipated? Explain.
2. Would a less ambitious plan have had a greater likelihood of successful implementation? Discuss.
3. Where does responsibility lie for this failure? With:
   a. Corporate management?
   b. Computer center management?
   c. Project management?
   d. Systems analysts?
   e. The MIS planning committee?

Source: Jane Linder,"Harnessing Corporate Culture, *Computerworld*, vol. 19, no. 38 (September 23, 1985), pp. ID/6–7.

CASE: A DATA BASE SERVICE CONTRIBUTES TO STRATEGIC PLANNING

PIMS (Profit Impact of Market Strategy) is a service that is offered by the Strategic Planning Institute (SPI) of Cambridge, Massachusetts. It consists of data on the actual experiences (both good and bad) of some 2,500 diverse business units. Most use of the service consists of queries. A client might ask, "If we change X (a variable, such as price), what would be the probable impact on Y (a result variable, such as profit)?" The computer will search the data base for a record of the business experience of units that resemble the client (sell similar products or services, have the same type of customers, and face similar competition) in order to provide the answer to the query. In other words, PIMS provides a way to analyze the effects of alternative strategic decisions, utilizing the experience of other companies.

The PIMS methodology originated at the General Electric Co. in the 1960s; at that time, GE was searching for "laws of the marketplace." During the 1970s, the project was refined at Harvard Business School. Today, the service is offered by SPI, a nonprofit institute, and serves about 200 participating corporations.

Questions

1. Is this a good use of simulation for planning? Explain.
2. What decision rules should be used to decide whether simulation for planning is appropriate or not?
3. Who should have the responsibility for determining what variables to test? Why?
4. Who does the model serve: the planner, the corporate manager, or both? Discuss.
5. What is the role of the analyst in designing, running, and analyzing the results of simulation for planning?
6. Should simulation be a technique:
    a. With which managers are acquainted?
    b. In which analysts are experts?
    Explain.

STUDY KEYS

Ad hoc planning committee   **Business Systems Planning (BSP)**
Annual operational plan   **Corporate culture**

Corporate strategic plan	**Operating budget**
Information Quality Analysis (IQA)	**Planning**
	Priority setting
Information System Model and Architecture Generator (ISMOD)	**Risk**
	Strategic plan for information processing
Long-range operational plan	
MIS planning committee	**Top-down planning**

REVIEW AND DISCUSSION QUESTIONS

1. Is planning necessary for all computer projects? Why? What are the environmental prerequisites that make it:
   a. Essential?
   b. Desirable?
   c. Unnecessary?
2. Is planning for computer projects more difficult and complex than for noncomputer projects? Explain.
3. Consider the planning of a project for the implementation of a large computerized information system. Compared to a noncomputer system for the same purpose, would the computer system:
   a. Require a different planning process?
   b. Be more complex?
   c. Require different planning techniques and skills?
   Explain.
4. Is the planning for a software project different from planning a:
   a. Hardware (CPU equipment) project?
   b. Teleprocessing-oriented project?
   c. Distributed processing project?
   d. Turnkey system?
   e. Hardware and software project?
5. What is top-down planning?
6. Distinguish between the following terms:
   a. Corporate strategic plan.
   b. Strategic plan for information processing.
   c. Long-range operational plan.
   d. Operating budget.
7. What should be the role of an outside independent consultant or consulting company in the planning process?
8. Discuss the role of planning tools in developing an information processing strategic plan.
9. Should the computer processing manager be involved in corporate planning? To what degree? Under what conditions?
10. Is planning of computer systems best accomplished by an individual or by a committee? If the latter, how should it be constituted?

11. Should top management be concerned with the planning of a functional information system? Explain.

12. What is corporate culture? How does it relate to information systems planning?

13. In the planning of an information system, what are the unique problems in assessing and estimating:
    a. Risk?
    b. Time of completion?
    c. Cost of completion?
    d. Personnel resources needed?

14. What criteria would you use when setting project priorities for the development of information systems?

15. Should there be standards for computer planning? If so, suggest them.

16. In planning a computer information system, what are some of the main variables in each of the following:
    a. External environment?
    b. Technological environment?
    c. Political environment?
    d. Social environment?
    e. Crisis-prone environment?

SELECTED ANNOTATED BIBLIOGRAPHY

Alvarez, Joan. "A Business Systems Plan." *Journal of Information Management,* vol. 4, no. 2 (Winter 1982), pp. 19–37.
This is one of many available articles explaining experiences using IBM's Business Systems Planning.

Artis, Pat. "The Maturation of Capacity Planning." *Datamation,* vol. 31, no. 24 (December 15, 1985), pp. 53–57.
A superb overview of the evolution of capacity planning and the relationship of capacity planning (desired and de facto) to corporate planning. The author concludes that good communication with top management is crucial. Without it, no amount of hardware or tools will keep up with corporate needs.

Buckelew, B. R. "The System Planning Grid: A Model for Building Integrated Information Systems." *IBM Systems Journal,* vol. 4, nos. 3 and 4 (1985), pp. 294–306.
The systems planning grid is used to build a set of integrated architectural guidelines to ensure that a "system," not a collection of unintegrated applications, is built. The grid can also be used to set product standards and organizational responsibilities.

"Capacity Planning Issues." *EDP Performance Review,* vol. 11, no. 7 (July 1983), pp. 1–7.
This article includes a discussion of the relationship of capacity planning to long-range planning. Planning an information center and planning a distributed processing environment are also topics examined.

Cassese, Vita; W. Gruber; and M. Hughes. "Planning Amid Change." *Computerworld*, vol. 19, no. 48 (December 9, 1985), pp. 71–75.
The authors work at Pfizer, a pharmaceutical company, and describe how they "focused on the planning process and the ability to manage change rather than writing a static long-range plan." As a result, they were able to reap the benefits of ever-changing information technology.

IBM. *Business Systems Planning/Information Systems Planning Guide*, GE20–0527–4. White Plains, N.Y.: IBM Technical Publications, 1984, 146 pp.
This IBM manual is written in a matter-of-fact style. It has good diagrams and examples culled from the experience of planners of both large and small systems.

Kanter, Jerome. "MIS Long-Range Planning—Why Don't More Companies Do It?" *Infosystems*, vol. 29, no. 6 (June 1982), pp. 66–72.
Kanter distinguishes between three types of planning: project planning, capacity planning, and resource or budgetary planning. In the latter, he identifies 14 categories for MIS: corporate guidelines, current operations, mission/direction statement, objectives/goals, assumptions/risks, strategies, policies, program/projects, management control tools, transition plans, priorities and schedules, organization and delegation, resource projections, and operating budget.

Lief, Robert E.; Robert D. Dodge; and Ralph L. Ogden. "Adapting DP Strategy to Management Style." *Computerworld*, vol. 18, no. 49 (December 5, 1983), pp. ID/25–32.
The authors argue that corporate objectives should dictate DP objectives, which in turn determine DP operating goals and specific plans of action. This discussion is in the context of experience gained in implementing a formal DP planning process at Flour Corporation.

McKean, J. D., and Tor Guimaraes. "Selecting MIS Projects by Steering Committee." *Communications of the ACM*, vol. 28, no. 1 (December 1985), pp. 1344–51.
A survey of 92 projects from 32 organizations showed that the most popular combination of a selection mechanism was top management in conjunction with user departments. Other mechanisms and their implications for project portfolios are discussed.

Shank, Michael E., and Andrew C. Boynton. "Critical Success Factor Analysis as a Methodology for MIS Planning." *MIS Quarterly*, vol. 9, no. 2 (June 1985), pp. 121–29.
The use and benefits of critical success methodology (CSF) to identify corporate information needs and to develop a corporate information systems plan is discussed in this article. The conclusions are based on a CSF case study conducted at Financial Institutions Assurance Corporation.

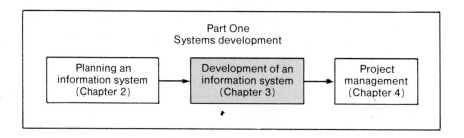

Part One
Systems development

| Planning an
information system
(Chapter 2) | → | Development of an
information system
(Chapter 3) | → | Project
management
(Chapter 4) |

Development of an information system

We build systems like the Wright brothers
built the airplane—build the whole thing,
push it off a cliff, let it crash, and start
all over again.

R. M. Graham

A computing time of a few seconds is all that is required for many reports produced by an information system. But the systems that generate these same reports may take months or years to develop. This is because systems development, which consists of planning, design, and implementation, can be a time-consuming process. Using a traditional development methodology, called the **system life cycle methodology,** developmental activities consist of a feasibility study, determination of systems requirements, systems design, systems implementation, testing, conversion and evaluation. This chapter opens with a discussion of these activities.

Another development methodology, one more recently introduced, is **prototyping.** An overview of the benefits and limitations of prototyping is also presented in this chapter. In addition, software tools that help speed development are examined.

The chapter concludes with a brief discussion on how to select a development methodology appropriate to a given development project.

SYSTEM LIFE CYCLE METHODOLOGY

Once the need for an information system has been perceived by persons working within an organization (users or EDP personnel), a request for that system's development will be forwarded to the planning committee. Chapter 2 described the way in which a planning committee evaluates requests for new systems and how it makes a decision whether

43

Figure 3–1   **Flowchart for system development**

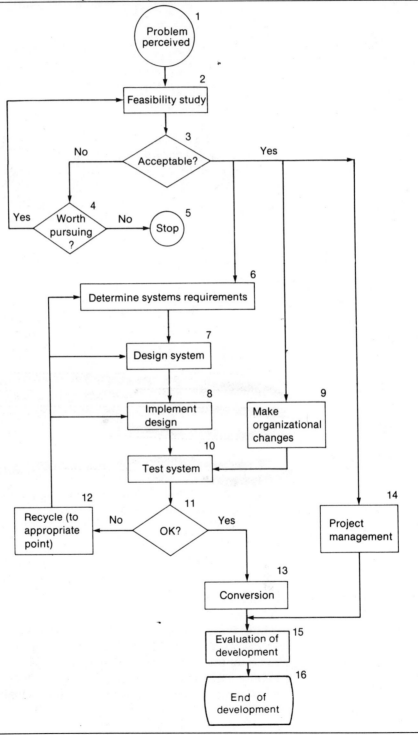

or not to implement systems development projects. In Chapter 3, our discussion assumes that the planning committee has given its approval for a new system and has scheduled its development.

A flowchart showing the activities in the system life cycle methodology of systems development is shown in Figure 3–1. Each of these activities will be discussed in the sections that follow.

Feasibility study

One purpose of a **feasibility study** (Box 2, Figure 3–1), the first activity in systems development using the system life cycle methodology, is to determine whether computer processing is the most effective way of generating requested information. (Sometimes, manual or electromechanical information processing is advisable.) Another purpose is to determine whether a computerized information system can be developed to meet desired objectives within expected constraints. In addition, the proposed information system's cost (monetary and organizational) is estimated during the study, and the benefits of the system are outlined. On the basis of the study, corporate management will decide whether to initiate development of the proposed system or discontinue its consideration. Feasibility studies are not required for each new report, but they are recommended when proposed systems require a large investment of the firm's resources or involve major change.

Although a feasibility study postulates a new system, it does not guarantee success: a custom-developed system may still fail when it is implemented. However, the study will identify economic, financial, technological, and organizational requirements and constraints to ensure that the company has the necessary resources for development. It will also identify problems that team members should be prepared to face.

A feasibility study has four phases: organization, search for a solution, feasibility analysis, and choice of a solution. Figure 3–2 is a flowchart showing, in detail, the activities in each phase.

Phase 1: Organizing for a feasibility study. The first phase of any feasibility study is organizing for the study itself. Once the need for change has been recognized (Box 2, Figure 3–2), the problem is defined and formulated by management (3). Then personnel are appointed to the feasibility study team (4). Members should be knowledgeable regarding computer systems. They should be able to work with people and be informed about the firm's structure, philosophy, objectives, policies, and operations. Including representatives from management will give the team the necessary status and authority to get cooperation at all organizational levels when information for the study is being collected. It may be necessary to add consultants to the team when members lack experience in the type of project under consideration.

Team size generally varies from two to eight. Large teams offer greater division of labor and more flexibility in staffing, which makes it easier

Figure 3–2   **Flowchart for feasibility study**

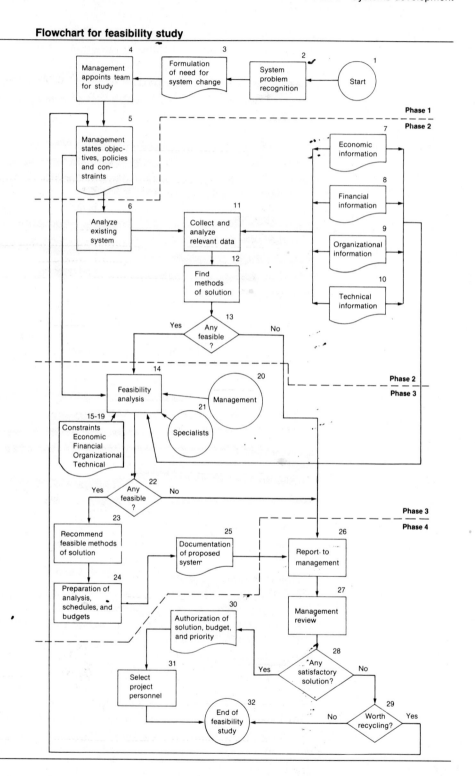

to ensure team expertise. But in large teams, personality conflicts may emerge that hinder the ability of the team to function effectively. When complex systems are under consideration, teams are generally more successful when the chair is drawn from the upper levels of management.

After the feasibility team has been appointed, management should state the objectives of the study. Policies and constraints that will affect development of the proposed system (5) should also be specified. Management usually waits until the feasibility study group has been assembled before doing so, because team members' questions regarding variables and their demands for clarification and elaboration assist management in defining the study objectives in operational terms. Because team members demand specifics, resource constraints for the project and the limits of acceptable organizational change are carefully defined. Without team-management interaction, the project's objectives, policies, and constraints are too often stated in ambiguous, generalized terms.

During this organizational phase, team members should be given authority to cross departmental boundaries when collecting information for the feasibility study. When complex systems development is proposed, this authorization should come from top management.

Phase 2: Search for solutions. The search for solutions usually begins with a study of current operations (6) and the collection and analysis of all relevant information on the processing environment (7–11). Then possible solutions to the problem are proposed (12). These solutions are reviewed to see whether any glaring reasons exist for declaring the project infeasible (13). For example, if management has allocated only $100,000 for the operation of a terminal system and the team discovers that the minimum equipment cost of such a system is in the range of $300,000, the team should submit its findings to management, and the study should be terminated. If proposed solutions pass this initial scrutiny, a detailed feasibility analysis should then take place.

Phase 3: Feasibility analysis. Feasibility analysis (14) is the formal testing of alternative solutions formulated in Phase 2. The development team, with the help of management (20) and specialists (21), tests solutions against economic, financial, organizational, and technological constraints (15–19).

Economic feasibility, testing to see whether expected benefits will equal or exceed expected costs, is easier said than done. It is difficult to assign a precise monetary value to benefits, because most benefits of information systems cannot easily be measured in dollars. For example, how can one measure the value of accurate, timely sales or production information that the new system will deliver, information that the firm has had no experience using? Stating costs accurately is a problem as well. User requirements are frequently underestimated during the initial stages of a project and escalate as the project develops. Because of such problems, many teams estimate a range of expected benefits and costs when making a benefits-cost analysis, with probability assessments for values within the range.

A proposed system with a good benefits-cost ratio may ultimately be rejected because lack of money prevents implementation. Although study teams often consider economic and financial constraints jointly, **financial feasibility** (checking costs against available funding) is a separate decision. Whereas computer analysts determine costs, users in consultation with financial advisors determine whether borrowed money will be available for the project, internal financing will suffice, or a combination of external and internal financing can be arranged. Other projects may be in competition for the company's limited financial resources. The time value of money, the accounting rate of return on investment, and the profitability index are examples of calculations that will be made during a study of financial feasibility. Such calculations may be decisive in recommending a proposed system's implementation or rejection.

Organizational feasibility is testing proposed solutions against organizational constraints. Is there support at operational and middle management levels? Are qualified systems personnel available? Will employee resistance to change undermine the effectiveness of utilizing computer technology in decision making?

Decision tables, such as the one in Table 3–1, can be used by teams in the determination of organizational feasibility when evaluating alternative solutions. Note that the condition statements and action statements listed in the left-hand column are separated by a double horizontal line. To the right, condition and action entries appear. Each rule column represents a set of conditions associated with a specific action (or set of actions). For example, if top, operational, and middle management support is lacking and experienced analysts are unavailable (see rule 4), then the project has little likelihood of success, and the feasibility study should be discontinued. Deciding what rules to apply is a decision of the feasibility team.

Finally, **technological feasibility** should be considered. Lack of equipment to perform certain types of operations, such as machine reading of handwriting, may rule out proposed solutions. In many unstructured decision-making situations, no mathematical or statistical techniques exist at the present time for determining optimal problem solutions. An information system is not technologically feasible for such problems.

When a number of solutions prove feasible (22—Exit Yes), the study

Table 3–1   **Decision table for testing organizational feasibility**

		Rule 1	Rule 2	Rule 3	Rule 4	Rule 5	Rule 6	Rule 7	Rule 8
Condition statements	Top manager support	N	N	N	N	Y	Y	Y	Y
	Operational and middle management support	Y	Y	N	N	Y	Y	N	N
	Experienced analysts available	Y	N	Y	N	Y	N	Y	N
Action statements	Discontinue study		X	X	X				
	Hire consultants (assume available)						X		X
	Train analysts						X		X
	Continue study with caution	X						X	X
	Continue with enthusiasm					X			

Key: Y = Yes
     N = No
     X = Action to be taken.

team should develop priorities for ranking solutions. The team should then recommend the top-ranked solution to management, also presenting alternatives in order of preference (23). A report accompanying the recommendation (24) should list anticipated benefits and consequences of the solution, dollar resources required for implementation, and problems that might be encountered by the development team. A time schedule should also be included. All proposals should be documented (25).

Phase 4: Choice of a solution. The fourth and last phase of the feasibility study is initiated when the study team presents its report to management (26). The findings in the report should then be carefully reviewed by corporate management (27). Management representatives should have participated in the team's deliberations when costs and benefits were weighted, values to intangible variables were imputed, effects of conflicting factors were estimated, and trade-offs were compared. But a reassessment of these value judgments should be made by management before final approval for a new system is given. Estimates also need to be recalculated, and a check should be made to ensure that all relevant variables have been specified. Should management decide that none of the proposed solutions are acceptable (28—Exit No), recycling of development activities may be initiated (29). Constraints might be relaxed or objectives scaled down in order to find an acceptable feasible solution.

Acceptance of a solution from the alternatives proposed by the study team (28—Exit Yes) is followed by decisions necessary for implementation: authorization of a budget, establishment of a time schedule for design and implementation, and formulation of development priorities (30). A project manager is appointed for the new system's development, and development team members are assigned (31). It will be the development team's responsibility to determine the requirements of the new system, to design it, then to oversee its implementation and conversion. The feasibility study is terminated once the development team is assigned, and the feasibility study team is disbanded (32).

Feasibility studies are costly and time consuming, but they are of value. Properly conducted, they reduce the risk of spending the company's resources on development projects that fail. When a recommended solution later proves infeasible, the cause can usually be attributed to one or more of the following errors:

- A crash approach that did not provide sufficient time for all of the phases of the study.
- A nonintegrated approach.
- Poor leadership and poor staffing of the feasibility team.
- Objectives and constraints not adequately specified.
- Lack of organizational support.
- Incorrect estimations, perhaps of the difficulty of the problem to be solved, requirements, organizational impact of the project, or resistance to change.
- Lack of participation by user management in the application area, either in review of project objectives or in development.

Determining system requirements

The next stage in an information system's development is **determination of system requirements** (Box 6, Figure 3–1). Figure 3–3 shows the steps followed during this stage, where user needs and system specifications that were stated in general terms in the feasibility study are restated in greater detail to provide the operational framework for the system's design.

The key to determining user requirements is data collection. Only by gathering facts and opinions about operating procedures and needed changes can the development team draw up a list of system specifications. The data collected during the feasibility study is used, but additional information is necessary at this stage. A literature search (2), interviews (3), meetings (4, 6, and 7), and the use of tools and techniques

Figure 3–3   . . .   **Determining system requirements**

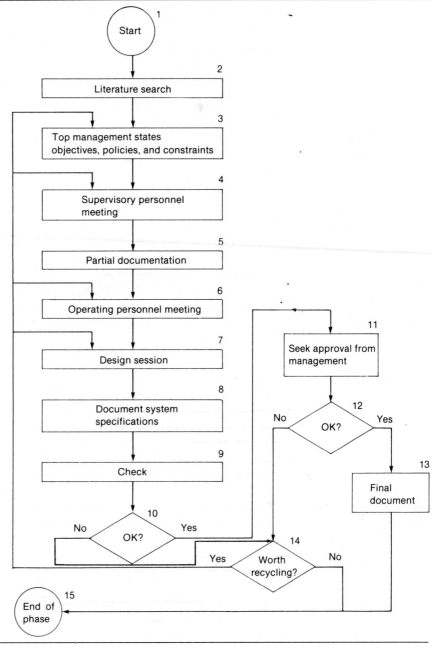

for data collection and analysis contribute to the process of defining system requirements.

Data collection and analysis. One technique of data collection is a **literature search.** Analysts on the development team can learn about the firm's organization, operations, products, internal structure, and stated objectives by studying the firm's annual reports, catalogs, and publicity material. To learn about systems used by other firms and to review and update knowledge about data processing equipment and capabilities, a search might also be made of:

- Monographs.
- Periodicals.
- Professional journals.
- House organs.
- Books.
- Promotional literature from manufacturers.

Interviews of management and users by the development team help the team assess user priorities. The views of management, systems personnel, and specialists (including consultants) can also be solicited

Table 3–2	Sample system analysis and design techniques by generation

Precomputer
 Time and motion studies
 Flowcharts
 Organization charts
 Linear algebra
 Gantt scheduling charts
 Board wiring diagram
	Third generation (1970–80)
	 Automated ADS, CPM/PERT,
	  decision tables
	 Hoskyns automated coding system
	 SODA (System Optimization and
	  Design Algorithm)
	 TAG (Time Automated Grid)
	 PSL/PSA (Problem Solver Language/
	  Problem Systems Analyzer)

First generation (1959–60) Point set theory MAP system charting technique Linear programming Applied statistical analysis	*Fourth generation (1980–85)* PSL/PSA II Structured methodology BSP (Business System Planning) SADT (Structured Analysis and Design Technique) Warner-Orr method

Second generation (1960–70)
 ADS (Accurately Defined System)
 SOP (Study Organization Plan)
 CPM/PERT (Critical Path Method/
  Program Evaluation Review
  Technique)
 Langefors methodology
 Decision tables technique
 Operations research/management
  science
	Fifth generation (1985–90)
	 ISDOS (Information System Design
	  Optimization System)

at **meetings.** The design sessions themselves are often a forum for data collection.

Over the years, a number of sophisticated tools and techniques have been developed to assist analysts in the collection of information about a system and in the analysis of this information.[1] Many of these tools are highly complex automated aids that serve design functions as well. As shown in Table 3–2, they are classified by generation, although the distinction from one generation to the next is not as clear-cut as the distinction between generations of hardware. And unlike early generations of hardware, early systems analysis and design techniques have not become obsolete over time but continue to be used.

Accurately Defined System (ADS), one of the data collection tools on the list, was designed by National Cash Register Corporation (NCR). It uses forms for collecting information on outputs, inputs, data files, computations, and systems logic. Gathering information with ADS is time consuming and costly. But the method is a systematic and thorough way to collect data needed to analyze bottleneck areas and to identify where change can bring added efficiency and effectiveness to processing. ADS provides the development team with information on which to base the design of a new system.

Process charts, flowcharts, data flow diagrams, and decision tables are additional instruments of data collection that are commonly used. An example of a process chart to analyze an accounts receivable procedure is shown in Figure 3–4. Each step is detailed, the time taken is recorded, and the volume handled is noted. An analysis of the chart will identify redundant steps and problems, helping the team to focus on areas in processing where improvements need to be made. For example, according to the chart, it takes from 40 to 120 hours (with an average of 60 hours) for errors to be corrected (Number 9). This will, in all likelihood, signal to the analyst that error correction procedures need revision. Perhaps a program can be written to speed error correction; perhaps revised control of data entry and data validation will reduce the occurrence of errors and, as a result, improve processing. Experienced analysts know how much time is reasonable for each processing activity. By studying process charts, they can determine where system weaknesses lie.

On the basis of collected data, user requirements are identified at each organizational level. (Refer back to Figure 3–3.) As mentioned earlier, meetings will be held with top management (3), supervisors (4), and operational personnel (6). At these meetings, objectives for the new system (what the user wishes to accomplish) will be defined. So will policies (guidelines that determine the course of action for accomplish-

---

[1]For an excellent survey of such approaches, see G. B. Davis, "Strategies for Information Requirements Determination," *Systems Journal*, vol. 21, no. 1 (1982), pp. 4–30.

Figure 3–4   **An example of a process chart**

PROCESS CHART WORK SHEET

Please read instructions on other side before completing this form.

Job: Accounts Receivables   Page __1__ of __1__

Charted by: __J. Williams__   Date: __02-05-87__

Procedure **Method**

Number	Details of Step	Delay / Operation / Transportation / Storage / Check/Control	Time / Required	Number	Comment
1	Wait for daily receipts and log them	○ ● □ △ ▽	2-3-4 h		
2	Wait for batch	● ○ □ △ ▽	2-3-4 d		
3	Glance verification	○ ○ □ △ ▽	50-90-120 m		
4	Corrections made	○ ● □ △ ▽	2-4-7 h		
5	Data entry	○ ● □ △ ▽	2-3-4 h		
6	Run edit program	○ ○ □ △ ▽	1-2-8 h		times at an
7	Return diagnostics to A/R	○ ○ ■ △ ▽	1-2-4 h		average
8	Errors await correction	● ○ □ △ ▽	1-4-16 h		
9	Correct errors	○ ● □ △ ▽	40-60-120 m		
10	When no errors, logged	○ ● □ △ ▽	5-10-12 m		
11	Records stored	○ ○ □ △ ▽	5-8-10 m		
12	Payment sent to bank	○ ● □ △ ▽	4-8-10 m		
13	Enroute to bank	○ ○ ■ △ ▽	4-4-8 hrs		
14		○ ○ □ △ ▽			
15		○ ○ □ △ ▽			
16		○ ○ □ △ ▽			
		○ ○ □ △ ▽			

Abbreviations used   d = days   h = hours   m = minutes

ing the objectives) and constraints. Theoretically, a study of stated policies should help clarify objectives. However, policy manuals are often outdated.

Frequently, unstated preferences, priority rankings, biases, and prejudices determine the success or failure of systems. The team should be sensitive to human factors and the political environment[2] in which the new system will operate. It should also be aware of economic, financial, and technological constraints.

---

[2]For an excellent discussion of political factors, see Richard K. Lindren, "Politics and System Justification," *Computerworld*, vol. 17, no. 2 (January 1983), pp. ID/1–8.

Determining performance specifications. The next step is to define user requirements in operational terms (7). That is, performance specifications should be listed in detail. These include:

- Output: Content, format, quantity, availability, response time, frequency, distribution list, retention.
- Processing; Decision rules, accuracy, significance of results, current and future capacity.
- Input source: Media, procedures, validity checks.
- Security: Input (organization, maintenance, decision rules), output (nature of access, list of those allowed access, control of access, identification), hardware, software, audit (general or specific, internal or external).
- Backup system: Items needing backup, nature of backup procedures, and maintenance.

Documentation of these specifications (8) should be completed soon after the specification sessions take place, while memories of events are still fresh. The documentation should include a record of discussions that has been verified by participants. Definitions of terms and the assumptions of the team should be included.

Approval procedures. When the system requirements statement has been completed and documented, the statement should be checked for factual and statistical accuracy (9). A check should also be made to ensure that the proposed system meets stated objectives. Then a series of approval decisions should be made. If users and systems personnel who participated in the project are satisfied (10—Exit Yes), management approval is sought (11). If management decides to implement the project (12—Exit Yes), documentation on system specifications will be finalized (13). Design of the system follows.

If dissatisfaction exists, recycling may be initiated (14—Exit Yes to 3, 4, 6, and 7) or the project is terminated (14—Exit No). Termination is not always a reflection on the quality of work of the development team. Altered environmental conditions—such as the unavailability of expected resources or changes in management priorities—may disallow project completion.

Design of the system

In the next stage of system development, system design (Box 7, Figure 3–1), two basic strategies can be used: **bottom-up design** or **top-down design**. In the bottom-up approach, the need for subsystems is identified and the modules are designed, tested as independent units, and then integrated into a total system. This approach is evolutionary in nature. For example, operational modules of transactions files can be designed first, and then modules for updating, control, and planning can be added as the need develops.

The top-down approach, also called **structured design,** starts by defining the goals of the organization. Then the means to achieve these goals is outlined, actions necessary to implement the means are prescribed, and finally the information needed for these actions is deter-

Figure 3–5   **Flowchart illustrating partial payroll program logic**

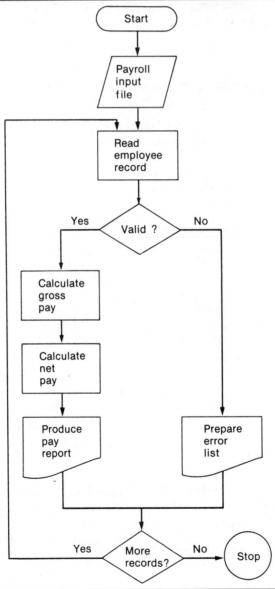

mined. This approach is one of elaboration and clarification. The skeletal version of the new system is designed before the system is subdivided into manageable components for development.

A decision on which of these two design approaches to use is made by the development team when the design phase begins. The top-down approach is generally favored.

As mentioned earlier in this chapter, a number of tools and techniques of analysis and design assist the development team in their design responsibilities. For example, **flowcharts** are one way of preparing a graphical representation of procedures or computer programs leading to problem solutions. (See Figure 3–5 for a sample flowchart.) Using symbols to represent data flow and operations, a flowchart diagrams the series of events that will achieve processing objectives. Such charts help the analyst organize the flow of data within a system. They also document design ideas on flow and convey these ideas to others working on the development project. (In large flowcharts, arrows may crisscross. These diagrams can be confusing to persons attempting to follow the flow of control, and the flowcharts can be difficult to redraw when changes in systems design occur during development.)

Another design tool is **structured English,** a subset of the English language that can be used to express systems logic. **Pseudocode,** an arbitrary code independent of hardware, serves the same purpose. It is a further formalization of structured English, often using IF–THEN–ELSE statements.

Analysts can also formulate decision tables that list conditions to be considered in the description of a problem together with actions to be taken for each set of conditions. Such tables help the analyst think through a problem and help express the problem in logical rules in a tabular format. (Decision tables were explained earlier in this chapter. See Table 3–1.) A similar design technique, but one that uses a tree structure instead of a table to show actions for a given set of conditions, is a **decision tree.** (See Figure 3–6 for a pseudocode and decision tree example.)

A **HIPO** (Hierarchy plus Input-Process-Output) **chart,** which is similar to process-oriented flowcharts, is still another documentation method often used in systems development. A HIPO package consists of three kinds of diagrams: a visual table of contents, overview diagrams, and detailed HIPO diagrams. This package graphically describes functions from the general to the detail level and helps illustrate the relationship between input, output, and processing as well.

Analysts can also take advantage of recent software technology that permits some automation of systems design. For example, SODA (Systems Optimization and Design Algorithm) generates an optimal design and a set of hardware specifications from a statement of processing requirements. SODA, along with PSL/PSA (Problem Statement Lan-

Figure 3–6   **Sample pseudocode and decision tree illustrating partial payroll program logic**

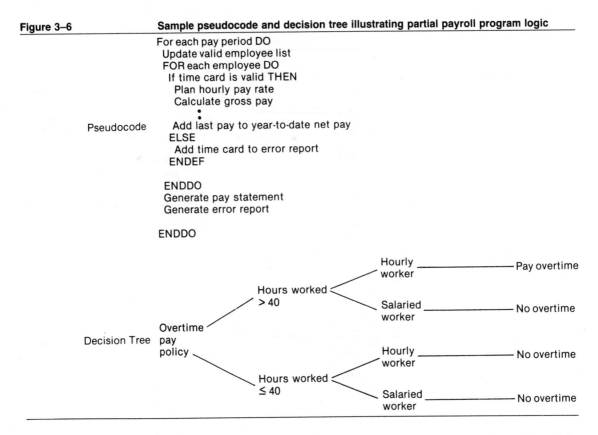

guage/Problem Statement Analyzer), is part of ISDOS (Information System Design and Optimization System), a system under development that attempts to automate the entire process of systems analysis, design, and implementation. Other software aids that facilitate the work of analysts include interactive screen generators, automated documentation, and high-function/high-default procedural languages.

It is beyond the scope of this textbook to explain in detail how these and other design tools and techniques work. But readers should appreciate that a large number of design methodologies, many of them highly complex automated aids, contribute to the design phase of systems development. Figure 3–7 is a network diagram of this design phase. Usually a number of design subcommittees are formed so that responsibility is distributed for the **design activities** described below.

a.   **Operational and hardware specifications.** Although overall operational and hardware specifications are decided when system requirements are determined, technical decisions regarding operational standards and hardware specifications are made at design sessions (Ac-

Figure 3–7   **Network diagram for design stage in system development process**

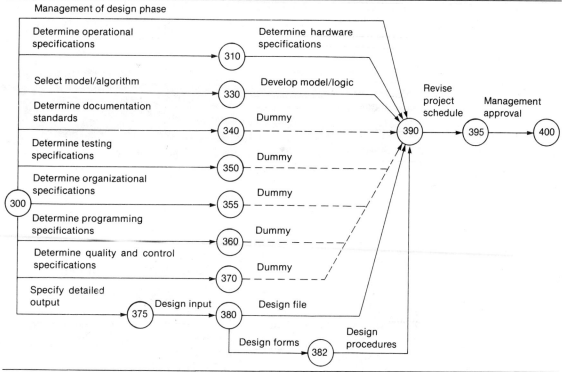

Note: In drawing a network diagram, "dummy" activities are labeled to provide unique numbering of parallel activities. These dummy activities do not use any resources.

tivities 300–310–390). For example, if scanning equipment for reading input data has been recommended, operational specifications prepared in the design phase might be:

Speed	> (more than) 1,600 documents/hour.
Error rate	≦ (less than or equal to) 1/10,000 markings.
Maintenance	≯ (no more than) 24 hours at any one time.
Cost	≯ (no more than) $4,000/year.
Capability	Read markings on document and convert to cards at least 400 markings per document. Document size should be $8\frac{1}{2}$ by 11 inches. Medium darkness of markings will suffice.

The development team generates a document with such detailed specifications for the use of technicians responsible for hardware selection, programming, and testing for the new system.

b. **Model selection and development.** The model required for problem solution has to be selected and developed (300–330–390). In simple applications such as payroll, accounts payable, or reports, flowcharts and decision tables can be used as long as relationships are stated in detail and all decision rules necessary for computation appear. Computer applications such as inventory control, queuing, scheduling, and planning require the development of complex mathematical models.

C. **Design of documentation specifications.** Two types of **documentation** exist: development and project control documentation. The former is a description of the system itself (objectives, characteristics, decision rules) and of choices and decisions made during the development process. The latter concerns project organization (personnel, time, materials, money). In the design of documentation specifications (300–340), the development team must decide:

- What documentation standards to require.
- What documentation manuals need be written.
- What manuals should include.
- How documentation will be tested.
- Who is responsible for documentation preparation.
- When documentation should be complete (time schedule).
- How documentation will be distributed.

d. **Testing of specifications.** Testing specifications to be determined in the design phase (300–350) include choice of testing approach. Some firms will design and test a pilot study. Others favor a parallel or dry run, testing the new system while the old is still in operation. Modular testing and conversion offer still another option.

Systems designers also decide what to test and how to test. They assign personnel to perform tests, identify control points where testing should take place, decide how to evaluate test results, and establish procedures for recording and distributing test results.

e. **Organizational specifications.** New systems may require changes in a firm's organizational structure: personnel may have to be retrained, transferred, hired, or fired. Such changes may result in a broadened (or narrowed) span of control for managers and altered departmental responsibilities. Unfortunately, not all staffing needs are known in the early stages of development. For example, the number and skills of operational personnel required for a new system will depend on equipment selected. But as soon as organizational requirements are determined (300–355), staffing and reorganization should begin because these activities have a long gestation period.

f. **Programming specifications.** Programming specifications (300–360) should include information on the capability, logic, and features of the programs to be written. The programming language(s) to be used should also be stated. In addition, systems designers are responsible for establishing program standards.

9. **Quality and control specifications.**   Quality and control are related because the function of control is to ensure specific levels of quality. During system design, quality standards for each system component are set for input, processing, and output. Control locations and methods of control to ensure that the standards are met are also determined (300–370). Design specifications are sent to the programming group so quality control capabilities can be programmed. They are also sent to personnel responsible for testing the system prior to conversion. (Chapter 8 discusses the subject of quality control at length.)

h. **Input and output specifications.**   In a functional sense, input comes before output. But from a design viewpoint, the order is reversed because input depends on output requirements.

Output.   Output specifications (300–375) should ensure that the new system provides all of the information that users need for current decision making. In addition, output that might be needed for decision making in the future should be projected and included in the specifications, since the incremental cost of producing added information at the design stage is small relative to the cost of redesigning the system at a later date. However, only essential information should be processed. Processing is costly, and data overload can impede users from locating and accessing the information that they need. The development team must, therefore, scrutinize proposed output closely and weigh proposed benefits against costs before determining exactly what output the new system will produce.

The format and content of output will depend upon the user's management style and need for information. The mode of processing (real time versus batch) and the nature of output (print versus terminal or print versus graphic) will also influence output design. Nevertheless, some basic **principles of design** apply to all output:

- Legends, headings, and output formats should be standardized whenever possible. Format consistency is an attribute of user-friendly output. Users feel comfortable with familiar layouts.
- Acronyms, abbreviations, and terms used in the output should be defined. Examples and explanations may serve this purpose, or a glossary can be appended.
- Algorithms and assumptions on which calculations are based should be available to users of the output. This assures correct interpretation of output.
- Output should be hierarchical and logical in presentation so that the user can locate needed information quickly without having to search through all of the data.

- Users' needs should govern the level of aggregation of output.
- Exceptional data should be displayed in a manner that facilitates comparison of actual values with expected values, and the comparison should be in meaningful units. For example, percentage increase or decrease in dollar sales might be more useful than absolute dollar values.
- Psychological and intellectual limitations of users in absorbing output should be taken into consideration when designing how output is displayed, including the amount of output and its format.

Output specifications, once determined, are sent to personnel involved in programming, physical preparation, and testing. The specifications are also needed by team members responsible for input specifications.

Input. In designing input (375–380), the development team must decide what data must be collected in order to produce the output that users desire. Too much data leads to inefficiency in storage and processing. Too little will lead to ineffectiveness because the desired output will not be available.

Once the scope of the data base has been determined, the data must be organized in files and stored so that it can be readily retrieved and used as a shared resource by many managers. This sharing across divisional and departmental lines complicates design specifications because not all users have equal needs for reliability, validity, integrity, and security of data. Should files be integrated horizontally, vertically, and longitudinally? What about backup? How will files be updated? These decisions are part of file design (380–390).

Another aspect of input development is the design of forms for input data collection (380–382).[3] Procedures for preparing input and disseminating output should also be designed and documented in a procedures manual for users (382–390).

Project schedule revision. An additional activity in the design phase is to revise the project schedule (390–395). Once detailed design specifications have been determined, time for completing activities can be estimated more accurately. Also, some activities may have been added that were not anticipated when the schedule was first drafted. This revision is the responsibility of the project manager.

Management approval. The revised schedule, the system definition, and the design specifications documents are presented to management for approval at the conclusion of the design phase (395–400).

---

[3]See Jack D. Harpool, *Business Data Systems* (Dubuque, Iowa: Wm. C. Brown, 1978), pp. 196–205. This is an excellent collection of many types of printed forms. Although the source is from the 1970s, the principles of form design discussed in the text have not become outdated.

Although management may have participated in design sessions, a review of the total design package by management is needed at this stage, and a formal decision must be made on implementation. Lack of approval means either termination of development or recycling those activities designated unsatisfactory. Approval is followed by implementation of the design.

Implementation

A major activity in the **implementation** of a computerized information system (Box 8, Figure 3–1) is programming. The main program(s) must be written (or software packages purchased) so that the system produces the information expected. In addition, programs must be prepared for storing, checking, and maintaining data. Since a fine line exists between programming design and implementation, it is not always possible to state where the latter begins. Some development teams provide so much detail in the design phase that programmers need only translate each design specification into a computer instruction. Other design teams merely specify logic in general terms, giving programmers responsibility for detailing this logic.

Hardware selection is also an implementation activity. Formerly, this activity was delegated to hardware and systems personnel. But today, the responsibility for selection of minis, micros, and input-output equipment is often assumed by operational managers. Site preparation, installation of new equipment, and equipment testing follow. Other implementation activities include:

- File preparation (creating new files or restructuring the old ones).
- Orientation and training programs so that employees are familiar with the new system and know how to operate it.
- Completion of company reorganization when the new system alters the span of control of existing departments (9).

Testing the system

The testing process (10) involves a comparison of desired performance (as stated in the users' requirements specifications) with actual performance. Problems should be identified and corrections made if tolerances are exceeded.

First, tests must be planned. This means test data must be prepared and staff selected to perform the tests. Testing is usually done at four levels. **Component testing** is checking the parts of the system, such as a piece of equipment, the performance of an individual operator, or the effectiveness of a form, procedure, or program. **Functional testing** is at a higher level of aggregation. It measures the performance of related components in a functional subsystem. **Subsystem testing** checks the interrelationships of functions tested individually in the preceding test. Finally, **system testing** checks overall results. This can be done by pilot tests, parallel runs, or simulation.

Figure 3–8   **Levels of testing for a financial system**

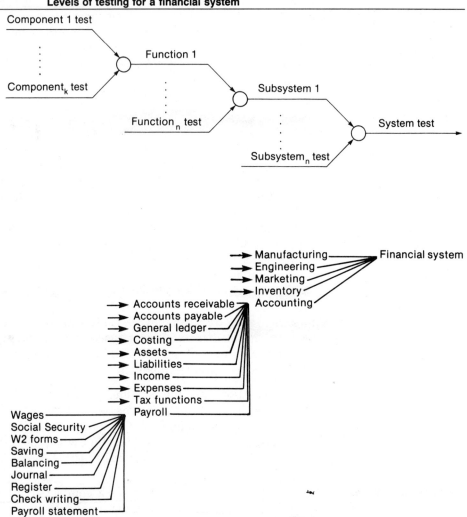

Perhaps a practical example will help make the concept of testing levels meaningful. Figure 3–8 shows how testing of a financial system is subdivided into subsystems. The figure further illustrates how a sample subsystem, accounting, is subdivided into functions for testing. In addition, the components of one of these functions, payroll, are listed. Testing would begin at the component level of this hierarchy, continue to higher levels of aggregation, and end with the total system check.

Recycling.   The testing phase ends when test results at each level are satisfactory. Unsatisfactory testing at any level requires recycling (12), as shown in Figure 3–1. Figure 3–9 illustrates the recycling pro-

Figure 3–9 **Recycling of testing process**

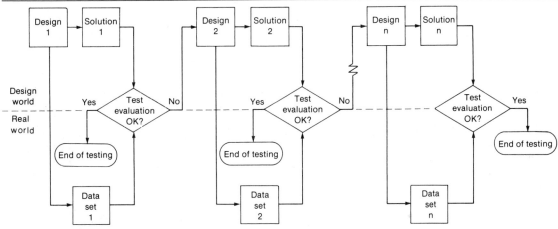

cess. Should Design 1 fail, the system's developers must search for flaws and correct them, then test the revised system design. In complex systems, the value of n (the number of revisions) may be 3 or 4. If n is large, responsibility may lie with users who have failed to adequately specify needs, systems personnel who did a poor design job, or a development process that was not carefully planned and controlled.

The value of n is seldom 1, even with capable personnel. Management should recognize that recycling is a part of the development process and be prepared for it. Formal recycling controls should be established. For example, procedures should be specified for recording the need for change and for documenting the modifications completed. Information about these changes should then be channeled to affected groups.

At the conclusion of favorable testing, the test results should be presented to end-user management. This is the final check to see that the system satisfies goals and objectives. At this stage, a sign-off procedure should formalize user acceptance of the new system.

Conversion

The development process concludes with the cutover, or **conversion**, from the old system to the new (Box 13, Figure 3–1). Of the many approaches to conversion, four of the most common are shown in Figure 3–10. Sequential conversion means that the complete switchover from the old to new system is made on a given date. Sometimes a small group of users runs a pilot system before total conversion takes place. Sometimes, old and new systems are run in parallel for a period of time. Large and complex systems are generally phased in, one module or subsystem at a time. This reduces the workload on personnel responsible for conversion and, at the same time, helps isolate problems

Figure 3–10   **Approaches to conversion**

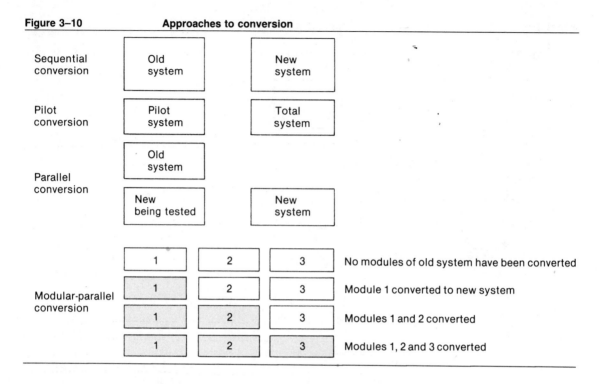

of the new system while minimizing the consequences of potential systems failure.

Evaluating the system development process

Before the development team is dispersed, evaluation of the system development process (Box 15, Figure 3–1) should take place. Mistakes should be identified and analyzed to see why they were made and how they could have been avoided. The purpose of such an analysis is not to exchange accusations and recriminations but to help future development teams. They can learn from the mistakes of others.

The development team should also evaluate the benefits and cost of the new system. It should critically review the need for recycling during the development process. It should identify communication problems that arose and reasons for schedule slippage. The evaluation process should lead to improved procedures and approaches for other projects.

PROTOTYPING

Let us now turn to a relatively new approach to systems development: prototyping. Whereas the system life cycle methodology requires the user to think through requirements before systems design begins, the prototype methodology begins with a "rough" initial system. That is, a model system is built, on the basis of the analyst's experience and perception, as a preliminary solution to the user's problem. This prototype performs only basic functions, using a small representative data base in order to provide information about the system's behavior. The user views how the model works and identifies deficiencies and shortcomings. The prototype is then modified and again presented to the user for comment. This iterative process is repeated until no new requirements are identified by the user. In effect, analysis, design, and implementation (separate steps in the life cycle methodology) are combined into one phase that is repeated several times.

A simple prototype might be nothing more than a mock-up of system outputs. A more elaborate prototype might be a functional throwaway model. The purpose of this model is to help users clarify what it is that they want the system under development to do. A third type of prototyping model, called an evolutionary system, has recently become feasible as a result of advances in fourth-generation software tools. This prototype can be refined into a final system.

Prototypes are sometimes constructed with tools designed for broader tasks, such as application generators or data base management systems. A query language capable of generating quick, ad hoc inquiries is useful as well. Some software packages, commonly called programmer-productivity tools, are also appropriate for the task, including fourth-generation languages supported by documentation generators.

A major benefit of development using the prototyping methodology is that user satisfaction is usually higher than for systems developed using the life cycle methodology. As refinements take place, performance evolves to match user expectations. Another advantage is that prototyping generally lowers the cost of designing systems. Cost reductions can be attributed to a decrease in time spent on analysis and design and to the use of sophisticated software tools rather than standard programming languages. These tools result in an increase in productivity.

However, the result is often a less efficient system than one developed by the life cycle methodology. Project management and project control also become more difficult because:

> The form of the evolving system, the number of revisions to the prototype, and some of the users requirements are unknown at the outset. Lack of explicit planning and control guidelines may bring about a reduction in the discipline needed for proper management (i.e., documentation and testing activities may be bypassed or superficially performed).[4]

---

[4]Maryam Alavi, "An Assessment of the Prototyping Approach to Information Systems Development," *Communications of the ACM*, vol. 27, no. 6 (June 1984), pp. 556–63.

MIXED METHODOLOGY

The system life cycle methodology and prototyping are not mutually exclusive. A mixed methodology may be used that integrates both approaches to systems development. When this occurs, prototyping is generally the strategy to help users clarify their requirements in the initial stages of systems development. Once a prototype is working satisfactorily, the model is used as a basis for writing system specifications. Then the system design and implementation phases of the life cycle follow.

Another development methodology is to design the framework for an information system, then to use prototyping in the development of subsystems.

SOFTWARE TO IMPROVE SYSTEMS DEVELOPMENT

Not surprisingly, computer professionals are turning to the computer itself for help in streamlining the systems development process. As mentioned earlier in this chapter, a number of automated tools for analysis and design are on the market. In addition, the 1980s has been characterized by the introduction of powerful software for program creation. This software contributes in two ways: it makes the work of the programmer easier, and it transfers some of the programming effort to software vendors and end-users.

Software that contributes to systems development falls into eight categories:

- Simple query facilities that let the programmer print stored records or display information in a suitable format.
- Data base user languages that enable programmers to access information that requires data base searching or the joining of multiple files or records.
- Report generators that can be used to extract data from a data base and format it into reports.
- Graphic languages that allow data to be displayed and charted according to programmer (or end-user) specifications.
- Application generators that enable a programmer to incorporate prewritten software modules in programs, or permit generation of an entire application using these modules.
- High-level, nonprocedural programming languages that permit fast applications development because they use a small number of powerful instructions.
- Generalized software (such as input/output subroutines or packages to sort, merge, or maintain files) that directs operations inside the computerized systems. Their use saves the programmer from having to program frequently used operations over and over again.

- Applications software packages, such as spreadsheets, word processing, or specialized programs for applications like inventory control and linear programming. These packages may serve as subsystems of a custom-developed information system and therefore reduce the work of professional programmers, or they may be acquired directly by end-users to avoid systems development by their data processing departments.

Although all of the **computerized aids** listed here can play an important role in systems development, computer professionals are already working on the next major plateau: automation of the entire system-building process. Such automation is classified as a fifth-generation systems development technique. Already some fifth-generation systems have been partially implemented, such as modules of ISDOS (cited earlier in this chapter).

Computerized systems development will reduce elapsed time from the statement of user requirements to an operational system. Many of the tasks analysts and programmers now do manually will be automated and done at computer speeds. It will be less important to get systems requirements right the first time and easier to accommodate change. Automated development will help to reduce the backlog of systems waiting to be developed.

CHOICE OF DESIGN METHODOLOGIES

In deciding whether to use the life cycle methodology or prototyping in developing a new system, both project complexity and project uncertainty should be taken into consideration.[5] Clearly, complexity increases when a large volume of new information is generated by the system for many different types of users and when a great deal of processing effort is required to produce this output. Project uncertainty is high when projects are not well structured, when users are not sure of their requirements, and when the systems development team is not familiar with the user's environment or the tools with which the system will be built.

In general, projects that have a high degree of complexity are good candidates for the life cycle methodology of systems development. They require detailed initial planning and cannot be designed in a few days. A structured approach is needed to integrate subsystems for large systems. It is important to minimize changes after system construction has begun because a single alteration can have so many ramifications in a

---

[5]For more on this subject, see G. B. Davis and M. H. Olson, *Management Information Systems: Conceptual Foundations, Structure, and Development* (New York: McGraw-Hill, 1985) and F. W. McFarlan, "Portfolio Approach to Information Systems," *Harvard Business Review* 59, no. 5 (September–October 1981), pp. 142–50.

Figure 3–11   **Project uncertainty-and-complexity**

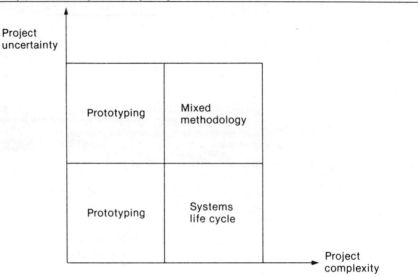

Figure 3–12   **Comparison of work effort using different development methodologies**

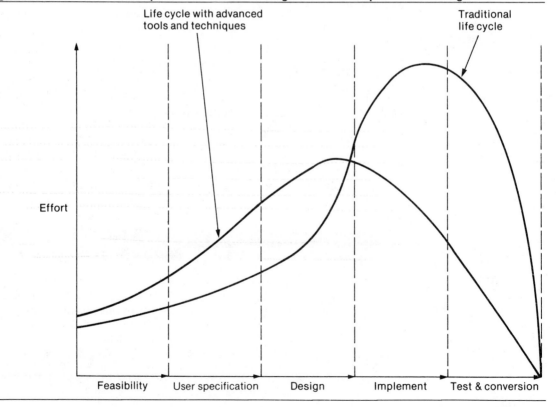

Figure 3–13   **Network diagram of the development of an information system**

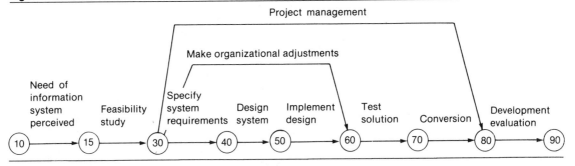

complex system. (A fluid design, user feedback, and change are the essentials of prototyping.)

For projects with a high degree of uncertainty, however, prototyping is a good choice. Its iterative nature is well suited to drawing out systems requirements when a user is unsure which functions should be automated, what types of output would be helpful, or how output might be used. When users are inarticulate about their needs and when developers have no experience in the area, prototyping can facilitate user-analyst communication. It is much easier for users to point out features of an existing model that they dislike or to indicate missing features than it is for them to describe an imaginary system.

For projects with both a high degree of uncertainty and a high degree of complexity, a mixed methodology is advisable. Prototyping might be used at the start of the project to identify user needs. But once users are satisfied with the model, the prototype can be discarded and the actual system developed, using the life cycle methodology.

Figure 3–11 is a matrix that shows the relationship of development methodologies to complexity and uncertainty. Of course, an actual choice of systems development methodology would depend not only on project characteristics but on the characteristics of the environment, the preferences of development personnel and management, and the time and computer specialists available for the development project.

Table 3–3   **Personnel with prime responsibility for development activities**

Development activity	Prime responsibility
Feasibility study	Management*
Determining system requirements	Management*
System design	Development team
Implementation	Development team
Testing system	Development team
Acceptance of tests	Management*
Organizational changes	Management*
Conversion	Development team
Evaluation of development	Mixed (management and team)

*Manager of the relevant application area, or manager directly involved.

Figure 3–14　　　　　　　**Lack of communication in project development**

As envisioned by the development team.

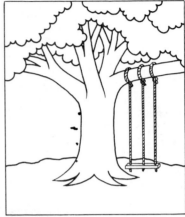

As specified in the product request.

As designed by the senior designer.

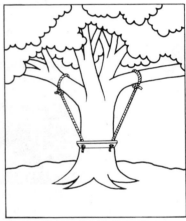

As perceived by the implementor.

As installed.

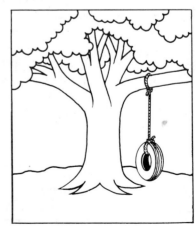

What the customer wanted.

Advanced tools, such as application generators, packages, or non-procedural languages, may be used both for the construction of a prototype and for traditional development activities, although modern techniques change the life cycle somewhat by combining some of the activities and altering the relationship of others. One noticeable effect of advanced technology is the redistribution of development effort during the life cycle, as illustrated in Figure 3–12. Note that less effort is expended by analysts today for implementation, testing, and conversion than in the past, thanks to automated tools, fourth-generation languages, and packages. But the effort required for systems specification and design is greater. This can be attributed, in part, to the fact that information systems today are far more complex than formerly, so that specifying "correct" requirements and design takes longer.

SUMMING UP

The development of an information system using the traditional life cycle methodology consists of the following activities: perception of need, the feasibility study, specification of system requirements, design, implementation, testing, conversion, and development evaluation. Figure 3–13 is a network diagram of these activities. Note that organizational adjustments (30–60) are done in parallel to specification, design, and implementation stages. Project management likewise parallels development activities from the feasibility study through conversion. The reason for this is that each activity needs to be scheduled, to have resources allocated, and to be controlled to see that requirements are met and to ensure that the project is completed within time and budgetary constraints. (Project management is the subject of the next chapter.)

Each numbered activity in Figure 3–13 can be divided into a number of subactivities. For example, Activity 40–50 (design system) consists of selection of the model/algorithm and the determination of specifications for testing, programming, quality, control, output, and so on. Each of these subactivities might be further disaggregated into a more detailed listing of tasks. Network diagrams expanded to four levels of detail listing hundreds of activities are not uncommon.[6]

End-user management has prime responsibility for certain development activities when using the life cycle methodology, as shown in Table 3–3. Activities that are delegated to the development team are also listed in the table. However, throughout the development process,

---

[6]When Western Airlines planned to move its data center, a PERT chart proved essential because timing and interdependencies of move activities were critical. An overall network diagram developed early in the planning phase was eventually expanded to include 1,200 activities. In fact, several detailed layouts had to be created separately for complex activities.

corporate end-user management should work in harmony with technicians to ensure that the system that results meets managerial and organizational needs. Because managers and technicians differ in background, training, and perspective, communication between the two can become strained during systems development. Disagreements may arise over what can be done and what should be done. The cartoon in Figure 3–14 shows what happens when communication during development is lacking. One of the purposes of this chapter (and of this book) is to provide managers and technical personnel with a common vocabulary and basic knowledge of information systems, so that misunderstandings do not arise.

The names given to life cycle development activities described in this chapter may vary from one organization to another. There is no standardization of such terms among authors or industries because of the newness of computerized information systems themselves. Nevertheless, most life cycle development schemas follow the stages of development described in this text, although they may combine several activities, add activities, or use other names. One development sequence is expressed in poetry:

(Canto the first: Proposal)

"An information system," said the president, J.B.,
"Is what this company sorely needs, or so it seems to me:
An automated, integrated system that embraces
All the proper people in all the proper places,
So that the proper people, by communications linked,
Can manage by exception instead of by instinct."

(Canto the second: Feasibility study)

They called in the consultants then, to see what they could see
And to tell them how to optimize their use of EDP.
The consultants studied hard and long (their fee for this was sizable)
And concluded that an information system was quite feasible.
"Such a system," they repeated, "will not only give you speed,
It will give you whole new kinds of information that you need."

(Canto the third: Installation)

So an information system was developed and installed,
And all the proper people were properly enthralled.
They thought of all the many kinds of facts it could transmit
And predicted higher profits would indeed result from it.
They agreed the information that it would communicate
Would never be too little, and would never be too late.

(Canto the last: Output)

Yet when the system went on line, there was no great hurrah,
For it soon became apparent that it had one fatal flaw:

Though the system functioned perfectly, it couldn't quite atone
For the information it revealed—which was better left unknown.[7]

The system life cycle is not the only development methodology.
Prototyping, a methodology that includes the development of a tentative
version of a system that is subsequently refined through user feedback
to evolve into a final model, has received considerable attention lately.[8]
Also possible is a mixed development methodology, which combines
the system life cycle approach with prototyping. Even the traditional
approach to applications development is being altered by advanced
tools and techniques for systems analysis and design.[9]

CASE: DEVELOPMENT OF THE SABRE SYSTEM

American Airlines recognized the need for a computerized information system in 1954. The company was finding it increasingly difficult to maintain accurate and timely records on passengers manually.
The conventional system of assigning agents quotas for seats was unsatisfactory. When local agents sold out their seat allotments, passengers were often lost to the airline as a result of delays in locating a
vacancy held by an agent in another part of the country. Lost revenues
resulted.

At the time the specifications for the system were drawn up, the
response time requirements seemed technologically infeasible. It actually took 10 years of development and more than $30 million to make
the desired computerized central reservation system operational. The
SABRE system is in use today, although it has been modified considerably since it was put into service.

SABRE includes control as well as reservation functions. For example, the system will not accept incorrect data, such as incomplete
input or a code for a nonexistent flight. Reservation information is used
to provide caterers with estimates of the number of meals to be prepared;

---

[7]Marilyn Driscoll, "An Information System," *Arthur Young Journal*, Winter 1968, p.
318.

[8]For a synthesis of recent articles about prototyping in contrast to the more traditional
system life cycle approach to applications development, see R. N. Burns and A. R. Dennis,
"Selecting the Appropriate Application Development Methodology," *Data Base*, vol. 17,
no. 1 (Fall 1985), pp. 19–23.

[9]For a discussion of the relationship of program maintainability to systems development methodology, see Tor Guimaraes, "A Study of Application Program Development
Techniques," *Communications of the ACM*, vol. 28, no. 5 (May 1985), pp. 494–99.

arrival and departure desks receive passenger lists; and flight control is given weight and loading information that also guides management in assigning crew and maintenance personnel. Furthermore, the system keeps accounts of funds receivable for each day, month, flight, and route. SABRE processes all flight information received from dispatch centers, adjusting scheduled flights and stops as well.

SABRE was developed using the life cycle approach. The chronology of development was as follows:

Preliminary study	1954–1958
Precontractual analysis	1958–1959
Contract	1959
Functional requirements	1960–1962
Program specifications	1960–1962
Program coding	1961–1964
Single-path testing	1961 on
Equipment arrival	January 1962
Package testing	1961–1962
Final checkout	October–December 1962
Test-city parallel operation	December 1962–March 1963
First firm cutover	April 1963
Several more cities cutover	May 1963
Further cutover delayed pending addition of memory to 7090	June–November 1963
Remainder of American cities added to system	November 1963–December 1964

Source: R. W. Parker, "The SABRE System," *Datamation,* vol. 11, no. 9 (September 1965), p. 52.

SABRE is a museum piece today, both literally and figuratively. (A Washington, D.C., museum has a display on SABRE.) The experience gained from this "first" large-scale, real-time commercial information system has contributed to the development of the more advanced reservation systems in current use among airlines, hotels, car rentals, and theaters.

Questions

1. What SABRE development activities are uncommon? Has the development cycle changed greatly in the last 35 years?
2. Why did SABRE's development cycle take so long and cost so much?
3. Suppose a new airline wishes to have a computerized reservation system. Will it cost the airline as much time and money as the SABRE system cost American Airlines? Explain.

CASE: A PROTOTYPING PROJECT AT SUPERIOR OIL

Companies that explore for oil require both steel casing to keep the well bore clear during drilling and tubing to deliver the oil from its reservoir within the earth to a surface storage tank. Since the inventory of casing and tubing (called tubular goods) for a single 18,000-foot well is valued at about $7 million, a large inventory of tubular goods ties up considerable capital. However, a procurement lead time of nine months to a year for tubular goods is common in tight supply periods. A company cannot afford low stocks at a time when drilling activity increases in response to favorable market conditions.

Superior Oil Company, a Texas firm, decided it needed to improve its purchasing system for materials in order to be more responsive to the dynamics of oil pricing and consequent drilling activity. They developed a new information system for both purchase order writing and materials control. For the latter, rapid prototyping software was used to prepare screens to handle keyboard data input and file inquiry. Then users were asked to evaluate the screens and identify missing features. Within a day, the draft set of screens was revised to include the new requirements that the users uncovered. The screens eventually evolved into the final operational screens. In other words, the design-program-implement cycle was repeated until the prototype satisfied users' needs.

The development project, starting with analysis, took eight months and a total labor investment of $27\frac{1}{2}$ work-months. (This included $15\frac{1}{2}$ work-months of MIS staff.) Here is how the time was spent:

Analysis	End of May to mid-August.
Design	End of June to end of August.
Programming	Mid-August to end of October.
Implementation	End of October to end of December.
Enhancement and correction	Mid-November to end of December.

Note that there is an overlap in the development stages as a result of the iterative nature of prototyping. According to management estimates, using the traditional life cycle methodology to develop the same system would have required approximately 20 months.

The speed of prototype development contributed to considerable savings for the firm. For example, in the first 11 months of operation,

Source: T. R. Young, "Superior Prototypes," *Datamation*, vol. 30, no. 7 (May 15, 1984), pp. 152–56.

the new system contributed directly to an inventory reduction of $100 million, with more savings to come. (These 11 months would have been spent in systems development, using the life cycle methodology.) Furthermore, the company could take advantage of the new system and therefore ensure the best possible use of tubular goods during a period in which cost reduction pressure on the oil industry was critical.

Questions

1. Why is this a good application for prototyping?
2. What benefits did the firm reap by using the prototype methodology of development over the more traditional life cycle development methodology?
3. Why would the following people at Superior Oil favor prototyping?
    a. Planners.
    b. Corporate management.
    c. Users of the inventory system.
    d. Systems analysts assigned to the project.

STUDY KEYS

Accurately Defined System (ADS)

Bottom-up approach

Component testing

Computerized aids

Conversion

Decision tables

Decision tree

Design activities

Determination of system requirements

Documentation

Economic feasibility

Feasibility study

Financial feasibility

Flowchart

Functional testing

HIPO chart

Implementation

Interviews

Literature search

Meetings

Organizational feasibility

Principles of design

Prototyping

Pseudocode

Structured design

Structured English

Subsystem testing

System life cycle methodology

Systems requirements

System testing

Technological feasibility

Top-down design

DISCUSSION QUESTIONS

1. Do all information systems go through the same stages of development? Explain.
2. Why is the development of an information system a cycle?
3. Describe how you would organize a development team to design and implement an inventory control system for six warehouses and a $30 million volatile inventory. Would the team composition change if the system were to be online real time (OLRT) as opposed to a batch system?
4. How does prototyping differ from the traditional life cycle development methodology? Under what environmental conditions would you use each?
5. What techniques of development would be most appropriate for:
   a. A large batch system?
   b. A small query-type output subsystem to be used by top management?
   c. Specifying the logic of a system?
   d. Specifying user needs?
   e. Describing the logic of a program?
   In one or two sentences, justify your choices.
6. Is a feasibility study important in the development of an information system? Why? Is it essential for all information systems?
7. Describe the phases of a feasibility study.
8. Describe the difference between economic, financial, organizational, and technological feasibility.
9. What considerations lead to a "GO" decision following the feasibility study? Who makes that decision?
10. Why do some systems fail even though a feasibility study was successfully completed?
11. What information needs to be gathered and synthesized before users' needs can be specified?
12. Empirical studies have shown that the user specification stage is the most difficult developmental stage. Why is this true?
13. Describe the activities in the design phase of systems development.
14. Why is documentation important? What documentation specifications must be designed?
15. List principles of output design. Would these fit all applications, including output for production, marketing, finance, and use of a home personal computer?
16. Why does design of output precede input design?
17. What is the difference between design and implementation in the development of an information system?
18. What role should management play in systems development?
19. Describe the four levels of testing. What are the advantages and disadvantages of testing in this manner?
20. Describe different approaches to conversion.

21. What is the purpose of evaluating the system development process following conversion?
22. What are the limitations and dangers of prototyping? When should prototyping not be used?

SELECTED ANNOTATED BIBLIOGRAPHY

Ahituv, Niv; Michael Hadass; and Seev Neumann. "A Flexible Approach to Information System Development." *MIS Quarterly*, vol. 8, no. 2 (June 1984), pp. 69–78.
The sequence of activities in the systems development life cycle should not be rigid. The article distinguishes between factors derived from user and environmental requirements and those derived from the nature of the development project that might affect the traditional life cycle.

Alavi, Maryam. "An Assessment of the Prototyping Approach to Information Systems Development," *Communications of the ACM*, vol. 27, no. 6 (June 1984), pp. 556–63.
The author recommends the use of prototyping. However, she cautions that it requires a supportive organizational climate along with tools that will facilitate timely response to requests for changes by different users. Prototyping is recommended when user requirements are ambiguous. It requires experimentation and learning before system specifications are finalized.

Ballou, Donald, and Sung W. King. "A Systems Life Cycle for Office Automation." *Information and Management*, vol. 7, no. 6 (June 1984), pp. 111–19.
The authors argue that the existing approaches to development of information systems are not appropriate for an office environment. The unique factors in this environment are discussed and a life cycle methodology addressing these factors is described.

Burns, R. N., and A. R. Dennis. "Selecting the Appropriate Development Methodology." *Data Base*, vol. 17, no. 1 (Fall 1985), pp. 19–23.
A good comparison of the traditional development methodology and prototyping. Factors that should be considered when making a selection of development methodology, including project complexity and uncertainty, are also discussed.

Couger, J. Daniel; Mel A. Colter; and Robert W. Knapp. *Advanced Systems Development/Feasibility Techniques*. New York: John Wiley & Sons, 1982, 506 pp.
An excellent set of readings on techniques of analysis, including optimizing techniques for systems design and implementation. Specifically included are chapters on structured analysis, BSP, PLEXSYS, and PSL/PSA.

Frenkel, Karen A. "Towards Automating the Software-Development Cycle." *Communications of the ACM*, vol. 28, no. 6 (June 1985), pp. 578–89.
Discussed are research attempts to substitute knowledge-based tools and knowledge-intensive methodology for the current labor-intensive processes

in the software development cycle. According to the author, a significant increase in productivity would be achieved.

Hoffnagle, G. F., and W. E. Beregi. "Automating the Software Development Process." *IBM Systems Journal*, vol. 24, no. 12 (1985), pp. 102–19.
A superb article on the entire software development process, although the authors' primary focus is on automating that process. They argue that automation must be evolutionary. They also discuss needed "flexibility, total portability, tool and process integration, as well as process automation for a wide range of methodologies and tools."

Janson, Marius, and L. Douglas Smith. "Prototyping for Systems Development: A Critical Appraisal." *MIS Quarterly*, vol. 9, no. 4 (December 1985), pp. 305–16.
The application of prototyping to engineering systems is reviewed, and this engineering experience is related to the development of information systems.

Martin, James. *An Information Systems Manifesto*. Englewood, N.J.: Prentice-Hall, 1984, 300 pp.
Martin quotes the Random House dictionary definition of manifesto as "a public declaration of intentions, objectives, opinions, or motives." He then spends 13 chapters describing action that should be taken now and 4 chapters on entrepreneurial opportunities, the Japanese threat, and governmental strategies. One chapter (pages 177–94) is on the development life cycle change resulting from new front-end technologies, prototyping, and information centers.

Snyder, Charles. "A Dynamic Systems Development Life-Cycle Approach: A Project Management Information System." *Journal of Management Information Systems*, vol. 2 (Summer 1985), pp. 61–76.
Snyder criticizes traditional systems development life cycles for not providing a mechanism to incorporate change to proposed designs during the development process. He suggests the use of feedback/feedforward to ensure that analysts and users arrive at a fully satisfactory MIS design. An application of this methodology is also described.

Systems Development, vol. 5, no. 10 (October 1985).
This special issue is devoted to the subject of prototyping. It includes six articles presenting a variety of views on the subject. In general, prototyping is recommended but not as a substitute for sound systems design and development. Also, prototyping is not appropriate for large and complex systems.

Wetherbe, James C. "Advanced System Development Techniques Avoid 'Analysis Paralysis.'" *Data Management*, vol. 22, no. 1 (February 1984), pp. 49–52.
Wetherbe recommends the heuristic approach to systems development. Output is first planned, then input defined. The author also recommends the cognitive style of prototyping: the development of a sample system, then its refinement through iteration. According to Wetherbe, advanced techniques, such as prototyping, are particularly useful when getting a project started.

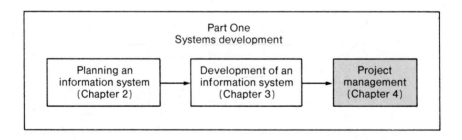

Part One
Systems development

| Planning an information system (Chapter 2) | → | Development of an information system (Chapter 3) | → | Project management (Chapter 4) |

CHAPTER 4

Project management

The genius of good leadership is to leave behind a situation in which common sense, even without the grace of genius, can deal successfully.

Walter Lippmann

A **project** is a temporary assemblage of resources (equipment and personnel) to solve a one-shot problem. Planning, organizing, and controlling these resources is called **project management**. To ensure the development of information systems within time and funding constraints, formal project management is advisable for all except simple systems.

Project management begins with the selection of a project manager and development team. It entails the definition of tasks and activities and the formulation of time estimates for project milestones. Scheduling, resource allocation, amendment control, progress evaluation, and quality control are also responsibilities of a project manager. Each of these subjects will be discussed in this chapter. The use of computerized project management tools will also be covered.

CHARACTERISTICS OF PROJECT MANAGEMENT

What distinguishes project management from ongoing management? Usually, projects have the following characteristics:[1]

- They have a specific objective; for example, the development of a sales order-entry system.
- They must be developed within a specific time period.
- Development must be accomplished within a given budget for capital expenditures and operating expenses.

---

[1]The following discussion is based on George Glaser, "Managing Projects in the Computer Industry," *Computer*, vol. 17, no. 10 (October 1984), p. 46.

- An ad hoc team is assigned to the project. Some members will be part-time, depending on the need for their skills.

From this list, the management of a project appears to be straightforward and to involve fewer elements than ongoing management. Why then, do so many systems development projects fail to meet users' needs? Why are time and cost overruns for development projects so common?

One reason is that project objectives frequently are poorly defined at the start of a system development project. Many users are unable to explain clearly and concisely what computer system is needed and what functions it should perform. Most system failures (60–80 percent) can be traced to an inadequate understanding of user requirements by both analysts and users at the start of the project.

In addition, project deadlines are often unrealistic, arbitrarily imposed by administrative fiat on the basis of external events. Even data processing managers and analysts with experience in systems development sometimes have difficulty estimating realistic time and costs at the start of a project. Generally, schedules need to be readjusted and costs recalculated after a development project is under way and problems are encountered. Furthermore, staffing for a development project is often determined by availability rather than technical competence.

To these complications, one must add the fact that information systems can be highly complex. Many development projects incorporate advanced technology. Many explore "uncharted territory." The detailed steps to be taken cannot be identified at the outset of the project, and progress therefore, cannot be realistically assessed. The development of an information system at the frontiers of knowledge has a high risk of failure.

None of the above factors, in isolation, presents insurmountable obstacles to project management. But taken together, they can sorely test the skill of a project manager when an information system is under development.

SELECTION OF A PROJECT MANAGER

The **project manager**, a key resource in successful project management, is appointed once the development of an information system has been approved by corporate management. (In the life cycle approach to development, this appointment follows management approval of the project (see Box 10, Figure 4–1).

Formerly, choice of a project manager was based on the technical knowledge of candidates. But today, managerial skill—in particular, interactive personnel skills and business experience—is valued as well. It is recognized that a project manager needs to be a leader, able to

Figure 4–1 **Steps leading to project management**

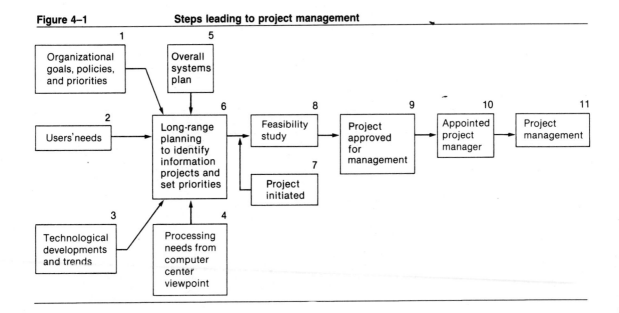

direct and motivate a team chosen from different functional departments and status levels within the organization. A project manager must be able to coordinate the various aspects of development and to interact with users, often in the role of counselor. After all, the real economic value of a computer system depends upon its effectiveness in meeting user needs. Both technical and managerial direction are needed to make that happen.[2]

Project managers generally report to a special committee appointed by corporate management to oversee the project. This committee may have a variety of names: for example, Project Review Committee, Steering Committee, or User and Administrative Committee. It's function is to assist the project manager in interpreting the firm's policies, to clarify users' needs, and to monitor the progress of the project.

The project manager will also have input and support from user management, the data base administrator, and the computer center director in a staff relationship, as illustrated in Figure 4–2. User representatives and technical personnel will have a line relationship. Consultants and accounting department representatives assigned to the project

---

[2]For large, complex information systems, both a project director and a project manager may be appointed. In such cases, the director might assume total project responsibility, make major decisions, set priorities, and provide the motivation for successful project completion. The project manager, on the other hand, would be responsible for day-to-day activities, monitor and report on progress, and keep the project moving. See Kenneth D. Meyers, "Total Project Planning," *Datamation*, vol. 30, no. 4 (April 1, 1984), p. 144.

Figure 4–2   **Project organization**

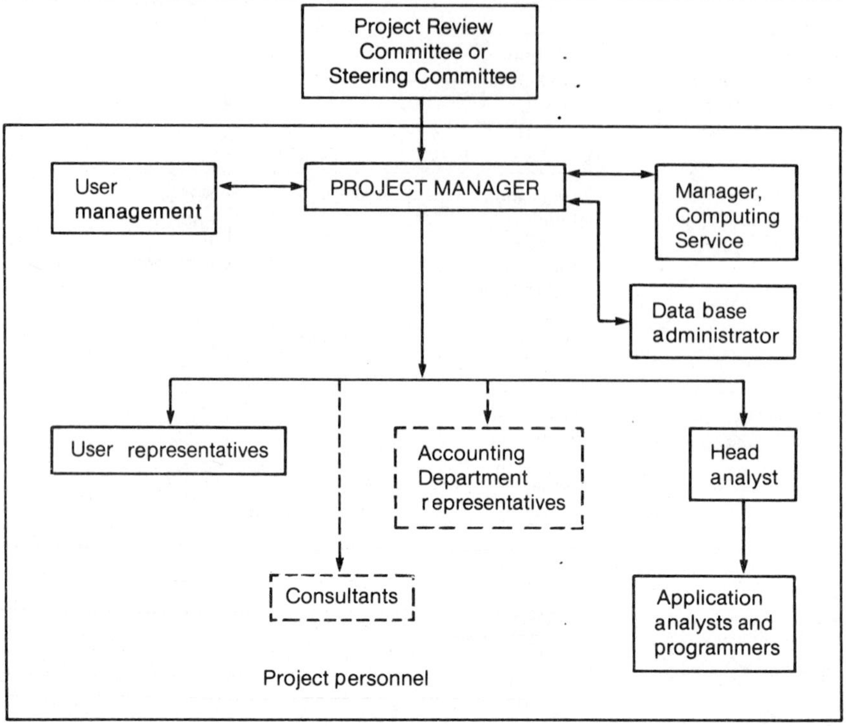

```
                        ┌─────────────────────┐
                        │   Project Review    │
                        │   Committee or      │
                        │  Steering Committee │
                        └─────────────────────┘
```

Project personnel

may also fall in this latter category. Typically, 70 percent or more of the total resources needed for a project must be within the project manager's direct control for a successful project.

Project managers plan and staff the project, analyze risk, monitor progress, adjust schedules, report project status, control budgets and salaries, prepare performance appraisals, and manage changes. They also must motivate, communicate, sell, counsel, delegate, and interact with users (for whom the system is being developed), corporate management, and project personnel. Unfortunately, few project managers receive formal training in project management. Too often, they must acquire needed project management skills on the job.

TEAM STRUCTURE

One of the first acts of a project manager is to structure the project development team. Several approaches to the organization of such teams are possible: organization by function, project organization, and matrix organization.

Functional organization generally keeps traditional line-staff relationships, with a vertical flow of authority and responsibility. For some projects, this type of organization does not work well, because the projects require the cooperation and use of resources from many line units. In fact:

> The essence of project management is that it cuts across, and in a sense conflicts with the natural organization structure. . . . Because a project usually requires decisions and actions from a number of functional areas at once, the main inter-dependencies and the main flow of information in a project are not vertical but lateral . . . . Projects are characterized by exceptionally strong lateral working relationships, requiring closely related activity and decisions by many individuals in different functional departments.[3]

Project organization is the creation of a unit with responsibility for all aspects of project development. In this schema, professional, technical, and administrative staff are hired for the duration of the project. When systems development projects are organized in this manner, serious problems can arise in attracting competent personnel. Many computer professionals are unwilling to join projects that offer no job security, and they dislike jobs of this nature because of a fluctuating workload.

A **matrix organization** combines functional and project approaches to project management. The staff is "borrowed" from functional divisions. In the case of a development team, members might be drawn from accounting, marketing, operations research, and data processing departments. Which employees are borrowed is negotiated by the project manager with functional department heads. The choice is usually based on the availability of personnel and the qualifications demanded by the project. Sometimes, department heads are reluctant to release competent personnel. However, most recognize that having staff members assigned to the development team can be advantageous to them. Departmental interests are protected by having staff representatives on the team, and staff experience in the development process will be beneficial when future information systems for the department are planned.

One problem with matrix organization is that project members have two bosses. They are responsible to the project manager for work assignments, yet their permanent supervisors retain jurisdiction over personnel matters such as salary and promotions. The two bosses may clash in values and objectives, with the project member caught in between. Such potentially explosive situations can be defused if, before

[3]M. Stewart, "Making Project Management Work," in *Systems Organizations, Analysis Management: A Book of Readings*, ed. D. I. Cleland and W. R. King (New York: McGraw-Hill, 1969), pp. 295–96.

the team is constituted, ground rules are negotiated between the project manager and functional heads regarding shared authority and responsibility over project members.

In summary, a matrix organization is advantageous because it:

- Allows a project manager to cut across vertical organizational divisions.
- Involves functional departments and is responsive to their needs because representatives are on the project staff.
- Has access to the resources in all functional departments (on a negotiated basis).
- Provides a "home" for project personnel after the completion of the project.
- Does not permanently disrupt organizational subgroupings or the continuity of seniority, fringe benefits, and so on.

Table 4–1   **A sample matrix organization of project teams**

Personnel assigned	Project					
	B19	B20	P5	P7	...	S3 ...
User Representatives Manufacturing Dept. Smith	X		X			X
Rogers		X	X			
Marketing Dept.		X				
Finance Williams		X	X			
Baker	X		X			X
R&D Dept.						X
Support Personnel Accounting/Finance	X		X	X		X
Lead Analysts Adams			X			
Campbell	X					X
Robinson				X		
Programmers	X	X	X	X		X
Other: Consultants		X				

Figure 4–3   **Choice of project organization**

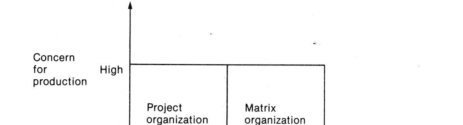

An example of matrix organization shown in Table 4–1 illustrates the concept that both individuals and departments may be assigned to development teams and may participate in several projects simultaneously.

Management style may be one factor in the choice of project organization. As shown in Figure 4–3, a functional organization is appropriate when people are the primary concern of a project manager. Project organization is appropriate when more importance is placed on production than on people. A matrix organization balances high concern for both people and production.

There is much anecdotal material on teams but little hard data identifying environmental variables that affect team performance. This section has suggested some factors in team structure that affect development efforts, but wide disagreement exists on what makes projects, especially programming projects, successful.

TEAM SIZE

Once team structure is decided, team members are appointed. A decision on optimal team size has to be made at this juncture. This problem plagued operations research workers as far back as the 1940s and 50s and still haunts projects. Studies in group dynamics have suggested that an optimal team size is 5–7 members and that as group size increases, job satisfaction drops, with absenteeism and turnover increasing. But some computer development projects are far too complex to have such small teams. The design of software for IBM's System 360, for example, required 5,000 man-years for completion. Teams need to be large enough to complete projects within a reasonable time frame. And should completion by a specific date be a constraint, a large rather than small team may be needed in order to have sufficient work-days of effort to complete the project on time.

Regardless of size, teams should have a balance of theoreticians and practitioners, idealists and realists, scientists and humanists, and generalists and specialists. The problem with small development teams is that they may be unable to achieve such a balance. As teams enlarge, however, many agree with the humor of Northcote Parkinson's third law that states that expansion means complexity, and complexity decay. Certainly, crosscurrents increase as teams grow in size. Members must spend more and more of their time communicating with one another. The following formula can be used to compute the possible number of interactions (I), assuming that there is a two-way interaction between each and every member:

$$I = \frac{K\,(K-1)}{2}$$

where K = number of persons on the team.

Figure 4–4 shows a curve plotted according to this formula. One can see from this curve that the number of potential interchanges increases

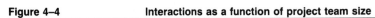

Figure 4–4   **Interactions as a function of project team size**

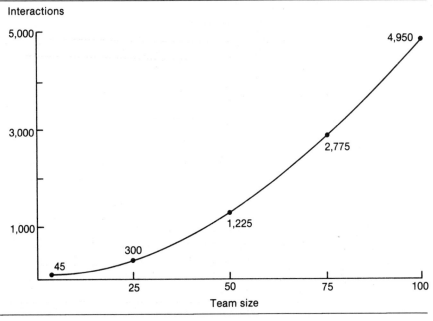

Interactions

nonlinearly as teams enlarge.[4] Dividing a large team into small work groups may not solve the problem, because coordination of these groups requires additional levels of management, thereby increasing the number of superior-subordinate relationships.

Empirical research on the effect of the curve in Figure 4–4 confirms Fried's law: there is an inverse relationship between effectiveness (production) and group size in complex technical projects (programming, electronic design, engineering, etc.). As Louis Fried points out, people organized into groups are not productive 100 percent of the time. Over an extended period of time, perhaps 25 percent of the workweek is spent on vacations, sick leave, coffee breaks, organizational meetings, training, and so on. Another 10 percent of the time may be unproductive because of "idle" time: time waiting for others to complete tasks that are essential to ongoing projects, time lost as a result of poor scheduling, or simple daydreaming. Add to these figures the time spent on intergroup communication. Fried estimates that in groups of 10, individuals spend about 10 percent of their time communicating with others. As size increases, he adds .01 percent more time for each member of the group over 10.

On the basis of the above figures, an estimated 55 percent of each calendar workweek is productive for a group of 10. For larger groups, productivity can be calculated by the formula:

$$P_1 = K\left(T\left[.55 - .0001\left\{\frac{K(K-1)}{2}\right\}\right]\right)$$

where

P_1 = Productive time.
T = Individual employee hours per work period.
K = The number of people in the group.

According to this formula, when working a 40-hour week, the productivity of a team of 94 is less than that of a team of 20.[5] Productivity peaks with a team size of 70. Figure 4–5 shows a productivity curve based on Fried's formula and demonstrates the fallacy in the reasoning that if the life cycle of development is 200 man-years, then 100 persons will take 2 years, or 200 persons 1 year.[6]

Another factor to take into consideration when organizing a devel-

---

[4]For more on teams, see Philip C. Semprevivo, *Teams in Information Systems Development* (New York: Yourdon, 1980), 130 pp.

[5]Frederick Brooks, the "father" and project manager of the IBM 360 system, reaches much the same conclusion. His curve of time versus number of workers for tasks with complex relationships shows that the time spent on the project increases as the number of people working on it increases. See Frederick P. Brooks, *The Mythical Man-Month* (Reading, Mass.: Addison-Wesley Publishing, 1975), p. 19.

[6]For more details on this subject, see Louis Fried, *Practical Data Processing Management* (Reston, Va.: Reston Publishing, 1979), pp. 142–46.

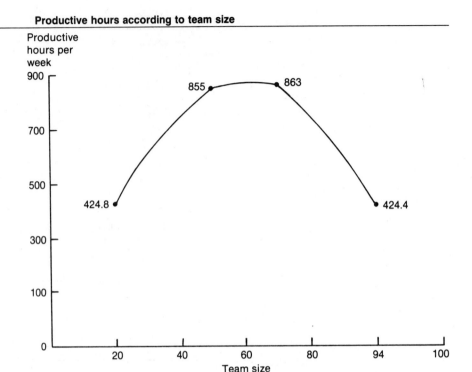

Figure 4–5   **Productive hours according to team size**

opment team is that certain project activities during systems development have to be completed before others can begin. For example, hardware must be acquired and installed before the test phase can begin. The number of persons assigned to testing cannot hasten project completion if hardware delivery is delayed.

It is also a generally accepted axiom that adding people to late projects only tends to make the project later.[7] In addition, crash development teams also have a high cost as a result of lower productivity, overtime, overcrowding, and so on. Figure 4–6 shows the relationship of cost and efficiency to time of completion, based on past experience with projects.

Once team size is determined, working groups of programmers, analysts, and users can be organized for specific tasks. The exact organization and size of each group will depend on the project. For programming teams, some project managers organize programmers under a chief programmer who is the market designer and architect of the system, who supervises structured walkthroughs and formal reviews of design and coding. This type of organization reportedly achieves

---

[7]This axiom is attributed to Frederick Brooks, mentioned in footnote 5.

Figure 4–6   **Project cost as a function of time for completion**

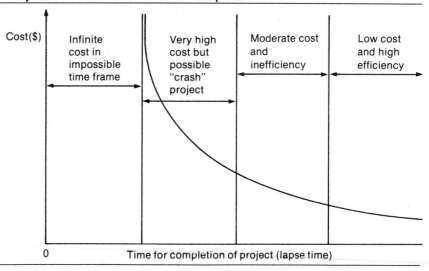

high technical standards and produces programs that are simple, obvious, and transparent. The team effort minimizes problems with egocentric programmers who want to save a millisecond here, an instruction there to prove their brilliance. A more democratic approach rotates leadership according to the problem at hand; opponents of this system call it "structured anomaly."

PROJECT PLAN

When a project is launched, the project manager divides the work into phases and the phases into tasks. One way to get started is to identify project **milestones** representing significant progress toward the project's objectives. These milestones can then be used to identify tasks that precede and follow them.

Next, the skills needed for each task are identified and the effort is calculated for task completion, based on the expected performance of available staff. The cost of completing each task (or group of tasks) should then be estimated by the individual or group responsible for completing it.

Task definition is the basis of a detailed **project plan**, which specifies what activities need to be completed and in what order. It states what end product is expected, designates which individuals (or departments) are responsible, and estimates "time to complete" and project cost.

The plan should be as comprehensive as possible, since schedules and budgets are based on it. It is also used in tracking project progress. The omission of tasks in the plan is a common cause of project time and cost overruns. Frequently overlooked or underestimated are project orientation, training, validation and review, production of reports, and correction of errors and omissions. It is wise to add a contingency factor to allow for unexpected tasks or amended user requirements during the course of the project.

When making the project plan, useful information can be gleaned from project control records of past projects. Such records may provide information on how long it took to produce program specifications, ratios of elapsed time to expended effort for different activities, and data on programmer productivity related to line of code. Many project managers keep a day-to-day log, a mine of information on systems development events, problems, and decisions that can serve as a useful reference when other projects are being planned.

SCHEDULING

On the basis of the system plan, a project schedule is prepared and resources are assigned to each activity. Some scheduling is straightforward sequencing, but when parallel activities are scheduled, care must be taken to ensure that adequate resources are available. For example, if two software activities are scheduled for simultaneous development, will an adequate number of programmers be available? The schedule should also keep employees working, avoiding lulls with idle personnel. Minimizing peaks and troughs of worker demand is known as **manpower leveling**. Such leveling does not mean merely juggling numbers (employees in the aggregate), because special skills may be needed for a given task. It does no good to assign a programmer who knows only FORTRAN to a project to be written in COBOL.

Project time completion and total project cost are recalculated once scheduling is completed, to see if they fit within the time/cost constraints in the project authorization document. If not, rescheduling is necessary, dropping desired but not essential activities and reshuffling resources. In some cases, the constraints themselves may be reviewed and revised.

PLANNING TOOLS[8]

A number of management tools are available to assist a project manager in resource and time analysis during the planning phase. The

[8]This section introduces planning tools but does not discuss them in depth. The interested reader should turn to books on operations research and management science for more information. One detailed text on the application of the critical path method (CPM) and program evaluation review technique (PERT) to project management is H. W. Handy and K. M. Hussain, *Network Analysis for Educational Management* (Englewood Cliffs, N.J.: Prentice-Hall, 1969), 186 pp.

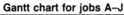

Figure 4–7 **Gantt chart for jobs A–J**

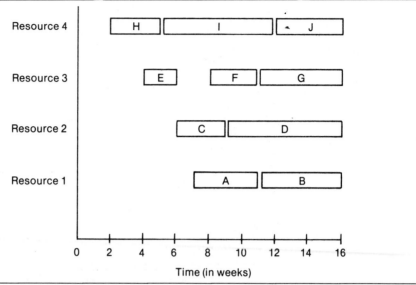

simplest is a **Gantt chart**, where every activity is represented by a horizontal bar on a time scale, as illustrated in Figure 4–7. A major limitation of a Gantt chart is that this graphic representation of a time-line cannot answer questions regarding activity interrelationships. For example, if one activity is delayed, there is no way of telling from the chart which other activity or activities would be affected.

A path or network diagram may be used for this purpose. These diagrams show interrelationships, clearly establishing which activities must be completed before others can begin. The **critical path** (that is, the set of activities where delay retards the entire project) can also be calculated. This information is needed to determine how long the project will take. For simple tasks, path and network diagrams can be drawn by hand, as illustrated in Figure 4–8. For complex projects, however, a manual drawing is a major undertaking. Fortunately, we now have software tools and high-speed flatbed or drum plotters able to produce a wide variety of graphic outputs showing time and sequence involving thousands of activities.

For example, **CPM (Critical Path Method)** is a scheduling technique for which computer programs now exist. This technique is commonly used in project management when the length of time for each activity's completion is known for certain. When times can only be estimated, **PERT (Program Evaluation Review Technique)** can be applied. It allows for three types of time estimates; optimistic time, most likely time, and pessimistic time. PERT is more appropriate than CPM for project

Figure 4–8   **Path diagram***

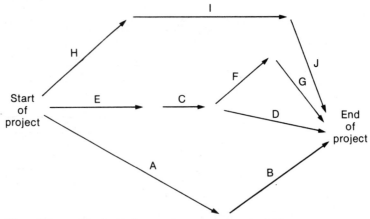

*Also called an activity diagram because the arrows represent activities.

management of information systems because the time needed for development activities is seldom known with certainty.

Another computerized scheduling technique frequently used in systems development projects is the **Graphic Evaluation Review Technique (GERT)**. The advantage of GERT is that it allows looping. A loop is exemplified when three activities (A,B, and C) must be completed before another (D) is initiated, but A must be done before B, B before C, and C before A, as depicted in Figure 4–9. Such loops frequently occur in information systems development. GERT also allows alternative paths (either E or F in Figure 4–9), whereas PERT conventions require that all activities be performed in a set sequence. That is, PERT allows "AND" relationships, whereas using GERT, one can specify the probability of alternative paths in an "OR" relationship (such as E or F) in addition to the "AND" relationship.

Another advantage of GERT is that the time of project completion is calculated with probability (p) associations. For example, the completion time might be 20 weeks with p = 0.6 and 26 weeks with p = 0.8.

GERT has disadvantages, however. It requires more data than PERT

Figure 4–9   **Illustration of GERT**

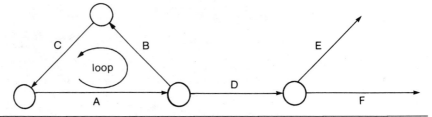

(data on probabilities, which may be expensive to collect), and GERT computer programs are not readily available. Vendors more commonly supply computer programs for PERT, many with refinements such as optimization (of cost and time) and both personnel and equipment leveling. As a result, PERT is more often used for information systems development. It is perfectly adequate as long as the user makes allowances for its limitations. For example, when calculating time estimates, the PERT user should include time estimates for possible looping.

Gantt, PERT, and CPM software for mainframes and minis has been available for some time. Now, software packages with project management capabilities are available for personal computers and are easy to learn and use. Although less powerful than project management software for mainframes, such packages break down projects into tasks, schedule tasks, assign resources, and provide information for time and cost control.

Each vendor that produces planning software has a different approach to solving project management problems. For example, one package may calculate the critical path of a project, listing constraints on the network. Another may show alternative paths should one or more constraints be relaxed. Some programs optimize personnel loading or cost. Others allow managers to ask "what-if" questions in testing how a change in the sequence of activities or a change in time estimates might affect the ultimate cost of the project and date of completion. Some software makes calculations interactively, showing the consequences for each of many alternatives.

One recent buyer's guide for project management software lists 58 different programs that run on PCs and 49 different software producers of such products. They differ in:

- Price.
- Operating systems.
- Memory requirements.
- Number of resources, activities, and projects they can schedule.
- Ability to represent numbers graphically that have been created and manipulated within a spreadsheet or data base.
- Manner in which information is displayed on the screen.
- Type of output produced.
- Peripheral requirements.
- Security features.
- Help routines.
- Error handling.

With so many options, selection of project management PC software requires managers to analyze their needs and research the market before making a purchase.

Project managers can also aquire software packages to generate reports for project control. The types of reports that most project managers desire are:

Activity status reports sorted by:
  Organizational units.
  Activity.
  Overruns.
  Time.
  Cost.
Budget:
  Standard.
  Exceptional.
  Comparisons.
  Costing.
  Loading.
    Personnel.
    Equipment.
Work schedules sorted by:
  Start date.
  Finish date.
  Float/slack.

With the aid of these computer-generated reports, the project manager can identify potential bottlenecks or problems. The output can also provide information that the manager uses in solving problems. For example, budgetary reports provide a powerful cost control capability, identifying how much has been spent by each person or organizational unit and for what task. The project manager can then compare these expenditures with the target budget. Some computer-generated reports are sent to project personnel and users to keep them informed on the status of the project.

PROJECT REVIEWS

In general, the schedules for most systems development projects need constant updating and revision during the life cycle of the project. It is important to have a formal **review process** for evaluating the progress of development so that this can be done. Review sessions serve a number of other purposes as well. They:[9]

- Measure development against project objectives to make sure that the project is on track.

---

[9]This list and the review recommendations that follow are drawn from George Glaser, "Managing Projects in the Computer Industry," *Computer*, vol. 17, no. 10 (October 1984), pp. 45–46.

- Interject general-management awareness, concern, and support.
- Reaffirm the correctness and completeness of current plans and schedules.
- Identify potential problems and assign responsibility and deadlines for resolution.
- Foster cooperation and communication among project staff and users.
- Create a sense of enthusiasm, cohesiveness, and importance.

How often such reviews are held depends on the nature and length of the project. For projects longer than six months, biweekly reviews at the project team level are recommended. Formal reviews with top management should be held at least monthly.

The project leader should also receive periodic progress reports. For example, at the end of each week, team members might hand in time sheets reporting which tasks have been completed with estimates regarding the amount of time necessary to complete partially finished tasks. These reports can be compiled in numerical summaries, bar charts, written reports, or some other fashion. A full progress report should be prepared at least once a month.

SLIPPAGE

In spite of reviews and reports, vast discrepancies often exist between estimations of the time and cost of a project and the actual completion date and development cost. A number of factors can contribute to this situation. Sometimes, activities are so innovative that no one with expertise is available in-house to make accurate time estimates. Sometimes, excessive pressure to keep to schedules and budgets makes team members hesitant to report stumbling blocks. Sometimes, no clear guidelines exist for assessing the degree of completeness of a given task. Sometimes, the scope of a project is changed midstream. Time and cost estimates will also require revision when system specifications change.

Of all project development activities, software preparation (both systems and applications software) has the worst record for accuracy in time estimates, even though many formulas exist for calculating needed programming time. One such formula, proposed by Lawrence Putnam, is:

$$t_d = \frac{S_s}{C_k \, K^{1/3}}$$

where

t_d = Development time.

S_s = Number of end product lines of source code delivered.

C_k = State of technology constant.

K = Life cycle in man-years.

Although experts disagree about how to measure programming time variables and about the relationship between these variables, such formulas do help to identify what variables should be considered.

When a record exists of past productivity of employees on development projects, a project manager can use such data in making target estimates. But with the high mobility of analysts and programmers, new personnel of untested ability will always be assigned to projects, and even known workers will not necessarily have stable productivity. Studies have shown that productivity may vary by as much as a factor of 10, even among experienced programmers. A few software firms with permanent staffs that use standardized methodology have completed up to 88 percent of their projects within 20 percent of their time/cost estimates, but firms not specializing in software are doing very well to come even close to this performance. At best, team members can only approximate the time needed for activity completion. The project manager must be prepared to revise the project completion date as development moves forward.

In many projects, schedule slippage is unavoidable. However, in all projects, a point is reached when specification and design should be frozen and no further modifications allowed. It is important that project managers have the authority to overrule users (even users in high levels, who otherwise outrank the project manager) that wish to add system features after the cutoff date.

To ensure that development progress is being reported by the project team as accurately as possible:

- Precise criteria for what constitutes task completion should be provided.
- More severe penalties should be imposed for misreporting progress than for reporting slippage or other problems.
- Guidelines should be provided for the proportion of effort to be allocated to standard tasks.
- The project manager should occasionally participate in team review sessions to ensure that task completion estimations are taken seriously.
- When a wide variance exists between estimates and actual time and cost figures for a given task, the figures of related tasks should be carefully reviewed to ensure that they, too, have not been underestimated.[10]

The proper response of a project manager to **schedule slippage** should be to try to determine ways to make up for lost ground. Alternatives

---

[10]See Rainer Burchett, "Avoiding Disaster in Project Control," *ICP Software Journal*, vol. 3, no. 1 (Spring 1982), pp. 22–27.

might include the reordering of task sequences and priorities. Functions may be deleted and "gingerbread" features eliminated. Another option is to introduce additional resources, such as extra staff or more computer run time during testing. Perhaps overtime work is an answer; perhaps workloads can be readjusted to make teams more productive.

The temptation to do a less thorough job should be strenuously avoided. If there is no way to make up for schedule slippage, a project manager should reluctantly accept the inevitable: a deadline should never take precedence over quality. If saddled with intense pressure to meet an impossible delivery date, the first responsibility of the project manager is to protect the development team from destructive pressure; the second is to get top-level management and users to negotiate a compromise. If system requirements are reduced, with some of the expected benefits excised, perhaps the deadline can be met. Perhaps a minimal system can be implemented on time, with additional subsystems added later. Another alternative is throwaway code, a temporary system to meet user demand. If, after explaining the problems of development and the reasons for delay, an unrealistic deadline is still imposed, the project manager should consider asking to be reassigned to another project. One manager in this situation told his boss, "If you think the project can be done in less time than I estimate, you may be a better person for this job."

SELECTING A PROJECT MANAGEMENT APPROACH

Much literature and conventional wisdom to the contrary, there is no single right way to manage a project. In deciding what **management tools** to use, a project manager must first consider how each tool contributes to project planning and control. Project management tools fall into four general categories:[11]

- External integration tools—includes organizational and other communicational devices to link the development team with users.
- Internal integration tools—devices that enable the team to work as an integrated unit.
- Formal planning tools—methods of defining tasks and planning their sequence, cost, and resource needs.
- Formal control mechanisms—tools used to evaluate progress and identify problems that need correction.

---

[11]The following discussion is based on F. Warren McFarlan, "Portfolio Approach to Information Systems," *Harvard Business Review*, vol. 59, no. 3 (September–October 1981), pp. 142–50.

Table 4–2   **Tools of project managment**

External integration tools	Internal integration tools
Selection of user as project manager	Selection of experienced DP professional leadership team
Creation of user steering committee	
Frequency and depth of meetings of this committee	Selection of manager to lead time
	Frequent team meetings
User-managed change control process	Regular preparation and distribution of minutes within team on key design evolution decision
Frequency and detail of distribution of project team minutes to key users	
	Regular technical status reviews
Selection of users as team members	Managed low turnover of team members
Formal user specification approval process	
	Selection of high percentage of team members with significant previous work relationships
Progress reports prepared for corporate steering committee	
	Participation of team members in goal setting and deadline establishment
Users responsible for education and installation of system	
Users manage decision on key action dates	Outside technical assistance

Formal planning tasks	Formal control tasks
PERT, critical path, etc., networking	Periodic formal status reports versus plan
Milestone phases selection	
Systems specification standards	Change control disciplines
Feasibility study specifications	Regular milestone presentation meetings
Project approval processes	
Project postaudit procedures	Deviations from plan

Source: F. Warren McFarlan, "Portfolio Approach to Information Systems," *Harvard Business Review*, vol. 59, no. 3 (September–October 1981), p. 149.

Table 4–2 lists sample tools in each category. For example, PERT contributes to formal planning tasks. Project reviews contribute to internal integration.

A decision on which tools to use will depend on the environment of the development project. For example, some projects are highly structured and present familiar technical problems. That is, the nature of the task is clearly defined. Users know what outputs they want, they are unlikely to change their minds, and they have no difficulty explaining their needs to analysts. As a result, a project manager has little need for external integration devices such as an elaborate approval procedure for system specifications. Since the firm has had experience with the technology, milestone dates will likely be met. But there still will be a need for control techniques to measure progress and spot problems that might lead to schedule slippage.

Now consider a project with low structure and high technology. In projects of this nature, it is very important to involve users in order to get their formal approval for both system requirements and design documentation and to retain their commitment to the design during implementation. External integration tools are extremely important in such

Table 4–3			Project types and relative contribution of tools to ensuring success		
Project type	Project description	External integration	Internal integration	Formal planning	Formal control
I	High structure low technology, large	Low	Medium	High	High
II	High structure, low technology, small	Low	Low	Medium	High
III	High structure, high technology, large	Low	High	Medium	Medium
IV	High structure, high technology, small	Low	High	Low	Low
V	Low structure, low technology, large	High	Medium	High	High
VI	Low structure, low technology, small	High	Low	Medium	High
VII	Low structure, high technology, large	High	High	Low +	Low +
VIII	Low structure, high technology, small	High	High	Low	Low

Source: F. Warren McFarlan, "Portfolio Approach to Information Systems," *Harvard Business Review* vol. 59, no. 3 (September–November 1981), p. 147.

situations. A users' steering committee might be formed to evaluate the design. A user might be assigned as either project leader or second in command. It will be wise to distribute minutes of all key design meetings to users.

In such projects, however, network analysis may be of little value. Tasks that appear simple at the start of the project may be found to be complex once analysts begin work on them. For this reason, the use of formal planning techniques may be inappropriate at the start of the project, and it may not be possible to make accurate time and cost estimates using these techniques early in the cycle of development.

Table 4–3 shows the relative contribution of each of the four groups of project management tools to projects classified by structure, technology, and size. One might make the framework more complex by adding other project descriptors. To do so would only confirm the premise that there is no "best" approach to project management. Rather, the choice of tools for a given project will depend on the characteristics of the information system under development and on the project personnel's knowledge of and familiarity with the available options.

SUMMING UP

Project management attempts to bring order and control to projects. (Some computer scientists downgrade the importance of project man-

Figure 4–10   **Responsibilities of a project manager**

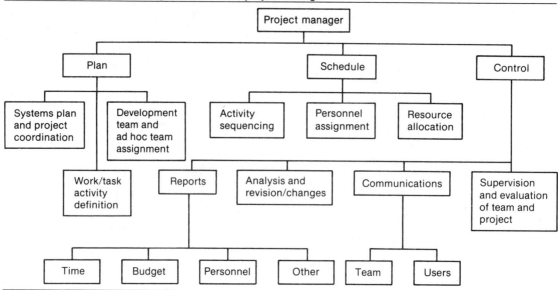

agement, an opinion not widely shared.) The choice of most project managers today is not based on technical competence alone but on the communication skills, business knowledge, and organizational ability of candidates. As illustrated in Figure 4–10, the work of a project manager falls into three general categories: planning, scheduling, and control. In each category, the project manager must serve as a negotiator, coordinator, and counselor as well as a technical advisor.

Figure 4–11 identifies the sequence of project management activities

Figure 4–11   **Network diagram for project management**

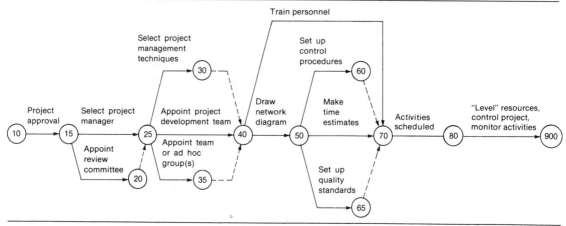

that have been discussed in this chapter, beginning with the selection of the project manager. Next, a development team is appointed, tasks are defined, a project map is developed that includes time and cost estimates, activities are scheduled, and development activities are monitored. One observer, N. J. Reza, states that successful project development is accomplished "not through providential guidance nor through any unique expertise, but rather through the application of time tested methods which are wholly dependent on adequate resources, both personnel and financial, and a well developed plan."

CASE: PROJECT MANAGEMENT SOFTWARE FOR PERSONAL COMPUTERS

Microcomputer software packages for project management are currently on the market that are well suited to the needs of both small businesses and large corporations. Here are some examples of the software in use.

Ben Armstrong Associates, Ltd., a firm located in Scottsdale, Arizona, provides financial counseling to professional athletes. The company uses a program called Harvard Project Managers (from Harvard Software) to create a "road map" of possible investments for clients for a given period of time, with milestones indicating when the investments need to be made.

Jeff Robinson, technical consultant for Union Bank of Los Angeles, has used Timeline (from Breakthrough Software) to manage a project involving the installation of software at the bank, ported over from another computer system. The program sorted tasks associated with the project by function and by date, giving Robinson an overall view of the project.

Lane Ward, director of planning and development at the Missionary Training Center of Brigham Young University, uses ProjectMaster (from Simple Software) to help plan a training program at his center. Ward loads all the tasks associated with training, the resources needed for the tasks, and three different time estimates for each task. The output includes a statistical analysis that details the best- and worst-case scenarios for time of training.

Price Waterhouse used MacProject (on a Macintosh computer) to

Source: David Needle, "Managing Time and Resources," *Personal Computing*, vol. 9, no. 5 (May 1985), pp. 85–93.

help prepare a bid for the California Department of Transportation to develop new ways to issue highway permits for extra-large vehicles. Gantt and PERT charts were produced that detailed each step of how Price Waterhouse would help the department set up the program.

Questions

1. Is the software used in these examples portable? Might the software designed for counseling athletes be adapted to investment planning? For what other applications might it be used?
2. Which of the three software packages would you use to:
    a. Control a project to install a large mainframe?
    b. Control complex systems development projects?
    c. Plan and control an accounts receivable application?
    Do you have enough information to decide what software to use on each of these projects? If not, what information do you need?
3. What advantages are there in using these software packages rather than mainframe programs for these same applications?
4. What are the limitations of using a microcomputer package for project management?

STUDY KEYS

CPM (Critical Path Method)
Critical path
Functional organization
Gantt chart
GERT (Graphic Evaluation Review Technique)
Management tools
Manpower leveling
Matrix organization
Milestones

PERT (Program Evaluation Review Technique)
Project
Project management
Project manager
Project organization
Project plan
Review process
Slippage

DISCUSSION QUESTIONS

1. What are the main responsibilities, functions, and activities of project management? Which of these should be assigned to:
    a. Project manager.
    b. Project review committee?
    c. Permanent computer department staff?
    d. Project team?

2. Should a committee be responsible for project control and management? What should the committee's relationship be to the project manager? What should be its functions? What skills should members have? How many should be on the committee? You may wish to qualify your answers by specifying the project environment.
3. To what extent is project management essentially crisis management? Can this be changed? If so, how?
4. What should be the composition of a project team for each of the following development projects?
   a. Application of accounts receivable project.
   b. Integrated application of accounts receivable, purchasing, and production.
   c. Implementation of a data base management system.
   d. Automation on the factory floor.
   e. Use of numerical control machines.
   f. Implementation of computer-aided design.
   g. Information retrieval for a company library containing books on technology, patent rights, and industries similar to the company.
   h. Automation of the offices in the marketing division.
   i. Acquisition and installation of a medium-sized computer.
   j. Decentralization and distribution of computing to three distributed sites.
   k. Design and implementation of a system of internal control for EDP.
5. What project control techniques (CPM, Gantt, etc.) would you use in each part of Question 4?
6. List special problems and dangers in project management for each of the projects in Question 4.
7. What mode of organization (functional, matrix, or project) would you recommend for each of the projects in Question 4?
8. What qualities in a project manager would be required in each project in Question 4?
9. Should project management itself be controlled? If so, why and how?
10. Why is management of computer projects different from noncomputer projects? What special approaches or cautions are required?
11. Computer projects are notorious for cost overruns and time schedule slippages. Why? How can these be minimized without a loss in the quality of the final product?
12. What is the role of top corporate management in relation to project management?
13. What is the role, if any, of outside consultants and consulting houses in project management?
14. When should computer software be used for project management? Explain.
15. What purpose is served by project review sessions?
16. Project management tools can be divided into four categories. What are they? What determines which tools are used in a given project?
17. Give examples of systems development projects that belong to each project type listed in Table 4–3.

SELECTED ANNOTATED BIBLIOGRAPHY

Block, Robert. *The Politics of Projects*. New York: Yourdon, 1983, 131 pp.
This book explores the political component of project and system failures. Although the concepts of political interaction discussed in this text extend to any political environment, this book centers on software development projects.

Brandon, Dick H., and Max Gray. *Project Control Standards*. Huntington, N.Y.: Robert E. Krieger, 1980, 204 pp.
A discussion of the basic fundamentals, procedures, and tools that comprise project management. The chapters are short, so that readers can easily pinpoint topics of interest and quickly retrieve the information they want.

Burchett, Rainer. "Avoiding Disaster in Project Control." *ICP Software Journal*, vol. 3, no. 1 (Spring 1982), pp. 22–27.
A good distillation of many years of project management, this article discusses the reasons why projects tend to cost more and take longer than expected. The importance of staff career development and training is examined, ways to ensure accurate progress reporting are proposed, and techniques to improve estimations are given.

Dauphinais, Bill and Leonard Darnell. "Task Force." *PC World*, vol. 2, no. 9 (September 1984), pp. 135–48.
Belying its nondescript title, this article discusses software available on small computers for project management. Two examples are given: Micro GANTT for small projects and the Primavera Project Planner for larger projects. The latter is a batch-oriented, menu-driven program that facilitates rather sophisticated planning, monitoring, scheduling, and handling of complex task interrelationships.

Glaser, George. "Managing Projects in the Computer Industry." *Computer*, vol. 17, no. 10 (October 1984), pp. 45–53.
This article is not restricted to projects in the computer industry, despite the title. The principles of project control discussed in the article apply to all industries. It is the author's premise that management skills as well as technical skills are needed by a project manager.

Gourd, Roger S. "Self-Assessment Procedure X." *Communications of the ACM*, vol. 25, no. 12 (December 1982), pp. 883–87.
Thirty multiple-choice questions are given on the subject of tasks, planning, personnel, and project control. Readers are invited to answer the questions and compare their answers with suggested responses. The purpose is to help readers appraise their own knowledge about project management.

Journal of Systems Management.
This journal is oriented toward project management. Readers will find updated articles on subjects such as computer programs for project control, and techniques for personnel appraisal and time estimations.

Keen, Jeffrey. *Managing Systems Development*. New York: John Wiley & Sons, 1981, 334 pp.

An excellent comprehensive coverage of the subject, with a nonacademic but management and end-product orientation.

Oliver, Linda. "Major Systems Project Planning and Control: Updating the Techniques." *Interpreter*, vol. 42, no. 7 (July 1983), pp. 26–30.
The best part of this article is the discussion of the role of the project manager as negotiator and coordinator. According to the author, successful project managers understand the organizational and the end-user's environment and have the ability to communicate with everyone.

Semprevivo, Philip C. *Teams in Information Systems Development.* New York: Yourdon, 1980, 130 pp.
This text examines the research literature and theory of teams and develops a methodology for applying that theory. The text is directed toward technical and nontechnical managers of computer software projects.

Strehlo, Kevin. "When the Objective Is Efficient Project Management." *Personal Computing*, vol. 8, no. 1 (January 1981), pp 132–94.
A long but well-presented view of project management. The author both praises project management techniques and identifies their limitations. The focus is on project management software used on personal computers. Strehlo is concerned that most supervisory-level people using project management software do not comprehend the significance of basic concepts like slack time and noncritical paths.

Thomsett, Rob. *People and Project Management.* New York: Yourdon, 1980, 106 pp.
This book, based on Thomsett's experience as a member of an education/consulting team, discusses the system of building systems. The fundamental issues of project management are discussed. So are recent developments in the areas of individual motivation, job satisfaction, performance, and attitudes toward work. Other topics covered include systems development methodologies, the process of project planning, and how to integrate the processes and people management techniques.

Turner, W. S. *Project Auditing Methodology.* New York: Elsevier–North Holland Publishing, 1980, 454 pp.
This book will interest all levels of data processing management, especially project management, consultant groups, teachers, and project auditors. It is filled with practical ideas of ways to evaluate projects. Included are extensive checklists that can be used to ensure project completeness and to communicate with the many parties involved about what is happening.

PART TWO

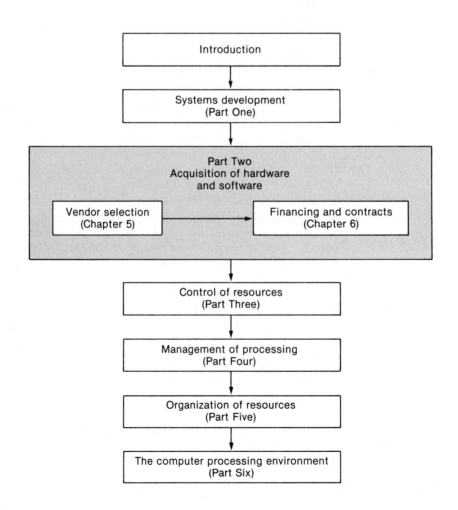

```
                    ┌─────────────────────────────┐
                    │        Introduction          │
                    └─────────────────────────────┘
                                  │
                                  ▼
                    ┌─────────────────────────────┐
                    │   Systems development        │
                    │       (Part One)             │
                    └─────────────────────────────┘
                                  │
                                  ▼
        ┌─────────────────────────────────────────────────┐
        │                  Part Two                         │
        │          Acquisition of hardware                  │
        │               and software                        │
        │                                                   │
        │  ┌──────────────────┐      ┌──────────────────┐  │
        │  │ Vendor selection │─────▶│ Financing and    │  │
        │  │   (Chapter 5)    │      │ contracts        │  │
        │  │                  │      │ (Chapter 6)      │  │
        │  └──────────────────┘      └──────────────────┘  │
        └─────────────────────────────────────────────────┘
                                  │
                                  ▼
                    ┌─────────────────────────────┐
                    │   Control of resources       │
                    │      (Part Three)            │
                    └─────────────────────────────┘
                                  │
                                  ▼
                    ┌─────────────────────────────┐
                    │ Management of processing     │
                    │      (Part Four)             │
                    └─────────────────────────────┘
                                  │
                                  ▼
                    ┌─────────────────────────────┐
                    │ Organization of resources    │
                    │      (Part Five)             │
                    └─────────────────────────────┘
                                  │
                                  ▼
                    ┌─────────────────────────────┐
                    │ The computer processing      │
                    │ environment  (Part Six)      │
                    └─────────────────────────────┘
```

ACQUISITION OF HARDWARE
AND SOFTWARE

Introduction to Part Two

The implementation of information systems may require the acquisition of computer resources. This part of the book describes the acquisition process. It tells how to request bids, evaluate proposals, and select a vendor (Chapter 5). Alternative methods of financing are also reviewed, and contract negotiations are discussed (Chapter 6).

The procedures recommended in this part apply not only to the acquisition of hardware. Software should be selected with equal care. (Not all software is written in-house. Some is purchased off-the-shelf, some contracted to an outside group for development.) Indeed, today's complex software, such as data base management systems, requires a major capital outlay and costly support services in terms of maintenance, personnel, and training. The selection principles outlined in this part are as valid in reaching a cost-effective acquisition decision for software as they are for hardware. The principles also apply to both large and small acquisitions, although analysis of options may be less formal and less rigorous in the latter case.

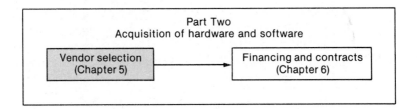

Part Two
Acquisition of hardware and software

| Vendor selection (Chapter 5) | → | Financing and contracts (Chapter 6) |

CHAPTER 5

Vendor selection

An investment in knowledge always pays the best interest.
Benjamin Franklin

During the design phase of the development of an information system, a list of equipment and software for the new system is prepared. Some of these resources may already be available in-house. For example, the firm may have a computer center with many of the required peripherals. But should the firm lack necessary software or should mandated equipment be fully committed to other projects, acquisition of resources will be necessary.

This chapter describes the preliminary steps in the acquisition process. Included are sections on how to translate needs into vendor proposals, how to evaluate alternative proposals and vendor claims, and criteria for selection of a vendor. The subject of computer resource acquisition is continued in Chapter 6 with a discussion of methods of finance, contract negotiations, and liaison with vendors during implementation. Figure 5–1 outlines the sequence of the acquisition process, showing which steps are considered in each chapter. Two chapters have been devoted to acquisitions because of the complexity of the process and the importance of procurement decisions. Indeed, the ultimate performance of an information system may depend on quality of acquisitions, and large capital investments can be at stake.

In large business corporations, procurement procedures may be formal, involving a full-time staff. In smaller firms, acquisition decisions are often made informally, even secretly, by one individual. But in both cases, the steps in the procurement process described in these two chapters apply since the principles involved are not related to corporate size or degree of formality in decision making.

Figure 5–1   **Procurement process for computer resources**

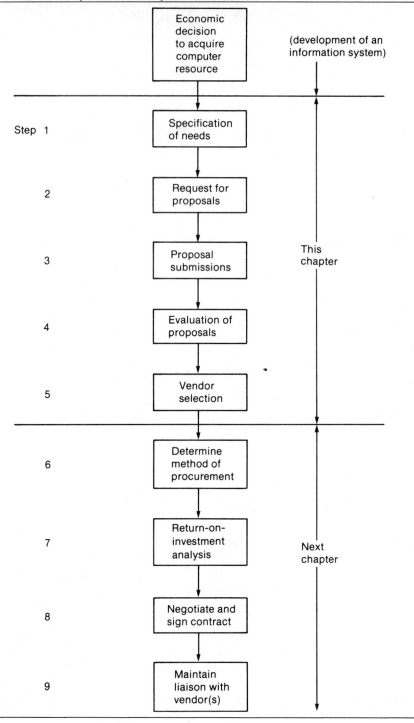

REQUEST FOR PROPOSALS

The first step in procuring computer resources is the preparation of a document that outlines specifications for needed hardware or software. This document, called a **Request for Proposals (RFP)**, is similar to and an extension of user specifications drawn up in the development cycle of an information system. It is important that the buyer list requirements in clear, unambiguous terms so that the vendor cannot misinterpret the specifications or manipulate the buyer into purchasing an inappropriate product.

Who decides what specifications are to be included in the RFP? That will depend on the resource to be procured and the size and structure of the firm. If only a small peripheral for exclusive use by one department is needed, the department head alone may write the specifications. At the other extreme, specifications for a major acquisition affecting many users and requiring a large capital outlay (a data base management system, for example) would probably be made by a team including user representatives, technical personnel, a financial officer, and someone from the upper levels of corporate management. Often, outside consultants are included as well.

When specifying needs in the RFP, the buyer should indicate mandatory features (for example, minimum capability in a computer) that must be included in the bid. These requirements should not be so restrictive that no vendor has a product that qualifies or so lax that a large number of vendors respond. Processing proposals is a time-consuming task: three to six submitted proposals is optimal.

Consulting with vendors is often helpful when drawing up mandatory requirements. Vendors can help evaluate the legitimacy and validity of requirements, although firms should be cautious of vendor bias. Vendors can also indicate whether their companies would be in a position to submit a bid. This, in effect, acts as a preselection process, reducing the number of RFPs that need to be sent.

Canvassing vendors can be done informally (on the telephone, for example) or by a document called **Request for Information (RFI)**. On the basis of the information collected, a matrix (such as the one in Table 5–1) can be compiled to show which vendors have the capability of meeting requirements requested. If, upon examination of the matrix, it is noted that most vendors fail to qualify, requirements can be relaxed. If too many qualify, additional mandatory features can be added for ease in processing proposals.

Once mandatory requirements are set, noncritical but "nice to have" features should be determined—for example, many users want terminal screens to have a color capability. Some features have a functional value, others may be wanted "to keep up with the Jones." Buyers should

Table 5–1   **Vendors' ability to meet mandatory requirements**

Vendor	1	2	3	4	... ...	15	16
Capability to meet current needs in one shift and 5-year future needs in three shifts	X	X	X	X		X	X
Real-time response of 35 seconds for 95 percent of the time	X	X	X	X		X	
Communication facilities	X		X	X		X	X
COBOL and FORTRAN IV compiler	X		X	X		X	X

distinguish between these two categories when evaluating proposals with optional features.

Sometimes, requirements show a bias toward one supplier that other vendors consider unfair. Complaints may be strong enough to force buyers to reevaluate mandatory requirements. To avoid ill will, clients should not write their specifications to fit the product of a particular vendor but instead should require minimum acceptable values for parameters that more than one vendor can meet.

OTHER COMPONENTS OF THE RFP

Although a major portion of the RFP is delegated to need specification, information should be given on procedures, schedules, and the user environment. In addition, required documentation should be explained. Table 5–2 is a sample list of contents showing what items a RFP should include.

General information on the buyer (Item 8), needed to help vendors

Table 5–2   **Sample contents of an RFP**

1. Needs specifications
2. Mandatory features
3. Desired features
4. Performance data wanted
5. Cost data needed
6. Information needed on vendor
7. Documentation required from vendor
8. General information on buyer

9. Request for vendor demonstration or presentation
10. Procedural details:
    How to handle questions
    Liaison
11. Schedule:
    Bidder's conference
    Proposal due date
    Award date
12. General comments

Table 5–3	Information to be supplied by vendor	

1. Experience of firm with computer resources:
   Recent mainframe and micro technology
   Inquiry and response capabilities
   Communication capabilities
   Graphics
2. Systems development expertise and experience:
   Design
   Implementation
   Human engineering
3. Technical assistance available:
   Systems support
   Engineering support
      Nature
      Experience
      Response time
      Maintenance
4. Training to be provided:
   Facilities
   Courses
   Materials
   Instructors available
   Media used
5. Research and technical programs of firm:
   Human engineering
   Education and training
6. Names and addresses of recent customers
7. Financial summary statement on assets and liabilities
8. Annual report (optional)

understand the environment in which the product under consideration will operate, should consist of:

- Resumé of firm and product(s).
- Projected rates of growth.
- Data volumes—maximum, minimum, and average.
- File characteristics.
- Input/output characteristics.
- Response time—maximum, minimum, and average.
- Constraints.

Table 5–3 is a further elaboration of Item 6 of the RFP sample contents. It lists the data that the vendor should supply to help the buyer evaluate whether the vendor is reliable and has the necessary expertise and support facilities to back up a bid.

PROPOSAL SUBMISSION

Vendors, upon receipt of a RFP, will prepare their bids. During this preparation period, it is useful for the buyer to keep in close contact with the vendor in order to answer questions and clarify the RFP if necessary. Sometimes, the RFP will be altered during this period as a result of vendor comments or objections. If so, all vendors receiving the RFP should be so informed.

This liaison and dialog with vendors can be very educational for the acquisition committee. It can teach them about advances in the computer industry and help them identify and weigh the importance of various features. Such knowledge will prove of value when proposals are later evaluated.

VALIDATION OF PROPOSALS

When the acquisition is a minor piece of equipment, validation of proposals can easily be done by technicians in the user department. But when a computer or computer system is to be purchased, checking proposals and validating vendor claims may take an acquisition team many months. There are two basic approaches to validation: a literature search and a study of vendor justifications. When performance is crucial, hand timing, benchmarks, and simulation are also useful tests.

1. *Literature search*

With reference to validation of proposals, a **literature search** does not mean a book survey, because the time lag in book production means books cannot keep current with computer advances. Rather, publications such as *DataWorld* (published by Auerbach) or *DataPro* (by McGraw-Hill) should be studied. In a service similar to that of consumer bulletins, magazines provide up-to-date evaluations of computer resources, especially peripherals and packaged software.

Literature searches are time consuming. One needs to locate relevant articles and to find a common basis for comparing equipment (or software) described in articles written by different authors. Another limitation is that a literature search can only be done after a product has been on the market for some time. Should the acquisitions committee be interested in recently developed computer resources, enough time may not have elapsed for evaluation of these resources to reach print. (Risks in acquiring new technology should not be underestimated. Hardware may still have bugs, delivery may fall behind schedule, software may prove unavailable, etc.)

One can supplement a literature search by asking other customers of the vendor how they evaluate the vendor's products and services. For this reason, a list of customer names is requested in the RFP. Usually, only the names of satisfied customers will be supplied, but those customers may refer the buyer to dissatisfied firms, which should be consulted as well.

2. *Vendor justification*

Another technique used by acquisition committees to validate vendor proposals is to ask vendors to appear before the committee or to submit documentation to justify their proposals. When using this approach, the committee must be careful that it is not swayed by a slick sales promotion instead of carefully evaluating the merits of the vendor's proposal. Many managers are "**satisficers**" and prefer to deal with vendors who have proved reliable, helpful, and satisfactory in the past.

Such managers are particularly receptive to this method of proposal validation. "**Optimizers**," those who attempt optimization, usually choose the more time-consuming literature search and validation (which require more technical expertise as well).

Hand timing

In **hand timing**, the engineering time to perform each set of operations is multiplied by the number of these sets in each applications program in order to determine run time. This calculation is matched with the vendor's time claims in order to verify the performance capability stated in the vendor's proposal. Hand timing is feasible in simple processing but is beyond present capabilities for complex processing configurations, such as parallel processing or multiprocessing.

Benchmarks

A **benchmark** test measures hardware or software performance under typical conditions, using a small set of programs selected to represent the work stream. The problem is in defining "typical" conditions. In a bank, the number of transactions processed on a single midweek day might be a fairly accurate sample of transactions throughout the year. But in a manufacturing plant, the workload may vary from day to day or week to week. The choice of a representative workload must, therefore, be made with care. The set of programs selected for the benchmark should include all important functions of processing, such as sorting, matching, updating, and queries.

Table 5–4 lists some of the factors to be included in a benchmark. Note that not only time, equipment, and processing must be representative but that current workload and future projections should be considered. One can allow for growth by multiplying test-run time by a multiplier called an **extension factor**. This factor varies according to each class of programs.

Benchmark testing may mean running the test programs on several

Table 5–4	Factors to be considered when preparing a benchmark

Representative workload:
   Current
     Normal
     Peak
   Future
     Normal
     Peak
 Representative equipment requirements:
   Memory
     Internal (core)
     External
   Input/output channels
   Communication equipment
   Peripherals
	Representative time requirements:
	   Compile
	   Execute
	   Input/output
	
	 Representative processing:
	   Files
	   Functions and types of processing
	     Sort/merge
	     Update
	     Computing
	     Matrix
	     Simulation

different computers for the purpose of comparing execution speed, throughput, and so on. If the buyer doesn't have the equipment, this means arranging with others for the testing. The problem is to find a firm willing to lend its hardware for testing, one with the exact combination of CPU features, peripherals, and software needed for the testing. Vendors may assist buyers in locating equipment for benchmark tests. They may contact clients (on contract to provide testing facilities) on the buyer's behalf or allow use of their own equipment for testing, as does IBM at its regional centers.

Another problem with benchmark testing is that the applications programs in the benchmark (programs in current use) may be in a different language than the system to be evaluated. For example, the benchmark programs may be in COBOL, whereas the new system under consideration uses APL. In such cases, new programs must be written for test purposes. Although preparing special benchmark programs has a high learning value, the effort is not trivial. The time spent on programming can be quite costly.

Simulation

An alternative to benchmark testing is to lease or purchase a special **simulation program**, such as SCERT, CASE, or SAM, that can be run on equipment already available in-house to simulate workload processing on equipment configurations under consideration. Or a computer service organization can be contracted to run the simulation.

A simplified representation of the flow of a SCERT simulation can be seen in Figure 5–2. This figure does not show all the stages within each phase, nor does it show all phases necessary for complex modes of operation, such as multiprogramming or real-time processing. However, the basic logic of the simulation is illustrated.

The first phase of simulation is to develop a mathematical model of the desired information system (Box 2), based on data that define the environment, system, and files (1). In parallel, a mathematical model of the hardware and software systems under consideration is developed (5), based on the configuration to be tested (4) and on information on resource capabilities stored in SCERT's factor library (3). The simulation is then run (6). The output (7) will include not only information on utilization of each main hardware component but information on core requirements, software performance, and costs as well. When output proves unsatisfactory (Exit No, 9), changes can be made to the resources in the configuration (4) or to the model itself (5), and the simulation will be rerun (6).

By definition, simulation will not give an optimal solution. It only provides information on different alternatives. The committee needs to exercise judgment when deciding which configurations (and how many) to test, since simulation runs are expensive. In making a choice among alternatives tested by simulation, the committee should be sure that no

Figure 5–2   **Simplified flow of SCERT**

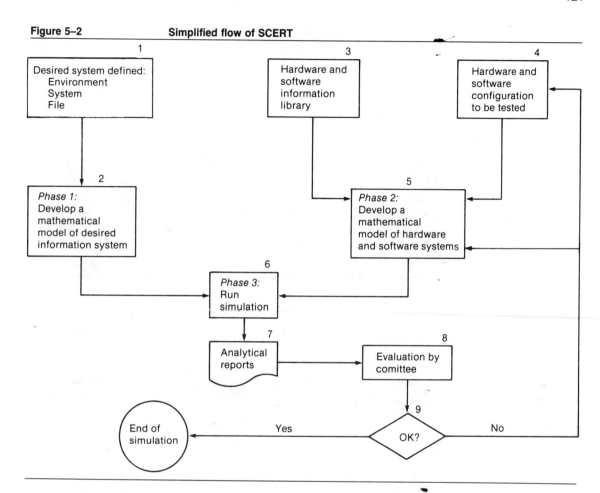

constraints have been violated. For example, a desirable solution may cost more than can be allocated to the system. The most satisfactory solution may turn out to be one vendor's central processing unit (CPU) combined with another vendor's peripherals.

Simulation is useful when validating a vendor's claims, but a significant difference generally exists between predicted and actual levels of performance. To minimize error in predicted performance levels, updated, correct, and complete information on equipment and software capabilities must be included in the simulation run.

CHOICE OF VENDOR

For simple equipment, a quick review of proposals may suffice when choosing a **vendor**. Even when purchasing complex equipment, many buyers are tempted to avoid a long, formal selection process. They opt instead to deal with vendors with whom they have had satisfactory dealings in the past, as long as the vendors submit proposals that meet objectives. However, a formal review of proposals would lead to the "best" choice, resulting in a system with high efficiency and effectiveness. For this reason, formal evaluation of proposals is often firm policy. It may even be required by law, as is the case with governmental acquisitions.

The weighted-score method and cost-value method are two techniques that can assist an acquisitions team in vendor selection.

Weighted-score method

The **weighted-score method** is used to evaluate all vendors that meet mandatory requirements. In this system, desired features are weighted, and each vendor is scored (from 1 to 10) according to how well each feature meets buyer expectations. A vendor's score on a feature is then multiplied by its weight to give a weighted score per feature. By adding all weighted scores, a total score for each vendor can be derived.

A worksheet utilizing this technique is presented in Table 5–5. Column 1 lists decision criteria. Weights are shown in Column 2 that reflect the relative importance of each criterion as evaluated by the acquisition team. In this table, for example, ability of hardware to meet growth needs is ranked three times higher than a real-time capability.

Assignment of weights is subjective and may cause disagreements among team members given the responsibility for calculating the table. Should top management intervene when a stalemate is reached? Have veto power? To reach consensus, long and heated discussions may sometimes take place, with arm-twisting and power politics playing a role.

The next step is scoring vendors. For example, according to Table 5–5, Vendor A's hardware rates an 8 for storage capacity, whereas Vendor B's system is only given a 6. Scoring is also a subjective activity, sometimes even more difficult than assigning weights. Often an individual or group with expertise on a given feature will be given responsibility for scoring that feature. When newly developed systems are being evaluated, fair scoring may require considerable effort, involving literature searches, calculations, and customer satisfaction checks.

The weighted score for each vendor for each criterion is calculated by multiplying the values in the weight column (Column 2) by the values in each vendor's score column (Column 3 for Vendor A, Column 5 for Vendor B, Column 7 for Vendor C). The total score for a given vendor is calculated by adding all of the values in the vendor's weighted-score column. According to Table 5–5, Vendor C has the highest score.

In addition to the problem of subjectivity in assigning weights and scores, additional weaknesses of the weighted-score method should be recognized. One problem is that each criterion is given a separate value

Table 5–5   **Worksheet for the weighted-score method**

(1)	(2)	(3)	(4)	(5)	(6)	(7)	(8)
		Vendor A		Vendor B		Vendor C	
Decision criterion	Weight	Score	Wtd. score	Score	Wtd. score	Score	Wtd. score
Hardware							
Meet needs of growth	3	7	21	7	21	5	15
Throughput/$	5	8	40	6	30	5	25
Communications	2	4	8	8	16	6	12
Real-time capability	1	1	1	5	5	3	3
Storage	2	8	16	6	12	7	14
Input/output interface	2	6	12	6	12	6	12
Site restrictions	1	4	4	6	6	8	8
Reliability	3	9	27	6	18	8	24
Ease of use	1	6	6	8	8	6	6
Total for hardware			135		128		119
Software							
Monitors	5	8	40	9	45	4	20
Compilers	4	7	28	9	36	3	12
Multiprogramming	1	8	8	8	8	6	6
Query capability	1	7	7	6	6	5	5
Data management	3	7	21	9	27	4	12
Reliability	3	8	24	9	27	6	18
Packaged software	2	8	16	9	18	5	10
Utility software	2	8	16	9	18	6	12
Documentation	4	7	28	7	28	8	32
Total for software			188		213		127
Other							
Cost	40	4.5	180	3	120	9	360
Engineering support	3	9	27	7	21	3	9
Systems support	4	9	36	6	24	1	4
Education	5	7	35	7	35	5	25
Reputation and stability	2	10	20	7	14	5	10
Delivery date	1	6	6	5	5	9	9
Total for other items			304		219		417
Total for each vendor			627		560		663

and assumed to be independent. But many features have a greater value when linked than the sum of their values when separate. The classic example of this used in economics concerns beehives and fields of clover. The higher yields due to synergism when bees and clover are brought into proximity can be compared to the higher production of computers when features (such as telecommunications and minicomputers) are connected. The weighted-score method may not take this causality into account, although there is no reason why telecommunications and minicomputers can not be listed as required features.

Table 5–6   **Cost elements of proposals**

One-time costs	*Recurring costs*
Cost of computer resources to be acquired	Personnel
Cost of auxiliary resources to be acquired	Program development
Site preparation:	Operations
Electricity	Maintenance
Facilities, such as false floor	Supplies
Security facilities	Communication
Transportation:	Insurance
Freight	Backup
Insurance	
Installation	
Conversion:	
Programs	
File	
Personnel	
Documentation	

Another major weakness is that the assignment of weights does not include cost considerations, such as those listed in Table 5–6. The vendor receiving the highest weighted score may not have the best proposal when cost-benefit ratios are analyzed. A lower weighted score may, in fact, give more value per dollar. One solution is to use the weighted-score method only when evaluating proposals with the same total costs. In practice, however, proposals identical in cost are rarely submitted. Those that vary slightly in price seldom include exactly the same features.

2. **Cost-value method**

The **cost-value method** attempts to equalize bids of features so that costs can be compared. Costs of desired features not included in proposals are added to each vendor's bid. The cost of each feature is based on the lowest cost estimate of acceptable alternatives available when making the calculations. A dollar value should also be calculated for operating the system without the desired feature, and this figure used if it is less than the cost of the feature itself. Total costs are then compared, selection being based on the bid with the least cost.

For example, suppose a proposal is submitted that does not include

Table 5–7   **Value template for the desired software (for one vendor only)**

Developing the software in-house	$12,000
Maintenance for life of system	4,000
	16,000
Development of software by software company	15,000
Maintenance for life of system	4,000
	19,000
Cost of doing without the software (i.e., degraded system and decreased efficiency)	12,000

Table 5–8 **Value template for delivery dates**

Vendor	Delivery date	Value
A	June	$ 0
B	September	+4,000
C	March	−2,000

a software feature that the buyer wishes to have. This software can either be developed in-house or purchased. To this initial expenditure, the cost of maintaining the software for the life of the system is added. In Table 5–7, a value template shows figures for this hypothetical software omission: the cost of developing the software in-house plus maintenance would be $16,000; the cost of software purchased and maintained, $19,000. The buyer estimates $12,000 as the cost of degraded service without the desired software. Of the three figures, the $12,000 is lowest, so this figure is the amount to be added to the basic price of the vendor's bid when alternative bids are compared during the selection process.

Sometimes, a value can be subtracted when a requirement is over-fulfilled. If June 1989 is the specified delivery date, a vendor who promises delivery in March, three months early, is given credit. A vendor who can't deliver until September 1989 is penalized. In the value template in Table 5–8, the buyer estimates that the March delivery will result in $2,000 in savings to the company. This value is then subtracted from Vendor C's proposal cost. Late delivery (September 1989) is assessed as costing the company $4,000, a figure added to Vendor B's bid.

Table 5–9 shows the cost-value method applied to an actual case: acquisition of a data base management system (DBMS). This case dem-

Table 5–9 **Cost calculations for selection of a DBMS ($000)**

Cost items	Vendor A	Vendor B
Cost of vendor proposal	$208	$102
Interface to a higher-level language (i.e., BASIC)	42	18
Natural language query facility, including communications interface	20	50
Equipment interdependence (52k/machine)	51	104
Data element dictionary	—	57
Supporting equipment necessary	—	20
Inverted file	—	70
Recovery procedures	—	55
Security	55.5	5
Conversion of data base	34	95
Total	$410.5	$596

onstrates that the cost-value method, usually applied to hardware acquisition, is equally valid for software, and it lists the features many companies seek when choosing software. The costs are genuine, although the table has been simplified for use in this text. (For example, 36 features have been consolidated into 10.) Note that Vendor A's proposal price is twice that of Vendor B but that when the value of omitted features is added, the total cost of A's system is lower than B's system. Also notice the high cost of conversion listed in the table. Conversion costs should be considered when acquiring new hardware, since existing applications programs may have to be altered to run on the new equipment. The most efficient hardware may turn out to be unacceptable because of such conversion costs.

The cost-value method does away with weighted value judgments and scores. It takes into consideration costs and feature interactions. But the problem of subjectivity still remains when estimating the life of a system, the cost of degraded service as a result of lack of features, or the benefits to be gained from overfulfilled requirements. Nevertheless, fewer subjective judgments are required than for the weighted-score method.

A major disadvantage with the cost-value approach to vendor selection is that it requires much time and effort to complete the evaluation. The DBMS selection effort cited in Table 5–9 took three and a half man-years of effort for a team of seven (head of information systems, consultant, three systems programmers, two applications programmers). Note that no representative of corporate management was on the team. In this case, management delegated selection responsibility because the choice of a DBMS requires considerable technical expertise. Other firms commonly include a management representative in the selection process, regardless of the technical nature of the acquisition decision.

REVIEW OF ACQUISITION RECOMMENDATIONS

When a large investment is involved, the final decision on the acquisition of information resources rests with top management. Usually, the recommendations of the acquisition committee are followed. However, it is the responsibility of management to ensure that proposed acquisitions are, indeed, in the best interests of the firm and consistent with the corporate strategic plan. Before acquisition approval is given, management should receive satisfactory answers to the following questions:

- Does the acquisition meet all essential system and user requirements?
- Is the acquisition appropriate, given the priorities stated in the corporate and data processing strategic plan?

- Is technical staff available to implement the acquisition? Did the staff participate in the decision process and recommend acquisition?
- Is the vendor reliable? Does the vendor have the ability to provide required support services?
- Will users accept the new acquisition?
- Can the company absorb the new technology? Will there be organizational disruption? How will conversion be managed?
- How long will it take before the acquisition can be put to use? Will it survive as long as needed?

The cost of proposed acquisitions should also receive close scrutiny by top management before acquisitions are approved. Once management accepts the committee's recommendations, financing and contract arrangements can be made. (These subjects are discussed in Chapter 6.)

SUMMING UP

Although the computer industry did not grow during the 1980s as fast as predicted by pundits at the start of the decade, the computer industry is still accelerating the introduction of new, advanced-technology products that make old products obsolete. In addition, software for an expanded range of applications is on the market, and prices for computer resources are continuing to drop, bringing the computer revolution to the doorstep of an ever-growing number of organizations. The acquisition of needed computer resources remains one of the major responsibilities of management in American business and industry today.

One problem for managers is the large number of acquisition options and the proliferation of computer vendors. Questions such as the following need to be answered:

- Should our firm implement a real-time system, replacing the batch mode?
- Should we replace current hardware with the latest model on the market or wait for new models being developed?
- Should we use minis in a network and distributed processing mode?
- Should we implement a DBMS or wait for the debate on data models to be settled?

Acquisition decisions are often made by a team, appointed by corporate management, that determines need specifications, sends out RFPs, evaluates returns, and selects vendors. The network diagram in Figure

5–3 traces this process. (This diagram is consistent with Figure 5–1 but has greater detail.)

Validation of proposals may include a literature search and vendor justification. Hand timing, benchmark tests, and simulation are techniques for verifying performance claims. Two procedures for evaluating proposals have been explained in this chapter: the weighted-score method and the cost-value approach. Once a decision is reached, all vendors submitting proposals should be notified of the choice.

At all stages in the acquisition process, judgmental decisions are made, and they are subject to error. One cannot state future computer needs with certainty nor predict a company's growth with accuracy. Assigning values to developmental costs or desired features is difficult at best. However, the procedures outlined in this chapter should help reduce the risk in acquisitions and should help firms reach cost-effective procurement decisions.

Vendor selection is a time-consuming activity requiring technical

Figure 5–3   **Critical path diagram of the acquisition process**

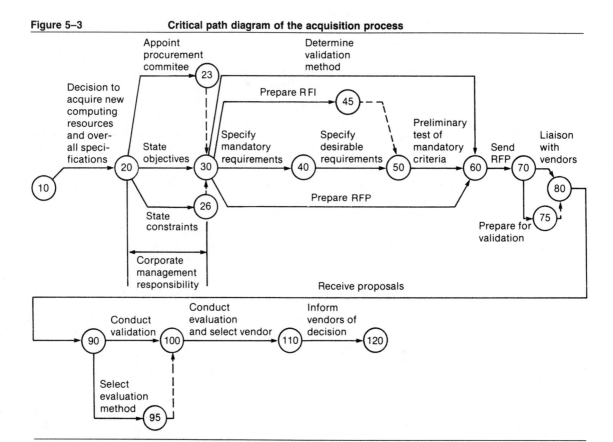

expertise. Constantly changing technology and the large number of possible hardware configurations available complicate the problem of choosing the best vendor proposal. The acquisition process does not end with vendor selection, because there are financial decisions to be made and contracts to be negotiated. Chapter 6 continues the discussion on acquisitions, dealing with these latter topics.

CASE: BUYING MICROCOMPUTERS AT NORTH DAKOTA STATE UNIVERSITY

When North Dakota State University received permission to spend up to $500,000 for microcomputers and associated peripheral hardware, an acquisitions committee was formed that consisted of representatives from the faculty, computer center staff, and central administration. This committee soon learned that the acquisition process was much more complicated, time consuming, technical, and frustrating than expected.

The committee's first hurdle was to develop a bidding procedure to acquire needed components at the lowest prices. It didn't take long before members recognized their need for technical support and turned to the university's purchasing agent for help. But other problems soon surfaced, such as problems of scheduling. For example, the committee discovered that it underestimated the amount of time required to prepare equipment specifications and to evaluate proffered bids. When the field was narrowed to four bidders and the testing phase of proposed equipment was to begin, the committee found that not enough time had been allowed to prepare for testing. Additional schedule slippage occurred when trying to get the equipment being tested to work as a system. The project fell four months behind even the "worst-case scenario" of the committee before the acquisition process was completed.

The committee faced some other problems. Not enough resources (time and people) were allocated to testing. Recordkeeping requirements during testing were initially too lax. (Comprehensive documentation on testing is needed to compare sample machines.) Many of the machines tested did not interface with the university's mainframe computer. Some vendors had versions of popular software that

Source: Harris Jorgensen, Andy Keogh, Sandy Sprafka, and Val Tareski, "Do's and Don'ts in Buying Microcomputers," *Cause/Effect*, vol. 9, no. 1 (January 1986), pp. 18–19.

would run only on their machines. Not all products had the same processor clock speeds. Communication problems between committee members and vendors arose. (For example, many of the vendors were unable to supply the committee with technical information on their products.)

As a result of their experience, the committee has the following advice for organizations planning to purchase microcomputers.

- Allow more time than you think reasonable for the acquisition process.
- Be sure that specifications in the bid are complete.
- Structure the bid document so that systems and individual components (peripherals) are bid separately. (This gives the committee flexibility in purchasing the best combinations at the best price.)
- Reduce each section of the bid to a small number of components. (Otherwise, some vendors are excluded because they can't supply all of the components.)
- Require that all computer configurations come from a single vendor whenever possible. (This reduces interface problems.)
- Test and evaluate each piece and configuration of hardware.
- Examine each computer for reliability, durability, and ease of repair.
- Provide vendors with a single contact person, not committee members' names and phone numbers.

Questions

1. Do you think that the North Dakota State University experience is typical? Why? What purchasing problems did the university have that might not arise in a business organization?
2. How could the problems at North Dakota State have been:
   a. Anticipated?
   b. Avoided?
3. Was part of the problem the composition of the acquisitions committee that was formed to purchase the microcomputers? Who do you think should have been on the committee?
4. Suppose the university decides to buy:
   a. A mainframe.
   b. A peripheral costing $500.00.
   c. Data base management software.
   d. An application package costing $2,000.00.
   Do you think that the same type of purchasing process used to acquire the microcomputers should be followed for each of these acquisitions? If not, why not? What process would you recommend?

CASE: EVALUATING A MICRO BARGAIN

Persons in the market for a microcomputer can find IBM-compatibles advertised in magazine ads and direct mail fliers or by word of mouth for about half the IBM price. Many of the manufacturers are "no-name" companies that offer no support beyond the company's warranty. Should serious consideration be given to such a product?

For knowledgeable users, the purchase of a discounted copycat product may be a sound investment. In particular, the discount makes sense when the name-brand micro is nearing the end of its life cycle. The user who buys the copycat can take advantage of third-party products and services that have been developed for the original, yet save in the purchase price. After all, why pay a high price for technology that will soon be obsolete?

The person who purchases a low-cost micro with a limited useful life may have many reasons for making this choice. Perhaps the user can't wait for the introduction of a more advanced micro. The purchase of the discounted micro may be viewed as a temporary answer to an immediate need. Perhaps the user assumes that a shakedown period will be required to correct flaws before the advanced micro can demonstrate reliability. Perhaps the user fears that software support and services for the new product will take several years to emerge or that the new product will be in short supply. For such a buyer, an inexpensive, throwaway micro may be appropriate.

But not all persons in the micro market should be tempted by discounted prices. The vendor who cuts prices cannot afford to provide training or help with applications development. For persons buying their first micro, this type of assistance is important. There is also the question of repairs. Does the discounted price mean that the vendor is discontinuing support service? The buyer should check on the vendor's reliability. Does the discount mean that the vendor is going out of business, unable to back up the warranty? For organizations that require a long write-off period for physical equipment, it is advisable to wait until the next generation of the product is on the market. They should rent or lease hardware in the meantime.

Questions

1. What are the advantages of buying from a "no-name" company? What are the limitations?

2. Would you consider buying a copycat personal computer? Why or why not?

3. Would you investigate the reputation of a vendor from whom you planned to purchase a microcomputer? If so, why? How would you do it?

4. How would you go about an assessment of copycat hardware's reliability? How would you make an assessment of copycat software?

5. What information would you need to decide whether a product was becoming obsolete? How can you find out if new computing products are soon to be commercially available?

CASE: BENCHMARKING DATA BASE MANAGEMENT SYSTEMS

Benchmarking is commonly used to determine the suitability of a data base management system for a particular application. Unfortunately, benchmark teams—under pressure to predict performance for complex applications on little test data and to evaluate several DBMS's quickly and inexpensively—often make mistakes that range from asking the wrong questions to interpreting the answers incorrectly.

One common error is to benchmark software before the hardware on which it will be used is acquired. Clearly, a DBMS tested on a VAX in a single-user environment will perform quite differently when run in a multiuser environment on a smaller machine. Yet, a benchmark team too often will draw up a set of benchmark criteria that are well thought out and then run the benchmark on a computer system that will not be used for the application under development.

Another problem comes from measuring the wrong parts of the DBMS package. If the DBMS is to have a high input/output load (for example, it will process bank transactions by several tellers simultaneously), it is inappropriate to measure how the system responds to a single user making a single statistical query. An error of this nature was made by a group that wanted to simulate a work environment in which 10 operators entered a new record every 15 seconds. A test was designed to measure the time required to input 40 records into the data base. But instead of enlisting 10 operators to perform the test, the 40 records were bulk-loaded. In effect, the benchmark evaluated the efficiency of the bulk-load input program rather than the ability of the DBMS to handle terminal input/output overhead and random file access.

Sometimes, benchmark teams fail to give proper weight to test results. When comparing two data base management systems, suppose $DBMS_1$ runs twice as fast as $DBMS_2$ for a transaction-processing function but five times slower for a decision support function. It would be a mistake to conclude that $DBMS_2$ is the superior system without considering the environment in which the DBMS will be applied. In a bank, the speed of the DBMS in processing deposits and withdrawals may be much more important than the speed with which the bank manager can calculate a monthly report.

Too small a sample can also lead to erroneous results. When the real-life situation calls for a data base in excess of 100 megabytes of data and routine input from 12 terminals, a benchmark using a small test data base and one operator will give inaccurate test results.

To avoid all of these pitfalls, a benchmark should be carefully planned. A needs analysis should be performed, and performance-critical areas of the application should be simulated and weighted as to their relative value. Testing should reflect accurate file size and system loading conditions and be performed on the actual (or as similar as possible) hardware system for the application under development. These steps are necessary if an organization wants an appropriate and robust data base management system that performs efficiently at low cost.

Questions

1. Describe common errors in benchmarking to determine the suitability of a DBMS.
2. How can a small test sample lead to erroneous results?
3. Would you form a committee to do benchmarking? If so, who should be on the committee?
4. Who should be responsible to see that the pitfalls mentioned in this case do not occur?

STUDY KEYS

Benchmark	Request for Information (RFI)
Cost-value method	Request for Proposals (RFP)
Extension factor	Satisficers
Hand timing	Simulation program
Literature search	Vendor
Optimizers	Weighted-score method

DISCUSSION QUESTIONS

1. Under what circumstances would you use the weighted-score method as opposed to the cost-value approach? Under what circumstances would you use neither? Explain.

2. In taking the product of two subjectively ranked values in the weighted-score method, the results are worthless. Comment. Can the problem be eliminated or minimized? How?

3. Why is it difficult to determine weights and to score vendors in the weighted-score method? How can these difficulties be eliminated or at least reduced?

4. The cost-value approach is sound in its concept and in its implementation. Do you agree with this statement? If so, why?

5. If the weighted-score method were to be used in selecting computer resources, who should do the:
   a. Weighting?
   b. Scoring?

6. Should the composition of the group performing the weighting and scoring depend on:
   a. Size of institution?
   b. Complexity of resource to be selected?
   c. Cost of resources?
   d. Other factors?

7. Should the selection of vendors vary according to the type of computer resources being chosen? What selection process would you recommend for:
   a. Hardware selection, such as a central processing unit (CPU)?
   b. Applications software?
   c. Peripherals?
   d. A DBMS?

8. In the selection process for a medium-sized computer, who should be responsible for:
   a. The acquisition decision?
   b. Preparation of the RFP?
   c. Preparation of specs for a CPU?
   d. Liaison with vendor?

9. Would your answers differ in Question 8 for selection of:
   a. Software packages?
   b. Terminals?
   c. A DBMS?
   d. A microcomputer?
   Explain.

10. When and why is the selection process important to an organization?

11. In the selection process, what are some of the difficulties and frustrations faced by the:
    a. Selection committee?
    b. User?
    c. Technical personnel?

12. List and rank sources that you would trust when collecting data for the selection process.
13. What special problems arise when a company is selecting computer resources that are:
     a. Being developed and not yet commercially available?
     b. Only recently commercially available?
14. What main activities precede or follow the selection of computer resources in the development process? Could selection be a bottle-neck delaying the entire project?
15. Should the selection process be treated as a project and be subject to project planning and project control?
16. How can one best validate and evaluate a vendor's claims?
17. Should top management rubber-stamp an acquisition decision made by the selection committee? What role should top management play?
18. Is the selection process getting more difficult with more advanced computer technology? Explain.
19. Why must compatibility be considered when making selections?
20. Why and how can SCERT or other simulation programs help in the acquisition process?

SELECTED ANNOTATED BIBLIOGRAPHY

Allen, Randy L., and Michael Berkery. "Conducting the Cost/Benefit Analysis." *Small Systems World*, vol. 12, no. 10 (October 1984), pp. 38–43.
The authors are from the accounting firm of Touche Ross. They list eight well-defined activities in performing a cost-benefit analysis for mini or microcomputer acquisitions. Also discussed are five worksheets used for the cost-benefit calculations.

Cash, Charles H. "Evaluation and Selection of Mini and Microcomputer Software." *Interpreter*, vol. 43, no. 8 (August 1984), pp. 8–11.
This is a standard discussion on software selection. A well-placed emphasis is given to the time that should be spent checking references and visiting sites where proposed software is in use. The importance of training is also stressed, as is the need for the allocation of time and financial resources to training. According to the author, little variation, if any, exists in procedures for the selection of software for minis and micros.

Coggiola, Donald A. "Evaluating Software: A Methodical Process." *Interpreter*, vol. 40, no. 12 (December 1981), pp. 12–16.
Although this article was written for the insurance industry, the process discussed for the evaluation of software can be applied to organizations in any industry. How to define user needs and how to evaluate vendors as well as promised service and support are topics that are covered well.

Cohen, Jules A., and Catherine Scott McKinney. *How to Computerize Your Small Business*. Englewood Cliffs, N.J.: Prentice-Hall, 1980, 171 pp.
This is actually a guide to computer selection. More than half the book is an acquisition case study. Many completed forms and details on financial

and economic criteria are included. The book is well written and not too technical.

Hogan, Thomas. "First at the Finish Line with 1–2–3." *Business Software*, vol. 3, no. 1 (January 1985), pp. 34–37.
This article includes a discussion of the selection of software packages in general and spreadsheets in particular. The author's advice is to first determine the range of hardware to be used and then select software to run on the hardware.

Lipner, Leonard D. "The Overloaded CPU." *ICP Interface*, vol. 7 (Spring 1982), pp. 30–36.
Benchmarks and analytical modeling are discussed, and examples are given for both batch and online applications.

Loud, James F. "Software Selection for Non-DP Senior Management." *Bank Administration*, vol. 61, no. 1 (January 1985), pp. 34–40.
The author offers a list of 12 questions that must be answered by corporate senior management before approving acquisitions requests. A list of suggested management priorities when considering acquisitions is also given. According to Loud, effectiveness should be given priority over efficiency, and achieved measured success is far more valuable than a brilliant but risky breakthrough.

Pooch, Udo W., and Rahul Chattergy. *Minicomputers: Hardware, Software, and Selection*. St. Paul, Minn.: West Publishing, 1980, pp. 271–320.
Chapter 8 is an informative chapter on the acquisition of minicomputers.

Sharkley, Paul. "Develop vs. Buy Decision on DP Software." *Journal of Information Management*, vol. 4 (Winter 1983), pp. 1–8.
Sharkley recommends packaged software purchases for support functions but development for unique applications that automate business functions.

Sigal, Hillel, and Jesse Berst. *How to Select Your Small Computer*. Englewood Cliffs, N.J.: Prentice-Hall, 1983, 200 pp.
This book is written by the executive staff of the Association of Computer Users. Included are numerous tips, worksheets, checklists, and glossaries. The style is conversational; the pace is fast.

Wiener, Hesh. "MIPS and Reality." *Datamation*, vol. 32, no. 1 (January 1, 1986), pp. 91–95.
This is a good discussion, although technical at times, on the acquisition of mainframes. The author explains the meaning of "Buy first or buy late." It is his advice that, regardless of the temptation to go for new equipment, it is better "to get more MIPS or storage capacity for the money than fewer MIPS or gigabytes when there is no other clear, concrete payoff for buying a newer machine."

Woolcott, Carlos E. "How to Select the Right Software Package." *Canadian Datasystems*, vol. 13, no. 11 (November 1981), pp. 55–57.
This article includes a checklist of 17 factors to be considered when selecting software.

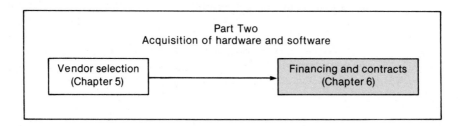

Part Two
Acquisition of hardware and software

Vendor selection
(Chapter 5)

Financing and contracts
(Chapter 6)

CHAPTER 6

Financing and contracts

Better one safe way than a hundred on which you cannot reckon.

Aesop

This chapter continues Chapter 5's discussion on acquisitions. Once resource needs are specified, requests for proposals sent out, submissions evaluated, and a vendor selected (all covered in Chapter 5), financing must be arranged and a contract signed. This chapter considers the pros and cons of rental, purchase, and lease alternatives. It concludes with sections on contract negotiations and contract preparation. The emphasis is on hardware financing and contracts, although some pointers on software acquisition are also given.

APPROACHES TO FINANCING

How should acquisitions be financed? Rental, purchase, or lease? A decision on financing computer resources differs from conventional acquisition decisions because unique pricing patterns have evolved in the computer industry over the years.

The industry was monopolistic at the beginning, with **rental** the only option. This changed in the 1950s, following antitrust litigation. At that time, the Justice Department set price guidelines and prodded IBM to offer users a **purchase** choice. But users continued to favor rentals because of the continual improvement in performance and the decrease in price of new models reaching the market. In effect, the high technology of the industry discouraged users from investing in the purchase of equipment that would quickly become obsolete.

Leasing became an alternative in the 1960s. IBM, pressured by the government to lease equipment, began to do so but at a high price. Other computer manufacturers soon followed suit. Recognizing a business opportunity, entrepreneurs stepped in and formed leasing companies of their own. These entrepreneurs first purchased equipment,

139

then leased it to users at a lower cost than the manufacturers asked. The new leasing companies were able to compete by depreciating equipment over a longer lifetime than computer manufacturers, relying on the premise that equipment could be kept in service far longer than manufacturers allowed and could be leased to a sequence of users. The favorable investment climate of the early 1970s also fostered the growth of leasing companies. Today, leasing firms are thriving, although their market is volatile. The introduction of each new family of IBM computers, for example, tends to disrupt the market, at least temporarily, as users wait for new equipment instead of leasing the old.

In this section, the advantages and limitations of rental, purchase, and lease options will be discussed. Numerical examples will illustrate the computations to be made when considering each alternative.

Rentals

When computing was limited to unit record punched card equipment, rental was the only user option. This changed in 1956 with the IBM consent decree, an out-of-court settlement of an antitrust suit against IBM filed by the government because of IBM's alleged monopolistic control over much of the existing data processing equipment. In the decree, IBM agreed to allow customers to purchase computing equipment, and a reasonable ratio between rentals and purchase price was established. Although ratio obligations have since expired, they have been maintained by IBM under the watchful eye of the Justice Department.

Today, the rental option is used by companies that want data processing equipment for only a short period of time (usually less than 12 months). Rental is also advantageous when user demand is unstable or uncertain. (In most cases, only 30 days' notice to the vendor is required to return equipment.) However, the vendor charges a premium for the flexibility of a rental contract, as much as 20 to 30 percent higher than an operating lease. One reason for this high cost is that the vendor must allow a margin to cover reconditioning or relocation of returned equipment.

Rental payments are tax deductible, an additional benefit to rental clients. Many vendors offer their clients a purchase accrual option that enables them to apply rental payments to purchase of their rented equipment. Another advantage of renting is that the vendor usually assumes responsibility for maintenance and insurance. However, the price of rental is high, so that renting for more than two or three years will cost more than the purchase price. Another drawback is a customary charge for overtime use beyond a specific number of hours a month, as much as 40 percent higher than the regular rental fee.

Purchase

Many users hesitate to purchase computer equipment because they fear **obsolescence.** This fear is justified. Computers have made quantum jumps in speed and performance in recent years, and competitive pressures often require firms to take advantage of the latest technology available. In the airline industry, for example, once American Airlines went online with reservations, all major airlines had to follow suit to retain their customers.

The continual drop in computer prices is another reason many users are hesitant to buy. Indeed, the **price-performance ratio** has dramatically improved over time. An industry rule of thumb is that prices drop arithmetically while performance increases geometrically. No wonder many companies are unwilling to commit themselves to a major capital outlay when they know that the capability they need will cost considerably less in the future.

Still another reason why many firms are reluctant to purchase computer resources is that their financial resources are limited: competing projects may be given funding priority. Furthermore, many firms choose to rent (or lease) because the bureaucratic procedures required to make a purchase are so involved that hardware can become outdated or obsolete before a purchase transaction is completed.

In spite of these problems, many considerations make purchase more attractive than rental or leasing. For example, purchasing equipment has an impact on a company's balance sheet. The purchased equipment is recorded as an asset, while the financing is recorded as a liability. There are also tax benefits to be considered. The purchaser might be eligible for investment tax credits (depending on the existence of such credits under current tax law) as well as interest expenses from financing the purchase, depreciation expenses, and maintenance expenses. (Credits are more powerful than expense deductions because they reduce tax by $1 for every dollar of credit. The amount and type of equipment for which credits are allowed vary according to the business climate and prevailing tax laws.)

The fact that new computer technology is continually being introduced to the market does not make all systems in use obsolete. Some computer equipment has a **useful life** of up to 10 years in the United States and even longer abroad, which justifies the purchase price. (Useful life can be operationally defined as the time period during which the required workload can be economically processed by the equipment in question.) After all, not all firms require the latest technology. Even when equipment must be upgraded, firms can capitalize on the **salvage value** of discarded hardware, which is sometimes as high as 40 percent of purchase price. (Not all equipment will find buyers, as owners of RCA, Memorex, General Electric, or XDS systems can attest!)

At first glance, purchase is also very much cheaper than rental. A $1.6 million computer might cost $593,244 in rent per year, making three years' rent more than the purchase price. Such a comparison is simplistic, however, because it does not allow for tax advantages and maintenance depreciation, which benefit the purchaser; nor does it discount for the present value (PV) of cash flows for each of the years of useful life. (The discounted rate used for calculating present value is the average rate of return on investment.)

Other factors that have a bearing when comparing the advantages of purchase versus rental are:

- Life expectancy of computer resource.
- Time expected until next generation.
- Reliability of resource (tried and proven?).
- Expected hours of usage.
- Stability of applications and usage.
- Likelihood of modification or updating of resource.
- Borrowing rate.
- Discount rate.
- Depreciation method.
- Depreciation rate.
- Property tax rate.
- Corporate tax rate.

Calculations for rental and purchase of a medium- to large-sized computer that take into consideration some of the variables cited above are shown in Table 6–1. Data on which the calculations are based appears in the first section of the table. Calculations for purchase and rental are then shown. In these two sections, each column represents one year of transactions. A positive number indicates outflow or cost; a negative number (in parentheses) indicates inflows or savings. The total net outflow equals the sum of costs less inflows.

To represent future costs as a present value so they can be compared with the present purchase price, the totals must be multiplied by a present value factor (as shown in the table). The present value of purchase and the present value of all other related costs after income tax are then totaled. The $637,988 represents the PV of purchase outflows. This figure should then be compared with cash outflows for rentals over the same time period, discounted to their present value. In Table 6–1, rental equals $1,124,406. Purchase, therefore, costs $486,418 less than rental in present value. According to the table, the **cutover point** is about three years. That is, if the useful life of the system is longer than three years, buying would be cheaper than renting.

The rent-purchase comparison in Table 6–1 is just an example. In an actual case, the cutover point might be two to three years. Variables also differ from one situation to another, although purchase is always less than rental over a period of five years, even when maintenance costs are included. Many of the variables affecting the calculations are

Table 6–1 **Purchase versus rent calculations**

A. Data on which purchase calculations are based

1. Purchase basic price	$1,600,000
2. Estimated useful life	5 years
3. Maintenance contract	$3,040 per month
4. Property tax	12,960 per year
5. Investment tax credit	10%
6. Depreciation (ACRS*)	Taken over 5 years, with annual rates 15, 22, 21, 21, and 21%.
7. Discount rate	10%
8. Tax rate (state and federal)	50%
9. Salvage value at end of fifth year	$500,000

Maintenance per year	$36,480
Tax savings per year at 50%	18,240
Net cost on maintenance	$18,240 per year

B. Calculations for purchase (inflows in parentheses)

		Year 1	Year 2	Year 3	Year 4	Year 5
Original purchase price	$1,600,000	$ 0	$ 0	$ 0	$ 0	$ 0
Maintenance		0	18,240	18,240	18,240	18,240	18,240
Property tax (net)		0	6,480	6,480	6,480	6,480	6,480
Cash savings from depreciation		0	(120,000)	(176,000)	(168,000)	(168,000)	(168,000)
Investment tax credit		0	(100,000)	0	0	0	0
Salvage value		0	0	0	0	0	(500,000)
Total cash outflow	$1,600,000	($255,280)	($151,280)	($143,280)	($143,280)	($643,280)
Present value (PV) factor	1.0	.9091	.8264	.7513	.6830	.6209
PV of cash outflow	$1,600,000	(232,075)	($125,018)	($107,646)	($ 97,860)	($399,412)

Total PV of cash outflow for five years: $637,988

C. Calculations for rental (inflows in parentheses)

	Year 1	Year 2	Year 3	Year 4	Year 5
Rental	$593,244	$593,244	$593,244	$593,244	$593,244
Tax savings from rental (50%)	(296,622)	(296,622)	(296,622)	(296,622)	(296,622)
Total outflow	$296,622	$296,622	$296,622	$296,622	$296,622
Present value (PV) factor	.9091	.8264	.7513	.6830	.6209
PV of cash outflow	$269,659	$245,128	$222,852	$202,593	$184,172

PV of cash outflow for five years: $1,124,406

*ACRS = Accelerated cost recovery system.

exogenous (external)—that is, beyond a firm's control. Borrowing rates, tax rates, or investment tax credit rates fall in this category. Other variables, although internal, are not always easy to estimate or manage. For example, demand for applications and debugging programs may mean more run time is spent than anticipated, raising rental costs because of overtime fees. When this occurs, the cutover period is affected.

Usually, a stable demand for a computer resource over its calculated payback period is needed before purchase (instead of rental) can be economically justified. There is obviously no point in buying unneeded equipment or software. Sometimes, firms are able to rectify purchase errors by passing inappropriate or redundant resources to other departments or subsidiaries. Sometimes, vendors allow clients to modify or upgrade purchased hardware that fails to meet user needs because of environmental changes or because equipment is outgrown.

In brief, clients should have a solid understanding of both their present and future information processing needs before a purchase decision is made. The purchase of a computer system is less costly than rental (or lease, as will be described in the next section) for long-term use. It represents a solid investment that can be capitalized and amortized over time. The purchaser may benefit from tax advantages, pride of ownership, and ready access to known hardware resources. On the other hand, the purchase of a computer system is a major financial commitment that ties up capital and involves a certain amount of risk (potential obsolescence, uncertain resale). Another disadvantage is that once an ownership contract is signed, the purchaser has no way to pressure the vendor for upgraded service or support.

3. Leasing

Computer systems can be leased (an acquisitions option that began in 1961) as well as being rented or purchased. As with a rental, ownership of a leased system is retained by the vendor. The main difference from a rental is the length of time the lessee is committed to the system: usually from 12 to 36 months for an **operating lease** or from four to seven years for a **financial lease**. Monthly payments depend on the length of the lease: the longer the term of the lease, the lower the monthly payment.

Leasing hedges against obsolescence. At the end of a lease period (or sooner if the lease contract has a cancellation clause), the lessee can switch hardware to take advantage of new models that have been introduced to the market. (However, some leases have a penalty for early termination, typically a percentage of the monthly fee for each month remaining in the lease.) Although this same benefit exists with a rental, an operating lease is generally less expensive than renting when the contract is for more than a year. And few firms choose to switch systems yearly. Most find that it takes longer to develop an information system and to learn how to use the system effectively. If they switch systems after a short period of time, they face the trauma of conversion before being experienced with the equipment at hand. Most computer personnel favor three to four years to develop a system before a change in equipment is made. For that length of time, leasing is more economical than renting.

Leasing is also advantageous when a company lacks the cash or credit required to purchase needed hardware or wants to conserve capital. Often, a lease with the option to buy can be arranged so that firms that have limited funds or are uncertain of the demand for the resource can postpone a purchase decision, yet not be greatly penalized by this postponement. The lessee makes monthly lease payments for a specified period or up to a given amount and then can decide whether to continue leasing or take title. Normally, this approach costs little more than a straight lease. Sometimes, it costs even less.

Another benefit of leasing is that less time and effort are generally needed for approval for a lease than for the purchase of equipment. Furthermore, equipment can usually be obtained without a long wait. Unlike rentals, a leased computer can often be used 24 hours a day without penalty. Some lease contracts allow upgrading of equipment with no penalty by simply adding the new amount onto the existing lease.

A decision to lease, with or without the option to buy, should be based on a **discounted cash-flow analysis.** Calculations showing costs for a straight lease for a period of five years appear in Table 6–2. A lease-purchase decision (purchase after a one-year lease) is figured in Table 6–3. The calculations are similar to those made earlier when comparing rental and purchase (Table 6–1), although more variables

Table 6–2	Calculations for lease

A. Data on lease environment

1. Lease payment	$600,000 per year
2. Period of lease	5 years
3. Maintenance	$24,000 per year
4. Property tax	Lessee pays
5. Investment credit	Tax benefit to lessor
6. Depreciation	Tax benefit to lessor
7. Discount rate	10%
8. Marginal tax rate	50%

Lease payments	$600,000 per year
Tax savings (50%)	300,000
Net lease cost	$300,000 per year
Maintenance	$24,000 per year
Tax savings (50%)	12,000
Net cost on maintenance	$12,000 per year

B. Calculations

After-tax cash outflow	Year 1	Year 2	Year 3	Year 4	Year 5
Lease	$300,000	$300,000	$300,000	$300,000	$300,000
Maintenance	12,000	12,000	12,000	12,000	12,000
Property tax	5,265	5,265	5,265	5,265	5,265
Total outflow	$317,265	$317,265	$317,265	$317,265	$317,265
Present value (PV) factor formula	$\frac{1}{(1.10)^1}$	$\frac{1}{(1.10)^2}$	$\frac{1}{(1.10)^3}$	$\frac{1}{(1.10)^4}$	$\frac{1}{(1.10)^5}$
PV factor	.9091	.8264	.7513	.6830	.6206
PV of total after-tax cash outflow	$288,426	$262,188	$238,361	$216,692	$196,895

Total PV of cash outflow for five years: $1,202,562

Table 6–3   **Calculations for lease/purchase**

A. Data on environment

Lease payments	$600,000 per year
Period of lease	1 year
Maintenance	$24,000 per year (note difference from purchase case)
Property tax	$10,530 per year after purchase
Investment credit	10% claimed on purchase
Depreciation	Straight line on five years after acquisition
Discount rate	10%
Tax rate	50%
Useful life	5 years
Portion of rentals deducted from purchase price	$320,000
Purchase price	$1,600,000 − 320,000 = $1,280,000
Resale value at end of 5 years	$300,000

B. Calculations (inflows in parentheses)

Cash outflows	Year 1	Year 2	Year 3	Year 4	Year 5
Lease	$300,000	$ 0	$ 0	$ 0	$ 0
Purchase price	0	1,280,000	0	0	0
Maintenance	12,000	12,000	12,000	12,000	12,000
Property tax	0	5,265	5,265	5,265	5,265
Tax savings from depreciation	0	(160,000)	(160,000)	(160,000)	(160,000)
Investment tax credit	0	(128,000)	0	0	0
Resale value	0	0	0	0	(300,000)
Total outflow	$312,000	$1,009,265	($142,735)	($142,735)	($442,735)
Present value (PV) factor	.9091	.8264	.7513	.6830	.6209
PV of cash outflow	$283,639	$ 834,057	$107,237	($ 97,488)	(274,894)

Total PV of cash outflow for five years: $638,077

are involved in leasing (see Table 6–4). Again, each column in the tables represents a year of transactions, with costs discounted to present value. Straight lease has a PV of $1,202,562 (according to Figure 6–2), compared to the lease-purchase alternative costing $638,077 (Table 6–3). According to these calculations (given the assumptions of the problem), lease-purchase is the better alternative, saving $564,485 ($1,202,562 − 638,077).[1]

Table 6–4   **Variables in leasing**

Lease payments	Costs for system checking and integration
Leasing period	Conditions for upgrading and updating
Maintenance cost	Conditions for renewal
Discount rate	Depreciation rate
Tax rate	Investment tax credit rate
Costs for installation	Recipient of investment tax credit
Costs for shipping	(either lessor or lessee)

---

[1]Calculations of present value may lead to erroneous conclusions when comparing different kinds of equipment with different useful lives. In such cases, the total cost of equipment alternatives should be converted to annuities over the lives of the respective alternatives and a comparison then made of these annuities.

Some of the variables used in these two sets of calculations differ from the rental-purchase variables in Table 6–1. (For example, the depreciation rate has been altered.) This is to show the reader that calculations are not always made on the basis of the same variables. Indeed, in an actual case, few of the variables or values of the variables listed may be applicable because a change in government in Washington can affect tax laws, discount rates, and useful life allowances. Also, the length of the lease period will affect calculations.

In addition, leasing vendors differ in their charges. Rates will be higher if a vendor has both developed and manufactured the equipment to be leased, because it will be necessary to recover research and development costs. Rates are also affected by the payback period and how often lease equipment is updated. The lowest rates are charged by **third-party leasing** firms, which purchase equipment directly from a manufacturer. They set a low rate structure (made possible, in part, by the tax benefits they derive from the purchase) and operate at a low profit margin. Rates are usually based on a computer life of from 8 to 12 years and the expectation that equipment will be leased to three or more consecutive users. (Manufacturers calculate a shorter life, approximately three to five years.)

The third-party lessor gambles on the firm's marketing ability to find users for older models in addition to users for up-to-date equipment. The lessor knows that firms are allocating an increasing share of revenues to computer processing and that the pool of potential customers is growing. Because of advances in technology, new equipment is becoming increasingly modular, flexible, reliable, and upwardly compatible. This makes it easier for leasing companies to find clients for their equipment and reduces the risk of unused inventories.

Nevertheless, lessors are cautious. If uncertain about the market for re-leasing equipment, they may simply choose not to buy a given model to lease. In 1979, for example, the only leasing company to offer IBM's 303K series (introduced in 1978) was Itel and then for a minimum of seven years, reflecting lessor uncertainty about the residual value of the series. Lessors want innovations in computer technology but models that have demonstrated their market value. Their perception of the market and degree of aversion to risk will determine what equipment is bought and placed on lease.

Unfortunately, in recent years, a number of leasing scandals have received publicity. As a result, many data processing managers are wary of the leasing option. But common sense, careful scrutiny of vendor promises and reputation, and legal expertise when negotiating a contract should help companies avoid leasing problems. For example, it is important to deal with respected leasing firms that have the financial standing and the business reputation to back up their lease obligations. A company that is planning to lease should review audited and certified financial statements of the lessor, check its credit rating, and choose a vendor that is likely to survive competitive leasing wars. Proposals from a number of competing vendors should be requested and compared. Legal counsel should carefully review contracts, especially for penalties for early termination of the lease and purchase options at the end. When negotiating with a third-party leasing firm, it is wise to have a clear understanding of the actual equipment price paid the manufacturer for the equipment being leased. Lessees should understand payment calculations and should consider the option of leasing certain system components but renting or buying others to reduce costs.

In addition, lessees should be suspicious of a deal that is "too good to be true." Before signing a lease that appears to be a bargain, consider how the leasing company can make that kind of offer. Perhaps the vendor will be unable to deliver what is promised. Perhaps the favorable terms mean that the system is not technologically up-to-date. Short-term and flexible leases should be given special scrutiny. The economic and competitive conditions in the leasing industry are such that users should be alert for deceptive marketing ploys.

CONTRACT NEGOTIATIONS

Objectives

Negotiations should begin the moment the acquisition process is set in motion, not when lawyers sit down to prepare a written contract. If a company selects resources and commits itself to a vendor before beginning to negotiate terms, leverage in obtaining meaningful contract concessions is lost. The purpose of negotiations is to identify problems and forge consensus before the contract is drawn up.

During negotiations, both parties will try to improve their economic position. A vendor trying to break into the market may have to accept less favorable terms than a well-established vendor and may come out the loser in a zero-sum game (buyer gains at the expense of the vendor). But it is possible for both negotiating parties to settle on a mutually advantageous contract. For example, a firm may inform a third-party leasing company of its interest in particular equipment, which the leasing company then purchases.

The client should control the negotiation process to gain maximum concessions from a vendor. The best way to do so is to:

- Form an interdisciplinary negotiating team that includes persons with contract experience.
- Use a well-designed Request for Proposals.
- Maintain multivendor competition.
- Set the negotiating agenda. Do not use the vendor's standard agreement form as the basis of negotiations. (The vendor is generally a pro in such negotiations, and such an agreement may be weighted in the vendor's favor.)

- Refuse to negotiate with vendor representatives that do not have final negotiating authority.

Contracts ultimately depend on the goodwill of both sides, but skilled negotiators and legal advice (either in-house lawyers or consultants experienced in computer acquisition contracts) are recommended. Having computer technicians and financial personnel on the negotiating team is also useful. Many buyers take the initiative and prepare a contract well in advance to be used as a basis of discussion during the negotiations. They recognize that vendors are experienced adversaries who may not include in their contract proposals all the clauses the buyer considers mandatory. At best, negotiations are a bargaining dialogue. Confrontation is in the interest of neither party.

Contents

Misunderstandings sometimes exist in vendor-client relationships because the two parties have dissimilar backgrounds and use different terminologies. A primary objective of a **contract** is to specify in legally binding, unambiguous terms the rights and obligations of both vendor and client. Detailed specifications will help produce a workable, enforceable document and help avoid disagreements that can lead to ill will or litigation.

Contracts will vary according to the nature of the product (hardware or software), the complexity of the system, and the personalities and past experiences of the negotiators. The basic contents of an acquisition contract should include the following:

Requirement specifications.
Critical commitments implied in demonstration and presentations.
Acceptance criteria.
Remedies for vendor nonperformance.
Penalties.
Arbitration provisions.
Warranties.
Guarantees.
Performance bonds.
Maintenance provisions.
Services:
  Training.
  Documentation.
  Systems and engineering help.
Financing.
Payment schedule.
Patents/proprietary rights.

Limitations and disclaimers.

Insurance.

In addition, the contract should specify date and method of delivery and the vendor's responsibility with regard to site preparation, installation, documentation, training, security, and confidentiality of user's data. The contract should also clarify what the user will do regarding provision for electric power, a proper environment (for example, air conditioning), and qualified staff.

When the acquisition is software, the contract should address the issue of software ownership. Is acquisition merely a license to use the software, or is the client purchasing proprietary rights? If the former, is the license perpetual or for a limited term? Who controls assignment and sublicense rights? Can the software be moved from one location to another? Does the client have the right to let others use the software? To avoid future disputes over extra site or use charges, the contract must fully document all restrictions on use.

Because the development of custom software is generally plagued by delays and cost overruns, three key elements should be included in a software contract: price, timing, and quality. Realistic acceptance procedures should be specified: tests should be designed both separately for modules or subsystems and collectively as a system. The agreement should also include warranty and maintenance provisions that provide for ongoing software performance, including routine and critical fixes, enhancements, and upgrades.

One cannot generalize on the level of detail or specificity required in the contract. Even definitions of terms may be subject to misinterpretation. It is a good idea to attach to the contract a copy of the Request for Proposals (RFP), incorporating it by reference.

A major problem with computer contracts is that few laws specifically regulate computer transactions. Equipment sales do fall under an article of the Uniform Commercial Code adopted by most states, but few specific legal guidelines govern the sale of separate software systems. This is unfortunate since software companies have less stability and maturity than hardware firms and need a legal framework. For the buyer, this means that a software firm's reputation is very important in vendor selection.

CONTRACT IMPLEMENTATION

Once a contract is signed, its execution requires close **liaison** between buyer and vendor. When multiple vendors contribute to a computing system, liaison increases in complexity. Although a one-vendor proposition simplifies the acquisition process and eases detection and correction of malfunctions, the system will generally cost more than when components are supplied from a number of competing firms. Indeed, the 1969 unbundling decision by IBM has resulted in the establishment of many companies offering components and peripherals at a lower price, with better performance and more features, than many giant corporations offer. As a result, buyers today commonly contract with several vendors even though interfacing resources can add considerable time and effort to conversion and increase stress in the buyer-vendor relationship. For example, the end-user often gets caught in the crossfire between vendors when there are systems failures during installation and testing.

Fortunately, the computer industry is moving toward **plug-compatible machines**, especially for IBM equipment. This means that a plug-compatible manufacturer, such as Amdahl, is able to replace an IBM computer with one of their machines without affecting systems software, applications, or peripherals. A few bugs may develop, but in principle, plug compatibility reduces liaison headaches that formerly plagued buyers of multivendor computer resources.

SUMMING UP

In this chapter, the advantages and limitations of rent, purchase, and lease alternatives have been discussed. Possible alternatives are shown in Figure 6–1. Modifications of these basic choices are also offered by many firms. For example, IBM offers a fixed-term plan, an extended-term plan, and a term-lease plan.

Figure 6–1 **Rent, lease and purchase alternatives.**

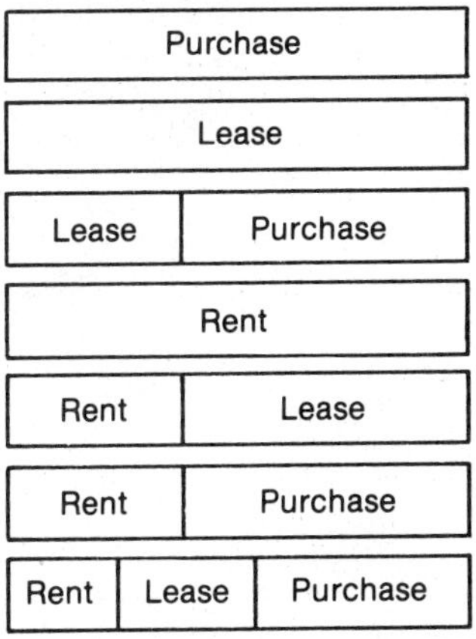

Purchase		
Lease		
Lease	Purchase	
Rent		
Rent	Lease	
Rent	Purchase	
Rent	Lease	Purchase

Table 6–5	Comparison of purchase, lease, and rent alternatives		
Factors	*Rent*	*Purchase*	*Straight lease*
Separate maintenance contract necessary?	No	Yes	No
Depreciation possible?	No	Yes	No
Rent/lease payments tax deductible as expense?	Yes	Not applicable	Yes
Useful life	1–2 years	More than 5–6 years	6 months to 6 years
Capital outlay needed?	No	Yes	No
Total cost for period of 5–6 years or more	Highest	Lowest	Higher than purchase

The decision of whether to rent, purchase, or lease is complex because many factors such as those in Table 6–5 must be considered. What is best for one firm will not necessarily be appropriate for another. As illustrated in Figure 6–2, trade-offs have to be made. The purchase of equipment gives a buyer less flexibility in upgrading equipment than

Figure 6–2   **Comparison of equipment cost and upgrading flexibility for purchase, lease, and rent.**

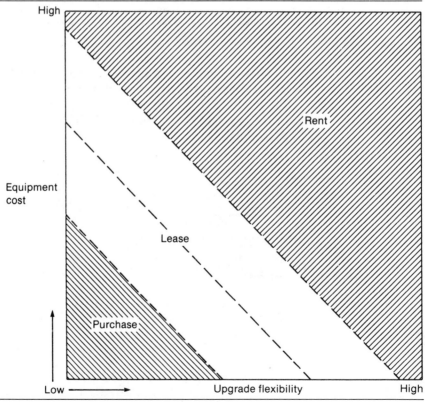

Source: F. Warren McFarlan and Richard L. Nolan, *The Information Systems Handbook* (Homewood, Ill.: Dow Jones-Irwin, 1975), p. 473.

rental or lease. However, the latter cost more. Each firm, after studying its environment, should base its acquisition choice on:

Financial climate. This includes availability of funds, both internal (opportunity costs) and external (banks and lending institutions); governmental policies on depreciation; and property taxes on purchases.

Anticipation of technological advances. Will more reliable, compatible, and cheaper computer resources soon be released? Will new innovative systems have a longer useful life, increasing their residual value to the lessor?

User demand projections. These include current and future user demand projections as well as predictions on the secondhand usefulness of the resources to other units in the organization when the original user updates.

Ability to maintain equipment. If the firm lacks maintenance knowledge and experience, rental or lease options may be advisable.

Decision-making structure. Renting or leasing may be expedient (though not necessarily economically sound) if firms have cumbersome procedures for letting bids and making acquisition decisions.

The future of leasing will depend on rental pricing policies of manufacturers, governmental policies regarding investments, and the speed with which new generations of computer resources are introduced to the market. The survival of individual leasing firms depends on how well they read industry trends, how they time purchases, and how successful they are in finding sequential users for leased resources.

Negotiation of acquisition contracts requires technical and legal expertise. When implementing contracts, close liaison with vendors may reduce the stress of conversion. Fortunately, interfacing equipment is becoming less of a problem with the introduction of plug-compatible machines.

CASE: OPM LEASING SCANDAL

When OPM Leasing Services, Inc. went bankrupt in 1981, more than $50 million was lost by American companies, including American Express, AT&T, Merrill Lynch, and dozens of other blue-chip corporations. They had signed computer lease contracts with OPM, typically for seven to nine years, but had the option of returning their computers earlier than the full term. OPM promised to find another client for the

Source: Hesh Wiener, "The OPM Scandal Unmasked," *Datamation*, vol. 29, no. 9 (September 1983), pp. 34–40.

returned equipment. The monthly payments of the second-lease clients would fulfill the obligations of the original lessee.

OPM's collapse resulted from the fact that they found few customers to accept second leases, and those customers paid a lower rate than anticipated. When bankruptcy was filed, companies that had expected to "walk away" from their contracts because they had returned equipment discovered that they had to pay whether they were using the leased equipment or not. From a legal standpoint, two unrelated, separately enforceable obligations were involved: the users' agreement to spread payments over a number of months and the leasing company's promise to cover payments of returned equipment. When OPM went under, the original lessees were required to pay their lease commitments to OPM creditors.

What went wrong? According to James P. Hassett, the court-appointed bankruptcy trustee, OPM was never solvent. It operated a pyramid scheme, maintaining its cash flow by gaining new customers and with bank loans obtained with forged computer leases as collateral. No client or creditor bothered to check the authenticity of the leases or the financial records of OPM.

A number of lessons can be learned from this leasing scandal. Before a lease contract is signed, review the financial records of the leasing company. Check to see whether the contract will give a reasonable return to the lessor or whether the terms might lead to the lessor's insolvency. Study sublease provisions. Since leasing arrangements can be very convoluted (sometimes, two to three leases are layered on top of the title), it is wise to file appropriate documents to secure lessee rights. For example, file a Uniform Commercial Code statement that secures an interest in the leased equipment. Get access to the payment stream coming from the ultimate lessee. Determine where the subleased machine is going, check the credit of the sublessee, and provide for repossession rights. Find out what happens if the leasing company goes bankrupt.

Perhaps clients of OPM would have subjected their leases to careful scrutiny if they had known what the initials stood for: Other People's Money.

Questions

1. Why do you suppose that the pyramid scheme went undetected for so long? Why didn't creditors or clients bother to check the financial records of OPM?
2. Should clients of OPM have been suspicious of the good leasing terms offered? Is this a case of the old adage, "Buyer beware"? Explain.

3. To ensure that legal complications, such as those that entangled OPM's clients, are avoided, who in a firm should review contracts before they are signed? Could the clients have taken steps that would have protected them from financial obligations following OPM's bankruptcy? If so, what steps?

CASE: FINANCING OPTIONS OFFERED BY IBM CREDIT CORPORATION

IBM Credit Corporation was established in 1981 to offer financing alternatives for IBM customers. At first, the corporation offered term leases and installment payment options for only IBM products. In 1984, however, it extended its services to the financing of non-IBM equipment as well. For example, the corporation has financed commercial and corporate aircraft and railroad rolling stock in addition to IBM typewriters, computers, software, and other products. Rolm Credit Corporation, with expertise in financing telecommunications equipment, became a subsidiary of IBM Credit in 1985.

It is the function of IBM marketing representatives to help customers select IBM equipment and also IBM Credit Corporation financing. Leasing has become an increasingly frequent choice for acquiring computer equipment. IBM Credit offers a Term Lease Master Agreement that, once signed, functions like a library card, enabling customers to acquire equipment as needed on a simple lease supplement to the agreement. A credit card is also offered that makes it easy for IBM customers to charge products at IBM's retail stores.

A broad menu of leasing options is available through IBM Credit. For example, a customer can choose from three standard commercial lease options that differ in monthly payments. Two lease options are available for state and local governments and lease-purchase customers. Furthermore, a software lease option is available, as is a volume-financing offering that permits the installation of additional selected equipment at predetermined lease rates. In addition, lease offerings in complex financing situations can be tailored to fit specific customer needs. In 1985, IBM Credit and its partners provided term-lease financing for IBM products valued at $1.984 billion.

Another financing option provided by IBM Credit is installment payment financing. In 1985, the company purchased $1.107 billion of in-

Source: IBM Credit Corporation Annual Report, 1985.

stallment payment agreements from IBM for computer hardware and software.

Questions

1. As a potential leasing client, how would you evaluate IBM Credit Corporation? How would you go about comparing the financial services of this company with other financing options?
2. Whose advice would you seek when deciding whether to take an IBM term lease or an installment payment option for a purchase?
3. Why does IBM offer so many leasing options through IBM Credit? Who benefits? How?
4. How does IBM Credit Corporation affect the competition among companies that manufacture computer equipment?

STUDY KEYS

Contract	**Operating lease**
Cutover point	**Plug-compatible machines**
Discounted cash-flow analysis	**Price-performance ratio**
Financial lease	**Purchase**
Leasing	**Rental**
Liaison	**Salvage value**
Negotiations	**Third-party leasing**
Obsolescence	**Useful life**

DISCUSSION QUESTIONS

1. Who should make the decision to purchase or lease? What factors determine the choice? When should a direct lease be favored over a third-party lease?
2. Is knowledge of the law necessary when selecting computing resources? Why? Who should provide this knowledge?
3. On what factors will the answers to Question 2 depend?
4. Compare the advantages and limitations of purchase, rent, and lease acquisitions of computer resources.
5. Under what circumstances in the acquisition process would you hire a:

     a. Consultant?

     b. Lawyer?

     What qualities and qualifications would you look for?

6. Here is a list of possible resources that can be acquired. For which of these would you employ a lawyer in the acquisition process? Why?

     a. Hardware.

     b. Software applications.

     c. Hardware and software systems.

     d. Turnkey system.

     e. Software, such as a data base management system.

7. Why is the preparation of a contract for computer resources different from the preparation of a contract for construction of a building or for equipment such as a lathe?

8. Do problems of acquisition vary depending on the source of the resource (i.e., hardware vendor, software house, or consulting company)? Explain.

9. Is planning necessary for the acquisition process? If so, why? Who should do it? At what stage of the development process should it be done?

10. How do the following factors affect the acquisition and implementation of computer resources? What special precautions and steps should be taken?

     a. Size of the organization acquiring the resource (i.e., small or large business).

     b. Value involved.

     c. Range of services to be offered by resource being acquired.

     d. Number of subcontractors involved.

11. Time is an important element in the acquisition process. Comment.

12. What are the problems of user-vendor liaison after an acquisition is made? How can these problems be minimized?

SELECTED ANNOTATED BIBLIOGRAPHY

Brandon, Dick H., and Sidney Segelstein. *Data Processing Contracts—Structures, Contents, and Negotiations.* New York: Van Nostrand Reinhold, 1984, 496 pp.

This excellent book should be on the shelf of anyone involved in computer resource acquisition. It is well organized and indexed for quick and comprehensive reference and use.

Franz, Charles R., and E. Ned Flynn. "Clarifying Warranties and Disclaimers in Computer Contracts." *Journal of Systems Management,* vol. 35, no. 12 (December 1984), pp. 32–37.

The author discusses the wording of warranties and disclaimers to protect both the vendor and customer from possible expensive litigation.

Goldberg, Alan L. "Financing Alternatives for Hardware and Software." *Small Systems World*, vol. 10, no. 12 (December 1982), pp. 30–34.
  Rental, operating lease, financial lease, and purchase are compared. An example of the acquisition of $70,000 of equipment is used to illustrate cash value flow analysis for the four alternatives.

Harris, Charles Edison. "Negotiating Software Contracts." *Datamation*, vol. 31, no. 14 (July 15, 1985), pp. 52–58.
  The author, editor of the journal *Computer Negotiations Report*, writes with knowledge and authority. He lists seven key steps in managing the legal and financial aspects of software acquisition.

Hilliard, Brook L. "How to Protect Yourself against One-Sided Computer Contracts." *Computers in Accounting*, vol. 1, no. 3 (May–June 1985), pp. 36–42.
  It takes a good consultant, an experienced computer contract lawyer, and a competent negotiator to protect against a one-sided contract favoring the vendor. Excellent examples of legal clauses and legal language are given to illustrate the pitfalls facing an inexperienced negotiator.

———. "Techniques for Negotiating a Computer System Acquisition." *Computers in Accounting*, vol. 1, no. 4 (July–August 1985), pp. 41–44.
  According to the author, the buyer should know what he wants and be willing to pay for it. When meeting with the vendor, the buyer should ask for general as well as specific concessions.

Keim, Robert T. *Business Computers: Planning, Selecting and Implementing Your First System*. Columbus, Ohio: Charles E. Merrill Publishing, 1985, 371 pp.
  Chapter 10 is on writing a performance contract; the information is applicable to any resource acquisition. Contract terms, language, and signing procedures are discussed.

"Litigation Avoidance Tips: Computers and Software Acquisition." *Computer Law and Tax Report*, vol. 11, no. 2 (February 1985), pp. 2–3.
  Reading this article will not guarantee that you will avoid litigation over computer resources, but it will certainly help sensitize you to acquisition dangers and how to avoid them.

Polis, Richard. "The Oath to Successful Procurement." *Infosystems*, vol. 22, no. 11 (November 1985), pp. 72–77.
  The author argues that successful vendor management requires a thorough understanding of the work to be done, a good contract, and strong monitoring of products.

Rummer, Patricia. "Making the Lease vs. Buy Decision." *Small Systems World*, vol. 12, no. 3 (March 1984), pp. 20–24.
  Leasing is a way to avoid obsolescence, and it facilitates upgrading. But before deciding to lease or buy, a detailed cash-flow or net present value analysis should be performed by clients.

Stamp, David. "A New Climate for Leasing." *Datamation*, vol. 32, no. 23 (December 1, 1986), pp. 85–88.

The impact of the 1986 tax law is explored. According to the author, there is a strong possibility that lease rates will increase, in part because of the repeal of the investment tax credit. This, in turn, may contribute to a decrease in leasing companies.

"An Update on the Lease-Buy Decision." *Computer Law and Tax Report*, vol. 10, no. 12 (December 1983), pp. 5–6.
Tax and capital consequences should be examined before deciding between lease and buy.

Watson, Hugh J., and Archie B. Carroll. *Computers for Business: A Managerial Emphasis*. Plano, Tex.: Business Publications, 1980, 530 pp.
Chapter 11 of this textbook discusses both selection and acquisition of computer resources. It integrates these topics backward with planning and forward with installation, appraisal, follow-up, and the review process. This integration is achieved at the expense of brevity, and some detail is lost in so broad a coverage. Assignments, a case study, and good references follow the chapter.

Weiner, Hesh. "Lessors on Leasing." *Datamation*, vol. 30, no. 7 (May 15, 1984), pp. 103–11.
Advice is given on selection of a lessor, long-term leases, early termination of a lease, and subleasing. According to the author, users should remember that lessors are financiers as well as computer dealers. "All that's not impossible is negotiable."

Yates, John C., and Henry W. Jones III. "Computer Acquisitions: The Role of Due Diligence." *Computer Negotiations Report*, vol. 8, no. 9 (1985), pp. 1–4.
Two lawyers give advice on the importance of knowing the vendor (including the litigation record) before signing a contract, and they suggest five ways of obtaining information about the vendor. The journal itself is a valuable source for articles on acquisitions and contracts but is difficult to obtain.

PART THREE

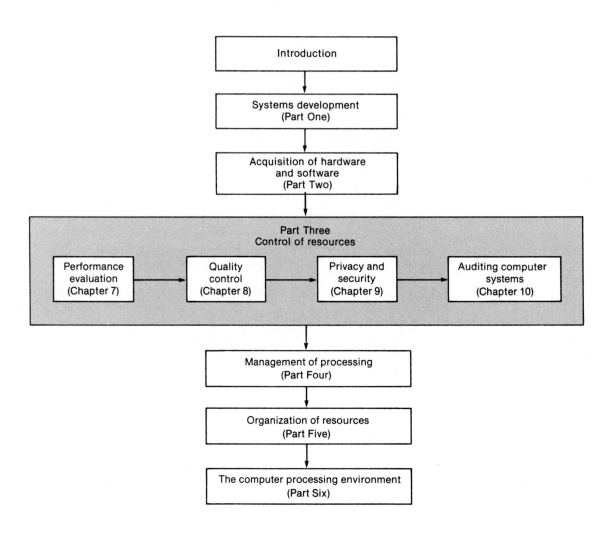

CONTROL OF RESOURCES

Introduction to Part Three

Part Three is closely related to Part Two insofar as all of the mechanisms of control described must be incorporated in systems design during systems development. Indeed, evaluation, quality, privacy, security, and control specifications must be included in the systems requirements statements.

The purpose of devoting a separate part of the book to control is to emphasize the importance of preventing errors and of protecting information from unauthorized access or illicit use in the business world today. The need for control and security of business data, of course, predates the use of computers. But the speed of computer transactions and the volume of confidential data processed by computers means that inadequate controls can lead to problems of a much higher magnitude than in the past. Consider, for example, the large sums of money being transferred daily with electronic fund transfer (EFT) and the scope for embezzlement if EFT security can be breached.

Chapter 7 discusses how a computer center evaluates its own performance and evaluation criteria and methods of collecting data on performance are outlined. Operations that need evaluation are also identified. Chapter 8 describes where control mechanisms should be located to monitor systems for human and machine error and suggests solutions to common problems.

Privacy and security issues are the subject of Chapter 9. Layers of protection are recommended, including access restrictions to computer resources, processing controls, physical safeguards, and organizational policies to discourage employee malfeasance. Finally, Chapter 10 describes computer audits by individuals not employed by the computer facility, so that a measure of objectivity in evaluating operations can be obtained. The role of auditors in controlling controls is also explained.

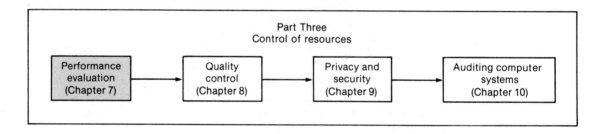

Part Three
Control of resources

| Performance evaluation (Chapter 7) | Quality control (Chapter 8) | Privacy and security (Chapter 9) | Auditing computer systems (Chapter 10) |

CHAPTER 7

Performance evaluation

The perfect computer has been developed.
You just feed in your problems—and they
never come out again.

Al Goodman

In order to ensure quality computing, the performance of an information systems department should be regularly evaluated. This evaluation, called **computer performance evaluation**,[1] consists of a comparison of actual performance with desired performance in resource utilization, operations, and service, as shown in Figure 7–1. When performance fails to measure up to prescribed standards, corrective action followed by reevaluation is required. A satisfactory performance evaluation indicates no immediate need for change but is no grounds for complacency. Computing is not a static field. New technology, an altered business climate, increased load, a change in users, demand for new applications, or delays in new systems development can suddenly turn contented clients into frustrated users. For this reason, evaluations should be scheduled at regular intervals so that systems weaknesses can be identified and rectified before they become chronic. Evaluation should also be initiated whenever problems arise.

Performance evaluation is, in effect, a control mechanism. Surprisingly, many information systems departments[2] that design and maintain financial and performance reporting systems for the organizations they serve treat performance evaluation of their own operations cas-

---

[1] Other terms frequently used as synonyms for computer performance evaluation are computer performance management and computer performance monitoring.

[2] Here again we have a terminology problem. The name of the organizational unit responsible for computing differs from one organization to another. Whereas some firms use the term *information systems department,* others call the unit the computer center, data center, EDP (electronic data processing) center, or some similar title.

Figure 7–1   **The process of performance evaluation**

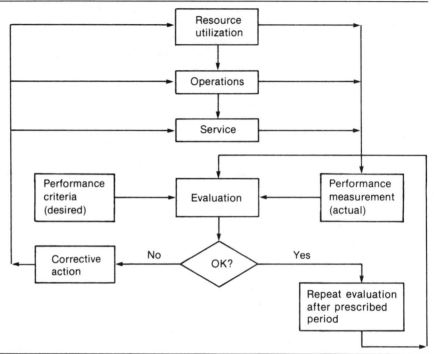

ually. This occurs even though improved computing performance would have a multiplier effect, enhancing the performance of other departments in turn. After all, an information system is a service function that exists to better the effectiveness of a firm's line functions. Systems are installed because they promise to deliver benefits that equal or exceed their cost. It follows, therefore, that any gain in the effectiveness of the information function would be magnified for the organization as a whole.

There are also financial reasons to focus on improved performance of computer operations. Information systems departments consume from 1 to 5 percent of the revenue generated by most manufacturing concerns. As much as 20 per cent of operating costs can be attributed to information systems for service organizations and public agencies that deal in information. What company would not welcome a way to reduce such expenditures? Performance evaluations lead to cost savings by identifying computing inefficiencies and tracking the results of corrective action.

This chapter describes the mechanisms of performance evaluation. First, critical performance variables that need to be evaluated are identified, and then evaluation criteria are described. This is followed by a discussion of how performance data are collected, measured, and analyzed. Finally, corrective action and evaluation of the evaluation process itself are considered. Sections in this chapter correspond to steps in the evaluation process as shown in Figure 7–2. Personnel, timing, and evaluation tools and techniques will be discussed at each step when relevant. This chapter deals with macroevaluation by departmental staff, the first level of performance control. The role of auditors external to the information systems department, who also evaluate performance, will be considered in Chapter 10.

Figure 7–2   **Steps in evaluation**

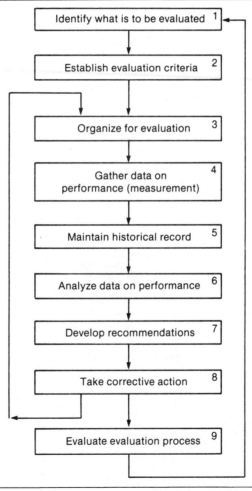

IDENTIFY WHAT IS TO BE EVALUATED

In computing, four areas comprise keys to performance:

- Financial management—management of the dollar resources allocated to the information systems function.
- Applications management—control and reporting of the design, implementation, and maintenance of applications systems.
- Productivity/operations management—ensuring availability and managing utilization of computers.
- Human resource management—productivity of personnel assigned to information systems.[3]

An organization that wants to improve its information function should collect performance variables in each of these four areas for analysis. The problem is to decide exactly which variables to collect and how to organize collected data for evaluation. Should data be gathered on expenditures by object of expense (salaries, supplies, and services)? By

Figure 7–3   **Performance components to be evaluated**

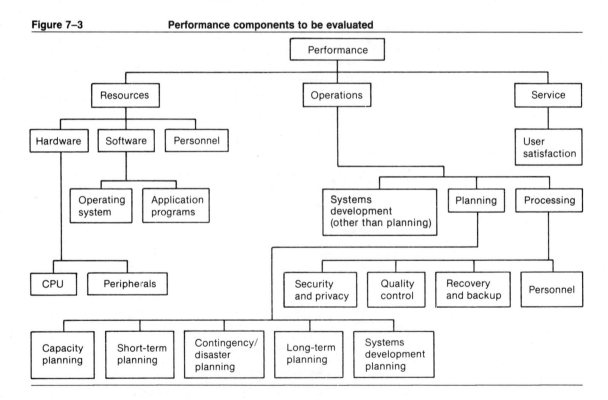

---

[3]This list and the discussion that follows are drawn from Kenneth G. Rau, "Performance Management," *Computerworld*, vol. 18, no. 34 (August 20, 1984), pp. ID/17–22.

activity? By the cost to run, maintain, and enhance applications programs? By customer? What aspects of production should be measured? On-time/in-budget delivery of systems? Resource consumption? Is an analysis of human productivity needed in order to evaluate performance, or would a study of the distribution of the workload and skill improvements through training suffice?

In deciding what performance variables to monitor and evaluate, corporate management, users, planning groups, data administrators, and EDP personnel should all have a voice. They should also participate in discussions of what performance objectives should be. Figure 7–3 shows commonly evaluated components of the information systems function.[4]

ESTABLISH EVALUATION CRITERIA

Efficiency of operations and effectiveness of product are basic evaluation criteria. Historically, information systems departments have focused on the computing process to ensure a high ratio of output to input (efficiency). Today, however, more emphasis is placed on effectiveness of the information function. The real issue, according to many corporate managers, is what level of service is being provided to computer users by the information systems department.

Let us now turn to a discussion of evaluation criteria in the two categories of efficiency and effectiveness.

Efficiency

Efficiency (η), a concept used in production management, is the ratio of output (O) to input (I) as expressed in the formula $\eta = {}^O/_I$. Unfortunately, the benefit of output in computing cannot always be calculated in tangible units. How can one measure the monetary value of a timely report, accuracy, or the absence of fraud? By keeping input constant, however, a change in output can be noted: if output increases, efficiency is increased; if output decreases, efficiency is decreased. Efficiency is generally measured in terms of throughput, productivity, resource utilization, and costs.

Throughput. The design of equipment, in part, determines computer **throughput**, the amount of work that can be performed during a given period of time. Throughput is advertised, known to the buyer at the time of purchase. Central processing unit (CPU) throughput may

---

[4]Usually, the evaluation of daily operations is distinct from the evaluation of systems development. Many firms consider planning so important that separate evaluations are held for capacity planning, contingency planning, long- and short-term planning, and systems development planning.

be measured in thousands of operations per second (KOPS) or millions of instructions per second (MIPS). Unfortunately, these measurements are not as standardized as horsepower or kilowatt hours, so one cannot always compare the throughput of computers sold by different vendors.[5]

CPU throughput, however, is rarely the prime processing constraint. Rather, efficiency is limited by peripheral devices used in pre- and postprocessing, such as optical recognition equipment, printers, bursters, decolators, and routing equipment. Such peripheral devices advertise throughput as a selling feature so that competing models can be compared by the buyer. When sales claims prove unsubstantiated, the vendor can be held accountable, provided that a well-written, detailed, legally binding contract has been signed.

Productivity. **Productivity** is the term usually applied to throughput performance of personnel—that is, the quantity of work produced by an individual in a unit of time. For example, the efficiency of data entry operators can be evaluated by comparing number of keystrokes per hour with standard tables. Lines of code (LOC) per programmer-day can measure a programmer's productivity. Other common productivity measures are documentation pages per documenter-month, cost per defect, CPU hours per programmer-month, and test cases developed and executed per programmer-month.

The problem is that the measurement of productivity in such work units can be misleading. For example, LOC is biased in favor of programmers who do not optimize their codes. This measure also penalizes high-level languages, making it harder to compare productivity between programmers. Many traditional productivity measures do not take program complexity, correctness, or reliability into account, nor whether the software is structured or not. They make little allowance for the program's size, for the organization of the programming team, or for the programmer's experience. Furthermore, some standard productivity measures are founded on unproven assumptions. As a result, the quantity of a programmer's work is somewhat discredited as a productivity measure. Many companies are in search of new ways to evaluate productivity.

One new technique that is currently attracting attention is function-point measurement, a method of characterizing the size and complexity of applications based on the amount of function delivered to the users.

---

[5]There is considerable debate whether improvements in system response times actually benefit all computer users. For example, it is questionable whether subsecond response time is needed for applications that are "human intensive," such as use of a text editor. Some studies indicate that such a fast system response can actually disrupt the human thought processes. See "The Great Response Time Debate," *EDP Performance Review*, vol. 13, no. 9 (September 1985), pp. 1–4 ff.

This method, under study at IBM, attempts to quantify the cost per function and assign a benefit to the function. Halstead metrics, another new technique, counts the number of action statements (operators) and data elements (operands) in a program. It has been demonstrated that the sum of the number of operators and operands is correlated with the error rate and productivity of a program.[6]

Unfortunately, flaws and errors in programs often take a long time to surface. A programmer who is rewarded for high productivity based on a measure such as lines of code may be writing software that requires excessive maintenance. (More discussion on the issue of productivity appears in Chapter 22, which is on staffing.)

Utilization. Another gauge of efficiency is **utilization,** the ratio of what is used to what is available. Unused capacity is a waste of resources; however, a high utilization value may indicate that bottlenecks in processing will occur in the near future. The same utilization data that is studied during performance evaluations can be used for capacity planning and scheduling as well.

Cost. Efficiency is increased when **cost,** with constant output, drops. One way to evaluate performance is by comparing budgeted with actual expenditures and reviewing trends in cost indexes:

$$\text{Material cost index} = \frac{\text{Cost of materials}}{\text{Total cost of computing center}}$$

$$\text{Personnel cost index} = \frac{\text{Cost of personnel}}{\text{Total cost of computing center}}$$

$$\text{Software maintenance index} = \frac{\text{Cost of maintenance (software)}}{\text{Total cost of computing center}}$$

In computing, inefficiency can often be traced to waste of materials (tapes, paper) and run time. Habits of waste frequently develop when user departments do not pay for computing services and computer time is not constrained. By charging for services, costs may be lowered dramatically—an example of a budgetary policy that may affect performance efficiency.

Effectiveness

Effectiveness evaluation is based on the objectives of the information function. An effective system is one that satisfies the expectations of users. When effectiveness is under study, the following questions are

[6]For more on these new measurement techniques, see Girish Parikh, "Techniques of Measuring Programmer Productivity," *Data Management*, vol. 23, no. 6 (June 1985), pp. 18–22 ff.; Steve Drummond, "Measuring Applications Development Performance," *Datamation*, vol. 31, no. 4 (February 1985), pp. 102–8.

asked: Are user needs being met by the information systems department? Does the output produced by applications programs meet user requirements? Are systems user friendly? Are users satisfied with their information systems?

When an organization focuses on effectiveness, the emphasis shifts from the technical aspects of information production to the problems that the computer can solve. Information specialists take on a business orientation, working closely with users and corporate management to ensure that information strategies fully support business plans. Performance is measured in terms of systems availability, information quality, timeliness, accuracy, and reliability, since user satisfaction is based on these criteria.

Availability.   Machine **availability** may be measured as the percent of time that equipment is in service. A company with three shifts that has half an hour daily downtime (for breakdowns or maintenance) has an availability index of roughly 98 percent $(^{23.5}/_{24})$. As downtime is reduced, systems effectiveness will increase. The problem with this index is that if the half-hour downtime remains fixed but the denominator changes, the index changes although the machine is no less available from the operational point of view. For example, if the half-hour downtime occurs during operations when the machine is utilized only 12 hours instead of 24, the index is roughly 96 percent $(^{11.5}/_{12})$ although no change has taken place in machine availability because of downtime. (Restrictions on availability as a result of priority scheduling or overloading is a separate problem of scheduling and capacity planning.)

One can also evaluate availability in absolute terms. If a job requires 300 minutes of machine time on a specific date, is that 300 minutes available when needed?

Quality.   Quantitive measures of **quality** are difficult to formulate, but one can identify costs associated with quality. For example, prevention cost is a measure of the money spent to prevent errors or do the job right the first time. Appraisal costs include the money spent for reviewing and testing systems to see that they meet systems requirements. Failure costs are those associated with defective systems. Evaluation teams should study these figures as they look for ways to help improve the information function.[7]

---

[7]For more on this subject, see "Trends in Performance Management," *EDP Performance Review*, vol. 12, no. 5 (May 1984), pp. 1–6.

Generally, quality is measured in terms of user satisfaction. Factors that will influence this satisfaction are:

- Ease of use of computer systems and software.
- Security and confidentiality of data.
- Technical support given users by computer specialists.
- Completeness, readability, and organization of documentation.
- User confidence that state-of-the-art technology is being applied.
- Ease with which systems can be maintained and upgraded.
- Portability and reusability.
- Ease with which a system can be audited and tested.

Timeliness.   There are really three measures for **timeliness:** turn-around time, response time, and schedule adherence. **Turnaround time** is the period of time between job submission to the information systems department and the return of output. This is usually a measure for batch work and will be measured in hours or days. **Response time** is a way of measuring the timeliness of interactive online activities and will typically be measured in fractions of a second. **Schedule adherence** refers to the ability of a computing facility to process applications on time and to deliver new systems that are under development when promised.

Other ways to evaluate timeliness would be to study waiting time, length of queue, number of days projects are delayed, and backlogs. It is often better to have 10 projects that are each delayed one day than to have one project 10 days late.

Accuracy.   **Accuracy** can be defined as the absence of error. But what constitutes an error? When a calculated value is 1.962256, one can truncate the number to 1.96 when the unit is dollars and cents but not when 1.962256 represents millions of dollars. A misspelled name on the mailing list for an advertising circular would be regrettable but not crucial. But suppose the misspelling were the name of the chairman of the board in a firm's annual report?

These examples illustrate that accuracy must be carefully defined when evaluating systems effectiveness. The permissible magnitude of error should be established, rate of acceptable error defined (for example, one in 1 million calculations), and error limits set in absolute terms (for example, number of allowable errors per month). Degree of accuracy should be set not only for computer processing but for peripherals, telecommunications, and data entry as well.

Since errors usually result in reruns, rerun data is one way to measure performance accuracy.

Reliability.   **Reliability** is an elusive concept although many formulas have been published to measure it. The problem is that too many variables in reliability calculations cannot be precisely measured. The relative importance of these variables in contributing to **systems reliability** is also difficult to impute. For example, what role do sickness, absenteeism, turnover, training, and operator motivation play in systems reliability? Should reliability be based on the effort, cost, or time required to keep a system operational?

Software reliability (a function of the complexity of the software, the competence of programmers, and viability of a given development approach) is also difficult to assess. The problem of identifying software errors compounds the difficulty of measuring systems effectiveness in terms of reliability. Systems may appear to function smoothly but be producing inaccurate output due to inherent, undetected software errors.

Users are generally interested not in a technical measure of reliability (involving statistics and probability theory) but rather in availability. They want to know whether they can count on the computer being operational when they need to use it.

Conflicts between evaluation criteria

Before concluding this section, a word should be said about the interrelationships that exist between performance criteria. In many cases, a high evaluation rating for one criterion precludes a high rating for another. For example, lowering response time may raise costs, and vice versa. Suppose the response time–cost curve for a given firm is as illustrated in Figure 7–4, with OC an acceptable response time according to management and OD an acceptable cost. Compromise is necessary since they yield different points on the curve. That is, both performance objectives cannot be met at the same time. At Point E, for example, the cost corresponds to DD', but the response time OF corresponding to FF' is slower than CC'. At Point B, the response time corresponds to CC', but the cost AA' is higher than DD'. One of the two variables has to give, or both may be compromised somewhat to fall within Points E and B on the curve. This means either a slower response time or higher cost than desired by management.

The same type of conflict may exist between other variables, such as quality and cost or quality and timeliness, as shown:

Quality control → Quality ↑ →   Desirable ⎫
                                             ⎬ Conflict
                   Costs ↑ →   Undesirable ⎭

Quality control → Quality ↑ →   Desirable ⎫
                                             ⎬ Conflict
                   Timeliness ↓ → Undesirable ⎭

Figure 7–4   **Response time–cost curve**

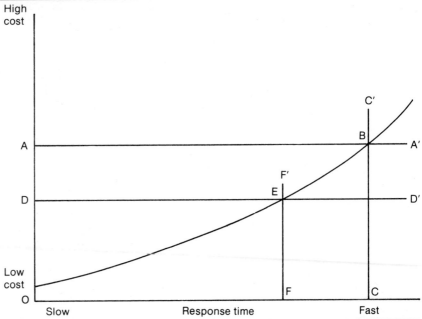

Indeed, more than two criteria may be in opposition in a given situation. Management must then search for a satisfactory or acceptable mix of controllable factors and set performance standards that minimize the effect of conflicts. This is not an easy task.

ORGANIZE FOR EVALUATION

Who evaluates the performance of an information systems department? Often, a staff member in the department is assigned the task, someone who is technically competent and also knowledgeable regarding organizational policies and procedures. Sometimes, more objectivity is sought. A person within the organization but working in another department—with no role in daily computer operations—will be given the responsibility of evaluating the information function. Still other firms hire a consultant to evaluate performance. For large organizations with complex information systems, an evaluation team may be required.

Performance evaluation should be a regularly scheduled activity. The staff member responsible for evaluation should be appointed, a budget for evaluation activities drawn up, and the purpose and scope of the evaluation publicized. Evaluations should be conducted openly, not secretly, with the evaluator and evaluation results known to workers. Employees can be helpful to evaluators in identifying and diagnosing poor performance, and their cooperation is needed when corrective procedures are initiated.

The frequency of evaluations will vary from one firm to another. Many organizations require the submission of monthly performance reports organized around financial management, applications management, productivity/operations management, and human resource management for study by the individual (or team) charged with performance evaluation. The reports may subsequently be reviewed at meetings with the information systems department head and staff.

Not all companies require such a rigid evaluation structure. Most corporate managers weigh the cost of evaluation effort, computer time, and organizational disruption against the potential costs of unidentified inefficiency and ineffectiveness. They then schedule evaluations accordingly.

GATHER DATA ON PERFORMANCE (MEASUREMENT)

Once performance criteria are specified and variables identified, data on the values of variables must be collected for analysis. This can be done by logging, using monitors, or canvassing users, as illustrated in Figure 7–5.

Logs

In many computer centers, manual **logs** are kept by operators. These logs are a source of information when evaluating performance. For example, data on the length of downtime for maintenance might be determined from an operator's log.

One disadvantage of such log use is that drawing information from a log is time consuming: a simple calculation, such as percent of jobs delivered on schedule, requires someone to search logs for relevant data. And human error is always possible in the calculation itself. Job accounting programs can replace manually collected statistics in some areas, but cost again is a factor, albeit much less so.

Monitors

Computer performance can also be measured using hardware and software monitors. (See Figure 7–6.)

Hardware monitors, equipment with sensors in input and output channels, record desired data on instrument panels or on tape for later analysis. An **accumulating monitor** is a counter used in simple computational environments. It might be used to count the number of jobs completed in a given time period, for example. A **logical monitor** is essentially a minicomputer used in more complex processing, such as

Figure 7–5 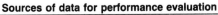 **Sources of data for performance evaluation**

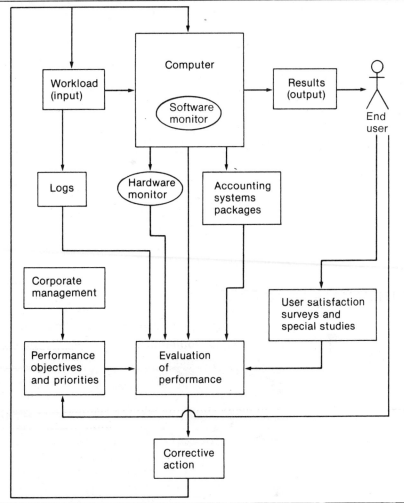

multiprogramming. Both types of hardware monitors are suitable for collecting utilization statistics and data on component conflicts—data needed for capacity planning.

A wide variety of counting measures are possible using hardware monitors. The monitors can accurately report data on short-term activities and measure systems overhead. However, hardware monitors are costly, have a long setup time, and require skilled personnel to operate. Probes and connections can be accidentally dislodged, damaged, or incorrectly connected, resulting in false data.

A **software monitor** is an application program that is part of the operating system or stored internally. The software contains a data

Figure 7–6   **Types of monitors**

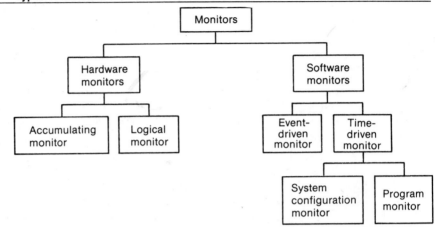

collector that takes time counts and gathers data by reading internal tables, status registers, memory maps, operating system control blocks, and so on. Then an analyzer/reporter reads the data and reduces, orders, groups, summarizes, and computes values of interest. Finally, the information is displayed in a logical manner. Sometimes, output is printed in hard copy; sometimes, it is displayed on a terminal screen.

Software monitors are of two types. An **event-driven monitor** interacts with the operating system's interrupt-handling mechanism and can monitor almost every occurrence of the event being studied. A **time-driven monitor** is a periodic sampling system activated at user-specified intervals. It is subdivided into system configuration monitors (which generate information on system components) and program monitors.

Software monitors can generate utilization figures, as hardware monitors do, and can also report on the performance of systems and applications programs. They are easy to use, low in cost, and allow flexibility in choosing options for data collection. However, the monitors may not be able to monitor concurrent events. The cost of CPU and storage overhead is also a disadvantage. In addition, these monitors generally have low priority for CPU access, and the software must be reprogrammed when changes are made to operating systems.[8]

User surveys

Data on user satisfaction with the performance of information systems can be collected in **user surveys** using questionnaires and inter-

---

[8]For more information on software monitors, see Jerry Gitomer, "Measuring System Performance with Software Monitors," *Journal of Information Systems Management*, vol. 1, no. 2 (Summer 1984), pp. 50–55.

views. The problem is designing relevant questions and framing them in a manner so that they are not misunderstood and resisted. In addition, the respondent must be motivated to reply candidly. Questions should be neutral, so that there are no implicit "right" answers, and nonthreatening. Otherwise, respondents will distort their replies for self-pro-

Figure 7–7	Questions from user satisfaction survey*

1. Please express your overall satisfaction with the service you receive from the computer center.
   ☐ Very good
   ☐ Good
   ☐ Fair
   ☐ Poor
   ☐ Very poor

2. For Report #20 (Cost Distribution by Department), please express your satisfaction in each of the areas listed on a scale of 1 to 10. (Low satisfaction would be indicated by a 1; high satisfaction by a 10.)

	For cost analysis	For fund management	For cost estimation	For decision making
Format				
Content				
Amount of detail				
Timeliness				
Overall rating				

3. How do you evaluate the charging policies for service at the data center?
   ☐ Very reasonable
   ☐ Reasonable
   ☐ Unreasonable
   ☐ Outrageous

4. Please express how charging policies affect your use of the computer center.
   ☐ No effect
   ☐ Discourage use
   ☐ Encourage use

5. Which of the following charging policies would you consider reasonable?
   ☐ Service at no cost
   ☐ Service at marginal cost
   ☐ Service at full cost
   ☐ Service at a cost that is competitive with external computing facilities.

*These representative questions are drawn from a survey to show how questions might be formatted. They are only sample questions, however, and the survey is by no means complete.

tection. That is, users must perceive their work environment as one in which they will not be penalized for making critical responses.

Questions might be asked on the following topics:

- Timeliness of operations and reports.
- Validity and completeness of reports.
- Achievement of predetermined acceptable levels of operations.
- Frequency of errors.
- Response time to meet users' requests.
- Protection of privacy.
- Data and systems security.
- Systems reliability.
- Achievement of long-range goals.
- Degree of incorporation of latest technology.
- Training availability and effectiveness.
- Quality of output and service.
- Lines of communication with EDP personnel.

This list is essentially a restatement of efficiency and effectiveness criteria described earlier in the chapter. Sample questions that might be used in evaluating systems performance appear in Figure 7–7. It is helpful if questionnaires are designed so answers can be mark-sensed or read by optical scanning equipment. A terminal might also be used, with answers collected by one-stroke responses or by touch-sensitive screens.

MAINTAIN HISTORICAL RECORD

When evaluating performance data, it is useful to compare current performance with records from the past. For this reason, historical records need to be maintained. Performance data stored in a data bank should help with longitudinal analysis, setting standards, identifying performance trends, and calculating moving averages.

ANALYZE DATA ON PERFORMANCE

Without analysis of collected performance data, the collection effort is wasted. Yet, too often, sheaves of performance data are stacked on an evaluator's desk waiting for analysis that never takes place. Time must be set aside to review and interpret data.

Analysis usually starts with a glance-check at data to see if the values of variables are reasonable. This may be followed by a trend analysis and a check to see how performance measures up to local, national, and industrial standards.

Figure 7–8 **Data on performance for analysis of CPU utilization**

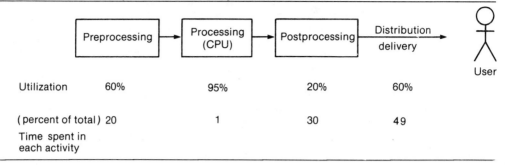

Utilization	60%	95%	20%	60%	
(percent of total)	20	1	30	49	
Time spent in each activity					

For example, let us look at the sample figures on CPU utilization listed in Figure 7–8. If the 95 percent were for three shifts, excluding preventive maintenance (often 5 percent), the computer would be running near full capacity. The person evaluating these figures would recognize that the figures indicate a need for system expansion or the acquisition of a larger system.

The 60 percent utilization figure for preprocessing and 20 percent for postprocessing is within an acceptable performance range. (The person who evaluates these figures should be well informed on standard performance statistics.) However, these figures may hide bottlenecks at specific equipment, so disaggregated data should be collected—for example, utilization statistics on all channel ports as well as utilization figures for tapes, disks, and other input/output devices. The 49 percent figure for distribution activities in this sample is high compared with other computer systems. The evaluator would recognize this to be one area of performance that could be upgraded if delivery procedures were changed.

DEVELOP RECOMMENDATIONS AND TAKE CORRECTIVE ACTION

On the basis of data analysis, evaluators should formulate a set of recommendations to improve performance, supported by reviews and reports. A sample listing of what should be included in these documents appears in Table 7–1.

Recommendations for corrective action may include changes in resource usage, new procedures and techniques, revised user interfaces, or perhaps alteration of the firm's planning process. The aim of corrective action should be not merely to bring performance to targeted levels but to raise it to higher standards.

Recommendations for action to correct an unacceptable service level situation are not the sole responsibility of the evaluator. In most com-

Table 7–1   **Reviews, reports, and recommendations by performance evaluators**

Reviews	*Reports*	*Recommendations*
Service levels	Exceptional	Cost-effective innovations
Priorities	Summary	Technical
Workloads	Technical	Organizational
Forecasts of:	Financial	Corrective actions to
Resource needs		improve performance
Personnel		
Acceptance levels		
Relevance and obsoleteness		
Cost effectiveness		

panies, managers meet with users and data processing personnel to consider evaluation reports and to devise strategies to improve the information function. Various tools and techniques may be called into play to help determine what changes to make. For example, job accounting packages, benchmarks, or modeling and simulation might be used to experiment with changes to the equipment configuration, the schedule, software, or any number of other variables that affect performance. The responsibility for selecting what performance improvements to make and how to implement these improvements rests with management.

EVALUATE EVALUATION PROCESS

A final responsibility of the evaluator is to evaluate the evaluation process itself. That is, problems in planning, organizing, and implementing the evaluation should be identified, changes in the basic premises or philosophy of evaluation suggested (if any are needed), and tools and techniques for future evaluations recommended. Such an evaluation is particularly important following a computer center performance evaluation, because firms are still learning how to conduct such evaluations. The speed with which technological advances take place in computing also complicates the evaluator's role, because new models of equipment and new applications software are continually being introduced.

SUMMING UP

Performance objectives are set by corporate management. To make sure that an information systems department meets performance objectives, periodic evaluations should be scheduled; they should also be triggered when problems arise.

Figure 7–9 **Components of performance**

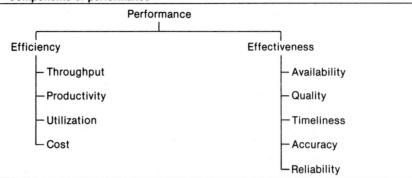

Performance

Efficiency
— Throughput
— Productivity
— Utilization
— Cost

Effectiveness
— Availability
— Quality
— Timeliness
— Accuracy
— Reliability

Evaluation begins by identifying what is to be evaluated and setting evaluation criteria. The number and nature of evaluation criteria will vary from firm to firm and depend on managerial preference and processing maturity. In most organizations, both efficiency of operations and systems effectiveness are evaluated. Figure 7–9 lists common evaluation criteria in each of these two categories.

An information systems department can run efficiently, yet still be ineffective, and vice versa. For example, the process of generating information may cost little and optimize resource use, yet deliver output

Figure 7–10 **Efficiency and effectiveness evaluation**

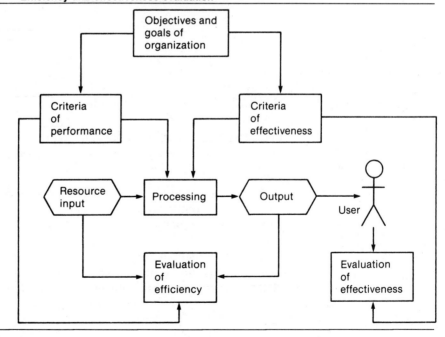

that fails to meet user needs. On the other hand, the department may provide quality information that improves the productivity of employees throughout the organization, yet take so much computer time to generate this information that the cost of the output is more than its value. The difference between efficiency and effectiveness as performance measures is illustrated in Figure 7–10.

Once performance criteria have been established, performance data in these areas are collected. The data are gathered primarily by logs, user questionnaires or interviews, and hardware and software monitors. It is the responsibility of the evaluator to study performance data in order to identify performance weaknesses and to report these weaknesses to management. The evaluator should also propose recommendations to improve the information function in accordance with processing objectives. Recommendations should also be solicited by management from users and data processing personnel. Which recommendations are adopted is a management decision. The implementation of accepted recommendations also rests with management.

The evaluation process should itself be evaluated. A report listing problems and mistakes as well as successful strategies of evaluation will be useful when the evaluation cycle is repeated. The evaluation process should be periodically scheduled and should also be initiated when major performance problems arise.

Evaluation, as described in this chapter, is one level of performance control. Chapter 14 deals with audits of the information function.

CASE: FINANCIAL TRANSACTIONS IN AN HOUR

Recently, Mr. Richard Braddock, head of Citicorp's individual-banking division, stated in a speech that the following transactions would take place in the next hour:

- 14 million personal checks would be written by Americans.
- 7,000 bank accounts would be opened.
- Approximately 6,000 consumer certificates of deposit would be negotiated.
- Using bank, travel, and entertainment cards, an estimated 22,000 airline tickets would be purchased.
- 45,000 people would take out insurance policies.

Source: "Wiring Main Street," *Economist*, vol. 298, no. 7438 (March 22, 1986), p. 16.

- More than 1,000 money-market fund and money-market deposit accounts would be opened.
- Over 12,000 transactions would take place in the U.S. stock market.
- 260,000 people would use automatic teller machines (ATMs) for financial transactions.
- 2 new ATMs would be opened to supplement the nearly 60,000 already in use throughout the country.

Questions

1. With reference to the above statistics, discuss the importance of efficiency and effectiveness evaluations of computer operations.
2. How would you go about evaluating the effectiveness and user satisfaction of 260,000 ATM transactions an hour?
3. Describe controls that you think should be in place to monitor processing of the 14 million checks written per hour?
4. What measures would you recommend to evaluate consumer and airline satisfaction with the use of credit cards for the purchase of flight tickets?

STUDY KEYS

Accumulating monitor	**Reliability**
Accuracy	**Resource utilization**
Availability	**Response time**
Computer performance evaluation	**Schedule adherence**
	Software monitor
Cost	**Software reliability**
Effectiveness	**Systems reliability**
Efficiency	**Throughput**
Event-driven monitor	**Time-driven monitor**
Hardware monitors	**Timeliness**
Logs	**Turnaround time**
Logical monitor	**User surveys**
Productivity	**Utilization**
Quality	

DISCUSSION QUESTIONS

1. Why and how is the performance evaluation of the development process different from the evaluation of:

        a.   Computer equipment?

        b.   User satisfaction of computing services?

        c.   Computer personnel?

2. What is necessary to initiate a program of performance evaluation for an information systems department?

3. Comment on the following statement: Mathematical formulas and models are not useful when evaluating performance in a computer center.

4. Performance appraisal of a computing activity is highly subjective. It should be conducted by a psychologist or sociologist rather than a computer scientist. Comment.

5. How is the performance evaluation of computing in a bank different from a similar evaluation in:

        a.   A manufacturing business?

        b.   A wholesale firm having a large warehouse?

        c.   A large office?

6. What is a monitor? What are the functions of monitors?

7. How can an information system's components, such as hardware, software, and procedures, be evaluated separately? Is such evaluation desirable?

8. When should evaluation take place? Who should be responsible?

9. What is the difference between the efficiency and effectiveness of an information system? How can they be evaluated?

10. What are the steps in the evaluation process?

11. Describe four common efficiency criteria.

12. What is the difference between the following effectiveness measures?

        a.   Availability and timeliness.

        b.   Quality and accuracy.

        c.   Completeness and correctness.

13. Can a conflict exist between performance criteria? Explain.

14. What is the difference between hardware and software monitors?

15. Comment on the statement: Operational efficiency should be given priority over systems effectiveness.

EXERCISES

1. Two programmers, A and B, have each completed programs of equal complexity. Statistics on their performance are:

	A	*B*
Lines of code	3,200	2,800
Number of output reports	5	4
Time taken (units of time)	6	5
Language used	PASCAL	FORTRAN
Response time	12	13

If you were manager, how would you evaluate each programmer on a scale of 1 to 5 (1 is lowest)? Explain the reasons for your evaluation.

2. Two CPUs are being operated in your shop. Which has a better performance, X or Y?

	X	Y
Cache memory	256K	512K
CPU cycle time	.3 microseconds	.2 microseconds
CPU memory	8 megabytes	10 megabytes
I/O channels	8	12
I/O channels at 3 megabytes	2	1
Manufacturer	A	B

SELECTED ANNOTATED BIBLIOGRAPHY

Arthur, Jay. "Software Quality Measurement." *Datamation*, vol. 30, no. 21 (December 15, 1984), pp. 115–20.
The components of quality and ways to measure quality are discussed.

Bromberg, Howard. "In Search of Productivity." *Datamation*, vol. 30, no. 13 (August 15, 1984), pp. 74–76.
The improvement of systems development, using new design methodologies and testing tools, can lead to better productivity. Bromberg states that the choice of a particular productivity aid is not as important as the decision to choose.

Brooks, Julie K. "Managing Data Processing through Standard Costs." *EDP Performance Review*, vol. 11, no. 6 (June 1983), pp. 1–6.
Brooks discusses standard budgeting and cost accounting procedures that could be used for a data processing organization.

Drummond, Steve. "Measuring Applications Development Performance." *Datamation*, vol. 31, no. 4 (February 15, 1985), pp. 102–8.
This article discusses the use of the function-point technique to enhance both internal and external performance reporting.

EDP Performance Review
This magazine has an annual survey of proprietary software packages that can help to measure productivity in a computer center. The software listed is not ranked. Caution is advised in selecting software, because a wide range of quality exists. Check a bibliographic reference for the issue in which the survey occurs.

Gitomer, Jerry. "Measuring System Performance with Software Monitors." *Journal of Information Systems Management*, vol. 1, no. 2 (Summer 1984), pp. 50–55.
The author recognizes that software monitors are costly but argues that monitors pay for themselves by the increased control and higher productivity that result from their use.

Heuser, Dick. "Maximizing Data Center Efficiency." *Infosystems*, vol. 32, no. 4 (April 1985), pp. 70–71.
    According to the author, both a customer service orientation and use of data center management software can improve data center efficiency, leading to improved customer satisfaction.

Howard, Phillip C. "Performance Management through User Service Levels." *Data Management*, vol. 19, no. 3 (March 1981), pp. 17–24.
    More attention is being paid today to the concept of user service. Howard states that computer professionals get into more trouble with management because of user complaints than as the result of specific inefficiency in the computer operation itself.

Kovach, Roger. "Performance-Measure Software Pinpoints System Bottlenecks." *Mini-Micro Systems*, vol. 17, no. 11 (April 1984), pp. 157–64.
    We now have improved technology for testing mainframe and large-scale systems for performance and have adapted performance measurement software to minicomputer systems.

Lambert, G. N. "A Comparative Study in System Response Time of Program Developer Productivity." *IBM Systems Journal*, vol. 23, no. 1 (1984).
    This is a report on a study to test the premise that added computer resources can decrease system response time and increase programmer productivity significantly. One of the findings was that individual group project offices lead to greater efficiency than large open rooms.

Parikh, Girish. "Techniques of Measuring Programmer Productivity." *Data Management*, vol. 23, no. 6 (June 1985), pp. 18–22.
    Although programming may not be measurable with mathematical accuracy, a number of systematic methods that allow reasonable assessments have been developed. This article introduces Parikh productivity metrics.

Performance Evaluation Review
    This is a publication of the ACM (Association for Computing Machinery) special-interest group on measurement and evaluation. It includes both mathematical and nonmathematical articles as well as reports on special workshops and conferences on the subject.

Schaeffer, Howard. *Data Center Operations*. Englewood Cliffs, N.J.: Prentice-Hall, 1981, pp. 301–67.
    This text has one chapter devoted to computer performance and another to computing center performance evaluation. Both are useful reading as an introduction to the subject, although the book would also be appropriate for a professional manager of a data center. The text has good illustrations and many samples of forms and reports used in performance evaluation. Appendix 1 has a comprehensive checklist for data center evaluation.

"Trends in Performance Management." *EDP Performance Review*, vol. 12, no. 5 (May 1984), pp. 1–6.
    An excellent discussion of technological changes that affect the practice of performance evaluation and capacity management. Also discussed is the effect of the proliferation of micros and improvements in software and cost-performance ratios.

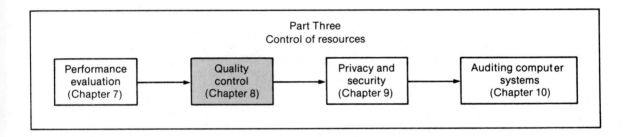

Part Three
Control of resources

| Performance evaluation (Chapter 7) | → | Quality control (Chapter 8) | → | Privacy and security (Chapter 9) | → | Auditing computer systems (Chapter 10) |

CHAPTER 8

Quality control

Sign on computer center wall: "Mistakes made while you wait."

Never before in history has it been possible to make so many mistakes in so short a period. Because of the rapidity of computer calculations and the repetitious nature of computer operations, undetected errors compound at an alarming rate. Some errors are built into systems by poor design. Some result from programming oversight. But many are procedural mistakes or the result of careless machine operation, such as the use of an outdated code, the wrong input tape, or incorrect output distribution.

The determination of technical control measures to ensure accuracy, timeliness, and completeness of data is generally the responsibility of computing personnel. However, management needs to identify which data needs protection and to specify standards of control after weighing monetary costs of control measures against the risk of inadvertent errors and security violations. The cost of delays and inconvenience to employees from controls must also be considered. For example, companies can go too far with controls, causing production to fall off because access to computers is made difficult for bona fide users or because procedures impede performance.

This chapter will describe how information systems should be monitored for human and machine error. Figure 8–1 shows where controls are necessary during processing. Potential threats to data quality and privacy at each location (circle) will be discussed, countermeasures to these threats will be suggested, and the personnel responsible for control will be identified. Systems security and the prevention of unauthorized access or illicit use of information are touched on briefly in this chapter. (They will be discussed in depth in Chapter 9.)

Figure 8–1   **Stages of processing (boxes) and quality control locations (circles)**

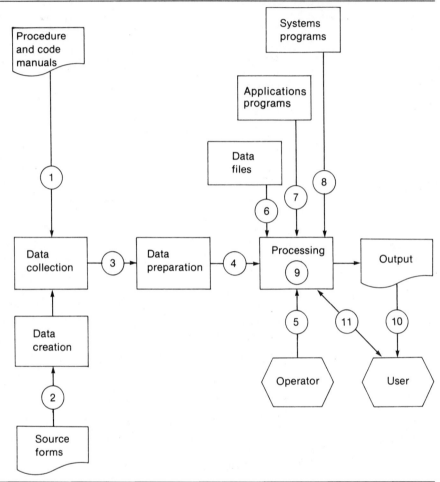

CONTROL LOCATIONS

**Control of
procedure and
code manuals
(Circle 1)**

    Table 8–1 summarizes common sources of error when using procedure and code manuals and suggests control solutions. In many firms, the data base administrator (DBA) or someone on the DBA's staff is responsible for establishing codes at the request of users and for coordinating assignment of codes so that redundant coding schemes do not occur. Publication, maintenance, and distribution of uniform code manuals are also delegated to this individual.

    Code users provide feedback to computing personnel regarding the effectiveness of procedures and codes. They may also initiate changes

Table 8–1   **Control of manuals**

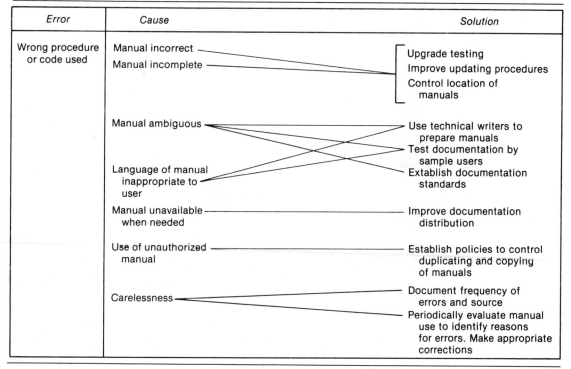

Error	Cause	Solution
Wrong procedure or code used	Manual incorrect Manual incomplete	Upgrade testing Improve updating procedures Control location of manuals
	Manual ambiguous Language of manual inappropriate to user	Use technical writers to prepare manuals Test documentation by sample users Extablish documentation standards
	Manual unavailable when needed	Improve documentation distribution
	Use of unauthorized manual	Establish policies to control duplicating and copying of manuals
	Carelessness	Document frequency of errors and source Periodically evaluate manual use to identify reasons for errors. Make appropriate corrections

when the manuals prove unsatisfactory. In this way, users contribute to control over procedures and codes.

Form control (2)

A common method of collecting data for an information processing system is through the use of forms. A well-designed form helps to ensure that collected data is error free. For example, banks usually provide customers with deposit slips that have the name, address, and customer account number preprinted on them so that only spaces for date and amount need to be filled. This **turnaround document** reduces the possibility of input errors entering the bank's processing system. (When customers write their own account numbers, they frequently interchange digits.) Other examples of turnaround documents are the tearoff sections of utility and credit card bills that accompany bill payment, and preprinted complaint forms that come with mail-order merchandise.

Error-free data collection may be impossible, but errors can be minimized by complying with the following principles of **form design:**

- Instructions should be easy to understand.
- Input codes (if used) should be unique and unambiguous.

- Adequate space, without crowding, should be allowed for completing information.
- Questions should be sequenced to avoid confusion and should be worded unambiguously.
- Lines for typed answers should conform to typewriter spacing.
- Vertical alignment on forms to be typewritten should enable clerks to use tabs.
- Larger spaces should be provided for handwritten data than for typewritten data.
- Only variable values should be requested.
- No information should be lost when the form is filed or bound.

In addition, the color of forms should be chosen for emphasis and ease of reading. (Light brown and light green print have been found empirically to be easy on the eye.) Some forms are printed on paper with shaded horizontal stripes to facilitate reading across columns of data without drifting of sight. The grouping of related data items on forms and spacing between data groups contribute to the ease with which forms can be read and collected information interpreted. These measures also facilitate accurate conversion when data on forms is readied by operators for the computer.

The importance of careful form design and pretesting cannot be overemphasized. Here is an example of how poor sequencing of questions and inadequate form directions resulted in the collection of incorrect data. One firm's application asked for name, address, birthdate, father's name, and date of high school graduation, in that order. Many applicants filled the form with their father's date of graduation, whereas the information desired was the applicant's own high school graduation date. Had the form been pretested by sample users, this sequencing problem might have been identified and, consequently, the order of the questions changed before the form was put into use.

The entry of numbers on forms is also a frequent source of errors. For example, handwritten ones and sevens often look alike. The use of boxes on forms for numerical data seems to encourage the user to write numbers legibly. Data processing personnel commonly use the European convention of placing a dash on the stem of a seven ($\mathcal{7}$) to distinguish it from a one. They also place a dash on the Z ($\mathcal{Z}$) so it won't be mistaken for a two, and a slash through the zero ($\emptyset$) to distinguish it from the letter O. (Unfortunately, this latter convention is the opposite of the practice in the military.)

Date entries, such as 3/1/52, can also cause problems of interpretation because the American convention of month/day is reversed in some European countries. For dates, the use of labeled boxes is advisable.[1]

---

[1] Boxes are also used for coding. Some forms have a space reserved in the right-hand column with boxes used by a coder to code information written on the left-hand side of the form. The form is then used as a document for direct data entry.

By using boxes, the danger of reversing the date order is eliminated. However, there still remains the possibility that "Mo," meaning Monday, might be filled in as day of birth instead of the desired date. One way to avoid the latter problem is to supplement form instructions with sample correct and incorrect responses.

Month	Day	Year

Another variation is a series of boxes that users check to indicate a condition. For example:

Marital status

1	2	3	4
☐	☐	☐	☐
Single	Married	Divorced	Other, specify _____

Input boxes are also used on forms that can be read by special machines, although the boxes may then have to be marked by a special pencil. This technique, called **mark-sensing,** reduces processing time and inaccuracies in processing, since data need not be manually converted into a machine-readable format.

Table 8–2 summarizes frequent causes of errors in filling out forms, and possible control solutions.

Data collection (3)

Data collection is not only the source of many careless errors but also the focus of much criminal activity. For example, a Blue Cross/Blue Shield claims examiner mailed forms to relatives who filled them in with real names and policy numbers to defraud the system of $128,000. In another recorded case of fraud, 11 employees of the Los Angeles County Department of Social Services issued checks to themselves, using terminated welfare accounts. Other cases of manipulation of input data include:

- An IRS clerk who awarded a relative unclaimed tax credits.
- The theft of $100,000 from a bank account, using the magnetic ink character recognition (MICR) number found on a discarded deposit slip.
- A conspiracy between an accounting clerk and a grocer resulting in a theft of more than $120,000 over the years by issuing false invoices for undelivered food.

Table 8–2   **Form control**

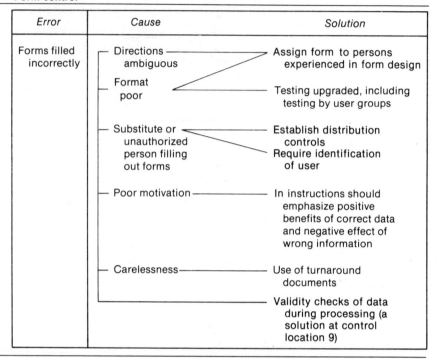

Error	Cause	Solution
Forms filled incorrectly	Directions ambiguous	Assign form to persons experienced in form design
	Format poor	Testing upgraded, including testing by user groups
	Substitute or unauthorized person filling out forms	Establish distribution controls / Require identification of user
	Poor motivation	In instructions should emphasize positive benefits of correct data and negative effect of wrong information
	Carelessness	Use of turnaround documents
		Validity checks of data during processing (a solution at control location 9)

Inadvertent errors can be equally harmful to an organization. In one firm, the code for equipment costing $20,000 was erroneously used to code the price of 50 manuals on that equipment. This mistake resulted in an inflated inventory value of $1 million.

Table 8–3 summarizes common errors in data collection and suggests possible control solutions.

Data preparation (4)   Errors in data preparation occur when data is incorrectly converted into machine-readable form. Control is exercised by the department responsible for the data preparation. Recommended control measures are summarized in Table 8–4.

Ways to detect error and procedures to correct mistakes are not all that is needed. The source of the errors should be traced and procedures amended so that the same errors do not recur.

Operations (5)   Employees can be trained in emergency procedures should flood, earthquake, fire, or an explosion interrupt operations. Although damage may be minimized as a result of such training, equipment may be destroyed and data lost in such disasters. To safeguard the information function against such adversity, **backup** is needed. That is, duplicate data files should be stored in a secure vault at another location, and

Table 8–3   **Data collection control**

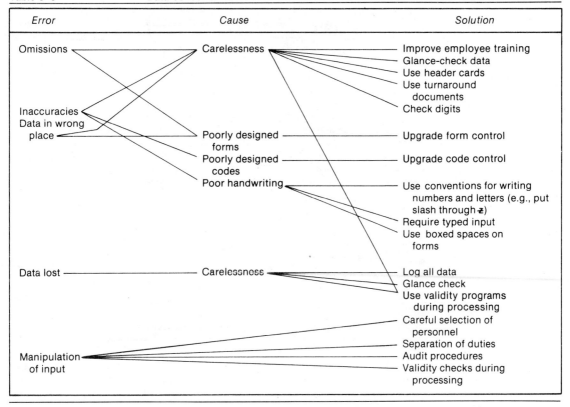

Table 8–4   **Summary of data preparation errors and solutions**

Error	Cause	Solution
Incorrect data	Poorly written data entry instructions	Upgrade procedures manual, include visual aides
	Hardware error	Proper maintenance
	Carelessness	Supervise data entry Periodically evaluate work of data entry clerks and operators
		Use check digits
Handling errors (Tapes or disks misplaced, put out of order, damaged, or duplicated inadvertently)	Carelessness	Glance check
		Validity programs
		Upgrade employee selection and training
	Poor procedure	Upgrade procedure testing
		Log data

backup processing facilities at a distant computer center should be available and tested for restart and recovery. Backup is also good insurance against intentional errors or willful damage, such as sabotage. Indeed, incidents of sabotage to computer equipment and data files have increased in recent years, particularly in industries engaged in research in politically sensitive areas such as nuclear energy or chemicals that might be used in warfare.

In handling sensitive information, the following basic operating precautions are recommended. Two operators should always be present. Work schedules should be changed frequently so that no single operator handles the same programs over a long period of time. No employees should be assigned processing tasks when a conflict of interest might arise. (For example, bank employees should not handle programming that will affect their own accounts.) In addition, proof of authorization and sign-in/sign out controls for handling sensitive files should be initiated. Finally, neither programmers nor analysts should be assigned routine operating tasks.

Although many controls are needed to prevent malicious intrusion during data preparation and operations, because information systems are vulnerable during these activities, most breakdowns and errors can be traced to lax procedures and careless operators. And these incidents can be costly indeed. For example, the running of an accounts payable program using an outdated price list cost one firm $100,000. In another expensive mistake, a bank employee fed a printout of sensitive data on depositors into a shredder with the line of print parallel to the blades instead of at right angles. As a result, strips of readable confidential data were thrown in the trash where they were spotted, retrieved, and peddled at a local bar by a drifter. The cost to the bank? Reward money for return of the strips and an incalculable loss of customer confidence.

More stringent control procedures could also have prevented the following incident. A Chicago hotel mixed address tapes, sending to vendors instead of to past guests letters explaining recent hotel renovations and urging the guests to return. Instead of goodwill, the hotel received irate calls from vendors whose spouses were citing the letters as evidence of their infidelity.

Failure to test control procedures produced this fiasco: When a fire broke out in a computer center, employees discovered that narrow doors barred passage of fire-extinguishing equipment. But who was to blame when a corrosive leak in an air-conditioning system destroyed a computer several floors below?

It simply isn't practical to devise control methods for all possible threats to an information system. Controls are costly, and too many controls can impede operations. The controls summarized in Table 8–5 are those most frequently adopted for operations.

Table 8–5   **Control of operations**

Error	Cause	Solution
Incorrect operation	Poor instructions Carelessness	Upgrade personnel selection, training, and procedure testing Check data file labels
Machine breakdown	Poor maintenance Careless operators	Upgrade maintenance Upgrade testing Upgrade personnel selection Upgrade training
	Act of nature (flood, storm)	Backup equipment Shutdown devices
	Fire	Emergency training Heat and smoke alarm Fire extinguishers Panic switches
Fraudulent operation	Sabotage	Intrusion detectors Police patrol
	Desire for personal gain	At least two people on duty Steel or steel mesh on windows and doors Control physical access Control access to files Remove conflict of interest Vary work schedules Strict supervision Upgrade personnel selection Bond personnel
Data not processed on time	Documents lost or misrouted	Establish documentation procedures (logging, checking record totals, etc.)

Data files (6)

If data files are centrally stored, a librarian generally is assigned responsibility for control. Otherwise, the owner of the data is responsible for their security.

Cited in computer literature are numerous cases of errors and fraud relating to data files. Stolen programs have been held for ransom. Disgruntled employees have maliciously scratched or destroyed tapes. At the Arizona State Finance Center, a backup card file was used for making Christmas decorations. In another organization, an employee moving files to storage wedged the vault open but forgot to remove the wedge after the move was complete. Although the vault was fireproof, a fire swept through the open door and destroyed hundreds of tapes.

In most cases, destruction of data files can be attributed to lax security. However, files are also vulnerable to industrial espionage. In

Table 8–6   **Summary of data file controls**

Error	Cause	Solution
Warped cards, dirty tapes or disks	Poor physical storage	Control storage humidity "Clean room" conditions Special cabinets Periodic cleaning
	Lack of clearly defined responsibility for data files	Centralize storage under a librarian
Destruction of files	Inadequate procedures	Upgrade storage procedures
	Natural disaster	Special vaults Back up data
	Theft, fraud, or sabotage	Control access to files: Data librarian Lock words Control labels

addition, they can be damaged by humidity, dust, or contaminants during storage. Table 8–6 summarizes the types of control needed to protect data files.

Programming controls (7,8)

Many mistakes in computerized systems can be attributed to faulty programming. One bank, for example, lost $300,000 by paying customers interest on 31-day months. A hyphen omitted from a programming card caused a rocket being tested to head for Rio. It had to be destroyed mid-flight at a loss of $18,500,000. Unintentional errors may result from an incorrect algorithm, erroneous programming logic, or a cause as minor as one out-of-sequence programming statement. Training, care, strict adherence to standard programming procedures, and proper documentation should minimize such problems.

The controls summarized in Table 8–7 should trace inadvertent errors and also help prevent fraud. Control measures should be initiated and enforced by computing personnel responsible for systems analysis and programming. Unfortunately, programming fraud is difficult to detect, and the crimes themselves are often quite ingenious. The first federal prosecution of computer crime in 1966 was against a bank programmer who programmed the system to omit his name from a list generated daily of overdrawn accounts. He withdrew large sums of money before being caught. Control measures, however, did not bring about his downfall. The overdrafts were detected when the computer broke down and the bank had to revert to manual processing.

Table 8–7 **Programming controls**

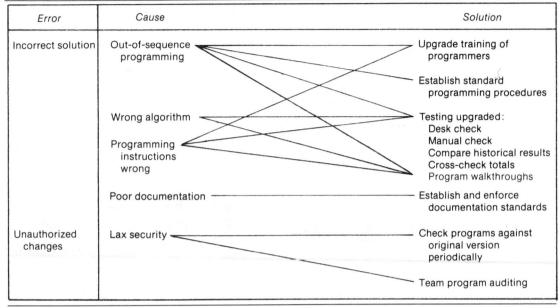

Error	Cause	Solution
Incorrect solution	Out-of-sequence programming	Upgrade training of programmers
		Establish standard programming procedures
	Wrong algorithm	Testing upgraded: Desk check, Manual check, Compare historical results, Cross-check totals, Program walkthroughs
	Programming instructions wrong	
	Poor documentation	Establish and enforce documentation standards
Unauthorized changes	Lax security	Check programs against original version periodically
		Team program auditing

Another programmer assessed a 10-cent service charge to each customer and put the amounts in a dummy account under the name of Zwicke. By chance, a public relations gimmick unmasked the bogus Zwicke. The fraud was discovered when it was decided to award a bonus to the first and last name on the firm's alphabetical list of customers.

Nibble theft, stealing small amounts of money over a period of time, is more difficult to detect than **bite-sized fraud,** the embezzlement of large sums. The latter can be uncovered by auditing and checking for unreasonable values or control totals. But no matter how well designed the controls, someone will think up a new technique for cheating the system. Constant vigilance is required.

Processing (9)

At the time of processing, many errors in data preparation that pass Controls 2, 3, and 4 can be caught by the computer itself, using stored **validation rules.** These rules, determined by users, need to be specified with care. Underspecification may lead to undetected errors, causing the system to produce unreliable information. On the other hand, overspecification adds unnecessarily to processing costs.

Validation tests include checks for completeness, format, range, reasonableness, consistency, sequence, transaction count, and recalculation of check digits. Some errors will still escape detection, such as data entry mistakes that fall within allowable ranges. But validation programs will help pinpoint invalid data resulting from:

- Entry error by data collector.
- Misinterpretation of documentation during input preparation.
- Coding errors.
- Operator errors in data conversion (largest single cause of input error).
- Errors in data transmission or data handling (for example, lost data or incorrect sequencing).

In the following sections, common validation rules and methods will be described.

Completeness. A validation rule for **completeness** requires that all characters be expressed before processing takes place in data that has a prescribed length, such as nine digits for a social security number. Completeness checks are necessary only when missing data will affect results, so completeness requirements should be carefully specified. For example, it would be necessary to halt processing of an order with a truncated product number or one with quantity blank, whereas the order could probably be filled if the client's middle initial were absent or if a digit were omitted from the client's phone number.

Format. Permuted characters can be specified in validation programs, and the data checked against these predetermined rules. For example, a validation program can be written to identify as an error an alphabetic character in a dollar data field or numeric data in names. The check can divide the **format** into subfields. An address may be assigned numeric fields for house number and zip code, but alphabetic blocks for street and city.

Range. A check rule may state that data entry is limited to predetermined values or a range of values. If M and F are used as sex codes, only these two characters would be valid in the sex code field. Any other letter or number would be listed as an error. Similarly, a **range of values** could be specified. If a firm's minimum wage per hour rate was $4 and the maximum $9, the computer could be programmed to identify as invalid any data with values under or over these amounts, errors called definite or **fatal errors.** The computer might also be programmed to identify possible or **suspected errors,** data near the limits of acceptable values. For example, if few employees earned over $8, a listing of employees in the $8–9 range could be provided for recheck. The validation rule would be:

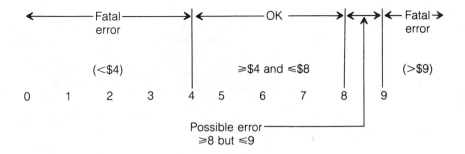

Fatal errors identified by the validation program would have to be traced and corrected. The data would then be reprocessed. Possible errors are checked and corrected, if necessary. An overriding code will permit processing of suspect data that proves valid.

Reasonableness. In any given situation, a number of checks for reasonableness can be postulated. Date of employment cannot predate a worker's birth, a probationary student cannot graduate with honors, and so forth. The cost of processing such checks must be weighed against losses (monetary and credibility) should errors pass undetected. Such decisions require management's judgment.

Consistency. One way to check data values is to compare the same raw data collected from two or more sources. Another way is to generate values of data elements from input and then match these generated values with keyed values for the same data elements. The latter method is used, for example, to check totals. If the information in Table 8–8 were keyed, a computer validity program could add $53.20, $32.80, and $39.90 in Batch 1 and match the total with the batch total $125.90 entered as input. Or each invoice total could be calculated by computer (price times quantity) and the product compared to the figure listed in

Table 8–8		Transaction data					
		Invoice number	Quantity (units)	Price ($)	Value ($)	Batch total ($)	Hash total
Batch 1	320	16	3.20	53.20		392.40
	321	8	4.10	32.80		365.90
	323	21	1.90	39.90	125.90	511.70
Batch 2	324	25	4.00	100.00		363.00
	325	31	4.20	130.20		490.40
	326	9	5.80	52.20		393.00
	327	5	6.10	30.50	312.90	681.60
					438.80	438.80

the value column. Any discrepancy would be identified on an error listing. Most frequently, invalid data is a mistake in keying the input.

A **hash total** entered as input is also a useful check for **consistency.** All the data in one transaction is totaled, even though the units are not the same. The computer then totals the "hash" independently (320 + 16 + 3.20 + 53.20 in the first transaction in Figure 8–8) and compares the total with the keyed hash total of 392.40. Since many transactions involve 80 to 100 characters, the hash total is an important validity check.

Duplicate processing is another method of checking for consistency. One firm needing to determine a coefficient to two decimal places (from complex calculations for the allocation of over \$4 million) used both COBOL and FORTRAN to make the calculations. Because of the large amount of money involved, it was helpful to compare calculations made by the two compilers, which differed in rounding and truncation rules.

Sequence.   In Table 8–8, Invoice 322 is missing. A validity test for **sequencing** would identify this situation. The document may have been mislaid or lost, in which case corrective action (such as recollection of the data) would take place. Often, an explanation will be found, such as a canceled order. In processing payrolls, logs are kept of checks damaged, destroyed by the printer, or left blank—a record that is searched when a sequence validity test flags an error.

Transaction count.   When a given number of transactions are to be processed, this total is entered as input. The transactions are again counted during processing. An invalid state will be identified if the totals do not match. **Transaction counts** will alert operators to a lost document, records stuck to one another, or possibly even multiple processing of the same transaction.

Self-checking codes.   A **self-checking code** is sometimes used to check for transposition of data or data entry errors, situations that often occur in data elements consisting of a long string of digits. This code, called a **check digit,** is calculated by a prescribed set of rules based on the value of the digits in the number and their locational relationships. The code is then added to the data element number and recalculated every time that data element is processed. If the recalculated value does not coincide with the original check digit, an error is identified.

Modulus 10 is one technique for calculating a check digit. In this technique, the position of digits in a number is significant. Digits in odd positions (such as first, third, fifth, etc.) are added for a subtotal.

Digits in even positions are multiplied by two, and the digits in the products added together for a second subtotal. The subtotals are then added and divided by 10. The number that must be added to the remainder to make it divisible by 10 is the check digit.

For the number 142796539, the check digit, according to these rules, is 2. To demonstrate the derivation of the check digit, the number will be aligned in two rows, digits in odd positions separated from digits in even positions. The calculations are then performed as follows:

	Multiplied by 2	Subtotal of digits in row
1 2 9 5 9	No	$1 + 2 + 9 + 5 + 9 \qquad = 26$
4 7 6 3	Yes	$8 + (1 + 4) + (1 + 2) + 6 = 22$
		Total $\qquad = 48$

Remainder when total is divided by 10 = 8
Number to be added to remainder to equal 10 = 2
New check digit = 2

New number = 1427965392

To test the working of the check digit, study the following example in which the value of one digit is changed.

Original number   1 4 2 7 9 6 5 3 9 | 2 |
New number   4 4 2 7 9 6 5 3 9 | 2 |

└→ error in value   └→ original
                                  check digit

	Multiplied by 2	Subtotal of digits in row
4 2 9 5 9	No	$4 + 2 + 9 + 5 + 9 \qquad = 29$
4 7 6 3	Yes	$8 + (1 + 4) + (1 + 2) + 3 = 22$
		Total $\qquad = 51$

Remainder after dividing total by 10 = 1
Number to be added to remainder to equal 10 = 9
New check digit = 9
Original check digit = 2

The new check digit does not equal the original check digit. Therefore, an error exists. In the next example, two adjacent digits are transposed:

Original number   1 4 2 7 9 6 5 3 9 2
New number   ④ ①2 7 9 6 5 3 9 2 ← check digit

└→error from single transposition

	Multiplied by 2	Subtotal of digits in row
4 2 9 5 9	No	4 + 2 + 9 + 5 + 9 = 29
1 7 6 3	Yes	2 + (1 + 4) + (1 + 2) + 6 = 16
		Total = 45

Remainder after dividing total by 10 = 5
Number to be added to remainer to equal 10 = 5
New check digit = 5
Original check digit = 2

The new check digit does not equal the original check digit. Therefore, an error exists.

The problem with Modulus 10 is that double transposition can take place without affecting the check digit (for instance, 5431 transposed as 3154). **Modulus 11,** another method of calculating a check digit, overcomes this problem. In Modulus 11, each digit in the value of the data element is assigned a separate weight, such as numbers in an ascending or descending scale. Each digit is then multiplied by its corresponding weighted value, and the products are totaled. The number that must be added to this total to make it divisible by 11 is the check digit. All types of transposition (double, triple, and so forth) and data entry errors are caught by this technique.

The use of a check digit has disadvantages. It adds to the length of numbers and increases data preparation effort, the time required for

Table 8–9   **Processing controls**

Error	Cause	Solution
Records lost	Carelessness	Validity checks Upgrade training of personnel Log jobs
Use of incorrect file	Carelessness	Use standard labels for all files Use program to automatically generated updated data
Lack of necessary supplies	Carelessness	Upgrade planning and inventory control

processing, and storage space requirements. The longer number is also harder to remember. But when reliability is important and the number is repeatedly used in processing, detection of errors may be worth the inconvenience and cost. Self-checking codes are commonly the last digit in identification numbers for employees, vendors, customers, accounts, and parts. Their use will identify posting of transactions to wrong accounts.

Other processing controls, the responsibility of computing personnel, are summarized in Table 8–9.

Output controls (10)

Output is the product of all input and processing. If proper control is exercised during both of these operational phases, the output should be free of error. But most firms add output controls in an information system's design to cross-check for errors that may have slipped past input and processing controls. Responsibility for these is divided between computing personnel responsible for output production and management using the output. Output controls are summarized in Table 8–10.

Many output mistakes can be caught by cursory sight checks. For example, a payroll run of paychecks issued without decimal points could be easily spotted by an alert operator, since the amounts would be unreasonable. In addition, many of the validation programs used for input can be run to control output.

Teleprocessing (11)

Access controls and the use of cryptography protocols (described in Chapter 9) are methods of protecting data during teleprocessing. **Parity checks** facilitate error detection. A bit of data is added to each set of

Table 8–10 **Output control**

Error	Cause	Solution
Inaccurate output	Processing errors	Audits
		Validation programs
		Interfile comparison
		Defer large-volume printing until proof data checked
		Sample check of output with corresponding input
	Operation error	Sight check
Incomplete output	Operation or processing error	Check page counts
		Check control totals for each process or report

bits representing a character so that the total number of 1 bits is odd (for an odd parity check) or even (even parity check). Upon receipt of the transmission, the bits are added and compared to the parity rule. When an error is detected, a signal is sent for retransmission of the data.

Checking for the use of a prescribed pattern of ones and zeros to represent characters is another method of tracing errors. Automatic checking of prescribed patterns can make this a self-checking code. This raises costs, however, since additional check bits must be transmitted and processed.

Fortunately, improved technology (such as large-scale integrated circuitry) is reducing the error rate in communications systems and is improving reliability.

CONTROL IN A MICROCOMPUTER ENVIRONMENT

The controls discussed in this chapter are appropriate for microcomputers as well as for business environments in which large computers predominate. However, responsibility for quality control varies in these two situations. Computer professionals generally install and monitor controls for mainframes and minis; the user is usually responsible for quality control in a microcomputer environment. Another difference is that much attention is placed on quality control at processing centers under the jurisdiction of computing professionals, whereas the microcomputer user often treats quality control casually. Indeed, many persons who use micros in their jobs have no training or knowledge regarding the management of computer resources. As a result, productivity using a micro may be poor, processing costs may be high, and micro output may be faulty.

One of the major problems facing businesses today is how to ensure quality at distributed processing nodes. Inaccurate, unreliable information generated by micros because quality controls are lacking can affect the work not only of individuals at the node but of the entire company. For example, the faulty information may be included in reports that are subsequently used as a data source for the work of other departments and thus pollute the company's data stream. The danger of such pollution is magnified with micro–mainframe intercommunication.

There is no easy solution to the problem. Rigid quality control administered by computer professionals undermines one of the major benefits of microcomputer use: user independence. But without such controls, how can a corporation be sure that its employees are using valid data and programs that actually do what they are supposed to do? One answer is to train micro users in the control measures outlined in this chapter and to motivate them to adhere to corporate standards for quality control. The subject of quality control at distributed nodes is of great concern to the computing profession at the present time because of the recent proliferation in microcomputer use.

SUMMING UP

This chapter examines controls for documentation, forms, data collection, data preparation, operations, data files, programming, processing, output, and teleprocessing. Deciding how much control is necessary is a management dilemma. Too much control is costly: it can impede work and affect morale. Too little control permits inaccuracies and security infractions, reducing the usefulness of systems.

The importance of carefully designed controls cannot be overstressed. Most readers will have personally experienced the frustration of trying to correct a billing error resulting from inadequate control procedures. Indeed, a major source of public distrust of computers can be traced to such experiences and the feeling of consumers that they are being victimized by computer systems. The reputation of a firm generally depends on the quality of its customer service. Inadequate controls over computerized information can lead to a decrease in clients, a decline in profits, and a loss of goodwill.

Control measures should be planned, implemented, tested, and evaluated during the development of information systems. Adding controls at a later date is both expensive and disruptive. This is especially true of online and real-time systems. This chapter has focused on batch systems, but the need for controls applies to all modes of operation. And quality controls are appropriate for all types of computers, from micros to mainframes.

Chapter 9 will discuss systems security, a subject closely related to quality control.

CASE: CHECK DIGIT ON BOOK NUMBERS

When publishers and book distributors began using computers in order processing and inventory control in the late 1960s, it became evident that unique identification numbers were needed for books. Several international conferences addressed the problem, and alternative numbering systems were proposed. The system chosen, the international standard book number (ISBN), is a 10-digit number with four parts consisting of a group identifier (national, geographic, or other grouping of publishers), publisher's prefix, title identifier, and check digit.

The check digit is used to detect errors in book numbers when processing orders. A calculation based on the other nine digits of the book number, using Modulus 11, is performed by the computer to check whether numbers have been transposed or miscopied, the source of the majority of ordering errors. Use of the check digit guards against more than 99 percent of these errors.

Here is an example of how the ISBN check digit was calculated for Hussain and Hussain, *Information Processing Systems for Management* (1985 edition).

ISBN number	0	2	5	6	0	3	2	0	9
ISBN weights	10	9	8	7	6	5	4	3	2
Weighted values (ISBN digits multiplied by ISBN weight)	0	18	40	42	0	15	8	0	18

Weighted total (sum of weighted values) = 141
Number added to make total divisible by 11 = 2
Check digit = 2
ISBN number = 0–256–03209–2

If the check digit had been calculated as 10, an X would have been used instead of the number, since only one character is assigned to the check digit. ISBN 0–256–02121–X, for James A. O'Brien's text *Computers in Business Management: An Introduction* (1979), fits this pattern.

Questions

1. What types of errors in placing orders will not be caught by the ISBN check digit? Which types of errors will be caught? Explain why.
2. Figure out the rules of Modulus 11 from this example. State the rules.
3. What do you suppose were some of the difficulties encountered in getting approval of an international publishing check digit standard in the United States and in different countries around the world?
4. What are the benefits of an international book standard?

CASE: ELECTRONIC TRADING SYSTEM FAILS AT THE LONDON STOCK EXCHANGE

A 1986 crash at the London Stock Exchange was not caused by the falling price of stocks. It was the crash of an electronic trading system—

consisting of five networked IBM PC ATs with an additional AT network controller—designed to handle options. (An option gives the holder the right to deal in a share at a future date at today's prices.) The failure of the system caused the exchange to halt options trading for a day in order to clear up the backlog left by the crash.

The purpose of the system is to match buyers and sellers, an activity previously carried out using a mainframe-based batch system at the London Options Clearing House. The crash occurred on the first day that the new system was in operation. Its cause? A hardware fault in one of the terminals locked up the network. Many brokers blamed the failure on inadequate testing: conversion to the new system took place after only three days of a parallel run. Another criticism heard at the exchange was that the system lacked a backup facility, although one had originally been specified.

An official inquiry has been initiated to find out why the system collapsed and what safeguards are needed to prevent future failures. The cost of the closure is also being assessed.

Questions

1. Who was responsible for this failure? Should or could a failure such as this one have been anticipated? By whom?
2. What type of testing should have taken place? If a system passes all tests, does that guarantee that no failure will ever take place? Explain.
3. Would periodic testing of the system be disruptive? How? Would you recommend such testing? Why?
4. How would you organize an official inquiry in this case? Whom would you appoint to conduct the inquiry? What resources would you allocate to the inquiry? What constraints (on funding and time) would you impose?

CASE: LOST REVENUE AT PACIFIC BELL BLAMED ON PROGRAM ERROR

A logic error in a program resulted in $29.3 million of lost revenue to Pacific Bell in early 1986. It appears that the rewrite of a switching-system program allowed more than 1.6 million Californians to make long-distance calls over a three-month period without being charged.

The programming change that caused the problem was a comparatively minor one. Prior to the rewrite, the company exempted customers from paying for calls shorter than one second. New Federal Communications Commission regulations raised the no-bill limit to two seconds, a change that forced Pacific Bell to rewrite programs controlling switching systems that "set the meter running." The logic error that was inadvertently introduced allowed the system to treat 12 percent of calls longer than two seconds as if they belonged to the no-charge category. The error went unnoticed until suspicions were aroused because of the low volume of calls billed in comparison with the volume of calls completed.

The bug apparently resulted because of the difficulty in writing software to control electromechanical switching systems, an older, less sophisticated technology than electronic switching systems. The fact that the error was not caught during a test phase after the program was rewritten suggests that software modification procedures at Pacific Bell need to be revised.

The billing problem has now been corrected. Pacific Bell hopes to recover its lost revenues by back-billing customers.

Questions

1. Who was at fault in this case?
2. How could the error have been:
   a. Avoided?
   b. Detected earlier?
3. To avoid similar errors in the future, what procedures might Pacific Bell adopt for:
   a. Writing programs?
   b. Testing programs?
   c. Maintaining programs?
   d. Controlling operations?

STUDY KEYS

Backup	**Modulus 11**
Bite-sized fraud	**Nibble theft**
Check digit	**Parity checks**
Completeness	**Range of values**
Consistency	**Reasonableness**
Duplicate processing	**Self-checking codes**
Fatal errors	**Sequencing**
Form design	**Suspected errors**
Format	**Transaction count**
Hash total	**Turnaround document**
Mark-sensing	**Validation rules**
Modulus 10	

DISCUSSION QUESTIONS

1. Distinguish between:
   a. External and internal control.
   b. Organizational and administrative control.
   c. Process and operational control.
2. Comment on the statement: A computer system adds to the probability of errors, fraud, and destruction of data and information.
3. Comment on the statement: Computers never make mistakes. People do.
4. What are some of the common causes of errors in computer systems? Classify them in terms of:
   a. Source.
   b. Motivation.
   c. Importance.
   d. Difficulty to trace.
   e. Difficulty to correct.
5. What is the difference between the design and implementation of controls? Where does each start and end? How do design and implementation overlap?
6. Can error-free data be guaranteed? Can error-free results be guaranteed? Explain your answers.
7. Identify control locations where measures should be taken to ensure security of data. Explain what measures you would require and why.
8. How can careless errors be reduced?
9. What are the need and significance of editing and validation? At what point in processing should they be performed? What resources are necessary?
10. Can the following errors be caught by validation? In each case, state the validation rule.
    a. $93A2.4.
    b. DR. HUSS3IN.
    c. $3 2.64.
    d. WAGE $1686 per hour.
    e. Account number incorrect.
    f. Age incorrect by one year.
    g. Age incorrect by 100 years.
11. When should a file be verified? Must all the contents be verified in each verification run?
12. What is the difference between verification of new data for content errors and editing for format errors? How is each done? Must each be done?
13. Explain six validation rules for data.
14. What are common causes for invalid data?
15. How does quality control in a distributed processing environment where microcomputers are in use differ from control of centralized processing?

SELECTED ANNOTATED BIBLIOGRAPHY*

Johnson, R. E. "How to Select and Implement a Data Security Product." *Infosystems*, vol. 31, no. 1 (January 1984), pp. 54–56.
Discussed are four principles of control: accountability, responsibility, separation of duties, and auditability. In addition, administrative, physical, and logical controls are described.

Mantz, Robert K.; Alan Merton; and Dennis G. Severance. "Corporate Computer Control Guide." *Financial Executive*, vol. 52, no. 6 (June 1984), pp. 25–36.
The authors present an excellent list of questions that should be asked to ensure that there is adequate control. The questions are meant for the senior corporate executive but could be asked by a director of a computer center as a self-assessment tool.

Menkus, Belden. "The Problem with 'Errors.'" *Journal of Systems Management*, vol. 34, no. 11 (November 1983), pp. 11–13.
The author argues that understanding errors is the first step in eliminating them. He then defines errors, classifies them, and discusses ways to reduce them.

Podolsky, Joseph L. "The Quest for Quality." *Datamation*, vol. 31, no. 5 (March 1, 1985), pp. 119–26.
Podolsky acknowledges the inadequacy of good formal quality assurance tools but still urges the use of what we have. He identifies seven measures that can build quality in the system through design, coding, systems operations, and striving for customer satisfaction.

---

*Additional references on quality control appear in the annotated bibliographies of Chapter 9 on security and Chapter 10 on auditing.

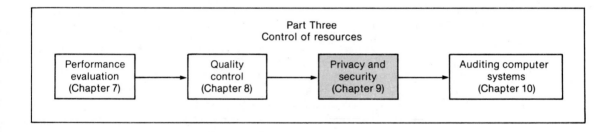

Part Three
Control of resources

| Performance evaluation (Chapter 7) | Quality control (Chapter 8) | Privacy and security (Chapter 9) | Auditing computer systems (Chapter 10) |

CHAPTER 9

Privacy and security

*Advanced technology has created new opportunities
for America as a nation, but it has also created
the possibility for new abuses of the individual American
citizen. Adequate safeguards must always
stand watch so that man remains master and never
the victim of the computer.*

Richard Nixon,
Address to the Nation,
February 23, 1974

Most commercial, industrial, and financial organizations process and transmit proprietary and sensitive information in the course of their daily activities. Protecting privacy and securing data from criminal access is a major concern. Equipment, software, manuals, forms, and other components of computer systems are also vulnerable to willful damage and theft.

This chapter examines the issue of privacy and outlines security measures that help safeguard the privacy not only of data but of all computing resources. Recovery following natural disasters is also discussed. Management's responsibility in planning and implementing security is presented, and the question "How much security is essential?" is addressed.

PRIVACY

Issues of privacy and computer abuse

American society is founded on the primacy of individual rights, none more sacrosanct than the right to **privacy.** No wonder that computer technology, which has fostered vast data banks, instantaneous

215

information retrieval, and worldwide data transmission through satellite networks, is viewed by the public with alarm. George Orwell's
1984 is a disquieting specter.

In modern society, data of a personal nature is collected by most
business units. For example:

- Employers keep personnel records that include data on the address,
  age, education, work experience, salary, dependents, sick leave, capabilities, and job performance of employees.
- Information on the status of customer accounts, including history of
  account aging, payment record, and personal credit data, is kept in
  the files of organizations involved in sales.
- Patient information on health history, allergies, disabilities, and prescribed medications is located in the files of physicians.
- Insurance companies store information on the number and cost of
  vehicles, types, accident record, and claims of clients.
- Banks keep records of loans, savings, deposits, and withdrawals of
  account holders.

The list could go on and on. Just about every salient fact about every
individual is in a computer file somewhere. (Figure 9–1 shows a sample
of the number of personal records in computer files, all of which are
subject to error or may be incomplete.)

Although recordkeeping has always been a part of organized society,
the amount of data collected in the past was constrained, due in part
to problems of storing and accessing data as well as to problems of
integrating and correlating data. Today, the ability of computers to
process, store, and retrieve vast quantities of data at high speeds has
led to a collection of pools of data that constitute comprehensive personal dossiers. The data need not be centralized in a single, all-inclusive

Figure 9–1   **Sampling of the number of personal records in computer files**

Selective Service	11 mil. young men
Medical Information Bureau	12 mil. patients
Private investigative agencies	14 mil. reports annually
Criminal records	60 mil. files
Credit bureaus	150 mil. subjects
State motor-vehicle agencies	152 mil. licensed drivers
U.S. government agencies	4 bil.

Source: *U.S. News & World Report*, April 30, 1984, pp. 46–47.

data bank. With the technology of linked data bases and telecommunications networks, bank records can be integrated with medical records, employment records can be linked with government records, and so on.

Few Americans want the intimate details of their private lives to be in the public domain. They believe they have a right to privacy, including the right to control the collection, dissemination, and use of information of a personal nature. The problem is to prevent privacy abuse while allowing organizations to collect and process personal data when they have a legitimate need to do so.

During the 1970s, the U.S. government first addressed the issue of privacy abuse by computers. An advisory group of the Department of Health, Education and Welfare (HEW) studied the problem and issued a 1973 report entitled "Records, Computers, and the Rights of Citizens," in which a **code of fair information practices** was proposed.[1] The HEW code states that privacy is a matter of mutual concern between record-keeper and subject. It affirms that the custodian of data is responsible for the timeliness, accuracy, and security of data. It also declares that personal information should not be used for a purpose other than that for which it is gathered. This report is credited with providing the intellectual foundation for much of the privacy legislation of the 1970s.

Accuracy.   How does the HEW code relate to business and to the management of computer processing within a business? **Accuracy** of stored data is a principal component of the privacy code. In the business world, required proof of data accuracy at the time of collection is common only when data is crucial to an organization's operation. For example, a birth certificate is not required when applying for a bank loan or credit card, since approval does not depend on the applicant's exact age. Yet, a birth date mistake in bank records is important if that mistake is passed on to another organization where an accurate birth date is vital. Suppose the mistake is incorporated in records that determine an individual's eligibility to benefits that are based on age, like retirement or Social Security benefits?

Most data base administrators claim that they have no obligation to determine the accuracy of information that they receive from others. This is the position of TRW Information Service, a company that sells 35 million credit reports each year to 24,000 subscribers throughout the country. Each month, TRW receives computer tapes containing the status of customer accounts from thousands of companies. TRW computers then lift, organize, and store information from the tapes so that credit history can be supplied to TRW clients making credit checks.

---

[1] See W. H. Ware, ed., *Report of the Secretary's Advisory Committee on Automated Personal Data Systems* (Washington, D.C.: U.S. Government Printing Office, 1973).

This service could not be provided if TRW were forced to check the accuracy of data elements on each tape. (It should be noted, however, that the company tries very hard to ensure the accuracy of its files.)

Inaccuracy of files is not a trivial problem. Each year, some 350,000 people register formal complaints about mistakes in TRW reports. Some 100,000 of these complaints annually result in changes to information stored in TRW computers. But how many incorrect entries are not noticed? How many mistakes are not corrected?

Unfortunately, one of the weak areas of computer systems is auditing for accuracy. Yet, mistakes are often made at the time of data collection, preparation, and input, as described in Chapter 8. A business with inaccurate personal data on file may be responsible for:

- Customer inconvenience and frustration. For example, a billing error may take numerous phone calls and letters to correct.
- The denial of goods and services to which individuals are entitled. For example, a car loan may be denied on the basis of inaccurate credit information.
- The ruining of reputations and disruption of lives. For example, mistakes in evaluation ratings may cost workers deserved promotions.

One way to reduce errors in data banks is to allow individuals the right to inspect personal records and to challenge mistakes that they find. However, there is no way for the challenger to know whether the mistakes have already been circulated to others and, if so, which organizations have copied the errors and stored them in their files. This explains why civil libertarians are concerned with the growth of computerized data banks, the unmonitored exchange of data, and the existence of stored data. It also raises the question of fair use of personal information.

Fair use of data.   To most Americans, privacy includes the right to control the use of personal data. In this country, we view secret files as a threat to individual freedom, and most of us want limits placed on data collection to prevent organizations from gathering data that has no relevance to their legitimate needs. Furthermore, we want to restrict access to stored personal data.

Personal information has a market value. For example, merchants can determine from such information where to direct their advertising. They can draw up lists of persons who like the outdoors, to whom camping equipment might appeal, or lists of Cadillac owners, who might be attracted to diamond jewelry. By gaining access to a data bank of personal information, a mailing list of prospective customers could be prepared. Would this activity constitute an invasion of privacy?

A fair-use restriction gives individuals the right to participate in this decision. **Fair use** means that consent must be obtained before personal data in a data bank are shared with others. After all, data pools are attractive targets for all types of groups. Consider how a thief might value information regarding who goes camping weekends or who likes diamond jewelry.

Fair-use restrictions also address the "gatekeeping" issue. **Gatekeeping** is controlled access to services, privileges, benefits, or opportunities. An example of gatekeeping is the point-scoring method—based on age, salary, duration of employment, and so forth—used by many credit agencies to determine whether an individual is a good credit risk. In this case, gatekeeping serves a legitimate business interest. But gatekeeping can also be used to discriminate. There is an ill-defined area of gatekeeping practices that go against the American grain.

Computer processing facilitates gatekeeping, just as it does the unrestricted exchange of personal data. As stated by the U.S. Privacy Protection Study Commission,

> The ability to search through hundreds of thousands, or even millions, of records to identify individuals with particular characteristics of interest is at once the most important gain and the most important source of potential harm stemming from the automation of large-scale personal data recordkeeping systems.[2]

Fair-use restrictions are an attempt to minimize this potential for harm.

Privacy legislation

The first legislative act to provide safeguards against privacy abuse by computers was the 1971 Fair Credit Reporting Act. The **Privacy Act of 1974** followed. It stated that the right to privacy is a personal and fundamental right protected by the Constitution of the United States, and it set guidelines for the collection, maintenance, use, and dissemination of personal information by federal agencies. Rights addressed in the act are discussed briefly here.

Right of notification. Each agency that maintains a system of records is required to publish in the *Federal Register* at least annually a notice of the existence and character of the records. This must include name and location of the information system, categories of records maintained, uses of the records, and policies regarding access and disposal. When records are disseminated to other agencies under compulsory legal processes, reasonable effort must be made to notify the individuals involved.

Right to accuracy and relevance. Agencies are charged with collecting and maintaining information that is current and accurate. They may only keep records that are relevant and necessary to accomplish their mandates.

---

[2]U.S. Privacy Protection Study Commission, Final Report, 1977.

Right to confidentiality. Agencies must establish administrative, technical, and physical safeguards to protect the security and confidentiality of records.

Right to access. Knowing the existence of recorded data is not sufficient if access to that data is restricted or the data is unintelligible (coded or recorded on magnetic tape, for example). The act recognizes an individual's right to access one's own record and to review and copy it.

Right to challenge. Amendment of records may be requested when an individual believes personal data is not accurate, relevant, timely, or complete.

Right for correction. The act states that procedures should be established for record amendment.

Right of control. No records may be made available for another purpose without an individual's consent. Only such information necessary to accomplish the purpose of the agency may be collected. (Exceptions are listed; for example, records for law enforcement or use by the Census Bureau.)

Right to redress. Individuals may bring civil action and be rewarded damages in district courts when agencies fail to comply with provisions of the act. Officers and employees of agencies are also liable to criminal penalties for willful disclosure of information to any person not entitled to it.

The act also created a Privacy Protection Study Commission to determine the extent to which provisions of the act should apply to the public sector and to recommend further standards and procedures to protect information in governmental, regional, and private organizations. In addition, the commission was asked to advise the President and Congress on further courses of action. During 18 months of study and testimony, the commission examined matters such as confidentiality of tax and bank records, the use/misuse of mailing lists, and the role of social security numbers in linking files. Although the commission, in its report to the president, counseled that the 1974 Privacy Act not be extended to the public sector, it recommended that the philosophy and principles of the act should be.[3]

The Privacy Act, though limited to federal agencies, changed the focus of public concern over privacy. Before the act, the issue debated was how to curb the harm of computer privacy abuse. After passage of the act, public concern broadened, focusing on the right of individuals, groups, and institutions to determine when, how, and to what extent

[3]The Commission's report to the President, *Personal Privacy in an Information System,* no. 052–003–00395–3 (Washington, D.C.: U.S. Government Printing Office), is available from the Superintendent of Documents, Washington, D.C., 20402.

personal information is communicated and shared with others without the knowledge or consent of the persons involved. The right to control the circulation of personal information is a cornerstone to personal freedom, according to many Americans today. Additional federal legislation to extend the protection of the 1974 act is currently being studied.

Active interest in privacy issues extends beyond the federal sphere. Most states have enacted privacy laws that supplement federal legislation to some degree. Some local laws on privacy also exist, as in

Figure 9–2   **IBM's policy on privacy**

Four Principles of Privacy

For some time now, there has been a growing effort in this country to preserve the individual's right to privacy in the face of expanding requirements for information by business, government and other organizations.

In searching for appropriate guidelines, private and governmental groups have explored many avenues and considered many aspects of the privacy question.

As a company with a vital interest in information and information handling, IBM endorses in their basic purpose four principles of privacy which have emerged from various studies, and which appear to be the cornerstones of sound public policy on this sensitive issue.

1. Individuals should have access to information about themselves in recordkeeping systems. And there should be some procedure for individuals to find out how this information is being used.
2. There should be some way for an individual to correct or amend an inaccurate record.
3. An individual should be able to prevent information from being improperly disclosed or used for other than authorized purposes without his or her consent unless required by law.
4. The custodian of data files containing sensitive information should take reasonable precautions to be sure that the data are reliable and not misused.

Translating such broad principles into specific and uniform guidelines will, of course, not be easy. They must be thoughtfully interpreted in terms of the widely varying purposes of information systems generally.

In particular, the proper balance must be found between limiting access to information for the protection of privacy on one hand, and allowing freedom of information to fulfill the needs of society on the other.

But solutions must be found. And they will call for the patient understanding and best efforts of everyone concerned in this search. IBM pledges its full and whole-hearted cooperation.

IBM

Source: Courtesy of International Business Machines Corp.

Berkeley, California. The Council of Europe and the Organization of Economic Cooperation and Development (OECD) are two bodies interested in international ramifications of privacy issues.[4] Recently, a number of firms have adopted privacy policies, showing their awareness of public concern over privacy issues. IBM, for example, has endorsed the four principles of privacy listed in Figure 9–2.

In all likelihood, the privacy issue is going to become more intense in the coming decade. Many citizens see privacy as one of the central "quality of life" issues of our times and believe that computers make it far too easy to obtain confidential information. They want to ensure that privacy controls are placed on both business and government, whose powers to process and store personal data have been vastly increased by computers in the last 20 years.

Privacy implementation

Managers in business firms, although not bound by the 1974 Privacy Act, should be cognizant of and sensitive to privacy issues. The following measures will help ensure that individual rights are respected when personal data are collected, maintained, and used in the course of a firm's daily operations.

Store only essential data.   Purge irrelevant and outdated information, or data that are unnecessary but "nice to have." This not only will reduce the danger of privacy invasion but will diminish the information glut that plagues many firms and lower storage costs as a consequence.

Improve the security of data.   Periodically review and update physical safeguards and carefully screen personnel. Many computer systems in use today were designed before the rise of widespread concern over privacy issues. Hence, they lack adequate data protection. Future legislation addressed to privacy in the business sector will undoubtedly spur manufacturers to produce security technology sufficiently rugged to resist determined attack and sufficiently economical to encourage use.

Identify which data elements are "sensitive."   Add data descriptions to these elements so they can be easily extracted from the data stream for control inspections and correction. Require management approval when use of these elements is extended to new applications.

State as policy that personal data should be complete, accurate, and timely.   This requirement is good business, irrespective of privacy ramifications. One reason it is difficult to isolate and assess the cost of privacy measures is that all sound information processing practices serve the interests of privacy.

Establish procedures to implement notification and challenge rights.   Authorization forms for consent for use or release of infor-

---

[4]See Organization of Economic Cooperation and Development, *Transborder Data Flow and the Protection of Privacy* (Paris, France: OECD, 1979), 335 pp.

mation may be required. Appeal routines need to be established. In many cases, procedures can be automated; but in each organization, at least one individual should be given responsibility for planning security and privacy measures, coordinating privacy policies with legal requirements, and overseeing privacy policy implementation.

Anticipate privacy legislation. Design new information systems to report on sensitive data and to log and monitor use of the data, since such controls will undoubtedly be requirements of the future. Privacy features can be added to systems under development at low marginal cost, whereas adding them after a system is operational involves expensive redesign. Furthermore, companies will be spared the disruption of redevelopment when privacy legislation is eventually passed.

Cost of privacy

Two types of expenditures are involved when implementing corporate privacy policies: one-time development costs and recurring operational disbursements.

Development costs include analysis and design of procedures for privacy protection and the acquisition of equipment and software dedicated to that purpose. The main component of operations is salaries, primarily for clerks handling notification, access, challenge, correction, and erasures. The cost of a manager's time to monitor procedures and standards and to resolve disputes should be added to this category, as should fees paid for legal advice. Other operational costs are for computer time, data storage, data transmission, rental or maintenance of security equipment, and supplies. Operational costs will peak after passage of privacy legislation, when many people exercise new rights of access and challenge, and then stabilize at a lower level.

One problem in determining costs is that so many implementation strategies exist for privacy policies. Some companies may require written consent from each data subject for each application. Others may use a single release for all applications. If companies discontinue (or do not initiate) applications because of privacy considerations, should operational costs include estimates for degraded service?

Another problem is that the value of many variables used in making estimates is unknown. When the Fair Credit Reporting Act was passed in 1971, one credit agency reported the number of access requests rose by a factor of 2,000. Would a similar increase occur if the 1974 Privacy Act were extended to the private sector?

Cost allocation is a problem when practices that affect privacy also serve other business interests. For example, security measures that protect personal data reduce the danger of lost records, guard trade secrets, and circumvent sabotage of facilities. How can the cost of privacy policies be isolated from security costs?

Robert Goldstein has developed a model to simulate cost components and total costs, given different assumptions of privacy protection requirements and different management strategies. Goldstein's model is based on the premise that privacy costs do not come "out of the blue" but rather arise in response to various events. Each time one of these events occurs, certain actions are taken to comply with privacy regulations. These actions consume resources and, hence, generate costs. The model includes 22 events and 19 requirements (laws are represented as sets of requirements) and can calculate a potential of 7,500 different actions from the 18 most useful combinations of strategy variables. In spite of the complexity of this model, however, the costs produced will not be accurate figures for any given organization because of the many unproven assumptions on which the model is based. The model's usefulness is for comparing relative costs of various strategies and for identifying variable relationships and assumptions.

SECURITY

To ensure privacy of information, computer systems must be secure. That is, data must be protected against unauthorized modification, capture, destruction, or disclosure. Personal data are not the only vulnerable data. Confidential data on market strategies and product development must be kept from the eyes of competitors. The large sums of money transferred daily by electronic fund transfer (EFT) must be protected against theft. The very volume of business information processed by computers today means that the rewards for industrial espionage and fraud are of a much higher magnitude than in the past and are still increasing.

Records must also be protected from accidents and natural disasters. For example, a breakdown in the air-conditioning system may cause a computer to overheat, resulting in loss of computing capabilities. Fire, floods, hurricanes, even a heavy snowfall causing a roof to collapse can cause destruction of data and valuable equipment.

The **security** measures described in the following sections are designed to guard information systems from all of the above threats. The measures can be envisioned as providing layers of protection, as shown in Figure 9–3. Some controls guard against infiltration for purposes of data manipulation, alteration of computer programs, pillage, or unauthorized use of the computer itself. Other measures guard the physical plant, monitor operations and telecommunications, and regulate personnel. All of the layers of protection shown in Figure 9–3 will be discussed, except for legislative deterrents (which are described in Chapter 24). Since control of inadvertent errors was the subject of Chapter 8, this chapter will focus on protection against calamities and criminal acts.

Figure 9–3   **Layers of control**

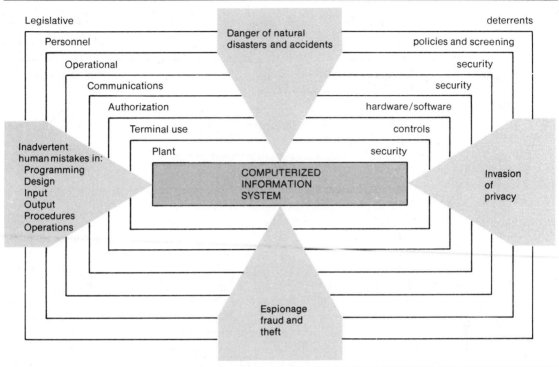

Legislative   deterrents

Personnel   Danger of natural   policies and screening
                                   disasters and accidents

Operational   security

Communications   security

Authorization   hardware/software

Terminal use   controls

Inadvertent
human mistakes in: Plant   security
Programming
Design
Input   COMPUTERIZED   Invasion
Output   INFORMATION   of
Procedures   SYSTEM   privacy
Operations

Espionage
fraud and
theft

Plant security

Many protective measures can be incorporated in the construction
or renovation of buildings to protect a computer from unlawful intrusion, sabotage, or destructive acts of nature such as fire, floods, or
earthquakes: for example, locks and window grills, alarms and panic
buttons, smoke detectors, earthquake-proof foundations, and automatic
fire extinguishers. (The fire extinguishers should be gas extinguishers,
not water. Water can be almost as destructive as fire to electronic equipment, particularly to magnetic storage.)

***Terminal use
controls***

Controlling the access to terminals is a common method of guarding
a system from illicit use. When all terminals are located in the computer
center, closing the center to unauthorized personnel will provide one
method of access control. Badge systems, physical barriers (locked doors,
window bars, electric fences), a buffer zone, guard dogs, and security
check stations are procedures common to restricted areas of manufacturing plants and government installations where work with secret or
classified materials takes place. A vault for storage of files and programs

and a librarian responsible for their checkout provide additional control.

With online systems using telecommunications, security is a greater problem, since stringent **access controls** to terminals may not exist at remote sites. The computer itself must, therefore, ascertain the identity of persons who wish to log on and must determine whether they are entitled to use the system. Identification can be based on:

- What the user has, such as an ID card or key.
- Who the user is, as determined by some biometric measure or physical characteristic.
- What the user knows, such as a password.

Keys and cards.   Locks on terminals that require a **key** before they can be operated are one way to restrict access to a computer. Another way is to require users to carry a **card** identifier that is inserted in a card reader when they want to use the computer. A microprocessor in the reader makes an accept or reject decision based on the card.

Many types of card systems are on the market. Some use plastic cards, similar to credit cards, with a strip of magnetically encoded data on the front or back. Some have a core of magnetized spots of encoded data. Proximity cards contain electronic circuitry sandwiched in the card; the reader for this card must include a transmitter and receiver. Optical cards encode data as a pattern of light spots that can be "read" or illuminated by specific light sources, such as infrared. In addition, there are smart ID cards that have an integrated-circuit chip embedded in the plastic. The chip has both coded memory, where personal identification codes can be stored, and microprocessor intelligence.

The disadvantage of both keys and cards is that they can be lost, stolen, or counterfeited. In other words, their possession does not absolutely identify the holder as an authorized system user. For this reason, the use of passwords is often an added security feature of key and card systems.

Biometric systems.   Some terminal control systems base identification on the physical attributes of system users. For example, an electronic scan may be made of the hand of the person requesting terminal access. This scan is then measured and compared by computer to scans previously made of authorized system users and stored in the computer's memory. Only a positive match will permit system access.

Fingerprints or palm prints can likewise be used to identify bona fide system users. Such security systems use electro-optical recognition and file matching of fingerprint or palm print minutia. Signature verification of the person wishing to log onto the computer is yet another security option. Such systems are based on the dynamics of pen motion related to time when the signer writes with a wired pen or on a sensitized pad. A biometric system can also be based on voiceprints. In this case, a voice profile of each authorized user is recorded as an analog signal, then converted into digital from which a set of measurements are derived that identify the voice pattern of each speaker. Again, identification depends on matching: the voice pattern of the person wishing computer access is compared with voice profiles in computer memory.

Biometric control systems, of special interest to defense industries and the FBI, have been under development for many years. Although technological breakthroughs that enable discrimination of complex patterns have been made recently, pattern recognition systems are still not problem free. Many have difficulty recognizing patterns under less than optimal conditions. For example, a blister, inflammation, cut, even sweat on hands can interfere with a fingerprint match. Health or mood that changes one's voice can prevent a voiceprint match. A combination of devices, such as voice plus hand analyzers, might ensure positive identification; but such equipment is too expensive at the present time to be cost effective for most operations in business.

Passwords.   The use of **passwords** is one of the more popular methods of restricting terminal access. One example of a password system is the required use of a personal identification number to gain access to an automated teller machine at a bank.

The problem with passwords is that they are subject to careless handling by users. Some users write the code on a sheet of paper that they carry in their wallet, or they tape the paper to the terminal itself. When given a choice, users frequently select a password that they can easily remember, such as their birth date or house number. Someone determined to access the computer will make guesses, trying such obvious passwords first. Even passwords as complex as algebraic transformations of a random number generated by the computer have been broken with the assistance of readily available microcomputers. Of course, the longer a password is in use, the greater the likelihood of its being compromised.

One-time passwords are a viable alternative. But systems of this nature are difficult to administer. First of all, each authorized user must be given a list of randomly selected passwords. Then there must be agreement on the method of selecting the next valid password from the list, a method that is synchronized between computer and user. Finally, storage of the list must be secure, a challenge when portable terminals are used by personnel in remote sites, where security may be lax.

Recently, a number of password systems have been put on the market that generate a new password unique to each user each time access is attempted. This is done with a central intelligent controller at the host site and a random **password generator** for each user. Typically, the system works as follows. To gain mainframe access, the user enters his or her name (or ID code) on a terminal keyboard. The computer responds with a "challenge number." This is input to the user's password generator. By applying a cryptographic algorithm and a secret key (a set of data unique to each password generator) to this challenge "seed," a one-time password is generated. The user then enters this password into the computer. The central controller simultaneously calculates the correct password and will grant access if a match occurs.

Such password management systems are difficult to compromise, because passwords are constantly changed. Only a short period of time is allowed for entry of the correct password. Furthermore, the control system is protocol dependent. This compounds the problems of a person trying to breach the system in a network having a variety of protocols. The advantage to the user is that the password generator is portable, usually a handheld device, and easy to use.

Authorization controls

In addition to the identification systems outlined in the preceding sections, control systems can be installed to verify whether a user is authorized to access files and data bases, and to ascertain what type of access is permitted (read, write, or update).

Data directory.   A computer can be programmed to reference a stored **data directory security matrix** to determine the security code needed to access specific data elements in files before processing a user's job. When the user lacks the proper security clearance, access will be denied. In a similar manner, the computer might be programmed to reference a table that specifies the type of access permitted or the time of day when access is permitted.

The data elements accessible from each terminal can likewise be regulated. For example, according to a programmed rule, the terminal in the data base administrator's office might be the only terminal permitted access to all files and programs and the only terminal with access to the security matrix itself. A sample printout from an access directory, sorted by user identification number, is shown in Table 9–1.

Table 9–1   Access directory

User identification: *076–835–5623*
Access limitation: *13 hours (of CPU time for current fiscal year)*
Account Number: *AS5842*

Data elements	Type of access	Security level	Terminal number	Time lock
Customer number	Read	10	04	08:00–17.00
Invoice number	Read	10	04	08.00–17.00
Cash receipt	Read/write	12	06	08.00–12.00

Assigning access levels to individuals within an organization can be a difficult task. Information is power, and the right to access it is a status symbol. Employees may vie for clearance even when they do not require such clearance for their jobs. Managers should recognize that security measures designed to protect confidential data and valuable computing resources may antagonize loyal employees. It is important that the need for security be understood by workers and that security controls be administered with tact.

Security kernel. Unfortunately, the use of a security matrix does not provide foolproof security. In a multiuser system, data in a file can be raided by installing a "Trojan horse" program. Figure 9–4 shows how this is done. Although the data directory does not authorize Brown to access File A, confidential data from that file is copied into another file that Brown is entitled to access, on the direction of a secret program, thereby circumventing system security.

The concept of a **security kernel** addresses the Trojan horse issue. A kernel is a hardware/software mechanism that implements a **reference monitor,** a systems component that checks each reference by a

Figure 9–4   **Raiding files: A Trojan horse program**

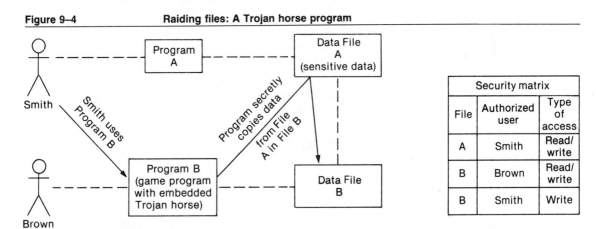

Suppose that Smith has read/write access to sensitive data in File A. Brown, who wishes access to that file but lacks the necessary clearance, first gains legitimate access to the computer and creates File B, giving himself read/write access and also setting the access control list to allow programs executed on Smith's behalf to write into it. (Smith is not told of this situation.)

Now Brown writes a program that Smith is likely to use, such as a game program. This program has secret embedded instructions (the Trojan horse) that tell the computer to copy data from File A and to write the data in File B when Smith plays the game. (The Trojan horse program is designed so that it can detect when Smith is the user.) The security matrix does not prevent this raid, since Smith has authorized access to File A.

Figure 9–5   **How a reference monitor blocks a Trojan horse raid**

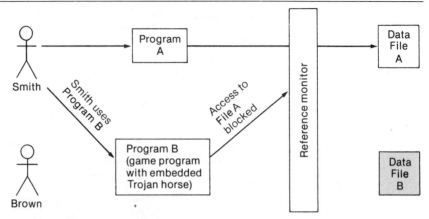

Suppose that there are two levels of security. One allows access to sensitive data (white) and one access to nonsensitive data only (grey). Suppose that the security monitor enforces the rule that states that a subject (a user or a program) cannot read a file at a higher security level nor can it write to a file at a lower security level.

Since Smith, Program A, and File A have the sensitive security rating, Smith can access File A. Brown, however, cannot. When Smith unknowingly triggers Brown's Trojan horse program, the program acquires his security rating. Nevertheless, the reference monitor blocks the computer from carrying out the raid instructions, because File B has a lower security rating than File A.

subject (user or program) to each object (file, device, or program) and determines whether the access is valid according to the system's security policy. Figure 9–5 shows how Brown is foiled by a reference monitor in his attempt to raid File A.

A security kernel represents new technology still in the developmental stage. Although a number of projects have attempted to demonstrate the practicality of this security approach, results thus far have been mixed.

Virtual machine.   An entirely different approach to security in a multiuser environment is a **virtual machine.** With this systems structure, each user loads and runs his or her own copy of an operating system. In effect, this isolates one user from another although they use the same physical machine, because each virtual machine can be operated at a separate security level. With a virtual memory structure, several user programs can reside in computer memory simultaneously without interference.

Communications security

Computer processing is today closely linked with telecommunications, which allows the transference of computer data between remote points. Protecting the confidentiality of this data at the initiating terminal, during transmission itself, or when transmission is received has required the development of sophisticated security techniques. For example, a **handshake,** a predetermined signal that the computer must recognize before initiating transmission, is one way to control communications. This prevents individuals from masquerading, pretending to be legitimate users of the system. Most companies use **callback boxes** that phone would-be users at preauthorized numbers to verify the access request before allowing the user to log on. A hacker who has learned the handshake code would be denied access with such a system. Protocols, conventions, and procedures for user identification (described earlier in this chapter) and dialogue termination also help maintain the confidentiality of data.

During transmission, messages are vulnerable to wiretapping, the electromagnetic pickup of messages on communication lines. This may be eavesdropping, passive listening, or active wiretapping involving alteration of data, such as piggybacking (the selective interception, modification, or substitution of messages). Another type of infiltration is reading between the lines. An illicit user taps the computer when a bona fide user is connected to the system and is paying for computer time but is "thinking," so the computer is idle. This and other uses of unauthorized time can be quite costly to a business firm.

One method of preventing message interception is to encode, or encrypt, data in order to render it incomprehensible or useless if intercepted. **Encryption,** from the Greek root "crypt" meaning to hide, can be done by either transposition or substitution.

In transposition, characters are exchanged by a set of rules. For example, the third and fourth characters might be switched so that 5289 becomes 5298. In substitution, characters are replaced. The number 1 may become a 3, so that 514 reads 534. Or the substitution may be more complex. A specified number might be added to a digit, such as a 2 added to the third digit, making 514 read 516. Decryption restores the data to its original value. Although the principles of encryption are relatively simple, most schemas are highly complex. Understanding them may require mathematical knowledge and technical expertise.

An illustration of encryption appears in Figure 9–6. A key is used to code the message, a key that both sender and receiver possess. It could be a random-number key or a key based on a formula or algorithm. As in all codes, the key must be difficult to break. Frequent changing of the key adds to the security of data, which explains why many systems have a key base with a large number of alternate keys.

The U.S. government is as concerned as business regarding security of telecommunications. The National Bureau of Standards, entrusted by the 1974 Privacy Act with the security of federal data, has produced a **Data Encryption Standard (DES),** which incorporates transposition and substitution repeatedly in each encryption. Since the adoption of

Figure 9–6   **Encrypting and decrypting data in teleprocessing**

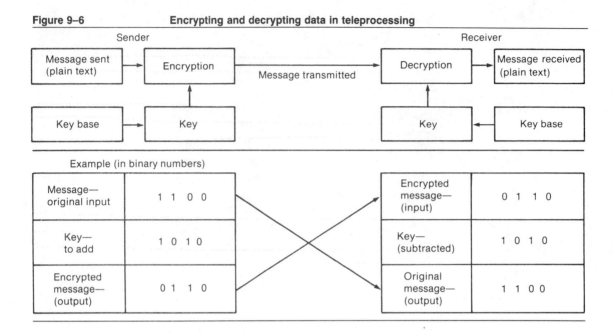

the DES algorithm as a federal standard in 1977, it has been approved by the American National Standards Institute and recommended for use by the American Bankers Association. Most manufacturers of teleprocessing equipment accept the standard as well, although some computer manufacturers have developed encryption products of their own.

In the past, the transportation of the encryption key to authorized users has been an Achilles' heel to systems security. An additional problem is that there sometimes is insufficient time to pass the key to a legitimate receiver. One solution is a multiple-access cipher in a public key cryptosystem. This system has two keys, an E public encryption key used by the sender, and a D secret decryption key used by the receiver. Each sender/receiver has a set of D and E keys. To code data to send to Firm X, for example, a business looks up Firm X's E key, published in a public directory, and then transmits a message in code over a public or insecure transmission line. Firm X alone has the secret D key for decryption. This system can be breached but not easily, since a tremendous number of computations would be needed to derive the secret of D. The code's security lies as much in the time required to crack the algorithm as in the computational complexity of the cipher, because the value of much data resides in timeliness. Often, there is no longer need for secrecy once a deal is made, the stock market closed, or a patent application is filed.

Cryptography, in effect, serves three purposes: identification (helps identify bona fide senders and receivers); control (prevents alteration

Table 9–3   **Who's been breaching the systems? (respondents total 160)**

Perpetrators	Responses*		Percentage of total by category
	Categories	Individuals	
Not identified	62		24%
Individuals within the organization	125		48
Executives, managers not directly involved with computers		21	
Computer operations supervisors		22	
Computer programmers, software personnel		67	
Nonsupervisory computer operations personnel		42	
Nonsupervisory personnel not directly involved with computers		40	
Other		18	
Individuals outside the organization	73		46
Competitors		16	
Customers/clients		11	
Outside consultants		22	
Individuals with no prior relationship with organization		37	
Other		16	
Total	260	312	100%

*Some respondents reported more than one crime. Some reported crimes involved more than one person.

Source: Task Force on Computer Crime, Section of Criminal Justice, American Bar Association, *Report on Computer Crime* (Washington, D.C.: American Bar Association, June 1984).

mers, computer operators, even vice presidents (see Table 9–3). Motives for criminal acts can be attributed to ego (the desire to demonstrate individual superiority over the system), revenge, financial gain, irrational behavior, and zealous adherence to a cause. When screening applicants, assigning duties, and supervising operations, managers should be cognizant of their vulnerability to internal security violations.

One well-known organizational principle that serves security is **separation of responsibility:** No employee should perform all the steps in a single transaction. For example, recordkeeping should be separated from the physical custodianship of records.

Computer systems can be divided into five basic functions:

- Programming and systems development.
- Handling input media.
- Operation of data processing equipment.
- Documentation and file library.
- Distribution of output.

It is advisable that the work assignment of no employee cross these functional lines. Separation of responsibility serves as a deterrent to crime, because a given job must pass through many hands, which facilitates many independent checks for accuracy and possible fraud. Although separation may not be feasible in small organizations because the limited number of employees means a single individual may have to perform many jobs, the principle should be followed whenever possible.

Security can also be promoted by rotating the duties and responsibilities of employees, by unannounced audits, by establishing a climate of honesty, and by close observation of disgruntled employees. Giving publicity to security measures may serve as a deterrent to attempted systems intrusions. Employees should be trained in security risks and procedures. In addition, the appropriateness, adequacy, and readiness of emergency planning should be periodically tested by drills. Many security officers state that the installation of security devices, such as alarms and detectors, is not the hard part of their jobs. What is difficult is motivating employees to be alert and sensitive to security issues.

Security in a microcomputer environment

Even though microcomputer systems process less volume of information than mainframes, they too must be protected from accidental or intentional data loss. Most of the measures described in this chapter for guarding the privacy of data and ensuring systems security are as appropriate in a microcomputer environment as in a computer center housing minis and mainframes.

However, a number of factors do contribute to unique problems in administering a microcomputer security program. For example, many micro users have limited computing experience and, unlike data processing professionals, are not aware of or alert to possible security infractions. Contingency planning is frequently ignored, regular backup procedures are lacking, provisions for audit trails are uncommon, and few local networks monitor network activity. Unfortunately, the current generation of micro hardware and software does not support effective security for the most part. The low cost of micro systems, in effect, limits the amount of system resources devoted to security. What's more, microcomputer hardware seems to present a temptation to thieves, while software theft for personal use on other machines is a common problem.

One solution to the security of micros is the use of Bernoulli drives. These have removable cartridges that can store an entire data base and the source code that generates that data. After use, the disks can be secured under lock and key. Passwords and encryption are two other protective measures frequently used with microcomputer systems. Ironically, one of the principal reasons for the spread of micros—to let more people benefit from computer capabilities—is the very advantage that creates so many security problems.

Who is responsible?

Figure 9–7 summarizes management's role in planning, implementing, monitoring, and evaluating security measures. A firm's survival is at stake when losses must be absorbed due to sabotage or theft. Its reputation for quality service may be imperiled and years of accumu-

Figure 9–7   **Security overview and action process**

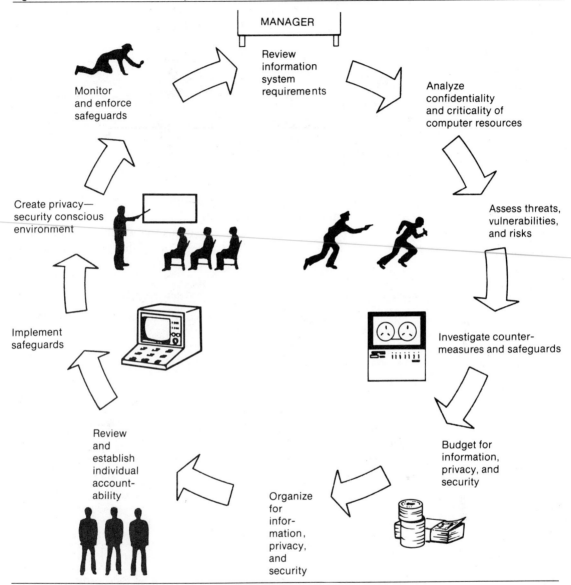

Source: Adapted from IBM Document G320–I372 (1974), pp. 35, 42–43.

lated goodwill endangered when security proves inadequate. Although EDP personnel should participate in technical control decisions, corporate management has the responsibility to identify vital data, establish security points, outline security procedures, assign enforcement personnel, allocate needed resources, and take corrective action when

security is violated. Management is also responsible for training programs to make employees sensitive to privacy and security issues. Clearly,
all security measures adopted should be flexible, effective, and enforceable.

***How much
security?***

Security is costly. In addition to the expense of equipment and personnel to safeguard computing resources, other costs must be considered, such as employee dissatisfaction and loss of morale when security
precautions delay or impede operations. In deciding how much security
is needed, management should analyze **risk.** How exposed and vulnerable are the systems to physical damage, delayed processing, fraud,
disclosure of data, or physical threats? What threat scenarios are possible?

As illustrated in Figure 9–8, systems and user characteristics should
be assessed when evaluating risk. Opportunities for systems invasion,
motives of a possible invader, and resources that might be allocated to
invasion should be considered. The resources available to deter or counter

Figure 9–8   **Factors in assessing expected losses from systems intrusion**

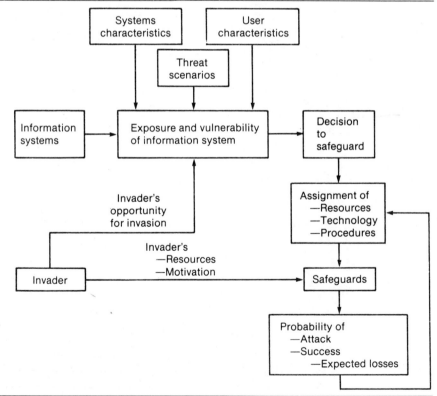

a security breach should also be appraised. The amount of security that should be given to systems should be based, in part, on evaluation of expected losses should the systems be breached. One way to calculate expected losses from intrusion is by application of the formula:

$$\text{Expected loss} = L \times P_A \times P_B$$

where

L = Potential loss.
P_A = Probability of attack.
P_B = Probability of success.

An insurance company or computer vendor can help management determine the value of L. Probability values are more difficult to obtain. Rather than attempting to assign a specific value (.045 or even .05 may be of spurious accuracy), relative risk (high, medium, or low) should first be determined and a numerical value assigned to each of these relative probabilities (for example, 0.8, 0.5, and 0.2, respectively). The risk costs can now be calculated according to the formula. For example:

Exposure	L	×	P_A	×	P_B	=	Expected loss
1	$500,000		1.0		0.2		$100,000
2	200,000		0.6		0.5		60,000
3	50,000		0.2		0.8		8,000
Total expected loss							$168,000

Loss is determined for each exposure; the sum of the expected losses is the total risk value to the system. If P_A and P_B are probabilities for the year, expected loss is $168,000 per year.

The application of this formula will help management determine whether the addition of security measures is worth the cost and where the greatest reduction of expected losses could occur by improving security.

The figures derived from the formula are approximations at best. We simply do not have the data to calculate reliable probabilities, because the computer industry is too new to have a long historical record of invasions on which to base probability assessments. Furthermore, firms are reluctant to publicize how their security has been breached lest their credibility suffer, so news of security invasions is seldom broadcast. This means data on security infractions are incomplete. More serious, persons who design security measures are not always aware of the tricks and techniques used by perpetrators of crime to break systems security and so cannot plan countermeasures.

SUMMING UP

Computer technology poses a threat to personal privacy because of the speed of processing, the collection of vast data banks, instantaneous retrieval capabilities, and the worldwide network of data transmission through teleprocessing. The 1974 Privacy Act has imposed use restrictions on personal data collected for U.S. federal agencies, but the debate continues over privacy requirements for the private sector.

Privacy is closely linked to systems security. No one disputes that information systems must be guarded from unlawful intrusion, that human errors should be detected, and that damage from natural disasters must be minimized. Management's dilemma is not whether security is needed but how much. Computer crime is increasing at an alarming rate. This can be attributed, in part, to the temptation arising from the large sums being transferred by EFT and to the fact that more criminals are becoming knowledgeable about computer technology and equipped with computers to help them plan and execute their crimes. There are also individuals who are challenged simply to "beat the system." For example, an Oregon youth used a remote terminal to gain access to the computer of the Department of Motor Vehicles, then put the system into irreversible disarray just to illustrate its vulnerability.

The American Bar Association estimates that the cost of computer-related crime may already exceed $3 billion. According to commentators, crime figures are destined to rise unless the computer industry and organizations that use computers pay greater attention to security issues and devote more resources to the protection of information systems. All known protective mechanisms can be broken, given enough time, resources, and ingenuity. Perhaps the major objective of security systems should be to make intrusion too expensive (in equipment costs and risk) and too time consuming (in planning effort and time needed to actually breach safeguards) to make attempted violations worthwhile.

Risk analysis is one method of helping management determine which security strategies are most cost effective, given budgetary constraints. Systems security can be provided by access controls, physical safeguards, personnel screening and policies, and operational controls as discussed in this chapter and in Chapter 8. (Legal deterrents will be discussed in Chapter 24.)

CASE: PROTECTION AGAINST WATER DAMAGE

More computer insurance claims are made for water damage than for fraud or anything else. The damage occurs as a result of water infiltration from air-conditioners, drains, sprinklers, and even newly washed floors.

One product recently introduced to the market is a device that continuously monitors the area under raised floors to detect the presence of leaks. (Raised floors are commonly found in computer installations.) The system consists of a water-sensing polymer connected to an alarm that sounds when moisture is detected. Sensitivity of the device can be adjusted according to client specifications.

Questions

1. Is water damage the fault of:
   a. Systems design?
   b. Daily operations?
   c. Other?
   Explain.
2. How can an organization protect itself against water damage?
3. Why don't many organizations take advantage of new technology, such as this water alarm, to protect their computer resources?

CASE: MALICIOUS DAMAGE

In recent years. much publicity has been given to hackers (usually youths) who derive malicious pleasure from outsmarting computer security. Here are examples of willful damage that can be caused when spurious software is secretly inserted in a computer. Only a few lines of code are needed to cause problems. When buried in complex programs, the secret instructions are virtually invisible, even to expert programmers.

"Worm." A software "worm" inserted by a hacker can alter a system's fundamental operations by deleting specific portions of a computer's memory.

"Virus." Another software demon, called a "virus," destroys stored files. In one case on record, Dick Streeter's screen went blank as he was transferring a free program from a computer bulletin board into his machine. Then the following message appeared: "Arf, arf. Got you." Nearly 900 accounting, word processing, and game files that were stored in Streeter's machine were erased.

"Trapdoor." A "trapdoor" collects users' passwords as they log on, giving the hacker an updated list of access codes. This technique was used to gain unauthorized access to hospital records at Manhattan's Memorial Sloan-Kettering Cancer Center.

"*Logic bomb.*"   At the Los Angeles department of water and power, a "logic bomb" (secret software) froze the utility's internal files at a preassigned time, bringing work to a standstill.

Questions

1.   How would you plan security against malicious software?
2.   Is the problem of malicious software one of:
     a. Design?
     b. Testing?
     c. Operations?
     d. Control?
     e. Procedures?
     Explain.
3.   Is insurance an answer? Discuss.
4.   Sometimes, computer personnel are responsible for malice. How can this be avoided?
5.   Can backup help to protect software? How?

STUDY KEYS

Access controls

Accuracy

Biometric control systems

Callback box

Card

Code of fair information practices

Data directory security matrix

Data Encryption Standard (DES)

Encryption

Fair use

Gatekeeping

Handshake

Key

Password generator

Passwords

Privacy

Privacy Act of 1974

Recovery

Reference monitor

Risk

Security

Security kernel

Separation of responsibility

Virtual machine

DISCUSSION QUESTIONS

1.   Comment on the statement: A computer system adds significantly to the probability of errors, fraud, and destruction of data and information.

2. Describe types of crimes perpetrated against computerized systems.
3. Describe five situations in which personal identification might be required before access to a computer is granted. In each case, which of the following methods would you recommend?
   a. I.D. card.
   b. Password.
   c. Signature identification.
   d. Hand form identification.
   e. Voice identification.
   f. Handprint identification.
4. Why is privacy of data important to business clients and customers? What other segments in business are affected, and why? How can each privacy problem be successfully approached?
5. How can the conflict between need for data privacy and need for data access be resolved? What trade-offs can be made?
6. In your judgment, is the Privacy Act of 1974 adequate? Should it be extended to state governments, universities, businesses, and other organizations?
7. If you were the head of an organization not bound by a privacy code, would you institute privacy measures? What measures? What obligation do you believe private organizations have regarding the privacy of client records?
8. Who should decide what information is sensitive and must not be collected because it violates the privacy of individuals?
9. Should the verification of the accuracy of data files be mandatory? What are the advantages and disadvantages of such a requirement?
10. What is meant by the term *gatekeeping*? Is gatekeeping in the interests of business? Explain your answer.
11. What is a password? Do password systems guarantee the security of data? What are some of the pitfalls?
12. How does a password generator work?
13. Give two examples of unexpected results that might be produced because of:
    a. Malfunction.
    b. Mistakes.
    c. Fraud.
    d. Theft.
    e. Sabotage.
    How might security be improved to prevent incorrect results caused by each of the above?
14. What are some common abuses of computerized information systems? How can these abuses be prevented?
15. Has your privacy been invaded by business computers? How can such invasion of privacy be prevented?
16. Can a computer system ever be completely secure? What are the trade-offs in costs? What are the social and nonmonetary costs?
17. Identify control points where measures should be taken to ensure security of data. Explain what measures you would require and why.
18. What should be management's role in planning systems security?

19. What makes particular industries more vulnerable to security violations than the average? What makes a particular firm within an industry more vulnerable than others? How can this vulnerability be reduced, if not eliminated?

20. What would you do if you suspected a fellow employee of being a computer criminal? Should your action depend on your industry? Would your action differ if you were working in a:
    a. Bank?
    b. Retail store?
    c. Multinational firm?
    d. Insurance company?

21. Are laws in the United States adequate for detecting, discouraging, and punishing:
    a. Computer crime?
    b. Privacy violations?

22. Is the cost of privacy excessive? How can a firm decide what security precautions to ensure privacy are worth the cost?

23. Explain the concept of a security kernel.

24. How does data encryption add to systems security? What is the purpose of encrypting data if coding schemes can be broken?

25. Describe controls that can protect a computing facility from natural disasters, such as earthquakes, floods, fire, or lightning.

SELECTED ANNOTATED BIBLIOGRAPHY

"Computer Matching: New Tools for Controlling Fraud and Abuse." *Government Executive*, vol. 17, no. 1 (January 1985), p. 43 ff.
This article discusses the advantages of matching to both state and federal programs, including lower cost, fewer errors, and a reduction of fraud. These benefits, however, must be weighed against the danger of violating individual privacy and the HEW code of fair information practices.

Finn, Nancy, et al. "Don't Rely on the Law to Stop Computer Crime." *Computerworld*, vol. 18, no. 51 (December 17, 1984), pp. ID/11–15.
The authors lament the absence of adequate state and federal legislation against computer crime. They urge organizations to adopt stringent policies and security systems to protect their computing resources.

Hoffman, Lance J., ed. *Computers and Privacy in the Next Decade*. New York: Academic Press, 1980, 250 pp.
This book is a set of readings and commentary written by well-known experts in the field (e.g., W. H. Ware, Paul Armer, Rein Turn, Abbe Mowshowitz). The topics are balanced and very provocative. Included are articles on privacy, the personal computer, EFT, transborder flow, and nonuniform privacy laws. Also addressed are problems and issues arising from the preservation of individual autonomy and the protection of public order in future decades.

Landwehr, Carl E. "The Best Technologies for Computer Security." *Computer*, vol. 16, no. 7 (July 1983), pp. 86–95.
A good discussion of "trusted" systems and advice for the developer involved in the design, implementation, verification, and testing of secure systems.

Murray, William. "Good Computer Security Practices for Two Areas of Current Concern: Personal Computers and Dial-Up Systems." *Computer Security Journal*, vol. 2, no. 2 (Fall–Winter 1983), pp. 77–88.
Topics discussed include log-on and dial-back, personnel policies, and protective storage. A critical problem in controlling access to large, centralized, common data bases is to establish procedures that do not make bona fide users pay penalties in delays.

St. Clair, Linda. "Security for Small Computer Systems." *EDPACS*, vol. 11, no. 11 (November 1983), pp. 1–10.
The author painstakingly identifies the differences in the security of small and large systems. Ways are suggested to achieve small systems security, including hardware, software, and contingency control.

Steinauer, Dennis D. "Security for Personal Computers: A Growing Concern." *Computer Security Journal*, vol. 1, no. 1 (Summer 1982), pp. 33–40.
To compensate for the lack of hardware security features and operating systems, management must put greater emphasis on access restrictions, encryption, and data control.

Westin, Alan F. "New Eyes on Privacy." *Computerworld*, vol. 17, no. 48 (November 28, 1983), pp. ID/10–17.
Westin focuses on privacy issues arising from the use of personal computers and cathode ray tube terminals. He evaluates different privacy policies and controls in terms of fair information practices.

Zimmerman, Joel S. "Is Your Computer Insecure?" *Datamation*, vol. 31, no. 10 (May 15, 1985), pp. 119–28.
The author argues that security systems should not be based on cost-effectiveness but on confidence in the protection they offer.

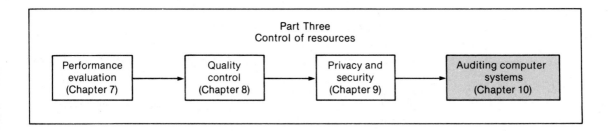

Part Three
Control of resources

| Performance evaluation (Chapter 7) | Quality control (Chapter 8) | Privacy and security (Chapter 9) | Auditing computer systems (Chapter 10) |

CHAPTER 10

Auditing computer systems

*Here and elsewhere we shall not obtain
the best insight into things until we
actually see them growing from the
beginning.*

Aristotle

Every computer system should be monitored for performance and evaluated for efficiency and effectiveness. Control locations should be established and control measures implemented to ensure protection of computing resources and to minimize error. Chapters 7–9 have dealt with these topics.

Auditing is yet another level of control. In this chapter, the function of an auditor is described, and approaches to computer auditing are considered. Since auditing requires professional training, no attempt is made to explain in detail how auditing is done, but the scope of an auditor's control over computing is discussed at length. Sections are also devoted to the role of auditors in the development of new information systems and to auditing benefits and problems.

AUDITOR'S ROLE

The function of an **auditor** in a firm is twofold:

- To ensure that controls to protect corporate resources are in place.
- To ensure that transactions are processed according to desired procedures and decision rules.

Traditionally, the auditor's primary focus was accounts and financial records prepared by hand under the jurisdiction of a firm's comptroller or financial officer, and hard-copy audit trails. Today, because sales, accounts receivable and payable, payroll, and inventory are all processed by computers, auditors have an added area of concern: electronic data processing (EDP) centers. Furthermore, computer-based systems do not leave a paper trail, so auditing methods have had to change.

As a result, computing skill is required in addition to accounting expertise to monitor modern recordkeeping systems. What's more, the auditor's job is complicated by that fact that error-free transactions processed by computer depend on procedures, standards, decision rules, and security that are embodied in the design of computer systems. For this reason, auditors generally participate in the development of new systems to make sure that adequate controls are a part of systems design. They also oversee development to be sure that new systems are auditable. Still another way in which the auditor's role has changed is that data, manuals, software, peripherals, and processors have been added to the list of corporate resources that need to be audited.

In the two preceding chapters, strategies of control, control locations, threats, and countermeasures were discussed. Also explained were the responsibilities of the computer center manager and EDP personnel with regard to control implementation and evaluation during daily processing. Auditors provide supplementary levels of control. For example, in most organizations, an **internal auditor** is assigned the task of evaluating both processing and the effectiveness of the controls implemented by the computer center to protect computing resources from error, unauthorized intrusion, or damage. To preserve the objectivity and independence of this **internal audit**, the auditor (an employee of the firm) generally reports directly to a senior executive such as the firm's financial vice president and is not a member of the computer center staff.

Many companies add yet a third level of control, an **external auditor** hired from outside the organization. This auditor looks at computer

Figure 10–1   **Layers of control**

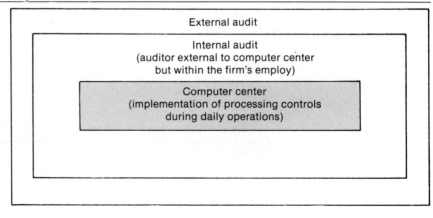

center processing and controls once again and, in addition, audits the internal auditor's report. Such a procedure is called an **external audit**.

Figure 10–1 illustrates these three levels of control. Management's responsibility in a given firm is to evaluate a computer center's exposure, the potential magnitude of loss, and the probability of systems intrusion when deciding whether all three levels of control are necessary. The depth of coverage and frequency of audits is also a management decision.

APPROACHES TO AUDITING

There are two main approaches to auditing computer-based applications: auditing around and auditing through the computer.

Auditing around the computer

In **audits around the computer**, output is checked for a given input. Presumably, if input is correct and reflected in the output, then the processing itself is also correct. Hence, the audit does not check computer processing directly. This type of audit uses traditional auditing methods and techniques, tracing who did what, when, and in what sequence.

The problem with this approach is that processing errors may exist even though no errors are apparent when checking output against input. For example, there might be compensatory processing errors that do not show in the output. Unfortunately, computer calculations provide few intermediate results for auditors to check processing accuracy by traditional trailing methods.

Auditing through the computer

To check both input and process, **audits through the computer** can be made. This auditing approach may use test data, auditor-prepared programs, auditor software packages, or special-purpose audit programming languages. The logic of an applications program may also be reviewed.

Use of test data. An auditor may design and process simple transactions, using test data in order to see how systems handle different transactions and whether programmed controls are part of the systems. In other words, the accuracy of a computer program in performing calculations is examined, and operating procedures used by the firm are scrutinized and checked for consistency with corporate policies. Auditors search for extreme conditions, out-of-sequence data, out-of-balance batches, and so forth, the types of errors frequently found when testing applications programs.

Auditor-prepared programs.   In this approach, specially written programs prepared by the auditors are used to check specific conditions and to identify situations that need further study and analysis. The programs also spot-check for unauthorized manipulations by programmers and operators and provide listings of "before" and "after" changes that facilitate auditing.

Auditor software packages.   Standard **audit programs** can be purchased. These are not as specialized as programs written by auditors for a specific information system, but they are less expensive and relatively easy to use.

Audit programming languages.   Special **audit programming languages** can be used to generate output needed by auditors. System 2170, for example, developed by the accounting firm Peat, Marwick, Mitchell & Co., is a language that can be learned in about one week and has 21 audit commands.

Review of logic.   The logic of an applications program can be reviewed to determine whether the program algorithm is appropriate.

Unfortunately, through-the-computer auditing can create problems when used on real-time systems. Unless extreme care is taken and expensive precautions are adopted, sample data can get mixed with the live data stream. One solution to this problem is to create a representative set of data for the company and to use it for auditing independent of the live data system. This approach is referred to as the **minicompany approach**, since the test data base is a miniature representation of the company.

It is beyond the scope of this text to explain auditing techniques of computer systems in greater detail. The subject is very complex and requires the skills of a professional accountant. What needs to be stressed here is that auditors of today use computers when auditing information systems. Unfortunately, current computer audit techniques are not as advanced as the technology being audited, and the computer profession shows no signs of slowing its pace to wait until auditors catch up.

AUDITOR PARTICIPATION IN NEW SYSTEMS DEVELOPMENT

Audit standards issued by the U.S. Government Accounting Office state:

The auditor shall actively participate in reviewing the design and development of new data processing systems or applications, and significant modifications, thereto, as a normal part of the audit function.[1]

The purpose of this standard is to ensure that features to facilitate auditing are incorporated in new or modified systems. Auditors are interested in documentation standards, testing samples, and recovery procedures. They want a voice in specifying programming decision rules, establishing logs, and determining backup. Table 10–1, which lists the type of features that auditors assist analysts in designing, is merely a sample: Lists will vary according to the firm, auditor, and type of application. One could expect greater auditor involvement in development of applications involving monetary transactions, funds, or assets than, for example, of a mailing list application.

The **auditor's role in systems development** activities may begin with the feasibility study if expensive audits are anticipated. Usually, however, the auditor's prime development function is user specification and design. A role is also played in testing to ensure that audit controls and security features work. Sometimes, conflicts arise between project staff and auditors due to different points of view with regard to development. For example, EDP staff may favor operational ease and expediency over rigid controls and standards. In such cases, the auditor is usually given the authority to prevail.

Auditors have no assigned responsibility during conversion but should oversee the process to be sure that only the tested and authorized ver-

Table 10–1	Design features of interest to auditors
Decision rules	Standards:
Rounding rules	Documentation
Consistency rules	Security
Validation rules	Control
Control points	Backup and recovery
Control procedures for trace	Special auditing reports:
and trail features	Reliability performance reports
Access rules:	Cost indexes
Who	Resource utilization reports
When	Logs:
Why	Data access log
What	System access log
	Invalid access log
	Sensitive file access log
	Secondary storage access log
	Program access log
	Data transmission log

---

[1] *Additional GAO Standards: Auditing Computer-Based Systems* (Washington, D.C.: U.S. Government Accounting Office, March 1979), p. 4.

Figure 10–2   **Role of auditor in development**

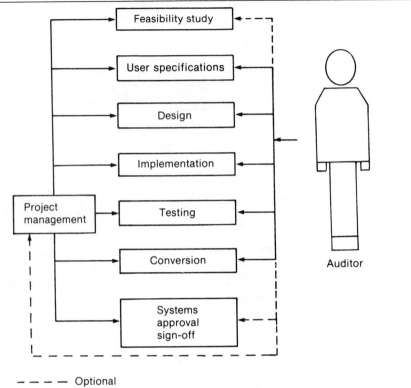

– – – – Optional

sions of new systems are implemented. Experience has shown that systems are vulnerable to malicious or fraudulent intrusion in this phase of development. Because of the confusion of the transition period and the staff's euphoria at a job completed, a computer center may be less attentive than usual to attempts to breach security. This is one reason why many firms require an auditor's sign-off approval after conversion is completed.

Whether auditors participate in project management or not depends on the industry and application. One would expect an auditor to assist in evaluation and review of the developmental activities for a complex accounting-oriented project, for instance. But practices differ among firms. Figure 10–2 summarizes in graphic form which developmental activities fall within an auditor's purview.

Auditing features can be added to systems once they are operational, although this practice is costly in time and effort and very disruptive. However, it is done when the need for a feature is overlooked during development or changed circumstances require added measures of control.

Table 10–2	Audit-related facilities in a DBMS	
	Subtotals and final totals	Comparisons:
	Testing footings and extension	Records
	Record selection based on:	Files
	Simple logical expression	Table lookup
	Complex logical expression	Account aging
	Sorting	Statistical sampling
		Categorization
		Stratification
		Automatic preparation of notices

The auditor's role in the development of new systems is increasing in difficulty because data bases are expanding, data structures are becoming more complex, operating systems are growing in sophistication, and both computers and peripherals continue to add advanced features with each new model. But new technology has also contributed auditing aids. For example, a data base management system (DBMS) offers monitoring facilities, data element dictionary and directory information, utility programs, and special descriptive and manipulative languages. Table 10–2 lists still other auditing features of a DBMS. As research increases DBMS capabilities, auditors will undoubtedly be better able to perform their control function.

SCOPE OF AUDITING

What should be audited? Table 10–3 lists aspects of computer processing that concern auditors. Attention is focused on the adequacy of controls in:

- Budgeting and finance.
- New systems development.
- Applications.
- Operations.
- Data security and privacy.
- Recovery.

To evaluate the efficiency and effectiveness of information processing in each of these areas, an auditor uses many of the same criteria that data processing professionals use during performance evaluation (discussed in Chapter 7). However, an auditor's perspective may differ. For example, both analysts and auditors are concerned with error rates, but an auditor may focus on the total dollar value of errors rather than the frequency of errors per se. Auditors are also much less worried about user satisfaction than about ensuring that expenditures fall within allocated amounts. Whereas computer personnel use monitors to iden-

Table 10–3   **Auditing concerns**

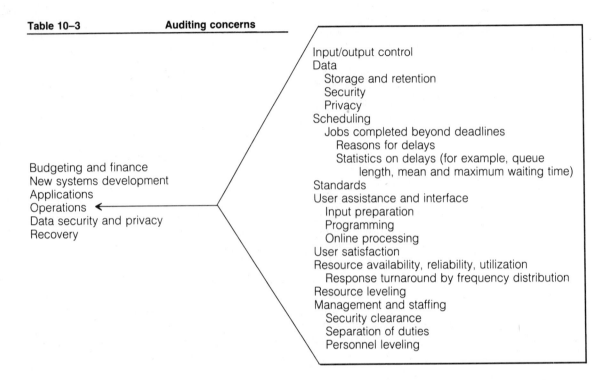

Budgeting and finance
New systems development
Applications
Operations ◄───────────
Data security and privacy
Recovery

Input/output control
Data
    Storage and retention
    Security
    Privacy
Scheduling
    Jobs completed beyond deadlines
        Reasons for delays
        Statistics on delays (for example, queue
            length, mean and maximum waiting time)
Standards
User assistance and interface
    Input preparation
    Programming
    Online processing
User satisfaction
Resource availability, reliability, utilization
    Response turnaround by frequency distribution
Resource leveling
Management and staffing
    Security clearance
    Separation of duties
    Personnel leveling

tify specific problems that need correction, auditors search for weaknesses, test extreme values, and may attempt to break a system to test its limits. Indeed, a major responsibility of auditors is to evaluate the adequacy and sufficiency of systems, not only for normal and peak workloads but for projected needs. In identifying areas where demand will exceed capacity in the future, the auditor's report is a valuable tool in long-range planning.

Each of the auditing concerns listed in Table 10–3 falls within the **audit scope**, and each has numerous subsets of activities. This table shows a blowup of one subset: activities that are evaluated by auditors with regard to operations. Some of the information required for the audit is provided by operating systems. In-house programs can also be written to collect the needed data, but auditors will also have to examine logs and records.

To give an example, analysis of delays will include examination of statistics on average delay time, maximum delay time, average length of queue, maximum length of queue, and so forth—data that can be collected by monitors. But to find reasons for delays, the auditor will have to examine the work flow from input submission, input preparation, preprocessing (for example, validation of data), processing, and postprocessing (for example, decollating and bursting) to distribution. Unless the cause is traced—be it faulty distribution procedures, poorly written manuals, inadequate training of operating personnel, or un-derstaffing—corrective action cannot be taken, and the purpose of the audit will be defeated.

An important task in an operations audit is to look at job assignments to ensure that checks and balances exist. That is, no single individual should participate in both programming and program approval or in testing and test approval. The likelihood that unintentional errors or malicious intrusion will pass unnoticed is diminished when the following jobs are handled by different persons on the computing staff:

- Source document preparation.
- Input preparation.
- File library.
- Output distribution.
- Systems programming.
- Hardware maintenance.
- Data base administration.
- Error corrections.
- Machine operation.

The auditor should also be concerned with computer center output. Possibly, needed information is not being generated, two reports might be more efficiently combined into one, or certain reports have outlived their usefulness. Questions such as those presented in Table 10–4 might

Table 10–4	User questionnaire on reports
	1. How useful do you consider this report?
	2. How often do you use this report?
	3. How many persons in your department use this report? How and why (briefly)?
	4. How much of the data in this report do you use?
	5. Can this report be:
	a. Subsumed in another report?
	b. Eliminated?
	6. If this report were eliminated, would you easily find equivalent information elsewhere?
	7. How do you store this report?
	8. How long do you keep this report?
	9. Is the report timely (available when needed)?
	10. Is the report used for:
	a. Reference?
	b. Action and decision making?
	c. Exceptional reporting?
	d. Planning?
	e. Control?
	f. Operations?
	g. Analysis?
	11. Do you consider the mode of processing satisfactory? Which mode would you prefer? Why?
	12. Is the report likely to be useful to you in the future? For how long?

be asked of users to ascertain the value of given reports. The answers might lead to report alternatives not previously considered.

When controlling output, the following questions should be asked. Are reports economically justifiable? Relevant? Timely? Accurate? Complete? Are reports effective in their presentation and easy to use? Are they packaged logically? Used frequently so that their cost can be justified? The expense of space, equipment, utilities, insurance, and security to store reports may be more costly than the value of report retention. Or perhaps the storage media should be changed to computer output on microfilm for more efficient storage and retrieval.

At one computer center, a serious breakdown resulted in an entire week of processing being lost. An alert auditor questioned users and found that 34 percent missed a report and complained, 24 percent missed a report but did not complain, and 42 percent weren't even aware of reports not processed. This analysis led to canceling many superfluous reports. Another auditor determined that information included in a regularly scheduled report could be generated as efficiently at one third of the cost if produced on a "need to know" basis on a terminal. These examples illustrate that an auditor can help identify system weaknesses that may slip past users or computer center personnel too immersed in daily operations to recognize macro problems of control.

FACILITATING AN AUDITOR'S WORK

Areas of conflict

The role of an auditor is to evaluate the way in which computing resources are managed, operated, and monitored. Even in a data center that runs smoothly, an auditor can raise difficult questions that cause discomfort. Furthermore, many subjective judgments made during the course of an auditor's work may be challenged by computer technicians or data processing managers. In the event of a dispute regarding an acceptable response time, level of utilization, or cost per unit of service, should the auditor's viewpoint prevail? Who should arbitrate controversy? Though management may intervene, most firms give auditors authority to both initiate and tighten controls when problem areas are identified.

Trade-offs are another area where differences of opinion between auditors and computer center personnel may surface. Sometimes, one objective must be degraded in order to achieve a secondary objective. For example, greater accuracy may require increased response time. Here again, the auditor's recommendations may conflict with the viewpoint of computer technicians, creating friction in their working relationships. Auditors can also raise hackles by questioning the value of reports favored by analysts or by recommending changes in procedures.

EDP staff cooperation

As a result of such conflicts of interest, auditors may not get the cooperation of EDP personnel during audits. Yet, assistance in identifying problems and explaining discrepancies is needed. It is management's responsibility to promote a harmonious working relationship between auditors and computing staff. **Auditor-staff harmony** and cooperation are, in fact, in the best interests of all concerned. After all, the purpose of an audit is better utilization of resources and improved efficiency and effectiveness. Since responsibility for establishing strong control systems lies with management and professional staff, an audit report that assesses weaknesses is very helpful: it can be used as the basis of a plan to improve the information processing function.

A number of ways exist in which data processing managers can facilitate the work of auditors and help them perform their duties with the cooperation of computing staff:

- Hold preaudit meetings with the auditor and data processing staff to discuss the objectives of the pending audit. Areas of high risk can be identified and managerial concerns aired.
- Have EDP staff help the auditor review and evaluate audit software to extract information on systems performance. Staff might also help develop audit modules that cannot be purchased as a package.
- Assign auditors to systems development teams to make sure that control issues are fully considered in systems design.
- Sponsor educational programs for both auditors and computer professionals to learn about evolving hardware and software technology and how that technology might impact on control systems.
- Inform auditors when new technology is being considered that may affect how existing systems are monitored.
- Joint auditor–data processing staff review of the audit report before it is finalized. Factual errors or erroneous assessments can be corrected before the report reaches corporate management. An exchange of ideas regarding control problems discussed in the report should foster the view among data processing personnel that the auditor is a co-worker whose expertise is of value in improving the data processing function.

COST

Audits are expensive, and with each new advance in information technology, the cost of maintaining an audit program is rising. This increasing **cost** reflects escalating salaries, training, use of hardware and software to monitor performance, maintenance of logs and other control documents, and computer time to collect and process audit data that may be available only in electronic form. It also reflects management's increasing commitment to the establishment and maintenance of quality control systems.

The frequency of audits is another cost factor. Although there is no rule of thumb regarding frequency, regularly scheduled audits and surprise audits are indeed the norm, and they may be called for when problems arise that require thorough, objective analysis. Also, the cost of disruption must be considered when users and overburdened technicians are interrupted from their usual tasks to participate in interviews and to provide audit assistance.

In spite of these costs, many executives would not consider managing a firm without audits. As the primary benefits that their corporations derive, they cite reduced operational errors and omissions, reduced criminal loss/exposure, better control over inefficiency and overruns, and increased user confidence and satisfaction.

SUMMING UP

Daily operations in a computer center are the responsibility of the data processing manager, who supervises processing to ensure quality performance and systems security.

A second level of control is provided by an internal auditor, who periodically reviews processing and the effectiveness of designed controls. To bring a measure of objectivity to the audit and to ensure the auditor's independence, the auditor should not be a member of the computer staff. Instead, it is recommended that the internal auditor

Figure 10–3   **Audit structure**

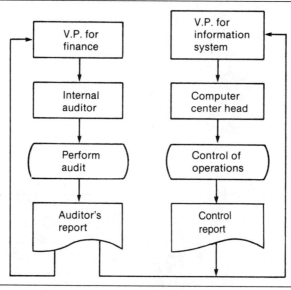

report directly to a corporation executive, such as the vice president of finance, whose authority parallels that of the vice president to whom the computer center director reports. This proposed organizational structure is illustrated in Figure 10–3. An external auditor hired from outside the organization can provide a third level of control.

Auditors examine both micro and macro controls. They review and control components of the systems, such as administrative procedures regarding input and output, and applications controls, such as audit trails. (These are micro controls.) Auditors also evaluate the system as a whole, looking into contingency and disaster planning and separation of duties (macro controls).

A computer center can be characterized as a "high payoff" audit area because of the concentration of records and activities to be audited. Furthermore, computer centers have a record of poor control, with many past operational and developmental disasters. It is in a manager's interest to see that audits take place, if only for self-protection, because responsibility for systems security and error-free computing is ultimately management's.

It may seem to some readers that this chapter has been merely a restatement of Chapter 7 on systems evaluation. True, auditors are concerned with the same processing controls that are scrutinized in performance evaluation. But the auditor's responsibility extends one step further, to control of controls. It is the auditor who reviews the effectiveness of control measures and recommends new controls when existing controls prove insufficient.

Auditors of computerized information systems need more than accounting skills and auditing experience. They must be knowledgeable about computer systems, especially the implementation of data bases, documentation, data security, and recovery. In addition, programming skills are needed, not only to check the decision rules incorporated in a program but also because computer programs are used in the audits themselves. (COBOL is the language most commonly employed in business programs and audits.) Audit programs can control calculations, comparisons, and verifications; perform intermediary operations, such as sampling and extractions; and also perform the functions of monitors, collecting data on operations. The number of practicing and proclaimed EDP auditors is on the increase, but the shortage of auditors experienced in computing is still a major problem.

Unfortunately, auditing techniques have failed to keep pace with advances in computer technology. Computer input, for example, is the source of many inadvertent errors and the point where theft and fraud are often attempted. In order to design input control strategies, computer scientists have spent many years analyzing the source and nature of errors and intrusions during input. Today, however, chips to receive voice input are being developed that will require controls quite different from those used for card or terminal input. In all probability, by the time adequate controls for the chips have been designed and implemented, the technology will have changed once again. This lag is one of the major problems facing the computer industry and auditors today.

CASE: AUDITING OFF-SITE STORAGE

To help explain what an auditor does, here are some of the review activities that take place when an audit is conducted of an off-site facility for the storage of computer tapes:

- An inventory is made of the off-site facility. The physical count of the tapes is matched with the log kept at the main computer center that lists tapes in storage.
- Government and corporate retention standards are examined to see if the standards need to be updated. Then a check is made of ways standards are enforced.
- The physical security of the tapes is evaluated. Fire alarms are tested. Temperature and humidity controls are examined. Addressed are questions such as: Is access restricted? How? What security measures are in place?
- A disaster may be simulated to test whether tapes stored at the off-site facility are adequate for recovery of the main computer center. Or specific applications may be tested to see if the use of off-site data would be sufficient to restore operations from a specific point in time.
- Delivery procedures to off-site storage are checked. Are backup tapes delivered to storage on holidays? What security measures are in force during transit?
- Older files are examined to make sure that data can still be read on them.
- Tape reel labels are sampled to be sure that they correctly identify data on the tape.
- The method by which tapes are arranged in storage is studied. Is the method efficient? Can a specific tape be quickly located?
- Procedures for requesting a tape in storage are reviewed. Who has authority to access tape?
- Responsibility for the off-site facility is evaluated. Who is accountable? What supervisory structure is in existence?

Questions

1. At a tape storage facility, how should an auditor test:
   a. Fire alarms?
   b. Disaster plan?
   c. Backup adequacy of stored files?
   d. Control procedures?
2. Who should have authority to access tape files in storage? What access controls should be installed?
3. What structure of accountability should be in place at an off-site storage facility?
4. Who should the auditor be? What training does the auditor need? To whom should the auditor report?

STUDY KEYS

Audit programming languages   Audits through the computer
Audit programs   Cost
Audit scope   External audit
Auditor   External auditor
Auditor's role in systems   Internal audit
  development   Internal auditor
Auditor-staff harmony   Minicompany approach
Audits around the computer

DISCUSSION QUESTIONS

1. Should computer operations be audited? If so, at what level or levels?
2. Consider a manufacturing plant with 1,200 employees and a computer system employing 30 people that processes 15 main applications.
   a. What level or levels should be audited?
   b. Would you recommend an internal auditor, an external auditor, or both?
   c. Would you also recommend internal control by the computer center itself?
3. When is an external auditor advisable?
4. In what ways do internal auditors, external auditors, and control personnel within a computing center complement or overlap one another?

5. Why should an auditor participate in the development of a computer application? What are the advantages and disadvantages of such participation?

6. What are the differences between auditing a computer application and a noncomputer application?

7. How are EDP auditors different from other auditors? Why are they in scarce supply?

8. How can an auditor help prevent:
    a. Input errors?
    b. Design errors?
    c. Computer fraud through unauthorized modification of a program?
    d. Theft of computer time?
    e. Theft of a data tape?
    f. Unauthorized access to a data base through a terminal?
    g. Theft of manuals?
    h. Dishonest computer operation?
    i. Dishonest management?

9. How can an auditor help a firm recover from natural disasters or fire?

10. Do computers make internal controls easier or more difficult? How?

11. Do computers aid auditors or make their jobs more difficult? How?

12. List the steps in the auditing of:
    a. A computer application.
    b. Computer systems development.
    c. A computer center.
    d. Computer personnel.
    e. A computer library.

13. How does one compensate for the fact that an audit trail is not available in a computer system?

14. Design procedures for auditing the effectiveness of a schedule for a computer center.

15. How could audit requirements be incorporated in the design of an accounting-oriented information subsystem?

16. How can an auditor defeat collusion among computer center staff? What types of clues might there be to such collusion?

17. Is it possible to overaudit? How could one detect an overaudit and prevent it from happening again?

18. Discuss ways that the director of a computing facility can promote a harmonious working relationship between computer personnel and an EDP auditor.

SELECTED ANNOTATED BIBLIOGRAPHY

Beitman, Lawrence. "Transaction Testing: A Systems Approach that Works." *EDPACS*, vol. 12, no. 3 (March 1985), pp. 1–3.

Transaction testing not only can aid auditors in detecting errors in computer processing but can also perform preventive maintenance by identifying weaknesses in applications controls.

Cornick, Delroy L. *Auditing in the Electronic Environment.* Mt. Airy, Md: Lomond Books, 1981, 316 pp.
This book discusses the EDP environment and the auditor's trade, tools, techniques, and role in EDP auditing. A chapter is also included on training and developing EDP auditing competence, an important topic in light of the shortage of EDP auditors. The second half of the book is devoted to an annotated bibliography and collection of auditing references.

Eva, Keith D. "EDP Auditing and Offsite Storage." *EDP Auditor,* Summer 1983, pp. 41–45.
The importance of auditing off-site storage is convincingly made. Backup, recovery, physical security, and efficiency should all be audited.

Farrell, D. J. "Applying an Integrated Test Facility—An Example" *COM–SAC,* vol. 10, no. 1 (January 1982), pp. A9-–12.
An integrated test facility, developed by the U.S. firm SDC, was used in Australia and shown to test successfully online production programs as part of the production environment, without any data contamination.

Holley, Charles L. and F. Millar. "Auditing the On-Line, Real-Time Computer System." *Journal of Systems Management,* vol. 34, no. 1, (June 1983), pp. 14–19.
Problems of auditing data files, output, transmission, systems failure, and recovery of online real-time (OLRT) systems are discussed.

Loebbecke, James K., John F. Mullarky; and George R. Zuber. "Auditing in a Computer Environment." *Journal of Accountancy,* vol. 155, no. 1(January 1983), pp. 68–78.
Three certified public accountants give advice on how to identify potential errors and irregularities and then how to adapt procedures and audit tools to control them. The emphasis is on transaction processing.

Menkus, Belden. "A New Approach Needed to 'Controls.'" *Data Processing Audit Report,* no. 21 (January 1985), pp. 3–5.
Because of the proliferation of microcomputers and networks, a new approach to controls is needed. Six controls, including dynamic real-time audit trails, are proposed.

Sardinas, Joseph, John G. Burch; and Richard Asebrook. *EDP Auditing: A Primer.* New York: John Wiley & Sons, 1981, 209 pp.
This introduction to EDP auditing discusses tagging, tracing, computer-assisted audit techniques, audit software, integrated test facility (ITF) and parallel test facility (PTF). There are also good sections on controls for operations, administration, documentation, and security.

Shudrna, Vincent J., and Frank J. Lackner. "The Implementation of Concurrent Audit." *EDPACS,* vol. 11, no. 4 (April 1984), pp. 1–6.
The authors discuss the futility of after-the-fact conventional audit techniques in advanced computing OLRT environments and recommend concurrent audit systems. They also suggest that the optimal time

to consider auditability and control requirements is during the design stage.

Ward, Gerald M., and Richard D. Paterson. "Surviving (and Profiting from) the Audit." *Computerworld*, vol. 18, no. 40 (September 24, 1984), pp. ID/13–23.

The authors urge the director of a computing facility to welcome and cooperate with an EDP auditor because auditing is in the director's best interest. Identifying systems weaknesses before a breakdown occurs has distinct advantages.

Weber, Ron. *EDP Auditing: Conceptual Foundation and Practice*. New York: McGraw-Hill, 1982, 643 pp.

The author focuses on control. He discusses how to evaluate a control framework, the techniques of evidence collection, and how evidence itself should be evaluated. The author's premise is that a good auditor must be better at business than clients. Many detailed and technical aspects of EDP control are discussed, such as concurrency, cryptography, kernel programs, and data dictionary. This is a very impressive text.

Winters, C. M. "Auditing Data Communication Networks." *COM-SAC* vol. 9, no. 7 (July 1982), pp. A1–4.

This is a tutorial on telecommunications networks and their exposure to a security breach. The author suggests policies and procedures for securing networks and for auditing them.

PART FOUR

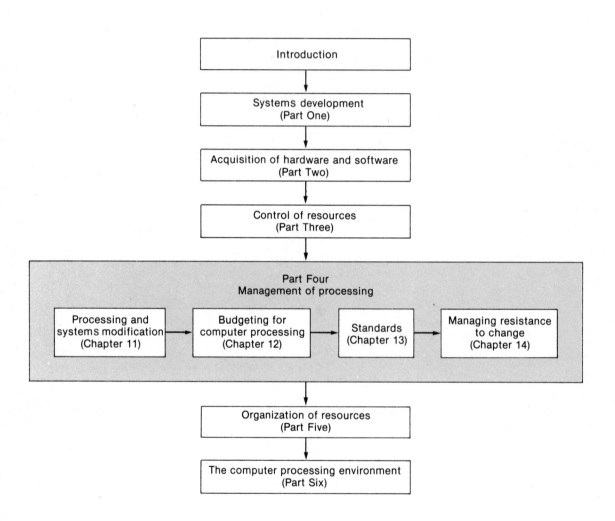

Introduction

Systems development
(Part One)

Acquisition of hardware and software
(Part Two)

Control of resources
(Part Three)

Part Four
Management of processing

Processing and systems modification
(Chapter 11)

Budgeting for computer processing
(Chapter 12)

Standards
(Chapter 13)

Managing resistance to change
(Chapter 14)

Organization of resources
(Part Five)

The computer processing environment
(Part Six)

**Introduction to
Part Four**

Part Four concerns the management of computer resources in daily operations. It focuses on the day-to-day responsibilities of a computer center head and suggests ways to prepare employees in a firm for changes that occur when the role of computers is expanded.

Most of the issues raised in Part Four need to be considered during the development of information systems. However, subjects discussed in this part—such as scheduling and production controls, the supervision of maintenance and systems modification, the preparation of computing budgets, the establishment and enforcement of standards, and the motivation of personnel—are matters that occupy management long after the development team is disbanded and conversion to the new information system has taken place. For this reason, a separate part has been devoted to management of processing instead of adding the chapters to Part One on systems development.

Chapter 11 describes the flow of a job through computer processing, from scheduling to output control and distribution. When output proves unsatisfactory, systems modification may be required, a process also examined in the chapter. Chapter 12 introduces budgetary approaches—examining elements and cost trends in computing budgets and alternative revenue schemes. This chapter also suggests methods of controlling budgets so that discrepancies between budgeted and actual expenditures are minimized.

The need for standards in computing is examined in Chapter 13, and the role of a standards committee in setting standards is explained. In addition, industry, professional, national, and international sources of standards are described.

The last chapter in this part, Chapter 14, deals with managing resistance to change. In this case, change means the introduction of computerized systems in a given firm. Strategies to foster positive employee attitudes toward computers are suggested.

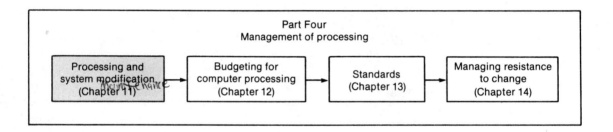

Part Four
Management of processing

| Processing and system modification (Chapter 11) | Budgeting for computer processing (Chapter 12) | Standards (Chapter 13) | Managing resistance to change (Chapter 14) |

CHAPTER 11

Processing and systems maintenance

Leave room in the system for the feedback of experience to redesign the system itself.

Max Ways

If an applications package is purchased or custom-developed for a microcomputer system, the user will store the program until it is needed, then load it into a micro for use. Data processing staff will typically have no responsibility for processing the application unless the user asks for assistance because the program fails to work or the microcomputer itself breaks down. However, the processing of software purchased or developed in-house for large computer systems falls under the jurisdiction of a computer department. Computer operators will be on duty at the time the job is run to oversee processing, perform manual operating tasks (such as loading peripherals), and troubleshoot if a processing malfunction occurs. Throughout processing, controls ensure the efficiency and effectiveness of processing and protect the security of computing resources.

Once the user is satisfied with output, the processing responsibility of the computer department ends. But should output fail to meet user needs or departmental standards, corrections will have to be made. Often, operational personnel can identify the cause of errors, make the necessary adjustments, and schedule a rerun. (Perhaps a peripheral device had an incorrect setting or the wrong output paper was used.) Sometimes, however, operators do not know how to correct the problem, or they lack the authorization to make necessary changes. In such cases, the job is sent to the group or department responsible for systems maintenance.

The first half of this chapter is on processing, the steps of which are shown in Figure 11–1. Topics discussed are scheduling, job run, output

Figure 11–1   **Flow of a job through operations**

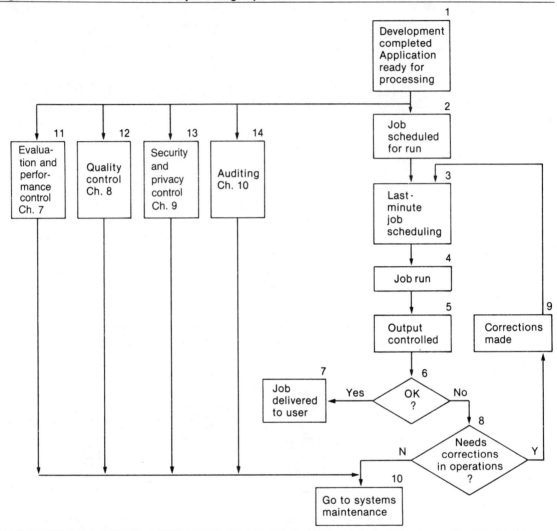

control and distribution, and production controls. Then the chapter addresses the issue of unsatisfactory output. Is hardware or software at fault? Does the system need modification or extensive redevelopment? Maintenance in both small and large systems environments will be considered.

PROCESSING

Scheduling (Boxes 2 and 3)

Ideally, there should be no constraints on processing. Run time should be available whenever needed. In practice, however, processing conflicts invariably arise in multiuser computer systems. (This explains, in part, the appeal of microcomputers.) Demand Curve A in Figure 11–2, typical when a computer is a shared resource, shows that capacity is exceeded at certain hours of the day. In such situations, jobs must be staggered to equalize the workload, to flatten Curve A to Curve B. (Curve C, with demand consistently higher than capacity, shows bad forecasting and poor capacity planning.)

Multiuser systems that are exclusively batch require a **master schedule**. In mixed systems, the online real-time uses are controlled by internal computer scheduling mechanisms, while the batch processing is still regulated by a master schedule. Most firms form a **user committee** to establish scheduling procedures, guidelines, and priorities, although the actual scheduling will be delegated to someone in operations, such as a **schedule officer** or production manager.

Scheduling is not as easy is it may seem. Problems generally arise because of limited resources. Some computers are peripheral-bound, with the speed of processing restrained by an input reader, printer, or other peripheral, causing jobs to backlog. Processing demand is often unpredictable, with unexpected peaks of demand. The availability of resources can be difficult to forecast as well. For example, delivery of new equipment may fall behind schedule, or a breakdown may wreak

Figure 11–2   **Different patterns of processing demand**

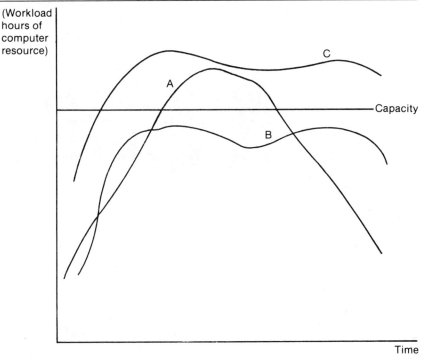

(Workload hours of computer resource)

havoc with the master schedule. When users are competing for computer time, tensions can build and tempers flare.

A master schedule includes batch jobs that are processed on a regular basis. Because the volume of input for such a job and the length of time required for processing are generally known, as is the time that the job will be submitted for processing, the job can be scheduled well in advance. For example, if payroll is regularly received by operations at 12 noon the last working day of the month, payroll processing can be blocked on the master schedule weeks, even months, ahead.

Not all batch jobs processed on a regular basis need to be as rigidly scheduled as payroll. Many weekly or monthly reports can be placed on the master schedule wherever there are open time blocks, as long as they are scheduled within a given time period (for instance, within the last week of the month). Other blocks of time can be allocated to regular users on the master schedule. Secretaries may be given one hour of processing time mornings and afternoons, for instance, and programmers assigned two hours daily.

Many jobs received by a computer center, however, cannot be planned in advance, so day-to-day scheduling within the master schedule framework is also needed. Perhaps the need for a special report arises during a bargaining session with union representatives; perhaps last-minute information is required to complete a sales bid; perhaps a programmer needs extra run time to meet a deadline. Maybe a user has forgotten to request computer time in advance; maybe the master schedule has been thrown out of kilter because a job scheduled months ahead is not ready for processing. A crisis atmosphere always seems to pervade computer centers when it comes to scheduling.

To illustrate the dilemma of a schedule officer, let us consider the problem of deciding how to schedule the four jobs listed in Table 11–1. One **scheduling algorithm** is *first come, first served*, also called *first in, first out (FIFO)*, an algorithm used in inventory control. Another option is *least processing time first*. This is a very common decision rule when the amount of processing time required for some jobs is much less than for others. The rationale behind this algorithm is that

Table 11–1   **Data on four jobs competing for priority scheduling**

Job	Processing time required (units of time)	Arrival	Due date Target	Due date Deadline	Priority class (1 = urgent)
A	3	09.00	Monday	Tuesday	1
B	5	09.15	Monday	Monday	1
C	1	09.10	Tuesday	Thursday	4
D	4	09.20	Wednesday	Friday	3

Table 11–2	Criteria used for scheduling jobs in Table 11–1					
	First come, first served	Least processing time first	Least slack time first	Earliest target date first	Earliest deadline date first	Highest-priority classification first
	A	C	B	A or B	B	A or B
	C	A	A		A	
	B	D	C or D	C	C	D
	D	B		D	D	C

users demanding only a second or fraction of a second of scarce processing time should be given priority over a single user wanting to "hog" the computer.

Yet another scheduling possibility is to give priority to the job that has the *least slack time* between target date and deadline. Sometimes, the job with the *earliest target date* (or *earliest deadline date*) is processed first. Using still another decision rule, scheduling can be based on urgency. Each job is assigned a numerical rating according to its urgency as assessed by the user, a rating that is reviewed by the schedule officer or user committee. According to the priority rule, jobs classified as 1 in Table 11–1 would be run before the jobs with a 2 rating, 2s would be run before jobs with a 3 classification, and so on.

In Table 11–2, priorities are assigned to each of the jobs listed in Table 11–1, using a variety of decision rules. Note that processing order is not always clear-cut, since some of the decision rules result in ties. In such cases, more than one rule has to be applied.

Table 11–2 lists only four jobs competing for processing time. In reality, scheduling is far more complex. Hundreds of jobs need to be scheduled per day in large computer centers, and scheduling algorithm possibilities are not limited to the six used in the table. Jobs might be

Table 11–3	Performance criteria used in scheduling	
	Category	Criteria
	User oriented	Minimum mean job lateness (completion time minus due time). Minimum mean job throughtime (job completion time minus job arrival time). Maximum mean earliness (amount of time job completed before deadline).
	Data center oriented	Maximum mean throughput (number of jobs processed in a fixed time period). Minimum number of jobs waiting to be processed. Maximum percentage of resource utilization. Minimum total processing cost.

Source: Howard Schaeffer, *Data Center Operations* (Englewood Cliffs, N.J.: Prentice-Hall, 1981), pp. 238–39.

processed on a round-robin basis. Priority might be based on length of wait, elapsed time from request to deadline, processing cost, status of user, length of advance notice to computer center, or any number of factors.

Scheduling algorithms can be categorized as either *user oriented* or *data center oriented*: some stress service while others minimize cost or optimize use of computing resources. In most computer centers, the user committee weighs the value and effectiveness of possible algorithms, decides what performance criteria are important to the computer center, and ranks the relative importance of selected criteria. (Table 11–3 lists performance criteria that are commonly used to evaluate scheduling algorithms.)

Once the priority rules are established, software internal to the operating system of the computer can help with the scheduling, or software packages can be purchased so that scheduling can take place automatically within parameters defined by the committee.[1] Such software can be overridden manually, enabling an operator to interrupt and change priorities when special circumstances arise. Although guidelines for scheduling are the responsibility of the user committee, authority is generally delegated to the schedule officer to make on-the-spot decisions when conflicts or problems arise.

Users should be informed of the decision rules on which scheduling is based and have access to processing schedules. Since the master schedule is prepared weeks or months in advance, it can be distributed in hard copy. The updated daily schedule should be available on a need-to-know basis at a conveniently located console or terminal, so that users can keep track of the status of their jobs. Many systems provide enhancements to this status output. For example, users may be able to interrogate the system for processing information, such as estimated time a given job run will start or reasons why a job is being delayed.

Job run (4)

Once scheduled, a job is run. Assuming that the operator's manual (written as part of systems documentation) is complete, that the operations staff is well trained, and that hardware and software are well maintained, the **job run** should be problem free. Before processing begins, pertinent data and relevant programs are assembled, and the computer and needed peripherals are assigned to the job. Job control (operational parameters) can be automated, manual, or a combination of the two, depending on the sophistication of the computer center. The sequence of run activities is illustrated in Figure 11–3.

Most systems require operators to fill out a number of forms when

---

[1]See Harold Lorin and Harvey M. Deitel, *Operating Systems* (Reading, Mass.: Addison-Wesley Publishing, 1981), chap. 15.

Figure 11–3   **Job run sequence**

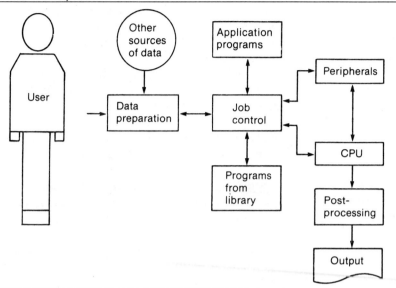

jobs are run. Some are checklists describing what steps to take, how and when. Others are control forms used to log operations and collect processing data. Table 11–4 is a list of common processing forms. Run information that is collected on the forms is later used by performance evaluators and auditors and may be referenced by analysts when seeking the solution to processing problems.

The list in Table 11–4 is not all-inclusive. Many firms have supplemental forms to collect processing data for unique needs. Unfortunately, forms tend to proliferate. Management should recognize the cost involved in designing and implementing forms and in training personnel in their use. Storage of information and forms is also expensive. The need for new forms should be carefully reviewed by management, form

Table 11–4   **Forms used in processing**

Batch ticket	Output distribution log
Computer problem log	Problem statement log
Data conversion instructions	Production control log
Data preparation instructions	Program maintenance instructions
Data validation instructions	Request form for computing services
Distribution control sheet	Routing tickets
Input data log sheet	Shift turnover log sheet
Job control instructions	Software problem report
Job monitoring log	Storage maintenance instructions
Job scheduling instructions	Usage log sheet
Job setup sheet	

design should be assigned to professionals, and strict control should be exercised by evaluators and auditors over each form used. Consolidation and elimination of forms without a loss of processing efficiency and effectiveness should be the goal.

In addition to forms, processing reports assist in control of operations. Some can be generated by the operating system. Others are prepared by computer center staff. These should include information on scheduling, work flow, job execution, downtime, resource utilization, and the status of workstations. Like forms, reports have a tendency to multiply. They should be subject to the same stringent standards as forms, so that only needed information is processed.

Output control and distribution (5 and 7)

In the batch mode, **output control** following a job run consists of checking to see that output specifications formulated during development and listed in systems documentation are met. Some controls, such as accuracy or completeness validation, can be exercised by software. The scrutiny of operators is also invaluable because their eyes can readily spot many errors, such as wrong format or size of a report, incorrect number of copies, or faulty packaging.

An example of a costly error that could have been avoided by an attentive operator was the mailing of 14,000 duplicate grade reports to a single individual, Mr. L. C. Abel, the first name on a list of students at a university. A programming error caused the output to be a repetition of Mr. Abel's grade report instead of a report for each of the 14,000 students on the list. A simple glance at the output by an operator or control clerk would have caught the mistake and saved the university embarrassment and the expense of materials, labor, and postage for the mailing. Numerous anecdotes of a similar nature surface in computer literature. Humorous to the reader but not to those involved, these anecdotes demonstrate the importance of output control in batch processing. Many computer centers give an internal control clerk the responsibility of checking all output.

Output distribution is an additional responsibility of computer personnel in batch systems. Delay in a user's receipt of a run can often be traced to inefficient distribution procedures rather than to an overloaded computer. Since privacy of output is valued as highly as timeliness by many users, both security of output and speed should be priorities in delivery systems.

Online output is not reviewed by computer center personnel, since processed results are delivered directly to the user. Although software will monitor and control processing to some extent, checking to ensure that output satisfies run specifications is the responsibility of the user.

Production control

In batch processing, a **production manager** supervises and controls processing activities from scheduling through output distribution to a satisfied customer. The manger also oversees most phases of online processing, though the user will control online input and output.

The following fall under the production manager's jurisdiction:

Input/output (batch).	Costs.
Processing.	Documentation.
Data.	Library.
Privacy.	Supplies.
Security.	

Most of these subjects have been (or will be) discussed in other sections of this book, with the exception of library and supplies, discussed next.

Library. A computer center **library** is the repository of data, programs, and documentation. Although security measures are the responsibility of management, a librarian must enforce these measures so that stored materials are protected, and must control access to the resources to bona fide users only.

One of the librarian's primary duties is guarding resources from fraudulent use. Badges, logging, and checkout systems can be used to keep resources from the hands of unauthorized users. A need-to-know policy might restrict individuals to certain resources. For example, an analyst might be permitted to withdraw documentation and programs, but not the operator's manual. In theory, the analyst would then lack the operational know-how to run equipment, which would prevent illicit processing. Restrictive policies may not be practical in small organizations where a single employee wears many hats; but in large firms, a need-to-know policy is a useful control.

Table 11–5 summarizes the control responsibilities of a computer librarian.

Supplies. Control of supplies in a computer center is similar to inventory control of supplies in other departments. The computer, however, can resolve shortages of printed header forms if headers are in computer programs and a multifont printer is available for printing needed forms.

Table 11–5	Responsibilities of a computer librarian
	Safekeep resources (data programs and documentation) and backup
	Ensure resources are updated
	Control access to resources to authorized personnel
	Maintain resources in usable condition
	Record errors and malfunctions experienced by users of library resources
	Charge, discharge, and log resource use
	Keep statistics on library uses

Security must be tight for many computer supplies, such as unprinted payroll checks or stock certificates. These must be counted upon receipt, tallied when printed, and a careful log kept of any damaged or destroyed during operations.

UNSATISFACTORY OUTPUT (6, 8, AND 9)

Thus far in this chapter, we have assumed that output meets specifications. Not all jobs pass output control successfully, however. Many need to be rerun because of hardware failure (central processing unit or peripheral breakdown), software problems (bugs, such as mistakes in programming logic), input errors, operator blunders, inadequate documentation, faulty procedures, or lack of controls. Sometimes the environment can be blamed, such as when electrical power is lost. To trace what is the matter or why output fails to meet specifications is not always easy, particularly when a combination of circumstances is responsible for errors. Also, to isolate the problem, make corrections, then repeat processing can be an expensive proposition, raising the question: Should users be assessed the cost of finding problem solutions and charged for reruns?

Charging users the cost of **reprocessing** when they are at fault has advantages. Too often, users are careless in their input preparation and shift the responsibility for finding errors to the computer center instead of controlling input before a job is submitted for processing. For example, a receptionist in one user department was responsible for data preparation in free moments when the phone was not ringing or clients were not at the desk. The need for job reruns dropped significantly when a charge system for reruns was initiated. To avoid payment, the department hired a trained data entry clerk and took control measures to ensure that input was correct prior to submission.

User responsibility for errors is not always so clear-cut, however. Should users be charged for program errors caused by inadequate user specifications or for errors traced to poor documentation? It would certainly be unfair to charge users for equipment breakdown or operator mistakes.

Since computer centers usually absorb the cost of most reruns, it is in their interest to plan strategies that minimize the need for and cost of reprocessing. Stringent operating controls are advisable. The establishment of procedures for failure diagnosis and failure recovery is useful. For example, careful analysis of rerun trends may help identify causes. One firm found that the rush during peak periods of demand reduced operator efficiency. By scheduling new jobs in off-hours, when personnel had more time for handling and troubleshooting unfamiliar reports, the number of reruns dropped.

Preventive maintenance of equipment is a necessity. When hardware design or hardware manufacture causes a recurring problem, some firms prod the vendor into corrective action by complaining to a person one step higher in the vendor's organizational hierarchy each time the problem arises.

Each firm has a unique environment, so measures taken to ensure satisfactory output will vary from firm to firm. But all firms should make a determined effort to find ways to reduce the need for reruns.

Sometimes, error correction requires the expertise of a computer specialist. Hardware may need repair; perhaps the software requires modification or redevelopment. This chapter closes with a look at the problems of systems maintenance.

SYSTEMS MAINTENANCE (10)

**Hardware
breakdown**

Although hardware is becoming increasingly reliable, computer systems do malfunction on occasion. To minimize downtime, a corporation has the following options.

Internal service. A **service department** to maintain hardware can be set up within the company. Some companies even offer repair service to other computer owners outside of their organization. Only organizations with many computers choose this option.

Manufacturer's fixed fee. A **manufacturer's maintenance agreement** may be signed. For a fixed monthly fee, the manufacturer agrees to repair most equipment malfunctions during specified hours of the day.

Time and materials charges. Equipment can be serviced by the manufacturer under a time and materials arrangement. That is, a charge will be made for each service call.

Third-party service. Maintenance can be contracted to a **third party maintenance** firm. This arrangement resembles a manufacturer's maintenance agreement but generally costs 10–25 percent less. For large customers, spare parts are commonly stocked at the site by third-party providers, which helps speed repairs.

Combining service systems. A **hybrid maintenance system** is also possible. A maintenance contract may be signed for major problems, but a company may rely on self-maintenance for minor ones. For example, they may stock replacement parts, such as logic boards and keyboards. Some hardware manufacturers provide customers with self-help maintenance manuals and supplement this instruction with a technical answering service.

Much of the growth in the third-party maintenance market can be attributed to this service arrangement's popularity with microcomputer owners. In fact, some PC dealers offer service contracts with third-party companies instead of doing repairs themselves. Individuals who own microcomputers like the fact that many third-party companies pick up machines that are out of order; others will accept defective machines through the mail. A corporation with many microcomputers purchased from different manufacturers may find that only an independent maintenance company can service their whole product line. And only a national service company can easily contract for maintenance when a corporation has microcomputers in offices scattered throughout a wide geographical area.[2] (A typical micro system needs repair once or twice a year, at the minimum. Disk drives and printers cause the most problems.)

Negotiating a maintenance agreement is generally advisable when deciding to acquire a new system. The quality and quantity of maintenance personnel should be a major consideration. Check references. Find out how many different sites are serviced by the company, also the number of service people available. Ask what happens when service is requested during off-hours. Is backup support offered? What is the company's relationship to manufacturers? How about spare parts? Does the maintenance agreement allow relocation of equipment without the vendor's consent? Be sure to examine the contract agreement carefully to determine exactly what is covered. Customers can protect themselves by explicitly spelling out service requirements in maintenance contracts.

Software maintenance

The failure of output to meet user needs may lie with software. In such cases, software maintenance is required. The term *software maintenance* is used to describe any work done on an existing system or program. Many other terms are used in computer literature as synonyms, including program maintenance, systems maintenance, production monitoring and control, systems control, systems tuning, and even postimplementation development. What is important, is not the name but the maintenance function. There are four types:

- **Corrective maintenance** occurs when a program is not meeting the requirements in the original specifications: for example, the correction of latent software design errors or program bugs.
- **Adaptive maintenance** means that software is altered to meet changing external requirements: for example, updating in response to changed environmental conditions such as new government regulations.

---

[2]For more on the subject of third-party maintenance, see Robert J. Rich, Jr., "The Pros and Cons of Third-Party Maintenance," *Small Systems World*, vol. 8, no. 1 (January 1981), pp. 32–35.

- **Upgrading** is needed when changes in hardware, software, or protocols—for example, a new operating system—necessitate program modifications.
- **Enhancement** takes place when user specifications themselves change, requiring corresponding changes in programs and systems design.[3]

Maintenance is costly. It is estimated that maintenance work constitutes more than half of the work of the typical information systems department, that 50 percent of data processing budgets are allocated to maintenance, and that more than $30 billion is spent on maintenance annually worldwide. According to a recent study by the Department of Defense, the cost of developing U.S. Air Force avionics software is approximately $75 per instruction; the cost of maintenance of deployed software ranges up to $4,000 per instruction. What's more, by every indication, maintenance expenditures are growing.

The problem is not always the nature of software but current programming practices and the tools that programmers use. Many experts believe that more effort should be spent during systems development to make software reliable and modifiable. They stress the need for improved modification techniques as well. For example, a methodology is needed that permits code reuse without risk and the separate storage of unique and reusable code so that each can be maintained independently.[4]

Many corporations are replacing software that has "aged." One reason is that old software systems are written in languages that are no longer commonly used by today's programmers, such as assembly language. The software may use outdated programming and design practices, factors that complicate maintenance, Programs may have been extensively "patched," with changes poorly documented, or they may have been increased in size beyond what their structure was originally designed to bear. Few people who worked on the original systems may be available to answer questions or explain how the programs work.[5] One might compare an old system to an old car that becomes increas-

---

[3]According to Bennet Lientz and E. Burton Swanson, software maintenance requires 45 percent of systems and programming resources in most companies. They divide maintenance into three categories: corrective maintenance (20 percent), adaptive maintenance (25 percent), and enhancement (55 percent). See their book, *Software Maintenance Management* (Reading, Mass.: Addison-Wesley Publishing, 1980), 220 pp.

[4]For a discussion of frame technology, whereby unique code is stored separately from reusable code, see Paul Bassett and Scott Rankine, "The Maintenance Challenge," *Computerworld*, vol. 17 (May 16, 1983), pp. 42–48.

[5]See Gerald M. Berns, "Assessing Software Maintainability," *Communications of the ACM*, vol. 27, no. 1 (January 1984), pp. 14–23, for a discussion of a maintainability analysis tool. It is the author's premise that program difficulty represents the sum of the difficulties of its constituent elements and that these elements can be quantified by the use of carefully selected weights and factors.

ingly unreliable and costly to maintain with age. Besides, most users (like car owners) want the latest technology. They favor the use of software that takes advantage of streamlined facilities and standard routines. They may even choose to redevelop software before the replacement of old systems can be economically justified.

Maintenance/
redevelopment life
cycle

Every firm needs a maintenance policy and procedures to identify maintenance problems and their solutions. A committee generally decides when maintenance or redevelopment is needed. In general, maintenance is defined as a change that affects few users and does not require much effort or many resources (not more than two weeks of a programmer's time, for example). Redevelopment, on the other hand, requires a major allocation of resources and personnel.

Figure 11–4 illustrates that the **maintenance/redevelopment life cycle** is similar to that of in-house systems development. First, the need for maintenance or redevelopment is identified. When change is under consideration, users should participate in discussions to ensure that proposed modifications meet their needs and that the final system will be accepted. When analysts are new to the organization and unfamiliar

Figure 11–4   **Development and maintenance/redevelopment cycle**

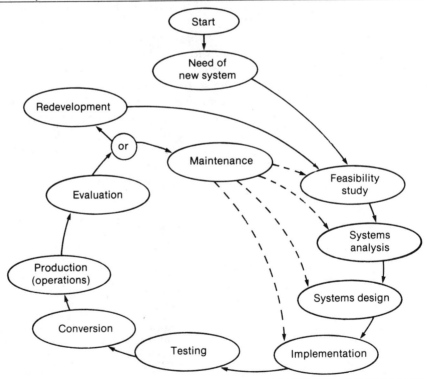

with the software that requires maintenance or redevelopment, the user can often save time for maintenance personnel by explaining how the system works and what problems to expect.

A feasibility assessment should be the next stage of the life cycle, including a cost estimate of the effort required to complete the change. Following management approval of the maintenance/redevelopment project, the job is scheduled and assigned to maintenance personnel. Once changes have been made, the modified software is tested to verify that it performs as expected. When both users and manager approve the test results, documentation must be completed, and the old software is replaced with the modified software.

Even routine maintenance should not skip steps in the development cycle. Too often, stages (such as need specification or testing) are omitted because of time pressures. This can lead to monumental blunders,

Figure 11–5   **Partial flowchart of a carelessly maintained program**

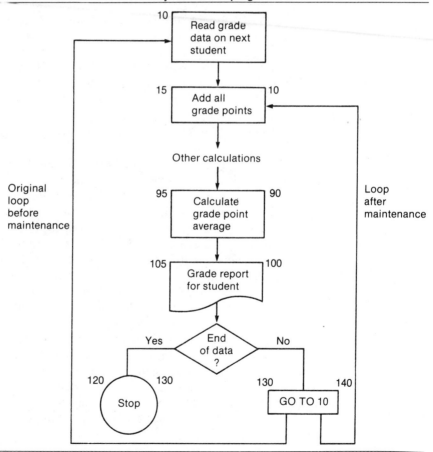

such as the error mentioned earlier: Mr. Abel's receipt of 14,000 duplicate grade reports. This happened because a programmer changed statement numbers when patching a program. Figure 11–5 shows the original statement numbers (to the left of each box) and modified numbers (to the right). Since the "GO TO 10" statement was unaltered but the statement numbers had been changed, the program skipped "Read grade data on next student." In this case, the maintenance programmer omitted an important step: testing. Output controls also proved inadequate; a supervisor should have caught the error. Mistakes of this nature can be expensive, disruptive, and ruin a firm's credibility.

The control principles outlined in Chapters 7 through 10 apply to software maintenance as well as to systems development and daily operations. The privacy of data needs to be protected, computing resources should be kept secure, and the performance of individuals working on maintenance should be monitored and periodically evaluated to ensure quality work within budgetary constraints.

What triggers software maintenance? The impetus for software modification may come from a number of factors:

Error in output. Debugging a program during a new system's development can never reveal the absence of errors, only their presence. Many design errors are not revealed until the program has been in use for some time. When a previously working system ceases to function, emergency maintenance is called for.

External environment. New laws and changed government regulations are two common reasons why systems must be modified. Also, competitors may so alter market conditions that systems redesign must be initiated. When regular changes in the external environment are anticipated, such as revision of tax rates, flexible programs can be written that make modification part of routine maintenance.

User management. Systems modification is sometimes triggered by a change in management. A different style of decision making may lead to the need for a different threshold of information (level of information detail). Or management may simply learn to use information systems more effectively. An increased awareness of a system's potential often causes management to place increased demands on the system. Policies of an organization may change, requiring new methods for calculations, such as new depreciation methods. Or frequent errors and inconsistencies resulting from poor systems specification, bad design, or hasty and incomplete testing may become apparent to management when the system is put into operation. User management may also have a wish list of features to be added to the system when finances permit.

EDP personnel. Systems generally require modification when new equipment is acquired. EDP personnel will alert management of the need for such modification. For example, more secondary storage would allow a larger data base, and increased processing would be feasible. Technological advance in the computer industry is swift-paced. Organizations adopting new technology or merely expanding their systems with more sophisticated computers will find that their information systems need modification.

Once systems are operational, analysts may detect errors resulting from poor design and implementation or invalid assumptions, errors that contribute to processing inefficiency or reduce systems effectiveness. Computer personnel, like users, may also have a wish list not included in the original development because the design was frozen or because development resources were lacking at the time. The list might include reorganization of data, new output form design, or even new programming solutions. Generally, these ideas were conceived and documented during development. Once the system is made operational, the suggestions are renewed and reevaluated.

Software maintenance management

Companies that rely on information technology all need to plan for software maintenance and to manage and control the process. **Maintenance management** entails a number of considerations.

Personnel. In spite of the large share of the data processing budget that is consumed by software maintenance, few companies are making a serious effort to reduce maintenance. It has earned the reputation of a second-class job and is typically delegated to junior programmers and programming trainees, not to the qualified senior-level programmers and analysts whose skills are often needed. Surveys reveal that maintenance work has only one half to two thirds of the motivating potential of other programming/analysis work and that the job is regarded as noncreative and nonchallenging. Persons assigned to maintenance tasks seldom receive status or professional recognition for their contributions. One indication of this fact is that few companies have even established the job classification of maintenance analyst or maintenance manager. Indeed, of all data processing technical personnel, the systems maintenance person is most prone to unhappiness and turnover.

A computer director might improve systems maintenance productivity by:

- Hiring persons with a flair for detective work and a preference for systems maintenance over other analysis/programming tasks.
- Enhancing maintenance jobs so that the motivational level and work status are comparable to new systems development.

Since the first suggestion is impractical because of the lack of candidates, let us focus on the second. Five variables (or job dimensions) typically motivate data processing personnel: skill variety, task identity, task significance, autonomy, and feedback from the job. The job of management in organizing systems maintenance is to design the work to enhance as many of these dimensions as possible.

For example, maintenance jobs may be rotated so that individuals work with a variety of software instead of specializing in one system. This will promote skill variety required by the job. Management should reward quality work, perhaps with monetary compensation. A career track should allow for professional advancement. Maintenance analysts and programmers should be challenged to apply new technology to their jobs and to try new maintenance methodologies. Chapter 20, which deals with computer department staffing, discusses still other ways to motivate data processing personnel.

Software maintenance contract.   Software maintenance is not always in-house maintenance. A company may enter into a license agreement for a software product, including maintenance. Key provisions of the contract that will affect cost are:

- User responsibility for escalation of charges.
- Overtime and traveling charge.
- Unsupported services or extras.
- Response time to maintenance requests.
- On- or off-site maintenance.
- Termination rights by user.
- Payment terms.
- User rights to source code.[6]

Chargeback policies.   The way in which maintenance costs are assessed and charged to users can be a source of ill feeling. If systems modifications are performed without charge by a computer center, users may be tempted to demand more maintenance than necessary. Users may also fail to include maintainability in their specifications for custom software or to approve maintenance features in the design of new systems because of their added cost.

On the other hand, a fair assessment of charges is difficult in an integrated system in which more than one user benefits from maintenance. Questions also arise about where the fault lies when maintenance is required: Are maintenance costs because of technical problems the responsibility of users? Is it fair to charge users for program modifications that are needed because the computer center installs a new operating system or institutes new procedures?

Computer centers vary in their charge structures. (See Chapter 12 for more on this subject.) A decision regarding which structure to adopt is the responsibility of data processing management.

---

[6]For more on this subject, see "Don't Underestimate Software Maintenance Costs," *Computer Law and Tax Report,* vol. 11, no. 9 (September 1984), pp. 1–3.

The microcomputer environment.   Software for microcomputer users is often purchased as a package. In this context, **microcomputer maintenance** may be little more than showing the user how the system works and providing help when the user is unable to understand terminal messages or generate expected output.

Microcomputer users may also write their own programs. The development of nonprocedural languages, such as query languages, report generators, and very high-level programming languages, means that users now have tools that allow them to construct their own systems. Sometimes, users wish to modify packages that they have purchased as well.

To give these users maintenance assistance, many firms have established **information centers** staffed by data processing professionals. One role of the center may be to train users in program modification techniques. For example, center personnel may give courses on a particular fourth-generation language. After teaching how to write software using that language, they might then ask: "Suppose the conditions of your original problem change?" By doing exercises in rewriting code, users will gain maintenance experience and, in the process, will learn ways to write programs so that they can be more easily maintained.

Maintenance priorities.   Usually, a committee composed of the data base administrator, an auditor, and users' representatives assigns priorities to maintenance requests and reconciles conflicts between user departments, settling jurisdictional problems of maintenance when they arise. Ideally, maintenance priorities should be decided on the basis of benefits-cost and benefits-performance ratios. The availability of personnel is, of course, an important consideration. Since most analysts and programmers prefer systems development, personnel with the skills and interest in maintaining old systems may be in short supply. Some firms base maintenance priority on the worst-first rule, clearly a subjective judgment. Too often, the assignment of priorities is based on corporate politics (for example, preference given to the boss or to the person who shouts the loudest and longest), not on economic or technological grounds.

SUMMING UP

Processing begins with scheduling and input preparation. Jobs must be run, their output checked, and results delivered to users. Responsibility for these operations differs in a batch environment from responsibility in an interactive online environment, as shown in Table 11–6.

Table 11–6   **Responsibilities for operations in batch and interactive environments**

	Responsibility	
Function	*Batch environment*	*Interactive online environment*
Determination of priorities	User committee	User committee
Scheduling algorithm and procedure determination	User committee	User committee
Scheduling jobs	Job scheduling software or production staff	Job scheduling software
Preparing input	User or data entry staff	User or data entry staff
Running jobs	Production staff	Computer (automatic)
Postprocessing	Production staff	User
Check output	User or control staff	User
Output distribution	Production staff	Job dispatch software

When output proves unsatisfactory, the problem must be identified. If it is a minor operational error, the correction can be made by operating personnel and the job rescheduled. When major hardware or software problems arise, maintenance personnel will have to be called in. Equipment may have to be repaired or the software modified or redeveloped. Software maintenance and redevelopment should follow the systems development cycle described in Chapter 3.

Control over maintenance activities is exceedingly important, since statistics show that security violations often occur during maintenance procedures. There is also a tendency to cut corners in maintenance work to get to more exciting projects. Control procedures should ensure that one job is completed before the next is begun.

Maintenance is very costly and takes a large share of effort, compared to the effort spent in the initial development of information systems. Managers should recognize the strong correlation between high standards in the original development process and low maintenance. To reduce the need for maintenance, systems developers should plan ahead for equipment and software compatibility, test thoroughly for systems weaknesses, and maintain high standards of documentation so that the effort needed for future maintenance is minimized.

One major problem of software maintenance management is finding and retaining personnel with the skill and patience needed to trace errors and weaknesses of programs. Correcting, testing, and documenting changes is often less interesting work, from an analyst's point of view, than attacking a new project. The need for maintenance often results from inadequate documentation, bad design, and unrealistic procedures. Senior programmers and analysts, who should be engaged in maintenance because of their experience and skill, generally shun maintenance duties.

Job enlargement, giving analysts maintenance responsibilities in addition to other duties, is one solution to this problem. Rotation has advantages as well, for a pool of maintenance analysts provides systems backup and brings a variety of approaches and fresh solutions to maintenance problems.

CASE: SURVEY FINDS SEVERE MAINTENANCE PROBLEMS

According to survey results released by the Quality Assurance Institute in 1986, the software maintenance problem within large data centers has yet to be solved. Here are some of the highlights of the survey, which polled 37 Fortune 500 companies.

- In the companies surveyed, maintenance backlogs ranged from 2 to 60 months. The average was 23 months.
- Expenditures for maintenance ranged from 10 percent to 90 percent of data processing budgets. The average was 51 percent.
- Nearly 80 percent of the respondents had systems with logic that could only be understood by specific individuals. This prevented rotating maintenance responsibility among data processing personnel.
- Formal methods for deciding when to rewrite programs existed in less than 15 percent of the companies surveyed. That older systems conform to the same programming standards as newly developed systems was required in 16 percent of the firms.
- In all but 5 percent of the firms surveyed, it was acknowledged that a programmer working on new systems development had a more prestigious position than one assigned to maintenance.

Questions

1. Why do analysts have trouble understanding the logic of a system? What is the solution?

Source: John Gallant, "Survey Finds Maintenance Problem Still Escalating," *Computerworld*, vol. 20, no. 4 (January 27, 1986), p. 31.

2. Why should a company have formal methods for deciding when to rewrite programs?
3. The survey reveals that programmers working on new systems have a more prestigious position than programmers working on maintenance. Should this difference exist? Does it benefit the firm?
4. Are you surprised at the results of the survey? Appalled? Explain.
5. What conclusions do you draw from the survey?

STUDY KEYS

Adaptive maintenance

Corrective maintenance

Enhancement

Hybrid maintenance system

Information centers

Job run

Library

Maintenance management

Maintenance/redevelopment life cycle

Manufacturer's maintenance agreement

Master schedule

Microcomputer maintenance

Output control

Output distribution

Production manager

Reprocessing

Schedule officer

Scheduling algorithm

Service department

Third-party maintenance

Upgrading

User committee

DISCUSSION QUESTIONS

1. A computer center is like a firm: it has to produce a product (information). It needs resources (hardware and software) and raw materials (data) for production. It requires specialized and professional labor. It must price and market its product, and it must control costs. Comment.
2. Why is the scheduling at a computer center different from scheduling bus routes, policemen on patrol duty, or jobs on a factory lathe?
3. What are the differences in operations in a batch mode compared to online processing?
4. Why is forecasting of demand and supply of computing resources different from the forecasting done by wholesalers or retailers?
5. How would you organize rerun problem analysis and correction activities?

6. Who should receive control reports on:
   a. Input?
   b. Output?
   c. Library?
   The production officer? Someone independent of the computer center?
7. Describe the role of a computer librarian.
8. What service options are available to companies in the event of hardware malfunction or breakdown?
9. What is systems maintenance? What is systems redevelopment? How are they related?
10. Give some examples of systems maintenance. In each case, explain how maintenance was triggered.
11. Can decision rules or standards be developed for determining when maintenance must be performed, or will maintenance decisions always be subjective?
12. Who should make a maintenance or redevelopment decision? Should the process be formalized?
13. Why is it difficult to pinpoint the reasons for and costs of maintenance?
14. Why is maintenance:
   a. Costly?
   b. Important?
   c. Difficult?
   d. Unpopular?
15. Should users be charged for systems maintenance, or should maintenance be part of the overhead of the data processing department? Justify your position.
16. How does maintenance in a microcomputer environment differ from maintenance for mainframes?
17. How long can the life of an information system be extended by modification and redevelopment? How can the cost-effectiveness of these activities be determined?
18. What are the role and the importance of maintenance programmers?

SELECTED ANNOTATED BIBLIOGRAPHY

"Don't Underestimate Software Maintenance Costs." *Computer Law and Tax Report*, vol. 11, no. 9 (September 1984), pp. 1–3.
An excellent discussion of the legal implications of a maintenance contract for a software package, including the type of information to include in the contract. The article recommends that as much time and effort be devoted to contract negotiation as to selection of a software package.

Lapur, Gopal. "Software Maintenance." *Computerworld*, vol. 17, no. 20 (September 26, 1983), pp. 13–22.

In this discussion of software maintenance problems, Kapur identifies reasons for the lack of control over software quality. He suggests a maintenance plan that should reduce the percentage of staff time spent on software maintenance from a high of 80 percent to a low of 30 percent.

Leeson, Margorie. *Computer Operations Procedures and Management*. Chicago, Ill.: Science Research Associates, 1982, 608 pp.
This book describes the operations of a computing center, with detailed discussions on hardware, peripherals, operating systems, microsystems, and time-sharing. It is designed as a text, each chapter ending with a summary followed by discussion questions, team and group projects, a glossary, and a study guide.

McClure, Carma L. *Managing Software Development and Maintenance*. New York: Van Nostrand Reinhold, 1981, 203 pp.
This book emphasizes software maintenance rather than development, but the important relationship of maintenance to the design and development of software is made clear. The author's premise is that maintenance management, not technical problems, is most often the reason for software failure. McClure discusses the organization of good maintenance and ways to reduce maintenance costs, which constitute the majority of the cost of the life cycle of a computer application.

Nickoll, Bill. "Buying Maintenance from Independent Organizations." *Data Processing*, vol. 24, no. 12 (December 1982), pp. 6–8.
The many advantages (including economic) and some pitfalls of third-party maintenance are discussed. The Computer Service Association, with its strict code for members and its advice service, is also described.

Parikh, Girish. *Techniques of Program and System Maintenance*. Cambridge, Mass.: Winthrop, 1982, 281 pp.
This is a collection of articles and extracts from books and articles on maintenance. Well-known authorities are represented, including Barry Boehm, Tom Gilb, Gerald Weinberg, and Edward Yourdon. Topics covered include the concept of maintenance, the relationship of maintenance to structured methodology, tips for maintainers and managers, and predictions regarding maintenance in the future.

Peltŭ, Malcolm. "Future Challenges for Computer Operators." *Data Processing*, vol. 25, no. 5 (May 1983), pp. 6–9.
The changing role of computer operations is discussed. The author states that complex networks and telecommunications are part of operations today and many professional services are provided to users.

Peterson, Robert O. "Maintenance Isn't Maintenance Anymore." *Computerworld*, vol. 18, no. 24 (June 11, 1984), pp. ID/27–36.
Peterson feels that maintenance is too important to be downgraded to a second-class status and relegated to novice programmers. The maintenance process is discussed, the desirable qualities of maintenance personnel are identified, activities of the maintenance support group are described, and ways to motivate maintenance personnel are identified.

————. "Moving Operations out of the Cellar." *Datamation*, vol. 30, no. 17 (October 1984), pp. 162–66.

The operations function is no longer limited to changing tapes and keeping clerical logs. The job of an operator has become technical and encompasses many responsibilities, including scheduling and control.

Shaeffer, Howard. *Data Center Operations.* Englewood Cliffs, N.J.: Prentice-Hall, 1981, pp. 190–264.
This book has two chapters relevant to computer operations: Data Center Workflow and Job Scheduling, and Resource Allocation. Many samples of forms used in computer centers are included. The text is detailed, perhaps more appropriate for a professional computer center manager than for a corporate manager.

Software Maintenance News.
This monthly journal, started in 1983, discusses both maintenance methodology and tools.

Taute, Barbara J. "Maintenance Quality Assurance." *Journal of Information Systems Management*, vol. 2, no. 2 (Summer 1985), pp. 48–50.
Discusses management quality assurance (MQA), a series of procedures, checks, and tests that ensure production software functions as expected, with high reliability and quality.

Zvegintzov, Nicholas. "Immortal Software." *Datamation*, vol. 30, no. 9 (June 15, 1984), pp. 170–80.
The relationship of maintenance to design and development is discussed, as is why and when maintenance should take place. Also described is structured retrofit, a technique for keeping old systems software alive and vigorous.

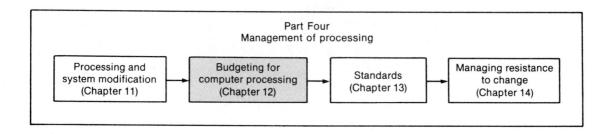

Part Four
Management of processing

| Processing and system modification (Chapter 11) | → | Budgeting for computer processing (Chapter 12) | → | Standards (Chapter 13) | → | Managing resistance to change (Chapter 14) |

CHAPTER 12

Budgeting for computer processing

More people should learn to tell
their dollars where to go instead
of asking them where they went.
Roger Babson

Although one-time costs of computing have been treated in earlier chapters, this is the first chapter to deal with budgeting of recurring and operational expenditures. It discusses approaches to budgeting, elements of an electronic data processing (EDP) budget, problems in costing and pricing computer services, and control measures to keep actual computing expenditures in line with budgeted figures.

APPROACHES TO BUDGETING

Three **approaches to computer budgeting** are possible. An EDP manager can (1) ask for needed resources, (2) be told the amount to be allocated, or (3) negotiate a budget based on changing demands and priorities from one year to the next.

In the early days of computing, an "asking budget" was common. Since corporate executives had neither background in computing nor experience managing computer centers, the EDP department would present a list of needs, which would then be budgeted if the firm had sufficient monetary resources. This method of funding was not very satisfactory, because it encouraged EDP managers to overstate basic requirements while it denied top management the type of budgetary control commonly exercised over other departments within the organization.

The opposite extreme, a "telling budget," occurs when top management makes all decisions on spending for computer processing. This method may not provide sufficient resources for efficient computing. Should funding be generous, panic spending may result to prevent budget cuts the following year.

Although dialogues may take place between top management and technical personnel when both asking and telling budgets are being formulated, a negotiated budget based on periodic reevaluation of hardware/software requirements and operational costs is most responsive to EDP needs and managerial constraints. This latter method of budget preparation is better able to take into consideration the difficulty of making estimates and projections in the field of computing, and it allows for periodic reassessment of budgets. It also allows for fluctuation in computing expenses and changes in priorities (for example, a large budget one year for acquisitions, the next for development expenditures). A disadvantage is that top management and the EDP head must spend a great deal of time and effort in budget preparation. But the time is well spent if it contributes to efficient utilization of data processing resources.

ELEMENTS OF A BUDGET

Table 12–1, an example of **object class accounting,** lists elements to be found in EDP budgets and shows what percentage of the total EDP budget is allocated to each element, based on 1986 U.S. industry figures. Some of the elements are fixed costs. Others are line items that vary according to load. For instance, if the computer is fully saturated during normal hours, extra hours of work will involve overtime pay, a variable cost.

The biggest budget category is personnel, partly because computer personnel are a scarce resource and premium salaries have to be paid to attract and retain experienced staff. This helps explain why EDP salary expenditures may be higher than in other departments of the firm. Education may also be a costly EDP line item. Many firms sponsor in-house educational programs to train needed analysts, programmers, data specialists, and operators or give employees subsidies to work toward a degree in outside classes.

When preparing an EDP budget, estimating hardware expenditures is sometimes difficult because costs fluctuate from one year to the next. A new model that incorporates new features may be considerably more costly than existing models on the market. Or a dramatic drop in price may occur due to competitive pressures and savings resulting from innovative applications of technology. The final price will also depend on the type of financing decision reached (rent, purchase, lease) and negotiations over discounts, trade-ins, lease time, service contracts, and so on. Sometimes, budgeted hardware is not delivered when antici-

Table 12–1 **Elements of an EDP budget**

Category	Costs
Hardware (41.2%)*	Computer and peripherals (purchase, lease, or rent costs)
	Overtime charges
	Maintenance
	Insurance
Software (5.4%)	Operating systems
	Teleprocessing monitors
	Packages
Salaries (34.2%)	Wages and overtime
	Benefits (taxes, insurance, vacations, education, etc.)
	Education for personnel
	Hiring, firing, and moving expenses
Communications (4.3%)	Equipment (modems, concentrators, voice)
	Maintenance, insurance, and taxes
	Line charges
Supplies (6.4%)	Tapes, lists, microfilm
	Forms, cards, stock paper, binders
	Office supplies
Other (8.4%)	Travel, conventions, and conference costs
	Printing, postage
	Utilities
	Journals
	Consulting
	Outside services (time-sharing, contract programming, etc.)

*Percentage values are for Fortune 1,000 sites in the United States in 1986.

Source: Percentages drawn from John W. Verity, "1986 DP Budget Survey," *Datamation*, vol. 32, no. 7 (April 1, 1986), p. 76.

pated, because manufacturers do not release new models when expected or they may fall behind in delivery schedules. In such cases, the expenditure may fall in the next fiscal year instead.

A measure of uncertainty is involved when budgeting for software as well. Software purchased with hardware may not fulfill needs. One firm, for example, spent $500,000 to develop a FORTRAN and COBOL compiler more appropriate to its command-and-control system than the compiler that was supplied. Whether supplementary packaged software will be available is also uncertain. On the other hand, estimating costs for in-house applications development (the alternative to a package) is an inexact art at best. The time required and corporate resources that will have to be assigned to the project are hard to predict: systems development projects are well known for cost overruns.

Development does not appear as a separate cost item in Table 12–1, because the salaries of programmers, analysts, and technicians appear under personnel expenses in object class accounting. Equipment and purchased software used in development are charged to the year that the expenditure was incurred or amortized. One cannot easily ascertain the cost of a project or isolate the expense of project implementation when spending is reported by object of expense.

In **expenditure accounting,** on the other hand, an effort is made to assign a cost to data processing (DP) activities. Typically, four main activities are identified:

Development.   Production.
Maintenance.   Administration.

Table 12–2 shows the percentage of a data processing budget that should be spent on each of these categories, according to some computer specialists. In practice, many companies spend a higher percentage of effort on maintenance than is listed in the table. This often can be attributed, in part, to a few culprit application systems that consume a disproportionate share of maintenance effort and should probably be replaced. (By one rule of thumb, 20 percent of software generally requires 80 percent of the maintenance effort.)

Software enhancement in this table is categorized as a development activity, not maintenance. (In Chapter 11, we considered enhancement an integral part of maintenance.) The problem of definitions limits the usefulness of the table. For example, many organizations charge feasibility studies to EDP overhead (administration) instead of listing them as an expense of development. The lack of standard definitions for terms such as maintenance and development hampers information exchange and dialogue in the computing field.

Another problem with Table 12–2 is that the activity labels themselves are somewhat misleading. For example, many hidden or indirect costs of project development are not generally included in the development category. These include the cost of data management or statistical packages ostensibly provided free by manufacturers when equipment is acquired but actually included in the rental, lease, or purchase price.

Problems in reporting personnel costs may also lead to inaccurate reporting of development expenditures. In a given project, development effort is not spent in discrete units nor is effort distributed evenly

Table 12–2	Expenditures by activity (as percent of total data processing spending)	
Activity	*Percent of budget*	
Development	0–20% ⎤ 1:1	
Maintenance	10–20 ⎦	
Production	40–60 ⎤ 1:2½	
Administration	5–20 ⎦	

Figure 12–1   **Effort distribution of analyst and programmer during systems development**

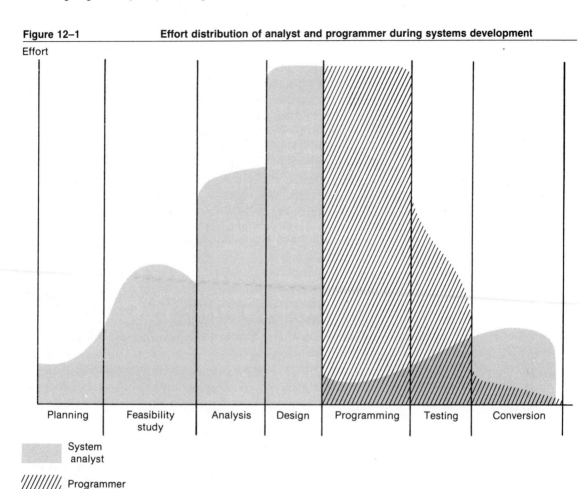

Effort

| Planning | Feasibility study | Analysis | Design | Programming | Testing | Conversion |

System analyst

Programmer

throughout the period of development. Figure 12–1 shows how the need for analysts and programmers changes as development progresses. Of course, this pattern may vary, depending on the nature of a specific project, but the figure does illustrate that it would be incorrect to charge a project for full-time services of analysts or programmers throughout development. Most companies plan so that personnel can work on more than one project simultaneously. They schedule development so that the peak demand for the services of an analyst or programmer in one project coincides with troughs of demand in another. Also, maintenance, documentation, and redevelopment tasks can be assigned during periods when the services of programmers and analysts are not needed for development work.

COSTING AND PRICING CONCERNS

Cost trends
Although comparing surveys based on diverse industry samples, different methods of off-loading computing costs to the end-user, different assumptions regarding cost categories is difficult, **cost trends** for components of EDP budgets are, nevertheless, apparent. Unit costs of mainframe computers are dropping. But total equipment expenditures in many firms are on the rise, since there is a demand for more powerful central processing units (CPUs) and for more sophisticated peripherals. For example, clients today demand intelligent terminals, and they want color and graphic capabilities, voice synthesizers, attached printers, and connections to retrieval units with access to large data bases. The budget category of data communications (local networks, private branch exchanges, and other connection schemes) shows strong growth as users move to connect the many stand-alone systems they have installed in recent years.

All the same, the budget slice allocated to hardware is still smaller than formerly, because other cost components are making proportionately greater demands on budgetary resources. Also, the total pie is getting larger every year, which means that the increase in equipment expenditures can be absorbed without requiring a larger slice of the total budget. (Growth in data processing spending slowed significantly in the mid-1980s. Even so, data processing budgets rose 4.2 percent in 1986, according to a *Datamation* budget survey, while many other sectors of the economy remained stagnant.[1])

Personnel costs, the biggest budget category, appear to be leveling in the mid-1980s. Cost cutting in the computer industry has slowed employment growth, so that the percentage of the total DP budget that goes to salaries is up only slightly. However, many persons who formerly were employed by the computer center for data entry, operations, and analysis are now on user department payrolls. The growing popularity of distributed data processing may have shifted computer specialists to user departments. It is, therefore, somewhat misleading to look only at the budget of a data processing department to assess DP personnel costs.

Table 12–3, a comparison of computer processing budget components for 1972 and 1986, illustrates budgetary trends. Note that software costs are gaining increased budget attention. The budget percentage for software may actually be higher than shown, because software development costs are often buried in personnel costs or distributed to the budgets of processing nodes. Also, the figures in Table 12–3 fail to

---

[1]John W. Verity, "1986 DP Budget Survey," *Datamation*, vol. 32, no. 7 (April 1, 1986), pp. 74–78.

Table 12–3   **Computer processing budget breakdown, comparing 1972 and 1986**

Budget items	1972	1986*
Personnel	47%	34%
Hardware	39	41
Software	1	5
Communication services	5	4
Media and supplies	6	6
Outside services	2	4
Miscellaneous	0	5
	100%	99%

*Values in this column have been rounded.

Source: Englebert Kirchner, "1982 Budget Survey," *Datamation*, vol. 28, no. 7 (July 1982), p. 59; John W. Verity, "1986 DP Budget Survey," *Datamation*, vol. 32, no. 7 (April 1, 1986), p. 76.

reflect the rising cost of teleprocessing (especially distributed data processing and word processing), software packages, minicomputers, small business systems, and educational services assumed by end-users.

Planning an operational budget

Chapter 2 explained that the **one-year operating budget** of a data processing department should implement strategic and long-range information processing objectives. To make the translation from long-range plans to an annual budget, a data processing manager must first:

- Review ongoing activities and long-range information processing plans.
- Select projects for the coming year that can be implemented within budgetary constraints and will help fulfill information processing goals.

Then, a one-year data processing operational plan is prepared. This plan should identify the application systems agenda, including ongoing applications, maintenance of existing systems, enhancements, and new systems development. Services and support for this applications agenda should be described; that is, plans for disaster preparedness, security, and control should be detailed. Finally, the EDP manager must outline resource requirements for implementing both applications and services, including hardware, software, staffing, environmental facilities, supplies, administration, outside services (consulting, time-sharing, service bureau), and training.

Actual budget preparation begins when costs are estimated in each resource category for each application project and for each service and support function. Then, estimates similar to those in Table 12–4 are inserted in budget worksheets. (Instead of filling out a paper worksheet, spreadsheet software may be used.) Last year's actual expenditures provide a basis for projecting ongoing costs for the coming year. Past experience, feasibility studies, historical records, and reports can help the budgeters estimate new-project expenditures.

Table 12-4 Simulation of a budget ($000)

	Fiscal year 1988				Fiscal year 1989				Fiscal year 1990			
	1st Qtr	2d Qtr	3d Qtr	4th Qtr	1st Qtr	2d Qtr	3d Qtr	4th Qtr	1st Qtr	2d Qtr	3d Qtr	4th Qtr
Revenues	$11,617	$13,233	$13,013	$14,211	$14,913	$15,023	$18,397	$15,968	$17,787	$18,470	$16,842	$19,727
Cost of sales	5,095	5,747	5,595	6,355	6,541	6,202	8,306	6,259	7,257	7,314	6,880	8,822
Net revenue	6,522	7,486	7,417	7,856	8,372	8,822	10,091	9,709	10,530	11,156	9,962	10,905
Selling and administrative expenses	2,323	2,647	2,603	2,842	2,983	3,005	3,679	3,194	3,557	3,694	3,368	3,945
Other overhead	1,452	1,654	1,627	1,776	1,864	1,878	2,300	1,996	2,223	2,309	2,105	2,466
Net profit	$ 2,746	$ 3,185	$ 3,188	$ 3,237	$ 3,525	$ 3,939	$ 4,112	$ 4,519	$ 4,749	$ 5,153	$ 4,488	$ 4,494
Percent of revenues	23.6%	24.1%	24.5%	22.8%	23.6%	26.2%	22.4%	28.3%	26.7%	27.9%	26.7%	22.8%

**Expenditure
analysis**

Corporate executives, who ultimately approve or reject data processing budgets, want to know whether too many or too few corporate resources are devoted to data processing and whether the money is spent on the right things. Commonly, 1 percent of total corporate revenues is spent on data processing.[2] Wide variations from this norm exist among industries and even within specific industries. For example, capital-intensive heavy industries tend to spend less. So do very small firms. Companies that want to be on the leading edge of technology tend to spend more.

An organization that establishes a data base of financial information on the data processing function, including historical data for comparative purposes, can perform an analysis of expenditures with the help of data management systems such as popular spreadsheet programs. For example, using cost figures collected by project or product, by user area, and by activity, the ratio between development and operations might be ascertained. Line cost ratios, such as the relationship of DP administrative costs to total expenses, might also be determined. Financial analysis tools can help senior management develop a model for **expenditure analysis** to fit the unique needs of the corporate environment. Such tools facilitate cost control and help managers make cost projections for the future.

Revenues

Data processing budgets must deal with constraints on **funding,** a very controversial aspect of computer management. Many firms assign computing costs to overhead and do not charge internal user departments. Others develop formulas so that departments can be charged for computing services. These two approaches will be discussed next.

Overhead accounting. In the early days of computing, potential users were skeptical about the benefits of electronic processing and needed an incentive to switch from traditional manual processing methods to EDP. Management in many corporations decided to offer free computer services to user departments to help reduce resistance to the new technology. The expense of computing was charged to overhead. Although users were not required to pay for computer runs, they generally received notification of the dollar value of their share of computer time. This often had the salutary effect of reducing wastage of computer resources, because users tried to use the computer efficiently once they were aware of the cost.

The problem with **overhead accounting** was that demand soon outstripped available overhead resources in most organizations. In order

---

[2]See Kenneth Rau, "Accounting for Computers," *Computerworld*, vol. 19, no. 40 (October 21, 1985), p. 61.

to generate income to expand computing facilities, many organizations switched to chargeback systems. Nevertheless, some companies today still retain their EDP departments as part of corporate overhead for the following reasons:

- Overhead accounting has organizational and accounting simplicity.
- The overhead system places responsibility for DP costs in the EDP department.
- The EDP department must account for its funds in a straightforward manner. Costs do not get buried under other department budgets. This helps restrain ungoverned growth of the DP function.
- The corporate controller feels that better control over all department expenditures can be exercised under overhead accounting.
- The EDP department will not experience a sharp drop in requested service from user departments during periods of economic stress. Stability is important because of the long lead time required for systems development and because budgetary continuity is needed to plan for the acquisition (or enhancement) of hardware/software resources.

Chargeback systems.   One of the main advantages of charging user departments for computing services is that users are not likely to consume computing resources on projects that do not demand data processing. Furthermore, they will cooperate with EDP personnel in the development of efficient and effective applications in order to minimize processing costs. With competing demands on departmental budgets, efforts will be made to prevent the wasteful use of processing time. Other advantages of a **chargeback system** include:

- Top management receives information on how EDP services are used by different departments within the organization.
- All of the expenditures of departments (including EDP expenditures) are known. This helps management evaluate the efficiency and capability of departments.
- Economic data is available to help management make a decision whether to centralize or decentralize processing.
- Revenues can be generated to finance growth in the EDP function.

For chargeback systems, the problem is how to establish an equitable rate structure. What happens when a department in need of electronic processing cannot afford to pay for computing services? Should selected users be subsidized? Partial costing is one answer. For example, development costs might be assigned to computer overhead, with users

Figure 12–2  **Who pays for what?**

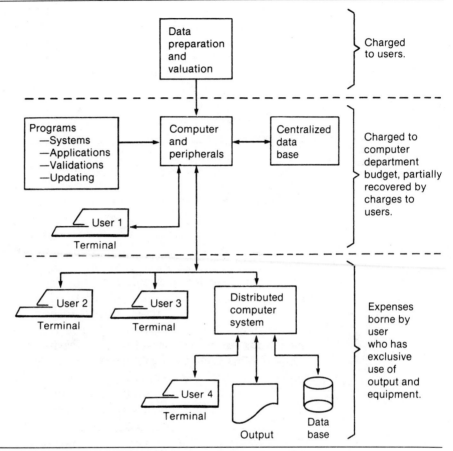

charged only for operational costs.[3] Integrated applications also raise questions. How does one assess individual departments for shared resources? Maintenance poses another dilemma. Some firms assign it to the computer department. Others, to discourage unnecessary maintenance, charge users. What happens when input data is collected by one department for use by others? Practices vary, but many firms compensate the data collector to ensure quality collection and input preparation on schedule.

---

[3]It is the premise of Haim Mendelson in "Pricing Computer Services: Queueing Effects," *Communications of the ACM,* vol. 28, no. 3 (March 1985), pp. 312–21, that organizing the computing center as a profit center leads to significant underinvestment of capacity, coupled with significant underutilization of this capacity. He suggests that a company would benefit from prices that lead to a computing center deficit.

Few companies have computing-charge formulas that generate profit, although they may seek external jobs to spread overhead costs. It is common for computer departments to bear a portion of computing costs or to draw from the firm's reserve funds when computing costs do not balance revenues. Figure 12–2 is an example of one firm's chargeback structure. Of course, many other schemes are also feasible.

Rates

Rate structures can range from a fixed flat fee per department per month/quarter for computing services to charges based on formulas for milliseconds of computer time, input read, lines printed, units of data stored, or other such services. During the 1970s, users were commonly charged for the CPU cycles they consumed. This proved to be a reasonably equitable form of accounting, since the CPU was the largest cost component in processing departments at that time.

In recent years, the cost characteristics of computing have changed. Improved data base management technology now allows users to store vast data bases. Computer centers have actually become data storage centers. According to surveys conducted by IBM and other disk manufacturers, data storage requirements in the average processing center have grown an average of 40 percent to 60 percent per year since the mid-1970s. At the same time, network technology has allowed the migration of input/output functions to users at remote locations, and CPUs have been put on the market with increasingly fast processing speeds. These factors have led to the consideration of new rate structures for processing-chargeback systems.

For example, some computer centers total network-associated costs, then divide this figure by the number of terminals using the network, to determine a network subscription fee. For some, rate structures for mainframe processing are based on the type of information processed. "Survival information"—information required for the long-term operation of a company—being most important, is charged the highest rate. Project information—that which loses its value after a period of time and is, hence, less important—is assessed at a lower rate. Still another rate structure used by some centers is to charge for data storage. The assumption here is that users with large data bases consume more computing resources than users with small data bases.

When determining rate structures, some firms run simulation programs to see how different rates affect revenues, and they establish highly complex chargeback schemes. Others engage in a long period of trial and error before management is satisfied with pricing. Since firms differ in their equipment configurations, stages of growth, levels of sophistication, and intensity of computer use, it is not surprising that rate structures vary widely.

Rate structures can do more than simply provide revenues. They can encourage efficient utilization of resources (for example, by charging low rates for night processing, surcharges for rush jobs) and can be used to support corporate policy. An example of the latter would be setting teleprocessing charges artificially low to encourage the switch from centralized to decentralized processing.

A major problem in pricing computer services is that there is no market mechanism to help corporate management assess the value of information, no competitive structure to regulate charges. In the manufacture of an automobile, costs must be kept low so models will sell. Information is a product too, but the market doesn't provide cost guidelines such as for manufactured goods. What's more, since computing rate structures may be set to reflect corporate policy, pricing of services can be totally unrealistic from a strictly economic viewpoint.

One control that pressures computer departments to be competitive in service and price is to allow user departments the option of going outside the firm to have their jobs processed by a computer service bureau. This forces the in-house computer center to root out inefficiency and keep rates low. Many firms also allow processing departments to take on external jobs when they have excess capacity, to sell their services on the open market like a utility. Both practices introduce market mechanisms in rate setting.

A great deal of controversy surrounds rate setting in the field of computing. Philosophical differences exist over such questions as: Should computing be a service or a profit maker? Should computer departments have a monopoly, or should users be allowed to process jobs on the outside? Should rates be set to foster centralization or decentralization? Whatever structure is chosen, it should meet two accounting goals: equitability and simplicity. Procedures for reviewing rates should also be established. A firm's environment will change in time, as will, perhaps, management's viewpoint. The rate structure adopted today may be totally inappropriate in the future.

CONTROL OF OPERATIONAL EXPENDITURES

Once an EDP budget has been formulated, approved, and implemented, it becomes the responsibility of the EDP manager to keep expenditures within targeted amounts. For **control of expenditures,** the manager needs to receive from staff members periodic financial reports on work in progress. Then expenditures are reviewed and compared to costs that were estimated at the time the budget was drawn up. Figure 12–3 is an example of how costs might be analyzed. In this graph, the absolute values of salaries (budgeted and actual) are plotted; but percentage values or variances might be used instead.

After studying the graph, the EDP manager should try to ascertain reasons why actual expenditures deviate from budgeted amounts. Per-

Figure 12–3   **Comparison of budgeted and actual salaries, by month**

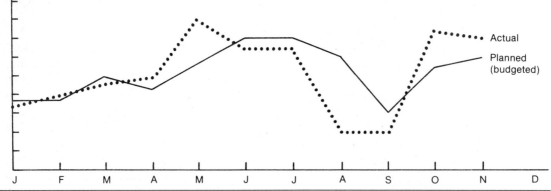

Salaries ($)

Actual

Planned
(budgeted)

J   F   M   A   M   J   J   A   S   O   N   D

haps a delay from August to October in a planned subsystem explains why expenditures were lower than expected in August and higher than anticipated in October. Perhaps November was a month with high overtime.

Similar graphs might be prepared for other expenditures (for example, teleprocessing or software) or for costs by function (such as data entry or maintenance). Sometimes, reasons for variances can be determined by using control software provided by manufacturers at the time of equipment purchase or programs bought from software houses or developed in-house. Finance and accounting staffs can often help explain reasons for discrepancies. Auditors and consultants can also provide insights.

When variances pinpoint a problem, the EDP manager must take corrective action. Examples of such actions are file consolidation, simplification of procedures, or the revamping of rate structures to give users incentives to save. To collect and analyze control data and then to plan changes in operations involve a cost in staff time (and possibly computer time) that should be recognized. But most large installations and those that find that planned budgets deviate greatly from actual expenditures justify this expense by the savings generated when problems are identified and measures taken to improve operating efficiency.

Control data should also be used to identify mistakes made in planning the budget. For example, when **feedback data** on budget overruns are sent to the development team, the team can analyze whether faulty procedures were used in formulation of the budget or whether incorrect budget assumptions were made. The team can then make recommendations to future development teams that may help avoid a repetition of budgeting errors. This feedback cycle is illustrated in Figure 12–4.

By analyzing overrun data, one firm learned that changes in user

Figure 12–4   **Control feedback for operations budget**

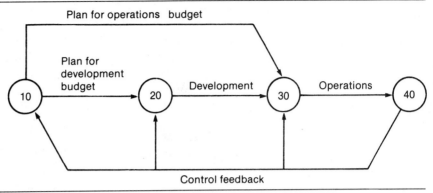

specifications during development were the main cause of overruns. Overruns in future projects were brought under control by setting a freeze date after which no respecifications were permitted. In another firm, an improved salary structure to attract and retrain competent personnel proved the solution to time overruns attributed to high programmer turnover. In both these examples, the corrective action was a policy decision requiring intervention by top management. But many problems can be resolved by changing the assumptions and priorities of budget planners or by measures that fall within the jurisdiction of computing departments.

SUMMING UP

Computer budgets are on the rise in spite of the mid-1980s slowdown of growth in the data processing industry as a whole. A noticeable trend is that the hardware and supplies costs as percentages of the budget have dropped, whereas communications, software packages, conferences, and training are today costing proportionately more.

The annual data processing budget will incorporate ongoing activities and new projects that are in keeping with the company's long-range management information systems (MIS) plan. The operations budget can be prepared from monthly financial reports of the past year, with the addition of known or estimated increases such as planned or negotiated salary increases or price escalations in goods or services. Effective budgeting is an iterative activity. The first version of the budget may prove untenable because it is not affordable. Budgets have to be reconciled with financial reality and other resource constraints.

Computing was originally conceived as a service, charged to overhead at no cost to user departments. This helped reduce employee resistance to computer use and fostered centralization of computing resources. Once demand started to outstrip resources and users were willing to pay for services rendered, chargeback structures developed. This has encouraged more efficient use of resources and helped finance the expansion of computing facilities. However, other problems have arisen, such as how to set equitable rates for all users.

Both development and operational expenditures should be periodically reviewed, and deviations from the budget should be analyzed. The budget itself may prove unrealistic, in which case the assumptions and priorities of the budget planners should be studied, the errors identified, and recommendations made to future budget planners so that mistakes won't be repeated. In other cases, corrective action (such as new budgetary controls) may bring expenditures in line.

Budgets should be viewed as guidelines to management preferences and constraints, not as something to "beat." Computer center budgeting is similar in principle to budgeting in other departments within a firm, although line items differ.

CASE: TURNING DATA PROCESSING INTO A PROFIT CENTER

Many DP/MIS managers are not interested in turning their computer centers into profit centers. They are too busy trying to keep up with corporate computing needs and burgeoning end-user demands. They fear that the time and effort spent trying to market their services externally will lead to degraded service within their own organizations. The revenue potential is limited, not worth the headache, they say. Besides, marketing is the key, and few data processing professionals have sales skill. Data processing managers claim that finding employees with needed technical qualifications is already hard. It would be even more difficult to hire computer specialists with the necessary entrepreneurial spirit to make a profit center work.

Nevertheless, a number of companies have turned their data processing departments into successful profit centers. Boeing is one. In the late 1960s, when the worldwide recession cut heavily into orders, the company was looking for ways to diversify and to prevent layoffs of key personnel. Boeing Computer Services Co. was launched with two missions: to service Boeing's internal processing needs and to generate external commercial business. In 1986, the services company, back in the corporate structure as a full division, employed 12,000 people and provided computer services to over 1,500 outside clients in government, energy, and manufacturing. The company would rank among the Fortune 500 if it were an independent firm.

Mellon Bank Corp. in Pittsburgh has sold data processing services for 25 years. At first, it merely marketed excess capacity on its mainframe. In 1986, its Data Center Division had an annual revenue of $55 million by selling a barrage of data processing services to bank clients. According to Kerry Ryan, senior vice president and manager of the division, offering leading-edge technology to customers has contributed to the success of the division. Another success factor has been the fact that the data center is an independent division, responsible for its own financial operations and employing its own sales force. The division is also big enough to leverage costs.

Caterpillar Tractor Co. of Peoria, Illinois, is attempting to launch a data processing profit center for reasons other than the usual profit motive. Because of the depressed farm market, the company has had to reduce its work force from 33,000 to 19,000 since the early 1980s. Concerned over the effect of these cutbacks on the community of Peoria, the company has created a spin-off group within its data processing department to train unemployed workers as computer professionals and then to sell their services to other data processing service companies.

Questions

1. Why is it difficult to attract computer specialists to work in a profit center?
2. What are the problems of running a computer center for profit?
3. What are the advantages of running a computer department for a profit? What are the disadvantages?
4. Does the head of a computer center run for profit need qualifications that are not required for the head of a center financed as overhead? Explain.

STUDY KEYS

Approaches to computer budgeting

Chargeback system

Control of expenditures

Cost trends

Expenditure accounting

Expenditure analysis

Feedback data

Funding

Object class accounting

One-year operating budget

Overhead accounting

Rate structures

DISCUSSION QUESTIONS

1. How does the preparation of a budget for a computing center differ from budget preparation for other departments in a firm?
2. What elements of a computer center budget are unstable and unpredictable? How can uncertainties be eliminated or reduced?
3. Is budget preparation in a distributed environment easier and more responsive to needs than budget preparation in a centralized environment? Explain.
4. Should a computer center budget be developed bottom-up or top-down? Why?
5. Why is the revenue of a computing center hard to estimate?
6. What is an equitable way to charge for computing services? What are the advantages and limitations of alternative charge systems?
7. Should a computer center budget be zero-based budgeting, or would you recommend some other approach, such as an incremental cost approach? Justify your choice.
8. Which computer center costs do you think should be charged to overhead? Why?
9. A computer center budget often has overruns. Why? How can overruns be controlled?
10. How can software costs be controlled?
11. What are the cost trends in computing? To what factors do you attribute them? Are the trends irreversible?
12. Why is it difficult, using standard costing methods, to cost each application and each job in a computer center?
13. How can the high personnel costs in computing be reduced?
14. How can developmental costs be reduced without affecting quality?
15. How is an annual operating budget prepared?
16. Should a firm actively seek jobs (inside or outside of the organization) to reduce overhead? Will this reduce quality of service?
17. What are the advantages and disadvantages of overhead accounting?
18. How might the rate structure of a computer center be used to promote corporate policy? Give examples.

SELECTED ANNOTATED BIBLIOGRAPHY

Boehm, Barry W. *Software Engineering Economics.* Englewood Cliffs, N.J.: Prentice-Hall, 1981, 767 pp.
  Software costs are often the most important component of development costs. This classic reference book includes a discussion of software maintenance cost estimates (chap. 30, pp. 533–55) and on software life cycle cost estimations (chap. 31, pp. 556–90). The constructive cost model (COCOMO) is the subject of chapters 5–9 (pp. 57–164) and 23–29 (pp. 344–51).

Churchman, John R. "Computerized Budgeting." *Data Management*, vol. 19, no. 5 (May 1981), pp. 33–35.
 Specialized computer software can use budget data and statistical forecasting techniques to analyze computer expenditures for management (data center or corporate). Available options are flexible report generations, hierarchial consolidation, and organizational analysis.

Cortado, James N. *Finance, Budgets and Cost Control in Data Processing*. Englewood Cliffs, N.J.: Prentice-Hall, 1980, 287 pp.
 This book includes sections on planning, justifying applications and hardware, DP contracts, dealing with vendors, service bureau facilities management, and development and control of a DP budget. The text is well organized, amply illustrated, and has a pleasing format.

Francl, Thomas J.; Thomas W. Lin; and Miklos A. Yasarhelyi. *Planning, Budgeting and Control for Data Processing: How to Make Zero Base Budgeting Work for You*. New York: Van Nostrand Reinhold, 1984, 192 pp.
 One point stressed is that an MIS plan must complement the corporate plan. The authors support zero-base budgeting, one approach to budgeting and control.

Loew, Gary Wayne. "Budgeting: A Top-Down, Bottom-Up, Top-Down Process." *Small Systems World*, vol. 13, no. 2 (February 1985), pp. 26–28.
 The title is unusually apt in describing the contents of this article. In addition to the budgeting process, some detailed line items are discussed.

Zorsch, Patrick D. "Creating and Using a DP Budget for Management Control." *Small Systems World*, vol. 11, no. 1 (January 1983), pp. 17–20.
 A good discussion of three approaches to keeping DP expenditures under control (traditional, cost allocations, and responsibility accounting).

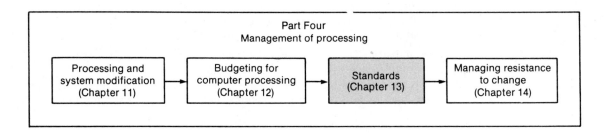

Part Four
Management of processing

Processing and system modification (Chapter 11) → Budgeting for computer processing (Chapter 12) → Standards (Chapter 13) → Managing resistance to change (Chapter 14)

CHAPTER 13

Standards

If you think of "standardization" as the
best that you know today, but which is to
be improved tomorrow—you get somewhere.

Henry Ford

When measuring weights, time, or distance, we adhere to standards—such as 16 ounces to a pound, 60 minutes to an hour, or 3 feet to a yard. We expect a dozen eggs to a carton, eight hours to a workday, 100 yards in a football field, and a holiday on the fourth of July. These are standards we all unconsciously acknowledge. **Standards** are accepted authorities or established measures for operations, behavior, or performance.

In the field of computing, standards are needed in programming languages, operating systems, electromechanical devices such as disks, printed circuit boards, chips and wafers, data base design, communications protocols, documentation, program development and testing methodology, data element representation—the list could go on and on. Without such standards, programs cannot be transferred from one computer to another. Computer customers cannot incorporate hardware and software marketed by different manufacturers into a single computer system. The interchange of information among computer users and computer professionals is hampered. Technological progress is slowed because competing computer manufacturers tie up critical resources by duplicating product development instead of building on past work.

The computer industry has been criticized for its lack of commitment to standardization. Many computer vendors favor proprietary systems rather than standardized ones in order to lock their customers into brand loyalty. Some entrepreneurs, in search of profits, hope to make their own proprietary systems the world's standard, as IBM has done so successfully in the past. Perhaps the high-tech slump of the 1980s can be attributed, in part, to customer unwillingness to invest in new system components that cannot communicate with the old, in new technology that makes obsolete what went before.

Computer standards are the subject of this chapter. The evolution of computer processing standards will be discussed first, followed by an explanation of how computer vendors and computer users create, implement, review, and enforce computing standards within their own organizations. A section on standards for documentation is included to illustrate problems in setting standards and the benefits that can be derived from them. The chapter closes with a look at the role played by industry, professional bodies, and both national and international organizations in the establishment of standards for the computer industry.

EVOLUTION OF STANDARDS

When computers were first introduced, no generally accepted guidelines existed for writing programs, designing forms, or processing output. In order to use software, the premises of the programmer had to be accepted. As a result,

> Patterns of behavior arose which, with sanction of time . . . became standards accepted by the bulk of programmers.
>
> Eventually somebody discovered that we were de facto using standards, but that they weren't written down and given formal blessing. So the scribes got to work, created standards committees, and offered long careers to their members.[1]

Critics charge that much of the inefficiency, duplication, and incompatibility found in the computer industry can be traced to this slapdash approach to the development of standards in the early days of computing. Today, computer professionals are far more aware of the need for standards, and a large number of groups (described later in this chapter) are making a concerted effort to develop standards for the industry. For example, we could not have plug-compatible systems, common today, without standards.

TYPES OF STANDARDS

Standards can be classified as reactive, a response to a problem or situation; progressive, providing a framework for operations; or retro-

---

[1]Norman Sanders, *A Manager's Guide to Profitable Computers* (Manchester, England: AMACOM, 1978), pp. 120–21.

Table 13–1 — **File specification standard (data required in each file)**

File name	Record data for each:
File label	Record name
File number	Record code
Summary file description	Record description
Source of file	Record size
Disposition data	Record content for each:
Blocking factor	Element name
Prepared (initially) by	Element number
Revised by	Element size (in 8-bit bytes)

spective, based on historical data and experience. Within a single installation, even within a single stage of processing, all three types of standards may coexist.

A standard may be a constraint, such as a rule that limits "GO TO" statements in programming. It might be a procedure: for example, time sheets, work targets, and formal employee evaluation sessions for appraising employee performance. It might be a technical specification, such as networking protocols that allow telex and teletex terminals to exchange written messages. It might be merely a list of terms, definitions, or symbols. Some standards are strictly local standards. These may be nothing more than work guidelines, or they may be mandatory to provide management with a measure of control over performance. Other standards may be formulated by national committees of computer professionals. Whether or not an individual firm complies with such standards is usually voluntary.

Clearly, not all computer facilities will operate under an identical set of standards. Yet, a common core of standards, with unique varia-

Table 13–2 — **Standard for analyst findings in feasibility study**

Timing: Part of feasibility study
Preparation: By senior analyst assigned to project
Content: 1. Detailed and summary costs in work-hours and dollars for:
  Development of system
  Annual operation of system
 2. Nonmonetary cost of system for:
  Development
  Operations
 3. Listing of system benefits:
  Tangible
  Intangible
 4. Estimated duration of project with probability associations
 5. Anticipated problems of development
 6. Evaluation of and comments on:
  Data on which estimates are based
  Any further investigation warranted
 7. Recommendations, if any

Figure 13–1 **Sets of standards for computing**

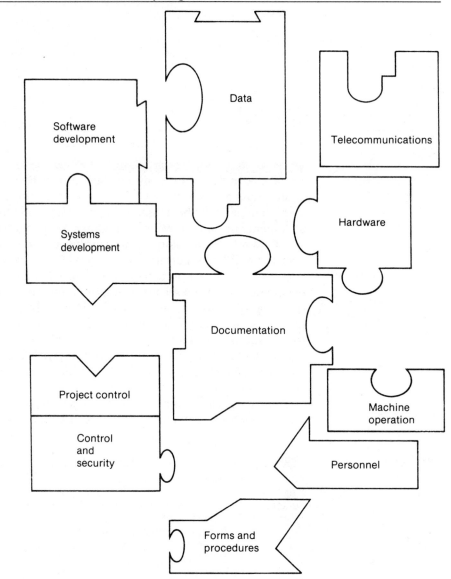

tions to fit local needs, is common. A description of this core would require more pages than have been allocated to standards in this text. In this chapter, we give only two samples, Tables 13–1 and 13–2. The first is an example of a standard for file specification; the second is a standard format to report the findings of a feasibility study.

Figure 13–1 identifies areas of computing that benefit from standards and illustrates the concept that standards in one area should mesh with standards in other functional areas. A three-dimensional figure would be an even better representation, since standards in nonbordering activities in the figure should also be coordinated.

STANDARDS COMMITTEE

In a firm that has a computer facility, the responsibility for establishing computing standards for the organization is commonly delegated to a committee. This **standards committee** should be a standing committee, not a special ad hoc assignment, because continual creation, revision, and updating of standards will be required as the firm expands, products change, or new technology is introduced. In addition to drawing up standards, the committee should assist management in explaining the need for standards to employees and in motivating employees to follow standards adopted by the firm. Standards should be viewed as helpful discipline, not resented, ignored, or bypassed.

Membership in the standards committee should be drawn from upper levels of management in the functional areas served by the firm's computers and should include both users and technical personnel. Sometimes, outside consultants are also members of the committee.

The first job of the committee is to develop standards that govern the formulation of standards. That is, the structure, modularization, and contents of standards manuals need to be decided. The format has be to designed, standards for indexing and cross-referencing have to be approved, and conventions for writing standards must be established. Once this groundwork has been laid, the computing standards themselves can be created and documented in the manuals.

Generally, implementation, maintenance, and operational control of standards are delegated by the committee to a part- or full-time **standards officer**. By one rule of thumb, one employee-week per year is required to create and maintain standards for each standard area. Some firms partially automate the control of standards. For example, a manufacturing firm may establish time and cost standards for given tasks, then monitor these tasks by computer through a badge or terminal check-in, check-out process. When operations consistently deviate from a prescribed standard, the standard is automatically revised, or a computer report is sent to the standards officer, who then reviews the work. This review may lead to changed procedures, a reprimand to employees, or a recommendation to the standards committee that certain standards be revised.

SETTING STANDARDS

In firms with a standards committee and a standards officer, the formulation and evaluation of new standards typically follow the flow-chart in Figure 13–2. The standards committee receives input from users, computing staff, and consultants when new standards are under consideration. Once a new standard has been formulated, approved, and put into operation, a formal evaluation is made of that standard by the standards officer and data processing staff to ensure that it is effective and that employees are using the standard in their work. When problems are observed, the committee should be notified so that the standard can be reconsidered. All standards should be periodically evaluated, even though they have been effective in the past. The environment of the firm may change over time so that old standards may no longer be appropriate.

To be sure, not all firms are organized in the same manner. In some firms, managers establish and implement standards in their areas of responsibility; other firms have no formal modus operandi for adopting

Figure 13–2   **Organization for setting and evaluating standards**

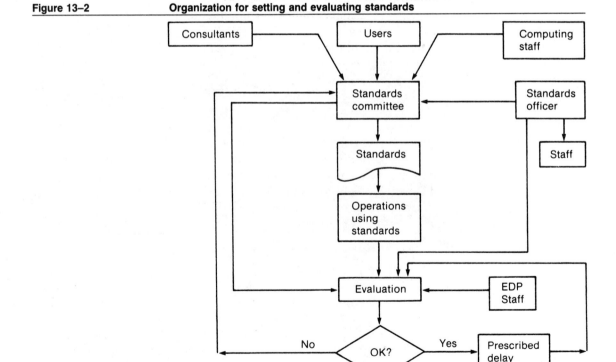

Figure 13–3   **Activities relating to standards formulation**

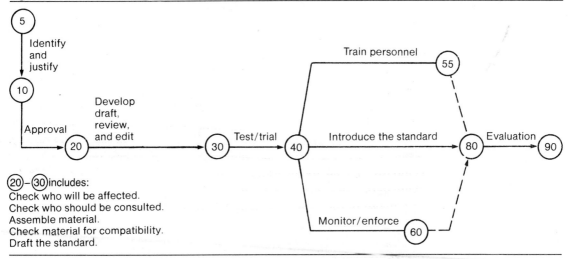

standards. More and more firms are forming standards committees, however, because experience has proven their value.

The network diagram in Figure 13–3 shows the activities associated with the development of standards. First, the area where standards are lacking must be identified (Activity 5–10). Then management should approve the purpose and potential scope of the new standards (10–20) before they are actually developed. This approval helps control the number of new standards that are introduced (systems should not become encumbered with needless standards) and focuses the attention of the committee on management priorities. In general, priority is given to standards that affect accuracy (as in data preparation), promote communication (as in documentation), or show immediate returns in terms of efficiency (as in programming).

Ideas about what the standards should encompass are next solicited from personnel in the functional areas for which standards are being developed (20–30). Since cooperation is essential if standards are to serve their purpose, employees should have a voice in standards formulation. Often, the very process of assisting in the development of standards makes employees aware of the need for, and value of, standards. They then willingly follow standards in their work. A draft of the new standards is then prepared (20–30) and tested (30–40). If satisfactory, the standards are introduced (40–80), monitors are set in place for their enforcement (40–60), and employees are trained in their use (40–50). Periodically, the standards should be evaluated. If unsatisfactory, they should be modified or withdrawn (80–90).

Documentation is an activity that is generally unpopular at computer facilities but is essential to communication and systems continuation. Many tales are told in computer literature of systems having to be redeveloped because an analyst or programmer resigned without leaving adequate documentation for successors to maintain the existing system. Only by setting standards for documentation and enforcing them can such problems be avoided.

A standards committee, assigned the task of developing documentation standards, has to decide how to structure documentation and what level of detail is needed. Modular documentation is generally favored at medium- and large-sized computer installations. That is, four manuals are typically designed to include all of the documentation on operations for the computer center. These manuals include a:

- Systems manual, with general information on the system and its objectives.
- Programmer's manual, containing descriptions of programs.
- Operator's manual, giving directions for running programs.
- User's manual, detailing procedures for use of the system, including data flow diagrams, decision tables, and program descriptions written in terms that users understand.

This division allows groups with differing needs to have simultaneous access to documentation information.

Next, the material to be contained in each manual is prescribed by the standards committee. (This task is sometimes delegated to the development team.) Usually, each manual is designed to contain abstract, detailed, and summary documentation.

The level of detail of the standards for documentation may include symbol shapes for flowcharts. (International shape conventions differ from the IBM template commonly used in the United States.) Because of the inaccuracies that can result in reading and interpreting alphanumeric data and codes, documentation standards generally include character shape specifications as well. (The look-alikes 5 and S sometimes cause confusion, as do the letter I and numeral 1, or the letter O and numeral 0. The Department of Defense convention is to slash the letter O [Ø], but many analysts slash the zero. Abroad, the letter O is frequently underlined [O].)

Another detail that may be addressed when setting the documentation standards is paragraph structure. Some installations require that the main paragraphs in manuals be headed by sequential decimal codes to identify topics and subtopics. Other organizations do not prescribe paragraph structure, the premise being that such a standard inhibits creativity, lowers morale, and causes problems in enforcement.

A standard on the timing of documentation may be set. For example, completion of documentation may be required one month after a job

Figure 13–4   **Documentation at different stages of development**

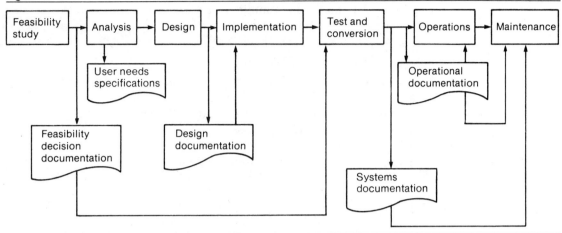

is operational or six weeks after acceptance testing. Figure 13–4 shows a documentation standard that prescribes progressive documentation after milestones in the development process. According to this standard, documentation prepared following the feasibility study is used in testing to ensure that the expectations of the system are fulfilled; design documentation is used during implementation; and the final documentations (operational and system) serve as the basis for operations and maintenance.

Few standards committees have the competence to set standards for all functional areas of an installation, so they delegate this responsibility to others. The problem is deciding who should set, evaluate, and implement standards. Formulation of documentation standards might be delegated to an analyst, programmer, user, or outside consultant. Perhaps documentation will be automated with a computer program, such as AUTOFLOW in flowcharting. (In effect, the programmer who writes such software sets documentation standards.) A decision must be made regarding who should evaluate and test documentation, take custody of manuals, assign and control manual access, and be responsible for updating and revisions. Generally, the committee (or person) that writes documentation standards also makes such decisions.

Programmers and systems analysts generally dislike documentation, because it is a tedious and time-consuming task. They often argue that they are too busy or that documentation should wait until the system stabilizes. Since systems are constantly redesigned, such stabilization rarely occurs; documentation may be indefinitely postponed. Some companies will contract for systems development at a 20 percent reduction in cost if no documentation is required. Acceptance of such a proposition is penny-wise and pound-foolish because documentation is too important to be compromised in this manner. A major responsibility of a standards committee is to educate both employees and management regarding the importance of documentation standards. For example, in pointing out their value, the committee should stress that documentation standards:

- Ensure that all commitments and expectations are on record.
- Help initiate and train newcomers to the system.
- Provide information needed to change the system should the environment or management's needs alter.
- Prevent systems dislocation and cost that might otherwise occur if knowledge of the system were centered in a few individuals who might resign, relocate, or be subsequently reassigned to other duties.
- Facilitate routine evaluation, auditing, and control.

An equally strong case could be made regarding the importance of standards for all of the components of an information system. It is obvious that no firm can permit secretaries to organize unique filing systems or allow programmers to use unique symbol sets. The problem is recognizing the fine line between standards that promote productivity and those that stifle creativity. The objective should be a set of standards that facilitate communication, control, and compatibility—standards that promote efficiency and effectiveness in operations and are recognized by employees as doing so.

COST AND BENEFITS OF STANDARDS

In assessing the **cost** of standards, the salary of the standards officer, committee time, and secretarial expenses in drafting, typing, editing, and reviewing/updating standards should be calculated. Also included are the expense of testing standards and the costs associated with enforcement of standards and training employees in their use. In addition, the cost of conformity and reduction of choices should be considered, though the latter is particularly difficult to quantify.

Benefits, in addition to those discussed earlier in the section on documentation, include:

- Better communication.
- Improved utilization of computing resources.
- Portability of data, procedures, equipment, software, personnel, and sometimes even subsystems or entire systems.
- Greater ease and speed in maintaining programs and systems at lower cost.
- Improved planning, control, and security.

EXTERNAL SOURCES OF STANDARDS

Thus far in this chapter, we have discussed standards developed in-house. In deciding what standards are appropriate, a standards committee can benefit from the experience of other organizations with a similar environment or turn for guidance to books and manuals devoted to the subject of standards. It can also adopt standards set by committees formed by industry representatives or by professional groups. In addition, many standards recommendations come from national institutes, the federal government, and international bodies. The advantage of adopting standards set externally is that compatibility with the operations and products of other firms may result.

This chapter closes with a look at national groups and international organizations having an interest in computer standards.

Industry standards

One example of an industry standard is the magnetic ink character found on the base of checks, a coding standard adopted by the banking industry to facilitate computerized processing of banking transactions. Use of this code speeds processing because checks can pass through a machine that reads the data, then sorts and routes the checks according to the preprinted magnetic ink block codes.

Another industry standard familiar to most readers is the Universal Product Code (UPC) found in retailing. This standard was developed by the Symbol Standardization Subcommittee of the Uniform Grocery Product Code Council Inc. to speed grocery checkouts. Scanning equipment reads the product identification code, which is fed to a computer to ascertain retail price.

Sometimes, industry representatives will agree on technical standards for new products. For example, in the 1980s, a standard was reached in the electronics industry for wiring office machines together. Usually, such agreements require the backing of a major company. When small firms attempted to get a standard accepted for the size of disk memories for microcomputers, the attempt failed.

Professional organizations

Among professional organizations concerned with standards in computing, the **Conference on Data Systems Languages (CODASYL)** is perhaps best known. This group has contributed widely accepted basic concepts to COBOL. CODASYL has also worked somewhat less successfully on the development of specifications for data base management systems.

The IEEE Computer Society has many technical committees working on computing standards. Here is a partial list of subjects of interest to the society:

- Computer dictionary.
- Semiconductor memory test pattern language.
- Microprocessor instruction sets.
- Software quality assurance plans.
- Floating-point arithmetic for microprocessors.
- Ada as a program design language.
- Operating system kernel.
- Logical link control.
- Token bus.

Other professional groups at work on the development of computing standards include the Computer and Business Equipment Manufacturers Association, the Electronic Industries Association, the Radio Technical Committee on Aeronautics, and the IEEE Instrumentation and Measurement Society.

National institutes

A national, private-sector organization with an interest in computing standards (and in other scientific and technical fields) is the **American National Standards Institute (ANSI)**, a nonprofit organization with 750 companies as dues-paying members. Although ANSI was founded only in 1969, it had forerunners under different names: the American Engineering Standards Committee founded in 1918; the American Standards Association founded in 1928; and the United States Standards Institute founded in 1966. ANSI is the instrument for U.S. participation in international standards bodies.

Figure 13–5 shows the broad range of ANSI activities in developing standards for computers and information processing. Of special interest to business programmers is the subcommittee X3J4 on COBOL, which is working in close affiliation with CODASYL to revise COBOL. Table 13–3 is just a sample list of some of the areas in which standards have been developed by ANSI that affect businesses with computer installations. It should be pointed out that corporations' compliance with ANSI standards is voluntary.

Federal government

Government activities in the field of computing standards are primarily under the aegis of the **National Bureau of Standards (NBS)** and the **Department of Defense (DOD).** Standards developed by the NBS focus on documentation, data base organization, office automation, interchange media, and communications. The Department of Defense, on the other hand, emphasizes languages, instruction sets, software development and configuration, and software management.

Disagreement always seems to take place in professional circles when new standards are promulgated. Controversy over the **Data Encryption Standard (DES)**, a standard that IBM developed in 1974 for the National Bureau of Standards (NBS) for purposes of coding unclassified govern-

Figure 13–5 **Organization chart for ANSI**

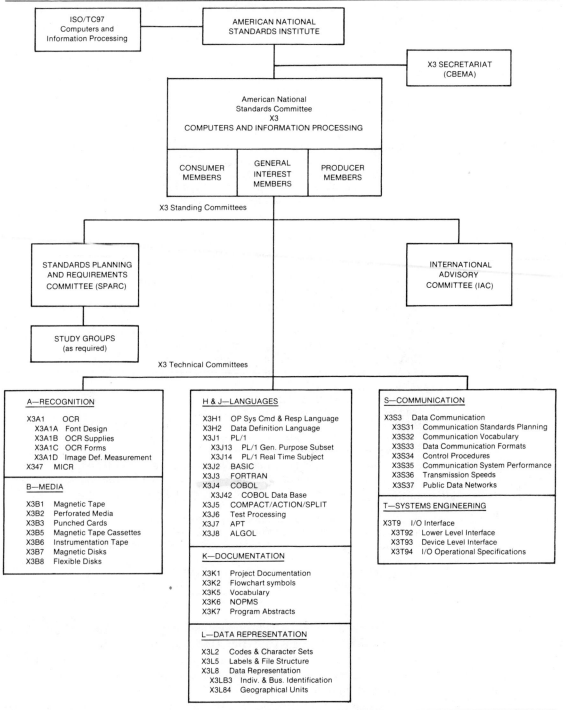

Table 13–3   **Partial list of areas covered by ANSI–X3 standards on computers and information processing**

Synchronous signaling rates for data transmission
Print specifications for magnetic ink character recognition
Bank check specifications for magnetic ink character recognition
Code for information interchange
Flowchart symbols and their usage in information processing
Perforated tape code for information interchange
FORTRAN
Basic FORTRAN
Specifications for general-purpose paper cards for information processing
Vocabulary for information processing
Recorded magnetic tape for information exchange
Code for information interchange in serial-by-bit data transmission
Character structure and character parity sense for serial-by-bit data
    communication in the American National Standard Code for information
    interchange
Character set for optical character recognition
One-inch perforated paper tape for information interchange
Eleven-sixteenths inch perforated paper tape for information interchange
Take-up reels for one-inch perforated tape for information interchange
Rectangular holes in 12-row punched cards
Recorded magnetic tape for information interchange (800 CPI, NRZI)
COBOL
Signal quality at interface between data processing terminal equipment and
    synchronous data communication equipment for serial data transmission
Character structure and character parity sense for parallel-by-bit
    communication in the American National Standard Code for information
    interchange
Hollerith punched card code
Magnetic tape labels for information interchange
Procedures for the use of the communication control characters of American
    National Standard Code for information interchange in specified data
    communication links
Specification for properties of unpunched paper perforator tape
Representation for calendar date and ordinal date for information interchange
Structure for the identification of the counties of the United States for
    information exchange
Graphic representation of control characters of ASCII
Interchange rolls of perforated tape for information interchange
Identification of states of the United States (including the District of Columbia)
    for information interchange
Recorded magnetic tape for information exchange
Unrecorded magnetic tape for information interchange

ment data, illustrates how hard it can be to gain widespread acceptance of a new national standard. When DES was first introduced, allegations were made that the code was too short, that pressure from the National Security Agency limited DES to a 56-bit code, when a key size of 64 bits would have been more secure. Though a Senate select committee on intelligence investigated the allegations and found the code to be free from any statistical or mathematical weakness, critics were not silenced. The claim that the code, with 100,000 million combinations, would require 2,000 years to test all possible keys at one test per microsecond was challenged by opponents such as Martin Hellman and W. Diffie.[2] They argued that with faster computers and parallel processing, the code could be broken in 12 hours.

The NBS then convened a panel of experts to reevaluate the code. They concluded that a computer costing $50–70 million might break the code, but the likelihood of success would be only 10–20 percent. Hellman was not satisfied. In 1978, he described to a national computer conference how a conventional computer costing $4 million could break DES in 24 hours. He argued that a 128-bit code was needed to ensure code security. IBM's response was that two DES chips can simulate a 128-bit code, so the 56-bit key in the DES cannot be called a weak link in the security chain.

The debate over DES continues to rage with cryptographers proposing alternatives, such as Hellman's public key system being developed at Stanford. Many firms have delayed adoption of a needed encryption standard because of the controversy, which may hurt the public interest in the long run.

International organizations

The **International Standards Organization (ISO)** is one of the principal international bodies concerned with computer standards. This is a private body affiliated with the United Nations, its membership drawn from most of the countries of the world. In the ISO, the most important technical committee is TC97 (Computers and Information Processing), which is organized into subcommittees, many of which are further subdivided into working groups. Figure 13–6 shows the wide range of topics under consideration by the subcommittees.

Other international organizations with an interest in computer standards include the International Electrotechnical Commission, the Consultative Committee on International Telephone and Telegraph, the European Computer Manufacturers Association, the International Federation for Information Processing, and the Organization of Economic Cooperation and Development.

Although many of the standards adopted in the United States have been embraced by other countries and accepted as international standards, not all American standards have foreign support. For example, COBOL, a standard for business processing in this country, is not a language favored by the Europeans. Getting international agreement on

---

[2]W. Diffie and Martin E. Hellman, "Exhaustive Cryptoanalysis of the NBS Data Encryption Standard," *Computer*, vol. 10, no. 6 (June 1977), p. 74. According to Peter Hage, *Government Computer News*, April 11, 1986, p. 70, the DES encryption algorithm today contains over 72 quadrillion encryptions keys to scramble data at the sending computer.

Figure 13–6   **Topics under consideration by subcommittees of the International Standards Organization, Technical Committee 97**

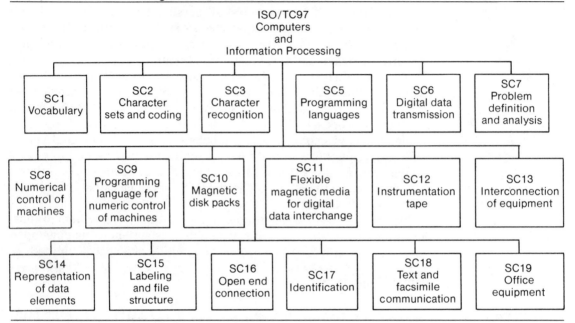

standards is a difficult process because delegates to international organizations have a vested interest in promoting standards that are implemented in their home countries. The speed of computer technology advances accentuates the problem, since the machinery for formulating international standards is too cumbersome to keep pace.

SUMMING UP

According to many experts, incompatibility of computer systems is a major problem in the computer industry. Standards are the answer.

Formulation of standards within a firm may be the responsibility of a standards committee, a standards officer, or both. Industry and professional groups and both national and international organizations also contribute to computing standards.

The term *standard* has a slightly different meaning at each of these levels. For in-house operations, firms develop procedures or guidelines that they call standards, such as standards for documentation. Businesses may sign an agreement to adopt a common method of operations, creating standards such as UPC. Sometimes, a manufacturer's product becomes a de facto standard; other companies design their product lines with the same or compatible specifications. (For example, Sony's 3½-

inch microfloppy may become an industry standard.) Industries, standards institutes, governments, and international bodies develop standards of a different nature. They concentrate on technical descriptions, rules for programming languages, and definitions of terms that will promote the interface of systems components, common measurements, and communication between persons working in the computer field.

In each of these cases, the nature of the standard, the procedure for setting the standard, and the obligation of individuals (or corporations) to follow the standard differ. But all standards have two common goals:

- To promote communication so that groups within and between firms can integrate operations and compare results.
- To contribute to productivity by providing guidelines for products or operations.

Perhaps too many groups compete with one another today in the setting of standards. Some critics suggest that there should be a way of selecting the best organizations and people to work on needed standards. Another problem is motivating individuals and corporations to follow standards, since conformity and discipline are not popular concepts. (Some managers explain that they do not impose standards, because strict enforcement seems to go against the American self-image.) There is also a cost to standards: staffing, training, implementation, and updating. But most computer professionals recognize that standards are a prerequisite to orderly, efficient, and effective growth of information processing.

CASE: UPC, A STANDARD IN RETAILING

The Universal Product Code (UPC), a bar code used for optical scanning of products in grocery stores, is one example of a national standard. This standard was developed when grocers throughout the country recognized their common interest in designing a nationally accepted code for precise point-of-sale data capture. Increased grocery checkout productivity and inventory control were two of the benefits that grocery store managers hoped to derive from the standard.

A subcommittee of the Uniform Grocery Product Code Council Inc., a council composed of representatives of grocery distributors and supermarket chains, was assigned responsibility for soliciting and re-

Source: D. Savir and G. J. Laurer, "The Characteristics and Decodability of the Universal Product Code System," *IBM Systems Journal* 14, no. 1 (December 1975), pp. 16–34.

viewing code proposals. The subcommittee engaged McKinsey and Co.,
Inc. as consultants and prepared code specifications:

Mode	Online real time
Size of code	12-decimal characters
Area of symbol	≯1.5 square inch
Speed of scanning	≯100 inch/second
Scanning reject rate	≯0.01 percent
Undetected error rate	≯0.0001 percent
Dirt and abrasion	Normal conditions allowed

Samples of designs submitted and the code selected by the council are
shown.

The UPC code is used extensively in the United States and Canada.
Many other countries have been considering adoption of the UPC standard as well.

Sample proposals

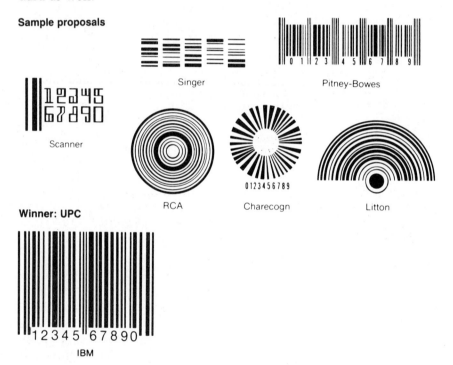

Singer

Pitney-Bowes

Scanner

RCA

Charecogn

Litton

Winner: UPC

12345 67890

IBM

Questions

1. How does the UPC relate to computer processing?
2. Why did grocers want a product code standard?
3. Suppose a grocer favored a code design other than the one chosen
    by the grocery council? Could it be used? Explain.
4. How do you suppose the council resolved differences among its
    members in selecting the code?

5.   What costs have been incurred to implement the UPC? Is the cost worth the benefits? How can the answer to this question be ascertained?

CASE: DEPARTMENT OF DEFENSE CAN'T WAIT FOR THE ISO

The U.S. Department of Defense (DOD) depends on distributed data processing and computer networking to fulfill its mandate. This requires that computers and peripherals purchased from multiple vendors and installed at remote sites be able to communicate with one another. To promote interoperability, the DOD has issued a set of military standards for communications protocols. In addition, to minimize communications costs and to increase security, the DOD has developed the Defense Data Network and issued interface standards for attaching components to the network.

It should be pointed out that the International Standards Organization is in the process of developing a framework for communications protocol standardization that, when completed, might meet the needs of the DOD. In all likelihood, the ISO standards will be widely accepted throughout the world. Why, then, has the DOD acted on its own?

The reason is that the Defense Department's needs are immediate: the department can't wait until ISO protocols evolve and stabilize. Furthermore, the DOD is particularly interested in security and robustness, concerns that are not top priority with the ISO developers.

DOD protocols include:

- Internet Protocol (to interconnect the Defense Data Network with local networks at local sites).
- Transmission Control Protocol (to provide a reliable data transport service).
- File Transfer Protocol (to send files from one system to another under user command).
- Simple Mail Transfer Protocol (an electronic mail facility).
- Telenet (a program to handle asynchronous as well as synchronous terminal traffic).

The Department of Defense has announced its intention to change from its own military standards to conform to international standards when they have been developed by the ISO and the Consultative Committee on International Telephony and Telegraphy. But until that time, vendors who wish to sell to the military must support the DOD's own standards.

IBM has developed its own Systems Network Architecture (SNA) in competition with the ISO standard. Already, SNA is a de facto standard in much of the United States.

Questions

1. Why are telecommunications standards needed?
2. We now have three standards in telecommunications: standards developed by the DOD, IBM's SNA, and standards of the ISO. Who gains and who loses in this competition between standards? How? Consider at least the following parties:
    a. Vendors.
    b. Government.
    c. Large business organizations.
    d. Small organizations.
3. If you were a manager in a company with plans for a large telecommunications sector, would you wait for standards to stabilize or not? What are the pros and cons of waiting?
4. Why is the development of standards a lengthy process?
5. What impedes the acceptance of standards, such as the SNA or ISO standards for telecommunications?

CASE: STANDARDS FOR MICROCOMPUTERS

When IBM introduced the personal computer in 1981, the groundwork for standards in microcomputers was laid. Within two years, the Compaq Portable and Compaq Plus reached the market. Both machines mimicked IBM's hardware and basic input/output system, BIOS, a version of MS–DOS. This meant that programs written for the IBM PC would run on the Compaqs.

Soon, almost all companies manufacturing personal computers followed Compaq's lead. The idea of compatibility in microcomputers took hold and exists even with today's 286-based machines. Software for the IBM PC XT will also run on a AT&T PC 6300 Plus, Tandy 1000, Sharp PC–7000, Leading Edge Model D, and Compaq Portable II. The machines are not clones; they vary in speeds, price, function keys, and features such as color graphics.

An important advantage to users of the open architecture that allows this compatibility is that by simply adding a board to their computers, users can take advantage of new technology. And John Wickser, a New York banker working on a spreadsheet using a PC XT at his office, can continue the work on his Compaq Plus at home after office hours, while Gorden MacPherson, a Maryland telephone consultant familiar with the Tandy 1000, has no problem operating his clients' IBM PCs.

Every time an independent company markets a compatible product, the standard becomes even stronger.

Questions

1. Do PC users take a chance that standards for PCs will change? Is Mr. Wickser more vulnerable than Mr. MacPherson in this regard?
2. How can a buyer of a PC determine when standards have stabilized and are "strong enough" not to change?
3. How has microcomputer standardization benefited the consumer?

STUDY KEYS

American National Standards Institute (ANSI)

Benefits

Conference on Data Systems Languages (CODASYL)

Cost

Data Encryption Standard (DES)

Department of Defense (DOD)

Documentation

International Standards Organization (ISO)

National Bureau of Standards (NBS)

Standards

Standards committee

Standards officer

DISCUSSION QUESTIONS

1. Standards are expensive to institute, difficult to enforce, unpopular with users, and cause disruption when they are implemented. Comment.
2. At what stage of the development of an information system should one start thinking of standards? Why?
3. Who should initiate standards for a computer center: someone within the computer center, someone within the organization but in another department, or an outside consultant? Explain.
4. Comment on the following statement: The benefits of standards are largely intangible. Does it matter that a cost-benefit ratio for standards cannot be calculated?

5. How can one determine whether expenses for a standards program are justifiable?

6. How do standards depend upon:
    a. Size of computing center?
    b. Complexity of applications portfolio?
    c. Number of users?
    d. Industry?
    e. Clients?
    f. Maturity of computing center?
    g. Computer executive?

7. Do we need standards for standards? Do we need to control standards? Explain.

8. Under what circumstances would a firm adopt local standards that differ from standards adopted by:
    a. The firm's own computer center?
    b. The industry the firm represents?
    c. National standards organizations?
    d. International standards organizations?

9. Under what circumstances should standards be mandated by:
    a. The industry of the firm?
    b. Computer professional organizations?
    c. National standards organizations?
    d. International standards organizations?

10. Who should be responsible for the enforcement of standards? Should this be an ongoing responsibility, should spot checks be the norm, or should controls wait until something goes wrong?

11. Explain how standards help to:
    a. Avoid disasters.
    b. Improve performance.
    c. Control operations.
    d. Assist in employee training.
    e. Contribute to good working habits.

12. Should we have standards for:
    a. Performance?
    b. Procedures?
    c. Design?
    Are these areas too intangible and variable to be standardized?

SELECTED ANNOTATED BIBLIOGRAPHY

Card, Chuck, R. Donald Prigge, Josephine L. Walkowicz, and Marjorie F. Hill. "The World of Standards." *Byte*, vol. 8, no. 2 (February 1983), pp. 130–42.
Excellent on the organization of national and international standards. The article helps the reader "better appreciate the importance of standards and the standard process to our technological world."

Dietrich, Mark, and Jennifer Stothers. "Toward a Graphics Standard." *PC World,* vol. 2, no. 12 (November 1984), pp. 264–74.

There are, of course, many specialized standards and many articles written about them. Often, the articles describe, as this one does, the time-consuming process required to reach consensus on standards. Diplomacy, patience, technical knowledge, and expertise in group dynamics all play an important role in reaching consensus.

Frank, Werner L. "Applications Backlog Begs for an Effective Solution." *Asian Computer Monthly,* November 1983, pp. 72–75.

Frank's solution to backlogs is standards, especially those in the area of data files and software portability.

Holmes, Fen. "The Standards Go Around." *System User,* vol. 2, no. 3 (March 1982), pp. 1, 10.

It is Holmes' premise that standards can be a mixed blessing. Most standards have been developed for a static world. We are in trouble if we don't adjust standards to the marketplace. Holmes points out that vendors play a role in the formulation of standards for hardware but have limited effect on language standards. Program development and documentation standards are open to those willing to develop them.

Smith, Joan M. "Text Structuring." *Data Processing,* vol. 25, no. 10 (October 1983), pp. 18–20.

This article on text processing standards discusses the work of various national and international committees on standards for document description, for office document architecture, and for office document interchange format. Considerations of security are also examined. The article should interest managers concerned with office automation.

Stibbens, Steve. "Buying a Desk-Top Computer? You're on the Road to a Dilemma." *Infosystems,* vol. 29, no. 12 (December 1982), pp. 40–44.

According to Stibbens, the main reason for the lack of integration of small computers in office automation is the lack of industry standards. Ways of playing a stopgap game are discussed.

Walsh, Willoughby Ann. "Solving the Standards Dilemma—Part 1: Defining the Need." *Office Administration and Automation,* vol. 44, no. 1 (January 1983), pp. 44–46.

Incompatible hardware, software, and communications are forcing the computer industry toward standards. First, needs have to be defined, and this requires negotiation, reasoned compromise, and a consensus.

Zeitler, Eddie L. "Developing Standards for Protecting Electronic Financial Data." *Bank Administration,* vol. 62, no. 10 (October 1986), pp. 38, 40.

Banking related, but the standards for encryption and message authentication may well spread to other industries.

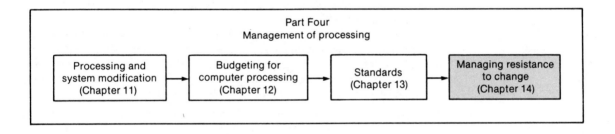

Part Four
Management of processing

| Processing and system modification (Chapter 11) | → | Budgeting for computer processing (Chapter 12) | → | Standards (Chapter 13) | → | Managing resistance to change (Chapter 14) |

CHAPTER 14

Managing resistance to change

More than machinery, we need humanity.
Charlie Chaplin, in the film *Modern Times*

Over 400 years ago, Machiavelli observed:

> It must be considered that there is nothing more difficult to carry out, nor more doubtful of success, nor more dangerous to handle, than to initiate a new order of things. For the reformer has enemies in all those who profit by the old order, and only lukewarm defenders in all those who could profit by the new order. This lukewarmness arises partly from fear of their adversaries, who have the laws in their favor, and partly from the incredulity of mankind, who do not truly believe in anything new until they have had an actual experience of it.[1]

Resistance to a new order has not lessened in this century. Indeed, the pace of the technological revolution has heightened fears that humans are becoming subservient to machines and stiffened resistance to technology that threatens to disrupt the status quo. This threat is perceived in information systems that incorporate advances in process control, microtechnology, teleprocessing, robotics, graphics, voice recognition, distributed processing, and word processing.

Implementation of **change** in computing does not require the guile of a Machiavelli. But implementers do need to identify and analyze why employees oppose innovations and to develop strategies to promote acceptance of change. Figure 14–1 is an overview of the stages in the management of change. These stages will be discussed in the following sections of this chapter.

---

[1]Niccolò Machiavelli, *The Prince*, translated by Luigi Rice, revised by E. R. P. Vincent (New York: New American Library, 1952), pp. 49–50.

Figure 14-1   **Stages in the management of change**

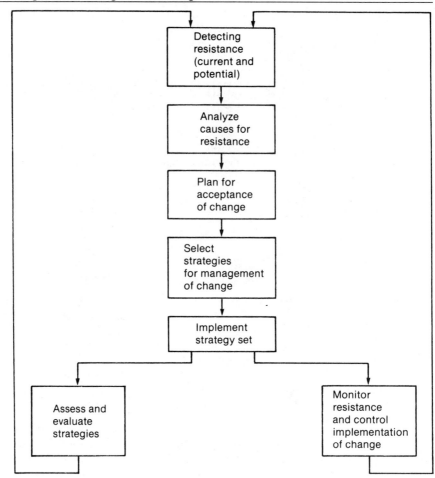

DETECTING RESISTANCE TO A COMPUTER ENVIRONMENT

A drop in production, failure to meet deadlines, absenteeism, mounting employee turnover, complaints and low morale, and a reluctance to learn new job skills are all symptoms of employee resistance to change. What makes human resistance to computers different from the antagonism felt toward machines (an antagonism that has existed since the industrial revolution) is that software adds a new dimension to the conflict. Today, as shown in Figure 14-2, one must add human-software interface (B) and human-machine-software interface (D) to the problem of human-machine interaction (C).

Figure 14–2   **Relationship between humans, machines, and software**

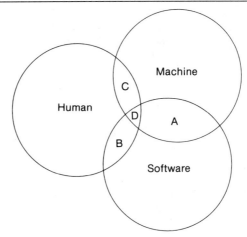

Area A = Machine-software interface.   Area C = Human-machine interface.
Area B = Human-software interface.   Area D = Human-machine-software interface.

Human factors, sometimes referred to as **human engineering** or **ergonomics,** is a field in which human-machine interrelationships are studied. European research focuses on physiological considerations, such as fatigue when operating machines, breathing rates, and pupil size, whereas the American emphasis is more on psychological factors. On both sides of the Atlantic, recommendations for improving the computing environment can sometimes seem quite mundane: for example, that workstations be comfortable and pleasing, since the arrangement of furniture and workspace around a terminal can affect user morale and an inconvenient layout may contribute to employee errors. The size of terminal keys, angle of the screen, flicker, and color of displays are all factors that may affect production.

When designing electronic data processing (EDP) equipment and developing software, many human engineering problems arise from the fact that users have a wide range of background knowledge and experience. For example, the same hardware devices may have to serve clerks (who use terminals primarily as input devices), professionals (analysts and programmers), managers (whose interest is primarily output), and specialists (such as product designers using computer-aided design). Nonprofessionals often have difficulty communicating with a computer. They may require interactive and conversational modes or special training materials and documentation in order to take full advantage of the potential of computers in problem solving. Users with a computing background, on the other hand, will have less need for special user-friendly features and may even prefer a "bare-bones" system (for example, a minimum of menus and help routines). Unfortu-

Figure 14–3   **Computer-human interaction**

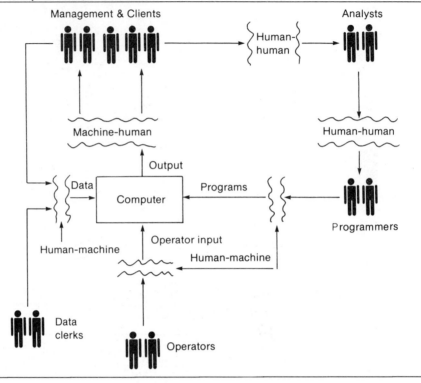

nately, many systems designers do not recognize the existence of individuals who see broad patterns and total pictures rather than well-bounded problems as they do, so they fail to incorporate features appropriate to all classes of users in the systems that they develop.

Growing recognition of the importance of human factors should help correct this shortcoming. The literature on human factors is, indeed, quite extensive. Management should follow research in this field because no computerized information system can achieve its full potential as a tool in management decision making when aspects of human engineering are ignored.

Figure 14–3 summarizes relationships in a computer environment. Human-machine relationships exist between the computer and management/clients. Human-human interchange takes place between management, computer personnel, and clients. This figure illustrates why information systems should not be categorized as machine systems or even as machine-dominated systems, since humans have a role in all aspects of processing. Because humans specify the need for information, design and implement systems, write programs, provide input, operate and monitor equipment, and use output, a climate receptive to the change is vital when new information technology is being introduced to an organization. Without human cooperation, the new technology will fail to live up to its productivity potential.

WHY RESISTANCE?

That employees resist change should come as no surprise to business managers, since this phenomenon has been well documented. For example, the Hawthorne Study at Western Electric in the late 1920s noted that factory conditions or salaries alone did not explain worker attitudes. Actions perceived as a threat to job security triggered a strong emotional response. According to the literature of operations research and management science, a similar negative reaction to change occurred at managerial levels when mathematical and statistical methods of decision making were first introduced.

Resistance to computers can be found at all levels of an organization. Employees at operational levels, such as assembly-line workers and technicians, may be as disturbed by disruption of the status quo as managers in the upper echelons of the company. People are creatures of habit and become upset when new technology jars their sense of control or disturbs their sense of purpose. They fear the change that the new technology will impose on their lives. Procedures may be altered, jobs may gain or lose status, and totally new relationships may have to be forged as departments are restructured in accordance with the expanded role of computers. Employees wonder how the technology will affect their jobs, their security, their authority, their access to information, their interaction with co-workers, and their values. They know that they may have to learn new job skills and that information technology can lead to job displacement and unemployment. Concerns such as these lead to resistance. Persons who see their power base eroding will, in self-interest, scheme to defeat the new technology. (On the other hand, employees who feel they will have an opportunity to attain privileged status because of their expertise in computers favor the introduction of information systems.)

Resistance to computer technology at managerial levels can often be traced to managers feeling that they are being hemmed in by information technology, that their choices are restricted because computer systems seem to centralize important decision making. Some local managers resent having daily goals defined, the action to achieve these goals specified, and performance evaluated by what they perceive as an impersonal machine. Computer systems may also provide data that managers prefer to suppress and may reveal staff incompetence. For example, a report by one company comparing monthly sales showed a correlation between low performance and deer-hunting season. Fore-

men lax in controlling unexcused absences of hunters were easily identified.

Perhaps the main reason managers oppose information systems is
that computers alter the decision-making process. Decisions in a computerized environment are largely based on data provided by systems
and supplemented by human judgment and experience. This method
of decision making requires a different type of conceptual thinking than
intuitive decision making, common in the past. Many managers find
their old style of reaching decisions under attack and yet are unable to
adjust to decision making that utilizes the new technology. Reasons for
resistance are summarized in Table 14–1.

Although resistance generally has adverse effects, not all resistance
is bad. If management examines the objections of employees and improves proposed systems by listening to constructive criticism, resistance can serve a useful purpose. Perhaps technicians have not paid
enough attention to human needs in designing the work environment.
Perhaps the stress has been on technology, ignoring the human-machine
interface on which success of new systems depends. Careful assessment
of employee objections may help avert costly flops. Those who assume

Table 14–1   **Effects of new technology on employee's reasons for resistance**

Reason for resistance \ Level primarily affected →	Operating personnel	Operating management	Middle management	Top management
Loss of status	XX	X		
Economic insecurity	XX			
Interpersonal relationships altered	X	X	X	X
Change in job content	XX	X	X	
Change in decision-making approach		X	X	X
Loss of power		X	X	
Uncertainty/ unfamiliarity/ misinformation	XX	X	X	X

Key
  X = Some affect
  XX = Strong affect

Key: X = Some effect.
     XX = Strong effect.

that all resistance is the grumbling of malcontents do their firm a disservice.

Tolerance to change depends on a number of variables. Some commentators suggest that resistance is greater among older employees with a long record of service to a company than among younger workers and is more likely among those with limited education and little background in computers. Resistance is generally proportional to the number of persons involved in the change and also increases as the rate of change increases. Rapid change has been known to produce dysfunctional behavior such as alienation, withdrawal, apathy, and depression, but even controlled change can lead to emotional stress and illness.

This phenomenon has been studied by psychologists T. S. and T. H. Holmes, who devised a system of scoring events in a person's life according to the amount of trauma they produce. For example, points are given for divorce, birth of a child, vacations, and a death in the family. It is significant that changes in employment, such as altered hours of work (20 points), new duties (29), or loss of a job (47), represent 20 percent of the list and have high score values. According to the Holmeses, a score of 200 at any given time is so disruptive that an individual is susceptible to disease or illness. Clearly, changed work conditions as a result of the introduction of an information system would score highly under this system, explaining the behavior of some individuals when their departments are computerized.

PLANNING FOR ATTITUDE CHANGE

Once resistance is identified, plans to change employee attitudes need to be made. Planning for change should resemble the planning of a project. That is, once the need for change is identified, strategies to implement the change should be developed, responsibilities for this implementation assigned, and a schedule for implementation adopted.

Often, a systems analyst is the change agent. But firms that have little experience in the management of change may hire a technical consultant to effect the change. The change agent should be technically competent and skilled in communication and procedural skills. The individual should also have expertise in human-machine interaction and human performance technology. In addition, knowledge about the integration of human factors with instructional technology is important, and the person should be schooled in industrial and organization psychology. The function of the change agent is to recommend policies that will smooth transition to new technology and to devise ways to alter the behavior and attitude of employees resisting change.

Skilled change agents know that employees must be made aware of a proposed change and have time to grapple with what the change means to them. Initial confusion, a lack of understanding of the ramifications of change, should not be misinterpreted as resistance. To avoid the heated, emotion-charged environment that accompanies sudden change, employees should be told early in a new system's development the reasons why new technology is being introduced and what will happen as a result. They will then have time to reflect on the change and will be able to evaluate the pros and cons of the project with greater objectivity. Given a period of adjustment, affected employees will have time to learn new job skills or to seek alternate employment. Firms can help smooth adjustment by providing in-house retraining and by offering the option of early retirement or severance pay to affected personnel.

Experienced change agents also recognize that an individual's assessment of new technology may be mixed, fluctuating between positive and negative emotional and intellectual judgments. At one moment, hope that work in a computerized environment will lead to professional advancement may dominate; at another, deep-felt anxiety about job displacement or unemployment may surface. The best expediters of technological change are adroit in accentuating positive reactions to the new technology. They know that when positive perceptions predominate, commitment to change will follow.

Initial commitment may be ephemeral, turning to pessimism when bugs in the new technology surface. It is the responsibility of the change agent to encourage employees to discuss systems faults so that bugs can be identified and efforts made to correct them. Often, the information obtained from disgruntled employees can be used to fine-tune the new system and, as a result, win back their support. The highest form of commitment occurs when employees, believing that the new technology is worthwhile, contribute to the design of new procedures or the molding of the technology for their own purposes. Cash incentives can help promote this involvement.

There is a cycle in an individual's attitude toward change, as depicted in Figure 14–4, that a change agent hopes to influence. Each person's emotional response to change is preconditioned by background, education, and past experience with change (Box 1). Emotional responses lead to attitudes (3) that affect whether the impact of innovation at work will be perceived as beneficial or as a threat (4). This perception, in turn, influences whether change will be accepted or opposed (5), and the degree of willing participation in the implementation of the change (6). This experience becomes part of the employee's background (1), conditioning future reaction to change.

The change agent hopes, by handling change in an equitable and humane manner (2), to interject new experience or knowledge into this cycle and reinforce positive responses to change. The employee's attitude toward change hopefully will be favorably altered, with resistance to change diminished in the future.

Figure 14–4   **Cycle in attitude toward change**

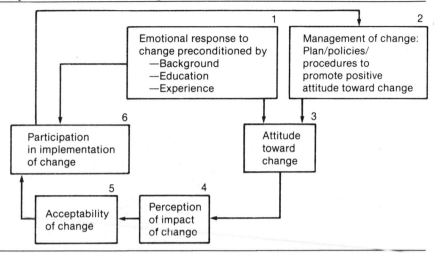

BEHAVIOR ALTERATION STRATEGIES

Two approaches to behavior alteration are possible when employees resist change: a **participative change,** which originates from within the individual, and a **directive change,** a response to management initiatives.

A participative change starts with new knowledge (formal education, self-instruction, or observation). This knowledge kindles new attitudes that, in turn, affect behavior—first individual, then group behavior. Such change can be nurtured by the environment. For example, time off may be given employees for class attendance or a bonus offered for joining educational programs.

A directive change is one imposed by management. Policies are formulated that require alteration of group behavior, which then modifies the knowledge and attitudes of individuals. For example, participation at orientation sessions may be compulsory, or employees may be told their jobs are in jeopardy if new job skills are not learned. A change in attitude can also be fostered by involving employees in systems development projects. Resisters can be co-opted, given an active role in identifying problems and planning solutions. Generally, individuals thus involved begin to see computers as valuable business aids, and their fears of a machine takeover fade.

Which of the two approaches to change, participative or directive, works best in an EDP environment? Generally, a participative change is most desirable. Self-motivated employees tend to imbue others with their enthusiasm, and their willingness to try new ideas often serves

Figure 14–5   **Participative and directive changes**

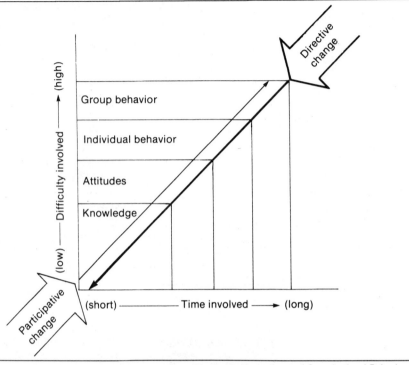

Source: Adapted from Paul Hersey and K. H. Blanchard, *Management of Organizational Behavior: Utilizing Human Resources* (Englewood Cliffs, N. J.: Prentice-Hall, 1977), pp. 281–82.

as a catalyst to a change in attitude of co-workers. The approach is also more appealing because it is open and democratic.

But when no employees voluntarily engage in activities that will transform behavior, management must implement strategies to encourage a positive attitude toward change even when these strategies smack of rigidity, formality, and bureaucratic authoritarianism. Time may also be a factor mandating the directive approach, since participative change is generally a slower process.

Figure 14–5 shows that the impetus for change comes from opposite directions in participative and directive change. That is, a participative change begins with the acquisition of knowledge and an attitude adjustment of individuals leading to altered group behavior. A directive change alters group behavior first in the expectation that the attitudes and knowledge of individuals will be changed accordingly.

STRATEGIES TO PROMOTE ACCEPTANCE OF CHANGE

Since every firm has a unique environment, appropriate techniques to promote acceptance of change and to ease the throes of conversion to new systems will vary from one organization to another. Common techniques to facilitate technological assimilation include:

- Conduct pilot study to determine impact of change.
- Assign responsibility for change to upper-level managers who possess the organizational power to legitimize change and assign agents to implement change.
- Identify individuals in the organization who must learn new behaviors, skills, or knowledge because of the change.
- Institute educational programs to provide employees with needed behaviors, skills, and knowledge.
- Involve employees in the development of new systems.
- Open up lines of communication between employees and management. For example, provide forums where employees can voice their concerns about new technologies.
- Publicize information regarding systems changes.
- Pace conversion to allow a readjustment period to new systems.
- Implement new systems in modules.
- Alter job titles to reflect increased responsibility.
- Reward ideas that will improve throughput.
- Document standards so that new procedures are easy to learn and reference.
- Clearly establish in advance the demarcations of authority that will exist following changeover.
- Upgrade the work environment following change, incorporating recommendations of human factor studies.
- Show sympathy and be receptive to complaints following conversion.
- Conduct orientation sessions.
- Arrange job transfers.
- Call a hiring freeze until all displaced personnel are reassigned.
- Provide job counseling.
- Offer separation pay.
- Organize group therapy.
- Initiate morale-boosting activities, such as a company newsletter and parties.

The key to success with these techniques lies in management's ability to demonstrate support and sympathy for employees adversely affected by the change and to show understanding when the disruption and dislocation caused by change produce anxiety and tension even among those not directly involved in the conversion. Management's skill in handling interpersonal relationships largely determines whether a firm can absorb technological advances in the field of computing.

Here is an example of what can happen when the introduction of new technology takes place without explaining the implications of the change to employees. One firm developing a computerized information system announced that installation would involve a reduction in the number of employees but failed to identify which individuals would be displaced. Fearing loss of work, 40 percent of the company resigned to seek secure employment. Many who left the firm were in positions that would have been unaffected by the change, and others left whose skills were vitally needed to run the new system. At a time when competent employees were sorely needed, the firm lost some of its best workers and was left with deadwood, persons with poor qualifications and hence little job mobility, to handle systems conversion.

RESISTANCE AMONG COMPUTER PROFESSIONALS

Before concluding this chapter, one other source of resistance should be discussed. Employees with no background in computing are not the only ones in a firm to resist the fast pace of information technology. Data processing professionals, like nontechnical workers, fear unemployment and powerlessness as advances in computer technology foster change in their work assignments.

For example, end-user computing and distributed data processing, which transfer responsibility to users for the operation and administration of computing resources, are often viewed with alarm by computer personnel. (End-user computing and distributed data processing are treated at length in Chapters 16 and 17.) Computer specialists claim that unauthorized and incompatible files will spring up, security will be lax, and applications will be ineffective and inefficient, all of which they will be blamed for. The realization that other employees can now interact with computers without the intermediary of the computer center is evidence that computing is no longer an exclusive club, that status and power have been lost. This helps explain some of the resistance to information technology that is found within the computer profession itself.

The same types of strategies are needed to promote acceptance of change in computer departments as in other departments of the firm. In general, resistance is short lived once data processing people realize that their jobs are not in jeopardy and that computing advances relieve them of many of the tedious duties associated with processing, freeing them for more challenging, exciting management information systems work.

SUMMING UP

In computing, information systems are commonly redeveloped every four to six years. New systems may affect the firm's organizational

Figure 14–6   **Responses to change over time**

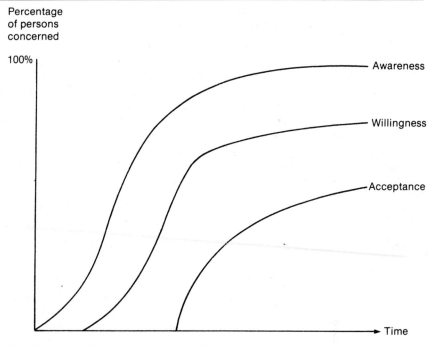

Note: The shapes of the curves (the starting point, slope gradient, and time horizon) will vary with
    a.   The complexity of technological change being implemented.
    b.   Education, training and communication (will especially affect awareness curve).
    c.   Strategies of change (will affect willigness and acceptance curves).

structure and require the forging of new interpersonal relationships among technical personnel, users, data providers, and clients. Resistance is an inevitable part of the change process. To prevent escalation of costs, disrupted production schedules, and lowered morale, change must be carefully planned, implemented, and controlled.

Management of change is more than merely supporting and sympathizing with workers adversely affected by new systems. Change agents should take an active role in systems development to ensure that human factors are incorporated in the design and implementation of proposed systems. They must help establish a work environment receptive to change, ready to "change with change so that when change comes, there will be no change."[2]

Figure 14–6 illustrates how people respond to change over time in terms of awareness, willingness and acceptance. Management can alter

[2]Advice given to the old patrician uncle at a time when Garibaldi's armies are overthrowing the old Sicilian order, in Giuseppe Lampedusa, *The Leopard.*

the starting point and gradient of the slopes of the curves by policies that create an atmosphere fostering change. The object of managing change is to shift the curves upward and to the left: that is, to increase awareness, willingness, and acceptance and to reduce the time it takes for employees to demonstrate these attributes. Orientation sessions, retraining programs, and modular conversion are examples of techniques that predispose employees to acceptance of technological innovations in computing. A major goal of these and other change strategies is to humanize computer systems, to make them friendlier and easy to use, and to ensure that no employee perceives computers as an economic or social threat.

CASE: WHAT'S HOLDING UP TELECOMMUTING?

The prophecy by futurists that 10 million information workers will be working, principally out of their homes, as telecommuters by the year 1990 seems unlikely to be fulfilled. In 1986, even the most liberal surveys reported only an estimated 50,000 telecommuters in the work force.

Lack of information technology to support telecommuting is not at fault. We now have advanced modems for direct-dial telephone connections and equipment for high-speed digital transmissions. In addition, telecommunications carriers like AT&T, MCI, ITT and others provide high-tech, low-cost network services.

It is the human element that is slowing growth in telecommuting. For example, many workers who have tried working out of their homes have had negative experiences. Here are some typical reactions:

> My professional and home life has become so intertwined that I can never get away from my work.

> I gained 60 pounds. My terminal was too close to the refrigerator.

> I feel isolated working at home. There is no incentive to work hard, no sense of personal accomplishment, no social contact, no feeling that I am part of a team.

> Everyone interrupts me—the dog, the kids, the mailman, the neighbors, even my spouse, who knows better. I'm just too available.

> There have been no raises, no promotions since I've had a home office. I'm afraid that I'm jeopardizing career advancement by being a teleworker.

> I'm getting claustrophobia (we simply lack the space), and my wife doesn't want me home during working hours.

A number of legal and economic considerations have given second thoughts about telecommuting to employers as well. The safety of expensive equipment kept at home is an issue. Who is liable if thieves steal a terminal from a home office? Privacy and security of data are also concerns.

Questions

1. Do you think that resistance to change is the reason why there is no "mad rush" toward telecommuting? Give your reasons.
2. Why might an employee resist telecommuting? For what reasons might an employer resist telecommuting?
3. What steps would you take to win the support of employees for a telecommuting program?

STUDY KEYS

Change	**Human factors**
Directive change	**Participative change**
Ergonomics	**Resistance**
Human engineering	

DISCUSSION QUESTIONS

1. Resistance to change resulting from the introduction of computer technology is not unusual and should be expected when implementing new information systems. Comment.
2. In a computing environment, resistance may occur not only when a change is first introduced but throughout the life of a system. Comment, and explain the reasons why.
3. Will the same types of resistance to computer applications be found in a bank, manufacturing plant, government office, warehouse, and retail outlet? Explain.
4. Will resistance differ in:
   a. Old and young employees?
   b. Skilled and unskilled workers?
   c. Management and workers?
   d. Top management and operational management?
   e. Small and large organizations?
      Explain.
5. A project that will displace 30 employees is kept secret until it is ready to be implemented. Comment on the ethical implications of such a strategy.

6. How is the management of change in a computer environment different from change in another technological environment, such as factory automation? Will resistance be of a different nature and magnitude?

7. How should strategies of change differ in the following situations?
   a. Implementation of a functional application.
   b. Implementation of an integrated system.
   c. Implementation of computer-aided design.
   d. Implementation of computer-assisted manufacturing.
   e. Implementation of a data base management system.
   f. Implementation of a network application.
   g. Implementation of a distributed processing environment.
   h. A change from decentralized to centralized computing.

8. Under what circumstances would you approach human resistance on an individual level rather than a group level?

9. Is the problem of management of change in computer systems going to become easier because of experience or harder because systems are becoming more complex? Explain.

10. In the future, we may have:
    a. Automated offices.
    b. Home computers connected to offices, with work done at home.
    c. Robot-driven factories.
    d. Cashless businesses and teleshopping.
    e. Telemail and telenewspapers.
    f. A wired city.
    g. Intelligent management information systems with artificial intelligence capabilities.
    In each of these cases, what unique problems of resistance should be expected? How would you plan to minimize adverse human factor effects?

11. Where should responsibility for human factors lie? With the vendor, analyst, or users?

12. What variables are important in anticipating, measuring, and dealing with resistance to organizational change?

13. Why do some computer professionals resist advances in information technology?

SELECTED ANNOTATED BIBLIOGRAPHY

Conner, Daryl. "Making Change." Computerworld, vol. 19, no. 42 (October 14, 1985), pp. ID/27–34.
    According to the author, it is not enough to design a new system and install new machines. Management must also create the environment for change that makes new technologies work. Ways to do this are described.

DeSanctis, Geraldine, and James F. Courtney. "Toward Friendly User MIS Implementation." Communications of the ACM, vol. 26, no. 10 (October 1983), pp. 732–38.

The authors advise readers how to lessen resistance to a computerized management information system. They argue that it is not enough to have a friendly technology to reduce resistance. One needs planned organizational change, survey feedback, group diagnostic meetings, communications training, and training labs as well.

Guarnieri, Harold, and Elizabeth Guarnieri. "The Psycho-Computer Syndrome." *Computerworld: Extra*, vol. 16 (November 17, 1982), pp. 11–15.
The eight stages from resistance to acceptance of change are identified and discussed.

Keen, Peter G. W. "Introducing Change." *Computerworld: Office Automation*, vol. 16 (September 28, 1982), pp. 10–13.
Technical personnel often lack awareness of the importance of nontechnical issues such as resistance. Ways of responding to resistance are explored.

Kotter, John P., and Leonard A. Schlesinger. "Choosing Strategies for Change." *Harvard Business Review*, vol. 57, no. 2 (March–April 1979), pp. 229–67.
An excellent article on the causes of resistance, and strategies for overcoming it.

"The Management of Change." *EDP Performance Review*, vol. 10, no. 11 (November 1982), pp. 1–7.
Many computer environments have constant change. Management must take explicit action to control such change. Otherwise, the organization will be exposed to and suffer from excessive errors, poor reliability, reduced productivity, and high user dissatisfaction and unhappiness.

Schneiderman, Ben. *Designing the User Interface*. Reading, Mass.: Addison-Wesley, 1987, 448 pp.
The author has written extensively on human-machine problems and interfaces. The book discusses ways of improving computer interfaces and thereby making computer systems more user friendly and reducing user resistance.

Tomeski, Edward A., and Harold Lazarus. *People-Oriented Computer Systems*. New York: Van Nostrand Reinhold, 1975, 229 pp.
The authors suggest that resistance is a function of rapid technological change and the limited capacity of humans to absorb change. They recommend that social as well as technical and economic factors should be taken into consideration when introducing and using computer technology.

Yarberry, William A. "Auditing the Change Control System." *EDPACS*, vol. 11, no. 6 (June 1984), pp. 1–5.
The control of change can add to an organization's security. Audit trails, quality assurance, and other control measures are discussed.

Zaltman, Gerald, and Robert Duncan. *Strategies for Planned Change*. New York: John Wiley & Sons, 1976, 404 pp.
This book is based on extensive interviews with over 75 professional change agents. The change to computer systems is discussed, as well as organizational change and innovation diffusion. Among the issues presented are planning change, issues of resistance to change, social problems, and ethical dilemmas resulting from change.

PART FIVE

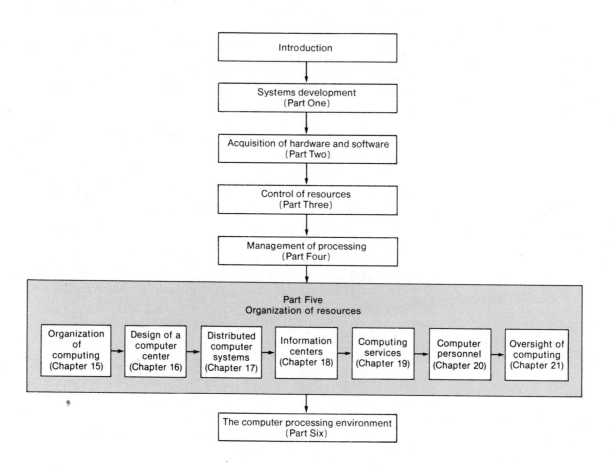

Introduction

Systems development
(Part One)

Acquisition of hardware and software
(Part Two)

Control of resources
(Part Three)

Management of processing
(Part Four)

Part Five
Organization of resources

Organization
of
computing
(Chapter 15)

Design of a
computer
center
(Chapter 16)

Distributed
computer
systems
(Chapter 17)

Information
centers
(Chapter 18)

Computing
services
(Chapter 19)

Computer
personnel
(Chapter 20)

Oversight of
computing
(Chapter 21)

The computer processing environment
(Part Six)

ORGANIZATION OF RESOURCES

Part Five describes how a firm organizes its computing resources. In Chapter 15, the opening chapter in this part, topics discussed include the location of computer departments within a firm's organizational hierarchy and problems of communication between computer departments, corporate management, and users.

Large computer systems are usually located in a computer center. The design of such a center is discussed in Chapter 16. Sometimes, computer resources (equipment and people) are located in dispersed sites, with hardware connected in a network. A mode of processing that uses such facilities is called distributed data processing, the subject of Chapter 17.

Still another mode of processing is end-user processing in which people who use computer output, many of whom have little or no data processing background, manage their own computers, such as stand-alone micros. Because these users often need advice and guidance from data processing professionals, many firms are establishing information centers to provide such services, as explained in Chapter 18.

Chapter 19 deals with service organizations that can supplement in-house computer resources. Considered are consultants, vendors, facilities management, service bureaus, remote processing, and utilities. Chapter 20 focuses on in-house computer staffing, job design, hiring, and turnover. Finally, Chapter 21 describes the role of management and steering committees in the oversight of computing.

Part Five includes a discussion of the organization of resources for both internal and external processing.

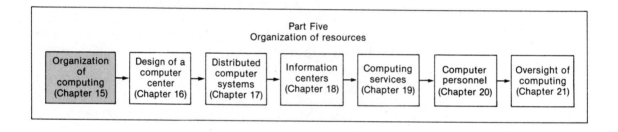

Part Five
Organization of resources

| Organization of computing (Chapter 15) | Design of a computer center (Chapter 16) | Distributed computer systems (Chapter 17) | Information centers (Chapter 18) | Computing services (Chapter 19) | Computer personnel (Chapter 20) | Oversight of computing (Chapter 21) |

CHAPTER 15

Organization of computing

You can't sit on the lid of progress.
If you do, you will be blown to pieces.

Henry Kaiser

Chapter 15 traces the organization of computing from the early days, when computer facilities were under the auspices of subdepartmental units, to the mix of processing locations commonly found in corporations today. The chapter describes a sample organizational structure in which several departments deliver information services and discusses problems of end-user computing.

Most organizations still retain an EDP (electronic data processing) department—sometimes called an MIS (management information system) center, EDP center, information processing center, or some similar name. This department may be assigned responsibility for planning and control of processing, maintenance, systems development, and applications. How EDP departments are organized for these purposes is also addressed here.

Problems of communication between data processing management and corporate executives are considered in this chapter, as well as sources of conflict between data processing technicians and users. Although the changing nature of responsibility of computer departments over time has kept these relationships in a constant state of flux, a number of solutions are offered for improving harmony between computer personnel, users, and corporate management.

LOCATION WITHIN ORGANIZATIONAL HIERARCHY

Many locations for a computer department are possible within the organizational structure of a firm. Six alternatives are shown in Figure 15–1.

359

Figure 15–1   **Alternative locations of EDP within a firm's organizational structure**

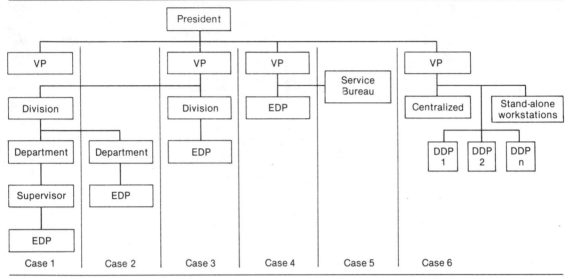

*Distributed data processing.

    When computing was in its infancy and computer applications were limited to basic data processing, EDP was commonly a subdepartmental unit. (Case 1 in Figure 15–1.) A company might have several computers located in dispersed departments, with no centralized authority to co-ordinate their activities. Data processed in this manner was slow to reach middle and top management and frequently failed to provide the information needed for decision making. In addition, the scarcity of qualified personnel meant that such centers were often poorly run.

    When more resources were devoted to computing and applications became diversified, EDP rose in the organizational hierarchy of most firms. This placed EDP personnel directly under a department head (Case 2) or a division chief (Case 3).

    Then, as the need for expensive data processing resources grew and applications extended to all functional areas, sharing of data and equipment across division lines was initiated to cut costs. This gave impetus to **centralized data processing,** the establishment of a single computer department reporting directly to top management (Case 4). Planning, computer operations, administration, and data base management were consolidated. Common data bases were established to be shared by analysts, programmers, and users. The expectation was that costs would drop. (Indeed, studies showed that a single large installation was less expensive to run than small dispersed centers.) It was also expected that information processing would be more responsive to management

needs than formerly, that the delivery speed of information would increase, that redundancy in processing and files would be eliminated,
and that security and control of information would be tightened.

Unfortunately, these expectations were not all realized. Lack of communication between users and analysts continued under centralization.
Users resented the hours required to justify and document requests for
service and felt isolated from computing facilities. They complained
that analysts were unresponsive to their needs. Analysts, in turn, chafed
at the criticism. They believed that the length of time required for
systems development was simply not understood by users. What's more,
the bureaucracy of centralization was often inept at mediating conflicting interests.

In spite of all these problems, centralized computing is the organizational structure in many firms today. To supplement internal computing capacity, firms may contract jobs with a service bureau as well
(Case 5).

In recent years, a large number of firms, disenchanted with centralized computer centers, have once again turned to **decentralized processing** (Case 6). A number of technological advances have made this
an attractive option. Computers have increased their power and dropped
dramatically in price. Today, stand-alone minis that users can operate
themselves are within budget range of many departments. Microcomputers, which provide the processing capability formerly offered by
much larger machines, can be placed on the desktops of employees in
all functional areas at low cost. This has led to **end-user computing**
(processing by noncomputer professionals). To train end-users in computer concepts, the mechanics of running specific packages, and how
to develop custom applications, more and more organizations are establishing information centers (a subject discussed in Chapter 18).

Furthermore, advances in networking and data base management
have made **distributed data processing (DDP)** an expeditious mode of
processing. Employees can access the computing power of distant computers by using terminals connected by telecommunications with the
far-off CPUs. The argument is now advanced that users are better served
and applications more easily implemented and maintained under DDP.

Figure 15–2 is a closer look at one configuration for distributed data
processing. Personnel are still needed at the corporate center to administer overall control of data processing. For example, dispersed sites
are counseled and coordinated from the center to ensure equipment
compatibility and to minimize duplication of effort. Control over budgets and auditing procedures is also still centralized, with headquarters
responsible for developing and enforcing performance standards for
equipment, software, and personnel at all DDP locations.

But under DDP, local systems development and operations are the
responsibility of managers at remote sites. These managers also make

Figure 15–2   **Sample DDP configuration**

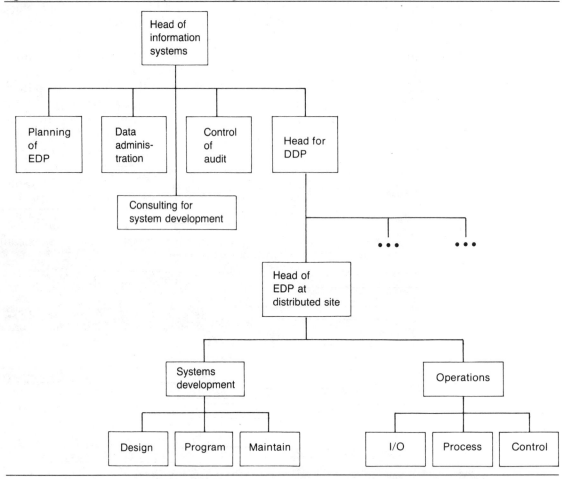

acquisition decisions, establish development priorities, and manage the
local data base. Firms are learning that one advantage to the distribution
of data files is that access control is easier to administer at small processing sites. In addition, the potential loss from fire or sabotage is
minimized when data files are not all stored in one place. However,
DDP is vulnerable to wiretapping and other transmission penetrations,
so security remains an issue.

To centralize or distribute processing is not an either/or proposition.
As shown in Table 15–1, a variety of combinations is possible. Alternative 4 has become increasingly popular in recent years. It allows
operations and developmental activities to take place under local control, but planning and data base control are centralized. Because of the
importance of DDP as a processing mode, this text includes an entire
chapter on the subject (Chapter 17).

Table 15–1 **Some alternative centralization-decentralization combinations**

Alternative	Development personnel	Equipment and operation	Development activities	Data base	Planning
1	C*	C	C	C	C
2	D†	C	C	C	C
3	D	D	C	C	C
4	D	D	D	C	C

*C = Centralized.
†D = Decentralized

PROBLEMS ASSOCIATED WITH END–USER COMPUTING

It is predicted that by 1990, 50 percent of the computer users will generate information without calling upon the services of computer professionals. They will access a distant mainframe through telecommunications or utilize stand-alone minis or micros, as described in the preceding section. They will purchase packages or write their own software instead of requesting systems development by their company's EDP department. Already, large numbers of employees belong to this category. They apply information technology to their jobs without the intermediary of trained data processing personnel, although most have no formal training in computer science.

In the effort to distinguish such users of computer resources from computer professionals, the term *end-user* has been coined. Not only is the name poorly chosen but agreement on its definition is lacking. Usually the term is applied to noncomputer professionals who design, program, purchase, and/or operate their own applications.

End-user computing is a relatively new phenomenon, attributed to recent advances in information technology that make modern computers easy to use, program, and administer. Corporate management has a responsibility to carefully plan for the expanded, productive use of end-user computing tools.

A number of risks associated with end-user computing can readily be identified:[1]

- Risks related to problem analysis. In developing applications, end-users may proceed without adequate problem specification and end up solving the wrong problem.
- Development risks. Persons who do not have systems development training and experience are more susceptible to modeling errors. They may fail to apply documentation standards and to test their solutions.

[1]The discussion that follows is based on Maryam Alavi and Ira R. Weiss, "Managing the Risks Associated with End-User Computing," *Journal of Management Information Systems*, vol. 1 (Winter 1985–86), pp. 5–20.

- Redundancy. End-users may spend time and effort developing applications that have already been developed.
- Unprofitable expenditure of time and effort. It is questionable whether people with professional skills should spend time developing applications rather than concentrating on their area of expertise.
- Waste of computing resources. End-users may be unaware of underlying operational costs as well as hardware/software costs. Without budgetary restraints, their use of computing resources may be uneconomical.
- Threat to data privacy and security. Physical access, custodianship controls, backup, and recovery issues are seldom addressed by end-users.
- Lack of computing efficiency and effectiveness. Few end-users establish procedures for performance evaluation of their systems or subject them to audits.
- Incompatibility of end-user tools and devices. Standards for acquisitions may be lacking.

The controls that need to be installed by management fall into three categories: preventive, detective, and corrective. The preventive category includes policies, procedures, and authorization structures to minimize the possibility that the risks will occur. For example, a cost-benefits analysis might be required before computer equipment is purchased by end-users; computer training might be mandatory; and rules on diskette access, storage, and backup might be promulgated. Detective controls might include procedures such as supervisory review of logs and performance. The changing of a password could be categorized as a corrective control.

This brief discussion points out that there are valid reasons to control end-user computing. What make controls difficult to install are the dispersed nature of end-user computing and the fact that control policies are often viewed as a frontal attack on employee/professional productivity. The organization and control of end-user computing are subjects widely discussed today in management circles and among data processing professionals. There is not yet consensus on how to resolve problems of organization and control, just recognition that problems exist.

INTEGRATION OF INFORMATION SERVICES

When information services are the responsibility of a number of departments, coordinating and integrating their activities becomes necessary. Many firms appoint a vice president of information services to oversee this integration. (The exact title of this position may vary from

Figure 15–3   **Horizontal integration under vice president for information services**

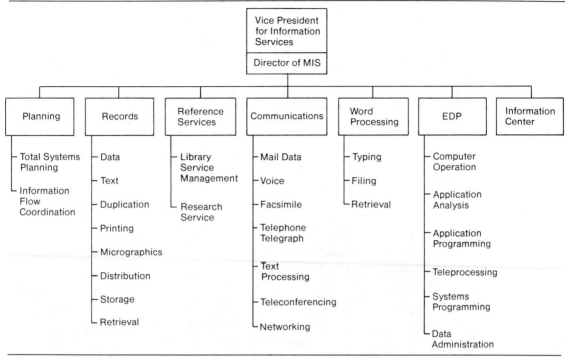

firm to firm. Vice president of information resource management is also frequently used.) Figure 15–3 is an example of an organizational structure for **integration of information services.** Of course, not all firms are organized in this manner. Some will combine recordkeeping with EDP; others will join word processing with reference services.

Whatever structure is chosen will be temporary at best, because advances in computer technology will undoubtedly lead to the development of new MIS applications in the future. Over time, it becomes necessary to restructure departments to incorporate new technology.

INTERNAL ORGANIZATION OF EDP DEPARTMENTS

Some companies structure computer development along project lines. Others are organized by function: systems development, operations, and support. Within each of these areas, personnel may be assigned to specific tasks. For example, as shown in Figure 15–4, systems development might be subdivided into analysis and design, programming, implementation, and maintenance units. The problem with such an organization is that personnel are too compartmentalized. Integration

Figure 15–4   **Functional organization for systems development**

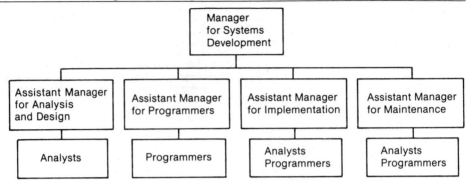

of development phases is impeded and development responsibility split, which often delays projects and leads to cost escalations.

In an alternative structure for the systems development function, development teams are organized to correspond with corporate departmental divisions, as illustrated in Figure 15–5. This configuration achieves integration of applications development and creates a close working relationship between analysts and clients, thereby helping to ensure that the EDP center is sensitive to users' needs. Problems with interface and split responsibility arise, however, when an integrated system under development crosses functional lines. Another disadvan-

Figure 15–5   **Systems development organization by functional departments under centralized EDP**

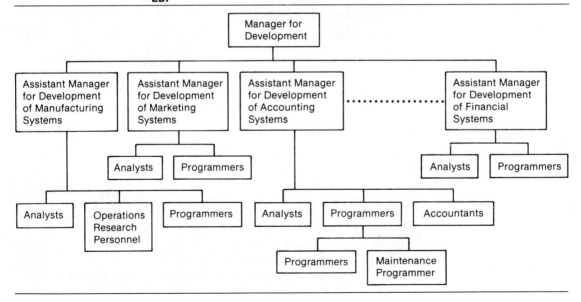

tage is that personnel become too specialized. For example, analysts and programmers assigned to the development of financial systems may find that they cannot assist marketing or manufacturing programmers because their expertise is too narrow.

DATA PROCESSING–CORPORATE MANAGEMENT RELATIONS

Organizational structure of computer departments is important because it establishes lines of communication between employees and management. Problems arise in every computing facility. Their resolution may well depend on harmony in the working **relations between data processing managers and top management,** which may in turn be a function of the level of communication between the two groups.

A major cause of misunderstandings is the background differences between data processing and corporate managers. The former generally have a technical background, the latter a business background. Table 15–2 shows that there is a wide divergence in how the two rank data

Table 15–2   **Courses needed by senior corporate executives and data processing executives in their jobs, ranked in order of importance**

Business management courses		Data processing courses	
Ranked by corporate presidents	*Ranked by data processing managers*	*Ranked by corporate executives*	*Ranked by data processing executives*
Economics	Decision making	Computer concepts	Computer concepts
Financial accounting	Problem solving	Using models	Data base concepts
Decision making	Business information	Data base concepts	Using models
Finance	systems	Project planning	Project planning
Writing	Writing	Estimating techniques	Systems analysis
Management psychology	Financial accounting	Introduction to	Introduction to
Problem solving	Management	teleprocessing	teleprocessing
Marketing	psychology	Systems analysis	Estimating techniques
Public speaking	Public speaking	Systems design	Systems design
Managerial accounting	Business policies	Programming concepts	Computer organization
Management theory	Managerial accounting	Data communications	Data communications
Business information	Management theory	Real-time systems	Real-time systems
systems	Finance	Computer organization	Programming concepts
Business policies	Statistics	Operating systems	Hardware configurations
Business cycles and	Economics	Hardware configurations	System simulation
forecasting	Business cycles and	System simulation	Operating systems
Statistics	forecasting	Algorithmic processes	Algorithmic processes
Operations research	Marketing	Computer systems	Computer systems
techniques	Principles of auditing	architecture	architecture
Theory of the firm	Operations research	FORTRAN	FORTRAN
Principles of auditing	techniques	COBOL	COBOL
	Theory of the firm	Assembler language	Assembler language

Source: Robert S. Hoberman, "The Billion-Dollar Chasm," *Computerworld*, vol. 14, no. 17 (April 28, 1980), p. 11.

processing and business management courses in relation to their jobs. No wonder the two groups often fail to view problems in the same light.

Another factor that affects the relationship between upper-echelon managers and data processing managers is attitude toward change. Corporate managers seek stability, whereas computer personnel are committed to change. Indeed, change and motion are viewed as constants in the field of computing. From an EDP manager's point of view, stability within change is a viable concept and not a contradiction of terms.

A divergence also exists in attitude toward the dissemination of information. Generally, corporate executives favor restrictions on the distribution of information, lest the information be misused. (The charge is often made that the real reason management wants information controlled is to keep unfavorable reports quiet). EDP personnel favor the free and wide distribution of information.

Friction between the two groups can often be attributed to the belief of computer personnel that corporate executives do not give them the recognition or status that is their due. Rarely are EDP managers included (as are other department heads) in key decisions on new products or budgets, although information processing can contribute analysis and decision support for such determinations. Too often, the road to other executive positions is blocked for computer managers, creating a dead-end career path: computer managers are seldom promoted to top managerial echelons of the firm, because corporate executives see them as computer technicians, disregarding their managerial skills.

Resentment against corporate management is further fueled by the manner by which the performance of EDP managers is commonly judged. The evaluation is based on quantitative measures (budget variances, for example) and general efficiency measures that poorly reflect important performance characteristics of EDP administration, according to the viewpoint of computer personnel. Moreover, corporate executives blame EDP management when embarrassing mistakes are made but rarely give those managers credit when the computer centers function well—at least, that is the perception of many persons in data processing. The belief of EDP managers that their services are unappreciated and undervalued is a source of much of the tension that exists in their relations with corporate management.

The first step in improving the working relationship between corporate executives and EDP managers is to determine the sources of friction. Only then can steps be taken to resolve misunderstandings. Although the action taken will depend on the nature of the problem, many companies look toward educational programs for answers. Presumably, an understanding of information processing on the part of corporate executives and an understanding of business management problems by EDP personnel will promote accord between the two groups.

Because it is easier and faster to train senior management about computers than for technicians to acquire the prerequisites for managing a firm, most companies provide in-house training programs on computer technology for high-level management, sponsoring group seminars or videotape programs acquired from consulting firms or software houses. Some firms release time for managers to attend educational programs in their home communities. Others organize pilot studies, demonstrations, and briefings. Another method of keeping management technically up-to-date is to circulate journals and pertinent literature.

All of these educational approaches attempt to smooth communication between corporate management and computer management. When the two groups use the same vocabulary and when corporate managers have enough background to understand computing problems, relations between the groups generally improve. Improved relations, in turn, can speed resolution of computer-related problems and raise employee morale, leading to higher productivity.

RELATIONS BETWEEN USER–EDP PERSONNEL

Another interaction that should be examined when considering how a computer department functions within the organizational structure of a firm is the **relationship between users and computer personnel.**

Unfortunately, most users (be they clerks or management) have a negative view of computer technicians, especially systems analysts and programmers. Users see such individuals as overzealous in changing existing procedures, disdainful of others (even of employees with years of experience in the firm), long on theory but short on common sense, and lacking in both humility and company loyalty. Computer personnel are also criticized for the impersonality of their reports, inability to relate to clientele, nonresponsiveness to inquiries, insensitivity to user desires, lack of functional involvement, and occasional dishonesty, such as the unauthorized sale of address lists or other information.

This long list of complaints makes all too evident the antagonism that is commonly directed toward computer specialists. Perhaps one factor contributing to this antagonism is that programmers and analysts have high job mobility. The rate with which they change jobs prevents them from forming deep interpersonal relationships with other corporate employees and gives them little time to improve their image.

On the other side of the coin, computer personnel complain that users often do not know what they want, fail to articulate their needs even when they do know, and keep changing their minds throughout systems development and implementation. Wouldn't it be unreasonable for a client to ask an architect to build a two-story building, then demand an additional story halfway through construction? Yet, the

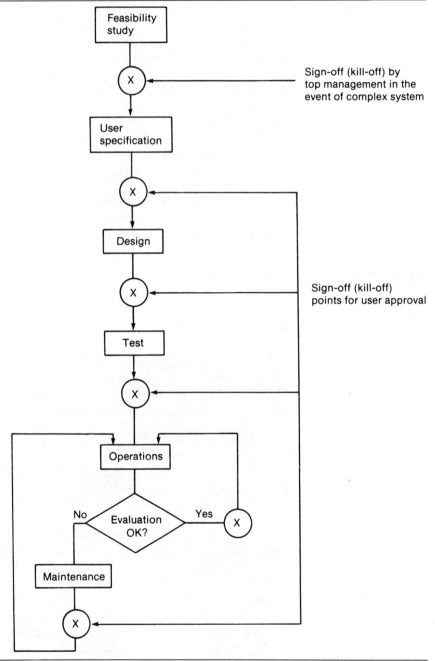

equivalent is commonly demanded of analysts and programmers during a systems development project, and the analysts and programmers get blamed for time/cost overruns that result.

One way of reducing friction between users and computer technicians is through educational programs. Such programs can teach users about computer technology and educate analysts about business management, so that each group understands the other's viewpoint and function. Another approach is to establish an ombudsman position to resolve or arbitrate complaints. Sometimes, development committees (such as a feasibility study group or project management group) mediate conflicts and provide interface between technicians and users.

A third approach to lessening friction during development is formal user approval of progress after specific stages of development. A **sign-off procedure** of this nature gives users a chance to monitor progress (and demand changes, if any are desired) when work is in progress and also protects the analyst from charges that the project, once completed, is not what was originally requested. Common sign-off locations (sometimes called kill-off points) are identified in Figure 15–6. Although sign-off procedures add to bureaucracy and delays, they help promote a harmonious working relationship between computer personnel and users.

Since problems in the operation and maintenance of newly developed systems can also cause friction between users and computer personnel, it is sometimes helpful to appoint a member of the development team to help implement new systems and to act as a liaison between the EDP department and users when things go wrong. Because of their familiarity with the new systems, such individuals can often trace the cause of problems quickly and recommend corrective action that will prevent a recurrence of problems.

Computing advances—nonprocedural languages, prototyping, software packages, applications generators, and other techniques—can help computer centers respond more quickly to users' requests for service. This helps to improve relationship between users and EDP departments. Furthermore, new technology encourages end-user computing, which reduces the need for interaction between computer personnel and users and, hence, lessens potential areas of discord.

The history of computing has been one of constant shifts in the relationship between EDP departments and users, as reflected in Figure 15–7. For example, note how responsibility for the data base has switched back and forth. Originally, local data was kept by users (1950–60). With the centralization of EDP and the advent of common data bases, data processing departments assumed jurisdiction over data (1960–75). Today's minis enable local sites to manage local data, while distributed data processing technology permits users to control replicated or seg-

Figure 15–7   **Changing responsibilities of users and computer departments**

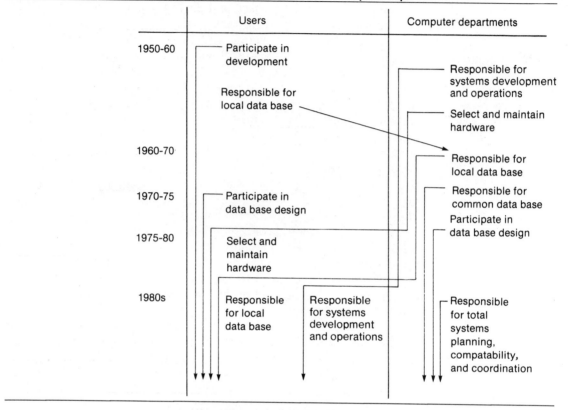

mented parts of the common data base as well. So again, responsibility
for data is reverting back to the user (since 1975).

Whenever changes in the responsibilities of computer professionals
occur, reorganization of computer departments is triggered. Such reorganizations keep relationships between users and computer personnel in a continual state of flux. Technological advances will certainly
bring still other organizational changes to computer departments in the
future, so one can expect that interaction between users and computer
personnel will always be volatile.

SUMMING UP

Describing where computer departments fit into a firm's organizational schema is no simple task, because technological advances have

changed the nature of EDP responsibilities over time and, as a consequence, altered the location of computer centers within the hierarchy of firms. In the 1950s, computers were generally found in subdepartmental units wherever data processing was needed. As more resources were allocated to computing, centralization was favored in order to take advantage of economies of scale and to ensure better integration and management of computer facilities. Today, distributed data processing is becoming popular, with local autonomy over development activities and operations, and centralization for planning, standards, and management of common systems. In fact, available today for the delivery of information services are a number of options, or combinations of options, including:

- Large, online, interactive, data base systems that operate under the direction of computer professionals.
- User-operated, stand-alone minicomputers.
- Distributed processing.
- Information centers, where computer staff train and support users in accessing, analyzing, and generating the information they need.
- Desktop microcomputers.

The problem for corporate managers is to choose and implement the computer systems that best match user requirements. In doing so, they alter the traditional relationship of EDP personnel with corporate management and users and create organizational problems and tensions that require resolution.

The position of computer departments within the organization is still evolving. Unfortunately, employee frustration and anger over the expanding role of computers is commonly vented on EDP personnel, who have demonstrated little sympathy for the nontechnician in the past, thereby exacerbating tensions. This chapter identifies many sources of misunderstandings and suggests ways to improve relations between computer personnel and management/users, such as educational programs, sign-off procedures, ombudsmen, or interface committees that provide a forum for airing problems and reaching collective decisions.

Crises in computing need not embitter relationships among employees of a firm. It has been noted that the Chinese expression for "crisis" has two characters. The first represents danger, the other opportunity.

CASE: ORGANIZATION OF COMPUTING AT THE COMMERCE DEPARTMENT

The chart below illustrates how information resources are organized by the U.S. government's Commerce Department.

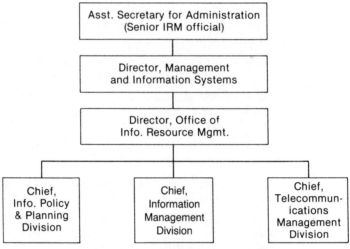

*Information Resources Management.

The senior official in charge of information resources is the Assistant Secretary for Administration. But daily operations are handled by the director of the Office of Information Resources Management, who reports to the director of Management and Information Systems.

Three divisions are responsible for information-related projects:

Information Policy and Planning Division.   All acquisitions over $1 million are reviewed by this division. It is also responsible for developing the Commerce Department's information technology plan, reviewing operating plans, and preparing budget requests. In addition, the division helps to formulate policy with regard to use of information resources.

Information Management Division.   This division administers the department's review program with regard to information resource management. For example, the division chief ensures that operating units comply with the government's Office of Management and Budget (OMB)

Source: "Commerce Has Full Schedule of Info-Related Projects," *Government Computer News,* March 28, 1986, p. 21.

guidelines. One recent project of the division has been to help bureaus eliminate unnecessary and duplicate forms.

Telecommunications Management Division. To understand the work of this division, consider the following 1986 projects: to develop an automated system to track the department's telecommunications assets, to provide cryptographic communications security to departmental units, and to evaluate the department's telecommunications needs.

Questions

1. How do you evaluate the Commerce Department's organizational structure?
2. Much of the data that the Commerce Department handles is sensitive. For example, data on economic trends, if leaked, is the kind of "insider" information that can be used to unfair advantage in the stock market. Census Bureau information is also confidential. Does the organizational structure of the department reflect security concerns? Explain.
3. Under the Paperwork Reduction Act, the Major Information Systems Review Council was recently created to support the work of the Office of Information Resources Management. This council will serve as the coordinating body to monitor the development of the Commerce Department's major new information systems. Is this another example of government bureaucracy, or is such a council needed? Comment on the organizational problems that are characteristic of government.

STUDY KEYS

Centralized data processing

Decentralized processing

End-user computing

Distributed data processing (DDP)

Integration of information services

Organizational structure of computer departments

Relations between data processing managers and top management

Relationship between users and computer personnel

Sign-off procedure

DISCUSSION QUESTIONS

1. What are the central issues in the controversy between centralization and decentralization?

2. Does the decision to centralize or decentralize depend on:
   a. Firm size?
   b. Whether the firm is multinational?
   c. Whether the firm has branch offices?
3. What are the merits of locating a computer department under a:
   a. Vice president of finance?
   b. Department of accounting?
   c. Executive vice president?
4. Should the location of the computer department in an organization be a function of:
   a. Size of the computer department and its maturity.?
   b. Organization's size?
   c. Power politics of the organization?
   d. Industry of the organization?.
   e. Computer executive's personality?
5. What are the risks associated with end-user computing? How can these risks be resolved?
6. Comment on the following statement. End-user computing frees employees from channeling all processing requests through EDP personnel; this independence, the main benefit of end-user computing, would be lost if end-user processing controls were installed.
7. What organizational structure would you recommend for end-user computing?
8. Should the computer department be a staff or a line department? What conflicts arise in each case? What organizational structure would avoid or minimize these conflicts?
9. Would you recommend integration of all departments that provide information services? Explain.
10. Would you favor internal organization of a computer department along functional or project lines? Justify your choice.
11. What measures should be taken to foster a smooth working relationship between computer personnel and users?
12. How can understanding between corporate management and computer personnel be promoted?
13. Do you agree with the concept of an ombudsman as an arbitrator and facilitator between the frustrated user and the computing center? If so, what qualifications should the ombudsman have?
14. Do you believe that computer technology will soon make users totally independent of computer departments? Explain.
15. Are conflicts between corporate management and computer personnel based on differences in educational background? Or do differing attitudes and biases contribute to dissension? Explain.

SELECTED ANNOTATED BIBLIOGRAPHY

Alavi, Maryam, and Ira R. Weiss. "Managing the Risks Associated with End-User Computing." *Journal of Management Information Systems*, vol. 1 (Winter 1985–86), pp. 5–20.

End-user computing activities require well-defined control processes because of the risks involved. Risks associated with conception, design of applications, operations, and maintenance are described.

Beaver, Jennifer E. "Bend or Be Broken." *Computer Decisions*, vol. 16, no. 12 (December 1984), pp. 130–38.
Policies should be adopted that will blend end-users with MIS/DP professionals. Better interfaces, friendly software, and information centers will help.

Borovits, Israel. *Management of Computer Operations.* Englewood Cliffs, N.J.: Prentice-Hall, 1984, 296 pp.
Chapter 4, "Organizing the Data Processing Activity," deals with the subject of alternative patterns of organization for data processing, DP functions, and positions.

Karten, Naomi. "Surviving the PC Challenge Demands Vigorous Management Skills." *Data Management*, vol. 23, no. 9 (September 1985), pp. 14–18.
Management must plan strategies for training, applications development, and support for end-user computing.

Klein, Mark. "Information Politics." *Datamation*, vol. 31, no. 15 (August 1, 1985), pp. 87–92.
Computer processing, traditionally associated with technology, increasingly is becoming an arena of politics. Klein discusses the new role of users in computing and the reconfiguration of responsibilities, organization, and power that has taken place with regard to information services in organizations.

Koch, Donald L., and Dolores W. Steinhauser. "Changing the Corporate Culture." *Datamation*, vol. 29, no. 10 (October 1983), pp. 247–56.
The old corporate culture valued standardization, procedures, and machines. The new corporate culture thrives on creativity, individuality, and flexibility, thereby using people and computers to their greatest potential.

Licker, Paul S. "Breaking Down the Wall: MIS–User Job Rotation." *Journal of Information Systems*, vol. 2 (Spring 1985), pp. 10–16.
Licker suggests a well-designed job rotation program for better distribution of labor and to help technicians and users get more familiar with each other's viewpoints and problems. Job rotation breaks down the "we-they" syndrome and improves interaction between two otherwise antagonistic groups.

Owen, Darrell E. "IRM: Obstacles Toward Success." *Journal of Systems Management*, vol. 38, no. 4 (April 1987), pp. 16–18.
The main roadblocks to the maturity of IRM are the lack of organizational location, organizational support, and the right people.

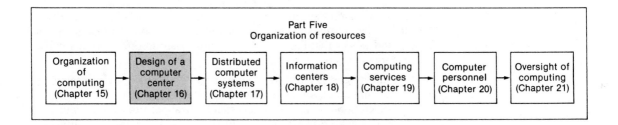

Part Five
Organization of resources

| Organization of computing (Chapter 15) | Design of a computer center (Chapter 16) | Distributed computer systems (Chapter 17) | Information centers (Chapter 18) | Computing services (Chapter 19) | Computer personnel (Chapter 20) | Oversight of computing (Chapter 21) |

CHAPTER 16

Design of a computer center

*When possible make the decisions now, even
if action is in the future. A reviewed
decision usually is better than one reached
at the last moment.*

William B. Given, Jr.

Computer departments, described in the preceding chapter, are responsible for computer systems that require the services of data processing professionals for their operation. Such systems are housed in a facility called a **computer center.** (The names data center, EDP center, and information processing center are also commonly used.) Mainframes, minis, communications equipment, printers, plotters, and other peripherals will be located there. This chapter describes how a computer center is planned, how the layout of the center is designed, and what problems must be resolved regarding site preparation before hardware is actually installed.

Not all of the computers in modern corporations are placed in a centralized computer center. Computer equipment may be located in functional departments but linked by telecommunications to the center, a processing mode called distributed data processing (discussed in Chapter 17). In addition, employees may have stand-alone microcomputers on their desks and manage their own computing resources.

Both of these modes of operation are relatively recent. Prior to the late 1970s, computer centers were the focus of computing activity; even today, the bulk of the information generated by many corporations is processed by computer centers. This explains the ordering of the chapters in this part of the book. We first address the problems of computer center organization and design, then consider alternative modes of processing.

PLANNING OVERVIEW FOR A COMPUTER CENTER

A new computer center—or one that is being relocated, renovated, or expanded—requires meticulous planning. The amount of floor space required will depend on the equipment to be installed, which in turn depends on the projected workload of the center. That is why the design of a computer center begins with **capacity planning** (Box 1 in Figure 16–1). Resource needs and area requirements are determined for both current and future information requirements. Next, the site is selected (2) and planning takes place for the physical layout of the center (3) and the room layout (4). Site preparation (5) will include consideration of special environmental support facilities such as air-conditioning, electrical power, and security measures. Each of these design stages is discussed. (Planning also includes the selection and acquisition of computing resources, the subject of Chapters 5 and 6.)

A full-time **project manager** is often needed to oversee a computer center overhaul or a new construction. This person should have 6 to 10 years of experience operating data centers and also have a technical background. The manager needs a thorough understanding of the operational aspects of a computer center, good project management skills,

---

Figure 16–1   **Planning process for a computer center**

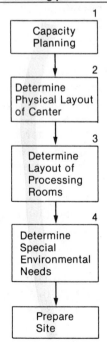

and some knowledge of structural problems that may be encountered in site preparation.

One of the first duties of a project manager, and one of the most critical to project success, is to identify personnel needed to support the project. Cooperation and assistance from data processing personnel who will work in the new center and from representatives of functional departments to be served by the center will be required when plans for the center are being formulated. The project manager will also need the expertise of electrical and mechanical engineers, vendors of computer equipment, persons from the local telephone company, an interior designer/architect, a lighting consultant, an acoustical consultant, a security specialist, a fire control consultant, insurance staff members, a telecommunications expert, and someone knowledgeable about local building codes. The role of each of these experts will become apparent as this chapter progresses and planning stages are discussed.

The services of many people are needed when a computer center, especially a large one, is designed. It is up to the project manager to make design decisions based on the recommendations of these experts and to oversee the actual construction and occupancy of the computer center in accordance with blueprints based on these decisions. What's more, the project manager must make sure that the construction does not interfere with the ongoing delivery of information services and is completed within funding and time constraints.

CAPACITY PLANNING

Once a decision has been made by corporate management to build (or expand) a computer center and a project manager has been chosen, planning can begin. The objective of **capacity planning,** the first planning stage, is to determine an efficient mix of resources in order to achieve and then sustain the level of information services expected by corporate management for workloads in the future. Generally, planners can only project usage two or three years ahead with any degree of accuracy, although estimates may be made for a longer time horizon.

Capacity planners first study the work processes and information needs of employees and how computer technology is presently used on the job. Then they look ahead, anticipating problems and how they might be solved using the information technology of tomorrow. This requires an in-depth knowledge of technological trends, coupled with the ability to make forecasts based on current data, estimates, hunches, intuition, and experience. Capacity planners must also consider possible future organizational changes that may increase computing load: for example, a merger or acquisition of another firm.

Clearly, capacity planning is a risky proposition. If planners fail to project the future environment with accuracy, the corporation may either lack adequate resources and processing power to meet information requests in coming years or have excess unused capacity, a costly waste.

Collecting data on goals and objectives

Projections for future computer center requirements are based on the answers to a number of basic questions. One of these questions is: What goods or services does the company plan to produce in the future?

The answer can be found by studying the organization's long-range plan, which outlines business goals and objectives. Departmental strategic plans (including those of the data processing department) will likewise provide insights into the expected direction of the company. From this information, the capacity planner must estimate what information resources will be needed to accomplish stated goals.

A simple source of estimates is other organizations that have already placed similar goods and services on the marketplace. If this is not feasible, the planner must determine what business transactions will be involved in producing and marketing the new goods and services. By analyzing these transactions, the role of information processing to support the transactions can be ascertained. Once this role is known, the planner can then extrapolate hardware, software, and personnel needs.

Questionnaires and interviews with end-users are also useful ways of gathering data on information resource requirements for the future. Suppose an end-user states that an online system to handle inventory queries is high on the department's applications wish list. Knowing applications priorities, the planner can map out which support resources should be available: inout/output devices, memory, communication facilities, and so on.

Gathering data from a large number of end-users can be time consuming and costly. Fortunately, this is not necessary. Only a small proportion of workers account for a major portion of a computer center's workload. According to one rule of thumb, the ratio is 80 to 20: that is, 80 percent of the resources are used by 20 percent of the users. Capacity planners can identify employees who place heavy demands on information services and direct questions to these users. On the basis of the information collected, a projection of service demands for the entire user population can be made.

Another data source on which to base projections is historical records. However, caution is in order here: straight-line projections from historical data have proven notoriously inaccurate. There are simply too many variables that can cause a dramatic alteration in computer center use. For example:

▪ Learning of new skills or changed attitudes toward information technology by the work force.

- Hiring of persons who use information services heavily.
- Demand for or introduction of new hardware and software products as a result of technological advances.
- Demand for new types of information to meet the challenge of competitors.

Software tools are available to help in the data collection and analysis phase of the planning process. Programs can be purchased for the task of matching, merging, and validating data from several different sources. Other packages help in determining the amount of information resources that will be required by new applications. Also available are performance/capacity planning software packages and capacity planning graphics/reporting software packages.

Service-level expectations

Another question that the capacity planner must consider is what level of service the computer center should provide. Client departments perceive service in terms of reliability, ease of use, and response time. They generally will give planners range estimates of service requirements. For example, an end-user may state that a 3-second response time is desirable, a 5-second response time is adequate, and a 10-second response time is intolerable.

The ability of the center to meet service requirements will depend, in part, on the volume of service the center will have to deliver. That is why workloads must be forecast. Many capacity planners subdivide current workload into major processing subsystems, then ask "what if" questions, using analytical modeling software tools to help them make their forecasts. They take into account activity periods (during both day and year) in which the workload may peak, as well as periods of nominal activity. An important decision of the capacity planner is whether to provide computer resources to fulfill all requests for service during **peak time zones** or whether to allow some of the demand to spill into **shoulder zones** (contiguous nonpeak zones). Since it requires less computing capacity, a spillover decision is one way to cut down the amount of funding that must be spent for information resources.

One of the difficulties in making workload projections is that workloads tend to rise with increased capacity, a phenomenon sometimes called the **latent workload.** This occurs because departments may not depend on the computer center for their information needs when service is poor but become clients when service improves.

Preliminary configuration of resources

The design of the resource mix for a new computer center can begin once the information demands that will be placed on the new computer center have been identified. The first step is to evaluate existing processing capacity. How reliable is the delivery of information services at the present? How much data is currently being processed? Are re-

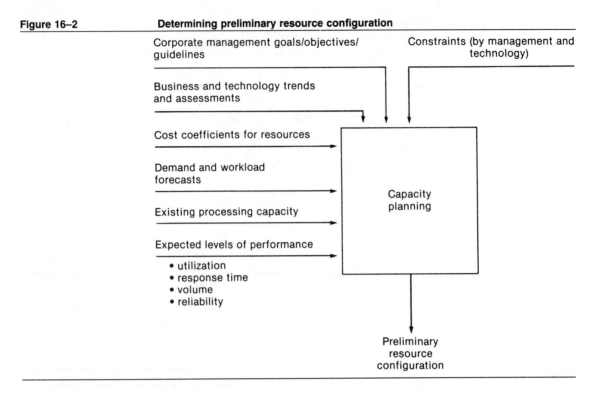

Figure 16–2   **Determining preliminary resource configuration**

sources on hand being used to full capacity? Could a reconfiguration of resources lead to a more effective utilization of facilities or personnel?

Next to be assessed are hardware and software in the marketplace, as well as products being readied for market introduction. Their features, limitations, and cost are examined, as are constraints imposed by management. How much money can be spent on the new computer facility? What is the time frame of the project? What will be the staff size and the qualifications of people working in the new center? What types of backup will be required? Note that planning issues faced by the project manager are similar to those facing a systems development team. That is, the configuration of information resources for a computer center will depend on technological, economic, financial, and organizational constraints similar to those that affect the design of new application systems.

Figure 16–2 summarizes the factors to be taken into consideration by the project manager determining the preliminary resource configuration for the new computer center.

Use of analytical and simulation models

Fortunately, software is on the market to assist planners in the evaluation of proposed **resource configurations.** For example, some programs will generate analytical standard reports on performance and service levels for given resource configurations. Others will make a technological assessment or financial analysis of a preliminary configuration. Some suggest configuration alternatives.

Simulation models can answer what-if questions, such as, "What if the demand for service of User B is increased by 100 percent?" The answer might be calculated in terms of the impact on other end-users with regard to average and maximum waiting times, length of queue, average and maximum response times, and so on. (ISERT and SCERT are models of this nature.) What-if questions might also be asked about a possible change in hardware or software resources: for example, what if a different model of a central processing unit (CPU) with different operating systems (or different peripherals) were used?

Contingency planning.   Simulation models are particularly helpful in **contingency planning**—planning for disaster or some abnormal shutdown of operations for an extended period of time. By asking what-if questions (for example, what if there were a power failure for six hours during a peak load period?), the planner can determine the effect on operations of an earthquake, flood, fire, bomb, or some other calamity, information that is needed in designing backup facilities for the center. (See Table 16–1 for a list of events that can cause confusion or havoc in a computer center.)

Consideration of **backup** is crucial at this planning stage because special equipment to warn against disaster (such as alarms, scanners,

Table 16–1	Potential calamities	
	Acts of God	*Other calamities*
	Dust storm	Collapse of structure
	Earthquake	Hardware operational faults
	Flood	Human errors, omissions,
	Hail	and negligence
	Hurricane	Industrial accidents and fires
	Intense cold weather	Mechanical failure
	Intense heat and/or humidity	Power failure
	Lightning	Software failure
	Rain	Telecommunications failure
	Snow	Utility (gas, water) failure
	Tidal waves	Arson
	Tornados	Bomb
	Volcanic eruptions	Holding hostage:
	Windstorms	Data
		Humans
		Programs
		Theft:
		Computer time
		Data
		Programs

or sensors) may require physical space within the center and funding from the center's budget. What's more, duplicate or supplementary resources placed in the center or in a separate facility may be essential in order to restore vital operations following a calamity. No corporation can protect itself from every possible disaster. In narrowing the field, in deciding what disasters are likely and what measures are most cost effective in protecting resources, simulation models are useful tools. They can also be used to calculate both the resources needed to restore vital operations and the cost of such recovery.

Usually, corporate management makes decisions regarding backup levels and policies. These decisions will be based on management's aversion to risk and a judgment on whether the cost of backup is worth the benefits. The responsibility of a project manager is to present contingency options to top management. It is important that backup strategies be decided before the resource configuration for the new computer center has been finalized, so that space for backup resources can be allocated and funds for their acquisition can be budgeted.

Analysis and consultation

Before finalizing the resource configuration of the new computer center, the project manager will analyze software results and consult with data processing professionals, future end-users, and corporate management.

Finalization of resource configuration

Sometimes, to avoid end-user disappointment or frustration should the plan require modification at a later date, no detailed disclosure is made of the finalized plan. More commonly, however, the **capacity plan** is publicly announced. This commits corporate management to the plan and makes the project manager accountable for its implementation.

Some organizations go a step further and formalize their commitment to the capacity plan with a **service-level agreement** (SLA), a document that guarantees users a given level of service in terms of transaction volumes and response times. The SLA may also specify the price structure for services. The advantage of this agreement is that end-users know what information services the center will deliver and planners know that they will not be accountable should end-users suddenly increase their service demands.

The most time-consuming and difficult stage of planning a computer center is capacity planning, the steps of which are reviewed in Figure 16–3. A capacity planner should keep a record of what scenarios are assumed, what information is collected, what planning tools are used, and what predictions are made. This record can guide future planners when the center needs further expansion. And should forecasts be off the mark, the record can be analyzed to determine what went wrong so that the mistakes won't be repeated.

Figure 16–3 **Stages in capacity planning**

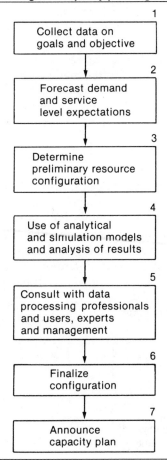

1
Collect data on
goals and objective

2
Forecast demand
and service
level expectations

3
Determine
preliminary resource
configuration

4
Use of analytical
and simulation models
and analysis of results

5
Consult with data
processing professionals
and users, experts
and management

6
Finalize
configuration

7
Announce
capacity plan

SITE SELECTION

Ideally, a decision regarding the location for a new computer center should follow capacity planning, so that adequate space will be allowed for current operations of the center and for projected growth. In companies building a new office facility that will include a computer center, the **site selection** team should include the project manager for the center to ensure that the special needs of the center are taken into consideration in the site decision. (For example, the desire of Shearson/American Express for a secure facility with controlled access led to the selection of a Lower Manhattan site large enough for a 10-story structure surrounded by considerable open space.)

Space allocation for the computer center within a new facility should be based on convenience of access for the users of the center and special construction requirements, such as floor load ratings, access to freight elevators, ceiling heights, and fire barriers. (More on computer center site preparation appears later in this chapter.) Here again, the expertise of the computer center project manager is invaluable. In practice, however, critical site decisions are often made without a computer specialist on the planning team. This can later lead to innumerable and costly problems in computer center construction.

FACILITY LAYOUT

The **layout** of a computer facility follows finalization of the resource configuration for the center. Figure 16–4 shows the layout of a typical small computer center, with rooms for job receipt, data conversion, library, job assembly, teleprocessing, CPUs and peripherals, output preparation and distribution, storage, and offices. In larger computer centers, more rooms for offices and support (such as rooms for vendors, customer engineers, or backup power) will be available.

Figure 16–4   **Layout of a small computer center**

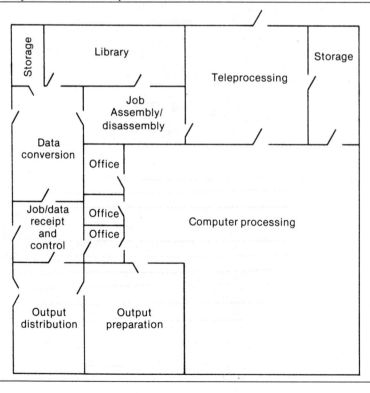

Figure 16–5   **Work flow in processing of a computer job**

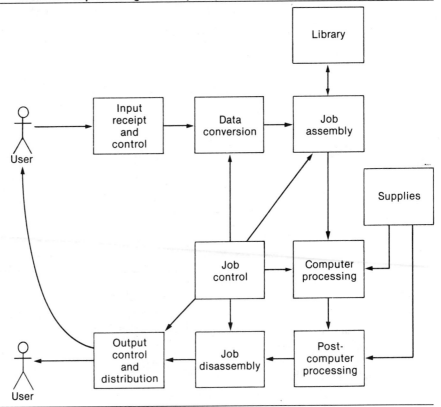

What decides the location of one room in relation to others? **Work flow.** Room placement is designed to facilitate the smooth and efficient movement of work from the time a processing job is received by the center to output distribution. For example, job assembly should take place near the room that houses processing hardware. Storage rooms for paper supplies should be in close proximity to the printers and plotters that use the paper. Although the offices for supervisory personnel should be near operations, access to these offices should not be through operational areas, to prevent the possibility of someone causing a malfunction by bumping into sensitive equipment.[1]

Figure 16–5 illustrates the order in which computer center tasks are performed. In general, this sequence of tasks dictates room assignments when computer centers are being designed. (Note that the computer center layout in Figure 16–4 is based on the workflow model in Figure 16–5.)

[1]For a good discussion of data center work flow, see Howard Schaeffer, *Data Center Operations* (Englewood Cliffs, N.J.: Prentice-Hall, 1981), pp. 190–230.

Sometimes, factors other than task sequence influence layout decisions. For example, the need for controlled access to CPUs may result in the placement of security checkpoints that interfere with a smooth, efficient work flow. Or the necessity of large outside doors for equipment delivery may dictate the location of the room in which processing takes place. The project manager may have to make compromises in workflow efficiency for a variety of reasons but will do so only with reluctance.

ROOM LAYOUT

After a decision is made regarding the arrangement of facilities in the computer center, the layout of individual rooms is planned. Here again, work flow is important. In equipment rooms, machines should be placed so that operators can move efficiently from one task to another. Vendors generally supply templates (like those in Figure 16–6) for their equipment, to be used when planning the location of machines. The shaded portion of each template in Figure 16–6 shows the machine in operation; the dotted and arced lines indicate the amount of space needed around each machine for opening equipment panels for maintenance and for ventilation and cooling.

SITE PREPARATION

A computer center has highly specific needs with regard to room construction, power supply, wiring, air-conditioning, fire protection, and security. Let us now turn to problems of this nature that confront a project manager in **site preparation.**

Room construction   The size and weight of computer hardware to be installed in the new center will dictate ceiling height, floor loading capacity, room dimensions, door size, and the location of loading docks. (Vendors will supply information on equipment requirements to the project manager.) Floors raised in height from 12 to 24 inches are standard in computer centers. This allows space for power cables, telecommunication lines, heavy-equipment supports, and air circulation under the floor and around pipes, wires, fire protection equipment, or whatever else needs to be installed there. In earthquake areas, sway bracing and flexible joints should be part of the room construction to ensure that equipment stays upright. Where flooding is a possibility, adequate drainage and sump pumps should be added at the time of construction.

In areas where radio frequency interference is a problem, the computer room will have to be shielded to suppress this interference. Even

Figure 16–6　　**Configuration of a computer room**

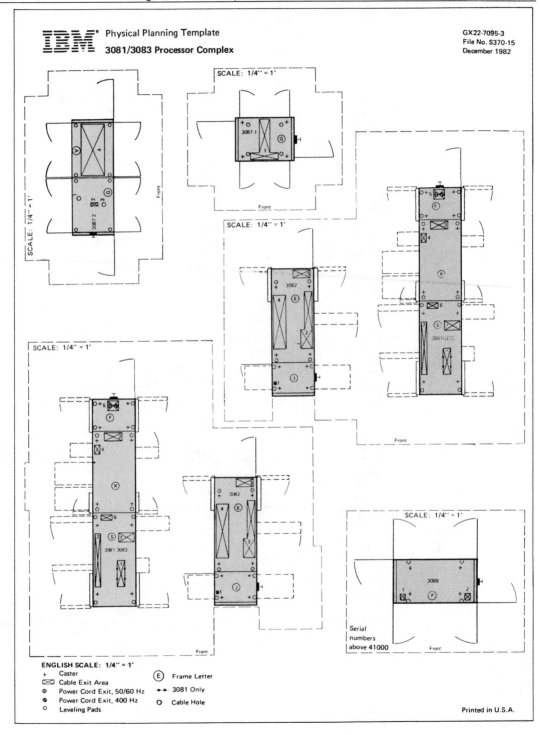

low to moderate levels of interference can cause read/write errors. High levels can be a hazard to operating personnel and equipment components. Shielding techniques include grounding computer equipment, using copper screens on windows, and installing equipment away from outside walls and windows.

Another special need is the inclusion of sound-absorbent materials in walls, ceilings, and room furnishings. Soundproofing will help reduce the noise level in operational areas and help isolate equipment noise from office areas and meeting rooms.

Chapter 9 described security precautions that should be taken at a computer center site, including restricted access through a single entrance, guard stations, locks, window grills, alarms, and so on. Many centers include three perimeter barriers: an outside wall or fence, interior walls, and locked cabinets and storage vaults within the center. Security is also taken into consideration in the design of manholes, door frames, ventilation ducts, and the roof.

A variety of detectors are available to protect facilities from intrusion. Some are triggered when an electric circuit is broken: for example, when a door is opened or when the lights are switched on. Others are activated when a light beam or laser beam is interrupted. Vibration monitors will detect a presence; ultrasonic and radar waves can be used to detect movement. Closed-circuit TV and time-lapse cameras, which snap frames at preset intervals, can assist security guards in surveillance of the center. Protective measures of this nature should be planned at the time the center is designed, not added later as an afterthought.

Power

The **power** requirements of a computer room will depend on the type and amount of equipment to be installed. Power needs for lighting, air-conditioning, heating, administrative office equipment, and future growth must also be taken into consideration.[2]

A backup power supply is commonly planned. There is always the danger that lightning or a storm will cause a blackout. A power outage for a period as short as four milliseconds can interrupt millions of computer operations and may result in equipment damage and data loss. Voltage problems, such as spikes, surges, dips, noise, or brownouts, can be equally destructive. If a computer center is to perform critical functions and must remain continuously online, then the purchase of a constant voltage transformer, motor generator, or uninterruptible power supply (UPS) is an answer. Some companies maintain large sets of batteries for power backup. Table 16–2 lists the causes and characteristics of common outage and voltage problems, describes their impact, and recommends solutions.

---

[2]For a guide to the power needs of computer sites, see Jesse J. Leaf, "Staying in Power," *Datamation*, vol. 32, no. 14 (July 15, 1986), pp. 67–72.

2

Table 16–2 | **Power disturbances in a computing center** | | | |

Type of problem	Characteristics	Cause	Impact	Solution
Spikes	Sudden rise in power	Lightning Heavy equipment switching	Burns electronic hardware Wipes out data	Voltage regulator
Surge	Increase in power	Opening or closing of switch Lightning	Burns electronic components	Suppressors Voltage regulator
Dip	Sudden drop in power	Voltage drops over distances	Erases data Causes CPU malfunction	Voltage regulator
Noise	High voltage High-frequency interference on power line	Lightning Ground faults Poor motor-brush contact Switching power supplies Heavy electrical equipment	System malfunction Data loss	Ultraisolation transformer
Brownout	Temporary reduction of voltage, ranging from 10 to 35 percent	Smoothing demand, causing 5–15 percent variation temporarily	Motors run hotter and slower on equipment designed for 10–15 percent variation	Backup system
Blackout	Complete loss of service	Storm Inadvertent shutoff	Data loss Computer damage	Standby power supply (SPS) or uninterrupted power supply (UPS) Backup system

Following a calculation of power requirements, the placement of power outlets and electrical conduits is decided. Floor sockets or roof sockets instead of wall sockets are useful. They allow the placement of equipment away from walls for ventilation without danger of employees tripping over and possibly damaging exposed cables. Electrical wiring can run under the floor when the room is designed with raised floors.

Air-conditioning   **Temperature regulation** of a computer center is a top priority because machine heat that is generated during computer operations can damage equipment and lead to the deterioration of tapes and disks. Excessive humidity can likewise cause damage. In designing a computer room, a project manager will consult vendors regarding the limits of heat and humidity for their products. It is the manager's responsibility to ensure that the site has adequate provision for air circulation, heating and cooling, and humidity control.[3]

Fire protection

In a computer center, **fire protection** is more than planning for fire extinguishers and sprinkler systems. It begins with room construction using fire-resistant materials, the erection of fire barriers such as fire doors, the placing of alarms, and the installation of fireproof vaults for the storage of critical records and documentation. The facility should have an independent air-conditioning system to minimize the possibility of a fire spreading from an external location. A decision on hardware location and density also has fire safety implications. To minimize potential fire damage, computer centers generally separate CPUs rather than place them side by side.

Heat-sensing devices that activate an alarm when room temperature rises suddenly or reaches a predetermined level may be installed. A drawback of this system in a computer environment is that electrical fires are generally localized. As a result, the alarm may not be triggered until extensive damage is done.

Smoke detectors are another fire prevention device. In general, such detectors are placed in ceilings, in ducts, and under the raised floors of computer centers. Unfortunately, smoke detectors are prone to false alarms. That is why some systems are designed to alert an operator of the presence of smoke rather than to set off automatic extinguishers and alarms. The operator is responsible for activating firefighting systems. Other smoke detection systems are controlled by a microprocessor and programmed to shut down computer equipment and air-conditioning, then release extinguishers following a short delay. The delay allows operators to override automatic firefighting systems in the case of a false alarm.

Sprinkler systems are recommended when the computer room is built of or stores combustible materials. Water cools a fire quickly, prevents flaskbacks, and is inexpensive to use. As long as equipment is deenergized, water will not cause permanent damage. But water sprinkled on machines with the power still on will create shorting and arcing and will ultimately damage equipment. The steam created can ruin magnetic media as well. What's more, the computer center will have to be cleaned up and dried out before it can go back online.

For this reason, some computer centers rely on carbon dioxide extinguishers to suffocate the fire. The danger is that humans will be suffocated as well, which is why carbon dioxide is used primarily to extinguish fires in unattended facilities. If used in areas where people

---

[3]For more on this subject, see Roger W. Haines, "Keeping Cool," *Datamation*, vol. 32, no. 14 (July 15, 1986), pp. 83–84.

work, safeguards will be added for their protection. For example, the room will have numerous exits, oxygen will be available, the gas will have a delayed release, and staff members will be highly trained in emergency procedures.

Another extinguisher is **halon gas,** a form of Freon that is safe for humans for short periods of time when in low concentrations. However, the gas does decompose into a toxic substance in the intense fire. A major disadvantage of halon is its expense. Whereas a water sprinkler system will generally protect a 20 × 20–foot area for $4,000, halon for the same area would cost $40,000.[4] Another problem is that halon pipes are custom-cut. They must be carefully cleaned of metal filings before installation, since the filings can cause electrical glitches in computer equipment.

Of course, hand-operated fire extinguishers should be placed in the computer center. In addition, space for storing waterproof and fireproof machine covers should be provided in all equipment rooms. Another fire safety feature is the placement of clearly marked and unobstructed master switches at all main doors to power down equipment.

Fire protection equipment should be carefully tested and properly maintained. When a fire occurred in one computer room, employees discovered that firefighting equipment installed just outside the computer center would not fit through the door.

Other features of special concern

Because of the importance of telecommunications to modern computer centers, consultants from the telephone company generally participate in the design of such centers. They help plan networks and the supporting communication facilities, including loop wiring, carrier lines, patch panels, and control centers. Sometimes, a special room for telecommunications equipment is strategically located in the computer center.

Lighting consultants help ensure that computer rooms are well lighted for daily operations, and they can offer advice on the ways to use lighting as an after-hours security measure.

Expert advice may also be sought regarding the installation of alarms to alert the police and fire departments of computer center emergencies. Sometimes, a center has special plumbing requirements. Water from leaks in pipes, air-conditioning units, or sprinkler systems can damage equipment; this water may collect under the raised floors, eventually seeping into cables and plugs. To prevent such damage, water detection systems may be installed.

---

[4]Eric Marcus, "Outfitting the Computer Room," *Datamation*, vol. 32, no. 14 (July 15, 1986), p. 62.

SUMMING UP

A subset of corporate planning is planning for the delivery of information services, a topic discussed in Chapter 2. The design of a computer center is just one of the activities in this category. To plan and oversee the construction of the center, a project manager will be appointed. Chapter 2 also described most of the planning tools and techniques used by this manager.

This chapter has dealt with planning issues that are unique to computer centers, such as how to determine capacity needs, decide on appropriate information resources, and design layouts. Special prob-

Figure 16–7   **Computer room layout**

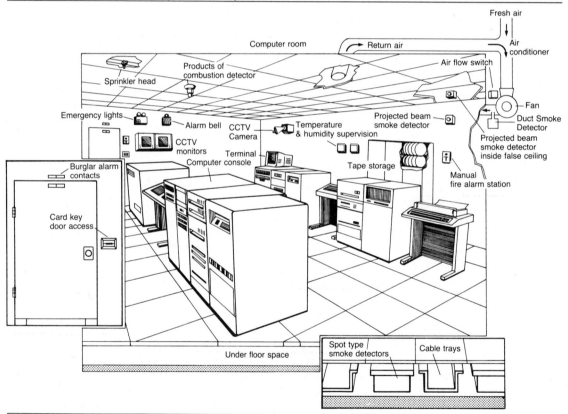

Note: Many means are shown for obtaining computer room security and safety, such as card-key door access and CCTV camera surveillance, and for detecting fire, such as smoke detectors, or in ceiling and air-conditioning ducts. A particularly interesting feature is automatic notification to a monitoring station of an emergency.

Source: ADT Security Systems, New York.

lems in site preparation have also been discussed. (See Figure 16–7 for a computer center that incorporates many of the features discussed in this chapter.) Because of the speed with which computer technology is advancing and because of escalating demand for information services, the design of a computer center is a continuous process. Quite often, planning for a new round of construction or remodeling begins as soon as the last round has been completed. In one center with which the authors are familiar, there were four changes in the CPU over a period of six years. And each required a new resource configuration and remodeling, including changes in the location of walls and false floors, a different power supply, altered ducts for air-conditioning, and so on.

The number of factors that a project manager has to take into account in site preparation makes the job a demanding one. Experience, technical knowledge, leadership, patience, the ability to listen to others, flexibility, organization, an instinct for cost control, and common sense are all needed to do the job well.

Fortunately, many technical manuals have been written to assist a project manager in designing a computer center. And many experts can be called in to consult on technical problems, such as the design of raised floors, the wiring for teleprocessing, or the installation of security devices.

CASE: TERRORIST ATTACKS ON COMPUTER CENTERS

In the last 10 years, U.S. and European computer centers have become targets for terrorist attacks. For example, IBM's facility in White Plains, New York, suffered considerable damage in the mid-1980s from a bomb explosion. Two companies in West Germany, MBP and SCS, were likewise victims of a bombing even though, tipped off by police that an attack was imminent, they had recently increased security. (During a raid, the police found the names of MBP, SCS, and 78 other companies on a terrorist hit list.) Protective measures taken at MBP included the hiring of a special guard to watch the offices of the firm and police to patrol the grounds every two hours. SCS, whose computer operations were visible from the street, installed reinforced glass in its windows. These measures did not prevent the terrorist attacks. At MBP, an explosion knocked a hole in the building and wrecked two mini-

Source: John Lamb and James Etheridge, "DP: The Terror Target," *Datamation*, vol. 32 no. 3 (February 1, 1986), pp. 44–46.

computers: at SCS, an explosion caused more than $760,000 in damages.

Even companies that do not believe they are targets are taking added security precautions in view of the increase in world terrorism. They fear that once terrorists realize how sensitive computer centers are in corporate operations, bombing attacks may escalate.

Questions

1. The SCS director Joachim Schweim reportedly has a philosophical attitude toward protection in general. He is quoted as saying, "There is a limit to how much of a 'fence' you can throw up around a building and still allow people to carry out their normal work." Comment.
2. What protective measures do you think SCS and BPM should have taken in view of the police tip-off that their names appeared on a target list?
3. What lies behind terrorist attacks on computing facilities?
4. If you were responsible for the design of a new computer center, what security features would you include to protect the facility from terrorism?

STUDY KEYS

Analytical and simulation models

Backup

Capacity plan

Capacity planning

Computer center

Contingency planning

Fire protection

Halon gas

Latent workload

Layout

Peak time zones

Power

Project manager

Resource configurations

Service-level agreement (SLA)

Shoulder zones

Site preparation

Site selection

Temperature regulation

Work flow

DISCUSSION QUESTIONS

1. Why are the planning and design of a computer center important? Who are the interested parties?
2. Because of the widespread use of stand-alone computers, are large computer centers becoming obsolete? Explain your answer.

3. Who should be responsible for the design of a computer center: a person from corporate management, a data processing professional, a user of computer services, or a consultant? Why?
4. Give some of the reasons why a new computer center may be needed.
5. What are the inputs and outputs of planning a new computer center?
6. What is capacity planning for a computer center? How can one predict future capacity needs?
7. How can computer programs like SCERT help in planning a computer center configuration? Does use of the model help with hardware only or also with software planning? What types of reports from SCERT are relevant to capacity planning?
8. What are the advantages, dangers, and limitations of gathering information from computer users regarding their expected future computing needs?
9. What, if any, should be the role of consultants in designing and implementing a new computer center?
10. What are the dangers of making straight-line projections of computer demand?
11. What is disaster planning? Why is it needed? How do you check to ensure that planning for disaster is adequate?
12. Discuss security issues in planning a computer center.
13. What is the relevance of a service-level agreement? Whom does it protect and how?
14. What are some of the factors to be considered in the layout of a:
    a. Computer center building?
    b. Computer center room?
15. What is the importance of work flow in the design of a computer center? Give examples of how work flow can be impeded or facilitated by room design.
16. What is a template? How can it be used in layout? Where can one get templates?
17. How can a computer center be designed to detect or prevent:
    a. Fire?
    b. Water leaks?
    c. Power failures?
    d. Security violations?
    e. Air-conditioning failure?
    Should these events occur despite protective measures, how would you deal with them?
18. Why is an uninterrupted power supply necessary to a computer center? How can it be obtained?

SELECTED ANNOTATED BIBLIOGRAPHY

Bhagah, D. B.; H. E. Brandmaier; and J. E. Ford. "More Power to You." *Datamation*, vol. 29, no. 10 (October 1983), pp. 121–30.
    A detailed and technical explanation of the issues involved in getting clean and reliable power for computer operations. The need for expert advice

on this subject when planning a computer center is explained to the reader.

"Capacity Planning and User Service Fulfillment." *EDP Performance Review,* vol. 9, no. 8 (August 1981), pp. 1–6.
A good discussion of timeliness, capacity trade-offs, and how pricing incentives affect load patterns. The article also discusses the user's viewpoint regarding capacity planning.

"Capacity Planning Issues." *EDP Performance Review,* vol. 11, no. 7 (July 1983), pp. 1–7.
This article is based on the issues raised at a conference on capacity management held by the Institute of Software Engineering in April 1983. Topics covered are capacity management of distributed data processing, decision support systems, information centers, and free-standing computers. The skills and experience needed for capacity management are also discussed.

Chandy, K. Mani. "Capacity Planning: The Art of Reasonable Decision-Making." *Infosystems,* vol. 29, no. 4 (April 1982), pp. 88–90.
The methodology and process of capacity planning, including contingency planning, are covered in this article.

Computer Security Manual. Hudson, Massachusetts: Computer Security Institute, 1980, 507 pp.
A very detailed manual that covers security management, physical security, hardware and software security, auditing of security, privacy, and computer abuse.

Datamation, vol. 32, no. 14 (July 15, 1986).
This issue has four articles on planning the computer room: Eric Marcus, "Outfitting the Computer Room;" Jesse J. Leaf, "Staying in Power;" William Sharon, "A Moving Experience;" and Roger W. Haines, "Keeping Cool."

Floch, George, "Sad Experiences because of an Earthquake." *Data Processing Digest,* vol. 31, no. 12 (December 1985), pp. 1–3.
The author, who was in Mexico City at the time of the September 19, 1985 earthquake, reports on the damage sustained by computer facilities in the city.

GTE Computer Systems Technology Group. "Capacity Management: We've Never Run out of Gas." *Computer Decisions,* vol. 16, no. 6 (July 1984), pp. 138–45.
Capacity planning at GTE saved $100 million over 10 years, achieved mainly through centralized management and purchasing.

Haack, James L. "Upgrading a DP Center." *Datamation,* vol. 29, no. 10 (October 1983), pp. 108–16.
In upgrading or building anew, thought must be given to the needs for storage, cooling power, fire prevention, security, and employee relaxation.

Howe, Douglas J. "A Basic Approach to Capacity Planning Methodology." Parts 1 and 2. *EDP Performance Review,* vol. 13, nos. 3 and 4 (March and April 1985).
Part 1 concentrates on practical considerations in capacity planning methodology. In Part 2, Howe discusses capacity planning formulas but states

that informal methods can sometimes be as effective in planning as the use of formulas.

IBM. *Data Center Relocation Workshop Guide.* DAPS–0894, ZZ05–0384–00. White Plains, N.Y.: IBM, December 1980, 471 pp.
A guide to relocation, including both a checklist for site planning and information on hardware planning, personnel considerations, vendor interface, and contract support services.

Mentzer, John W. "Paving the Way for Productivity Improvement." *Journal of Information Systems Management,* vol. 4, no. 1 (Winter 1987), pp. 82–84.
In addition to physical design considerations for improving productivity, it is important that the MIS manager review the internal working of the MIS organization and create an image that MIS is a progressive organization.

Morrison, David. "May the Power Be with You." Part II. *Computer Decisions,* vol. 17, no. 4 (April 23, 1985), pp. 116–39.
Morrison discusses power problems in computer centers, how they can be anticipated, and protective measures, including surge suppressors, line conditioners, and power distribution units.

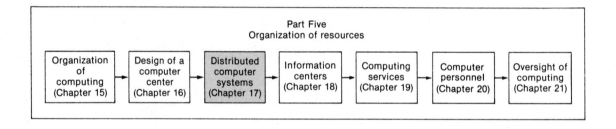

Part Five
Organization of resources

| Organization of computing (Chapter 15) | → | Design of a computer center (Chapter 16) | → | Distributed computer systems (Chapter 17) | → | Information centers (Chapter 18) | → | Computing services (Chapter 19) | → | Computer personnel (Chapter 20) | → | Oversight of computing (Chapter 21) |

CHAPTER 17

Distributed computer systems

Decentralization evokes deep-seated reactions.

Simon Nora and A. Minc

Distributed data processing (DDP)—the decentralization of processing to dispersed locations of an organization (branch offices, regional warehouses, or plants distant from corporate headquarters) by computers connected in a network—is one way of organizing equipment and personnel to implement a management information system. The computer **network** permits coordination and control of operations by corporate management, even though processing takes place at a number of locations. Ideally, a decision to utilize this processing structure is made during the developmental stages of a new information system, but an ongoing system is sometimes converted to DDP.

This chapter describes the evolution of DDP equipment configurations, and how data bases can be distributed. Sections on DDP planning, implementation, and management are also included. The material is an extension of Chapter 15 but merits a separate chapter because of the newness and growing popularity of this mode of operation. The purpose of the chapter is to explain how DDP affects the management of equipment, software, and personnel.

EVOLUTION OF DISTRIBUTED COMPUTER SYSTEMS

As described in Chapter 15, the first EDP centers were physically dispersed and had no centralized authority coordinating their activities. It soon became apparent that such centers were inefficient. There was redundancy in data collection, files, and processing. The centers were unresponsive to corporate management needs, and processed information was slow to reach decision makers.

As a result, a move toward centralization of computing facilities took place. It was hoped that costs would drop, that duplication of effort would be eliminated, and that tighter control of processing would produce more timely, more relevant information for management. However, large centralized systems soon became too complex to manage well. Users complained because they were unable to get service tailored to their needs, and communication problems between technical personnel and users were not resolved.

Dissatisfaction with centralized processing led to reconsideration of dispersed processing. Technological developments in the meantime made distributed data processing practical and economically feasible. Micro- and minicomputers with capabilities exceeding many former large computers were now on the market at low cost. Chip technology had increased central processing unit and memory capacity while reducing computer size and price. Strides in telecommunications meant processing networks could be established, linking dispersed processing sites. In addition, experience with data processing had given users confidence that they could manage and operate their own processing systems.

A primary advantage of DDP is that network linkage of processing sites permits centralized control over policies and processing, yet the system retains the flexibility of decentralization. Each site is under operational control of local management and may have unique equipment configurations according to local processing needs. The popularity of DDP as a mode of operation is growing.

WHAT IS DDP?

Among computer scientists, the definition of DDP is still evolving. For the purposes of this text, we shall define distributed data processing as dispersing a single, logically related set of tasks among a group of processing centers, called **nodes,** that belong to a single organization. Each node has computer facilities for program execution and data storage, and each is geographically separate. Yet, linkage between the nodes and the central computer (or between the node computers themselves) enables them to cooperate in processing tasks.[1] A DDP network can be spread over a large or small area: some DDP systems are global (for example, the U.S air traffic control system); others may fit within a single building or room.

The distributed computer concept applies age-old management principles to new technology. For example, DDP permits division of labor,

---

[1]Note that this definition excludes computer networks such as ARPA (Advanced Research Projects Agency) and EFT (Electronic Fund Transfer) because they serve many clients in business, industry, and government.

the increase of productivity through parallelism. It incorporates the concept of specialization of labor, since computers (like people) vary in the tasks that they do best. Furthermore, DDP promotes the delegation of responsibility. (Management at the remote nodes commonly controls acquisitions, operations, and systems development.)

Distributed computing seems simple in principle. However, it is not simple to put into practice. More than relocating hardware from a centralized computer center to dispersed locations, DDP affects the design of operating systems and data bases, applications, how departments within the organization are structured, the flow of corporate information, relationships between management and workers, and the decision-making process itself.

EQUIPMENT CONFIGURATIONS

The difference between distributed data processing and earlier dispersed processing is linkage: DDP involves a communications network to link decentralized processors. Figure 17–1 shows sample DDP net-

Figure 17–1 **Sample DDP network configurations**

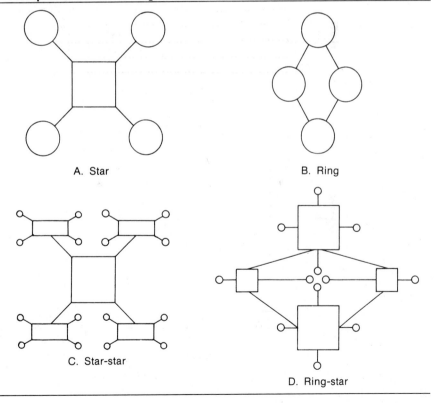

A. Star

B. Ring

C. Star-star

D. Ring-star

work configurations. In a **star network,** failure of the central computer impairs the entire system. The **ring network** structure overcomes this problem, because rerouting is possible should one processing center or its link fail. A ring network allows interaction and offloading (the transference of processing from one site to another) without dependence on a central host.

Both star and ring configurations are essentially horizontal systems. That is, each node processor is equal. The hardware may be unique at each node, which means that equipment may be purchased from several vendors. The advantage is that users can acquire computer resources that incorporate the latest technology on the market. But this flexibility has a negative aspect: it increases problems of linkage and compatibility between nodes. Many variations of ring and star networks are possible, such as the star-star and ring-star configurations shown in Figure 17–1.

Hierarchical distribution is the configuration that many firms prefer because, corresponding to the hierarchical structure already in existence within many corporations, it requires the least reorganization. This configuration, illustrated in Figure 17–2, has a central host com-

Figure 17–2   **Hierarchical distributed data processing**

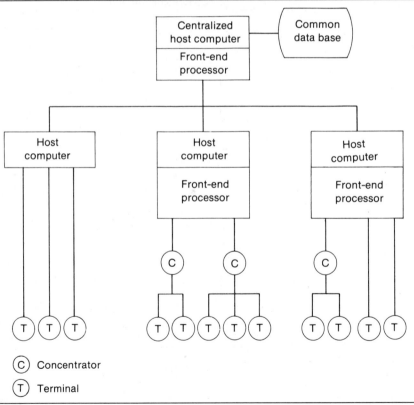

Ⓒ Concentrator

Ⓣ Terminal

puter and common data base with minis and micros at dispersed sites. Generally, all equipment and software in hierarchical systems are supplied by the same vendor, minimizing problems of compatibility between nodes. Because many computers have either a **fail-safe capability** (ability to continue operations, in spite of breakdown, due to the existence of backup) or a **fail-soft capability** (the ability to continue with a degraded level of operations), a breakdown in the hierarchy should not incapacitate the entire system.

Of course, Figure 17–2 is merely a model. Firms will design hierarchical configurations according to their needs.

Micro–mainframe link technology

Although microcomputer use for stand-alone processing has been common in the business world since the early 1980s, recent advances in technology (such as IBM's LU6.2 protocol for the personal computer and its token-ring network) have integrated microcomputers into distributed processing networks. Sales in **micro–mainframe link** products, including software, modems, and emulation boards, are on the rise. The number of vendors for such products is also increasing.

The original impetus for linkage was the desire of users to download data from mainframes to micros. But today, uploading is viewed as a major application of the technology as well. In the future, mainframes may be used as data base machines, while much local processing will take place on network microcomputers.[2]

Many technological problems still must be resolved. Software to facilitate micro–mainframe communications is needed, as are ways to handle different people working on the data base at the same time. Security is a major issue. Corporate proprietary data that is downloaded to portable floppy disks is in jeopardy. How can access to data (and disks) be controlled? The possibility that users may upload incorrect information processed on their microcomputers is also a concern. Ways to check and verify data before it is uploaded need to be devised.

Other problems that affect microcomputer–mainframe linkage are:

- The cost of micro–mainframe products and the speed with which such products are developed for the marketplace.
- Problems of incompatible data formats. Data downloaded from the mainframe may require processing before it can be used for microcomputer applications.
- Lack of open-architecture links. At present, most micro–mainframe systems are based on proprietary architectures. The micro–host software will only access data residing on the same vendor's mainframe software.

---

[2]The discussion in this section is based on James Martin, "Micro-to-Mainframe Links: An Uphill Climb to a Data Access Solution," *Computerworld*, vol. 28 no. 51 (December 20, 1985), pp. 77–82.

- The inability to use the processing power of a microcomputer while it is communicating with the mainframe. Currently, the micro can serve only as a terminal during emulation. Its own processor is turned off.
- The complexity of the technology. Learning to use link packages and how to access mainframe data bases takes time and effort.

Workstations in the future may include a built-in micro–mainframe communications capability. But perhaps technology will take another direction. One suggestion for the future includes a midlevel processor placed between the microcomputer and mainframe to handle requests for data access. This schema may prove more efficient than a direct micro–mainframe link.

DISTRIBUTED DATA BASE CONFIGURATIONS

With distributed processing networks, a decision needs to be made regarding the organization of the company's data bases. In such networks, should all data be centralized, or should processing nodes store data base segments that they need for daily operations? Perhaps data stored centrally should be replicated for use at local sites. Options for data organization are discussed next.

Centralized data base

Centralization of data is possible under DDP, but costs are high when all data must be transmitted to distributed nodes for processing. A centralized data base is appropriate when infrequent access to that data is needed or when updating needs to be strictly controlled.

Segmented distributed data base

The storage of parts of the data base at local nodes is called **segmented distributed data base** organization. The segments might be data from a function or data pertaining to the geographic area—data that allows the node to be virtually independent, although other nodes may also use the data as a shared resource.

Replicated distributed data base

When more than one dispersed processor needs the same data, a common approach to data base organization is to store the data base at a central repository with duplicate segments needed for local processing stored at each node. A data base organized in this fashion is called a **replicated distributed data base.** The local bases used for processing, including online real-time operations, are then periodically used to update the centralized data base. From the updated centralized base, the replicated data bases at distributed sites are updated in turn.

Large regional banks frequently adopt this form of data base organization. Central processing takes place after banking hours, and replicated distributed data bases are then created for branch offices. These replicated data bases consist essentially of working files used for local transactions, such as deposits and withdrawals. At the end of each working day, the central data base is again updated by incorporating data on transactions conducted at the branches during the day. Then the cycle begins once again with the creation of updated data bases for distribution to the branch offices.

In general, the centralized data base includes all control and summary data, whereas transactional data and local data are in the replicated distributed data bases. Branch offices still have to access the centralized data during the course of the day. This occurs if a customer of the bank wishes to cash a check at a branch that does not have a record of his or her account. In this case, the transaction has to be routed through the central data base.

One advantage of replicated data bases is that they provide backup. As a result, the system is less vulnerable should failure occur at the central location. An additional advantage is that systems are more responsive to local needs when data is managed locally (an advantage that applies to segmented data bases as well). In particular, maintenance and updating of large and complex data bases are more effective when portions of the base are under local control. Certain types of processing are also more efficient. For example, retrieval by indexes requires careful cross-indexing. Personnel on location with a need for the retrieved data will be more highly motivated to update and maintain indexes and retrieval software and are more knowledgeable about user needs than programmers at a centralized data base.

A major problem with replicated distributed data bases is redundancy. For efficient processing, no more data than absolutely necessary should be stored at remote sites. Unfortunately, the distributed centers' exact need for data is not easily determined.

Hybrid approach

Some firms both segment and replicate their data bases. This is the **hybrid approach** to data base organization. For example, a large national business may segment its data base geographically, giving regional headquarters segments relevant to their operations. Replicated data from these headquarters is then distributed to branch offices within each region. Warehouse inventories are often controlled in this manner.

In a data base management system (DBMS) environment, both distributed and central systems are possible. Although the distributed systems may satisfy local needs, the central DBMS would have the overall schema of the entire logical data base and would be concerned with problems of security, integrity, and recovery of data, including data at distributed centers.

WHEN TO IMPLEMENT DDP

Distributed data processing is not applicable to all organizations. How does a firm decide whether it is appropriate? What **organizational considerations** are important in the decision? Unfortunately, no formula or precise decision rule exists to guide management in reaching a DDP implementation decision. However, firms with geographically dispersed outlets, firms with a matrix structure rather than functional organization, multinationals, project-based companies (such as construction firms), and conglomerates have organizational structures that lead naturally to decentralization and the distributed mode.

In less obvious cases, a grid analysis may help determine the appropriateness of DDP. A sample is shown in Table 17–1. Here, a hypothetical firm with Sites A, B, C, and D has informational needs satisfied by Processes 1–3 and Files 1–3. The informational requirements of each site are marked on the grid. Since Process 1 and File 2 are required by all sites, centralization of their processing is indicated. Since Process 2 and File 1 are needed by only a single site, they are clear candidates for the distributed mode. Process 3 and File 3 are possible candidates.

However, before implementation, management should assess DDP's impact on the firm. How will DDP affect corporate decision making? Is DDP economically feasible? If a firm has centralized processing, a switch to DDP is usually not considered unless there is dissatisfaction with centralization. It is up to management to decide whether this dissatisfaction with operations can be remedied by DDP and whether the benefits of DDP will be worth the cost and disruption that reorganization entails.

Costs

Before making a decision to implement DDP, the **costs** of distributed processing should be appraised. One component of cost is CPU hardware. Today's micros and minis are dropping in price while increasing

Table 17–1 **Illustration of grid analysis**

Informational Sites / Needs	A	B	C	D
Process 1	X	X	X	X
2	X			
3			X	X
Files 1	X			
2	X	X	X	X
3			X	X

in computing power as a result of recent technological advances. This means DDP is economically feasible for many businesses that formerly could not afford dispersed processors. Terminal hardware is also dropping in cost; but as users demand more sophisticated units, such as intelligent terminals with local processing capabilities, actual terminal expenditures may rise.

At the present time, transmission costs are not dropping as dramatically as the cost of hardware, so it is tempting to install additional processors in the distributed mode rather than transmit data to a centralized computer. High transmission costs are due, in part, to the monopolistic character of the transmission industry. However, changes in federal regulations may alter this situation in the future. Firms that implement DDP should periodically make a financial reassessment of transmission costs and how they affect their equipment configurations.

Cost elements other than hardware and data communication facilities are software, personnel, and training. As a norm, 0.5 to 1.0 percent of a firm's budget is allocated to data processing in largely centralized organizations. When a firm chooses DDP, costs may increase to as much as 5.0 percent. In general, DDP proves economically feasible when:

- A high remote transaction rate exists.
- Remote sites have a total mass data storage capability of at least 40 megabytes.
- A distributed local data base will handle most local needs (no more than 20–30 percent of data base access requirements from other locations).
- Data transmitted is much smaller than local data use.
- Distribution of processing would improve overall organizational efficiency.

EDP reorganization
Distributed data processing requires that electronic data processing (EDP) personnel be shifted to dispersed centers for operations. Responsibility for systems development, security, and acquisitions may also be transferred to local managers. The EDP staff at the corporate center will be dismantled, managers will lose "empires," and new sets of interpersonal relationships will have to be forged. How far to go with decentralization may often depend on human factors rather than economic and technological considerations. Will managers accept a redefinition of their responsibilities, or will jealousies undermine DDP service? Is competent staff available to manage and operate local computing sites? Will employees agree to transfer to distributed centers? Will distributed processing promote greater efficiency and happier staff relationships once the trauma of reorganization is passed?

Conversion to DDP is much easier in a receptive environment, but the key to DDP success in all firms is careful DDP planning and competent management of DDP networks. The next sections of this chapter will discuss these topics.

PLANNING FOR DDP

The planning process described in Chapter 2 applies to **planning** for distributed data processing as well as planning for a centralized processing system. Once in operation, both types of processing centers continually engage in planning activities, such as planning for new systems development or for expansion of facilities. This section focuses on planning issues that are unique to DDP: how to decide the jurisdiction of local nodes and how to coordinate operations and management in a firm with semiautonomous processing centers.

A cardinal rule in establishing a DDP center is to include users in the planning task force. This task force should develop a series of master plans that describe the intended flow of information within the organization under DDP and how responsibility for this flow is to be divided. These should include:[3]

1. A master plan that outlines goals, functions, schedules, performance levels, and expenditures for each node and the center.
2. A master systems design that details the structural relationship of nodes to center, the communications subsystems to be used, standards for hardware and software, and protocols for synchronization and security.
3. A master management plan that describes the degree of autonomy granted node managers, training plans, career development paths, possible job rotations, and control procedures.

Planning for DDP structures is largely dependent on the technology available and on forecasts of equipment to be expected in both the short and long term. The nature of the business, top management's organizational philosophy, stage of growth of the firm, existing organizational structure, and management style also have a bearing. Here are the types of questions that must be asked when deciding DDP structure:[4]

- What are the hardware and software configurations (CPU, channels, disks, operating system, data base types) required at the various locations?

---

[3]George A. Champine, Ronald D. Coop, and Russell C. Heinselman, *Distributed Computer Systems: Impact on Management, Design, and Analysis* (New York: Elsevier–North Holland Publishing, 1980), pp. 318–19.

[4]This list is drawn from S. Agassi, "Performance Considerations for a Distributed Data Processing System Designed for High Availability," *IBM Systems Journal*, vol. 24. no. 3 and 4 (1985), p. 200.

- What communication network connections are best suited for the specified requirements?
- What will be the response time of the transactions?
- What effect will the various backup configurations have on the response times?
- How will the data base distribution technique affect response times?
- How can data base synchronization be ensured?
- How will the growth in the number of users or in the transaction rate impact the system?
- How can systems security be ensured?

Answers to these questions lead to planning three organizational variables: degree of centralized control, hardware configurations, and data base distribution. At one extreme, a firm might choose to distribute only limited functions; at the other, total distribution and decentralization of processing with complete profit and loss responsibility assigned to local managers. In most cases, a firm will choose a position somewhere in between.[5]

The hypothetical firm described in Table 17–2 is one example of DDP. Here, the central staff has global responsibilities. That is, central management sets standards for planning and controls, is responsible for systems maintenance and network design, prepares budgets, and

Table 17–2	Hypothetical DDP structure with distribution of activities between center and nodes		
	Activity	*Center*	*Distributed node*
	Overall planning	Corporate systems Policy determination Resource needs Compatibility	Local processing
	Planning and control	Major software Global security Global standards Common data base	Local software Local security Local standards Local data base
	Management and control	Central resources	Local resources
	Network management	Design Operations and control Maintenance	
	Budgeting	Central and network expenditures	Local spending
	Quality control	Systems	Local
	Audits	Systems	Local
	Personnel	Hiring/coordinating systems personnel	Local personnel management

---

[5]For a good discussion of alternatives, see Grayce M. Booth, *The Distributed System Environment: Some Practical Approaches* (New York: McGraw-Hill, 1981).

Table 17-3

Sample DDP structure (distributed functions)

Function \ Site	New York	Chicago	San Francisco	London
Need assessment	X			
Policy determination	X			
Resource	X			
Compatibility	X			
Acquisitions	X			
Major spending				
Common data base		X		
Standards			X	
Major software development				X
Network management			X	
Quality control		X		
Auditing	X			

assigns staff. This results in uniform standards throughout the organization, flexibility in personnel placement and utilization (small processing centers do not need and cannot afford the full-time services of on-site hiring and maintenance personnel), systems backup, and centralization of major financial decisions. On-site managers have control over local planning, local resources, and local processing. Figure 15–2 in Chapter 15 is basically this DDP configuration.

Another approach is to assign specific functions to individual nodes. For example, the New York office of a firm might be responsible for policy and resource planning, the Chicago office for the common data base and quality control, San Francisco for standards and network management, and so on. Table 17–3 shows this concept. Under this structure, duties assigned to the center in Table 17–2 are distributed among the nodes.

These two examples are oversimplifications. In practice, many firms have mixed processing modes that combine features of centralized, decentralized,[6] and distributed processing. For example, materials, services, legal reporting, and employee benefits might be centralized; customer service, inventories, payroll, and personnel might be decentralized; with production information, orders, and accounts receivable handled by the distributed mode.

---

[6]Decentralized processing refers to physically separated, stand-alone processing entities.

MANAGEMENT OF DDP

The management of distributed data processing can be divided into the areas of static and dynamic control. Because firms may differ in network configurations, the location of managers responsible for these controls may vary from one firm to another, but both types of control are necessary in DDP systems. **Static control** deals with equipment, data base structure, and applications, whereas **dynamic control** concerns monitoring, testing, interfacing, and security.

In static control, compatibility is the key issue. Equipment guidelines and language standards are essential. For example, management might decide that all equipment should support an American National Standards Institute (ANSI) standard version of COBOL or that all hardware used for scientific processing should provide a standard FORTRAN compiler. Data bases for applications must be designed for integration and interface protocols established for information exchange. Above all, management should check to see that duplication of effort is avoided.

Dynamic control involves monitoring the network so that problems or failures at each node can be detected and corrected. Each component of a DDP system should have self-test facilities to assist in isolating the source of problems. A veritable arsenal of security measures is needed to manage the transmission of data over long distances, because the possibility of wiretapping and electrical interference must be added to conventional security issues, such as access, integrity of data, privacy, threat monitoring, and auditing. In addition, statistics should be collected on the system and patterns of usage analyzed to help identify potential network weakness.

Because of the complexity of distributed data processing, many firms today assign one person from top management the responsibility for network administration. Obviously, a person in this position needs managerial and technical skills of the highest order, because issues that affect the entire operation of the firm are within the **network administrator**'s jurisdiction (for example, hardware compatibility, language choice, division of the data base, systems security, error detection and correction, and traffic monitoring).

REWARDS AND RISKS OF DDP

Improved systems reliability is one of the primary functional advantages of DDP. The fact that work is modularized means that tasks are less complex and therefore less vulnerable to failure. Furthermore, natural compartmentalization can reduce the scope of errors, failures, and damage. Should one module fail, another can provide backup service.

A DDP system facilitates growth without disruption of service. System upgrades can take place in small increments. For example, modules can be replaced or modernized one at a time so that conversion can be easily managed. There is built-in flexibility that allows systems to meet new requirements, to bypass failed components, to integrate new services or new technologies, and to extend systems life expectancy. What's more, throughput and response time are improved because communication delays and queueing are avoided when local nodes process local data bases. Less complex software is required, a fact that reduces the cost of systems development, maintenance, and training.

With on-site processing, the need for communications with a centralized processor is lessened. This helps to reduce costs, as does improved systems response. Shared resources minimize the need for duplication of resources. Modularity can improve procurement competition and can likewise improve cost-performance ratios because of economies of specialization. (A system can cater to the needs of a particular group rather than service the complex needs of diverse groups.)

Certainly, this list of benefits should include increased motivation among distributed staff, resulting from greater independence and local control of processing. With a smaller user base, fewer political and priority conflicts need to be resolved. Staff can concentrate on systems optimization instead. There is also a psychological advantage when users find services tailored to their needs and have more voice in computing decisions, such as hardware and software upgrades. In addition, the geographical location of facilities is no longer an important factor.

In spite of these advantages, the initiation of DDP involves multiple risks. Among the more common are poor systems design resulting from inexperience, redundancy among nodes, problems with interface, costs that are hidden or that escalate, and employee resistance to change. For example, distributed computing requires more planning than centralized systems. More attention must be paid to the efficiency of information flow and distribution. Standards for data elements and interfaces need to be designed, monitored, and enforced. Four thorny data distribution issues need to be resolved:

- Where to store data.
- How to find needed data efficiently.
- How to keep data synchronized and maintain integrity.
- How to protect data from security and privacy abuse and fraud.

Distributed architectures are still in the early stages of development. To date, most of the work has centered on how to connect hardware components. A number of issues, such as how to build a distributed network operating system, still need more research. Clearly, new technology means new potential yet also heightens risk. And designing a multiple-processor system is much more difficult than designing a single-processor system.

DDP IN THE FUTURE

The future of DDP is cloudy because of uncertainty regarding federal communications regulations. (The stance of the Federal Communications Commission on DDP is unclear.) There is also lack of agreement in the computer industry regarding network standards, which is an impediment to DDP research and development. For example, the Europeans utilize the X.25 standard, the Americans use Systems Network Architecture (SNA) and Synchronous Data Link Control (SDLC). DDP will not be widely implemented until universal standards are adopted so that the DDP equipment and software of competing manufacturers can be integrated into a single DDP system.

Once DDP is cost effective and hardware, systems architecture, and communications are integrated into reliable and robust systems, DDP will become more viable. Advances are being made in DDP technology and software so that data can be accessed with ease, no matter where it is stored in the distributed network. Solutions to problems of deadlock and optimal routing of queries are presently being researched. Future systems must be less vulnerable to failure and more easily restructured in response to growth or changed informational needs. DDP applications will undoubtedly broaden from current use for data entry and validation to full office automation and shop floor control in the near future.

SUMMING UP

DDP takes computing power from one large, centralized computer and disperses this power to sites where processing demand is generated. The equipment used is a mix of terminals, mainframes, minis, and small business computers integrated by appropriate systems architecture. (Some computers are being specially designed for DDP applications.)

Distributed processing offers firms an increasingly wide range of organizational alternatives, as opposed to the former black-and-white choice of centralization or decentralization. Computers in a DDP network can be linked in a variety of configurations, such as star, ring, or hybrid designs, although the hierarchical structure with fail-soft capability is more common. Technological advances (such as improvements in chip technology and telecommunications) and the willingness

Table 17–4   **Advantages of distributed data processing**

1. Offers decentralized processing and satisfies desire for local autonomy and local applications development. Facilitates user access to computer centers.
2. Local control over needed segments of the data base is retained at the distributed centers.
3. Improved quality of input and processing because of greater sensitivity to local conditions.
4. Users feel analysts at dispersed sites are more responsive to their needs.
5. Enables modular growth with little disruption at central site.
6. Enables use of different equipment at sites, provided interface problems are resolved.
7. Provides stand-alone operations with fail-soft capability for hierarchical structures and alternative routes for ring structures.
8. Provides middle management at distributed level with unique, relevant, and timely information and, consequently, a measure of independence from top management.
9. Enables use of heterogeneous equipment and resource sharing, including dynamic load balancing (by moving around and distributing load) to maximize throughput.
10. Systems can be more easily designed and developed in modules.
11. Reduced duplication of resources.
12. System can be aligned with organizational patterns and goals.

and ability of EDP personnel to manage local computer centers have made DDP feasible.

Deciding when to distribute depends on how much processed data is needed by the corporate center and how much is utilized at branches. One rule of thumb states that distributed processing is indicated when 20 percent of the processed information is needed by the center and 80 percent at local sites. Other factors indicating the need for DDP are decentralization of responsibility, distributed functions, and limited information flow to headquarters.

Table 17–5   **Limitations of DDP**

1. Can be more expensive than centralized processing in spite of low-cost minis, largely because of the cost of transmission, necessary software, and overlapping of equipment (especially disks in cases of replicated data bases).
2. The interface of expensive equipment from different vendors at dispersed nodes is a problem, for equipment may differ in instruction sets and operating systems.
3. Most existing software packages are designed for stand-alone computers and need to be adapted for DDP.
4. Communication systems of DDP are vulnerable to security violations.
5. National and international standards for network communication do not exist, causing problems of interfacing and implementing DDP.
6. With autonomous distributed sites, corporate standards for development, integration, and data base are more difficult to enforce.
7. Although each individual module may be less complex than a centralized system, design of a distributed computer system as a whole is very complex.
8. Being newer technology, DDP has greater risk than centralized processing.
9. Modularity restricts local applications' size and complexity.

A major advantage of DDP is that systems can begin simply and grow modularly. DDP can also be adapted to various organization structures and modified when necessary to adapt to changing patterns in the flow of information. These and other advantages are summarized in Table 17–4; limitations appear in Table 17–5. Most of the technological limitations will be overcome in time. The computer industry is already researching systems architecture, equipment, software, and data base management systems. Resistance to change will slow the spread of DDP, but once a firm restructures its data processing and new relationships and power structures are forged, DDP will prove its value to users as well as to technical personnel.

One final word. DDP requires the total commitment of top management. Special staffing and new positions, such as data base administrator and network administrator, should ease systems implementation and operations, but the involvement of management in planning for DDP and setting standards and controls is essential to ensure that the system meets the firm's needs. Although many of the planning decisions are technical, they should not be delegated exclusively to technicians. Coordination, integration, and control are keystones to DDP success, and these are the responsibility of management.

CASE: DDP AT STAMFORD HOSPITAL

Stamford Hospital in Stamford, Connecticut, is a 320-bed, private, nonprofit hospital. Dissatisfied with its data processing, hospital management drew up a five-year computerization plan in the early 1980s. The ultimate goal: a complete order-entry system that would be able to enter all medical orders (diet, tests, medicine) through terminals distributed in different locations in the hospital.

The local network chosen for the system was ARC (Attached Resource Computer), produced by Datapoint Corporation of San Antonio, Texas. Medical Scientific International Corp., a firm specializing in hospital systems, was selected to put together the software.

Three years into the project, Stamford had 12 processors, 14 printers, and 41 terminals on its ARC network, with system components connected by coaxial cable. Three pieces of lab equipment, a card embosser, and an optical character reader were also part of the system. Implementation of the final phase of the computerization plan is on schedule and proceeding smoothly, according to hospital officials.

Questions

1. How will Stamford Hospital benefit from its DDP system?
2. Why do you think DDP was chosen instead of decentralization?
3. What personnel will be needed to run Stamford's DDP system?
4. Hospitals have been slower than the business sector to implement advances in computer technology for administrative purposes. Why do you suppose this is true?

STUDY KEYS

Centralization	Network
Costs	Network administrator
Distributed data base	Nodes
Distributed data processing (DDP)	Organizational considerations
	Planning
Dynamic control	Replicated distributed data base
Fail-safe capability	Ring network
Fail-soft capability	Segmented distributed data base
Hierarchical distribution	Star network
Hybrid approach	Static control
Micro–mainframe link	

DISCUSSION QUESTIONS

1. Describe the essential elements of a distributed processing system.
2. What are the characteristics of DDP? Which activities should be distributed? Which centralized? Would this distribution change with:
    a. Size of organization?
    b. Organizational structure of firm?
    c. Geographical distribution of branches?
3. Would you select a star computer configuration in preference to a ring or hierarchical configuration? Why? Give examples of each in business and industry.
4. What configuration of computer equipment in a DDP environment would you select for the following situations:
    a. A bank with many branches?
    b. A wholesaler with many warehouses?
    c. A factory with distributed plants, each of which manufactures a different component?

5. What problems arising out of personnel conflicts and power struggles should be expected in the transition from centralized EDP to DDP? What can be done to minimize the harmful effects of such conflicts?

6. Why is a micro–mainframe linkage more difficult technologically than linkage between two mainframes?

7. Give examples of business usage for micro–mainframe linkage.

8. What management problems are unique to micro–mainframe linkage?

9. What are the problems of control, security, and privacy to be expected in a DDP environment? How can one overcome such problems?

10. What is the role of telecommunications and teleprocessing in a DDP environment? How will costs and regulation of telecommunications affect DDP?

11. What type of business or industrial environment lends itself to DDP?

12. What factors should be taken into consideration in deciding whether to implement DDP?

13. In planning for DDP, what types of master plans should be formulated?

14. Describe the difference between dynamic and static control in DDP. Does the type and degree of control vary among businesses and among different firms within an industry?

15. What is the role of a network administrator? When is a network administrator needed?

16. Discuss the disadvantages and risks in distributed computer systems.

17. Discuss the benefits of DDP.

SELECTED ANNOTATED BIBLIOGRAPHY

Ahituv, Niv, and Batami, Sadan. "Learning to Live in a Distributed World." *Datamation*, vol. 31, no. 18 (September 15, 1985), pp. 139–48.
A very detailed and scholarly discussion of the range of choices of organizational structure. The authors give many pointers on how to set up a policy for distributed processing.

Booth, Grayce M. *The Distributed System Environment: Some Practical Approaches.* New York: McGraw-Hill, 1981, 286 pp.
This book, written by a practitioner from Honeywell, has neither an IBM bias nor the theoretical bias of an academician. Good sections on distributed network architectures, distributed systems structures, and design considerations are included.

Champine, George A. *Distributed Computer Systems: Impact on Management, Design, and Analysis.* New York: Elsevier–North Holland Publishing, 1980, 380 pp.

Comprehensive coverage of distributed processing, including excellent chapters on human interface in distributed systems (Chapter 6) and the management of distributed systems (Chapter 15).

Colony, George F. "New Ports of Call." *Datamation*, vol. 32, no. 22 (November 15, 1986), pp. 69–74.
This is a good discussion of departmental resource processors and departmental computing as one twist to DDP. "Medium-sized computers will be ferries between the micro and the mainframe, and a means of harmonizing large populations of PCs with corporate information, especially centralized data bases."

Kleinrock, Leonard. "Distributed Systems." *Computer*, vol. 18, no. 11 (November 1985), pp. 90–103.
The discussion of performance and behavior is rather technical and mathematical. However, the rest of the article is not as difficult to read. Recommended are the sections on introduction to DDP, DDP architecture and algorithms, and likely future developments.

Mariani, M. P., ed. *Distributed Data Processing—Technology and Critical Issues*. New York: Elsevier Science, 1984, 217 pp.
This book discusses baseline tools and techniques, critical implementation issues, architectural concepts, and areas that need to be researched.

Patrick, Robert L. "A Checklist for System Design." *Datamation*, vol. 26, no. 1 (January 1980), pp. 147–53.
This article is an excerpted version of the author's *Design Handbook for Distributed Systems*, discussing 15 ideas on systems design (out of 186 ideas in the book). He describes how each idea has been successfully implemented in practice. The article is especially good on the human factors of designing and implementing a distributed system.

Rademacher, Robert A. "Distributed Processing with Microcomputers." *Small Systems World*, vol. 11, no. 2 (February 1983), pp. 22–26.
Microcomputers are too slow for many applications, and their software is inadequate. Both of these problems can be overcome by adding microcomputers to a DDP network.

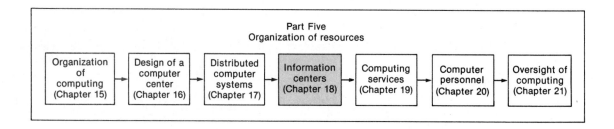

Part Five
Organization of resources

| Organization of computing (Chapter 15) | Design of a computer center (Chapter 16) | Distributed computer systems (Chapter 17) | Information centers (Chapter 18) | Computing services (Chapter 19) | Computer personnel (Chapter 20) | Oversight of computing (Chapter 21) |

CHAPTER 18

Information centers

Knowledge exists to be imparted.
Ralph Waldo Emerson

As early as the 1960s, when the introduction of computers in business organizations surged forward, there was discussion in professional circles about ways to help computer users get the most out of their computer resources. Over time, the concept of a computer support group evolved to provide users with guidance and training as well as hardware and software tools. To describe this concept, a number of expressions have been used, such as client service center, solution center, resource center, and business systems support center. However, the term **information center,** coined by IBM Canada in 1976, is the name most widely used today.

Growth in the number of corporate information centers has been fueled in the 1980s by the increased use of microcomputers for business processing. Many of the people who today work on these machines have neither background nor experience in corporate computing. Management recognizes that training and consulting services, coupled with easy access to packaged tools and data availability, are required if the potential of microcomputer resources is to be realized. For this reason, more and more information centers are being established. Regardless of how these centers are organized, the goal is the same: to support users in various information systems activities so that they can solve their own business problems.[1]

---

[1] In Canada, a support group called the Information Centre Exchange has been established to help data processing professionals learn how to manage end-user services. See Lida Kozlowsky, "Info Centre Provides Users with 'Tools' and Services," *CIPS Review,* vol. 7 (November–December 1983), pp. 24–25.

MISSION STATEMENT

The first step in organizing an information center is for corporate management to decide exactly what role the center is to play. Then, to define the function of the center, a **mission statement** is prepared, such as, "The information center's mission is to improve user self-sufficiency and effectiveness in order to maximize the profitable use of computing."

A detailed **operating plan** should be attached to the mission statement. It should contain information regarding the structure, environment, and activities of the center, including:

- Justification and strategic direction.
- Placement in the organization.
- Support and services.
- Physical facilities.
- Staffing.
- Financing.

In the sections of this chapter that follow, each of these topics will be considered. The future of information centers will also be discussed.

JUSTIFICATION

An information center is generally a centrally located facility staffed with computer specialists who can communicate effectively with **end-users,** persons who use computers but are unskilled in data processing. End-users may be executives, managers, professional staff, secretaries, officeworkers, sales representatives, or other employees who use information technology in their jobs. Most definitions of an end-user exclude computer professionals. However, some information centers do provide service to programmers, analysts, and other data processing personnel.

By studying the factors that contribute to the frustrations of both users and data processing personnel working in a computerized business environment, justification for an information center can be established. No business environment is static. Yet, artificial stability is created when systems specifications are frozen during a systems development project. By the time the development cycle is completed, there is often a mismatch between the user's needs and what is delivered. The alterations required may be minor. However, because of scheduling priorities and project backlogs, modifications cannot be made to the system in what the user considers a reasonable time frame.

This situation leads to strain in the relationship between end-users and the data processing department. From the user's viewpoint, the department is unresponsive and inflexible. The complaint of computer specialists, on the other hand, is that users seldom know what they want, make unreasonable modification requests, and do not appreciate services rendered.

End-users have high expectations regarding systems output, even though most do not understand how computers process information. (Although some users have been involved in development projects, the typical user today merely supplies data to the system, receives reports, and makes error corrections.) This explains user frustration when the need for special information arises that cannot be supplied by systems in use. In such cases, the user has several options:

- Ask computer specialists to write a new program (or modify an existing one).
- Purchase packaged software to do the job.
- Manually compile data to obtain the desired information.

None of these options is satisfactory if the need for the information is immediate. To ask the data processing department to write or modify a program may take too long and cost too much. An appropriate package may not be on the market. Even if available, acquisition procedures are generally time consuming, and budget restrictions may preclude package purchase. To compile the data manually may interfere with ongoing responsibilities and require overtime.

Assuming that the request for information is reasonable and that data exists, the answer to this dilemma is for the user to generate the required information by computer without involving analysts and programmers. The purpose of an information center is to provide the support—training, consultation, software tools, and data availability—so that the user can do so. Benefits to users include more control over their work and timely solutions to their needs.

From the standpoint of data processing personnel, the center helps solve user problems, contributes to a reduction in backlogs, reduces a substantial portion of maintenance work, and abates friction with users. The organization as a whole benefits because information resources are used in an effective and productive manner. In addition, a harmonious relationship is fostered between users and the community of information specialists.

The implementation of an information center is a business decision. Management must be able to justify investment in the center, as it justifies investment in other projects or business opportunities. For this reason, a cost-benefit analysis is common practice when a center is under consideration.

Sometimes, sites are started by first deciding which interactive software products will be supported. Then the business potential that will be derived from such tools is surveyed, and the benefits that will be realized from the products are identified. Other firms examine information systems backlogs and determine which projects can be developed by users with the assistance of an information center. Then a cost-benefits analysis is made of this mode of operations compared to traditional development by data processing personnel. Many companies establish pilot information centers and use a sort of scorecard or evaluation document to record expenditures and benefits. On the basis of this data, continuation or expansion of the center is justified.[2]

In general, top management will not support the establishment of an information center whose sole mission is to train users. It must be demonstrated that the center will give the company a competitive edge and help people make faster, better decisions.

PLACEMENT IN THE COMPANY

Organizational An information center has a mission statement and operating plan, as mentioned earlier, and its own management and staff. In the organizational hierarchy of a company, the center is usually placed under the data processing director, who monitors and controls the center's usage and growth. **Organizational placement** can be a critical factor in the center's success. If placed too high in the company's organizational chart—for example, directly below the vice president for information

Figure 18–1   **Information center placement in organization**

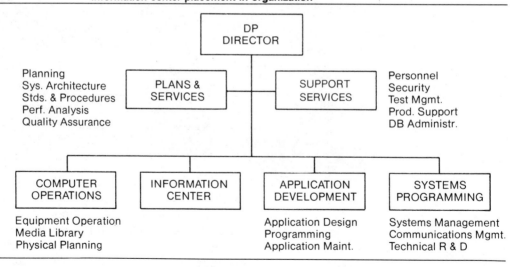

[2]D. A. Gregory, *IS Information Centre* (Ontario, Canada: IBM Canada, 1983), p. 38.

services—the center may be viewed as a tool of top management, not of users. If placed too low—reporting to a functional area manager—it may be viewed as belonging to that function and manager, not to the organization as a whole. A satisfactory solution is to give the center equal status to computer operations, applications development, and systems programming within the data processing department, as illustrated in Figure 18–1.

One reason for separating the information center from other information services is to prevent staff, whose primary responsibility is user assistance, from being distracted by other assignments (such as crisis "fire fighting," an activity in which most analysts and programmers are continually engaged). Another reason is to overcome the psychological inhibition that many users have toward working with computer technicians, an inhibition that may result from unsatisfactory dealings with the data processing department in the past.

Physical

A separate unit (perhaps located in offices apart from other data processing services) will encourage hesitant employees to give the information center a try. One company located its information center next to the employee lounge. This site helped to advertise the center's existence. The fact that drop-ins were encouraged helped to broadcast the services offered. This is an example of how location can affect center effectiveness. Clearly, potential benefits of an information center will not be realized unless employees are induced to utilize the facility.

SUPPORT AND SERVICES

Figure 18–2 is representative of the internal organization of an information center. It will typically be divided into groups with responsibility for technical support, consultation, education, product support, and administrative services. In this section, the **support and services** available from the information center will be explored.

Troubleshooting, consulting, and training are core services offered by most information centers. According to a 1985 survey of information center users in five Fortune 1,000 companies, these services are valued much more highly by users than any other services that an information center can offer.[3] After describing activities in these categories, other functions of information centers will be examined.[4]

---

[3]James C. Brancheau, Douglas R. Vogel, and James C. Wetherbe, "An Investigation of the Information Center from the User's Perspective," vol. 16, no. 1 *Data Base* (Fall 1985), pp. 4–14.

[4]For a good article on services, see John R. Vacca, "The Information Center's Critical Post-Start-Up Phase," *Journal of Information Systems Management*, vol. 2, no. 2 (Spring 1985), pp. 50–56.

Figure 18–2   **Internal organization of information center**

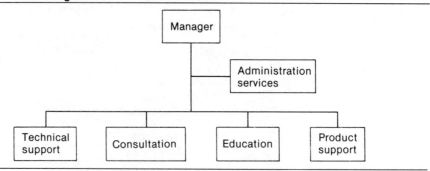

Aid in problem resolution

User assistance usually begins by staffing a telephone hot line and a help desk. Requests for service may range from a simple query regarding the meaning of a message on a computer screen to an appeal for help when a system malfunctions or breaks down. When a problem cannot be quickly resolved, the user will be referred to a staff member with expertise in that area.

Consultation

Typically, the role of a consultant in an information center is to help users plan for effective use of their computing resources, to advise them in ways to computerize their work, to evaluate proposed computer applications, to assist in product selection, and to answer specific questions regarding hardware and software.

Training

Computer literacy is the main objective of educational programs. Training may consist of self-study methods, such as computer-based training and audiovisual presentations, or be instructor led. Self-study is favored when:

- Immediate training is required and the center does not have time to plan and deliver a course on the subject.
- The schedule of the employee in need of training precludes class attendance.
- Training is needed at a remote site that instructors cannot reach.

Individualized instruction may be given when an employee needs to develop a specialized skill not needed by others. More commonly, workshops and classroom instruction are the teaching mode. Popular courses include word processing, file creation, electronic mail, and how to use software such as Lotus 1–2–3, Multimate, Omnilink, and dBase III. Classes may last a half-day (for example, an introduction to the personal computer) or for as long as a week to 10 days (for example, application engineering to teach techniques in prototyping, data modeling, and structured analysis).[5]

Technical support

Technical assistance is provided by the center when user problems are too large or complex to be solved without the aid of computer specialists, but only if the solution is not extensive modification of a large applications system or new systems development. (Those problems will be referred to persons in the data processing department responsible for development projects.) "Fast-response report group," a name some information centers give to their technical support team, helps explain the team's assignment. In addition to problem solving, staff may be asked to help audit systems performance, establish backup and recovery procedures, plan data access, assist with the design of security, plan projects, or document user requirements. In effect, technical support is an extension of the center's consulting service.

Product support

Software packages may reside at the information center to provide users with services such as graphics, spreadsheets, decision support, modeling capability, financial analysis, fourth-generation query languages, data base management, applications generators, and so on. Staff may demonstrate how the software is used, perhaps by providing a sample problem solution walkthrough. In addition, they may help users interpret reference manuals, suggest tips and techniques for using the product, and give debugging assistance if needed. Aid of this nature will also be given to users when they purchase new software.

Hardware access

Terminals, microcomputers, printers, plotters, microfilm and microfiche readers, and other equipment may be available for use, or hardware may be on exhibition to help end-users decide what equipment to acquire. Sometimes the information center serves as an in-house computer store. End-users can try out equipment, receive advice about the relative merits of models produced by different manufacturers, and then lease or purchase the equipment directly from the center. This eliminates the lengthy acquisition procedures that are required when dealing with outside vendors. The center offers "one-stop shopping," and the prices may be lower than those of retail stores. Furthermore, the center can provide training, configuration assistance, and maintenance after the lease or purchase.

Staffing

Some information centers provide backup assistance for users who have a temporary need for information processing personnel.

---

[5]Sample training programs are described by Craig Zarley in "Training People to Use Their Computers," *Personal Computing*, vol. 8, no. 1 (January 1984), pp. 124–201.

**Computer resource
planning and
justification**

The center can help end-users analyze their workloads, make projections of future needs, and prepare (and justify) requests for additional funding for computer resources. One of the more important roles of the center is to nurture user awareness of the importance of standardization and integration of resources.

**New-service
evaluation**

In order to provide better services to end-users, center staff will keep abreast of users' needs. When new products (both hardware and software) come on the market, these products will be evaluated to see whether they will increase end-user self-sufficiency and productivity. If appropriate, the center may then initiate a proposal to management for acquisition of the product.

**Administrative
services**

This category of service commonly includes:

- Promotion and advertising of information center activities (for example, a newsletter or bulletin board notices).
- Orientation workshops or open houses to introduce users to the information center.
- New-product announcements.
- A library of computer-related materials.
- Equipment maintenance and service.
- Accounting and billing for center use.

**Service
implementation**

Some information centers are reactive; others are proactive. A **reactive center** models its services around identifiable user demand. For example, if a large number of Apple computers are being requisitioned, the center will organize classes that train users on this machine. If a strong interest in graphics is exhibited by the engineering department, then graphics software and hardware will be acquired by the center and supported. The **proactive center** takes the opposite approach. It aggressively seeks to introduce new technology that will enhance employee performance and result in increased job productivity. In other words, it leads rather than follows.

There are variations in how services are delivered. In some centers, a person on the staff will work with a user from start to finish. That is, the staff member will analyze the user's problem and requirements, select appropriate packages, train the user if needed, and support the user in developing the problem solution. In this way, the staff member will have time to become thoroughly familiar with the end-user's environment (perhaps even be able to identify hidden problems) and will be able to develop a close working relationship with the end-user. The drawback is that a single individual may lack some of the skills needed to solve the problem.

At other centers, someone at the help desk may first analyze the user's problem, then pass the user to staff members who have expertise in that specific problem area. A number of specialists from the center may work with the user over a period of time.

Most information centers being opened today are microcomputer oriented. But training is not limited to stand-alone computing: remote computing is supported as well, since microcomputers are often used as intelligent terminals when connected with minis or mainframes. Within the center, computers may belong to a local area network or be networked with computers in other departments. An important role of many information centers is to promote the acquisition of computers with a set of data communication standards, so that linkage of all corporate computers will be facilitated in the future.

FACILITIES

Physical facilities to support an information center include space for staff offices, a work area with terminals for general use, a resource center, and classrooms. Usually, these components are at a central location. However, classrooms may be located elsewhere, particularly when shared with other departments that provide training.

In the typical information center, staff members have individual cubicles where they can work quietly with end-users without being disturbed. An open area contains workstations, anywhere from three to a dozen, where computers and software packages can be displayed and demonstrated. Partitions to separate the workstations are advisable because users, especially neophytes, may be reluctant to demonstrate their lack of knowledge in front of others. (Managers are especially sensitive in this regard.) To promote space flexibility, the partitions should be easily movable. This allows enlargement of the workstations to accommodate small groups attending demonstrations.

The resource center may be in one corner of the work area or in an adjacent room. It should contain a library of books, periodicals, vendor literature, and self-help instructional material. In addition, both software packages and videocassette equipment may be available for loan.

The last essential component is the classroom facility. Most of the rooms should contain workstations so that students can have hands-on use of equipment. Terminals with large-screen displays or TV-type screen extenders are useful for classes that are too large to provide individual terminals for every student.

In all likelihood, end-users will bring problems to the center that involve personal and proprietary data. For this reason, the security officer of the firm should be involved in planning the center so that security considerations can be addressed from the start. Passwords, sign-ons, hardware locks, classification of data security levels, protocols for sharing of data between functions—indeed, all of the types of controls discussed in Chapter 9 should be considered. It is up to the staff of the center to ensure that security works and to observe and enforce all security measures.

STAFF

Information centers often start with a small **staff,** a manager and two or three consultants, then add new members as the center builds its clientele and as demands for service increase. From 12 to 50 employees may work in a well-established center. In addition, the temporary services of data processing personnel (or personnel from functional departments) may occasionally be added on a loan basis.

Staff members require computer expertise; technical competence is a prerequisite for the job. However, business experience is important as well. In hiring, most corporations look for data processing professionals who understand business problems, and many like to include M.B.A. graduates, who can "speak management's language." Teachers are also excellent candidates for employment, since education is the focus of much information center activity.

Information center personnel need to possess a number of personal characteristics. Foremost, they require interpersonal communications skills. All staff members play a teaching role, although not all teach in a formal classroom. They must be able to present their ideas clearly and at a level of difficulty appropriate to the user's background and experience. They must have patience and persistence as they impart the knowledge that will lead to user self-sufficiency, building the user's self-confidence all the while. They also need selling talents, the ability to solve problems, a willingness to develop new skills (such as applications and package skills), and the capacity to act as a self-starter.

Staff roles should be well thought out before hiring begins. In all likelihood, the manager will be responsible for personnel and financial management of the center and for planning, control of resources, and liaison with other departments. The manager will also be expected to make periodic reports to superiors (for example, the data processing department head or the chief information officer) regarding the activities of the center.

Staff composition will depend on the mission of the center and the extent to which outside, part-time consultants are used for training and technical support. Usually, analysts, consultants, product specialists, teachers, and clerical personnel are hired. (In small centers, a single individual may perform several of these roles.) Analysts and consultants help users define their problems and offer guidance in ways to reach solutions. (See Chapter 20 for more information on these positions.) Product specialists are experts in the uses and functions of the packages that the center supports. They direct users to appropriate packages, provide training in package use, and will structure interfaces between packages, if needed. Teachers help users develop the necessary skills to utilize computer resources effectively. Clerical personnel provide secretarial support, keep financial records, prepare schedules, maintain manuals, and so on.

Job descriptions of information center personnel will vary from one organization to another. Assignment of duties will depend on how the center is organized and what services are offered.

FINANCING: WHO PAYS?

Many corporations have a "no charge" structure for information center services, which are counted as overhead. One reason for such a policy is to make the center available to all departments, even those with tight budgets. The more common reason for no charge is to encourage end-users to use the information center when it first opens. Once demand for the services of the center builds, a payment schedule may be initiated.

So that all costs can be allocated to users, most large information centers have elaborate **chargeback** systems based on complex algorithms. One objective of a chargeback system is to ensure that persons who use the center realize the benefits they receive and what it would mean if the center were not available. By assessing the cost of service, benefits are quantified. Another objective is to encourage responsible use of the center. A person is less likely to make frivolous or excessive demands on the center when required to pay service charges. (Note that the rationale behind chargeback schemes for data processing departments, discussed in Chapter 12, is repeated here.)

Chargeback financial data can be used to justify the center's existence to top management. The figures establish the value of the services offered to end-users. In addition, the figures can document use trends and are helpful in making capacity-planning projections.

Functional departments may be charged a fixed flat rate for information center service (often a percentage charge based on department size, since use is generally proportionate to size), or they pay according to connect time, CPU cycles, disk space, hard-copy output, or some other cost algorithm. The problem is to create a charge structure that is fair to all users. Sometimes, algorithms are used to control and monitor user demands. For example, an information center that is operating its computers at near capacity may impose time-of-day charges to encourage use of the center at off-peak hours.

Training is usually charged by the hour. The problem is that users need a lot of help and support when they are first introduced to new equipment or software. However, the need tapers off in time. This pattern of uneven demand means that the center may lose money in slack times and be forced to cut back the number of persons assigned to training and support as a result. Then, when new hardware or software becomes available, the center will be understaffed.

Whether or not an information center implements a chargeback system, the end-user should be informed of the expenses incurred by the center for the services it provides. Such information is needed by the end-user in order to make a cost-benefits analysis of services received. In conducting this analysis, intangible benefits should not be overlooked. Perhaps the most important benefit in this category would be the improved ability to find rapid and rational solutions to information-oriented business problems, because of the availability of tools and the support of the information center staff.

FUTURE OF INFORMATION CENTERS

Since the inception of information centers, a debate has ranged in professional circles over the following question: Are the centers here to stay, or are they a temporary phenomenon? It is generally agreed that end-users will always need troubleshooting, training, and consultation in order to take full advantage of their computing resources. The focus of the controversy is whether such services will be the responsibility of departmental experts working in functional areas or whether they will remain in the information center in the future.

Judging by the content (and number) of current articles on the subject, information centers are not likely to disappear soon. One reads of the need to expand the services that the centers offer, not of center dissolution. It would appear that for this decade at least, reliance on information centers will continue to grow. What's more, the centers may remain the central focus for guiding and supporting end-user computing in the 1990s, as long as centers keep up-to-date on new applications and technology, maintain quality staff, and address issues of user concern.

SUMMING UP

The primary goal of an information center is to develop end-user self-sufficiency. The center offers technical assistance, consulting services, product support, and training. It focuses on short-term (often

Table 18–1   **Who uses an information center?**

Users	Percent of sites surveyed*
Business management staff	95%
Clerical staff	70
Data processing staff	66
Engineers	43
Production staff	25
Commercial staff	13
Other	16

*Figures are based on a user survey reported in Wayne L. Rhodes, Jr., "The Information Center: Harvesting the Potential," *Infosystems*, vol. 32, no. 11 (November 1985), p. 54.

one-shot) computer-related problems that can be immediately resolved and on the teaching of computer literacy.

Users benefit because they are taught the skills they need to solve their own problems, and they are given timely advice when they need technical assistance. (See Table 18–1 for survey results showing which employee groups use the services of the information center heavily.) The data processing department benefits because it can now concentrate on systems development and long-range projects. Backlogs are also reduced once users learn to use packages and ways to modify and maintain programs on their own. The corporate organization, as a whole, benefits because the center promotes efficient and effective use of the company's information resources. (Table 18–2 lists reasons why end-users require professional assistance to take full advantage of their information resources.)

Table 18–2   **Reasons why end-user computing requires guidance and direction**

End-users tend to "reinvent the wheel." That is, they waste time and computer resources duplicating work that has already been done.

Learning by trial and error how to use computer resources and how to negotiate with vendors is unnecessarily costly.

Hardware and software vendors do not support end-users adequately.

Corporate data bases may become contaminated by users who lack proper training.

End-user requests for professional assistance are overwhelming data processing departments, leaving them little time to devote to long-range development projects.

End-users lack sensitivity to security issues and are not adequately trained to deal with them.

It takes technical knowledge to plan for the standardization and integration of computing resources. Both are essential if computer potential is to be realized, but most end-users are not well informed on these subjects.

The volume of computer products on the market bewilders the novice. To select appropriate hardware and software and to evaluate and compare options require knowledge of the market and some technical know-how.

End-users cannot be expected to keep abreast of new technological advances in the computing field.

Information centers are commonly a separate organizational entity under the data processing manager. Competent staff is a key to success. Employees should have technical expertise and a high level of communication skills, since all staff members—be they analysts, product specialists, or educators—will be teaching much of the time.

When an information center is being organized, decisions regarding the center's role will be made by top management. Included will be a decision on what approach to the transfer of information technology the center will take. A mission statement that tells the function of the center and the roles and responsibilities of both users and staff is then prepared. It should be accompanied by detailed information on how the center will meet its mission, tools and data that will be available, and accountability and chargeback considerations.

CASE: INFORMATION CENTER GIVES ADVICE ON MICROCOMPUTER SECURITY

The security of microcomputers and data processed on PCs is a growing problem for large organizations. Although office theft is nothing new (electronic products with an estimated worth of $10 billion were stolen in 1986), PCs now rank as the number one target. The unfortunate fact is that many employees are the thieves. According to the U.S. Department of Commerce, in-house dishonesty cost businesses in this country an estimated $40 billion in 1985.

In one large cosmetic company, one of the duties of the information center is to advise departmental managers on ways to make office PCs secure. Recommended are devices for both physical security of the micros and security of telecommunications. For example, departments are advised to use cable lockdowns. Some PCs in the company are permanently affixed to an aluminum plate by a superstrength adhesive. A lockdown device that the company hopes to use in the future is a product that transmits a signal to a security checkpoint if someone tries to remove the PC.

Other protective measures recommended by the information center include:

- A motion-detecting device that emits an alarm when PCs are moved.
- A power switch that can be locked into an off position so that no unauthorized person can access the interior of the machine.
- Point-to-point and file encryption devices.
- Access-control software, such as passwords and time locks.

Questions

1. What methods can be used by the information center to alert employees to security issues? How can the information center make employees aware of available security devices?
2. Why not assign responsibility for the security of PCs to computer center staff instead of the information center?
3. How can corporate management make sure that its information center keeps up-to-date on technological advances in areas such as security?
4. What other end-user issues should concern the information center in addition to security?

STUDY KEYS

Chargeback

End-user

Information center

Mission statement

Operating plan

Organizational placement

Physical facilities

Proactive center

Reactive center

Security

Staff

Support and services

DISCUSSION QUESTIONS

1. Although the concept of a support center for end-users is not new, it was not until the 1980s that the concept gained widespread support. Why?
2. What is the difference between a user and an end-user? Should an information center distinguish between the two? Why? What distinction should be made?
3. Can an information center reduce end-user frustration in the use of computer resources? How?
4. How does the data processing department benefit from the establishment of an information center?
5. What is a mission statement? What documents should accompany the statement?
6. Where should an information center be placed in the organizational hierarchy of a firm? What are the options? What factors should be taken into consideration when deciding placement?
7. Discuss the services that information centers commonly provide.
8. Who should decide whether a request for information center service is legitimate and reasonable? What criteria should be used?

9. What measures should be taken at the information center to ensure that training is appropriate to the audience?

10. Suppose that the advice given to the end-user by the information center conflicts with the view of the end-user's supervisor. How should the conflict be resolved? Should the information center be passive or "battle" for what it believes?

11. What physical facilities are needed to support the mission of an information center?

12. In a corporation that is housed in a large number of buildings at one site, should the information center have offices in more than one building? Explain.

13. If you were given responsibility for hiring information center staff, what qualifications and personal characteristics would you look for?

14. In problem solving, should information centers utilize the services of outside consultants, in-house data processing professionals, and experts in functional departments? How should this be arranged?

15. Do end-users expect too much from information centers? Why? Can overexpectations be avoided? How?

16. Should the information center be free of bias toward vendors? How can this be achieved?

17. Should an information center be a closed shop, or should end-users have the option of seeking help outside the corporate organization?

18. What are the advantages and disadvantages of a chargeback policy?

19. Do you think that informations centers are here to stay or just a passing fad? Give your reasoning.

SELECTED ANNOTATED BIBLIOGRAPHY

Brancheau, James C.; Douglas R. Vogel; and James C. Wetherbe. "An Investigation of the Information Center from the User's Perspective." *Data Base*, vol. 17, no. 1 (Fall 1985), pp. 4–14.
This is a report on a survey conducted during 1985 that involved over 50 end-users in five Fortune 1,000 corporations regarding the importance of information centers, their effectiveness, critical success factors, and their future.

Brandt, Allen. "Make Information Systems Pay Its Way." *Harvard Business Review*, vol. 65, no. 1 (January–February, 1987), pp. 57–63.
The author argues that for an information center to achieve its strategic end in a business, it must have a flexible budget, a systematic policy for pricing its product, and capable management.

Cook, Rick. "Who Picks Up the Info-Center Tab?" *Computer Decisions*, vol. 17, no. 2 (January 29, 1985), pp. 94–98.
The author argues that an information center should charge users and suggests ways of doing so. Charge policies at Security Pacific are cited to illustrate some of the problems in setting an equitable fee structure.

"Future Effects of End User Computing." *EDP Analyzer*, vol. 21, no. 11 (November 1983), pp. 1–14.
Corporations can expect that end-users will be making more and more direct, hands-on use of computers in the future. Types of use, the preference for personal computers, and problems of growth in end-user computing are subjects addressed.

Henderson, John C., and Michael E. Treacy. "Managing End-User Computing for Competitive Advantage." *Sloan Management Review*, vol. 27, no. 2 (Winter 1986), pp. 3–13.
Both tight control and little or no control of end-user computering pose problems for management. This article discusses the challenge of meeting end-user demands while advancing an end-user computing strategy that will efficiently support the competitive position of the firm.

Hoshower, Leon B., and Anthony A. Verstraete. "Accounting for Information Center Costs." *Journal of Accounting and EDP*, vol. 1 (Winter 1986), pp. 4–9.
Cost accounting in a newly opened or underused information center should differ from that in a mature information center. The authors discuss why this is so and recommend appropriate accounting methods for growth stages.

Johnson, Richard T. "The Infocenter Experience." *Datamation*, vol. 30, no. 1 (January 1984), pp. 137–42.
This case study of Exxon Corp.'s experience with an information center helps to provide insights into end-user computing.

Karten, Naomi. "Adding Context to Computing." *Information Center*, vol. 2, no. 11 (November 1986), pp. 25–27.
The author argues that end-users in business need to understand more than product mechanics in order to become self-sufficient in the use of computers.

Mills, C. R. "Strategic Planning Generates Potent Power for Information Centers." *Data Management*, vol. 22, no. 2 (February 1984), pp. 23–25.
The author discusses how the information center can contribute to planning.

O'Mara, Janet. "Building an Information Center that Works." *ICP Data Processing Management*, vol. 9, no. 2 (Autumn 1984), pp. 24–27.
Types of activities that an information center should provide to foster user self-sufficiency are described.

Rhodes, Wayne L., Jr. "The Information Center: Harvesting the Potential." *Infosystems*, vol. 32, no. 11 (November 1985), pp. 48–54.
What an information center can accomplish depends on the quality of information center staff, the availability of hardware and software at the center, and the types of problems brought to the center by end-users.

Shidal, Jerry G. "Advice for the Budget Bound." *Information Center*, vol. 2, no. 3 (March 1986), pp. 38–42.
Interim solutions to budget limitations are suggested, including the hiring

of part-time help, relocation, the purchase of microcomputers rather than complete systems, and the use of modestly priced, medium-range query and retrieval software products.

Vacca, John R. "The Information Center's Critical Post-Start-Up Phase." *Journal of Information Systems Management,* vol. 2, no. 2 (Spring 1985), pp. 50–56.
The wide range of support services that an information center can provide is discussed.

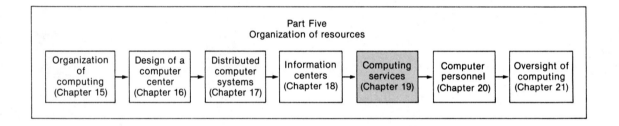

Part Five
Organization of resources

| Organization of computing (Chapter 15) | Design of a computer center (Chapter 16) | Distributed computer systems (Chapter 17) | Information centers (Chapter 18) | Computing services (Chapter 19) | Computer personnel (Chapter 20) | Oversight of computing (Chapter 21) |

CHAPTER 19

Computing services

If you want to make a long trip through
a far wilderness, find a guide who has made
the journey before.

Old proverb

A large computing service industry has developed over the years to provide organizations with computer expertise to supplement and enhance in-house processing capability. For example, a company may contract with an outside firm for remote processing. Data will be transmitted by telecommunications to this outside source for processing. Another segment of the computing service industry provides consulting services. When the problem is lack of personnel to manage and run a corporate computing facility, a facilities management company can be contracted on a short- or long-term basis to operate the center.

Firms with no computers of their own may turn to a service bureau or a utility for information processing. Such service firms are also used by companies that want access to computing power to supplement in-house capability and by those needing access to hardware or software that they lack in-house.

This chapter will discuss the advantages and disadvantages of each of the above types of computing services, stressing that these alternatives are not mutually exclusive. A variety of mixes is possible. For example, a firm with an in-house computer center may assign certain jobs to a service bureau. Or a firm that contracts for facilities management may also use remote processing to access a utility's specialized data base.

REMOTE PROCESSING

Remote processing is defined as the processing of computer programs through an input/output device that is remotely connected to a computer system. That is, jobs are submitted online to a computer from a terminal that is physically distant from the central processing unit (CPU).

With remote processing, a terminal may be used by an employee to access a company computer located in another room, on another floor, or in another company building. (The terminal will be connected to the CPU by in-house cable or by telecommunications.) Another type of remote processing is access to computing power from an external source, such as another firm with excess computing power or a utility that specializes in meeting the computing needs of clients. (Utilities will be described later in this chapter.) This latter type of remote processing is categorized as a computing service, the subject of this chapter.

Remote processing may be either **continuous processing** or **batch processing.** That is, data can be transmitted online as it is generated for instantaneous processing (**active online processing**) or can be stored upon receipt by the computer for later batch processing (**passive online processing**). An example of active online processing would be an airline system that allows a travel agent to ascertain seat availability for a given flight and to confirm a reservation for a client. An example of passive online processing is found in the automobile industry when a local car dealer sends sales data by remote job entry to headquarters in Detroit for overnight batch processing with sales data from other dealers around the country. Reports based on information so processed are then transmitted back to the dealers to aid in management decision making.

Active online processing may be subdivided into two parts: processing that does not require any updating of the data base (**nonmodifying**) and processing that does (**modifying**). A query to an existing data base or processing of scientific input data are examples of nonmodifying processing. Functional online real-time (OLRT) systems dedicated to process control or transaction processing in banking or reservations are examples of processing that modifies the data base. Modification is also required in some general-purpose online computing, such as when a manager or production engineer wants to know the effect of a certain parameter change. **Time-sharing,** which is sharing a computer with other users (although the speed of response may give one the illusion of being the sole user), is becoming an increasingly popular mode of remote processing in the business sector.

Figure 19–1 diagrams the relationship of the modes of remote processing discussed in this section.

Why remote processing?

Remote processing is a time saver. It allows a person to input data for computer processing without having to go to the location of the CPU. Sometimes, a company uses remote processing to an external source to supplement its own processing capability, taking advantage

Figure 19–1  **Classification of modes of remote processing**

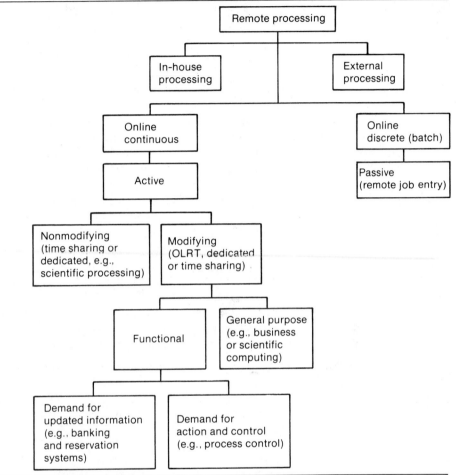

of the storage capacity, specialized data bases, or other processing services offered by the source. An additional reason to combine remote
with local processing is to cushion surges in processing demand. When
professional personnel and corporate management want the computational power of a large computer but need it only intermittently,
remote processing may be the most cost-effective answer.

Other firms choose remote processing as an alternative to developing
an in-house computing facility. They save space, equipment, and personnel resources that would otherwise have to be allocated to a computer center. Still other firms utilize remote processing as an interim
solution to their processing needs while developing an in-house processing capability.

Selection of an external remote processing service

Factors that should be considered when deciding whether external remote processing is advisable are listed in Table 19–1. Turnaround time, for example, may be critical, so benchmarks should test the response time of prospective suppliers during both supplier and user peak periods, as well as during hours with normal workloads. Teleprocessing costs may also be decisive. Pricing is usually based on transmission costs plus computing costs (per unit of connect time or per unit of computing time).

Most supplier firms have elaborate pricing algorithms that vary as much as 200 percent. These algorithms are based on type of use and length of job. Adjustments may be made for guaranteed minimum usage, and discounts given according to number of terminals or other considerations. Charges may drop 20 percent by simply mentioning a competitor. To help users understand pricing algorithms, many suppliers provide users with accounting reports so that expensive jobs can be identified. Often, by redesigning the jobs or rescheduling them to nonpeak periods, users can cut processing costs.

A decision to contract for remote processing with an external source should be based on a cost-benefits analysis, and care should be taken in selecting the supplier of this computing service. Over time, increases in transmission costs or changes in volume of service may reduce the economic viability of remote processing. Therefore, a financial review of remote processing should be periodically conducted.

Table 19–1   **Factors to be considered in deciding on external remote processing**

Type of assistance needed:
  Hardware
  Software
    Operating systems, DBMS's, etc.
    Applications packages
  Support
Financial payoff
Remote processing performance:
  Turnaround and response time
  Error rates and accuracy
Effect on credibility and public relations when work is not done in-house
In-house knowledge and experience with remote processing
Experience to be gained by contact with outside firm
Telecommunications problems
Possible loss of control over data
Possible need to submit to outside standards
Added vendor contacts and hassles
Human factor considerations
Organizational impact

CONSULTANTS

Using **consultants** is a thoroughly ingrained way of doing business in this country. Few firms can afford to staff their companies with experts in all technical fields. As a result, they face problems from time to time that no employee within the firm is qualified or competent to handle. The expertise of a consultant is invaluable when in-house experience is lacking. What is more, consultants can bring an independent viewpoint to problem solving. They often serve as mediators in internal politics and act as spark plugs to get projects moving.

In the field of computing, the need for consultants is accentuated by the fast pace of technological development. The typical data processing department is struggling to fill backlogged user demands. There is no time for internal staff to develop expertise in such technical areas as micro to mainframe links, local area networks, office automation, telecommunications, information systems architectures, or general systems integration. Just to keep abreast of vendor trends in both hardware and software may require outside help. According to one observer, "The computer industry has been characterized by phenomenol change, and change creates uncertainty, and uncertainty creates the demand for consultants."[1]

Even large firms with a wide range of specialists on the payroll often employ consultants. The need may arise because in-house personnel have ongoing commitments and do not have time to devote to new projects. Sometimes, a company wants the services of someone experienced in the problem at hand. For example, in applications development, a consultant who has had practical experience designing a similar system for another firm can be an invaluable member of a project team. Sometimes, the technicians a firm wants to hire are unavailable in the marketplace. Sometimes, a consultant rather than a full-time specialist is preferred because the latter's wage demands would distort the organization's wage and salary plan and create wage inequities.

An important advantage of consultants is that they are not a party to the internal power struggles within a firm and so can be more objective when seeking problem solutions. Their jobs and future promotions are not jeopardized by any recommendations they make. And not being bound to firm traditions or precedents, they should be able to evaluate vendors and systems without bias.

The outside consultant, on the other hand, will not be acquainted with the personalities in the firm and will not understand how de-

---

[1]Michale Hammer, president of Hammer Associates. Quoted in Glenn Rifkin, "Choosing and Using Consultants," *Computerworld*, September 2, 1985, p. Update/3.

partments interact or how the firm functions. Recommendations made without taking time to gain familiarity with the firm's unique environment may prove inappropriate. What is more, the presence of a consultant may be viewed as an intrusion and hamper smooth working relationships. The large hourly salary of the consultant may be resented by in-house staff. In addition, ruffled feelings may arise from the fact that advice received from internal staff members may have been ignored by top management while the same advice is accepted from the consultant. The question of security also arises. Should sensitive data be exposed to consultants who have not demonstrated loyalty to a firm? The possibility exists that the information the consultant learns about the business might later be sold to competitors.

The need for an outside opinion can arise in all phases of development and operations. For example, consultants often participate in feasibility studies, decisions of resource acquisition, systems specifications, and the design of new systems. They may be hired to set standards, to establish privacy and security procedures, to help select personnel, or to run training programs. They have even been known to function as project managers for short-term, highly technical development projects. Managerial consultants may also help organize de-

Figure 19–2   **Areas in which users tap management consultants**

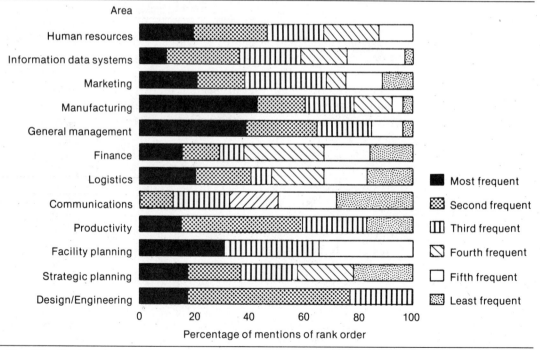

Source: Glenn Rifkin, "Choosing and Using Consultants," *Computerworld*, September 2, 1985, p. Update/3.

partments, assist in planning, or devise strategies to reduce resistance to change. (Figure 19–2 shows the areas in which management consultants are frequently employed.)

The broad range and critical nature of these activities require that consultants must be selected with care, with their qualifications and reputations carefully screened.

Selection

When searching for consultants, a good starting point is to ask professional associates to make recommendations based on their past experiences with consultants. Corporate executives may ask contacts at conferences or industry meetings to provide names of consultants with whom they have had successful dealings in the past. In addition, many professional organizations compile consulting lists. In the United States, the Independent Computer Consultants Association in St. Louis has a listing of more than 1,600 member firms representing more than 4,000 independent consultants. Other lists of consultants may be obtained from organizations such as:

Association of Management Consulting Firms.

JobNet Inc., Self Employed Professionals.

Professional & Technical Consultants Association.

Society of Telecommunications Consultants.

Software Consultant Brokers Association.

Many consultants advertise in newspapers and professional journals. Academia is another mine for consultants.

Unfortunately, no official body regulates or certifies consultants, so the selection of a suitable candidate can be a risky proposition. Here are some guidelines that should help narrow the field and control the consultant's work:

- Examine the consultant's personal and corporate background through reference checks and financial reviews.
- Draw up a detailed written project plan and schedule for the work the consultant is to do. Make sure that the consultant understands the assignment and can demonstrate competence in this area of work.
- Build checkpoints or milestones into the project.
- Conduct regular review meetings between milestones.
- Thoroughly test the work of the consultant.

These recommendations are basic hiring and project management techniques.

Consultants may be hired by the hour or by the job. Rates are high. Well-known consultants command $5,000 to $10,000 per day, plus expenses. Consulting firms may charge from $75 to $200 per hour: independents command fees that range from $40 per hour to the rates

cited earlier for superstars. Nevertheless, most firms feel the money is
well spent. Surprisingly, consulting firms find their clients mainly among
successful companies rather than companies in trouble. As stated by
Ira Gottfried, president of Gottfried Consultants, "The growing, profitable corporation recognizes its limitations and is able to spend the
money to gain additional assistance from outside the company."[2]

Future trends

The fast pace of technological advance in the computer industry
suggests that consulting work should continue to be plentiful in the
near future. As in the past, corporations will undoubtedly call upon
the services of consultants in order to keep up-to-date regarding developments in the computing field. However, many observers suggest
that the more important role of consultants in the future will be to help
corporations manage their information resources in order to gain a
competitive edge. For example, customers who have installed personal
computers, local area networks, and telecommunications equipment
will want to learn how best to integrate such technology in order to
meet business objectives, information no single vendor or technician
can provide. Consultants will be valued for their computer knowledge
plus their business expertise.

VENDORS

Vendors are often an underutilized source of technical expertise.
Unlike consultants, vendors have a bias in favor of their own products,
but this bias does not necessarily preclude sound advice on equipment
and systems. (A company would, however, be wise to check the literature and other users for corroborative opinion.)

Vendors can often provide technical information on controls, security, and even installation of equipment. For example, when a computer center is being planned, vendors frequently furnish an installation
expert to help design the layout. The expert may supply tables and
charts on clearances and power needs and even provide templates and
sample layout diagrams. For microcomputers, many computer stores
(such as ComputerLand, Radio Shack, and Future Information Services)
today offer a range of services, from maintenance and support to seminars and consulting. A store that sells both hardware and software may
be in a better position to know what is wrong and how to solve the
problem than either hardware or software vendors, who tend to waste
time blaming one another when something goes wrong. A classic ex-

---

[2]Quoted in Louis Fried, *Practical Data Processing Management* (Reston, Va.: Reston
Publishing, 1979), p. 285.

ample of vendor assistance with systems design was IBM's contribution to the first commercial airline reservation system for American Airlines.

Vendors commonly provide documentation and training on systems they supply. One vendor specializes in training programs featuring management games played at a country club, with golf interspersed between work sessions. This is good publicity for the vendor, while informative and fun for the trainee. Vendors often keep clients informed regarding industry scuttlebutt as well, such as who is in the job market and what new products are being launched.

Of course, not all vendors perform such roles, but many do offer valuable counsel. Establishing good rapport with vendors can speed up delivery dates of equipment, even result in visits by the vendor's analysts and engineers. Without doubt, most vendor representatives are knowledgeable in their respective fields, well supported by their companies, carefully trained, and well rehearsed. That they can be smooth talkers and high-pressure salesmen should come as no surprise. It is up to computer departments to be just as well prepared, know what questions to ask, and review responses critically, compensating for bias.

Sometimes, a vendor representative responsible for equipment maintenance is assigned to a given firm and is on-site daily. Such individuals become well acquainted with the staff and problems of the computer department and often act as informal consultants. On occasion, they take sides in disputes. Vendor representatives have even been known to appeal to corporate management to reverse computer department decisions and to win. Vendors have clout and sometimes use it.

FACILITIES MANAGEMENT

Facilities management (FM) is the use of an independent service organization to operate and manage the contracting firm's own data processing installation. Firms assign some or all of their computing to FM corporations for a variety of reasons. Some lack the technical personnel needed to run their data processing centers. Others do not want responsibility for operating computing equipment. Still others utilize facilities management because their firm's own computer department has been so badly mismanaged (dissatisfied users, missed deadlines, poorly utilized equipment, frequent time and cost overruns) that it must be reorganized, rebuilt, and restaffed. In the interim, the FM company is given responsibility for the center. Some firms also decide on a long-term facilities management contract because they believe that their centers will be better managed under FM than by in-house staff.

Advantages and disadvantages

Few firms can match FM corporations in the quality of their computing staff. This is one reason why companies turn to FM for computing assistance. Good salaries and challenging work attract highly qualified personnel to FM. Computer professionals are drawn by the range of experience that they can gain when employed by a FM firm, experience that helps them move quickly along their chosen career paths. Experts in fields such as teleprocessing, numerical control, and planning that use linear programming or simulation are also attracted to FM because they are able to concentrate on their specialities full-time in an FM job. In other firms, demand for their expertise might be limited, resulting in work assignments outside their fields of expertise.

Under facilities management, a computer center can often be operated more economically than when managed by a corporation's own computing staff, partly because FM firms buy in quantity lots and obtain bigger discounts from vendors than do other firms. The highly trained professionals who work for FM companies also get better efficiency, reliability, and utilization from computer resources than the average employee in a data processing center. What's more, FM employees can redesign systems, reorganize, and eliminate redundancies to achieve better performance in client firms without being encumbered by obligations to individuals or power blocks within that firm.

With FM, however, interface problems are compounded because computing is no longer organizationally in-house. The user must now interact with computer personnel whose primary loyalty lies with the FM company. New liaison procedures must be established, and new boundaries of authority and responsibility have to be defined between user and electronic data processing (EDP) personnel. Though obligations of the FM corporation should be detailed in the contract (see Table 19–2 for a list of subjects to be included in FM contracts), it takes time to develop smooth working relationships when a FM firm takes over management of a firm's computer center. Considerable disagreement between users and FM staff regarding performance under FM may surface as well, for evaluation of performance can be a highly subjective judgment. In such cases, relations are bound to be strained.

Table 19–2	Subjects for inclusion in facilities management contracts	
	Duration of contract	Standards
	Availability of personnel	Input requirements
	Availability of expertise	Documentation scope
	Lines of reporting for personnel	Output portfolio and schedule
	Liaison	Priorities
	Ownership of equipment	Changes
	Ownership of software	Payments
	Security	Limitation and liabilities
	Privacy of data	Right to audit FM firm's operations
	Property interests	Contract termination procedures
	Applications portfolio	Scope and level of effort of FM personnel
	Extension of applications	and contracting firm

Another disadvantage of FM is that users lose control over their data and worry about privacy and security, particularly when the FM company is also servicing a competitor. (FM companies must guard against legal violations in such cases.) User flexibility is lost as well. And how can clients ensure that FM employees are motivated to act in the client's best interest? Designing contract incentives can challenge a client's lawyer.

When negotiating for FM services, the length of the contract period will depend on what type of service is required. Activities that have a long period of gestation, such as development of integrated systems or training programs, can not be undertaken when the FM contract is short-term. (An FM company may prefer to omit training, since lack of training may extend the company's need for FM and hence create a dependency on FM.) A long contract period, however, may so entrench FM that it is hard for the client to take back management responsibility for processing. Most users do plan to manage their computer departments eventually, and they try to estimate the length of time needed to develop the technical expertise to do so, signing a FM contract for this interim period only. Indeed, many client firms find reliance on FM insulting to corporate management and believe their own personnel will be more responsive to internal processing needs than will FM staff. A compromise strategy is to take a short-term contract with an option to renew.

Cost

Cost of FM will depend on the size of the data processing configuration to be managed, scope of processing activities of the client firm, level of performance to be achieved, and ownership conditions. Contract length is also a factor (most run two to six years). The contract awarded Bunker Ramo by the National Association of Security Dealers to run the nationwide stock market quotations and trading for over-the-counter securities is one example of what facilities management costs: $10.5 million for a three-year contract. Though this figure may seem high, many firms find that FM is less expensive than the cost of developing equivalent in-house expertise and capability.

Cost-plus contracts are sometimes negotiated for facilities management. The problem is defining the "plus" component.

Variations

FM contracts are based on user needs. Although most facilities management means processing is on the client's hardware, some FM firms will also contract for services on their own equipment. (One third of a major FM corporation's 90 client firms, for example, use the FM company's hardware.) Advantages to the client include freeing equipment and personnel for other activities, and the creation of backup. Security and transportation are major problems in this arrangement.

Another variation is a contractual agreement whereby the FM company selects equipment, installs it, and makes it operational, providing the client with a **turnkey system.** The client takes possession and manages processing once all problems associated with systems development, data base implementation, programming, testing, and conversion have been resolved. This concept is popular in the Middle East, where technical expertise is in short supply but companies don't want outsiders, particularly Americans, responsible for daily operations.

SERVICE BUREAUS

Service bureaus can provide equipment, software, or personnel to clients according to their needs. For example, the firm under contract to the service bureau may have its own computer department but lack hardware or programs for specialized computations, such as linear programming. Perhaps more data storage capacity is needed for a prediction model. Perhaps a special compiler (like SIMSCRIPT) is required for a simulation run. The firm will contract with a service bureau for hardware/software access of this nature to supplement in-house resources.

Some bureaus provide access to specialized data bases, such as the full text of state and federal court decisions or updated daily lists of stock market transactions. One service bureau has a data base of extracts from Securities and Exchange Commission filings from over 12,000 publicly held companies; another has data on the Japanese economy, including a macro model and forecasts. Service bureaus can also prepare data, assist in data collection, consult, and even contract facilities management. A sample list of service bureau offerings appears in Table 19–3.

Table 19–3	Services offered by a service bureau	
	Contribute to one or more stages of development	Storage capacity
	Provide specialized data base	Facilities management
	Prepare firm's data base or assist in data conversion	Capacity for excess workload
		Unexpected
		Seasonal
	Prepare data for ongoing data base	Growth
	Provide programs	Handle processing when firm lacks:
	Standard functional programs (e.g., accounting)	Capital for hardware acquisition
		Space
	Programs for decision support systems	Personnel
		Time
	Industry-specialized programs	Processing capacity
	Customized programs	Miscellaneous
	Process data in a variety of modes	Data collection
	Batch	Output delivery
	Interactive batch	Consulting
	Online	
	Online real-time	

**Why service
bureaus?**

Many of the advantages of facilities management apply to service bureaus as well. Service bureaus can attract highly qualified personnel and specialists and can therefore operate at a higher level of efficiency and professionalism than the average firm. They can also operate at lower cost, taking advantage of economies of scale. For example, program development is less costly when shared by a large base of users. Because of this base, service bureaus can also maintain large computer installations, develop extensive data bases, and offer all modes of processing (batch, interactive batch, online, and online real-time). Firms that utilize service bureaus may not have the in-house capability of performing needed activities or may find it more economical to use a service bureau than to gear up for the activity. Even well-known large firms, including Boeing, Chase Manhattan, Control Data, GE, GTE, Lockheed, New York Times, Time Inc., and Xerox Corporation are service bureau customers. In some cases, these same firms sell services to others and buy services concurrently (for example, Boeing and Control Data).

Selection

A firm considering the option of a service bureau should first examine the economic feasibility of handling the activity in-house, then contact a number of service bureaus and compare their offerings, because service bureaus differ in their fee structures. Some charge a flat rate. Others base fees on the amount of resources used, how they are used, and for what applications. Before a service bureau contract is signed, costs should also be compared with other alternatives (for example, facilities management or acquisition of minis and software packages).

But cost of services should not be the only criterion for selection of a service bureau. Table 19–4 lists other factors that should be considered.

Table 19–4	Factors to be considered in service bureau selection	
	Services offered	Hardware configuration
	Reputation of service bureau	Arrangements for data transfer
	Years of operation	Time involved
	Experience with firm's industry	Convenience
	Competence of personnel	Frequency
	References	Availability for access
	Financial stability	Benchmark results
	Promptness record	Backup facilities
	Quality of service	Pricing algorithms
	Errors	Normal load
	Reruns	Offload
	Integrity	Reruns
	Security and privacy record	Liability and damage conditions
	Software portfolio	Discontinuation conditions
	Compatibility	

The challenge facing service bureaus

The availability of inexpensive microcomputers has enabled many firms to keep work in-house that was formally contracted to service bureaus. The bureaus have also lost clients because the cost of software is down. Many companies can afford to purchase all of the programs they need, so software availability is no longer a major service bureau attraction.

With revenue dropping, service bureaus are consolidating and redefining their role. Some industry observers predict that by the 1990s the field will be narrowed to a few gigantic superbureaus that emphasize information management instead of processing. These bureaus will offer services such as time-sharing, on-site microcomputers, and turnkey systems. They will help set up information centers and increase installation support and education. More emphasis may be placed on software-related consulting services. The companies may download software to customer microcomputers or act as distributors of small software developers. Electronic data interchange, the linking of buyers and suppliers, is a technology that may open new markets for service bureaus. Artificial intelligence and voice recognition may lead service bureaus in still other directions.

Change in the service bureau industry is nothing new. The industry today is radically different in appearance from that of the 1960s, when service bureaus were primarily hardware vendors. The industry has survived by meeting the evolving needs of clients, providing services that users have been unable to develop for themselves. According to the Yankee Group, a Boston-based research and consulting firm, the future of service bureaus will lie in their ability to offer:

> a combination of access to processing power; application specific software, standalone, on-line, and hybrid; value-added services; intercompany computer facilities; micro-to-mainframe links; variable bandwidth services; on-site hardware; and customized communications software.[3]

COMPUTER UTILITIES

A **computer utility** is a source of remote processing, selling computer time and services. Utilities offer unique processing features that distinguish them from service bureaus and other remote processing suppliers. Instead of contracting with a client for a specific service, time-sharing is available at any time, for as long as requested, to any user who can pay for it. The computer utility resembles an electric utility insofar as computing power, like electric power, must be continuously

---

[3]Edith Myers, "Here Come the Super Service Bureaus," *Datamation*, vol. 30, no. 16 (October 15, 1984), p. 110.

Figure 19–3   **Sample configuration of a utility**

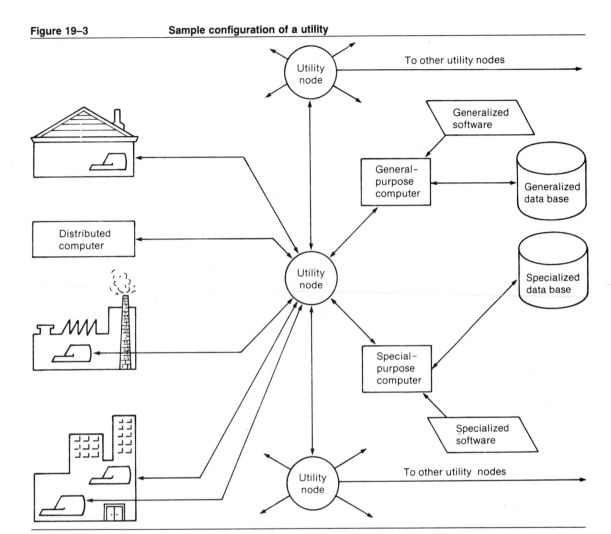

offered and be able to handle fluctuations of demand. This requires a grid or network, so that computing power can be accessed from a distant site if regional facilities are overloaded.

Figure 19–3 shows a sample utility configuration. Individual customers at home or business may be serviced by a utility node supported by a variety of resources (software, data bases, and computers), as illustrated. The node may draw on computing power from other nodes for special services or during peak periods of demand. Compatibility of hardware, software, and interfaces is therefore needed. Telecommunications and protocols to link utility nodes are also required.

A computer utility is an old concept, but because of regulation and networking problems, utilities offering comprehensive services are not too common in this country. However, recent court decisions (in relation to AT&T and IBM) that now allow the intersection of communications and computing may well spur the growth of this industry and foster fierce competition for customers. Conceivably, computer networks of the future may connect thousands of computers and service millions of users. They will undoubtedly carry both voice and video traffic, be fail-soft, and have sharing protocols for both terminal and file transfers. The X.25, a standard in communications, is a step in this direction.

Public fears over data security and privacy issues may slow public acceptance and use of utilities. Will proprietary data be safe from unauthorized intrusion when processed by a distant utility? Will linked utility data bases infringe upon individual privacy rights? How utilities should be regulated is also an unresolved question. The social implications of computer networks need to be addressed now by computer specialists, political theorists, and social scientists. The growth of utilities as a sector of the computer services industry will depend, to a large extent, on future legislation affecting network regulation and control.

SUMMING UP

This chapter has described segments of the computing service industry. Both consultants and vendors offer professional services based on their technical knowledge and experience. Consultants are more objective, have a broader base of experience and wider range of knowledge; but the services of vendors are usually free and, within narrow parameters, equally professional. Another difference between the two is that consultants may be hired to give advice to corporate management or the computer department, whereas vendors counsel mainly the latter and have a bias in favor of their own products, a difference illustrated in Figure 19–4.

Figure 19–4   **Relationship of consultants and vendors to the client**

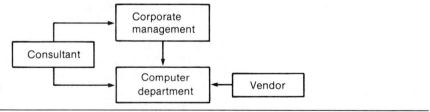

Table 19–5   **Professional services available to computing departments by source**

Source	Management consultants	Computer consultants	Auditors	Vendors	Facilities management	Software houses	Service bureaus	Utilities
Planning for computing	X	X		X	X		X	
Organization of computer department	X	X					X	
Phases of development		X	X		X		X	X
Standards		X	X		X		X	
Program implementation				X	X	X	X	
Control systems design		X	X	X	X		X	
Audit of efficiency and performance		X						
Hiring of computer personnel		X		X				
Training		X		X	X	X	X	
Planning for change	X	X		X	X			
Selection of computing resources		X					X	
Operations					X		X	X

Facilities management is useful when a firm owns equipment but does not wish to operate it. The firm may have had a bad experience with ineffectual internal management of computing in the past, or the shortage of qualified candidates means personnel capable of managing high technology cannot be hired. FM can be a short- or long-term solution to computing problems for small and medium-sized companies. Large firms are usually able to attract or generate the management necessary for their computing operations and so use FM less frequently.

Remote processing, service bureaus, and utilities may be contracted for external processing. Remote processing is appropriate for firms that want access to hardware, software, or data bases not available in-house, or that have occasional demand for a powerful computer. Remote job entry is also an alternative for firms that want to gain experience in computer processing before setting up an in-house processing facility.

Many small and medium-sized firms that want a full range of computer services are attracted to service bureaus.

Two other sources of professional assistance not discussed in the chapter deserve mention. One is auditors, whose functions are described in Chapter 10. The other is software houses, sellers of standard packages, which can also develop customized software and will, if paid, provide programmers and analysts to assist in software implementations, including documentation.

Table 19–5 summarizes, by source, professional services available to computer departments.

In selecting a supplier for computing services, cost-benefit studies should be conducted and bids from more than one vendor received, because pricing and services vary considerably. Alternatives should also be periodically reevaluated, since costs and benefits may change in time. For example, the availability of low-cost microcomputers means that many of the applications formerly contracted to outside service companies can now be done more cheaply in-house by many corporations.

CASE: EDS, A COMPUTER SERVICES COMPANY

In 1984, General Motors purchased Electronic Data Systems Corp. (EDS), a computer services company, for $2.5 billion in order to improve GM's data processing operations. The acquisition gives GM computer resources that it would have trouble developing from scratch. EDS will be responsible for integrating the automaker's facilities.

The experience gained from the work should put EDS in the forefront in two fast-growing computer service markets: telecommunications and factory automation. By the late 1980s, EDS expects to sell this expertise to outside clients.

EDS was founded in 1962 by Ross Perot, an IBM salesman who recognized that companies with mainframe computers would be willing to pay for help in operating their computer systems. Perot's company has expanded its service offerings as data processing has matured. Although EDS is now within the GM fold, the company will continue to keep its books separate and will issue its own financial statements. If EDS succeeds in its plans to automate GM's manufacturing plants and

Source: "How General Motors Is Bringing Up Ross Perot's Baby," *Business Week*, April 14, 1986, pp. 96–100.

to connect the company's far-flung operations with a large, sophisticated telecommunications network engineered to carry voice, video, and data, the company's leadership among computer service companies, particularly in the systems integration market, is assured.

Questions

1. Why did EDS keep its books separate once in the GM fold?
2. Why did GM purchase EDS instead of hiring computer professionals to help improve its data processing operations? Why not contract with an outside services company instead?
3. What are the benefits to EDS in being part of GM?
4. What advantages should EDS have in competing against other service companies when its expertise is sold to clients outside GM?

STUDY KEYS

Active online processing	**Passive online processing**
Batch processing	**Professional services**
Computer utility	**Remote processing**
Consultants	**Service bureaus**
Continuous processing	**Time-sharing**
Facilities management (FM)	**Turnkey system**
Modifying	**Vendors**
Nonmodifying	

DISCUSSION QUESTIONS

1. How can consultants be used by:
    a. Computer executives?
    b. Steering committees?
    c. Top management?
    d. User managers?
    e. Project managers?
    f. Planning personnel?
2. What are the problems and limitations of engaging a consultant? How can these be minimized?
3. What are the advantages of using a computer consultant? What environmental conditions must be created to maximize these advantages?

4. If you were top management, would you hire a computer consultant if you had a computer technician with equivalent experience and knowledge of your staff? Why or why not?

5. A consultant is a highly paid outsider and is therefore respected. An in-house expert is relatively underpaid and much less respected. Do you agree? Comment.

6. What are the advantages of contracting software development to a consultant or software house, as opposed to developing the software in-house? Would there be a difference in:
    a. Documentation?
    b. Run efficiency?
    c. Maintainability?
    d. Reliability?

7. Would you use vendors as sources of information to help with recruiting, training, and design; or as a sounding board on future developments? Why?

8. Comment on the statement: In dealing with FM, a lawyer is needed to protect the contracting firm's interests.

9. Do you believe that FM hinders the building of in-house processing capability? Comment.

10. List arguments for and against FM for the following businesses:
    a. Department store in a middle-sized town.
    b. Warehouse of shoes.
    c. Drugstore chain of 20 stores.
    d. Hospital with 450 beds.
    e. University with 7,000 full-time students.
    f. Racetrack.
    g. Stock broker.
    h. Restaurant.
    i. Grocery chain of 25 stores.

11. Is remote processing appropriate for firms or departments that have specialized tasks using special programming languages or data bases? Comment.

12. Is remote processing appropriate to supplement centralized processing for intermittent and one-shot jobs? Comment.

13. Compare the difference between online real-time and time-sharing service for a manufacturing business.

14. How does the interactive capability of time-sharing affect a user in business? Which type of use will be most affected?

15. Compare the advantages and disadvantages of time-sharing from a commercial outside source with time-sharing in-house?

16. Can remote processing be used profitably for testing programs remotely? What limitations exist?

17. What are the advantages and pitfalls of using a service bureau? Under what circumstances would you recommend such use?

18. Why might management choose an external computing service instead of developing an in-house processing capability?

19. Under what conditions might a firm decide to use:
    a. A service bureau?
    b. Remote processing?

       c.   A computer utility?

       d.   In-house computing?

       Identify the problems and pitfalls of each.

20. What future do you foresee for remote processing, utilities, and service bureaus?

21. Should the sale of computer services, like the sale of electricity, be regulated by federal law? Explain.

22. Comment on the following statement: The problem of privacy and security is difficult to control with time-sharing, a service bureau, or a utility, and the problems will get worse in the future, not better.

23. Do you think that the service industry has matured and is growing into a stable, important, and well-defined sector of the computer industry? Explain your answer.

SELECTED ANNOTATED BIBLIOGRAPHY

Ardle, Jack M. "What Do You Do after Choosing a Data Processing Consultant?" *Office*, vol. 99, no. 6 (June 1984), pp. 63–64.
    Ten suggestions are given on how to best use a consultant. The author discusses an office environment using microcomputers, but his advice is applicable to other computer environments as well.

Fersko-Weiss, Henry. "Managing Your Computer Consultant." *Personal Computing*, vol. 10, no. 1 (January 1986), pp. 75–85.
    The author recommends getting referrals before consultants are hired. He also suggests a well-written, detailed contract, milestones, and weekly project meetings.

Kile, Michael. "Going Outside for MIS Implementation." *Information and Management*, vol. 6, no. 10 (October 1983), pp. 261–68.
    Small businesses do not have the expertise for many computer applications. A good consultant can be very helpful to such companies. The author discusses principles for dealing with consultants and presents a case study of consultant use by a small technical company.

Myers, Edith. "Here Come the Super Service Bureaus." *Datamation*, vol. 30, no. 16 (October 15, 1984), pp. 110–18.
    This article focuses on the changes that service bureaus are making in order to survive.

"Organizing for the 1990s." *EDP Analyzer*, vol. 24, no. 12 (December 1986), 16 p.
    Three issues are identified as being crucial for the organization of future information systems: separate production from innovation, manage the technology rather than its use, and incorporate all types of data.

Rossotti, Charles O. "The Computer Alternative." *Infosystems*, vol. 29, no. 9 (September 1982), pp. 60–62.
    Eight factors are identified for consideration when choosing between an in-house computer or an outside service bureau.

Stamp, David. "Is Anyone Really Using Computer Consultants?" *Datamation*,
    vol. 32, no. 23 (October 15, 1986), pp. 99–102.
    According to software consulting firms and free-lance programmers, there
    is high demand for consultants. But managers of management information
    systems say they don't depend on outsiders.

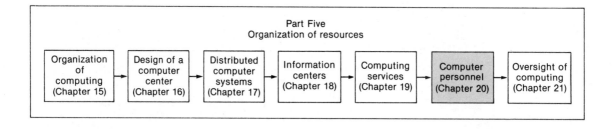

Part Five
Organization of resources

| Organization of computing (Chapter 15) | Design of a computer center (Chapter 16) | Distributed computer systems (Chapter 17) | Information centers (Chapter 18) | Computing services (Chapter 19) | Computer personnel (Chapter 20) | Oversight of computing (Chapter 21) |

CHAPTER 20

Computer personnel

The extension of man's intellect by machine, and the partnership of man and machine in handling information may well be the technological advance dominating this century.

Simon Ramo

Although computerized societies are often pictured as machine dominated, with humans subservient to technology, computers exist to serve people and to aid managers in reaching decisions. And they cannot execute given tasks without the assistance of a large number of professionals and support personnel.

For example, input—be it data, operating instructions, or applications programs—is initiated by humans. It takes analysts to assess the needs of users, and skilled programmers to convert these needs into bits, the only medium understood by machine. Collection and updating of data are an iterative human activity. Programmers are needed for the preparation of computer instructions, and many technicians are required for operating and servicing the computer itself. Without analysts, programmers, operators, managers, clerks, librarians, schedulers, and other support personnel, computers are unable to produce the information users request.

This chapter focuses on computer staffing. First, the duties and responsibilities of computer personnel are described. Job design, hiring, and turnover are discussed next. Since studies have shown that computer people place a high value on professional growth, both career development and training are also addressed in the chapter. The chapter closes with a section on job stress in the computing field.

469

JOBS IN COMPUTING

Who are the professionals and support personnel needed to run a computing facility? Data processing is usually subdivided into three functional areas: systems development, operations, and support, as shown in Figure 20–1. Programmers and analysts fall in the first category, operators in the second, with librarians, standards officers, schedulers, supply clerks, training coordinators, and others providing technical support in the third.

The schema in Figure 20–2 serves as an example of how a computer center can be organized and lists positions within these three functional areas. Figure 20–3 shows the typical mix of personnel in each area, in percentages. Of course, the mix will be adapted to the specific environment of each computer department. For example, a distributed processing configuration generally requires more operational and fewer support personnel at each node. A centralized computer installation has the opposite mix: more support and fewer operational personnel. Departmental organization, job titles, and job descriptions will vary from firm to firm.

Even within a given facility, positions are not static, since needs are constantly changing. A salary survey by *Datamation* in the early 1950s listed 27 computer positions. A similar survey in 1980 listed 55. This increase can be attributed to the growth of computing facilities and the complexity of computer operations today. Not all computer centers have 55 positions, however. Small companies may have far fewer positions, with a single individual filling several jobs.

Every year, the number of people choosing data processing careers grows. Since the Bureau of Labor Statistics (BLS) predicts that the average annual growth rate of the computer industry in the coming decade will be 3.7 percent, the choice appears to be a wise one. Indeed, of the 10 fastest-growing occupations, 7 are in the computer and electronic fields, according to the BLS (see Table 20–1). For example, the number of programmers is expected to rise 71.7 percent during the

Figure 20–1   **Organizational structure of a computer processing department**

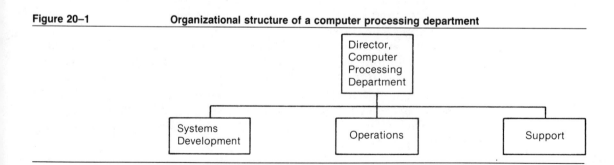

Figure 20–2   **Sample organization chart for a computer department**

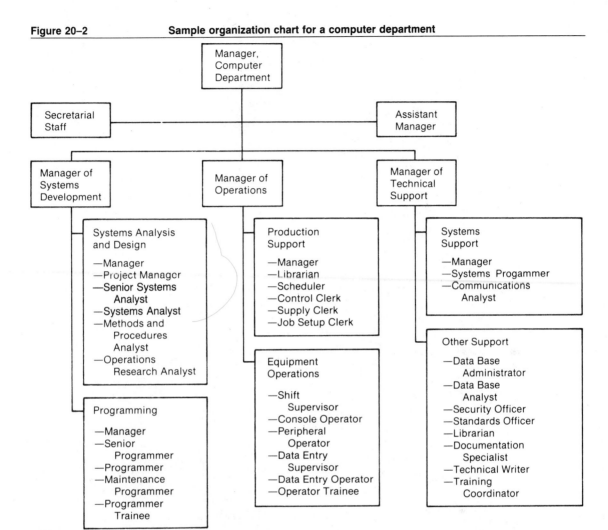

years 1984–1995, from 341,000 to 586,000. A similar increase is forecast for systems analysts, with computer operators and maintenance personnel showing significant gains as well.

Computing salaries are also on the rise. A salary survey conducted by the Administrative Management Society ascertained the average 1984–85 salary increase to be 5.3 percent.[1] (This increase occurred in spite of the fact that the industry suffered a slump during that period that forced many computer companies to make harsh cutbacks.) Average

---

[1] The survey drew its conclusion from a sample of 47,333 data processing employees in 2,085 companies in 99 cities in the United States and Canada.

Figure 20–3   **Percentage mix of computer personnel**

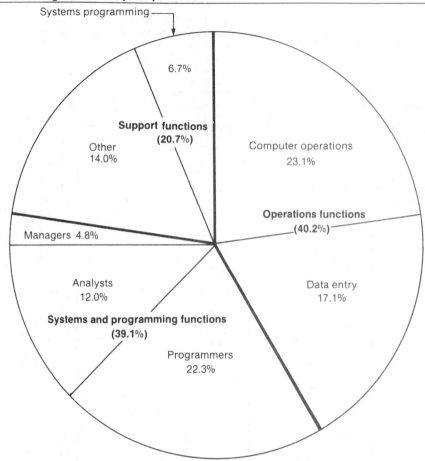

Systems programming

6.7%

**Support functions
(20.7%)**

Other
14.0%

Computer operations
23.1%

**Operations functions
(40.2%)**

Managers 4.8%

Analysts
12.0%

Data entry
17.1%

**Systems and programming functions
(39.1%)**

Programmers
22.3%

Source: Bruce Hoard, "Division of 250 Employees Found in Typical MIS Profile," *Computerworld*, vol.
14, no. 3414 (August 25, 1980), p. 4.

Table 20–1   **Fastest-growing occupations 1984–1995**

Occupation	Projected percent of increase
Paralegals	97.5%
Computer programmers	**71.7**
Computer systems analysts	**68.7**
Medical assistants	62.0
DP equipment repairers	**56.2**
Electrical and electronic engineers	**52.8**
Electrical and electronic technicians	**50.7**
Computer operators (except peripheral equipment)	**46.1**
Peripheral DP equipment operators	**45.0**
Travel agents	43.9

Note: Computer and electronics occupations are shown in boldface.

Source: U.S. Bureau of Labor Statistics.

Table 20–2   **Overall salaries by position, 1984–1985, U.S. summary**

Position	1984	1985	Percent of change
Computer operations			
Manager, computer operations	$35,400	$38,000	+7.3%
Supervisor, computer operations	25,900	27,800	+7.3
Lead computer operator	20,900	21,000	+0.5
Computer operator, Level A	17,600	18,400	+4.5
Computer operator, Level B	15,600	16,100	+3.2
Computer operations support staff			
Tape librarian	15,500	16,400	+5.8
Data quality control clerk	14,900	16,300	+9.4
Data entry operations			
Supervisor, data entry	20,200	22,100	+9.4
Lead data entry operator	16,000	16,800	+5.0
Data entry operator, Level A	13,600	14,400	+5.9
Data entry operator, Level B	12,800	13,100	+2.3
Applications programming			
Manager, applications programming	40,000	41,700	+4.3
Project leader (lead programmer/analyst)	35,600	37,400	+5.1
Systems analyst (senior programmer/ analyst)	30,900	32,600	+5.5
Programmer/analyst	26,300	27,400	+4.2
Programmer	21,600	22,800	+5.6
Software systems programming			
Manager, software systems programming	40,400	42,800	+5.9
Senior software systems programmer	34,700	36,200	+4.3
Software systems programmer	28,200	30,500	+8.2
Data base management			
Data base administrator	36,400	37,400	+2.7

Source: *Computerworld*, vol. 20, no. 10 (March 10, 1986), p. 12.

1984 and 1985 salaries in 20 computing positions, with percent of change, is shown in Table 20–2.

In the sections that follow, the work of analysts, programmers, operators, and technical writers is described. The duties of a data base administrator, data administrator, and chief information officer are also presented. Check the index to find where in the text the duties of other information processing personnel are discussed. For example, the responsibilities of schedule officers and librarians are covered in Chapter 11, the work of computer director in Chapter 21.

Systems analysts

A **systems analyst** is a technician who participates in the development, implementation, and maintenance of systems. The analyst studies a problem and decides what procedures, methods, or techniques are required for a computer solution to the problem. Analysts also gather and analyze data, document systems, design forms, and test systems.

In addition, analysts serve as the link between users and the com-

Figure 20–4   **Roles of systems analysts in development of a computer system**

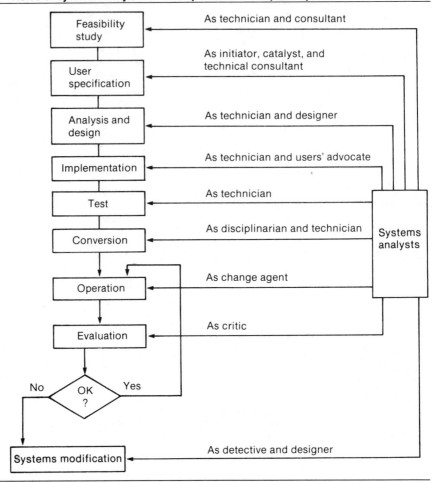

puting staff, interpreting client needs and formulating user specifications for systems development teams. Analysts are also responsible for explaining the capabilities and limitations of computing to users with no technical background. And analysts are the persons who resolve complaints and serve as mediators in user–EDP staff disputes. Indeed, the position of systems analyst was originally designed to bridge the gap between users and programmers in order to resolve the classic computing problem: how to develop computer systems when users (who want results) and programmers (who know how to make things happen) have difficulty communicating with one another. The idea was to train a computer professional with the knowledge of what computers can do, someone familiar with the jargon of programming, able to talk to and translate for end-users.

Figure 20–4 outlines the responsibilities of systems analysts in each phase of a computer system's development. During the feasibility study, analysts make cost-benefits estimates and advise the development team on the technological feasibility of proposals. During the user specifications phase, analysts take an active role in structuring the problem, quantifying objectives, and helping to synthesize and crystallize user desires so that systems specifications can be prepared. When conflicting user interests arise, analysts must find a compromise.

When the design phase is reached, analysts have technical concerns: design specifications for output, input, files, forms, and procedures. In implementation, analysts become users' advocates, working with programmers for solutions that consider human factors. During conversion, analysts may seem to switch sides. Their job is to prod reluctant users procrastinating over conversion and to refuse user requests for late specification changes, working on behalf of the computer center to resolve technical problems and speed conversion.

Although most analysts are assigned other projects when a system is finally operational, some may assist management in planning and implementing strategies to reduce employee resistance to the new system. Analysts can advise management as to how new technology will affect daily operations, and they may be astute in gauging the amount of change an organization can comfortably absorb. Analysts may also assist in orientation and training programs, effectively acting as change agents to promote favorable attitudes toward computing. Once systems are operational, analysts often participate in systems evaluation. They identify errors and recommend system modifications.

Most firms have a number of systems analysts so that no individual analyst would be assigned all of these functions. As a matter of fact, it is unwise for a single analyst to have prime responsibility for all stages of systems development. That would violate the principle of separation of duties, a management principle that stipulates that those who plan and design a system should not take part in testing and approval decisions. Since complex projects require the expertise of many analysts, this division of responsibility can usually be enforced. It is over the life of a number of projects that an individual analyst may be required to perform the spectrum of roles shown in Figure 20–4. However, small firms with limited personnel may require a single analyst to work on all phases of development.

The ideal systems analyst should have the characteristics listed in Table 20–3. One look at the list should explain why good analysts are in scarce supply. Because the ability to handle people is as important as technical competence and because knowledge of an organization, its power structure, policies, and procedures is essential to analysts, many firms like to hire analysts from their organization's labor pool. Individuals who have demonstrated aptitude for systems analysis and have

Table 20–3   **Desirable characteristics of a systems analyst**

Technical expertise in systems analysis and systems design.
Working knowledge of hardware, software, data bases, operating systems, and
    telecommunications.
Detailed knowledge of a programming language, such as COBOL for business
    applications.
Creative mind.
Ability to think in the abstract, to work with symbols and problem logic.
Receptivity to different approaches to problem solving, analysis, and design.
Ability and patience to teach and train both professionals and nontechnical
    users.
Good listening skills.
Project management skills.
Enjoys working with people.
Sensitivity to people and knowledge about human factors.
Knowledge about clients, their business, and industry.
Sensitivity to the company's power structure.
Ability to work in nonstructured, ill-defined, and conflict-prone environments.
Ability to function well under pressure, resolve conflicts, and balance
    trade-offs.
Ability to work in a team.
Halo—if possible.

the right temperament are hired even if they lack some of the skills needed in the job. They are then given appropriate technical training. It is thought by some that analysts hired and trained in this fashion are more quickly of value to the firm than analysts hired from outside who have technical qualifications but are unfamiliar with key personalities and how the company is run. Not everyone agrees with this viewpoint, however.

Programmers

The job of a **programmer** is to write and test the instructions that tell the computer what to do. Unlike analysts, who have to deal with the marriage between people and machines and often with unpredictable human emotions, programmers solve problems of logic in a more predictable environment—a machine environment. They first decide how to solve a problem, then prepare a logic chart, code instructions in a language the computer can understand, establish input/output formats, follow testing procedures, allocate storage, and prepare documentation.

Although some of a programmer's duties overlap with those of analysts, programmers do not require the social skills of analysts. Indeed, the typical programmer is reclusive, an individual who wants to work alone, without much social interaction or managerial direction. Many programmers are high strung and overspecialized and reject externally imposed structure and routine. Most have no desire to enter into managerial or executive ranks. A large number of young, mobile, unmarried people with technical bents enter the field, which helps explain why programming is a high-turnover profession.

Sometimes, small firms that cannot afford a large staff merge the responsibilities of analysts and programmers in one position. Even large firms like the analyst-programmer combination, since it helps reduce the misunderstandings that often arise between the two professional groups and eliminates finger pointing and blame shifting when things go wrong. The problem is finding qualified personnel. The development of special-purpose, high-level languages that makes programming easier has contributed to a number of analysts doing their own programming, so the analyst-programmer may become more common in the future.

With regard to programming skills, there is great diversity among programmers. Some specialize in COBOL, FORTRAN, or other high-level languages. Others specialize in packages for decision support systems (DSS) or languages for DSS, like GPSS and SIMSCRIPT. Still others, schooled in operations research, focus on simulation. Systems programmers with expertise in hardware deal with low-level languages (assembler or machine languages). These programmers work more closely with operations than with applications development.

Operators

Since the early days of computing, the job of **operator** has changed greatly for both peripheral and computer operators. Formerly, operators loaded machines with tapes, disks, or cards and monitored relatively simple machine consoles. Vocational or junior college training was adequate for the job. Today's operators, because they operate sophisticated systems, must be knowledgeable about hardware, software, and data bases. An estimated 80–90 percent of an operator's time is in software-related activities, where knowledge of the system's job control language is required in order to optimize the system's resources.

Operators have responsibility for the security and privacy of data and hardware as well. Operating errors can lead to damage to expensive equipment, necessitate reconstruction of the data base, require costly reruns, or result in lost business due to delay or inconvenience to users.

Data base administrator

The training of specialists to assist in systems development and implementation has arisen as information technology has grown more complex. For example, the position of **data base administrator (DBA)** has emerged in recent years. This administrator is responsible for the coordination and use of data stored under the control of a data base management system. For example, it is the job of the DBA to minimize the cost of the machinery or hardware involved in data management and to minimize disk space and the time it takes to access data.

The position entails the upkeep of data (updates, additions, deletions, and data base reorganizations), data maintenance (this may entail moving data from one storage media to another for quick and efficient

Table 20–4	**Functions of a data base administrator**

Data base design	Retrieval
Content	Search strategies
Create	Statistics
Reconcile differences	Access
Dictionary/directory	Frequency of processing
Create	Space use
Maintain	User utilization
Data compression	Response time
Data classification/coding	Operational
Data integrity	procedures design
Backup	Access to data base
Restart/recovery	Access for testing
	Interfaces
Data base operation	Testing system
Data element dictionary	
custodian/authority	
Maintain	*Monitoring*
Add	Data quality/validity
Purge	Performance
Data base maintenance	Efficiency
Integrity	Cost
Detect losses	Use/utilization
Repair losses	Security/privacy
Recovery	Audit
Access for testing	Compliance
Dumping	Standards
Software for Data element	Procedures
dictionary/data dictionary	
Utility programs	
Tables, indexes, etc., for	*Other functions*
end-user	Liaison/communications with:
Storage	End-users
Physical record structure	Analysts/programmers
Logical-physical mapping	Training on data base
Physical storage device	Consulting on file design
assignments	
Security/access	
Assign passwords	
Assign lock/key	
Modify passwords/keys	
Log	
Encrypt	
Modify	

access), maintenance of historical data (including modification of files when definitions of data elements and classifications change), and the purging of useless data. Any changes to the data base, data directories or data element dictionaries must also be approved and supervised by the DBA. In addition, the DBA resolves conflicts when users dispute data classifications or who should create data, establishes policies for segmented or replicated data bases, and determines the distribution of data.

The role of the DBA is both technical and nontechnical: mainly, the DBA interacts with technical staff (analysts and programmers) and with end-users. Persons in this job need training in data base management systems, physical and logical data base design, data planning, relationship modeling, data standardization, data dictionaries, data security, and operating systems.

Table 20–4 lists the numerous responsibilities of the DBA. Because of the scope of these activities, most large organizations provide DBAs with a staff including data specialists and analysts experienced in public relations and liaison with users. Usually, the DBA reports to the computing department head, but some firms give the position independent status, with the DBA reporting directly to a user committee.

Data administrator

A specialist who shares responsibility with the DBA for managing and controlling data is the **data administrator.** This individual generally handles the coordination and use of all data collected by an enterprise. In some organizations, the data administrator is allocated responsibility for the logical organization of data while the DBA focuses on physical data base design. That is, the data administrator may be responsible for the global management, control, and documentation of information that the organization uses, while the DBA designs, implements, and maintains data bases and data base management systems. In other organizations, however, the division of responsibility may be made along different lines.

The positions of DBA and data administrator are relatively new and still evolving. A great deal of variation still exists among firms in both job descriptions and titles of computer specialists assigned the task of data control and management. One of the challenges of a computer processing director is to organize and manage personnel in such a way that specialists (including data specialists) work in harmony as cohorts and co-workers, not as antagonists and competitors.

Technical writer

Today, computers are in the hands of many people who have no training in information technology. As a result, an increased responsibility has been placed on the developers of both hardware and software to provide clear and complete descriptions of their products and instructions for their use. **Technical writers** perform this role. In addition, they document computer and clerical procedures within an organization. This documentation helps to provide continuity when personnel turnover occurs and to facilitate operations, programming maintenance, and audits.

A new trend is to add technical writers to systems development teams. This helps the writer gain a clear knowledge of the product.

In addition, the writer's skill as a technical communicator can be used to improve the quality of the writing in systems specifications, planning documents, and analysis statements prepared by analysts and programmers.

Chief information officer

The position of **chief information officer (CIO)** is being introduced in organizations where information plays a key role. Usually, the CIO is a senior vice president who acts as an information resource representative and technology advisor to the chief executive officer and other members of the executive committee.

The job of CIO is generally a staff position, with no direct responsibility for line activity. Perhaps the term *technology facilitator* best describes the CIO's work. CIOs act as advisors and coordinators, relying on their ability to express and sell ideas to peers and subordinates to get things done. Most have a good technical background in data processing, knowledge of the industry, and management experience. Their exact role will differ from one organization to the next, but the key functions that usually fall under their jurisdiction are data processing, office automation, communications, and sometimes planning.

JOB DESIGN

As mentioned earlier, the responsibilities assigned to a given position will vary somewhat from firm to firm. When organizing a computing department, **job descriptions** will be prepared by management for each computing position, and these descriptions will be used when hiring and evaluating personnel. A sample job description, that of a maintenance programmer, appears in Figure 20–5.

How does the manager of a data processing department decide what duties to assign a given job? One design technique is to first draw up a list of all responsibilities of computer center staff, then to distribute the workload among the positions funded. A sample from such a **task list** appears in Table 20–5.

Many managers like to customize assignments to individuals in their employ, matching aptitude, skill, and preference while rotating unpopular duties. They prefer general job descriptions so that a change in a given employee's duties will not require a corresponding change in title and job. Figure 20–6 shows how such flexible assignments might be made. Note that although both Adams and Hawk are junior programmers, Hawk is not responsible for Task 223. This could be for any number of reasons. Perhaps Hawk is poor at documentation, or as a recent trainee, is still learning the firm's documentation standards. Maybe Hawk has just served as a maintenance programmer and is now being rotated to other duties. Perhaps Hawk strongly dislikes documentation.

Figure 20–5   **Sample job description: Maintenance programmer**

Data processing job description—Page 1	Classification No. 222

Job title: Maintenance programmer	Grade

Reports to: Manager of programming

Job titles supervised directly: None	Approximate no. of positions:

Narrative description
Performs maintenance and modification of programs currently in production to keep them responsive to user needs and to assure efficient operation in the production environment. Modifies or expands coding to accomplish specified processing changes. Tests modified programs to ensure that changes operate correctly and that changes have no adverse impact on program or system operation. Updates program historical and procedural documentation to reflect modifications. Creates special reports and file extracts from existing data bases, using generalized routines.

Responsibilities
1. Analyzing existing program logic to determine best method of accomplishing required changes or causes of program malfunction.
2. Designing change modules and adjustments to existing coding to accomplish correction or modifications.
3. Testing modified programs.
4. Maintaining installation test data base.

Duties
1. Analyze production programs to isolate problems or to determine more efficient methods.
2. Design program logic to eliminate problems, accomplish needed changes, or increase operational efficiency.
3. Expand test data to perform more thorough validation and to reflect requirements of program modifications.
4. Update program documentation to include changes.
5. Fulfill user requests for data extracts and special reports.
6. Fulfill administrative reporting requirements.

External job contacts
1. Systems designers and analysts.
2. EDP operations personnel.
3. Applications programmers.

Qualifying experience
1. High school diploma and two to four years of college.
2. Programming fundamentals.
3. Six to 12 months as a programmer trainee.
4. Proficient in at least one of the programming and job control languages used in the department.

Achievement criteria

Source: IBM, *Organizing the Data Processing Installations*, C20–1622–2 (White Plains, N.Y.: IBM).

Table 20–5   **Sample from task list**

Number	Task
1	Act as coordinating point for all data processing plans in the organization.
14	Be responsible for achieving the agreed annual data processing revenue.
44	Agree and maintain data processing priorities.
58	Maintain staff records.
117	Direct and control systems feasibility studies.
145	Prepare user procedure manuals for new systems.
223	Document written programs in accordance with departmental standards.
237	Prepare, agree on, and maintain the department's five-year hardware plan.
262	Control the process of hardware selection.
283	Direct induction training for recruits engaged in the systems function.
288	Ensure that computer run job streams are scheduled to obtain maximum utilization of equipment.
320	Conduct routine purges of files in order to release redundant files.
333	Record data preparation work done and maintain appropriate logs.

Source: Drawn from task list of Anthony Chandor, *Choosing and Keeping Computer Staff* (Winchester, Mass.: Allen & Unwin, 1976), pp. 165–200.

Making job assignments from a task list has many advantages. It serves as a checklist to ensure that all tasks are allocated and that backup for crucial tasks is assigned. In computing, where continual adjustment must be made to new hardware, software, and changed environmental conditions, new tasks are constantly being identified. The list helps a manager restructure jobs to incorporate the new tasks or plan changes to allow for job enlargement and job enrichment. In addition, the list can serve as a basis for evaluation when using the management-by-objective approach to evaluation.

Another useful managerial tool when designing jobs is a job diagnostic survey. Such surveys give employees an opportunity to express views on their own jobs and to recommend changes. Suggestions should be adopted for humanizing jobs, for making them more enjoyable as well as more challenging and efficient. A follow-up attitude survey will help managers evaluate the effectiveness of implemented changes. In computing, job redesign should be an ongoing process. Jobs cannot remain static when computer technology is moving at such a fast pace.

HIRING

Computer personnel, especially those in professional classifications, are in demand. The shortage of qualified professionals is creating delays

Figure 20–6   **Sample task assignments for systems development personnel**

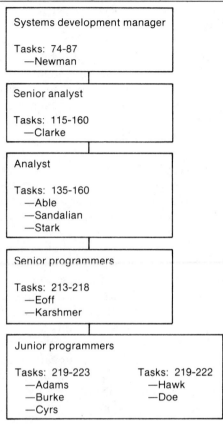

Systems development manager

Tasks: 74-87
—Newman

Senior analyst

Tasks: 115-160
—Clarke

Analyst

Tasks: 135-160
—Able
—Sandalian
—Stark

Senior programmers

Tasks: 213-218
—Eoff
—Karshmer

Junior programmers

Tasks: 219-223   Tasks: 219-222
—Adams   —Hawk
—Burke   —Doe
—Cyrs

in the development of new computer systems and means large financial rewards for professionals who are willing to job-hop. To find experienced personnel, organizations engage in a variety of **recruiting** practices. Openings are advertised in "Help Wanted" sections of national newspapers, in professional journals, and on the radio. Many companies send personnel representatives to recruit on college campuses and may also have members of their computing staff visit the schools to explain what kinds of work they are doing. This sparks student interest and helps sow the seeds for future hiring. Other firms turn to placement agencies and search firms, even though the agency fees are high for a referred prospect who is subsequently hired.

Corporations with a large number of openings in many departments may hold an open house for prospective employees. Sometimes, a computer director is looking for persons with a more diverse educational background than computer science (someone with a major in accounting, finance, or engineering and with some computing experience is often preferred over the pure computer science major). The open-house setting allows the director to interview candidates who might not realize that their backgrounds qualify them for data processing positions.

Setting up booths at professional job fairs is another recruiting technique. Most people find that a fair is a nonthreatening environment for job hunting and like being able to shop around and compare available jobs. Recruiters like the opportunity of meeting a large number of prospects face to face.

Some organizations have formalized internal employee referral services that have proven highly effective. They ask employees to inform recruiters when they learn of professional colleagues who have entered the job market. Succession planning, a form of internal recruitment, is another way to fill openings. It may be as simple as designating successors to key positions, or it can encompass detailed career planning and career ladders.

Because there are seldom enough qualified job applicants in computing, firms may have to hire inexperienced programmers and analysts or train people to fill openings. Unfortunately, predicting aptitude or potential is difficult for many computing positions. A few multiple-choice tests for programmers have been developed, but those in existence are used so often that applicants in the job market will probably be given the same test over and over. Before applying to firms of their choice, many try to gain experience with the test by first interviewing with companies low in their preference list. To make testing effective, a battery of tests is needed, or a large data base of questions should be prepared from which a test can be generated at random.

As a result of the demand for qualified personnel and the shortage of suitable candidates, the already high salaries for computer personnel are constantly rising. Personnel officers must guard against hiring new, inexperienced employees at a higher rate than the salary received by employees on the same job that were hired earlier. Compression, the reduction of salary differentials because of inflation, can also be the source of employee dissatisfaction if new employees are hired at high pay. Salaries should synchronize so that employees who change to other occupational ladders (switching from operator to programmer, for example) do not experience loss of pay.

Sometimes, a fringe benefit package that will attract applicants is negotiated, or an appealing career path or promotion schedule is offered. Competition for applicants may be so keen that companies may even give bounties ($2,000–$4,000) to employees who succeed in enticing (raiding) experienced computer personnel from competitors or other firms, although most managers consider this practice unethical.

TURNOVER

Lack of qualified personnel is not the only staffing problem of computer departments. **Turnover** is also a major concern. In the early 1980s, annual attrition of computing personnel was as high as 15–20 percent in many organizations. Although there has been a drop in turnover in recent years—to an average 5.6 percent in the mid-1980s, according to one survey[2]—corporate managers remain concerned about turnover, because qualified data processing replacements are so hard to find and so expensive to train. They recognize the importance of identifying positive and negative motivational work factors so that they can improve the corporate environment in ways that will encourage employees to remain on the payroll.

Although many studies have been done on employee motivation in the past, only recently have they addressed the question of whether factors motivating computer personnel are different from those for other employees in the work force. In 1978, for example, Jac Fitz-enz questioned 1,500 computer personnel on how they ranked a list of job

Table 20–6	Rankings by Herzberg and Fitz-enz on satisfiers and dissatisfiers		
Herzberg's criteria	Herzberg's ranking	Fitz-enz's ranking
Achievement	1	1
Recognition	2	4
Work itself	3	3
Responsibility	4	7
Advancement	5	5
Salary	6	10
Possibility of growth	7	2
Interpersonal relations, subordinate	8	9
Status	9	14
Interpersonal relations, supervisors	10	12
Interpersonal relations, peers	11	8
Supervision, technical	12	6
Company policy and administration	13	15
Working conditions	14	16
Personal life	15	11
Job security	16	13

Source: Adapted from Jac Fitz-enz, "Who Is the DP Professional?" *Datamation*, vol. 24, no. 9 (September 1978), p. 126.

[2]Glenn Rifkin, "Finding and Keeping DP/MIS Professionals," *Computerworld*, vol. 19, no. 22 (June 3, 1985), p. ID/15.

satisfiers and dissatisfiers,[3] criteria drawn from a previous study by Fred Herzberg,[4] whose work is still widely referenced in industrial training. A comparison of the responses in the two studies is shown in Table 20–6. Note that the rankings for three criteria (achievement, work itself, and advancement) are identical in the two surveys. However, significant divergence is apparent in other rankings. Computer personnel list recognition and salary as much less important than Herzberg's respondents, whereas growth possibilities and certain other criteria are valued more highly.

In another study, J. Daniel Couger and R. A. Zawacki[5] compared the attitudes of 2,500 computer employees with the findings in a survey done by J. R. Hackman and Greg Oldman, using the same diagnostic survey instrument. The two main findings of Couger and Zawacki are that analysts and programmers express a greater need for personal growth and development than the 500 other occupational groups surveyed and they express a lower social need strength (desire to interact with others) than any other job category analyzed. However, Couger hastens to add:

> Programmers and analysts are not anti-social; they will participate actively in meetings that are meaningful to them. But their high growth need also causes intolerance for group activities that are not well organized and conducted efficiently.[6]

More-recent studies agree that computer people seek personal fulfillment and growth from their work and are less motivated by money and job titles than other employee groups. The results of one such study, conducted by Columbia University researchers for *Business Week*, is shown in Figure 20–7. This study compares the different priorities of computer specialists and general managers in choosing a job.

In acknowledgment of such differences, corporate managers have developed new strategies to motivate and reward computer professionals. They realize that job satisfaction is the key to turnover reduction.

---

[3]Jac Fitz-enz, "Who Is the DP Professional?" *Datamation*, vol. 14, no. 9 (September 1978), p. 126. The sample came from a dozen companies in the western United States and was taken in the latter part of 1977. Fitz-enz's study also did rankings by job level and sex.

[4]Fred Herzberg, Fred B. Mausner, and B. S. Synderman, *The Motivation to Work*, 2d ed. (New York: John Wiley & Sons, 1959).

[5]J. Daniel Couger and R. A. Zawacki, *Motivating and Managing Computer Personnel* (New York: John Wiley & Sons, 1980). For a summary, see Couger and Zawacki, "What Motivates the DP Professional," *Datamation*, vol. 24, no. 9 (September 1978), p. 123; or Couger, "What Motivates MIS Managers," *Computerworld*, vol. 14, no. 1 (March 10, 1980), pp. ID/9–16. The sample used by Couger and Zawacki consisted of approximately 1,000 programmers and analysts and 1,500 data processing managers and staff from over 34 companies and 16 governmental organizations, each organization having a staff size ranging from 25 to 300 persons.

[6]Quoted in *EDP Analyser*, vol. 19, no. 4 (April 1981), p. 10.

Figure 20–7 | **Priorities in choosing a job: Technical innovators versus managers**

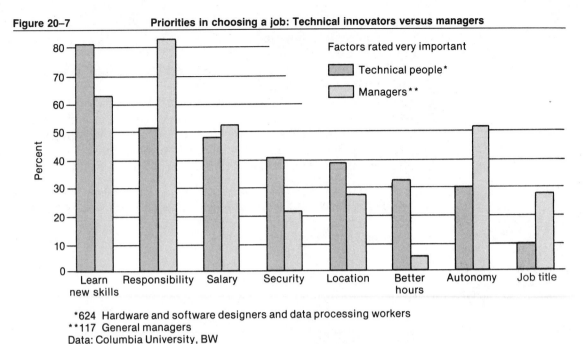

*624 Hardware and software designers and data processing workers
**117 General managers
Data: Columbia University, BW

Source: " 'Computer People': Yes, They Really Are Different," *Business Week*, no. 2827 (February 20, 1987) p. 72.

Here are some corporate managers' suggestions of ways to improve job satisfaction of computer specialists, other than the traditional rewards of pay, title, and promotion:

- Keep on the leading edge of technology. Most computing people prefer to create new systems than to spend their time maintaining outdated ones.
- Provide challenges. Reduce routine.
- Pay attention to the needs and desires of individual workers. When work tools are lacking, job-hopping may follow.
- Make sure that each employee sees that the work he or she does is used and that it plays an important role in making a product (or project) successful.
- Provide training and educational opportunities.
- Create attractive career paths that allow for individual growth.
- Work together with computing staff to develop equitable ways to measure and evaluate performance. (The problem of performance evaluation in the field of computing was discussed in Chapter 7.)
- Establish informal lines of communication with co-workers and management.
- Decentralize the company's structure to allow for more individual autonomy and decision making on the job.

- Recognize and reward contributions. When a cash bonus or promotion is not appropriate, how about two tickets to a Broadway show, a posh dinner, or a four-day weekend?
- Involve employees in planning. This instills a commitment on the part of the employee to make the plans work.
- Provide work that increases the number of skills used on the job.
- Rotate unpopular assignments, such as systems maintenance.
- Move people from project to project to keep them from getting bored.
- Institute flexible working hours. Explore telecommuting.
- Offer stock-purchase plans or profit sharing as long-term incentives.

Of course, good personnel administration is also needed, the features of which are found in general business texts and will not be repeated here.

Reasons why computer personnel commonly leave their jobs are summarized in Table 20–7.

CAREER DEVELOPMENT

Since computer personnel place a high value on professional development, a computing facility should offer employees career paths that progress in responsibility, authority, and compensation. These paths should allow employees to move from any position laterally or upward in the hierarchy of the computing department. (The possibility of a career track for technical employees that does not necessarily lead to promotion into management should be considered. Many computer specialists lack the interest in and aptitude for management.) The pipeline concept has been adopted by many firms: they encourage employees to prepare themselves for higher-level jobs and give employees first consideration for positions as they open up.

Figure 20–8 illustrates how such **career paths** work. An applicant's

Table 20–7   **Main reasons for loss of DP personnel***

Reason	Total percent
Lack of advancement	16–32%
Compensation	15–30
Other job opportunities	6–12
Challenges elsewhere	6–12
Changing environment	4–9
Location	3–6
Bad management, lack of planning	3–6
Competition	2–4

*Data: Burke Marketing Research. Information from base of 50 data processing respondents.

Source: Glenn Rifkin, "Finding and Keeping DP/MIS Professionals," *Computerworld*, vol. 19, no. 22 (June 3, 1985), p. ID/15.

Figure 20–8 **Career paths for punch operators**

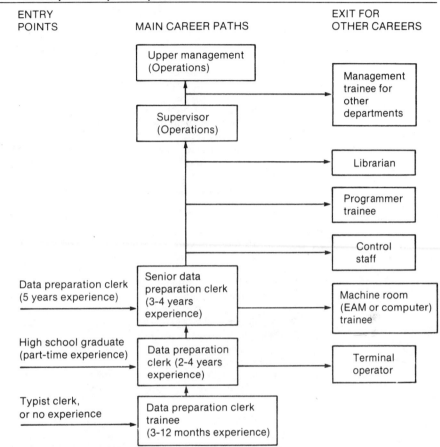

ENTRY
POINTS

MAIN CAREER PATHS

EXIT FOR
OTHER CAREERS

Upper management
(Operations)

Management
trainee for
other
departments

Supervisor
(Operations)

Librarian

Programmer
trainee

Control
staff

Data preparation clerk
(5 years experience)

Senior data
preparation clerk
(3-4 years
experience)

Machine room
(EAM or computer)
trainee*

High school graduate
(part-time experience)

Data preparation
clerk (2-4 years
experience)

Terminal
operator

Typist clerk,
or no experience

Data preparation clerk
trainee
(3-12 months experience)

*Electrical accounting machine.

education and previous experience determine level and salary when hiring a data preparation clerk. The different entries also mean that employees who transfer to the position from other jobs can be placed at a level with equal responsibility and authority, receiving a salary commensurate with or better than their former pay. Data preparation clerks can exit laterally to other computer jobs as they gain experience and learn new skills, or they can work up to a supervisory position and then switch to other departments as a management trainee.

Career ladders should be developed for all computing positions with entries and exits, and lists showing the body of knowledge and skills that belong to each professional position should be available to employees. These lists help employees select career paths and guide them in planning the training they need. Table 20–8 is an example of one such list. It ranks occupational prerequisites for systems analysts and

Table 20–8   **Knowledge required for job as systems analyst or programmer, by priority rankings**

Prerequisite	Systems analyst	Programmer
Introductory computer and information systems concepts	1	1
Computer security controls and auditing	13	13
Planning and controlling of systems development projects	9	14
Improving computer center productivity	18	18
Human relations in systems development	4	9
Software package analysis	15	17
Computer scheduling	16	16
Legal aspects of computing	19	19
Human factors in equipment design and layout	7	13
Telecommunications concepts	8	7
Hardware characteristics	10	8
Data base management systems	6	5
Operating systems characterization	11	4
Information-gathering techniques	2	11
Minicomputer characteristics and uses	14	2
Systems design topics	12	6
Applications programming languages	5	3
Computer simulation	17	19
File design	3	2
Job control languages	12	3
Introductory statistics	20	20
Statistical decision theory	23	21
Regression analysis and sampling theory	24	22
List processing	21	15
Sorting	22	10

Source: Adapted from Paul H. Cherney and Norman R. Lyons, "Information Systems Skill Requirements: A Survey," *MIS Quarterly*, vol. 4, no. 1 (March 1980), p. 42.

programmers in order of importance according to a survey of 32 information systems managers in the nation's largest organizations. Once introductory computer and information systems concepts are mastered, each job has different priorities of required knowledge.

Each job in a career ladder should also be associated with a set of required skills, so that an employee knows what training or experience is necessary to move up the ladder. Since computer technology is not static, these requirements are subject to frequent change. For example, analysts today have to know about personal computers, word processing, spreadsheets, graphics, and voice synthesizers—subjects not part of their jobs 10 years ago. In addition, since there are optimal times for switching from one job ladder to another, employees should be cognizant of how jobs mesh. For example, Figure 20–9 shows that an operator wishing to become a programmer should make the switch no

Figure 20-9   **Two career paths, with salaries***

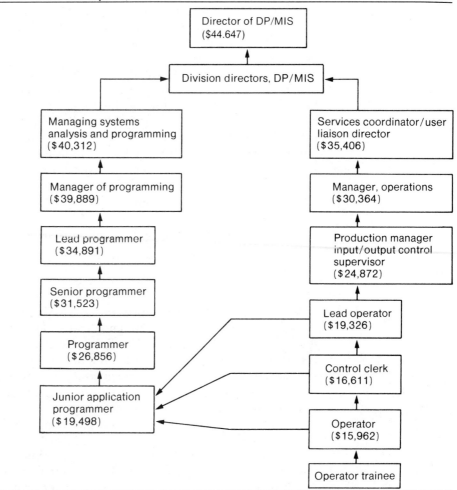

*Salary data from "1985 DP Salary Survey," *Datamation*, vol. 31, no. 18 (September 15, 1985), pp. 94–95.

later than senior operator or control clerk. If the operator has risen to the position of production manager, a switch to the programming ladder will result in a loss of pay, since the only level at which an inexperienced programmer can enter this ladder is as a junior application programmer.

Sometimes, certain courses or a college degree are prerequisites for advancement along a career path. Firms differ in their policies regarding released time or financial support for studies, but all should offer advice and encouragement to employees willing to make an educational commitment in order to advance their careers. Indeed, management should encourage job mobility, since it is in the interest of a firm to have an experienced core of employees who know the organization and can provide backup for a number of jobs. And since career development is a key to job satisfaction, advancement within the firm should help foster company loyalty and reduce job-hopping to other companies.

Although an employee should theoretically be able to cross over and move up career ladders to reach any desired position in computing by gaining qualifications and experience, openings must be available and management willing to promote or transfer the employee. Sometimes, however, managers turn down requests for promotion or transfer. For example, programmers who wish to switch to the more prestigious career ladder of systems analyst may lack the requisite temperament, although they may have the required technical competence. (Programmers tend to be loners who shun interpersonal relationships, whereas analysts need to be perceptive of group dynamics and at ease when dealing with people.) Such an individual may find a career path or choice blocked in some organizations, even though jobs have been designed to allow for vertical or lateral movement.

TRAINING

Many computer departments sponsor **training** programs to provide employees with the background knowledge, skills, and up-to-date information needed to support the firm's hardware and software. The programs may also be designed to promote career development of personnel. The justification for the expense of the career programs is that they help reduce turnover, improve productivity, instill cooperation and loyalty to the firm, attract applicants, and also help retrain at less cost than firing/hiring when new computer applications upset the job structure of the firm.

The approaches used by corporations in training computer personnel are much the same as those used to train employees in other departments of a firm. Programs range from on-the-job training, briefings, and seminars to course work that rivals degree programs at many universities.

Many software houses and manufacturers of hardware provide training materials, such as programmed instructions that come in manuals or a package for a terminal. The primary advantages of computer-based training over formal classwork is that the course is self-paced and can be scheduled at the employee's convenience. (Unfortunately, many people lack the self-discipline required to take a course of this nature.) Vendors many also sponsor training programs of their own at reasonable cost for their corporate clients.

Some firms organize training by setting up an educational matrix that identifies groups of employees and courses needed by those groups, scheduling courses on the basis of the matrix. Other firms build courses

Table 20–9	Sample training status report	
	Name	Karen Dallenbach
	Social security number	327–40–3216
	Current title	Programmer
	Manager's name	Marion Latch
	Interests	Working with people
	Personal dislikes	Documentation
	Future job	Systems analyst
	Training needs	
	Internal	Courses on systems analysis
		Basic course in accounting
		Assignment to development projects, especially accounting-oriented projects
	External	Computer auditing
	Other recommendations	Courses on DBMS
	Target date of achievement	1990
	Last date of update	5/2/87
	Date of run	12/6/87

around jobs, scheduling courses needed for becoming a programmer or manager, for example. Still others provide counseling to employees, customizing the training for individual career development. Table 20–9 shows a sample training status report of one employee under such a program. The company draws up a list of training needs prepared from the status reports and then plans and schedules courses accordingly.

Although training based on individual needs is expensive, it may prove the solution to firms otherwise unable to fill openings due to the low supply of and high demand for qualified computer personnel. Also, such training may be the only way to get needed specialists, such as employees trained in computer-aided design or in languages such as APL that are used in numerical control.

TECHNOSTRESS

Before closing this chapter, a few words are in order on the impact of **stress** (mental, emotional or physical tension) on workers in computer-related professions. Although moderate levels of stress can motivate and challenge, the negative effects of stress are becoming increasingly apparent in the computing field. Too often, stress is associated with low morale, decreased efficiency, hair-trigger tempers, ulcers, heart disease, nervous conditions, neuroses, and job-hopping.

Some stress can be attributed to physical discomforts in a computer environment. For example, eyestrain may result from screen flicker or from terminal glare. Backache may be triggered by poorly designed or positioned equipment. Many people are sensitive to the cold temperature of computer installations and to the loud noise of many peripherals, such as high-speed printers.

Other stress factors are attributed to the fast pace of the computer industry. Innovative products and technologies are continually emerging; computer professionals must keep abreast of advances in the field and adapt to them. Frequently, new procedures must be learned and new hardware mastered. The scope of computer jobs has to be altered and data processing departments reorganized. The tension that accompanies such changes is often compounded by unrealistic management and user demands, heavy workloads, and backlog pressures. Furthermore, many computer installations are run in a day-to-day crisis mode. Technostress, a "disease that results when the delicate balance between people and computers is violated,"[7] may also result from inadvertent disk erasure, system breakdown, slow response time, or similar frustrations associated with computer use.

An important role of management in a computerized organization is to identify the causes of stress and to initiate programs that will reduce it. For example, planning can help minimize strain during periods of heavy workload. Contingency planning and well-tested recovery procedures can lessen turmoil during and following system breakdown, while careful planning for project development should prevent unrealistic time schedules. It is no longer uncommon for firms to use the services of industrial psychologists and psychotherapists when planning social structures to relieve strain in the workplace.

Many companies also help employees learn how to alleviate stress. (For stress symptoms, see Table 20–10.) They offer seminars in stress

Table 20–10	Stress signs*
	Rapid breathing
	Heart rate increase
	Nervousness and tiredness
	Energy level lower or higher than usual
	Headaches
	Pain or irritation in neck, jaw, lower back, or outer body regions
	General tension of body muscles
	Changes in sleeping and eating patterns
	Feeling of fear, anger, and sadness
	Circular thought processes
	Excessive preoccupation with a single problem or situation

*Although the listed symptoms may occur when people are in stressful situations, no single sign is a good stress indicator. Consider the context in which these signs occur, and remember that the presence of injury or disease may cause many of these same signs.

Source: National Employee Services and Recreation Association.

---

[7]Craig Bond, *The Human Cost of the Computer Revolution* (Reading, Mass.: Addison-Wesley Publishing, 1984).

control that teach time management techniques and physical remedies, such as special exercises. At career workshops, employees may playact stressful situations and be counseled on ways to cope with job tensions. Since exercise is a good way to relax, firms may provide recreational facilities for their employees and sponsor sports teams.

The first step in alleviating computer-related stress is to acknowledge that the problem exists. Rather than debate whether information processing is more stressful than other professions, the focus should be on planning programs to control and alleviate pressures associated with computer use.

SUMMING UP

In the 1950s, when firms first introduced computing, a single employee may have acted as a programmer, analyst, and operator. As computing grew, more positions were added to computing departments. This is graphically portrayed in Figure 20–10. Note that the temporal evolution of computing corresponds with growth of firm size and that some jobs in the 70s and 80s are completely new. These include data base administrator, security officer, word processing specialists, problem analysts (who might be compared to earlier time-and-motion experts, tracing back to Taylor), and policy analysts (who evaluate data processing input and output for policy implications). Yet companies with limited electronic data processing today may still retain the computing structure of the 1950s, consolidating operations, programming, and analysis.

Computer personnel can be grouped in three categories: systems development, operations, and support. The systems development group, consisting of analysts and programmers, is concerned with long-term projects. Operations concerns daily activities. Maintenance programmers, production personnel, and operators of peripherals fall into this category. The support function includes system programmers, the DBA, security and standards officers, the librarian, and training personnel. This chapter has outlined the duties and responsibilities of some of these employees and described how their jobs are designed.

Hiring, motivation, evaluation, and training of computer department personnel should be consistent with traditional theories of personnel management, such as Fred Herzberg's theories on work (mentioned earlier), Abraham Maslow's on motivation,[8] and Edgar Schein's on or-

---

[8]Abraham Maslow, *Motivation and Personality* (New York: Harper & Row, 1954), 369 pp.

Figure 20–10   **Correlation of temporal and size evolution in computing personnel configurations**

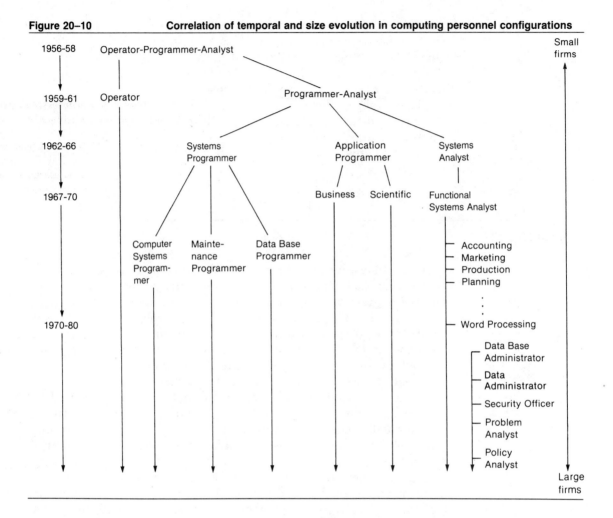

ganizational psychology.[9] Special attention, however, should be paid to the emphasis computer personnel place on challenging work and career development. Because many computer-related jobs are stressful, an important management concern in data centers is to implement strategies to control and alleviate job tensions.

Computer personnel in the 1990s will need skills and knowledge in data base management, networks, telecommunications, artificial intelligence, fourth-generation languages, multiprocessor systems, and ergonomics (human factors)—to name but a few areas where new technology is being introduced. This need will exacerbate shortages of

[9]Edgar Schein, *Organizational Psychology*, 3d ed. (Englewood Cliffs, N.J.: Prentice-Hall, 1970), 274 pp.

qualified personnel, although the increased level of computer literacy in schools and universities should lead to more persons entering the computer field. Unions for computer personnel may be in the offing, demanding higher salaries, shorter workweeks, and more employee participation in job-related decisions. Managing a computer department in the future should be quite a challenge.

CASE: LOW TURNOVER AT GUARDIAN LIFE INSURANCE

One reason that computer people switch jobs is to learn new skills. They like challenging work and realize that their expertise can quickly become outdated because of the fast pace of technological advance in the field of computing.

The fact that Guardian Life Insurance has had an astonishingly low turnover of its computer professionals in recent years can be attributed to the emphasis the company places on learning, according to John F. Kuemmerle, Guardian's senior vice president for administration. The company asks its employees to spend 40 percent of their time learning. This may be discussing the latest technological breakthroughs with vendors, reading books and magazines, attending seminars, or taking formal courses. Computing staff also study the insurance industry. This helps them frame the solution of technological problems in a business context, keeping in mind how solutions benefit the company financially.

Kuemmerle believes that his company gains from the 40 percent education time. The dedication of the computing staff and the work pace they set for themselves is evidence of that.

Questions

1. Do you think that all firms should have a learning program similar to that at Guardian Life? Explain your point of view.
2. How can a firm assess the benefits of educational programs?
3. How can Guardian Life ensure that employees are using their learning time effectively? Are they not daydreaming and wasting time instead of learning?

Source: " 'Computer People': Yes, They Really Are Different," *Business Week*, no. 2827 (February 20, 1984), p. 68.

4. What other factors might be contributing to low turnover at Guardian Life?

5. How does the company know what factors are decisive in low turnover? Who makes that assessment?

STUDY KEYS

Career paths	**Recruiting**
Chief information officer (CIO)	**Stress**
Data administrator	**Systems analyst**
Data base administrator (DBA)	**Task list**
Job descriptions	**Technical writers**
Operator	**Training**
Programmer	**Turnover**

DISCUSSION QUESTIONS

1. Are personnel concerns in a computer department different from personnel concerns in other departments of a firm? Explain.

2. Should authority over computing personnel reside within the computer department, or should the personnel office of a firm handle personnel matters for all departments of the firm?

3. Are computer staffs given privileges or special treatment? Explain. Does this create tension and dissatisfaction among other employees? How can a firm minimize or eliminate dissatisfaction arising from unequal treatment?

4. Once development, input preparation, and output generation are shifted to the user, the nature of personnel problems in computer departments will change. Comment.

5. Is it true that computer personnel do not mix well with other employees in a firm? Explain.

6. Is the danger of becoming professionally obsolete any different for a computer technician than for an engineer? How can computer professionals keep abreast of new technology?

7. Is the current shortage of computer personnel a temporary problem? How can this problem be solved?

8. Are employee-motivation personnel policies that are studied in personnel administration applicable to computer personnel? Explain.

9. Many employees believe evaluation procedures for computer jobs are irrelevant and unfair. Comment. What evaluation procedures and criteria would you use to evaluate the work of programmers,

analysts, computer managers, and other computer department personnel?

10. Why is there high turnover among computer personnel? How can turnover be reduced?

11. Is a user-friendly computer environment just a matter of improving personal relations between user and computer technicians, or does it also require the special design of hardware, software, and data systems in order to bridge the gulf between the user and computer personnel? Explain.

12. What is the role of a:
    a. Systems analyst?
    b. Programmer?
    c. Operator?
    d. Data base administrator?
    e. Technical writer?
    f. Chief information officer?
    Name other positions commonly found in large computer centers.

SELECTED ANNOTATED BIBLIOGRAPHY

Benjamin, Robert I.; Charles Dickinson, Jr.; and John F. Rockart. "Changing Role of the Corporate Information Systems Officer." *MIS Quarterly*, vol. 9, no. 3 (September 1985), pp. 177–88.
Responsibility for information is rapidly being distributed. As a result, the role of the chief information officer is evolving. Today, this executive is largely responsible for staff and for a proactive role in business strategy issues.

Bond, Craig. *The Human Cost of the Computer Revolution*. Reading, Mass.: Addison-Wesley Publishing, 1984.
Bond discusses the anxiety and fear people experience when attempting to master the computer.

Brod, Craig. *Technostress*. Reading, Mass.: Addison-Wesley Publishing, 1984, 242 pp.
This is a thorough treatment of the nature of stress and ways to overcome it.

Burton, Gene E. "Relax, DP Stress Isn't All that It's Cracked Up to Be." *Data Management*, vol. 23, no. 6 (June 1985), pp. 33–42.
Burton has an unusual viewpoint: he downplays the importance of stress in a computing environment.

Chadwin, Mark Lincoln, and Edward M. Cross. "Personnel Management for a Special Breed: The Data Processing Professional." *Personnel Administrator*, vol. 28, no. 8 (August 1983), pp. 53–59.
The reader is told that computer people are different from other employees in an organization and, consequently, require special techniques and ap-

proaches of management. These special techniques and approaches are then discussed.

Couger, J. Daniel. "Blue Skies Ahead." *Datamation*, vol. 30, no. 21 (December 15, 1984), pp. 107–10.
Coauthor of *Motivating and Managing Computer Personnel* (New York: John Wiley & Sons, 1980), Couger has done much research on computer staffing. In this article, he discusses career paths at all levels and for all types of computer personnel, noting that these paths are expanding both horizontally and vertically.

Hartog, Curt. "Of Commerce and Academe." *Datamation*, vol. 31, no. 17 (September 1, 1985), pp. 68–78.
Hartog discusses the gap between business needs and university curricula with regard to training students for work in a data processing environment. Too often what is taught is technologically obsolete by the time students enter the job market.

Kearby, D'Ann B. "Personnel Policies, Procedures and Practices—The Key to Computer Security." *Computer Security Journal*, vol. 4, no. 1 (January 1986), pp. 63–68.
The author argues that computer-related losses can be controlled and even reduced through the implementation of a good program for human resource security. The author then outlines such a program.

Kerns, L. Stevens. "What End Users Don't Know May Hurt You." *Computerworld*, vol. 18 (October 8, 1984), pp. ID/31–36.
According to the author, people in the organization who need to know about computers should first be identified (including executive management and professional, technical, secretarial, and clerical staff). Then the education and training should be provided that are suited to their needs, level of education, and skill.

Licker, Paul. "The Japanese Approach: A Better Way to Manage Programmers." *Communications of the ACM*, vol. 26, no. 9 (September 1983), pp. 631–36.
Added to the U.S. management Theories X and Y comes Theory Z, based on experiences in Japan. The Japanese stress lifetime employment, nonspecialized career paths, collective decision making, and a holistic view. Can U.S. programmers work comfortably and productively under Theory Z? Licker says yes, through a climate of support, training, and monitoring.

Lucas, Henry C., Jr. *The Analysis, Design and Implementation of Information Systems*. 2d ed. New York: McGraw-Hill, 1981, 419 pp.
Chapter 17 discusses the organization and staffing of a computer department, its relationship with users, security, control of processing, management of computer operations and the computer room, and charging for services.

———. "Organizational Power and the Information Services Department." *Communications of the ACM*, vol. 27, no. 1 (January 1984), pp. 58–65.
A survey of 40 manufacturing plants show that the information services department is perceived as having low levels of power and influence in

an organization. Reasons for this are discussed, and recommendations are offered to improve departmental status.

Lyons, Michael. "The DP Psyche." *Datamation*, vol. 31, no. 16 (August 15, 1985). pp. 103–10.
Many computer professionals consider themselves different from the rest of humanity. A survey of 1,129 individuals tells us how different they think they are.

Marks, Shirley. "High Tech, High Stress?" *Datamation*, vol. 31, no. 8 (April 15, 1985), pp. 97–100.
Most computer people show symptoms of high stress. Causes of stress, its manifestations, and ways to overcome, if not avoid, stress are discussed. This same issue has another article entitled "Stress," by D.D. Warrick, Donald G. Gardner, J. Daniel Couger, and Robert A. Zawacki, which discusses the stress process in terms of stressors, personal characteristics, coping responses, and stress effects.

Proceedings of the Twentieth Annual Computer Personnel Research Conference, ACM–SIGCPR.
These proceedings contain many research papers, most by academicians, on the subject of the conference. Available from ACM, P.O. Box 64145, Baltimore, MD 21264.

Salvendy, Gabriel, ed. *Advances in Human Factors/Ergonomics*. New York: Elsevier–North Holland Publishing, 1984, 488 pp.
This book contains a section on stress, health, and psychological issues in computerized work. Recommended are the articles by Michael Smith, G. Johansson, and M. Dainoff.

Verity, John W. "Empowering Programmers." *Datamation*, vol. 31, no. 16 (August 15, 1985), pp. 68–78.
A resident commentator at *Datamation* discusses how programmers may be displaced by the transformation of the programming task and by advanced software development tools.

Wilson, Glenn T. "Workforce Strategies: Hire, Win, Hire, Lose." *Data Management*, vol. 19, no. 12 (December 1981), pp. 27–29.
Four strategies of hiring are discussed: (1) hire, train, and keep; (2) hire, train, and lose; (3) hire experienced people; and (4) pirate from other firms, including competitors. Piracy is not recommended, and its disadvantages are identified.

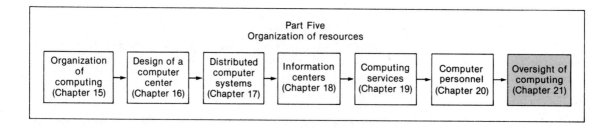

Part Five
Organization of resources

| Organization of computing (Chapter 15) | Design of a computer center (Chapter 16) | Distributed computer systems (Chapter 17) | Information centers (Chapter 18) | Computing services (Chapter 19) | Computer personnel (Chapter 20) | Oversight of computing (Chapter 21) |

CHAPTER 21

Oversight of computing

*All the time the Guard was looking for her, first
through a telescope, then through a microscope, and then
through an opera-glass. At last he said, "You are
travelling the wrong way"*

Lewis Carroll, *Through the Looking-Glass*

Computer departments have often been called "**a business within a business.**" But for reasons described in this chapter, they are under the direction of corporate management. User departments also exercise a measure of control over computer departments through their representatives on steering committees and project development teams. The sections that follow will describe the many ways in which activities of computer departments are subject to supervision and how steering committees, top management, users and computer department directors interact in their oversight roles.

Each firm has a unique environment. Although this chapter describes how the **oversight function** is typically carried out, companies vary considerably regarding supervisory practices.

A BUSINESS WITHIN A BUSINESS

Within the organizational framework of a firm, a computer department is merely one of many departments. In structure, however, it resembles an independent business. Indeed, the department can be compared to a manufacturing concern, since it operates as a job shop (in batch mode) or a continuous-production shop (real-time processing) to provide a product (information). There is a correlation in specific activities as well, as shown in Table 21–1. For example, facilities planning in manufacturing could be compared to computer configuration

Table 21–1   **Parallel computer center and manufacturing business activities**

Manufacturing business	Information processing center
Product planning	Information systems planning
Facilities planning	Computer configuration and network planning
Market research	Computing demand forecasting
Product research	Keeping abreast with computer technology
Market development	User education
Product design	Systems design
Problem analysis	Systems analysis
Tooling	Programming
Production scheduling	Job scheduling
Production	Computing and operations
Production control	Production/operations control
Inventory control	Supplies inventory
Quality control	Input/output and information quality control
Consumer survey	User satisfaction survey
Consumer services liaison	User liaison
Personnel management	Personnel management
Administration	Administration
Product for sale	Information (sold or as a service)
Product line strategy	Applications development strategy
Product cost analysis	Applications project estimation
Pricing policy	Charge policy

and network planning, tooling might be compared to programming, and a product line resembles the department's applications portfolio. The primary difference is product disposal: computer departments do not have to rely on market mechanisms for pricing or selling. Their product is often for a captured market, when sold to other departments in the company, or considered as a service when provided to user departments without charge.

Nevertheless, computer departments do seek to provide a product that is competitive with outside information processing centers. To do so, they must be managed with efficiency and effectiveness. Usually, a steering committee plays an oversight role.

STEERING COMMITTEE AND SUBCOMMITTEES

A **steering committee** might be considered a board of directors for computing: it ensures that computing strategy is in line with corporate strategic planning objectives. That is, the steering committee usually establishes corporate policy toward information systems, makes long- and short-range plans for the computer department, sets data processing priorities, and allocates computing resources. It may also set standards and performance levels; schedule, monitor, and control operations; approve acquisitions; evaluate interfunctional applications; and resolve conflicts concerning user needs.

See Table 21–2 for a summary of the responsibilities of a typical steering committee. These functions can be classified in five general areas:

- Direction setting—links corporate strategy with computer strategy.
- Rationing—reconciles the commitment of corporate resources to information systems with commitments to other business activities.
- Structuring—settles the centralization versus decentralization issue and charters various organizational units.
- Staffing—selects top computer managers.
- Advising and auditing—assists in problem solving and checks to ensure that the department's activities are on track.

Top management should be represented on steering committees, as should management representatives from user groups. Sometimes, consultants will be added to a committee to ensure a balance between technically oriented members and those knowledgeable about the goals, objectives, and policies of the organization. A balance between line and staff representatives is also advisable, as is a balance between planners,

Table 21–2	Functions of a typical steering committee
	Establishes corporate policy for information systems.
	Formulates strategy to reach corporate objectives.
	Assures coordination of information systems policy with corporate goals, objectives, and policies.
	Approves strategic, tactical, long- and short-range plans.
	Recommends to top management the allocation of resources (budgetary decisions).
	Designs organizational structure to ensure effective use of computers within the company.
	Evaluates and approves proposals for resource acquisition and development of projects.
	Reviews and monitors milestones of major development projects.
	Establishes criteria and levels of performance for computing operations.
	Establishes evaluation procedures.
	Monitors and controls operations and schedules.
	Resolves and arbitrates conflicts on priorities and schedules.
	Formulates standards, guidelines, and constraints for both development and operations.
	Allocates scarce resources.
	Exercises funding discipline over major expenditures.
	Oversees staffing.
	Provides communication link between computer center and corporate management.
	Provides forum for feedback from users.

production personnel, and individuals from accounting and finance. With such representation, committees become a forum for computer management and user departments to express their views, air their problems, and reconcile their differences with regard to information systems.

Some steering committees are more successful than others. (Many data processing managers consider them bureaucratic nonsense, rubber-stamp committees of little value.) Those that function effectively do so because they involve senior management as well as EDP personnel and users. Indeed, most steering committees today are chaired by a corporate manager, and it is probable that as information technology becomes more intertwined with corporate strategy, the trend toward top management chairmanship will continue. Another characteristic of successful steering committees is that they make long-range plans instead of approving projects singly. Furthermore, they involve users in project planning and require them to justify their requests for information services.

According to some observers and practitioners, steering committees that meet too frequently get bogged down in details and find that they do not have enough knowledge to deal with the issues. Quarterly meetings that focus on strategic issues work best. The ideal committee size

Table 21–3	List of committees and their reporting units	
	Committee	*Responsible to:*
	Standing committees	
	Steering committee	Top management
	Tactical steering committee	
	Operating committee	
	Users' committee for operations	
	Project priority committee (for	Steering committee
	development, maintenance,	
	and redevelopment)	
	Resource planning committee	
	Data base committee	Steering committee or
		director of systems
	Ad hoc committees	
	Resource selection committee	
	Hardware committee	
	Software committee	
	Resource acquisition and	
	implementation committee	Steering committee
	Security advisory committee	
	Privacy advisory committee	
	Control advisory committee	
	Project team	Project manager and project
		review committee

seems to range between 5 and 10 members. Larger committees often result in one-way communication, not an open discussion of problems.

Organizations with a small computing facility may find that a single steering committee suffices. But organizations with large computer departments that offer complex services will undoubtedly require a hierarchy of lower-level steering committees. For example, a project review committee may be given responsibility for project development, while a tactical steering committee has responsibility for operations. Other common subcommittees and their reporting units are listed in Table 21–3. The function of standing committees differs from that of ad hoc committees, which are created to solve an immediate problem, then dissolved after a solution is reached. The former have ongoing responsibilities.

At times, the steering committee may act as a crisis center. Ideally, however, problems should be brought to the attention of the committee before reaching crisis proportions. Computing activities should be constantly monitored by steering subcommittees. Feedback and control systems (such as exception reporting) should alert committee members to problems. In addition, the computer director has the responsibility of bringing problems to the committee before they get out of hand.

OVERSIGHT ROLE OF TOP MANAGEMENT

Let us now focus on **senior management oversight** of computer departments. As explained in the preceding section, representatives from senior management serve on steering committees. Although user representatives and EDP personnel are also on the committees, two factors add weight to management's importance: (1) usually, the chair is drawn from senior management and (2) corporate management oversees the steering committees themselves. That is, the function of steering committees is decided by corporate managers, and they are the persons who appoint committee members in the first place.

Since corporate managers are also users of information systems, representatives from the top echelons of the firm participate in the development activities of many projects. For example, managers, as future systems users, will participate in feasibility studies and help draw up systems specifications when new applications are initiated. They will help evaluate testing to see that systems that are developed do, in fact, meet managerial needs. As illustrated in Figure 21–1, senior managers have an oversight role in computing through development team membership as well as through steering committee stewardship. Furthermore, corporate management has budgetary control over development activities. It makes Go/No Go decisions following feasibility studies,

508

Figure 21–1 **Management's oversight role in development**

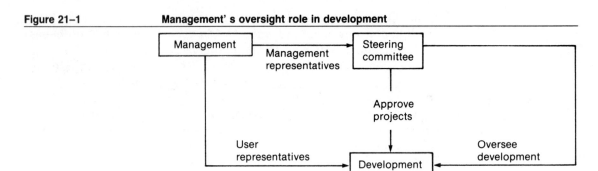

Figure 21–2 **Role of management and EDP staff at various developmental stages**

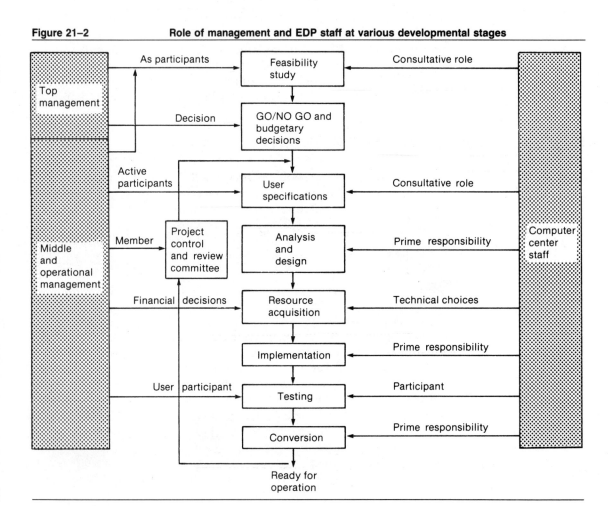

Figure 21–3   **Corporate management's role in computer operations**

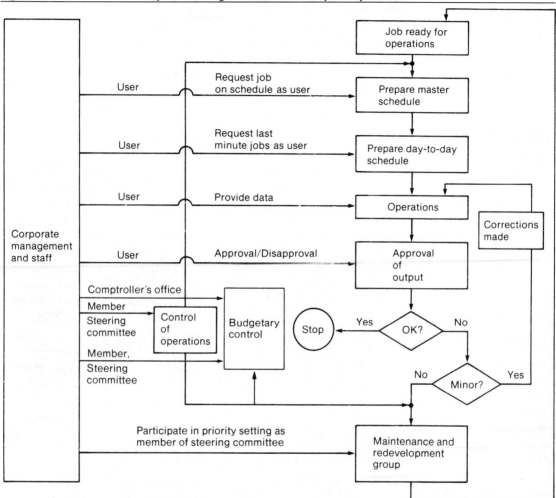

selects methods of financing projects, and approves major resource acquisitions. This can be seen in Figure 21–2, which also clarifies the relationship of top management and computer center staff to each stage of development.

With regard to daily operations, management again has multiple supervisory roles. As a user of information services, management can exercise a measure of control by refusing to accept output that fails to adhere to systems specifications. Through membership in the steering committee, management will appoint auditors to evaluate efficiency and effectiveness of daily operations. Approval of maintenance or redevelopment and the setting of priorities are also responsibilities of the steering committee, which gives management control over operations. Finally, management supervises the activities of a computer department through the budgetary process. Expenditures for ongoing operations require the approval of the financial officers of the firm. By holding the purse strings, top management controls operations. Figure 21–3 illustrates the many ways in which management participates in daily operations as a user while engaging in a supervisory role at the same time.

OVERSIGHT ROLE OF USERS

This chapter has already discussed the role of senior managers as users of computer services. Users are also found in nonmanagerial levels of an organization. They may be clerks, accountants, programmers, secretaries, warehouse personnel, engineers, sales representatives, planners—the list could go on and on. At all levels in the organizational hierarchy of a firm, there is **user oversight** of computing. For example, user representatives serve as members of the steering committee and participate in the development of new systems, just as management representatives do. They also provide feedback to the steering committee and to the computer director regarding weaknesses in processing systems that they use in their jobs.

To collect and act on user feedback requires (1) mechanisms for identifying and classifying users, (2) instruments for determining user satisfaction, and (3) procedures for evaluating user criticisms and improving service.

Identification and classification of users

Opinion regarding effectiveness of operations is sought from all users, regardless of their level in the organizational hierarchy of a firm. But organizations do attempt to classify users according to:

- Skill level in computing use (novice, intermediate, expert).
- Intensity of computing use (frequent, occasional, infrequent).
- Position of the user in the organization's hierarchy.
- Type of systems used. Static systems (e.g., data base searches, programming, text editing) versus dynamic systems (e.g., process control).

Users' opinions are then weighed according to classification and problem at hand. For example, data entry clerks would have more voice in workstation layout than infrequent management users. However, experienced users would have more say than novices in the development of a data base management system (DBMS). (The classifications also aid computer center staff in identifying major user groups so that services can be tailored to their needs.)

User satisfaction
determination

In small companies, word of mouth may be adequate to determine user satisfaction. In organizations where users are free to choose between in-house computing and an external facility, market mechanisms are at play. Satisfied users remain customers. Dissatisfied users demand improved service or take their business elsewhere. Large organizations that do all their own computing usually rely on formal **survey instruments** to gauge user satisfaction. Such surveys may be designed for

Figure 21–4   **Sample user satisfaction questionnaire**

A. *User inventory*
   Name:
   Department:
   Position:
   Relationship to computer center:
   Participation in computer center organization (committees):
   Computer center resources used:

Resource	*Frequency and degree of usage*

   Knowledge of computing:
   Interest in computing:

B. *Satisfaction survey* (You may wish to answer some of the questions below for each output you use.)
   Development:
      Was your project developed on time?
      Was your project adequately tested?
      Did your project meet your initial needs? Changing needs?
      Is your application using the most recent technology available?
      Is your application satisfactorily integrated with other applications?

   Operations:
      Is your report:
      a. Timely?
      b. Accurate?
      c. Well packaged?
      d. Corrected promptly when errors occur?
      e. Available in mode desired?
      f. Easy to use/understand/verify for accuracy?
      Are computer center personnel helpful and cooperative?
      How can your existing reports be improved?
      How can the service to you be improved?
      How can the computer center be more responsive to your needs?
      How can the structure of the computer center be changed to improve:
      a. Performance?
      b. Responsiveness?
      Is user orientation and training:
      a. Adequate?
      b. Timely?

specific user classifications or for specific computing environments, such as inventory control or word processing. Some may survey user attitudes toward service, while others may concentrate on evaluation of performance criteria.

Whatever the instrument's approach, the purpose should be to help the steering committee and computing staff identify areas where efforts to improve quality of service should be concentrated. Figure 21–4 is a sample survey instrument, showing the types of questions that users might be asked.

Corrective action   Usually, an individual (or committee) from the computer department will be assigned responsibility for analyzing the responses to user surveys. Problems that can be quickly solved are differentiated from those requiring long-term solutions. The former are sent to the appropriate staff member for action, the latter to the steering committee or relevant project team for study.

Surveys may indicate a demand for an added peripheral, such as a faster printer or plotter. They may identify problems that require program maintenance or point to the need for development of a new application. A common user complaint is lengthy turnaround time. In response, many computer departments (especially those with a DBMS environment) institute a quick-response service for users needing fast service for short, simple reports—the equivalent of the express lane in a grocery store. Many complaints can be resolved at small incremental cost, yet yield a high payoff in user goodwill. The computing center can then count on the support and cooperation of users when tackling problems that have long-term solutions.

In summary, user opinion helps the steering committee and the computer director determine how computer service might be improved. User representatives on the steering committee are in a position to see that user concerns, once identified, are followed by corrective action. So users perform an oversight role in two ways: by reporting problems and by participating as members of steering committees.

ROLE OF COMPUTER DIRECTOR

The **computer director** (also called a data processing manager) is responsible for daily operations of the computer department. In some companies with a steering committee, the computer director is hired/fired by the committee and may approach top management only through the committee. In others, the director is directly responsible to senior management, reporting to a vice president of information services or some similar officer.

Oversight function   Like other departmental managers in a firm, the computer director must plan departmental activities, prepare and control budgets, schedule work assignments, monitor work in progress, and select, hire, train, and evaluate personnel. The personnel roster of a computer department includes individuals with a wide range of skills: from clerks engaged in repetitive tasks and having hourly deadlines and a short-term outlook to highly trained professionals engaged in experimental systems design with long-term vision. Such diversity complicates management. So does the fact that many of the people working in high-tech fields are task-oriented, creative individuals who like working alone, dislike interruptions and small talk, and work with a sense of urgency that makes them insensitive to the status quo.

It is up to the computer director to establish a work environment that provides freedom of creative expression, yet promotes orderly organizational processes at the same time. The director has to command the technical respect of employees and be responsive to innovative ideas. Yet, the manager's knowledge must extend beyond technology to people, equipment resources, user relations, and budgeting and capital expenditures. At the same time, the director needs to understand the corporate environment outside of the department, be comfortable in relationships with senior management, and be knowledgeable about the industry to which the company belongs. The director should be prepared to make and stand behind a decision, willing to get involved in risky projects or play the role of a change agent.

Clearly from this list, the director needs both behavioral and technical skills. Unfortunately, many computer directors have been promoted from systems engineering ranks and have no managerial training other than on the job. Only recently have universities begun to add information management to their master of business administration programs.

The relative importance of behavioral and technical skills on the job is determined to some degree by the size of the applications portfolio that a computer director must oversee. When the portfolio is limited (a small budget and few computer employees), the director's job is more technical and less managerial. As the size and complexity of applications increase, however, technical tasks will be delegated to analysts and specialists, freeing the executive for managerial concerns associated with an enlarged staff and budget. Figure 21–5 shows that the skill requirements of a director's job are a function of portfolio size and complexity.

The position of computer director is very stressful and has a high turnover. This can be attributed largely to the element of risk in the job. Technical risks are run when trying to incorporate the latest computer advances in new systems. Financial risks are high due to the

Figure 21–5   **Required computer director skills as a function of application portfolio size**

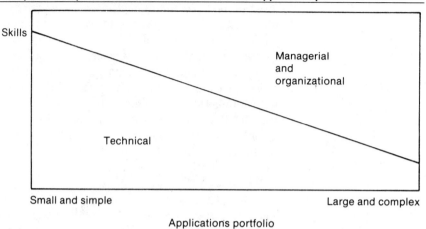

probability of time and cost overruns in systems development. Security of computer resources and privacy of data are vulnerable to assault, while reputation and credibility depend on user satisfaction.

Tension in the job can also be attributed to the fact that computer technology tends to upset traditional organizational and operational patterns, sending disruptive reverberations throughout the firm. It is the computer director who is responsible for orchestrating the introduction of new computer applications, for setting up interface committees to interpret technology to users, and for smoothing conversion to new systems. Hostility may be exhibited toward the computer department, and toward the computer director in particular, by persons who resent the intrusion of computers in their work spheres.

The computer director cannot seek solace from other department heads, who may themselves harbor resentment against the computer department. They are piqued that computing is given favored status, yet produces no tangible product or benefit of ascertainable market value. They are embittered that the failure rate accepted in computer projects would cost them their jobs.

A strain may also exist in the relationship between the computer director and corporate management. This strain is based, in part, on differences in their backgrounds, technical orientations, and objectives but can also be traced to problems in communication. Technical jargon and computer acronyms are not always understood outside the computing field. "Talking down" to senior management is also inappropriate, for management is becoming increasingly knowledgeable about computer capabilities. A genuine dialogue should be sought: corporate management sharing its vision of the firm's future, the computer director explaining in nontechnical terms how computer advances (such as microtechnology, telecommunications, networking, office automation, computer-aided design and manufacturing, and robots) can further corporate goals. Corporate management can help moderate the pressure on the computer director by being accessible for counsel and by establishing a fair approach to evaluation of the director's performance.

The new breed of computer managers

Because of the large funds involved in computer processing and the long lead time required for equipment delivery and systems development, planning has always been a major concern of computer directors. "What can the computer department do for you?" was the question traditionally asked of users. Today, however, the style of computer management is becoming more aggressive. Directors, as change agents, offer innovative ideas instead of waiting for service requests, saying, "Here is what we can do and should do for you."

The new breed of computer directors is more political, able to recognize power bases and win converts. Such directors are also integrators, able to merge computers, communications, and data bases into effective delivery systems. But not all have the same outlook regarding the primary function of their computer departments. Some endorse the concept that computer departments should be profit centers and that users should determine what services are offered by their willingness to pay. Others view their departments as service agencies. They are less concerned with departmental profits than with developing systems to improve corporate performance. Perhaps, the ideal computer director would be a combination of the two: a profit-conscious, service-oriented manager.

SUMMING UP

Computing involves a web of relationships between corporate management, computing personnel, and users. This chapter has focused on committees that provide the formal structure for interaction between these groups in the oversight of computing. In Figure 21–6, which diagrams a sample configuration of oversight relationships, the computer department director reports directly to a steering committee. The steering committee also receives reports on performance from subcommittees that oversee developmental activities and operations. Some steering committees require that all computing be done in-house. Others allow users within the firm to request bids for jobs, placing in-house computing facilities in competition with outside service centers.

Top management controls computing by chartering the steering committee, making budgetary decisions, and serving with other users as

Figure 21–6   **Sample configuration of a steering committee and subcommittees in relation to corporate management and the computer director**

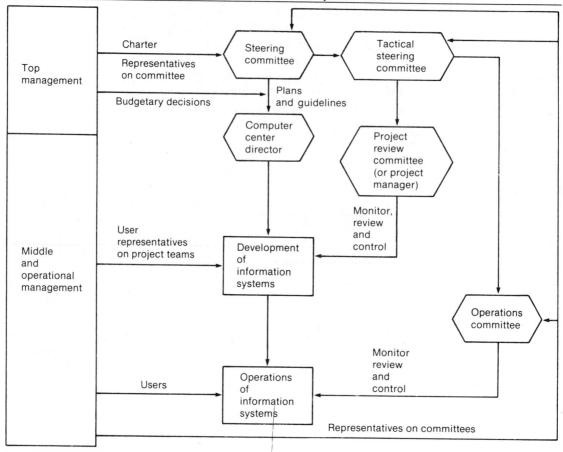

members of the steering committee and subcommittees. Management is also a receiver of computing services and so participates in development projects as a team member and criticizes output, just as other users do.

Users are found at all levels of an organization, from data clerks to company presidents. The steering committee and computer director need a method of determining whether the services offered meet users' needs. Many firms conduct user surveys for this purpose.

New responsibilities are continually being added to the job of computer center director. The expansion of applications, the addition of word processing to traditional data processing, and the movement toward distributed processing centers require technical expertise and business skills that former EDP heads did not need when computing was a mere back-shop operation. The computer director of the future will be an information manager who takes the initiative in business information planning, one who discovers opportunities for improving the effectiveness of information utilization and "sells" these options when appropriate and beneficial to the company.

Computer directors with demonstrated proficiency in managing modern computing centers have administrative talent that should not be wasted. Director of computing should not be a dead-end job but should have a career path leading to corporate management.

CASE: OVERSIGHT AT A BANK

In a regional bank in the United States, management was dissatisfied with the bank's data processing, as were departmental users within the bank. The bank officers were concerned about the data processing budget. User departments felt that data processing should be of greater service but weren't sure how. Computing management worried about staff turnover and how best to allocate computing resources. There was general agreement that the bank needed an organizational body to provide direction and control to computing.

The first step in setting up a guiding body was to establish objectives for such a group. It was agreed that the group would be responsible for setting data processing directions and services and for the establishment of priorities for data processing activities and development.

An Executive Steering Committee (ESC) was then chartered. It asked a consulting firm to assist bank personnel in evaluating the bank's data processing. Systems maintenance and enhancement were found to be inadequate, and efficiency pressures had gone too far, resulting in damage to many systems and technical resources. The ESC then formulated a data processing funding evaluation strategy and established new funding directions for the bank's data processing. In time, the committee broadened its scope to include more technical oversight of data processing.

The ESC has proved effective in its oversight role. One key to the committee's success is that the ESC members have developed (1) a working relationship with employees and (2) analysis procedures that lead to consensus regarding the current status of data processing, issues,

Source: Richard L. Nolan, ed. *Managing the Data Resource Function*, 2nd ed. (St. Paul, Minn.: West Publishing, 1982), pp. 381–83.

and resolution of problems. They are also able to communicate this consensus in business language and business structure to bank officers.

Questions

1. Why do you suppose that the ESC turned to a consulting firm for oversight assistance?
2. Should the establishment of procedures for oversight wait until problems become apparent? Explain.
3. Why do some companies fail to provide oversight of computing?
4. What lessons can be drawn from this case?

STUDY KEYS

Business within a business   **Steering committee**
Computer director   **Survey instruments**
Oversight function   **User oversight**
Senior management oversight

DISCUSSION QUESTIONS

1. How does corporate management oversee computer department operations?
2. How can the following functions be controlled in a computer department?
   a. Spending.
   b. Standards.
   c. Scheduling.
   d. Integration of systems.
   e. Honesty and integrity of staff.
   f. Priorities for maintenance jobs.
   g. Computing center director.
3. In what ways do computing departments differ from:
   a. Wholesale business?
   b. University?
   c. Government office?
   d. Public library?
4. What mechanisms should be implemented to achieve a satisfactory interface with users in:
   a. Conversion?
   b. Debugging user programs?
   c. Meeting user hardware needs?

5. Can the same user interface mechanisms be used in centralized and decentralized processing?
6. When managing a computer department, is the element of risk the same for both:
   a. Small and large computing systems?
   b. Centralized and distributed systems?
   c. Functional and integrated systems?
   d. Batch and online systems?
   e. A large computer and a network of minis?
7. At what point and under what circumstances should a steering committee delegate its authority and responsibility to other committees?
8. What is the purpose of classifying users? How best can this be done?
9. What qualities and qualifications are desirable in a computer director?
10. Should computer directors have technical or business management backgrounds? Explain.
11. What qualifications would you recommend for appointees to a steering committee?
12. What are the main risks faced by computer directors and steering committees? How can they be minimized or eliminated?
13. What role (if any) should the computer director play in corporate policy decision making?
14. How should user satisfaction be determined?

SELECTED ANNOTATED BIBLIOGRAPHY

Crane, Jane. "The Changing Role of the DP Manager." *Datamation*, vol. 28, no. 7 (June 1982), pp. 96–108.
This article reports on opinions on the changing role of data processing managers collected in interviews with DP consultants and managers.

Hargraves, Robert F., Jr. "Corporate Strategies and DP Tactics." *Datamation*, vol. 29, no. 8 (August 1983), pp. 204–16.
The job of a manager of management information systems is more than operational management. It involves planning for activities that fit into corporate management's strategic plans.

Ives, Blake; Margrethe Olsen; and Jack Baroudi. "The Measurement of User Information Satisfactions." *Communications of the ACM*, vol. 26, no. 10 (October 1983), pp. 785–93.
The authors critically examine various instruments for determining user satisfaction and eliminate scales that they consider psychometrically unsound. They propose using a short form that requires only an overall assessment of satisfaction when survey time is limited.

Karten, Naomi. "Surviving the PC Challenge Demands Management Skills." *Data Management*, vol. 23, no. 9 (September 1985), pp. 14–18.
An environment with personal computers makes new demands on a manager of computing resources. Training, MIS management support, and ap-

plications development are required. Oversight is needed to avoid the "do-it-all" syndrome.

McKeen, J. D., and Tor Guimaraes. "Selecting MIS Projects by Steering Committee." *Communications of the ACM*, vol. 28, no. 12 (November 1985), pp. 1344–51.
A survey of 92 projects shows alternative ways that projects are selected. The best method appears to be a management decision in conjunction with user departments. Other studies on project selection are reviewed, and the impact of steering committees on project portfolios is discussed.

Nolan, Richard L. "Managing Information Systems by Committee." *Harvard Business Review*, vol. 60, no. 4 (July–August 1982), pp. 73–79.
The author writes with authority on the committee approach to managing a computer facility. Discussed are direction setting, rationing, structuring, staffing, and empirical guidelines.

Rogan , Winnie R., and Herbert W. Perkins III. "Steering Committees." In *Managing the Data Resource Function*, ed. Richard L. Nolan. St. Paul, Minn.: West Publishing, 1982, 417 pp.
This book has several chapters of interest. "Steering Committees" (pp. 370–83) describes the role of the committee in direction setting, budgeting, bridging the user-provider gap, and providing management controls. Another recommended chapter is "Towards a Theory of Data Processing Leadership" (pp. 361–69).

Umbaugh, Robert E. "Corporate Responsibility and the MIS Manager." *Journal of Information Systems Management*, vol. 4, no. 1 (Winter 1987), pp. 58–62.
With the increasing strategic importance of MIS to the competitiveness of a business, it is important that managers learn new lessons about performing responsibly from an organizational viewpoint.

Zmud, Robert W. "Design Alternatives for Organizing Information Systems Activities." *MIS Quarterly*, vol. 8, no. 2 (June 1984), pp. 79–93.
Tasks associated with acquiring, deploying, and managing information technologies are in a considerable state of flux in many organizations. The evolving nature of these activities and alternative ways of organizing them are presented in this article.

PART SIX

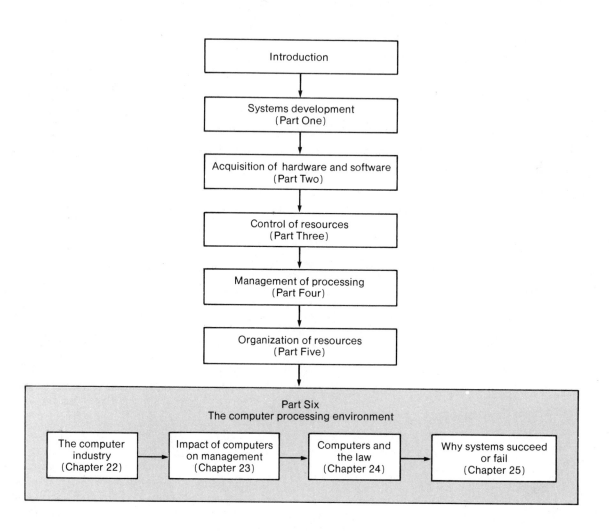

Introduction

Systems development
(Part One)

Acquisition of hardware and software
(Part Two)

Control of resources
(Part Three)

Management of processing
(Part Four)

Organization of resources
(Part Five)

Part Six
The computer processing environment

The computer industry (Chapter 22)

Impact of computers on management (Chapter 23)

Computers and the law (Chapter 24)

Why systems succeed or fail (Chapter 25)

THE COMPUTER PROCESSING ENVIRONMENT

The chapters in this final part do not fit together under a topic heading as nicely as chapters in preceding sections, yet they are all important to business managers. They address issues of concern regarding the data processing environment.

Chapter 22 is an overview of the computer industry, discussing growth sectors of the industry, competition among equipment manufacturers, and pricing strategies of vendors. It is suggested that social issues and the merging of communications with computing will have more impact on the direction of computing in the near future than will technological advances.

Chapter 23 discusses the impact of computers on management and organization. How computers have changed management decision making, job responsibility, and span of control is addressed. So is the subject of information technology as a competitive weapon. The chapter also explores whether jobs at the managerial level are jeopardized by computers and how modern corporations are being restructured because of the computer revolution.

Computers and the law is the subject of Chapter 24. Firms engaged in computing must be cognizant of antitrust statutes, copyright provisions, and laws regulating contracts, patents, trade secrets, tort, and computer crime. This chapter discusses statutes and common law relevant to computing in each of these areas. It also reviews cases that have set guidelines for computer operations and helped to create new sectors of the computer industry.

The book closes with Chapter 25, "Why Systems Succeed or Fail." Factors critical to systems success (factors identified in earlier chapters) are reviewed and summarized. Stressed is the importance of focusing on human needs when creating information systems rather than concentrating solely on technological considerations. The chapter also introduces the concept that firms must pass through stages of growth in order to implement advanced technology.

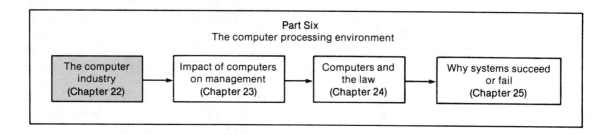

Part Six
The computer processing environment

| The computer industry (Chapter 22) | Impact of computers on management (Chapter 23) | Computers and the law (Chapter 24) | Why systems succeed or fail (Chapter 25) |

CHAPTER 22

The computer industry

*Wherever we are, it is but a stage on
the way to somewhere else, and whatever
we do, however well we do it, it is only
a preparation to do something else that
shall be different.*

Robert Louis Stevenson

Will recovery from the data processing slump in the 1980s leave the
computer industry stronger than ever? Can newcomers to the computing
field find a market niche and successfully compete with established
firms? Is the industry overregulated? Should IBM be constrained, or
should its dominance be allowed because the company's success contributes to U.S. world leadership in information technology? In what
directions is the computer industry moving?

Because of the computer industry's importance to the health of the
American economy, these questions are debated in Washington whenever economic forecasts are made, trade regulations are proposed, or
business legislation is introduced on Capitol Hill. This chapter presents
background information on the industry so that readers can participate
in the debate. Knowledge of the status of the industry is a prerequisite
to informed opinion and to effective management of information resources.

The chapter first presents an overview of the computer industry,
then discusses in detail several sectors of the industry (semiconductors,
supercomputers, mainframes, small systems, peripherals, software, service, and electronic information). Pricing strategies within the industry
are examined, constraints on innovation are described, and the future
of information technology is explored.

OVERVIEW OF THE COMPUTER INDUSTRY

The **computer industry** is big business. In 1985, the top 100 data processing companies worldwide had total revenues of $150.8 billion.[1] (This figure represents 92 percent of the total data processing market that year.) When speaking of the industry, one is talking about firms with diversified computer products, including mainframes, minis, microcomputers, peripherals, software, data communications, maintenance, service, and accessories and supplies. The relative market share of each of these products for the top 100 computer firms is listed in Table 22–1.

Although the computer industry includes many companies, a few firms dominate it. For example, the top 15 companies, listed in Table 22–2, generated 65 percent of the revenue in data processing in 1985. Note that IBM is the industry leader, exceeding others in both computing income and employment. Its 1985 data processing revenue was approximately 6.9 times greater than next-ranked Digital Equipment Corp. This figure is significant because a measure economists frequently use to identify a monopoly is whether an industry leader exceeds its nearest rival by twice its revenue. In no other American industry does such a a wide gap exist between top competitors.

Even though IBM is often accused of monopolistic practices, the company cannot be said to have exclusive control of the market. (Table 22–3 indicates the large number of data processing firms that traded stock in the United States in 1986.) Thirty-one of IBM's competitors

Table 22–1	Market shares of computer industry products (based on top 100 organizations in data processing)	
	Market share ($ billions)	*Percent of market*
Mainframes	$ 25.3	16.80%
Peripherals	41.1	27.25
Minis	16.8	11.14
Micros	15.3	10.15
Software	11.5	7.63
Data communications	11.2	7.43
Services	8.6	5.70
Maintenance	17.4	11.54
Other	3.2	2.10
Total	$150.4	99.74%

Source: Pamela Archbold and Parker Hodges, "The Datamation 100," *Datamation*, vol. 32, no. 12 (June 15, 1986), p. 44.

---

[1]Pamela Archbold and Parker Hodges, "The Datamation 100," *Datamation*, vol. 32, no. 12 (June 15, 1986), p. 43.

Table 22-2   **Top 15 companies worldwide with data processing revenues of more than $1 billion, 1985**

	Company	Country	Data processing revenue ($ billion)	Percent of total revenue	Number of employees
1.	IBM	U.S.A.	$48,554	97%	405,535
2.	Digital Equipment Corp.	U.S.A.	7,029.4	100	91,000
3.	Sperry	U.S.A.	4,755.1	86	67,000
4.	Burroughs	U.S.A.	4,685.3	93	60,500
5.	Fujitsu	Japan	4,309.5	66	74,187
6.	NCR	U.S.A.	3,885.5	90	62,000
7.	NEC	Japan	3,761.8	38	90,102
8.	Control Data	U.S.A.	3,679.7	100	44,300
9.	Hewlett-Packard	U.S.A.	3,675.0	56	84,000
10.	Siemens	West Germany	3,265.0	18	348,000
11.	Hitachi	Japan	2,885.4	14	164,951
12.	Olivetti	Italy	2,518.2	82	48,944
13.	Wang Laboratories	U.S.A.	2,428.3	100	31,000
14.	Xerox	U.S.A.	1,959.0	22	102,896
15.	Honeywell	U.S.A.	1,951.9	29	94,022

Note: Three of the top 15 firms are Japanese (Fujitsu, NEC, Hitachi) and two are European (Siemens, Olivetti). Many of the companies in this list are large conglomerates that draw only a portion of their revenues from data processing.

Source: Pamela Archbold and Parker Hodges, "The Datamation 100," *Datamation,* vol. 32, no. 12 (June 15, 1986), p. 56.

have annual data processing revenues greater than $1 billion.[2] These companies are leviathans in their own right. Most earn considerably more than $1 billion, drawing income from other products and services as well. For example, less than one fifth of the revenue of Siemens (see Table 22–2) was derived from data processing in 1985; for Hitachi, the figure was closer to one seventh.

However, no overview of the industry would be complete without acknowledging that IBM towers over competitors. IBM is the world's most profitable industrial company. It sets standards and new directions in computing. In all countries except Japan, it exceeds every other data processing company in revenues. The very size of IBM helped it weather the slowdown in industry growth that led to layoffs, losses, and collapsing stock prices among computer makers and suppliers in the mid-1980s. (Industry revenue growth decreased from 30 percent a year in the early 1980s to 15 percent in 1985.)

A number of factors other than the normal boom-and-bust business cycle were blamed for the computer slump of the 80s. Sales slowed as businesses tried to figure out what to do with machines acquired during earlier buying sprees. Lack of systems integration caused dissatisfaction. Most companies wanted to tie their computers together in order

---

[2]Ibid., p. 58.

Table 22–3   **Summary of data processing firms selling stock in the United States in 1986**

Exchange	Computer systems	Exchange	Software and data processing services	Exchange	Peripherals and subsystems
O	Alpha Microsystems	O	Advanced Comp. Tech.	A	Am Intl.
O	Altos Computer Sys.	N	Advanced Sys.	A	Anderson Jacobson
A	Amdahl	N	AGS Computers	O	AST Resh
O	Apollo	O	American Mgmt. Sys.	O	Autotrol
O	Apple	O	American Software	O	Avant Grade Computing
N	AT&T	N	Anacomp	O	Banctec
N	Burroughs	O	Analysts Intl.	N	Bolt Beranek & Newman
O	CPT	O	Ashton Tate	O	Cambex
N	Compaq	O	Ask Computer Sys.	N	Centronics Data
A	Computer Consoles	O	Astradyne Comp.	A	Cetec
O	Concurrent Comp.	N	Automatic Data Proc.	A	Cognitronics
N	Control Data	O	Computer Assoc. Intl.	N	Compugraphic
O	Convergent Tech.	O	Computer Horizons	N	Computervision
N	Cray Resh.	O	Computer Network Tech.	N	Conrac
O	Daisy Sys.	N	Computer Sciences	A	Dataproducts
N	Data General	O	Computer Task Group	A	Dataram
N	Datapoint	O	Computone Sys.	O	Data Switch
N	Digital Equip. Corp.	O	Comshare	O	Datum
N	Electronic Assoc.	N	Cullinet Software	N	Decision Inds
N	Floating Point Sys.	O	Cycare Sys.	O	Endata
N	Gould	O	Duquesne Sys.	O	Evans & Sutherland
N	Harris	N	General Elec.	N	Floating Point Sys.
N	Hewlett-Packard	N	General Mtrs.	O	Gandalf Technologies
N	Honeywell	N	GTE	N	General Datacomm Ind
N	IBM	O	Hogan Sys.	N	Hazeltine
O	IPL Sys.	O	Information Sciences	O	ICOT
N	ITT	O	Infotron Sys.	O	Information Intl
N	M A Com.	O	Keane	O	Intecom
N	Matsushita Elec. Indl.	N	Logicon	O	Interleaf
O	Mentor Graphics	O	Lotus Dev. Corp.	O	Megadata
N	Modular Computer Sys.	O	Management Sci. Amer.	A	MSI Data
N	Mohawk Data Sci.	O	MCI Comm.	N	Nashua
N	NBI	O	Micom Sys.	O	Network Sys.
N	NCR	O	Micro Pro Intl.	N	North Amern. Philips
N	Prime Computer	O	Microsoft	N	Northern Telecom
N	Sperry	O	National Data	O	Novell
O	Stratus Computer	O	On Line Software Int.	O	Omex
O	Symbolics	O	Oracle Sys.	N	Paradyne
O	Tandem Computers	N	Pansophic Sys.	A	Penril
N	Tandy	N	Planning Resh.	N	Plessey Plc.
N	Texas Instrs.	O	Policy Mgmt. Sys.	O	Printronix
A	Ultimate	O	Programming & Sys.	O	QMS
A	Wang Labs.	O	Reynolds & Reynolds		
A	Wang Labs.	O	Scientific Computers	O	Ramtek
N	Xerox	O	SEI	N	Recognition Equip.

Table 22–3 (Concluded)

Exchange	Supplies and accessories	Exchange	Software and data processing services	Exchange	Peripherals and subsystems
N	Amer. Business Prods	O	Shared Med. Sys.	N	Sanders Assoc.
N	Barry Wright	O	Software AG Systems	O	Scan Tron
A	Duplex Prods.				
N	Ennis Business Forms	O	Software Pubg.	N	Scientific Atlanta
		A	Sterling Software	O	Seagate Technology
N	3M	N	Uccel	N	Storage Technology
N	Moore				
O	Standard Register	N	URS	O	Sun Microsystem
N	Wallace Computer Svcs.	O	VM Software	A	T-Bar
				A	Tab Prods
			Semiconductors	O	Tandon
		N	Advanced Micro Dev.		
				A	TEC
		N	Analog Devices	N	Tektronix
		O	Analogic	O	Televideo Sys.
		N	Applied Magnetics	N	Telex
		O	Avantek	N	Timeplex
		O	Hadco	N	Titan Corp.
		O	Intel	O	Visual Technology
		O	Micro Mask	O	Wyse Tech.
		N	Motorola		
		N	National Semiconductor		*Leasing companies*
		N	Teradyne	N	Comdisco
				N	Continental Info. Sys.
				O	Finalco Group
				O	Phoenix Amern
				O	Selecterm
				N	U.S. Leasing

Exchanges: N = New York; A = American; O = Over-the-counter.

to raise productivity. Sales were postponed, waiting for the industry to develop the technology to allow computers from mixed suppliers to "talk" to one another. Many customers chose to delay computer purchases until much-advertised new models were delivered. Others, disenchanted with the ability of computers to improve their business operations and effect cost savings, froze spending for new data processing equipment.

The state of the economy was also a factor in the slowdown of industry sales. Manufacturers—who usually buy one third of all computers—were not shopping, because manufacturing was in the doldrums. A glut in suppliers and products contributed to a slackening of customer interest. (There were 35 worldwide manufacturers of floppy-disk drives in the mid-1980s. The capacity of the top four companies was adequate to meet world demand.) The new way in which computers were being sold, as information networks, resulted in a lengthening of the acquisition process. Before making equipment purchases, customers now spent time designing new strategies for storing information and routing it throughout their companies. Because of the lack of clearly defined hardware and software standards, shopping for compatible resources was a time-consuming process.

The slump did have some beneficial effects. Firms lowered their overblown growth expectations, reduced inventory pileups, put a stop to excess hiring, and took measures to become more efficient. IBM, for example, was supporting 15 different computer architectures in the early 80s, none of which used the same software. It made the decision to eliminate losers from its product line and put its resources behind its three strongest architectures, the PC family, the System/36, and the System/370. The company also instituted rigorous cost controls (including cuts on travel and conferences), slimmed down its work force, and made organizational changes, moving toward greater decentralization.

INDUSTRY SECTORS

Semiconductors

Companies in the **semiconductor** business produce chips that contain integrated circuits. Recognizing that the semiconductor industry would have an impact beyond its own domain since chips are components of computers and electronic products, the U.S. government (particularly the Department of Defense and the space program) helped underwrite integrated circuit development costs, spending an estimated $1 billion between 1958 and 1974. Companies that began to manufacture integrated circuits grew rapidly, finding receptive markets for their chips. California's "Silicon Valley," where many of the companies established plants, has over the years became associated with innovation and expertise in microelectronic technology.

The Japanese got a strong foothold in the chip market in 1977–79, when U.S. manufacturers failed to expand to meet the increase in demand for 16K computer memory chips. At that time, U.S. manufacturers thought the increase was merely the upswing in a boom-and-bust cycle and underestimated potential semiconductor sales. The high cost of money during the late 70s also contributed to their reluctance to expand production. Even Intel, which held 40 percent of the 16K market, did not produce enough 16K chips to satisfy its customers, having diverted production to other products for which Intel was the sole supplier. Japanese manufacturers (notably, Hitachi, Fujitsu, and NEC, companies that had a more limited range of products), were able to shift their output to 16K chips and quickly fill the gap. By 1980, they were challenging U.S. domination of the semiconductor market, introducing new chips of their own with greater intensity of large- and very large-scale integration (LSI and VLSI, respectively) to match technological advances in American semiconductors.

The 1980s have been characterized by a semiconductor trade war. U.S. chip manufacturers charge that Japanese companies have engaged in predatory pricing tactics in an effort to increase semiconductor sales, even dumping chips on the U.S. market at below cost. Private patent and antitrust suits claiming damage from the Japanese have been brought before U.S. federal courts. Chipmakers have asked Washington to consider massive trade duties on Hitachi, Fujitsu, NEC, Toshiba, Mitsubishi, and Oaki, Japan's top producers of memory chips. (Memory chips comprised nearly half of Japan's semiconductor sales in the United States in 1985.) With Congress threatening to ban Japanese imports of chips and products containing them, from pocket calculators to telephone switchboards, top-level trade negotiations between Washington and Tokyo have been given high priority by the Reagan administration. U.S. semiconductor firms demand not only price relief but substantially wider access to the Japanese market.

A negotiated settlement will not come in time to save many U.S. makers of dynamic random-access memory chips (DRAMs), a target market of the Japanese. Motorola, National Semiconductor, Intel, and Mostek all left the business in 1985, a year in which prices for the most common DRAMs dropped 80 percent. These companies will not likely reenter the business: an efficient factory requires an estimated investment of $150 million. The erasable programmable read-only memory chip (EPROM) market has also been attacked by the Japanese. (One advanced type of EPROM plunged from about $17.50 to around $3 in 11 months in 1985: another, less-sophisticated type sold at one point for less than the cost of packaging and testing. Intel, AMD, Texas Instruments, National Semiconductor, and Seeq Technology lost an estimated $200 million on EPROMs in that year.)[3] But American companies stand on firmer ground with EPROM because they retain a lead in technology.

Why is the market for memory chips so important to Silicon Valley? Because memory chips are easy to test for defects, which means that they can be used to refine new production processes. These processes can subsequently be used in the manufacture of more-complex products. In other words, memory chips help manufacturers stay competitive in production technology.

A long-term settlement of the U.S.-Japanese semiconductor trade war may require structural changes in Japanese industry, some experts say.

---

[3]Bro Uttal, "A Respite in the Chip Price War," *Fortune*, Vol. 113, no. 10 (May 12, 1986), p. 88.

American firms want assurances that Japanese companies will not dump chips or subsidize their sale with profits from other products in the future. Americans also want the Japanese to open their doors to more imports.

Supercomputers

The largest and fastest computers belong to the **supercomputer** category. The U.S. has traditionally held a lead in both supercomputer technology and supercomputer use. The American government is a major purchaser, with most of its supercomputers placed in governmental agencies with defense missions, such as the National Security Agency and federal research laboratories. (The nuclear weapons laboratory at Los Alamos has 10.) But commercial use of supercomputers is growing. The machines are presently being used in fields such as automobile and aircraft design, seismic exploration, weather forecasting, cryptography, biomedical research, and movie production (special effects), where large-scale "number crunching" is called for.

Why is preeminence in supercomputers believed to be in the national interest? Market dominance in supercomputers means jobs and revenue to the computer industry, an important sector of the American economy. Supercomputer technology has a spillover effect, contributing to the development of more-powerful, lower-level computers—a spillover that benefits computer users and enhances American leadership in computing. Fields that depend on supercomputers to process massive amounts of information (such as aerodynamic design) have been transformed, and new technologies have been stimulated by the use of supercomputers. It is also argued that the country with the best supercomputers will lead all others in scholarship, industry, and government. (Consider, for example, the national security implications if the United States, which depends on supercomputers to develop weapons and plot defense strategies, falls behind in the supercomputer race.)

Two American companies have the main share of the supercomputer market: Cray Research and Control Data. (There are presently more than 100 of these machines in the workplace.) However, significant competition is beginning to appear from two Japanese manufacturers, Fujitsu and Hitachi, that have introduced IBM-compatible supercomputers. The Japanese have also announced that they are developing a fifth-generation computer for the 1990s, a machine that they hope will far surpass present-day supercomputers in performance. It is in the supercomputer marketplace that the battle for technical and industrial leadership in the worldwide information processing industry may be fought in the next 10 years.

Mainframes

Figure 22–1 illustrates which companies dominate the world market in large systems (costing more than $350,000) and shows that IBM leads in **mainframe** sales. The company commands more than 63 percent of

Figure 22–1   **1985 worldwide market share in large systems (more than $350,000 in cost)**

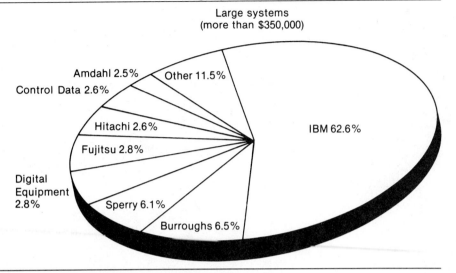

Large systems
(more than $350,000)

Amdahl 2.5%

Control Data 2.6%

Other 11.5%

Hitachi 2.6%

IBM 62.6%

Fujitsu 2.8%

Digital
Equipment
2.8%

Sperry 6.1%

Burroughs 6.5%

Source: Infocorp: Media General.

the mainframe market. Burroughs, its nearest competitor, has a 6.5 percent market share.

The top six U.S. mainframe manufacturers are IBM, Burroughs, Sperry, NCR, Control Data, and Honeywell. The six are called the "giant and five dwarfs" by insiders, but the dwarfs are small only when measured against the giant, IBM. In absolute terms, their data processing revenues are considerable (see Table 22–4), and each has a tradition of service in business, with a loyal cadre of customers. Burroughs, for example, has roots in adding and bookkeeping machines; NCR, long associated with cash registers, has a specialty in banking and retail markets; and Control Data, which debuted in large computers, draws clients through its service bureaus and its focus on energy applications.

IBM mainframe dominance can be traced to the early days of computing. In the 1960s, for example, the introduction of the IBM/360, with a revolutionary single architecture for a family of computers (leading to the 370), set a standard for computer architecture that all other mainframe manufacturers soon followed. IBM's leadership extended to mainframe pricing as well. Competitors operated under IBM's price umbrella, keeping their mainframe users captive by slightly undercutting IBM in price. Whenever new IBM models reached the market, competitors scrambled to introduce enhanced versions of their own computers with matching capability.

Though some jockeying for position did occur in the early 70s (Control Data made changes in its high-end computers, and both Burroughs and NCR introduced new series), IBM's dominance in mainframes re-

Table 22–4   Top ten in the U.S. by data processing revenues for 1985

	Ranking in terms of DP Revenue												Employment (1000)	R&D $ billions	R&D % of Revenue	DP Revenue	DP as % of total
	86	85	84	83	82	81	80	79	78	77	76	75					
IBM	1	1	1	1	1	1	1	1	1	1	1	1	405.5	4.723	9.4	48,554.0	97
Digital Equipment Corp.	3	2	2	2	2	2	4	6	6	6	7	7	91	770	10.9	7,029.4	100
Sperry	2*	3	6	6	6	6	5	5	5	5	3	4	67	504.9	9.1	4,755.1	86
Burroughs	2*	4	3	3	5	5	6	2	2	2	2	2	60.5	285.2	5.7	4,685.3	93
NCR	5	5	5	5	4	4	2	3	3	3	6	6	62	299.1	6.9	3,885.5	90
Control Data	6	6	4	4	3	3	3	4	4	4	5	5	44.3	438.3	11.9	3,679.7	100
Hewlett-Packard	4	7	7	7	7	7	8	8	8	9	8	9	84	685.0	10.5	3,675.0	56
Wang Laboratories	7	8	8	8	10	10	11	23	25	25	32	45	31	187	7.7	2,428.3	100
Xerox	8	9	11	10	9	9	9	12	19	15	22	19	102.4	603.1	6.9	1,959.0	22
Honeywell	11	10	10	9	8	8	7	7	7	7	4	3	94.02	451.4	6.8	1,951.9	29

*Under the name Unisys Corp. after the merger of Burroughs and Sperry.

mained uncontested throughout the 70s. This was true even though IBM's 370/168 was becoming technologically outdated as demand for high-end computers increased. Gene Amdahl, an IBM designer of high-end processors, had forecast this likelihood as early as the 60s and had recommended that IBM develop a new mainframe family with increased computing capacity. But IBM, committed to the price-performance ratio of the 370s and not seeing enough demand for the new series to make development profitable, did not heed Amdahl's advice.

Amdahl left IBM in 1970 and started a company of his own to manufacture mainframes compatible with software and peripherals developed for IBM computers. Though plug-compatible peripherals were common on the market, Amdahl was proposing an IBM **plug-compatible mainframe** that used IBM systems software. Crucial funding came from Fujitsu of Japan. The Amdahl mainframe was put on the market in 1976, and its success surprised both industry observers and economists who had not believed that demand for high-end computers was elastic. Amdahl proved such elasticity did exist. He also demonstrated "that it was possible to build compatible computers, . . . to obtain customer acceptance, to provide the hardware and software support adequate to synergize this acceptance, and to grow rapidly while doing it."[4]

What is more, Amdahl helped refute monopoly charges against IBM by demonstrating that a new company could surmount entry barriers in the mainframe market. Other companies to manufacture early plug-compatible mainframes (emulating Amdahl's activities) were Intel, Magnuson, Nanodata, Cambridge Memories, Citel, and NCSS. By the late 1980s, major plug-compatible contenders were Amdahl, Magnuson, National Advanced Systems, and IPL.

To meet mainframe competition, IBM has introduced new mainframe models with improved price-performance ratios. The company has also reduced the life cycle of its models and has tried to operate under a lower price umbrella while still retaining its lease base. It spends vast sums to upgrade its products and improve operating efficiency. (In 1985, for example, $4.7 billion was spent for research, development, and engineering. Another $3 billion was allocated to factory automation. These figures add up to more than the total 1985 sales of Digital Equipment Corp. (DEC), IBM's closest rival.)

IBM also has a well-trained sales force and aggressive marketing strategy. It times price cuts and new-machine deliveries to catch competitors off balance. It fosters confusion and doubt in the market by announcing new features and hinting of advances to come. Thousands

---

[4]Gene M. Amdahl, "The Early Chapters of the PCM Story," *Datamation*, vol. 25, no. 2 (February 1979), pp. 113–16.

of sales representatives descend on customers to convince them that any move away from IBM is foolhardy.

Despite these strategies, IBM's share of the mainframe market has dropped from 82 percent during the 60s and early 70s to 62 percent in 1985. Its competition today comes from foreign companies as well as from American firms. For example, Fujitsu and Hitachi are two formidable Japanese competitors. They are international organizations with ambitious long-term goals in computing and have large resources at their disposal. What's more, they benefit from Japanese government subsidies for the development of high technology. Although these companies have captured only a small share of the mainframe market to date, they may challenge IBM's mainframe dominance in the future.

IBM's revenues from mainframes are also threatened by superminicomputer competitors, whose machines, each year, grow in processing capability and demonstrate improved price-performance ratios. The fact that the distance between mainframes and minis is narrowing may undercut mainframe sales in the future. According to some industry observers, this trend is already apparent. They cite as evidence the stall of mainframe sales in the mid-80s even though sales for smaller machines continued to mount. (See Figure 22–2.) However, others believe

Figure 22–2   **Sales of mainframes, departmental minis, and personal computers from 1981 to 1985**

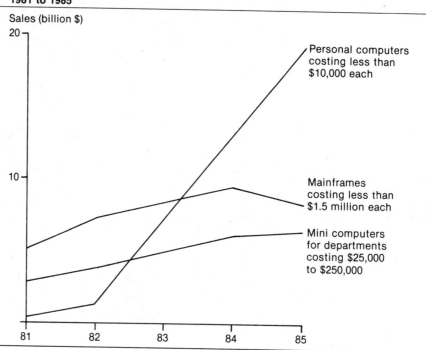

budget constraints and the existence of excess processing capacity explain the stall. They find little evidence of users shifting applications to smaller systems.

Small systems

In the small-systems market (systems costing from $12,000 to $349,999), IBM leads other companies once again but does not dominate as in mainframes. (Both Figure 22–3 and Table 22–5 show leaders in the field. The latter lists the top 15 companies in **minicomputer** revenues.) DEC's sales are rising; and in number of installed minis, the company does not lag behind IBM. However, DEC revenues are lower than IBM's because DEC minis are less costly than IBM models. In addition, IBM usually sells complete systems (computer, peripherals, and software), while DEC more often sells "stripped-down" models. DEC machines are commonly bought as data communication processors or are purchased by dealers who resell them after adding their own peripherals or proprietary software.

Microcomputers

When **microcomputers** were first introduced in the market for home, school, and business use in the late 1970s, Apple, Commodore, and Radio Shack (Tandy) dominated the market. Although IBM did introduce a small business computer series at that time, the microcomputer systems of its competitors were superior.

This changed in 1981, when IBM introduced the IBM PC, a technologically up-to-date machine with a 16-bit processor and good software, marketed through computer stores and business product centers.

Figure 22–3   **Market leaders in sales of small systems (costing $12,000–$349,999)**

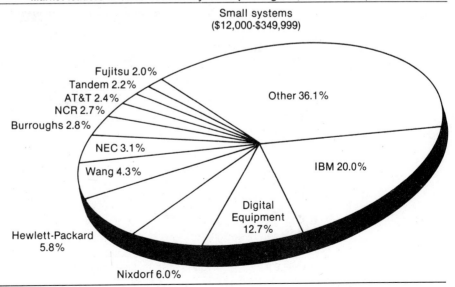

Small systems
($12,000-$349,999)

Fujitsu 2.0%
Tandem 2.2%
AT&T 2.4%
NCR 2.7%
Burroughs 2.8%
NEC 3.1%
Wang 4.3%
Hewlett-Packard 5.8%
Nixdorf 6.0%
Digital Equipment 12.7%
IBM 20.0%
Other 36.1%

Table 22–5   **Top 15 firms worldwide by minicomputer revenues, 1985**

Company	Revenue ($ millions)
IBM	$3,500.0
Digital Equipment Corp.	1,600.0
Hewlett-Packard	1,050.0
Wang Laboratories	870.9
Data General	799.7
Prime Computers	533.1
Harris	470.0
Fujitsu (Japan)	439.0
Nixdorf (West Germany)	407.9
Sperry	400.5
Burroughs	400.0
NCR	400.0
Volkswagen (West Germany)	366.7
Olivetti (Italy)	348.6

Source: Pamela Archbold and Parker Hodges, "The Datamation 100," *Datamation*, vol. 32, no. 12 (June 15, 1986), p. 45.

This machine soon gave IBM a leadership role in microcomputers. Today, IBM has more revenues from microcomputer sales than any other firm. However, the microcomputer market is divided into many segments (e.g., business and professional users, home users, scientific users, educational users). A number of companies have been able to establish a strong presence in one or more of these segments.

The microcomputer market has not met predictions made at the start of the 1980s. Sales to home users have been disappointing. On the other hand, the sales potential of microcomputers for business use was under-

Table 22–6   **Top 15 micro manufacturers worldwide by 1985 revenues**

Company	Revenue ($ millions)
IBM	$5,500.0
Apple	1,603.0
Olivetti (Italy)	884.5
Tandy	796.8
Sperry	742.8
Commodore	600.0
Compaq	503.9
Hewlett-Packard	400.0
Convergent Technologies	395.2
Zenith	352.0
NEC (Japan)	338.6
Apollo	295.6
Matsushita (Japan)	270.6
Ericsson (Sweden)	232.6
Digital Equipment Corp.	225.0

Source: Pamela Archbold and Parker Hodges, "The Datamation 100," *Datamation*, vol. 32, no. 12 (June 15, 1986), p. 45.

estimated. With improved speed and memory capability and refinement of the technology linking micros with mainframes, the future of microcomputers looks bright. However, the number of firms that have entered the industry and the success of large firms such as IBM mean that companies selling microcomputers must operate in an extremely competitive environment.

Table 22–6 lists the top 15 companies in micros. Although total market revenue was up in 1985, not all microcomputer firms are doing equally well. IBM's revenues have flattened, Olivetti and Tandy's have surged, and Commodore has suffered substantial losses.

Peripherals

Peripherals are units of equipment, distinct from the central processing unit, that provide a computer system with outside communication. Included are input/output devices, auxiliary storage units, and communications equipment.

Some of the devices that fall into the peripheral category illustrate the diversity of that market:

- Machines that read data stored on cards, tapes, disks, drums, or microfilm, such as magnetic ink character readers, disk drives, badge readers.
- Direct keyboard input devices, such as cathode ray tube (CRT) terminals, point-of-sale terminals, and touch-tone telephones.
- Pattern recognition devices, such as data tablets and voice recognition equipment.
- Output recording devices, such as printers, plotters, audio response units, and computer output on microfilm devices.
- Storage equipment, such as disk packs, Winchester disks, or mass storage systems with honeycomb cells containing cartridges of magnetic tape.
- Equipment to generate and receive electronic signals for the transmission of information from one computer system component to another, such as modems, concentrators, and multiplexers.

Peripherals are the biggest revenue producer in the data processing market, as shown by sales figures in Table 22–7. Some companies manufacture a single peripheral; others offer a range of products. The table lists the top 15 peripheral companies ranked by sales revenues. Note that in this market, IBM is again the leader, with $12.6 million in sales for 1985. The table also shows that more than one third of the top 15 are non-U.S. companies, many of which are growing rapidly.

Software

In the early days of computing, systems engineers who installed a new computer also developed the applications software to run on the new machine. However, it soon became the practice of clients who purchased computers to develop their own applications programs in-

Table 22–7   **Top 15 peripheral producers worldwide by 1985 sales revenues**

Company	Revenue ($ millions)
IBM	$12,676.0
Digital Equipment Corp.	2,750.0
Burroughs	1,479.0
Xerox	1,430.0
Hitachi (Japan)	1,416.7
Control Data	1,270.0
Wang Laboratories	1,229.5
Hewlett-Packard	1,100.0
Fujitsu (Japan)	1,084.3
NEC (Japan)	1,053.3
NCR	1,000.0
Siemens (West Germany)	816.2
Toshiba (Japan)	795.5
Groupe Bull (France)	699.1
Honeywell	656.0

Source: Pamela Archbold and Parker Hodges, "The Datamation 100," *Datamation*, vol. 32, no. 12 (June 15, 1986), p. 44.

house, and programmers were hired for this purpose. By the mid-1960s, entrepreneurs recognized that selling a program to many users would be profitable. IBM resisted this concept and continued to sell software bundled in a hardware purchase price until forced by Justice Department action to stop this practice in 1969. IBM's **unbundling** led to software becoming a viable business product.

As the software industry has matured, there has been a sharp distinction between systems and applications software firms. They have very different characteristics and cultures. Systems software products are sold to data processing management and must compete in areas where IBM is strong, such as in operating systems and languages. (Since IBM derives its revenue primarily from hardware sales, it is not surprising that it is more attuned to this market than to applications.)

Applications software is not sold exclusively to computer technicians. Much is purchased by end-users with little background or experience in computing. IBM lacks a strong presence in this market. A primary reason is that the breadth of IBM's customer base means that no single package could possibly fit all customer needs. Many IBM applications are semicustom: they require a great deal of modification by the buyer in order to adapt the package to the environment in which the software will be used. Many small, independent software houses compete by becoming industry specialists. They concentrate on a single applications area, with sales, marketing, and product development focused on the needs of the target market. This strategy has enabled these small vendors to find a market niche. Just two companies that produce only software appeared on the list of the top 100 data processing firms in 1985: Lotus Development and Sterling Software.

One reason the future of the software industry is uncertain is that firms that are applications specialists, which are intensely competitive and sales driven, are broadening their product lines in response to customer requests for integrated families of software. They are now considering data base management systems, environment-independent productivity tools, cross-industry applications, and microcomputer productivity software. If they move from industry-specific applications to generalist systems, they will face formidable competition from IBM.

Another problem for software firms is that the downturn in the computer industry of the mid-1980s has affected software sales. No longer is there enough software business for all software houses to win substantial sales increases, as at the start of the decade. Once-thriving software vendors have experienced slower growth, buyer resistance to new products, and fierce competition. This has led to price wars and the merger of many independent software houses into large, well-capitalized firms.

Computer services

The makeup of the **computer services** industry was described in Chapter 19. The top 15 companies in 1985 in this market are listed in Table 22–8.

Electronic information

The selling of information through terminals, personal computers, or television screens is a new arm of the computer industry. In the mid-1980s, more than 1,400 firms sold **electronic information** ranging from commodity and security quotes to news, abstracts, and professional/technical information. (See Table 22–9 for the major information categories.) For example, financial information (such as money-market and

Table 22–8   **Top 15 computer services firms by 1985 revenue**

Company	Revenue ($ millions)
Automatic Data Processing	$1,102.1
Control Data	1,058.7
General Motors	978.3
General Electric	950.0
Computer Sciences	800.7
McDonnel Douglas	650.0
Martin Marietta	429.9
Nippon Telegraph and Telephone (Japan)	382.0
Sperry	302.5
NCR	300.0
IBM	300.0
Boeing	270.0
Xerox	200.0
General Instruments	190.2
Quotron Systems	187.5

Source: Pamela Archbold and Parker Hodges, "The Datamation 100," *Datamation*, vol. 32, no. 12 (June 15, 1986), p. 46.

Table 22–9   **Types of electronic information that sold best in the United States in 1985**

Category	Sales ($ millions)	Percent of total
Securities and commodities quotes	$ 560	34.8%
Professional (legal, medical, etc.)	213	13.2
Scientific and technical	91	5.6
Abstracts, bibliographies, and other text	76	4.7
Nonbusiness consumer	48	3.0
Other numeric data bases, including financial	623	38.7
Total	$1,611	100.0%

Source: SRI International.

foreign currency rates) is sold by Telerate, a company that took six years to turn a profit. Lloyds Maritime Data Network keeps track of the movements of every commercial oceangoing vessel for its customers. The Institute for Scientific Information scans 7,000 scientific and medical journals and then sells indexes of these magazines to customers. For a listing of the top companies in electronic information, see Table 22–10.

The electronic information industry has been slow to develop. Experimental videotex information services aimed at a mass audience (such as Florida's Viewtron, which carried everything from news to restaurant reviews) have failed. For one reason, the fixed costs for gathering and organizing information have been higher than expected. Another problem has been marketing. The industry has learned that a broad base of customers will not pay for information that is readily accessible in the press. Only those for whom speed of information delivery is critical to operations will buy the service. This explains why

Table 22–10   **Top 8 companies providing electronic information (not ranked)**

Company	Type of information provided
Dow Jones	General business and securities
Dun & Bradstreet	Credit and miscellaneous business
McGraw-Hill	Financial
Mead	General business and legal
Quotron	Securities quotes
Reuters	News and quotes on commodities and securities
Telerate	Quotes on commodities and securities
TRW	Credit-worthiness

Source: Extracted from Anne R. Field and Catherine L. Harris, "The Information Business," *Business Week*, no. 2,961 (August 25, 1986), p. 84.

financial information accounts for nearly half of the electronic information sold in the United States. To money managers, rapid access to up-to-date information on stock and commodity prices and trading volume data means power and profit, because all relevant information needed to make sound financial decisions is readily available.

Companies that have succeeded in the electronic information industry have done so by:

- Targeting specific customers.
- Customizing data.
- Delivering information first.
- Choosing information technology that is familiar to customers and easy to use.
- Repackaging collected information for different clients according to their particular needs.
- Selling aggressively.

At present, the electronic information industry as a whole is only modestly profitable. The home and business market was $1.6 billion in 1985. Although demand is far lower than expected at the start of the decade, experts believe that refined marketing techniques and advances in computer and communications technology will foster industry growth in the future.

Change among the players

Any listing of leaders in computing (such as in Table 22–2) is quickly outdated because the industry is volatile, with many entries and exits. For example, the growing popularity of minis, word processors, and personal computers has enabled newcomers such as Apple, Radio Shack, and Wang to capture substantial market shares. Mergers have also brought new firms into computing (for example, GTE and Telenet, NCR and Comten, ITT and Qume), whereas acquisitions have strengthened certain competitors [for example, Telerate bought by Dow Jones, Satellite Business Systems (SBS) bought by MCI Communications, Siliconix bought by Westinghouse, and Synertek bought by Honeywell]. Marriages across international boundaries will undoubtedly cause further dislocation in the marketplace. (To give one example, in 1985, McDonnell Douglas, which sells computer services, bought Applied Research of the United Kingdom.)

In addition, some firms (such as Honeywell, Incotern, and Varian) already in one area of computing are diversifying. Others are retrenching. Exits from mainframe manufacture include such giants as GE, RCA, and Xerox. Itel has dropped from the peripheral market, and Singer has left the field of computing altogether, its computing division absorbed by TRW.

Furthermore, new technology in telecommunications has brought firms such as SBS into computing. So have court decisions, such as the

1982 out-of-court settlement that allowed AT&T to merge its communications with data services. The agreement also broke AT&T's monopoly in communications. It opened the door for IBM and such multibillion dollar firms as ITT, Exxon, RCA, and GTE to compete in data communications and to offer integrated office systems connected by communication networks. In effect, the settlement acknowledged what computer experts have maintained for a long time: computers are essential to modern communications, and communication facilities are essential to information processing. The settlement places IBM and AT&T in direct competition for the first time in history. The collision of these two giants will undoubtedly shape the computing industry in the years ahead.

AT&T will be a powerful antagonist. Since homes and offices are all wired for telephones, AT&T equipment is already on the premises of most potential customers for data services. Furthermore, AT&T's UNIX™ operating system is used by many small systems. IBM will have to displace the company from this entrenched position to gain control over data communications. AT&T's universal market presence is supported by an eminent research division (Bell Laboratories) and a production arm (Western Electric) that rivals IBM in size and product quality. AT&T has also demonstrated that it can raise vast sums of investment capital. If this capital is focused on new-product areas where IBM is weak, AT&T could threaten IBM's dominance in computing.

IBM's strength lies in the fact that the company has welded its software and hardware sales, manufacturing, distribution, and services into an integrated whole, giving the company worldwide marketing muscle. The company has a wide range of products and a record of applying its research and development to innovative product lines. IBM's data processing standards are another weapon in its arsenal. Customers that have invested in IBM equipment and software cannot readily switch vendors. AT&T may find it difficult to woo such customers away. Unless AT&T can find markets where IBM's presence is negligible or where no de facto standards exist, AT&T's challenge may well be limited to the development of plug-compatible products.

Figure 22–4 summarizes present areas of confrontation between AT&T and IBM. Competition between these corporations should ultimately benefit the user because it will foster a wider spectrum of cost-effective products and services than offered previously.

Since the 1982 settlement, however, AT&T has made little headway challenging IBM. Until 1985, it was unable to take advantage of its strength in the communications field, because of a ruling by the Federal Communications Commission that kept AT&T communications and the operations of AT&T Information Systems separate. It wasn't until September 1985 that this restraint was lifted, allowing the company the option of having one salesman (or team) offer both communications and computer products to the same customer.

Figure 22–4   **Areas of confrontation/competition between AT&T and IBM**

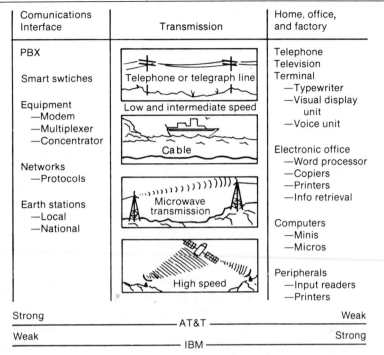

Comunications Interface	Transmission	Home, office, and factory
PBX Smart swtiches Equipment —Modem —Multiplexer —Concentrator Networks —Protocols Earth stations —Local —National	Telephone or telegraph line Low and intermediate speed Cable Microwave transmission High speed	Telephone Television Terminal —Typewriter —Visual display unit —Voice unit Electronic office —Word processor —Copiers —Printers —Info retrieval Computers —Minis —Micros Peripherals —Input readers —Printers

Strong	AT&T	Weak
Weak	IBM	Strong

The company appears to be focusing on the midrange market for its computers, a market that includes businesses with 1,000 or fewer employees and departments of large corporations. It is also striving to bring more UNIX applications to the market and to promote UNIX as a multiuser departmental interface. In local area network (LAN) technology, it is meeting IBM head-on. But overall, the performance of AT&T in the computer business has thus far been disappointing, and some analysts feel that AT&T may never become a computer powerhouse. Others believe it is too early in the game to see the outcome of this competitive battle.

All of the above entries and exits affect competition. In antitrust litigation, the volatile nature of the industry has been cited by both prosecutors and defendants in support of their cases. IBM has been under fire by the Justice Department since the 1950s for its alleged monopolistic practices (see Chapter 24). The exits of competitors, such as GE and Xerox, are cited as evidence of IBM's stranglehold on the market. IBM counters that its dominance is chiefly in mainframes and that in monopoly litigation, the industry as a whole should be considered, not just mainframes. If software, peripherals, maintenance, services, minis, micros, programmable hand calculators, military computers, and special-purpose computers (such as those used in process control) are taken into consideration, there is no evidence of monopoly. The number of new firms entering computing proves market entry is without barrier, according to IBM.

PRICING

An important strategy of computer firms when competing for markets is pricing. Amdahl proved the great elasticity of demand at the high end of the market for CPUs. Similar elasticity could exist all along the CPU spectrum and should affect price. But IBM's mainframe competitors operate under IBM's price umbrella, which allows for profit making and a payoff period of only 4–5 years. (The cost of IBM mainframes is estimated as only 15 percent of their selling price.) The mainframe market might be categorized as an oligopoly with price leadership.

The peripheral market is much more competitive in price. IBM tolerates competition within bounds, out of fear of the Justice Department. But the company reacts sharply when its market share is in jeopardy, using pricing strategies as one competitive tool. The problem is that there is a fine line between pricing in pursuance of profit maximization—a legitimate goal—and predatory pricing intended to restrict competition, which is a violation of the Sherman Act. Unfortunately, no legal definition of predatory pricing exists for the computer industry. (If predatory pricing is pricing below cost, should cost be defined as average total cost or short-run average, short-run marginal, or long-run marginal cost?) In the absence of such a definition, IBM and its competitors adopt various pricing strategies in accordance with what they perceive as the boundaries of the law.

Price tying

IBM originally combined (tied) hardware, software, education, documentation, and consulting in a single-price package. To counter critics and antitrust action, IBM "unbundled" its prices at the end of the 1960s. Though this helped some competitors, particularly software houses, IBM still had the advantage of economies of scale in software development. Other mainframe vendors, following IBM's lead, also separated software from mainframes, charging for what they had traditionally given away.

Despite unbundling, **price tying** is a strategy still commonly used when products can technically be justified as one unit. Critics charge that, too often, IBM uses the strategy in the face of fierce peripheral competition—tying vulnerable peripherals with a CPU (which has a high market entry barrier) and supportive software.

Price-cutting

Just before introducing a new product, firms often cut the price of the product being replaced. Competitors must respond with cuts of their own. Prices of IBM's 370/158 and 168 were slashed 30 percent before the introduction of the 3031 and 3032, for example. The new machines had only modest enhancements but cost even less than the reduced rates for the 158 and 168. (IBM refrained from more than a 30 percent reduction of the old models to prevent undercutting the rental of installed equipment.)

Price-cutting also occurs in peripherals. For example, a repackaged IBM disk pack was offered at a 26 percent discount. Knowing that old customers are often unwilling to make an equipment change or are oblivious of price differentials, IBM did not lower the price of the original disk pack. Disguising a price cut as a model change in this manner puts competitors on the defensive. They must be able to convince customers that their models match the new equipment in performance or must respond with modified models of their own.

An alternative price-cutting strategy is to reduce the price of products facing competition while raising the price of products with no competition.

Value pricing

Value pricing is charging a high price for an indispensable product to cover low profit margins for other products in a company's line. An inflated price for a disk drive is an example of value pricing, since customers do not have the ability to change disk drives and are "locked in" to their purchase.

Profit pricing

Sometimes, companies will alter their profit margins in response to competition, the market, or environmental conditions. It was expected that IBM might lower its profits while being tried for antitrust violations during the 70s, for example. But IBM continued to price aggressively, not linking its defense with profit pricing.

Price differentiation

Price differentiation is pricing a product in order to help favored customers or damage specific competitors. Allegedly, IBM used this strategy in pricing the 360 model 44 and model 90, taking an estimated loss of $100 million.

Pricing over a fixed term

Pricing over a fixed term was the strategy used by IBM when it offered customers a 16 percent discount for peripherals leased for a fixed term of two years without the usual option of a month's cancellation notice. This strategy was directed against plug-compatible manufacturers who have to wait until new IBM mainframes are on the market before they can start development of plug-compatible peripherals. Since peripherals have a limited life span due to the pace of technological change in computing, plug-compatible manufacturers (PCMs) have only a limited time to recoup their investments. With potential customers locked into two-year IBM leases, IBM hoped the

PCMs would decide it was not worth their while to risk developing plug-compatible peripherals in competition with IBM's own peripherals.

Are the above pricing strategies predatory and, hence, illegal? Charges of unfair competition in computing abound, and the courts are burdened with deciding questions such as whether IBM purposely sets lease/purchase prices to drive out third-party lessors. Most firms see pricing as just another card in the game of competition and employ pricing strategies to increase their share of the market within what they perceive as the boundaries of the law. IBM is as entitled as other firms to use pricing as a competitive tool.

Pricing is only one element of sales policy. A unique product, applications sales emphasis, stable charges for service, technological excellence of product, and good account management may be as important as pricing strategies in making sales.

INNOVATION IN COMPUTING

Innovation in business is closely linked to capital expenditures and outlays in research and development (R&D). This is particularly true in the computer industry, where technology quickly becomes obsolete and products have a short life span. As might be expected, IBM towers over competitors in such expenditures (see Table 22–11). Research is part of the company's broad marketing strategy. According to observers of the industry, IBM evaluates whether customers are ready to accept innovation, determines whether adequate profit from old technology has been milked, and decides where the benefits of research would most effectively throw competitors off stride.

Table 22–11   **Top 10 companies worldwide, by 1985 total R&D investments**

Company	Investment dollars (millions)	Percent of total revenue
IBM	$4,723.0	9.4%
AT&T	2,209.7	6.3
Siemens (West Germany)	1,632.5	8.8
NEC (Japan)	1,258.8	12.7
Hitachi (Japan)	1,223.9	5.9
Philips (West Germany)	1,208.1	6.6
Matsushita (Japan)	1,011.0	4.8
Toshiba (Japan)	862.7	6.0
Digital Equipment Corp.	770.0	10.9
Texas Instruments	769.0	15.6

Source: *Datamation*, vol. 32, no. 10 (August 1, 1986), pp. 56 ff.

Lack of capital is a major restraint to technological innovation in computing. Even large corporations, such as RCA, GE, and Xerox, have not had the success or the capital needed to be competitive and have consequently left the mainframe field. Government regulation is also a factor constraining the industry, particularly growth in the area of telecommunications. It is charged that FCC constraints are the reason why the United States has lagged behind France, Germany, and Japan in wired cities and videotex applications such as CEEFAX and PRES-TEL found in the United Kingdom.

FUTURE DIRECTIONS IN COMPUTING

The first four generations of computers have all shared a single basic design: the **von Neumann processor,** which executes simple instructions in sequence. Improvements have been achieved by making individual parts run faster and by increasing storage capacity. By the end of the 1980s, it is estimated that conventional systems should be able to execute 100 million sequential instructions per second and access gigabytes (billions of bytes) of memory. The problem is that the ability to process instructions with speed does not guarantee that a problem can be solved quickly. For one thing, increased processing capability can lead to tons of output, obscuring the solutions to problems. Systems designers are now addressing the issues of information indexing and data management, so that users in the future will not be overwhelmed by a glut of information.

Furthermore, computer scientists recognize that software must do more than fulfill the predetermined information needs of users. Programs must also help define information needs: They must help users recognize a problem, help them draw the problem's boundaries, help them access the information relevant to the problem's solution, and then solve the problem.

In 1981, the Japanese announced an ambitious plan to develop a new **fifth-generation computer.** These computers will run at faster speeds and have increased processing capability, machine intelligence, and enhanced input/output capabilities. Since the Japanese announcement, similar projects have been proposed in the United States and Europe. All of the programs are concentrating research in one or more of the same basic areas: very large-scale integrated circuits, new computer architectures, knowledge-based problem-solving systems, improved human-machine interfaces, and networking.

Very large-scale integrated circuits

Very large-scale integration (VLSI) is a basic field of fifth-generation research. (The term *ultra–large-scale integration (ULSI)* is used by some fifth-generation researchers.) Present design and fabrication techniques are not available to build the complex VLSI chips and wafers required for a new generation of machines. The first step, therefore, is development of VLSI design tools to assist in the design of next-generation chips and wafers and support of the manufacture of experimental designs during the course of the research.

Computer architectures

Unlike the monolithic supercomputer of today, fifth-generation computers will be compact, high-performance **multiprocessor systems.** They will consist of small, specialized units that operate in parallel, allowing the computer to perform many operations at once. Each unit will solve portions of the problem under the direction of a control unit that integrates the work of the specialized processors. The components of a fifth-generation computer will vary according to the needs of the user. If a vision system is required, for example, a vision system will be added, just as we add components to a stereo system today.

A lot of research still needs to be done on multiprocessor architectures. The main goal is to develop a usable, highly functional system that will increase processing speed as more components are added. This goal is dependent on concurrent, or parallel, programming—that is, the programming of systems components so that they execute two or more processes simultaneously—which no one yet knows how to do well. In addition, there is still only a limited understanding of task decomposition, which is the process of deciding how to subdivide a complex problem into small segments for parallel processing. Multiprocessor experiments to date have shown that additional processors may decrease performance because of the "too many cooks" syndrome. In effect, the processors start "tripping over each other's toes." The problem to be resolved is how to use a large number of processors effectively in a given application.

Disk storage is another area of systems architecture under research. Two promising technologies should contribute to increased memory: optical storage and vertical magnetic recording.

Knowledge-based problem-solving systems

Fifth-generation computers will use **intelligent software** (software that incorporates artificial intelligence features) to solve complex problems. The building blocks of such software will be:

- A **knowledge base**—a body of expert knowledge on a particular subject.
- **Context data**—information the system builds up about the situation in which the problem arises.
- An **inference engine**—a computer program that provides strategies to draw inferences about and produce solutions to the problem under analysis.

- A **knowledge-based management system**—a system to automatically organize, control, update, and retrieve knowledge (both data and rules) stored in memory.

When these building blocks are combined, the result will be a computer able to select an appropriate line of reasoning to solve a complex problem. The computer will then search for data relevant to the problem and arrive at a solution.

Intelligent programming is another software objective of researchers. Intelligent programming implies that the user tells the computer what to do, not how to do it. The computer itself writes the "how-to" instructions according to software that gives the machine instructions.

Finally, output display systems of the future will automatically determine how to present numbers, text, and graphic information according to the needs of the user.

Networks

Fundamental to fifth-generation computing will be **networks** that enable computers at dispersed locations to share resources. Computers will be connected in local area networks, which will be interconnected in a nationwide network.

Large-scale integrated circuits and telecommunications technology have already solved some of the hardware problems related to networks. We currently have LANs capable of carrying many megabytes of information. Satellites and fiber optics on land interconnect clusters of local area networks.

Various software-related problems, however, still need to be resolved. For example, work still is needed on the development of software to facilitate the interfacing of computers built by different manufacturers (computers that vary in architecture and protocols). The next generation of computers will also require distributed operating systems that synchronize processing when several nodes work on aspects of a given problem in parallel. Distributed data bases must also be implemented so that computers in the network can obtain information from any network node.

SUMMING UP

The computer industry is fragmented into segments: hardware, software, computer services, and electronic data. Although IBM's presence is felt in most computer markets, each industry segment has many players and is highly competitive—with the exception of mainframes, where IBM controls over 60 percent of the market. Table 22–12 lists

Table 22–12   **Top three leaders worldwide in different segments of the computer industry in 1985**

Industry segment	Dollars (millions)	Percent of change over 1984
Manufacturers		
IBM	$14,010.0	6.7%
Sperry	1,890.8	30.3
Fujitsu	1,618.6	5.4
Minis		
IBM	3,500.0	0
Digital Equipment Corp.	1,600.0	4.8
Hewlett-Packard	1,050.0	10.5
Micros		
IBM	5,500.0	0
Apple	1,603.0	−8.2
Olivetti	884.5	78.2
Peripherals		
IBM	12,676.0	8.8
Digital Equipment Corp.	2,750.0	10.0
Burroughs	1,479.0	4.7
Computer services		
Automatic Data Processing	1,102.1	14.9
Control Data	1,058.7	13.8
General Motors	978.3	24.4

Source: Pamela Archbold and Parker Hodges, "The Datamation 100," *Datamation*, vol. 32, no. 12 (June 15, 1986), pp. 44–46.

the top three industry leaders in mainframes, minis, micros, peripherals, and computer services.

Although IBM's 1985 revenues were greater than its next 12 competitors combined, its total share of the data processing market has dropped since the 1960s. This is due to the emergence of competitors such as Amdahl in mainframes, to plug-compatible manufacturers, and to market entry of many resource-rich foreign firms, such as Fujitsu, Siemens, and Hitachi. IBM has reacted to competition with product enhancements and pricing strategies such as tying and bundling prices, price-cutting, value pricing, profit pricing, and pricing over a fixed term. Furthermore, the software, services, and telecommunications sectors of the market (areas that IBM does not dominate) are growing.

Acquisitions and mergers, not only within the United States but between domestic and foreign companies, are changing the profile of the industry. Revision of governmental policy is also changing the nature of competition. For example, the fact that computer companies may now merge data processing with data transmission is placing AT&T and IBM, two industrial giants, in direct confrontation.

The Japanese have announced a fifth generation of computers to be introduced in the 1990s. The new computers will include very large-scale integrated circuits, advanced architectures, knowledge-based problem-solving systems, improved human-machine interfaces, and network integration. Companies throughout the world hope to meet the Japanese challenge by incorporating advanced information technology in their own computers.

Many critics charge that the computer industry is placing too much emphasis on information technology and not giving enough thought to problems such as:

- How computer information is used.
- The dehumanization of business transactions because of computer processing.
- The use of artificial intelligence, knowledge data bases, and expert systems for business computing.
- The optimum end-user computing environment.
- The social implications of computing in relation to corporate and data processing management.

They claim that the industry has lost sight of its primary objective: to serve users. It is time that the industry shifts its focus from technological concerns to people who feel "bent, stapled, and mutilated" by computer systems. Unless such a shift takes place, a ground swell of public reaction against the industry may occur.

CASE: AUTOMATION OF PRODUCTION AT IBM

In 1985, Americans bought 4 million low-priced computer printers, more than 80 percent coming from Japan. In order to gain a larger share of this market, IBM is using automated manufacturing techniques. The company's goal is to become the world's lowest-cost producer of computers and related equipment.

To compete with Japanese printers, IBM has a new automated plant in Charlotte, North Carolina, that is designed to build 1 million Proprinters a year. Few people are on the assembly line. Instead, conveyors take printer components to robots that fit the parts together. Finished goods are taken by conveyer to test areas and to a highly automated packing line. Computers control the process, flashing an error message to operators when a malfunction occurs, such as the inability of a robot

Source: John Marcom, Jr., "IBM Is Automating, Simplifying Products to Beat Asian Rivals," *The Wall Street Journal*, April 14, 1986, p. 1.

to insert a part. In a similar manner, robots assemble the IBM PC in Austin, Texas, and color monitors for IBM computer terminals in Raleigh, North Carolina.

Although many IBM competitors are also installing robotized assembly lines, few can match IBM's resources. For example, the design of the software for the robots, many of the robots themselves, and all of the computers used in IBM's automated factories are IBM products. In spite of the computer slump, IBM's outlay for new plants and property in 1985 was $6.1 billion.

The Proprinter was "designed for automation." That is, product designers, manufacturing managers, and information specialists worked together from the time the printer was first on the drawing board, so that the manufacture of the printer would lend itself to automation. For instance, the number of parts was reduced to 60 from the 150 parts in a comparable printer. The motor was designed to twist and lock in place, eliminating the need for screws, nuts, and washers. Each production task was analyzed to see whether the company should assign the work to employees, robots, special-purpose machine tools, or outside contractors.

Questions

1. Will automation by IBM make its products cheaper and more reliable? Will it cause companies that cannot afford such large capital outlays to exit from the industry?
2. Will automation in the computer industry lead to oligopoly? What are the advantages and disadvantages of having only a few large computer firms?
3. What are possible reasons why the Japanese have such a large share of the printer market? Do you think IBM's strategy to capture part of the market will work? Explain your reasons.
4. How can the Proprinter experience be used to the advantage of IBM in the manufacture of other products?

STUDY KEYS

Computer industry	Human-machine interface
Computer services	Inference engine
Context data	Intelligent programming
Electronic information	Intelligent software
Fifth-generation computer	Knowledge base

Knowledge-based management system

Mainframe

Microcomputers

Minicomputer

Multiprocessor systems

Networks

Peripherals

Plug-compatible mainframe

Price-cutting

Price differentiation

Price tying

Pricing over a fixed term

Profit pricing

Semiconductor

Software

Supercomputer

Unbundling

Value pricing

Very large-scale integration (VLSI)

Von Neumann processor

DISCUSSION QUESTIONS

1. Does free entry into the computer industry exist? Does it vary with the segment of the industry? Why is there variation? Does it serve the consumer and industry to have free entry in all segments? Explain.

2. What factors contributed to the slowdown of growth of the computer industry in the 1980s?

3. What led to the trade war in semiconductors?

4. Why is it important for the United States to lead in the technology for supercomputers?

5. Is IBM's dominance of the mainframe market a monopoly? How does IBM counter monopoly charges? Do you think government action should be taken to reduce IBM's market share?

6. What is the biggest revenue producer in the data processing industry? Why?

7. How have small, independent software houses carved a market niche?

8. At the beginning of the 1980s, it was predicted that the market for electronic information would produce revenues of $16 billion by 1990. Is this estimate proving to be accurate? Explain.

9. Describe pricing strategies used in the computer industry.

10. What are future directions in computing?

11. Would it be in the best interest of the consumer to have an unrestricted computer industry? Or should the computer industry be regulated by the government? If so, how?

12. Does the computer industry in the United States face a serious challenge from abroad? If so, in what sectors? What should be done to retain U.S. dominance in computing?

13. Must the U.S. computer industry be an oligopoly in order to provide strength to compete with nationalized computer industries abroad and, at the same time, provide consumers at home with both innovative and inexpensive products? Explain your answer.

14. What does the computer industry need most: entrepreneurs, capital, government protection, researchers and scientists, more R&D investment, or growth in computer applications? Justify your position.

15. What are the future prospects of the computer industry? Which segments will grow, and which will decline?

16. It is said that the computer industry spends too much effort developing new technology and not enough effort developing user interface or applications for the technology. Do you agree? How should the industry change?

17. Should the computer industry in the United States be protected by quotas and tariffs against competition from abroad? Comment.

18. Should the transfer of computer technology to friends and foes in the world be controlled? If so, by whom and how?

19. Should the computer industry be provided financial incentives and legal protection by the government to make U.S. computer firms competitive with foreign firms receiving such support? What incentives and protection do you recommend?

20. Should the Justice Department take a more active role in controlling pricing strategies and collusion in the computer industry or leave regulation of the industry to economic and competitive forces?

SELECTED ANNOTATED BIBLIOGRAPHY

Archbold, Pamela, and Parker Hodges. "The Datamation 100." *Datamation*, vol. 32, no. 12 (June 15, 1986), pp. 42–54.
The year 1985 was one of mixed results for the data processing industry. This article surveys each of the industry segments.

Datamation Staff Report. "Pushing the State of the Art." *Datamation*, vol. 31, no. 19 (October 1, 1985), pp. 68–84.
This report is on computer research projects by the United States, Esprit, France, Japan, the United Kingdom, Scandinavia, and the USSR.

Feigenbaum, Edward A., and Pamela McCorduck. *The Fifth Generation: Artificial Intelligence and Japan's Computer Challenge to the World.* Reading, Mass.: Addison-Wesley Publishing, 1983.
Artificial intelligence and Japanese–U.S. competition are both emotional issues. The authors suggest that the United States should not bet on the Japanese or against them but should instead take advantage of whatever research they accomplish and apply it at home.

Fishman, Katherine Davis. *The Computer Establishment.* New York: McGraw-Hill, 1983, 480 pp.
This book contains personality sketches of Seymour Gray and William Norris and also describes IBM's rise contrasted with RCA's and GE's fall.

Friberger, Paul, and Michael Swaine. *Fire in the Valley: The Making of the Personal Computer.* New York: Osborne/McGraw-Hill, 1984, 288 pp.

The valley referred to is the Silicon Valley, the birthplace and nursery of microcomputers. This is a history of the many entries and exits in the microcomputer industry, along with many personal glimpses of its players.

"The Great Debates: Technology and National Policy." *High Technology*, vol. 4, no. 10 (October 1984).

This section contains a number of articles on the efforts in the United States and abroad to develop and maintain a competitive edge in high technology. Especially recommended is "R&D Consortia: Can U.S. Industry Beat the Japanese at Their Own Game" (pp. 46–52).

Kidder, Tracy. *The Soul of a New Machine*. Boston: Atlantic/Little, Brown, 1981, 293 pp.

This is the story of the engineers who developed the 32-bit supermini for Data General, written by a reporter. It is almost an adventure story but has enough detail to make the book substantive and credible without being superficial. It deserves the Pulitzer Prize that it won.

"Management's Newest Star," *Business Week*, no. 2,968 (October 13, 1986), pp. 160–72.

This article is a special *Business Week* report on the new breed of manager surfacing in the executive suite: the chief information officer.

Moreau, R. *The Computer Comes of Age: The People, the Hardware and the Software*. Cambridge, Mass.: The MIT Press, 1986, 266 pp.

The author, the Director of Scientific Development of IBM in France, traces the history of computers from the early 1960s. The book makes fascinating reading despite the IBM bias. It is lucid in style and very readable.

Shafer, Dan. *Silicon Visions*. Englewood Cliffs, N.J.: Prentice-Hall, 1986, 311 pp.

Over 200 interviews, profiles, and technical explanations on the future of microcomputer technology are included in this book.

Tatsuno, Sheridan. *The Technopolis Strategy*. Englewood Cliffs, N.J.: Prentice-Hall, 1986, 298 pp.

Japan's Ministry of International Trade and Industry is planning to build 19 high-tech "Silicon Valleys" in Japan to spawn a new generation of creativity. This book describes Japan's "technopolis concept."

Uttal, Bro. "A Respite in the Chip Price War." *Fortune*, vol. 113, no. 10 (May 12, 1986), pp. 113–14.

U.S. manufacturers of memory chips are relieved that the government has concluded that the Japanese have been dumping. But to survive, they also need a share in the Japanese market.

Vallery, Nicholas. "High Technology." *Economist*, vol. 300, no. 7,460 (August 23, 1986), pp. 3–18.

Japan has begun to challenge American preeminence in high technology. The strengths and weaknesses of these two superpowers are explored.

Verity, John W. "1986 Mainframe Survey." *Datamation*, vol. 32, no. 9 (May 1, 1986), pp. 67–74.

A survey of 3,900 mainframe sites finds that single-user workstations now surpass minicomputers for scientific and engineering applications. Other reported trends include a movement toward departmentally based office systems and strong technical gains by DEC in minicomputer sectors.

Verity, John W., and Willie Schatz. "Fast Break in Armonk." *Datamation*, vol. 31, no. 1 (January 1, 1985), pp. 68–74.
   Another title for this article is "How Big Blue Keeps Winning." The article states that IBM is more relaxed since the Justice Department dropped its antitrust suit in 1982.

Weizer, Norman, and Frederic Withington. "IBM: Mainframes in 1990." *Datamation*, vol. 31, no. 1 (January 1, 1985), pp. 97–104.
   The 1990 IBM mainframe hardware architecture is described.

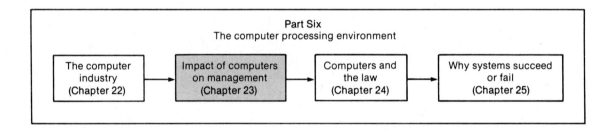

Part Six
The computer processing environment

| The computer industry (Chapter 22) | Impact of computers on management (Chapter 23) | Computers and the law (Chapter 24) | Why systems succeed or fail (Chapter 25) |

CHAPTER 23

Impact of computers on management

The purpose of computing is insight, not numbers.
Richard Hamming

Virtually no American business is untouched by the computer revolution. Payroll and accounting computer applications are common. Office work is being transformed by word processing, instantaneous data retrieval, and the storage of information and correspondence on disk and tape. Robots, numerical control, and process control affect many workers in the factory. Even firms that hand-process data undoubtedly deal with automated suppliers and clients. Certainly, no one escapes the clutches of the computerized Internal Revenue Service.

As the popular press and unions frequently call to our attention, the widespread use of computers is changing the nature of work for employees in the United States. The impact of computers on business management receives less notice. Are computers dictating the organizational structure of companies? Are they replacing humans in decision making? Are computer specialists indispensable to top management, or are they a dangerous elite?

This chapter begins by examining whether early predictions regarding the impact of computers on management have been realized. Then the ways in which information technology alters managerial style, span of control, and job content will be discussed. This leads to an analysis of new organizational structures that are evolving in order to manage information technology. The vulnerability of management to displacement by computers, the relation of information specialists to management, and computerization problems that managers must resolve are other topics covered.

The focus of this chapter is the impact of computers on corporate management. How this subject material relates to computer management will depend on the placement of computing in the organizational structure of a firm. Some companies have elevated the EDP manager to the status of vice president for information services, as described in Chapter 15. In such cases, the EDP manager has a major responsibility in the direction of the firm and in the utilization of information technology as a competitive weapon. In other firms, the EDP manager is a department head, part of middle management. However, this manager may be called upon to advise corporate management on technical issues and to help plan corporate use of information technology. In order to give sound advice and to plan for effective utilization of computer resources within the computer department, this manager also needs to understand how computers impact on corporate management.

CHANGE RESULTING FROM COMPUTERIZATION

Let us begin with a look at ways in which information technology has affected the organization of information in the corporation and the role and style of management. We will also discuss one method of quantifying the computer's impact on management.

New organizational options

In 1958, H. J. Leavitt and T. L. Whisler made a number of predictions regarding how computers would affect business management in the 1980s.[1] At that time, computers were usually found in subdepartmental units wherever data processing was needed. Leavitt and Whisler forecasted the need for centralized computer centers. They believed managers would be unable to cope with the large amount of information that computers would make available by the 1980s and that control over decision making in large organizations would necessitate centralization of computing.

In part, Leavitt and Whisler were correct. Centralization of computing was the organizational structure favored by most firms during the 60s and 70s. But Leavitt and Whisler failed to envisage the technological breakthroughs in microtechnology and telecommunications that have led, in recent years, to distributed data processing and the placement of microcomputers on workers' desks. Today, some companies choose centralization of computing, others choose decentralization or distributed processing, and still others choose a mix of processing structures (as described in Chapters 15 and 17). Advances in computer technology have given corporate managers **new organizational options** in determining the structure of their companies that were not envisioned by Leavitt and Whisler.

---

[1]H. J. Leavitt and T. L. Whisler, "Management in the 1980s," *Harvard Business Review*, vol. 36, no. 6 (November–December 1958), pp. 35–43.

Changes in managerial roles and styles

Another prediction by Leavitt and Whisler as well as other early commentators was that computers would be the managers of the future.[2] This has not happened. Managers continue to be indispensable, particularly at higher managerial levels. However, computers have altered management style in modern business. Solutions to many problems can now be programmed. Computers also provide more timely information than was formerly available, and the information is better in quality and wider in coverage. Managers are expected to utilize this information in making decisions, instead of relying largely on intuition which requires a different conceptual approach to problem solving.

Somewhere between 50 and 80 percent of all managerial decisions are programmable or semiprogrammable (given the current state of the art), especially in areas such as accounting, finance, and manufacturing. In actual practice, however, a much lower percentage of decision making is computerized, and the percentage varies from one industry to another. Figure 23–1 approximates current computer problem-solving effort in relation to decisions that could be programmed. Although managers do not maximize the potential of computers, computer technology has without question affected **style of management.**

Altered span of control and job content.   In many automated factories, computers have both altered managerial **span of control** by changing the number and level of employees a manager supervises and transformed the **content** of a manager's work. For example, drilling machines were formerly operated by workers following blueprints; the

Figure 23–1

Current problem-solving effort by computer, relative to programmable solutions possible with current technology

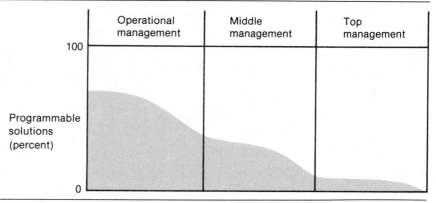

[2]Herbert Simon, *The Shape of Automation for Man and Management* (New York: Harper & Row, 1965).

Figure 23–2   **Traditional and computerized approaches to operating a drilling machine**

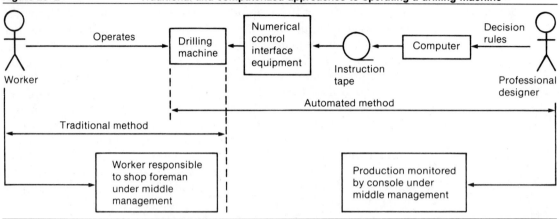

shop floor was managed by a person in a supervisory position. In many firms today, instruction tape (the blueprint) is fed into numerically controlled machines that do the drilling without worker intervention. The semiskilled or skilled workers who formerly operated the drilling machines have been replaced by professional designers who prepare the instruction tape. The supervisor has been replaced by a worker who monitors production on a machine console. Figure 23–2 illustrates how such changes have affected the worker and middle manager responsible for production in manufacturing.

The emergence of the electronic office is another example of how

Table 23–1   **Computer-induced changes in office work**

Area	Without a computer	With a computer
Information handling	Typing	Word processing
Memory	Human	Auxiliary memory of computer
Recordkeeping	Manual filing	Computerized
Information retrieval	Manual search and human recall	Computer search and retrieval
Calendar	Manual	Automated, with prompts
Written communication	Postal service	Teleprocessing
Estimation	From experience	Through quantitative models
Supervision & control	Manual	Exception reporting
Task distribution	Specialization of tasks	Functional and integrated system
Decision making	Judgment, intuition, and experience	Testing alternatives, simulation, and planning models
Graphics	Manual drawing	Graphic display; interactive displays
Data base	Old or current data	Real-time data
Conferences	Attendance (in person)	Teleconferences

computers are changing the job content and scope of control of managers. Word processing is replacing conventional office procedures for the creation of correspondence, documents, reports, and memos. Electronic processing is speeding computations and retrieval of data. Traditional office communication patterns are being altered by electronic mail. Teleprocessing enables some personnel to work out of their homes. The need for business travel is being reduced by teleconferencing. These and other activities that have been affected by the introduction of computers in the office are listed in Table 23–1. They have altered the duties of clerks, secretaries, and administrative assistants and, as a consequence, the responsibilities of office managers.

Productivity tools are not limited to the factory floor and clerical operations. They are being introduced in all departments at all organizational levels. Also, systems to coordinate and control operations now make it possible to manage large enterprises with fewer persons, particularly at middle management levels. There is evidence that computers are contributing to the shrinkage of the traditional management hierarchy.

Decision support systems. Top management is less affected by computer technology than is operational and middle management, because many decisions made in the higher echelons of a firm are what Herbert Simon calls "nonprogrammable" decisions. These are ill-structured problems (**"wicked" problems**), complex in nature, with variables that are not easily quantified. For example, personnel decisions (hiring and firing) fall into this category; so do decisions regarding goals and policies. Top management's business acumen in promoting innovation, motivating the work force, and resolving disputes cannot be programmed. Indeed, many areas of business decision making may never be automated. Table 23–2 shows that some management functions have had relatively little impact from computers.

Top management does receive reports based on operational and control information generated by computer, and the utilization of planning

Table 23–2	Impact of computers on functions of management		
Function	Top management	Middle management	Operational management
Identify areas of improvement	Scant	Scant	Some
Analyze these areas	None	Scant	Some
Develop alternate solutions	Scant	Moderate	Moderate
Evaluate alternate solutions	Scant	Moderate	Moderate
Implement decision	Some	Moderate	Heavy
Job content	Some	Moderate	Major
Job numbers	None	Scant	Moderate

Source: Adapted from Jerome Kanter, *Management-Oriented Management Information Systems* (Englewood Cliffs, N.J.: Prentice-Hall, 1982).

and control models is becoming more common. A computer **decision support system (DSS)** is of particular value to top management in finding solutions to semistructured problems, those for which the solution requires managerial judgment and subjective analysis of information derived from a large number of, or complex, computations. For such problems, the manager plus the DSS can provide a more effective solution than either alone.

One problem with DSS is that some modules (such as simulation) and some programs (such as spreadsheets) can generate reams of output in a few minutes just by changing a few parameters. In such cases, managers are faced with information overload, unable to evaluate or assimilate the output. This is why the use of charting programs and graphics output is of intense interest in managerial circles. (Charting and graphics programs can produce a pictorial representation of information: for example, output in the form of pie charts, bar and line graphs, or diagrams.) Many companies are now selling integrated packages that combine charting and graphics capabilities with spreadsheets, word processing, and communications facilities.

The development of **expert systems** can also help managers reach decisions. Expert systems are the electronic equivalent of consultation with a specialist. These systems, which have emerged from the discipline of artificial intelligence (AI), are programmed to ask managers to supply information on a problem. Computer processing of this information is based on facts and decision-making rules provided by an expert in the subject area. At present, such systems exist in only a few limited domains. Their potential is very great, however. They may well change the way in which managers collect and evaluate information in the future. The threat to managers is that expert systems, once they have a knowledge base of managerial expertise, may eventually replace some human managers on the job.

As a result of research in artificial intelligence, progress is being made in areas such as voice recognition, natural language processing, and computer vision that will also impact on the managerial role. For example, keyboards on terminals may be replaced with voice input, making it easier for managers to interact with computers. Natural language processing will help to eliminate the need for computer specialists to translate managerial requests for information into a programming language.[3] This will increase the speed with which results are obtained and reduce the "noise" of communicating through an inter-

---

[3]Microcomputers and data base management systems (DBMS's), advances unrelated to AI, have already reduced dependence on computer professionals. Managers can access some of the information they need from desktop micros without the intercession of programmers and analysts. They may even do simple programming on their own, using a DBMS language.

mediary. Projected for the future are intelligent computer systems with the ability to query a manager to find out what type of information is needed and, based on this determination, to self-program for the delivery of the required output.

A word of caution, however. The problems AI researchers must solve are formidable. As stated by Derek Partridge, a researcher in the field, "respect for the complexity and subtleties of human intelligence just keeps on growing." People working on AI projects continually have to scale down their goals and objectives as they encounter unexpected hurdles. Furthermore, the lead time between an AI prototype and a commerical product is proving to be quite lengthy.

Some commentators fear the increased reliance of managers on computers and processed information in decision making. The danger, they say, is that processed data filters out emotion, feeling, sentiment, mood, and all of the irrational nuances of human situations. Yet, effective management and decision making often depend on judgments based on the very elements that have been filtered out. The manager who makes intuitive decisions that are just below the level of consciousness often has a clearer vision of reality than managers who base decisions solely on data expressed in words or numbers. After all, not all information required for problem solving can be rationally condensed into lists, categories, formulas, or compact generalizations.

Quantifying the computer's impact on management

Can the impact of information technology on management be quantified? Jerome Kanter has attempted to do so. He divided management into five functions—planning, organizing, staffing, direction, and control—and gave each a number indicating susceptibility to computerization. He also assessed the percent of time spent in each function by operational, middle, and top management. A weighted value for each function was then determined and a computerized coefficient derived for each level of management. (See Table 23–3.) According to Kanter's calculations, 29 percent of top management's functions, 43 percent of middle management's functions, and 61 percent of operational management's functions can be computerized.[4]

This analysis is simplistic insofar as it did not allow for industry differences or variations over time. Kanter's conclusions were also based on highly subjective weight assignments. Nevertheless, many commentators would argue that Kanter's percentages are reasonable approximations of the actual contribution made by computers to decision making at the three levels of management at the present time. The analysis is also useful because it stresses that not all managerial func-

---

[4]Jerome Kanter. *Management-Oriented Management Information Systems* (Englewood Cliffs, N.J.: Prentice-Hall, 1982), p. 196.

Table 23–3   **Calculation of the computerization coefficient for different levels of management**

Function	Percent susceptible to computerization	Top management		Middle management		Operating management	
		Percent of total job	Weighted value	Percent of total job	Weighted value	Percent of total job	Weighted value
Planning	30%	70%	21 %	20%	6 %	5%	1.5%
Organizing	15	10	1.5	10	1.5	5	1.0
Staffing	25	10	2.5	10	2.5	5	1.5
Direction	5	5	—	20	1.0	20	1.0
Control	80	5	4	40	32.0	70	56.0
Computerization quotient			29 %		43 %		61 %

Source: Jerome Kanter. *Management-Oriented Management Information Systems* (Englewood Cliffs. N.J.: Prentice-Hall, 1982).

tions can be computerized and that the mix of functions at a given level is what determines the limits of computer assistance.

In coming years, as more operations research models are put into use and as progress is made in artificial intelligence, many functions not currently susceptible to computerization may become so, and Kanter's percentages will have to be changed. But we are not yet close to Norbert Weiner's prediction that whatever man can do, a computer will also do.[5] Managers are still needed to recognize and infer patterns from nonquantifiable variables—especially human variables—to interpret information, evaluate divergences between planned and actual performance, and determine corrective actions. Even programmed decision making requires managers initially to think through problems and establish decision rules for problem solutions. As Peter Drucker states:

> We are beginning to realize that the computer makes no decisions; it only carries out orders. It's a total moron, and herein has its strength. It forces us to think, to set the criteria. The stupider the tool, the brighter the master has to be—and this is the dumbest tool we have. . . . It shows us—in fact, it compels us—to think through what we are doing.[6]

INFORMATION TECHNOLOGY AS A COMPETITIVE WEAPON

Perhaps the greatest impact of computer technology on business has been the new opportunities created for managers. Information technology is changing the fundamental nature of industry, altering the structure of markets, and transforming daily operations, from product design to marketing and sales. In this section, we will explore modern managers' responsibility to capitalize on information resources, using them as a **competitive weapon** in order to improve competitive position.

Products and services

The life cycle of a product and the speed of its delivery in many industries is being changed by technological advances in computing. With computer-aided design, for example, a cathode ray tube replaces the engineer's drawing board. The computer can be used to produce conventional engineering drawings, make design calculations, and simulate operation of the device being designed. **Computer-aided design (CAD)** is used not only for original product design but also to make changes in response to factors such as revised contract specifications or altered marketplace preferences. The blueprints can then be drafted

---

[5]J. M. Bergy and R. C. Slover, "Administration in the 1980s," *S.A.M. Advanced Management Journal*, vol. 14, no. 2 (April 1969), p. 26.

[6]Peter Drucker, *Technology, Management and Society* (London, Heineman, 1970), pp. 147–48.

Table 23–4	Some CAD applications

To design and proportion bottle shapes; perform modeling and volume calculations for bottle molds; generate tooling of fixtures, jigs, and pumps; and prepare engineering drawings for bottle molding and manufacturing.

To generate technical illustrations, both two-dimensional and three-dimensional, for instrument housings, assemblies, and schematic and wiring diagrams; to generate layouts for use in technical manuals of an electronics company.

To perform the mechanical design and layout of gear boxes, axles, springs, drive shafts, and so forth, for the undercarriage of truck models.

To produce high-quality, accurate engineering drawings for sheet-metal parts, electrical schematics, wiring diagrams, and control panels.

by computerized equipment. (Sample CAD applications are listed in Table 23–4.) The use of these automated techniques speeds the turnaround time from design to production.

The manufacturing process can be aided by **process control,** the use of a computer to monitor a continuous activity such as the production of chemicals. (See Table 23–5 for examples of process control applications.) **Numerical control,** the automation of discrete operations, can also be used on the factory floor to control specific functions, such as boring, milling, planing, and pressing, in a production process. Today, many factories dedicate a small computer to each production machine. Robots are another way to automate manufacturing. They are commonly

Table 23–5	Process control applications		
	Production center	*Input*	*Sample output*
	Pharmaceutical factory	Mold	Penicillin
	Plastics factory	Ethane (gas)	Polyethylene (plastic)
	Rubber factory	Butane + benzine	Rubber
	Resource recycling	Domestic garbage	Fertilizer Mineral resource Energy
	Glass production	Silica + additives (e.g., sodium)	Glass
	Food factory	Crude oil	Synthetic steak
	Petroleum refinery	Oil	Gasoline
	Steel mill	Coke, coal, and iron	Steel wire
	Bakery	Flours, yeast, butter, and other ingredients	Bread

Figure 23–3   **Integration of CAD and numerical control with manufacturing process: CAD/CAM**

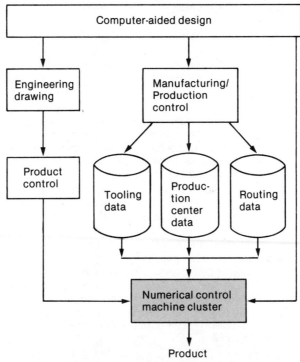

When a device designed by CAD is ready for manufacture, the computer can be programmed to produce codes necessary for numerical control of the machines that will be used in the product's manufacture. Routing data (that is, the sequence of operations) is prepared by manufacturing control. So are machine and work center requirements (that is, which machines in which work centers will produce the product), and tooling data (that is, what tools are needed for each production stage).

used on assembly lines to machine parts, spray-paint, load and unload furnaces, spot-weld, assemble goods, inspect products, pack cartons, and shelve merchandise by matching product codes with shelf codes.

The computer-stored data that defines a product's design is precisely the same data needed for various manufacturing purposes. As a result, computer-aided design can be integrated with the manufacturing process, in **computer-aided manufacturing (CAM),** as illustrated in Figure 23–3. Data bases of engineering designs that are part of **CAD/CAM** systems can also serve persons with planning, purchasing, inventory control, and production responsibilities.

Smart products are also being manufactured. They contain embedded microprocessor chips that enable the product to sense variables in the environment, compute, make choices, and control and time specific activities. For example, a microprocessor built into a postal scale can

Table 23–6   **Examples of smart products**

Smart taxi meter: Keeps track of charges for as many as five persons sharing a cab, even when passengers are traveling to different destinations. The meter automatically adds luggage-handling charges to each bill.

Smart thermostat: Automates control of heating, ventilation, and air-conditioning systems. To prevent energy surcharges during peak demand periods, the thermostat is programmed to switch systems off for short periods of time when energy demand reaches a predetermined level.

Smart crane: Includes a microprocessor-based monitoring system that computes safe machine operation, based on data supplied by the operator. A load chart stored in memory computes variables, such as safe boom acceleration and hook load. The operator can enter constraints such as the location of a power line or wall to be avoided. The range of the crane will be restricted accordingly.

Smart TV: Enables viewers to program entertainment for an evening. The correct channel for each program will be automatically selected. Captions for the deaf, transmitted in code and not visible on ordinary TV sets, can be decoded and displayed at the bottom of the screen. Favorite programs can be recorded and stored for later replay.

Smart camera: Focus is set by an embedded microprocessor after distance to the subject being photographed is calculated using sonar technology. That is, the camera emits ultrasonic waves, and the length of time it takes for these waves to reach the subject, bounce off, and return to the camera is used by the microprocessor to calculate distance. Camera focus is then automatically adjusted. (More than one microprocessor may be used in a single camera, each performing a different function.)

Smart watch: The wearer can enter dates of importance, such as birthdays and anniversaries. The watch will flash a reminder when each date arrives.

Smart calculator: A sequence of instructions can be programmed for execution when a given key is pressed. Special-purpose calculators are available for realtors, financial agents, persons planning diets, airline pilots, racetrack bettors, and so forth. These calculators will perform square roots, logarithms, and other trigonometric functions in a preset sequence according to the use for which the calculator is designed.

Smart car: Microprocessors in an automobile can be used for control of emissions, engine operation (e.g., air-fuel mixture, ignition timing), door locks, theft deterrent alarms, air-conditioning, belt buckling, braking, skidding, and speed control. Other uses are vehicle diagnosis, collision avoidance, maintenance analysis, and vehicle performance analysis.

Smart materials handler: Uses sensors to inspect certain materials passing on an assembly line. If materials are upside down or at the wrong angle for the next assembly stage, robot arms will correct the position. Materials can also be scanned and X-rayed in search of structural defects, such as air bubbles, and removed if they fail to meet manufacturing specifications.

determine the exact postage required for a weighed package once the destination is keyed by an operator or read by an optical scanner. Table 23–6 describes some of the smart products currently on the market.

The responsibility of managers is to assess customer preferences and needs, then to plan ways to produce an appropriate product while keeping costs competitive. The use of information technology is an important weapon in the competitive arsenal of a manager, who decides whether to introduce a product with embedded microprocessors, whether to design the product using automated techniques, and how the manufacturing process might be improved through use of robots and process and numerical controls.

Production economics

A major difference exists between businesses that have computerized warehousing and inventory control and those that rely on manual operations. The computer helps the former take advantage of economies of scale by monitoring, controlling, and coordinating deliveries and by processing warehouse records with speed and accuracy. The administration of the warehouse without a computer too often gets bogged down in paperwork, which impedes operating efficiency. Warehouse automation is a method used in many businesses today to reduce production costs.

Almost every business has areas where **production economics** can be enhanced by information resources. The challenge for the manager is to identify those areas and implement appropriate information technology. At the same time, the manager must resist pressures to use computers for status, for prestige, or to "keep up with the Jones" when computer use will not improve the competitive position of the firm.

Market expansion

Many modern customers are computer literate. In addition, communications technology has erased traditional geographic market limitations. By planning to meet the demand for electronically based goods and services and by looking beyond local markets, managers can gain a competitive advantage for their companies through **market expansion.**

To give an example, we now have automatic teller machines, home banking, and electronic transfer of funds. Bank managers who have not responded to the changing market for financial services are losing customers to institutions that offer electronic services. Likewise, a large number of hotels, airlines, and car rental companies today rely on computerized reservation systems. The ability of these companies to service customers throughout the nation has contributed to their growth. Competitors who have failed to implement computerized reservation systems of their own have lost a share of the market to these large chains.

Reduction of buyer/supplier power

In contract negotiations, strong buyer and supplier groups can demand favorable terms that reduce the profitability of companies. Buyers have power when they purchase large volumes relative to a company's total sales. These customers can threaten a company's survival by moving their business to competitors, which explains why concessions are given to them at the bargaining table.

Information technology can be used by management to counter **buyer/supplier power**. Buyer leverage is lost when a company makes switching costs expensive. To illustrate, consider a medical supply company that provides online order-entry terminals and inventory management software for customers. The order system essentially locks customers into a buyer relationship with the medical company. To switch business to a competitor, customers would have to develop new order procedures. These procedures would then have to be tested, and employees would have to be trained in their use. The cost of developing and implementing new procedures rules out an indiscriminate switch.

Information technology can also help a company identify the profit potential of different buyer groups. All industries have some customers that are more expensive to service than others. The problem for management is to identify which buyers bring in profits and which buyers should be pared from customer rosters (or charged more because they are expensive to service) in order to maximize profits. (Consider the insurance industry, which has traditionally provided full services to all business customers. Today, many insurance companies are building up extensive claims data bases for use in identifying service costs and profitable customer categories.) Buyer power may be diminished because of the information that the computer provides. Here, technology is used as a strategic weapon in buyer selection.

Like buyers, suppliers can reduce a company's potential profits. Suppliers can negotiate concessions in their favor when they control access to sources for raw materials, machinery, capital, or labor or when the cost of turning to an alternate supplier is high. Information technology is providing ways for managers to reduce the power of suppliers by introducing new products, services, and distribution channels. For instance, robots are a viable alternative for high-priced labor. In banking, computer systems help managers decide on optimal funds sourcing. (The systems help gather and process data on money markets and provide managers with information regarding the current and future money positions of their institutions.) No longer are bank managers at a strategic disadvantage in dealing with their major supplier: the financial markets.

Creation of entry barriers

When new competitors enter a market, the profits of established firms fall unless demand is growing fast enough to accommodate the new companies. This explains why most industries try to establish conditions that favor existing industry participants and slow or exclude new entrants.

Information technology can be used as a tool by management to create **entry barriers** and deterrents. Suppose a company installs a network to support its multilocational distribution facilities. The network helps to improve operations and, at the same time, makes it hard for a new entrant to be competitive without an equally efficient distribution system. Suppose a company's reputation has been built on its information technology capabilities. A newcomer has a formidable capital barrier to overcome.

Joint ventures

Information technology provides companies with ways to alter their relationships with rivals. It is not always necessary to engage in "guerrilla warfare" to gain a competitive advantage; cooperation may work as well. For example, small rival banks in some towns share ATMs, which helps them stand against large banks in their communities. Standardized data and communications networks between railroads have contributed to the upgrading of rail transportation, a factor that has helped entice customers from truckers. A strategic advantage may be obtained by sharing software or by establishing computer-to-computer connections with rivals. A modern manager needs to be alert to opportunities for joint information technology ventures.

Support of business objectives

Every company has business objectives. The challenge for management is to find ways to apply information technology to help realize these objectives. Suppose that high priority is given to the reduction of costs. The implementation of a computer system to transmit and process transactions might contribute to desired savings. Suppose a distinguished product is desired. The use of computerized machine tools might lead to manufacturing precision that no competitor can match.

Since most companies have many demands on their financial and personnel resources, management must identify the most cost-effective use of information technology to support corporate objectives. To illustrate the large number of options before management, see Table 23–7. It shows strategies that might be implemented for the objectives mentioned above: lower costs and product differentiation. Similar lists might be compiled for other corporate objectives. Of course, the burden on management is not limited to selection of appropriate systems. Managers must also oversee their implemention, integrate the use of the systems in the daily operations of the firm, and overcome resistance to innovation. For example, highly sophisticated computerized sales systems will not be effective if people are not hired, trained, and motivated to use them.

Table 23–7   **Strategies for cost reduction and product differentiation**

	Strategies	
Functional area	Cost reduction	Product differentiation
Administration	Planning and budgeting models	Office automation for integrative office functions
	Automation for staff reduction	
	Electronic mail	
Product design and development	Product engineering control systems	CAD
	Product budget control system	R&D data base access and use
	CAD workstations	
Marketing	Market research report analysis	Econometric models for marketing
	Market distribution control	Telemarketing system
		Service-oriented distribution system
Operations	Cost control system	CAM products
	Process control system	CAD/CAM
	Material resource planning (MRP)	Quality control system
	Inventory control system	Customer order-entry system
Sales	Sales control system	Customer support system
	Sales incentive control	Dealer support system
	Advertising control system	Customer/dealer/vendor OLRT system
Computer services	Budget control	Analysis for competitive advantage
	Cost control	

CORPORATE RESTRUCTURING

As mentioned at the beginning of this chapter, computers have affected management by making necessary the reorganization of the information function to accommodate modern information technology. When computers were first introduced in business organizations, data processing personnel spent much of their time trying to convince management of the value of computerized information systems. Today, there is little evidence of this former apathy. Corporate managers recognize that information systems are vital to business operations and have high expectations for the use of information technology. The problem is that the pace of technological advance in the computer industry often outstrips the ability of organizations to absorb the new technology.

In response to pressures for more and better information, management changes have been introduced. Formerly, management of computer resources was delegated to the computer center head or to the manager of the data processing department. Today, it is not uncommon to find information system managers elevated to upper management levels in positions such as corporate director of management information systems or vice president for information services (see Chapter 15). Persons in these positions are concerned with information as a corporate asset. Their positions acknowledge the importance of information as a strategic element in gaining a competitive advantage in the marketplace.

The creation of a new organizational entity, the information center (discussed in Chapter 18), is another structural adjustment many companies have made to promote better utilization of information technology. Clearly, this **corporate restructuring** has had an impact on the assignments and responsibilities of management. The question is, are these changes sufficient to accommodate pressures for more and better information?

Reasons for reorganization

The information systems manager today is customarily the data processing manager of the past. In other words, the person formally responsible for data processing operations has been moved to a higher organizational level and is now responsible for management of technology and its use as well as for management of the actual information generated. Many organizations fail to recognize that this has created a management gap. The job of information systems manager is simply too broad for a single individual. At a time when the technology of computer systems is growing ever more complex, the manager of data processing, who has assumed additional corporate responsibilities, lacks adequate time to devote to technological concerns.

What is more, many companies still organize their computer resources around operations and applications, with central processing, distributed processing, micros, office systems, communications, and now information systems fitted into a structure that was designed to accommodate the centralized process-oriented technology of 20 years ago. What is needed are structural accommodations to change the company from a data processing organization into an information systems organization.

Figure 23–4 suggests a way to restructure the management of information systems in order to take into account new roles and responsibilities in computing. In this chart, centralized data processing, office systems, communications, and distributed systems are organizationally separate, and the information center is one of the responsibilities of support staff. Of course, a company might modify this chart to fit traditions or unique environmental conditions. What the chart illustrates is that structural adjustments are needed to accommodate modern information technology. It is the responsibility of corporate management to provide an appropriate framework for managing modern technolo-

Figure 23–4   **Organization chart that restructures information systems management**

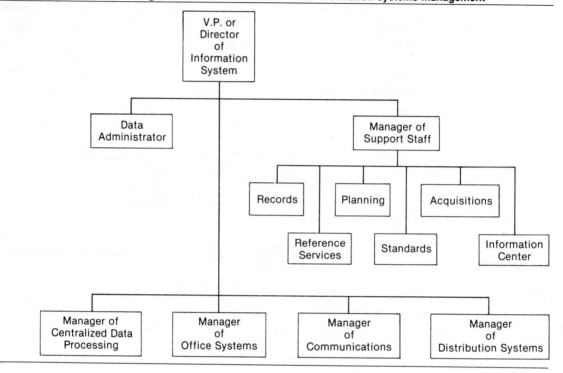

gies. Only then can new and changing technologies be effectively applied to the needs of the corporation as a whole.

INFORMATION SPECIALISTS

Failure to take full advantage of available computer systems can sometimes be traced to resistance to change. Unfortunately, managers as well as operational personnel may be reluctant to change familiar work patterns. More often, however, failure to maximize computer potential can be traced to lack of know-how. More and more business managers acknowledge that they do not know how to utilize effectively the computing resources at their disposal, and they are turning to information specialists for help.

Information specialists generally are computer scientists knowledgeable about business and management or are individuals drawn from operations research who have acquired an expertise in computers and data bases. The role of an information specialist is analogous to the role of the secretary in a traditional business organization in that both channel information to management. Secretaries control access to management; information specialists control the flow (and sometimes content) of computerized information to management.

Like secretaries, informational specialists wield far more power than is apparent from a firm's organizational chart. They often decide how information is presented (flashed on a terminal screen or buried in a printed report), how data should be correlated, what processing mode to use, the form of output, and which models are appropriate. (They do so because the manager wants information but fails to specify how it should be presented or because the manager delegates this decision making to the specialists.) Such decisions may subsequently limit the range of choices open to management. Though officially only technical advisors, information specialists may actually be decision makers of considerable importance.

It is important for managers to learn about computers and their limitations and to take an active role in defining variables and constraints in problem solving. If they fail to do so, they may, unaware and by default, lose decision-making prerogatives to information specialists. This is not to suggest that management should dispense with the services of information specialists. On the contrary, they are a valuable resource. But managers should both understand and authorize delegated decision making and should carefully define, monitor, and control the work of information specialists.

PROBLEMS ARISING FROM COMPUTERIZATION

Thus far, this chapter has focused on ways computers have changed organizational structure and methods of decision making. Before closing the chapter, a few comments are in order on **problems arising from computerization** and requiring mitigation by managers.

A firm's power base is altered as a result of computerization. According to organizational theorists, four variables are associated with corporate power: links to others, irreplaceability, dependency, and uncertainty. In all four areas, information technology scores highly, giving power to computer personnel. Applications such as payroll and accounting have become irreplaceable and link data processing personnel to many functional departments. These departments depend on computing, particularly when integrated systems have been implemented. Computer planning models and programs for control and decision making also reduce uncertainty among users. No wonder computer departments and their personnel have gained so much power.

Shifts in power, however, are accompanied by bruised egos, jealousy, and conflict as traditional power bases erode. Management skill in reducing tension and restoring harmonious interpersonal/interdepartmental relationships is taxed to the limit following computerization.

Resentment against computer personnel also stems from the fact that computer departments often win in competition for scarce corporate resources. Computers require major capital investments and large operating budgets. Few departments will admit being less deserving. Should hostility to computer personnel become overt, low priority to job requests may be assigned, a retaliation that reinforces and sustains resentment.

Users' unrealistic expectations, poorly drawn system specifications, or projects that have fallen behind schedule may also be the cause of hostility directed toward computer personnel. Often, computer professionals working in a crisis atmosphere fail to take the time to develop positive relationships with users. Unions may exacerbate existing tensions. The *London Times* first ceased publication, then was sold because of industrial strife over computerization. Modern management that proves inept in coping with and resolving the social and psychological tensions that accompany computerization may find the very survival of its firm at stake.

SUMMING UP

Computers are changing the nature of a manager's work and altering methods of decision making. Managers are also being displaced by computers, although the threat of unemployment is less acute at top levels of management than at operational levels and far fewer managerial jobs are jeopardized by computers than are workers' jobs (see Figure 23–5). There are still too many wicked problems for management to resolve, problems that defy programmed solutions because their variables cannot easily be quantified. However, research in artificial intelligence, data management, linguistics, and psychology will undoubtedly expand the role of computers in decision making in the future and lead to further managerial displacement.

The immediate concern of corporate management is to learn how to utilize information technology as a competitive weapon. Opportunities exist to use the technology in the manufacture of products and in the selling of services. It can contribute to production economics, market expansion, reduction of buyer/supplier power, creation of entry barriers, and formation of alliances. Corporate objectives can also be supported by computer systems. An important role of managers is to develop strategies to take advantage of information technology and to mitigate threats to the company because of the use of this technology by rivals. More and more managers are turning to information specialists for assistance in maximizing the use of computing resources.

Traditional organizational structures are not able to respond to grow-

Figure 23–5 **Displacement caused by computerization**

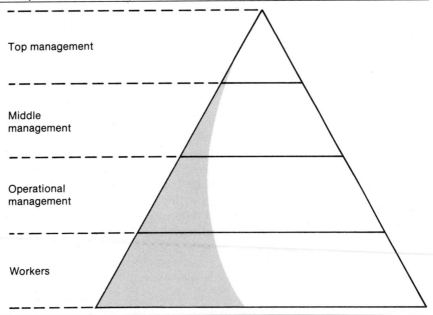

ing pressures for more and better information, nor are they able to manage new information technologies effectively. The organization chart in Figure 23–4 is one structure that accommodates the changing role and environment of information technology.

Computer departments and computer personnel today are becoming power centers indispensable to normal operations. This has upset the traditional power structure in most firms and has led to conflicts, rivalries, and corporate dissension. While computers have contributed to the problem-solving ability of management, they have created management headaches as well.

CASE: SEIZING AN OPPORTUNITY AT FRITO–LAY

Frito-Lay, which produces chips, Cheetos, and other snack foods, is equipping its sales representatives with handheld computers. The idea is to reduce the paperwork necessary to process orders and to improve

Source: Robert J. Crutchfield, "Getting a Leg Up by Using Handhelds," *Datamation*, vol. 33, no. 1 (January 1, 1987), pp. 32–34.

company productivity and services. For example, the computers will be used to reduce paperwork in ordering and, hence, speed the order process. Data collected by the handhelds will be used in the automation of inventory control. The processed data will give management a better understanding of the work flow on a day-to-day basis and should therefore contribute to improved decision making. (For example, sales data will be used to justify the share of shelving allotted to Frito-Lay products in grocery stores when competitors try to usurp that space.) In the future, the sales information may be used to control the production of chip types, based on demand.

The company has had to undertake a number of organizational adjustments in order to use the handheld computers. It is adding to the processing capacity of its management information systems department and distribution centers, in part to accommodate the handhelds. Shift assignments of data processing staff have changed. Training and support have been more of a problem than managing the network.

Questions

1. What do you think was the impetus for the change in the way in which Frito-Lay collects and processes information?
2. Who do you suppose initiated the new data collection system? Explain the reasons for your position.
3. How can Frito-Lay use the handhelds as a competitive weapon?
4. How does a change in the use of computer technology, such as the introduction of these handhelds, affect management at Frito-Lay?

STUDY KEYS

Buyer/supplier power	**Joint ventures**
CAD/CAM	**Market expansion**
Competitive weapon	**New organizational options**
Computer-aided design (CAD)	**Numerical control**
Computer-aided manufacturing (CAM)	**Problems arising from computerization**
Corporate restructuring	**Process control**
Decision support system (DSS)	**Production economics**
Entry barriers	**Smart products**
Expert systems	**Span of control**
Information specialists	**Style of management**
Job content	**Wicked problems**

DISCUSSION QUESTIONS

1. How have computers benefited management?
2. What negative impact on management have computers had?
3. How can the adverse effects of computers on decision making be minimized? How can benefits be enhanced?
4. How have computers altered decision making at the following management levels?
   - a. Top.
   - b. Middle.
   - c. Operational.
5. Would the impact of computers on management vary with:
   - a. Size of firm?
   - b. Style of management?
   - c. Content of management?
   - d. Qualifications of managers?
6. How do decision support systems aid management?
7. How can information technology be used as a competitive weapon by management?
8. What problems do managers have to face when implementing a computerized information system? How can these problems be minimized?
9. Do computers turn managers into conformists? Do managers lose their:
   - a. Individuality?
   - b. Creativity and innovativeness?
   - c. Self-confidence and self-assurance?
   - d. Independence in thinking?
10. Computers may solve technical problems for managers, but they create more problems than they solve (including human and social problems). Comment on this statement.
11. How are managers affected by the addition of a:
    - a. DBMS?
    - b. Online real-time system?
    - c. Query language and interactive processing?
    - d. Simulation language?
    - e. Word processing workstation for secretary?
    - f. Teleprocessing?
    - g. Artificial intelligence?
12. How has computer technology affected the quality of decision making? The quality of management?
13. How can a manager's knowledge of computing contribute to:
    - a. Decision making?
    - b. Control of the negative impact of computers?
    - c. Improved efficiency and effectiveness of computer usage?
14. Why do managers feel threatened by computer technology? What can be done to alleviate management fears?
15. Why do many firms need to restructure their companies to accommodate modern information technology?

16. Why are young managers more favorably oriented to computer systems than their seniors?
17. Which levels of management have been most and least affected by computer technology? Why? Do you expect this to change in the near future? Why?
18. What is an information specialist? Should management rely on them? What contribution do they make?

SELECTED ANNOTATED BIBLIOGRAPHY

Cash, James I., and Benn R. Konsynski. "IS Redraws Competitive Boundaries." *Harvard Business Review*, vol. 63, no. 2 (March–April 1985), pp. 134–42.
The authors discuss frameworks to help managers weigh the strategic benefits and possible costs of high-speed data exchange between companies.

Davis, David. "SMR Forum: Computers and Top Management." *Sloan Management Review*, vol. 25, no. 3 (Spring 1984), pp. 63–67.
PCs are useful tools for the top manager. With the availability of better software, the use of PCs by managers will increase.

Lucas, Henry. "Utilizing Information Technology: Guidelines for Managers," *Sloan Management Review*, vol. 28, no. 1 (Fall 1986), pp. 39–47.
Strong advice for corporate managers not to let computer technology drive corporate decisions but instead to actively manage computer technology.

Magee, John F. "What Information Technology Has in Store for Managers." *Sloan Management Review*, vol. 26, no. 2 (Winter 1985), pp. 45–49.
Discussed is the changing role of middle management and the impact of information technology on organizations and management careers. Magee holds the view that the traditional management hierarchy is shrinking and that the change is permanent. Information technology has made it possible to manage large enterprises with a smaller-sized management group.

McFarlan, F. Warren. "Information Technology Changes the Way You Compete." *Harvard Business Review*, vol. 62, no. 3 (May–June 1984), pp. 98–103.
The author points out that it is important for executives to assess how information technology can give a company a competitive opportunity in order to determine the proper level of expenditures and the proper management structure for computer systems.

McGarrah, Robert E. "Ironies of Our Computer Age." *Business Horizons*, vol. 27, no. 5 (September–October 1984), pp. 34–41.
The author believes that computerization can be used in planning and control and will overcome the problems of low productivity that plague American business today. Ironically, however, overindulgence with computers has led to the neglect of subjective information about values that it is not possible to computerize.

Owen, Darrell, "SMR Forum: Information Systems Organizations—Keeping Pace with the Pressures." *Sloan Management Review*, vol. 27, no. 3 (Spring 1986), pp. 59–68.

The author suggests various adjustments that organizations should make in order to cope with the pressures for more and better information.

Porter, Michael E., and Victor E. Millar. "How Information Gives You Competitive Advantage." *Harvard Business Review*, vol. 63, no. 4 (July–August 1985), pp. 149–59.

A framework for analyzing the strategic significance of new information technology is presented in this article. The authors show how and why information technology is changing the way companies operate internally as well as altering the relationships among companies and their suppliers, customers, and rivals.

Seligman, Daniel. "Life Will Be Different When We're All On-Line." *Fortune*, vol. 111, no. 3 (February 4, 1985), pp. 68–72.

Seligman predicts a future when all businesspersons will have access to online data bases such as Telerate, NewsNet, Nexis, and Dialog. These predictions are based on some current experiences at Lockheed, the Securities and Exchange Commission, and Reader's Digest.

Wiseman, Charles. *Strategy and Computers.* Homewood, Ill.: Dow Jones–Irwin, 1985, 246 pp.

This book is intended to be a practical guide to top executives and line managers on how computers can be used to support or shape competitive strategy.

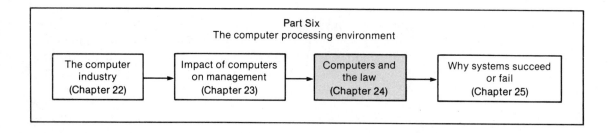

Part Six
The computer processing environment

| The computer industry (Chapter 22) | Impact of computers on management (Chapter 23) | Computers and the law (Chapter 24) | Why systems succeed or fail (Chapter 25) |

CHAPTER 24

Computers and the law

In a computer battle, lawyers fight with Latin phrases and DP persons retaliate with jargon.

Thomas K. Christo

The body of law governing the computer industry is complex. Managers must be cognizant of antitrust statutes, copyright provisions, and laws regulating contracts, patents, trade secrets, tort, privacy, theft, freedom of information, communications, and fair employment. But knowledge of written statutes is not enough, because the courts, in interpreting these laws when resolving disputes, have established precedents that have given shape to the industry.

This chapter discusses the application of general business laws to computing and reviews cases that have had an impact on the creation of new industry sectors or have set guidelines for computer operations. Both common law and statutes that relate to computer law are considered. **Common law** derives from custom, usage, and the decisions and opinions of the courts, whereas **statutes** are laws enacted by a legislative body. The two are complementary. When common law proves deficient or incomplete as a result of changed social conditions or the development of advanced technology, the need arises to establish new rules or principles of behavior. Unfortunately, the legislative process is slow. In a field as dynamic as computer science, the law simply can't keep pace with technological advances. As a result, the computer industry today lacks an adequate legal framework for operations.

Law categories discussed in this chapter appear at the top of Figure 24–1; connecting solid lines show the statutory counterparts of common law. Several of the preceding chapters have already touched on legal considerations. For example, Chapters 8 and 9 dealt with systems security and computer crime. The emphasis in this chapter is on laws protecting computing resources and laws regulating the operational

Figure 24–1 **Constituents of computer law**

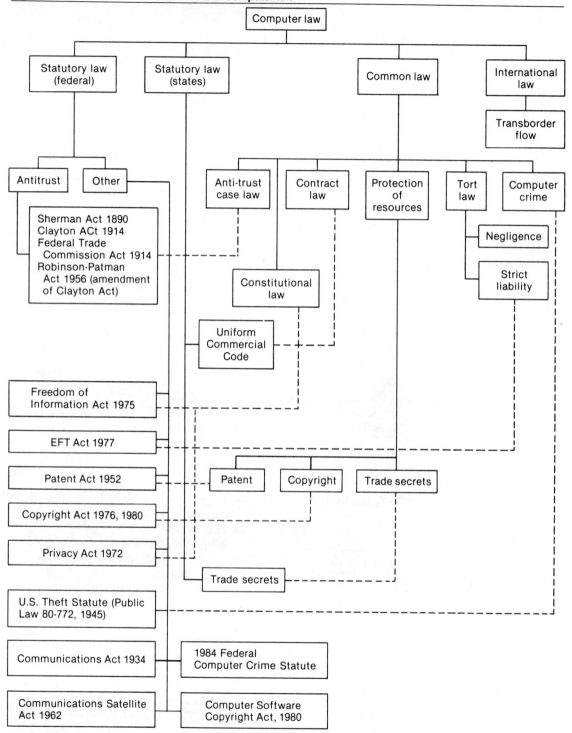

NOTE: The dashed lines indicate the complementary relationship between branches of common law and specific statutes.

environment of the industry. Sections appear on antitrust laws, communications, transborder flow, contracts, patents, copyrights, trade secrets, tort, and computer crime.

ANTITRUST LAWS

The basic framework of **antitrust laws** governing U.S. corporations is shown in Figure 24–1. Disputes over interpretation of these laws have resulted in much litigation, particularly in technological fields. IBM has been a defendant in a large number of the antitrust suits di-

Table 24–1   **Antitrust litigation against IBM**

Date initiated	Case	Action date	Action taken
1932	U.S. v. IBM and Remington Rand	1936	Court decision
1952	U.S. v. IBM	1956	Consent decree
1969	U.S. v. IBM	1971	Judge Edelstein assigned
		1975	Trial starts
		1977	IBM defense starts
		1982	Case dropped/withdrawn by U.S.
1971	Greyhound v. IBM	1972	Case dismissed
		1972	Greyhound appealed
		1981	Greyhound upheld
1971	Memorex v. IBM and IBM v. Memorex	1972	Cases dropped
1971	Symbolic v. IBM	1975	Case dismissed
1971	Advanced Memory v. IBM	1972	Case settled out of court
1972	Telex v. IBM	1973	Court decision totally favoring neither
		1974	Telex appeals settlement
		1975	Partial decision on appeal
		1978	Case settled out of court
1972	Marshall v. IBM	1975	Case settled out of court
1973	Calcomp v. IBM	1977	Court decision favoring IBM
		1977	Calcomp appeals
		1979	Appeal dismissed
1973	Memorex v. IBM	1979	Case dismissed
		1980	Case appealed but dismissed
1973	Transamerica v. IBM	1979	Case dismissed
		1983	Case appealed but dismissed
1974	Memory Tech. v. IBM	1976	Case settled
1975	Sanders v. IBM	1977	Case dismissed
		1979	Case appealed by Sanders
		1979	Sanders drops appeal

rected against firms in the computer industry since 1932. The company's size and leadership in pricing make it a natural target for the application of antitrust principles to computer manufacture and sales. Table 24–1 lists major suits involving IBM. The number of suits and the time elapsed before settlement are evidence of the massive effort and commitment of the corporation in fighting antitrust actions. The number of cases dropped, dismissed, or settled out of court shows IBM to be a formidable opponent.

Some of the cases against IBM have influenced the basic structure of the computer industry. The first landmark case was in the 1930s, when the federal government charged IBM and Remington Rand with restraint of trade for monopolizing the market for punched cards. (IBM dominated 85 percent of the market, Remington Rand 15 percent.) At that time, both firms required that their own cards be used in their tabulating units and card machines, tying card purchase with equipment purchase. A 1936 Supreme Court decision ruled against this practice. But the judgment proved academic, for IBM subsequently drew up such rigid card specifications for IBM machines that only their own rotary presses could manufacture the cards.

This led, in part, to a 1952 suit in which IBM was again charged by the government with restraint of trade for its restrictive leasing agreements and price discrimination. IBM was accused of violating the spirit, if not the letter, of the 1936 decision. An out-of-court settlement was reached, the **1956 IBM Consent Decree**[1] avoiding a court battle. Although a consent decree means that no judgment is made regarding innocence or guilt, IBM agreed to offer customers the option of buying or leasing equipment. This provided an opening for smaller companies to purchase computers from IBM for subsequent lease to customers. By depreciating equipment over a longer lifetime than IBM and by accepting a lower unit profit margin, these companies were able to establish themselves in the leasing market. In the consent decree, IBM also agreed to establish a separate service subsidiary and to release technical information on machine maintenance. These latter provisions led to the establishment of the independent services segment of the computer industry, a segment that today consists of over 1,000 companies, many of which have become substantial enterprises.

IBM was also required to reduce its share of the punched-card market and to sell some of its rotary presses. (By 1956, IBM controlled 90 percent of a greatly expanded card market.) This spurred the growth of independent card producers. Other provisions required IBM to sell equipment discounted for age and to make both current and future

---

[1] *United States* v. *IBM*, Civil No. 72–334 (S.D.N.Y., 1952). For details, see Bruce Gilchrist and Milton R. Wessel, *Government Regulation of the Computer Industry* (Montvale, N.J.: AFIPS Press, 1972), pp. 177–99.

Table 24–2   *CDC* v. *IBM*, Civil Action No. 3–68–312: Primary charges summarized

IBM:

    Monopolizes and attempts to monopolize markets and submarkets.
    Exploits size, profits, and pricing power, impeding competition.
    Engages in discriminatory and exclusionary pricing practices, including leasing at a loss.
    Misrepresents status of design, development, production, and performance software.
    Coerces employees and improperly influences customer procurements.
    Falsely disparages plaintiff's computers, software, maintenance policies, personnel, financial position,
       and overall capabilities.
    Engages in bait-and-switch methods to deceive customers and deprive plaintiff of sales.
    Violates the 1956 Consent Decree with its time-sharing service business.
    Uses its patent position to entrench its monopoly.

patents available on an unrestricted, nonexclusive basis, although reasonable royalties on new patents could be charged. A 1963 revision of
the decree limited IBM still further, requiring the company to divest
itself of 50 percent of the punched-card market.

Antitrust suits have been filed against IBM by competitors as well
as by the government. Such a suit was filed in 1968 by Control Data
Corporation (CDC) charging IBM with violation of the Sherman Act.[2]
(Charges are summarized in Table 24–2.) CDC hoped that its suit would
force IBM to divest itself of its Scientific Research Association, Service
Bureau Corporation, and Office Products Division and would force the
company out of terminal manufacture, education, and training.

Again, a settlement was reached out of court. IBM paid CDC $51
million and sold its service bureau far below its true value. But in
return, CDC destroyed a computerized index of 80,000–100,000 documents in support of its case, a data base compiled from over 1 million
documents at an estimated cost of $3 million. Plaintiffs in other cases
against IBM, the Justice Department in particular, were enraged. Lacking the financial resources to duplicate CDC's effort, they wanted to
use the documents in cases of their own. From the price IBM paid for
the destruction of CDC's data base, one can surmise that it did indeed
contain damaging evidence. Incidentally, CDC's use of a data base for
evidence is a computer application to be expected from a computer
manufacturer.

In January 1969, on the last business day of the Johnson administration, the Department of Justice again filed an antitrust action against
IBM for violation of the 1890 Sherman Act and the later Clayton and
Robinson-Patman Acts.[3] The government alleged that IBM had "pur-
sued a manufacturing and marketing policy that has prevented competing manufacturers of general-purpose digital computers from having

---

    [2]Ibid., pp. 211–28.
    [3]*United States* v. *IBM*, Action No. 62–200 (S.D.N.Y. 1969). See Gilchrist and Wessel,
Government Regulations, pp. 201–6.

Table 24–3   **Extract, 1969 *U.S.* v. *IBM* antitrust suit**

IBM:
a. Maintained a pricing policy whereby it quoted a single price for hardware, software, and related support, and, thereunder, *(i)* discriminated among customers by providing certain customers with extensive software and related support in a manner that unreasonably inhibited the entry or growth of competitors; and *(ii)* limited the development and scope of activities of an independent software and computer support industry as a result of which the ability of its competitors to compete effectively was unreasonably impaired;
b. Used its accumulated software and related support to preclude its competitors from effectively competing for various customer accounts;
c. Restrained and attempted to restrain competitors from entering or remaining in the general-purpose digital computer market by introducing selected computers, with unusually low profit expectations, in those segments of the market where competitors had or appeared likely to have unusual competitive success, and by announcing future production of new models for such markets when it knew that it was unlikely to be able to complete production within the announced time; and
d. Dominated the educational market for general-purpose digital computers, which was of unusual importance to the growth of competitors both by reason of this market's substantiality and by reason of its ultimate impact on the purchasing decisions in the commercial market, by granting exceptional discriminatory allowances in favor of universities and other educational institutions.

Source: *US* v. *IBM*, Civil No. 69–200 (S.D.N.Y., 1969).

an adequate opportunity effectively to compete." The complaint echoed familiar charges (that IBM had "monopolized, restrained, dominated, improperly deprived" others) and called for divestiture, divorcement, and reorganization of IBM as remedies. (See Table 24–3 for a list of formal charges.)

The case dragged through the 1970s at enormous cost to both IBM and the taxpayer. (IBM's defense in the shorter, less complex CDC suit cost an estimated $60 million.) By 1978, 80,000 pages of transcript had been recorded, yet the suit was still far from settlement. Many people charged that the government was at fault for lack of aggressive prosecution of the case. In 1977, Attorney General Griffin Bell suggested that major antitrust issues should perhaps be resolved through the legislative process, not by the courts. He acknowledged that: "the process would necessarily be more political but the questions at hand in a sense are political. They involve the basic restructuring of American Industry and the shape of the American Economy."[4]

In 1982, after 13 years of litigation, the 1969 antitrust suit against IBM was dismissed. IBM declared itself "totally vindicated." During

[4]Linda Flato, "Washington's Concern with Antitrust Stalemates," *Datamation*, vol. 25, no. 7 (July 1979), p. 88.

the course of the suit, the corporation had become bigger than ever, its annual revenues tripling. Most observers of the trial agreed that the suit had long outlived its relevance: monopoly in mainframes no longer was the issue. The focus of competition had shifted to other industry segments, including small computers, communications, computing services, and software. It is expected that IBM will expand into new markets now that it is unshackled by legal and political restrictions. Some observers suggest that IBM, because of its size, will restructure and split of its own accord, the very action the government antitrust action was trying to force.

COMMUNICATIONS AND THE LAW

Law in the field of communications also has an important bearing on the computer industry. At the time of enactment of the Communications Act of 1934, which established the **Federal Communications Commission (FCC)** to control all "interstate and foreign communications by wire or radio and all interstate and foreign transmission of energy by radio," the telecommunications linkage of computers was not envisioned. Nevertheless, the language of the law extends the jurisdiction of the FCC to computer applications that depend on telecommunications networks, such as electronic fund transfer (EFT), the electronic office, teleconferencing, and remote processing. The importance of telecommunications for transmission of computerized business data has given the FCC immense power. Some critics charge that this independent agency has become, in effect, the fourth branch of government.

By the mid-1960s, communications' growing importance to information systems led the FCC to initiate an inquiry into the question of the interdependence of communications and computers. Responses by individuals, associations, and government agencies were evaluated by Stanford Research Institute, which submitted a seven-volume report to the commission in 1969. At that time, the Department of Justice felt that the communications industry, unless restrained, might dominate or restrict competition in the computer industry.

A **Final Order,** issued by the FCC in 1971 at the conclusion of the inquiry, established that:

1. The FCC would retain jurisdiction over those aspects of the computer field related to communications.
2. **Maximum separation** would be a central doctrine to FCC regulatory schemata. According to this doctrine, a separation must exist between the generation and the flow of information. In other words, a firm in computing (information generation) would not be allowed

to enter the field of communications (information flow), or vice versa.

3. Common carriers could not give preferential treatment to their data processing affiliates.

Unfortunately, the Final Order left many questions unanswered. It was unclear whether the order nullified the 1956 IBM Consent Decree or preempted state regulations. Could AT&T and other common carriers offer "enhanced services"? How were intelligent terminals or micro-computers, when part of a communications network, to be classified? Were they to be regulated, like telephones, as customer premise equipment?

The lack of precise rulings by the FCC has hampered the development of a telecommunications infrastructure needed to maximize the potential of computers. More statutes like the Communications Satellite Act of 1962 need to be written to provide a legal framework for tele-processing, a fast-growing field of computing. Although the courts have contributed to the resolution of some telecommunications issues, the judicial process is slow and expensive, not an effective substitute for legislative action.

A recent case in telecommunications that will have far-reaching re-percussions in computing is the 1982 settlement of a government an-titrust suit against AT&T. The settlement freed AT&T from restrictive federal regulation and, in effect, repudiated the FCC doctrine of max-imum separation. AT&T is now free to compete in whatever business it chooses, including the fields of electronic information, office auto-mation, home banking, and computer manufacturing. The settlement also opens the way for computer firms to enter the communications field. (See Chapter 22 for a discussion of the effect of this case on the computer industry.) The AT&T case illustrates that the legal guidelines for computing are in a continual state of flux.

TRANSBORDER FLOW

Computer networks speed business transactions and enable com-panies to share data among affiliates. **Transborder data flow (TDF)** describes data that crosses national borders.

Many laws are on the books in both Europe and the Third World to govern TDF. In France, for example, a fine of $400,000 and five years in prison are the penalty for transborder data flow of information that is defined as sensitive. In England, the post office has the right to read all transmitted messages, a right implying that firms must share their cryptographic codes. Some countries require that all transborder data flow be handled by public carriers, which results in loss of control by the user and often means degraded service. A 1973 data act in Sweden empowers a data inspection board to approve all transmissions of personal data crossing its borders. Brazil has closed its borders altogether to foreign data processing and significant international data links.

Originally, such laws were designed to protect individual privacy. Today, however, foreign governments are beginning to use these laws as a way to control trade in information services for their own economic and political objectives. In complying with these laws, multinationals face two major difficulties:

1. The laws are not uniform. Restrictions for TDF vary widely.
2. Reciprocal legislation is lacking. Many countries will allow transmission of personal data only if the receiving country's legal protection for data is equivalent to the transmitting country's legislation. Often, U.S. privacy laws fail to meet this test.

Guidelines for transborder data flow have been established by the Organization for Economic Cooperation and Development (OECD), an organization of industrialized countries (mostly Western, although Japan is also a member). The developing countries have formed an organization of their own—the Intergovernmental Bureau of Informatics, or the Group of 77—in an effort to control TDF. Third World countries recognize that information has economic value. Their leaders believe that the West's dominance in computers and satellite technology gives it a political and technological advantage over their countries that jeopardizes their national sovereignty. They see a new form of colonialism forced upon them by information technology. Third World leaders also fear that the traditions of their countries, indeed their national identities, will be lost if their citizens are exposed to unrestricted foreign information.

With the exception of Brazil, however, the success of the less developed nations in restricting transborder data flow has been limited. The rules of TDF continue to be made by the OECD and the multinationals. Nevertheless, the West is not totally insensitive to the viewpoint of the Third World, and most firms that operate in international markets recognize the need for a TDF accord between developed and developing countries. Just how such an agreement will impede or promote growth of international trade and TDF networks remains to be seen.

COMPUTER CONTRACTS

The importance of well-written contracts and warranties governing the sale/lease of computer hardware and software cannot be overstressed. More than monetary losses is at stake if a poorly written contract leads to disputes and court battles. Time-consuming litigation can tie up personnel and resources needed for other projects.

The **Uniform Commerical Code (UCC)** is the law that governs the sale of hardware and software. (By judicial custom, this law includes the sale of computer services in most states as well.) The law states that products are covered by two implied warranties: mercantability and fitness for a particular purpose. Included in the code are a series of remedies to the buyer of defective products, including a requirement that the seller repair defects or replace the product. However, the UCC also permits the vendor to disclaim warranties and liability limitations, remedies, and damages in contracts.

Formerly, most contracts signed by companies for the purchase of computer resources were standard boilerplate agreements that were loaded in the vendor's favor—agreements that typically limited liability to the amount of the contract and severely restricted the vendor's exposure to consequential damages. Today, clients commonly bring their attorneys to the bargaining table and negotiate acquisition contracts with vendors rather than signing standardized forms. Most lawyers who specialize in computer **contract law** are in private practice. However, many companies with a major commitment to information systems have added such attorneys to their staffs. (In 1985, the American Bar Association's computer law division had about 800 members, almost 10 times as many as in 1980—evidence of the growing importance of this specialty.)

Attorneys are able to recognize whether or not the legitimate interests of a company are protected in a contract. For example, many vendor contracts end with a seemingly insignificant clause often referred to as the "entire agreement" clause. This clause states that the written contract is the entire agreement of the parties and that no other agreements or statements (written or oral) between vendor or customer are binding. In effect, this clause can repudiate all of the promises made by vendor sales representatives that led to selection of the product. An attorney will make sure that the meaning of this clause is understood by the buyer and that performance specifications are carefully spelled out in the contract.

The lawyer also helps the client understand what goods and services are being contracted for and makes sure that contract terms such as "satisfactory performance" are defined in the contract. They will review warranties, payment schedules, and provisions for acceptance testing.

Vendor-user contractual relations are complicated by the fact that hardware is becoming increasingly sophisticated. Users may not fully understand the shortcomings of advanced technology or how to apply that technology to business applications. And how can the buyer "beware" when software is a product that literally cannot be seen? Increasingly, users are going to court, claiming that the product bought does not work and that the vendor was aware of the fact when the product was sold. User dissatisfaction has also spilled into state legislatures. Special consumer-oriented legislation has been introduced in a number of states to curb unfair practices by high-technology vendors.

Sometimes, abuses in contractual relationships lie with customers. Many take advantage of their economic leverage and technical expertise to shift all of the risks in an acquisition to the vendor. Too often, the proprietary rights of the vendor are not respected. For example, software piracy, the unauthorized duplication of programs without payment of fees to the vendor, is a common user practice.

The failure of vendors and users to share risks in computer-related transactions is cited by computer experts as an impediment to growth in the computer industry. As stated by an attorney who has represented both vendors and buyers in the acquisition of computer systems:

> It makes sense now for each party to stop overprotecting itself from every conceivable risk. In a competitive market, vendors who eschew needless contractual limitations will surely gain a competitive edge. Similarly, customers who know that they can reasonably assume certain risks may find a better business deal than those who stonewall on all issues. Once the real risks are identified, . . . the actors in the marketplace can arrive at mutually beneficial solutions. But if they fail to act voluntarily, practices may be legislatively or judicially imposed that are not especially helpful to the industry or to computer users.[5]

PROTECTION OF COMPUTING RESOURCES

Computing resources can be protected by patent, copyright, or trade secret laws.

Patents

The **Patent Act of 1952,** a statutory law, gives inventors a legal monopoly over their inventions for a period of 17 years. This act clearly applies to computer hardware. Until the 1980s, however, efforts to obtain **patents** on software met with mixed success. Why? Because patents were viewed by the Patent Office as ideas expressed in mathematical algorithms, and ideas cannot be patented.

In 1981, the Supreme Court upheld software patentability, but its decision suggested that only software systems that directly control machinery could be patented. At first, this limitation appeared to exclude most applications software. But the Patent Office and patent appeals court have nevertheless adopted a liberal attitude toward patents: patents are being granted for applications programs. The problem is that

---

[5]Susan H. Nycum, Gaston Snow, and Ely Bartlett, "Let the Buyer—and the Seller—Beware," *High Technology,* vol. 6, no. 1 (January 1986), p. 14.

it typically takes three years for a patent application to be processed. This lengthly period is one reason why many software producers do not turn to the Patent Office for software protection.

Software patentability is a good example of a basic dilemma facing the computer industry. A large body of cases interpreting court rulings is needed by lawyers before they know the exact meaning of judicial decisions. Because the computer field is too new for such a body of rulings to exist, it is hard for lawyers to translate court decisions into practical advice for clients.

Copyrights

Computer programs are protected under both common and statutory **copyright laws.** Under common law, an author has the right to control the distribution of unpublished writing. The Copyright Office extended this common-law protection in 1964 by starting to accept computer programs for copyrights, provided the subject matter was patentable and the programs were original, novel, utilitarian, and nonobvious.

The **1976 Copyright Act** gave statutory protection to some computer software by classifying programs and data bases as nondramatic literature works under Class TX. According to the provisions of this act, a copy of the protected material had to be in a form visible to human beings without the use of a computer. The author's controlling rights were extended to death plus 50 years, with the copier liable for actual damages or an award of $250 to $10,000 in statutory damages should the author be unable to prove the exact amount of the damage.

In 1980, the 1976 copyright law was amended specifically to cover computer programs, providing that the software meets copyright requirements. That is, the programs must be original (recognizably the author's own) and creative (call upon judgment and skill in their production). The **Computer Software Protection Act of 1980** extends federal copyright protection to "computer source and object codes, data bases, screens, report formats, documentation, and any other manifestation of software that is fixed in a tangible medium of expression."[6]

However, copyright alone does not completely protect software, because it does not protect ideas, design, process, or algorithms. Only the expression of the idea can be copyrighted. Yet, for some types of programs, the idea itself is more valuable than the particular expression of the idea. For example, if a software house were to develop a new method of programming, that method could be copied by others without violating the copyright law, even though this might mean that the software house would be unable to recoup its development costs.

Another problem with copyrights is that detecting isolated acts of infringement is hard. What is more, the practice of making illegal copies

---

[6]Jerome Roberts and Michael Bronwell, "Copyright Protects Software Development Investment," *Computerworld*, September 2, 1985, p. 72.

is widespread among users. For a program author to sue everyone who violates the copyright law is clearly impractical. Also, U.S. copyrights are not honored in many foreign countries, so programs have little protection from international pirating.

Patents and copyrights are not mutually exclusive. Some computer systems are protected under both patent and copyright law: the ideas by patents and the expression of the ideas by copyright.

Trade secrets

A **trade secret** is defined by the courts "as any formulae, pattern, device or compilation of information which is used in one's business, and which gives him an opportunity to obtain an advantage over competitors who do not know or use it."[7] Clearly, trade secrets are not limited to blueprints or to the chemical formulas for new products. Marketing plans, customer names, financial data, even price lists may be classified as trade secrets in this age of information.

Common law is the basis of trade secret laws, although a dozen states have passed the **Uniform Trade Secrets Act**, which gives companies civil enforcement weapons when trade secrets are stolen. Most trade secret laws define intentional unauthorized use of a trade secret as a criminal offense. However, the firm that sues must prove that the violation was a trade secret, protected and treated by the firm as such.

Trade secret laws were originally drawn up to protect physical property. The laws are outdated and weak, inadequate protection against modern pirates who steal ideas. Another problem is that the courts are slow to act when a trade secret case is prosecuted, and penalties for theft are slight. This explains why many corporate lawyers believe that companies should not rely on the legal system for protection of their secrets but should try to put trade secret thieves out of business themselves by tightening their internal security. For example:

- Employees should be advised when they are working on confidential projects. Proprietary notices should be placed on important documents. Employees should sign nondisclosure agreements.
- Distribution of confidential material should be restricted on a need-to-know basis.
- Buildings and phone lines to computers that process trade secret information should be secured.
- Trade secret material should be kept in areas that cannot be accessed by the public and are locked up at night.
- A badge system for employee identification should be installed.
- Working data and programs should be encrypted.

Chapter 9 describes still other ways to protect computer resources, including trade secrets.

---

[7]*Kewewanee Oil Co. v. Bicron Corp.*, 416 U.S. 470 1974.

Unfortunately, current or former employees who steal information are more of a threat to companies than outside spies. Leaks are difficult to pinpoint and guilt difficult to establish. Also, what is legal (or ethical) is not always clear-cut. Suppose a programmer takes a flowchart to a new job. Does that constitute violation of a trade secret? How about remembered flowcharts or experience gained in solving particular programming problems? Students learn in their first programming class that plagiarism in programming is hard to prove. Changes in variable names, statement numbers, and comment cards make programs look quite different even though the programming logic may be "borrowed." The practice of hiring well-positioned employees in order to access knowledge acquired in their former companies is all too common. Pirating companies not only gain new ideas but are spared development costs and long lead times that are crucial in a competitive situation.

Contracts for systems engineers and programmers that disallow employment by a competitor for a given period after leaving the firm might help prevent the leakage of secrets. However, there are legal problems in enforcing such contractual provisions. In any case, many employees refuse to sign. Demand for their expertise is great enough that jobs without such restrictions are available.

COMPUTERS AND TORT

Tort deals with a wrongful act, injury, or damage (not involving breach of contract) for which a civil action can be brought. Tort law is based on the premise that manufacturers have a responsibility to make their products safe. Although the law regarding tort differs from one state to another, liability generally covers personal injury, property damage, and consequential damage for negligence, willful misconduct, and strict liability. (Some products are judged so dangerous that a higher standard of liability, called strict liability, is applied to them.) To give an example, a surge of lightning or loss of electric power that causes a computer to malfunction, producing erroneous bank balances or credit ratings, might be judged unintentional tort if the malfunction led to personal injury.

The danger of physical harm resulting from a computer system grows daily as more and more computers are introduced in the business world. The crucial question yet to be decided by the courts is who is responsible for software bugs. One can easily envision a scenario in which a software error causes serious property damage, loss of revenue, or loss of life: a doctor's misdiagnosis based on information returned from an expert-system program leads to faulty treatment and a patient's death; a glitch in an inventory program delays restocking and causes financial loss because customers turn to competitors for needed supplies; a program error in the control system for a nuclear plant leads to an explosion such as the one that occurred at Chernobyl. The potential for such events is certainly there. Manufacturers and programmers both acknowledge that it is impossible to make complex software completely bugproof.

There is not yet enough case law to know how product liability will be applied to software. Most software vendors are using "as is" clauses when they license their software to disclaim all responsibility for their products, including implied and express warranties. But some observers do not believe that as-in wording will stand up well in court. They believe that the tort law system needs to be revised to protect software manufacturers. Otherwise, lawsuits in the future may choke the software industry and stifle its entrepreneurial spirit.

COMPUTER CRIME

Computer crimes may involve fraud or theft or be physical actions, such as sabotage directed against a computer system. Unlike tort, where the injured party sues for compensation, victims of computer crimes are not granted awards or damages. Rather, sanctions such as fine or imprisonment are imposed on the perpetrator of the crime.

Until recently, most computer crimes were prosecuted under laws written for other purposes. (Laws applicable to computer crime depend on the exact nature of the case and vary from state to state. More than 40 sections of the U.S. Code can be cited to provide sanctions for computer-related criminal conduct.) The first federal computer crime statute, the **Counterfeit Access Device and Computer Fraud and Abuse Act of 1984,** prohibits:

- Unauthorized access and use of computers to obtain information to be used to harm the United States or to benefit a foreign nation.
- Unauthorized access and use of computers to obtain financial or credit information that is protected by federal financial privacy laws.
- Unauthorized access of a federal computer for use, modifications, or destruction of information or for preventing others from using the computer.

Any attempt or conspiracy to commit any one of these three offenses is also prohibited by the act.

The act is a narrow piece of legislation. It focuses on three specific types of criminal activity only, and it does not apply to computers outside of the government, except in the area of financial privacy. What is now needed is legislation for broader jurisdiction over computer crimes. This might include expanding the type of information protected by the act; outlawing certain uses of computers, whether they are authorized or not; repealing dollar thresholds necessary to trigger federal jurisdiction; and extending coverage to computers in the private sector.

In an effort to "flesh out the skeletal structure that was passed in 1984," the U.S. House of Representatives has passed the **Computer Fraud and Abuse Act of 1986**. This bill gives the federal government authority to prosecute interstate computer crimes involving private-sector computers. One indication of the bipartisan support for this statute is that the bill passed the House by a voice vote with no opposition, under expedited rules, after only about 20 minutes of floor discussion.

SUMMING UP

The law has had a profound impact on the structure of the computer industry. For example, antitrust legislation led to the 1956 IBM Consent Decree, which in turn helped give birth to the service and leasing sectors of the industry. Antitrust pressure is also cited as instrumental in IBM's 1969 unbundling decision to no longer price hardware offerings to

Table 24–4   **Comparison: Patent, copyright, and trade secret laws**

	Laws		
Characteristics	*Patent*	*Copyright*	*Trade secret*
Basic source	Statutory law	Statutory and common law	Common and state law
Administering body	Patent Office	Copyright Office	Management of the firm
Eligibility criteria	Original idea, useful, involving skill	Novelty, utility, originality of ideas	Gives firm competitive edge
Prohibitions	Making, selling, or using the embodiment of an inventive idea	Unauthorized use or copying of physical expression, not the concept of algorithm or approach	Unauthorized copy or use
Remedies provided	If successful court action, 50 percent of proven loss	Actual damages Statutory damages Injunctions Attorneys' fees	Damages, if proven in civil or criminal action
Systems protected	Hardware	Software (object and source programs)	Software, data base, design of system, procedures, mailing list
Implementation	Registration with Patent Office	Copyright notice; registration required for certain remedies	Controlled access and security
Primary application	Algorithms Inventions of high value When long period of protection is required	For large-volume multiple-copied products	Algorithms Businesses with high value, even with low dissemination

include software and services. This decision gave impetus to firms specializing in software, education, and maintenance. The 1982 settlement of the government suit against AT&T, which repudiated the principle of maximum separation (long the basis of FCC regulatory schemata), is leading to the merger of the computer industry with the communications industry.

Both common law and statutes form the basis of computer law. Table 24–4 shows how patent, copyright, and trade secret laws help to protect computer resources. Federal statutes such as the Privacy Act of 1974, the Information Act of 1975, the EFT Act of 1977, and, more specifically, the Counterfeit Access Device and Computer Fraud and Abuse Act of 1984 also relate to computer use. Although legislators recognize their responsibility to write appropriate laws to help fight computer crime and to provide a legal framework for business operations, they cannot keep pace with the speed of technological development in the computer industry. The industry is further handicapped by the lack of a body of court rulings to interpret laws and judicial decisions.

A number of newsletters help to keep users, vendors, and their lawyers abreast of the current status of computer law. A list of these publications appears at the end of the bibliography to this chapter.

CASE: DISPUTE OVER "SHRINK–WRAP LICENSES"

Most off-the-shelf software sold for microcomputers contains a document on the package that is often called a "shrink-wrap license." This document states that the act of opening the package is deemed consent to the terms of the license, the provisions of which are written by the manufacturer's lawyer.

Recently, a number of states have introduced legislation similar to Louisiana's Software License Enforcement Act of 1984, a law that validates shrink-wrap licenses. Backers of the bills claim that they are antipiracy legislation. They say that the bills are a way to protect the proprietary interests of software manufacturers, a way to combat violations of the copyright law.

Opponents argue that the bills undermine the rights of software users. According to their point of view, the shrink-wrap licenses are used by software manufacturers to limit warranties so that they do not have to stand behind their products. In effect, they allow the manufacturer to say, "If the software does not do what you expect it to do, too bad." User advocates claim that software license enforcement acts are special-interest legislation, masquerading as antipiracy legislation but designed to improve the economic position of software manufacturers.

This battle illustrates the difficulty of writing computer laws. Legislators cannot be expected to understand all of the ramifications of bills regarding high technology. In the case of shrink-wrap licenses, both the industry and consumer advocates are mounting campaigns for and against the introduction of laws similar to Louisiana's Software License Act in other states.

Questions

1. Are you in favor of the shrink-wrap license or against it? Defend your point of view.
2. How does a shrink-wrap license affect:
   a. Individual firms?
   b. The computer industry?
   c. Consumers?
3. What other ways can software be protected against piracy? Are they as effective? As controversial?
4. Who should advise legislators on the impact of legislation that relates to information technology? Computer specialists? Industry representatives? Users? Defend your position.

STUDY KEYS

Antitrust laws

Common law

Computer Software Protection
  Act of 1980

Contract law

Computer Fraud and Abuse Act
  of 1986

Copyright laws

Computer Fraud and Abuse Act
  of 1986

Counterfeit Access Device and
  Computer Fraud and Abuse
  Act of 1984

Federal Communications
  Commission (FCC)

Final Order

1956 IBM Consent Decree

1976 Copyright Act

Maximum separation

Patent Act of 1952

Patents

Statutes

Tort

Trade secret

Transborder data flow

Uniform Commercial Code
  (UCC)

Uniform Trade Secrets Act

DISCUSSION QUESTIONS

1. Has the law in the United States inhibited or protected the computer industry?

2. What is the difference between common law and statutory law?
3. Would the growth of IBM have been different without the constant threat of antitrust suits? Explain.
4. Has the overpowering size and power of IBM inhibited the growth of small firms in the computer industry? Should the law protect the small firm, or should the competitive market determine survival? Explain.
5. How has antitrust action against IBM altered the computer industry?
6. Have antitrust proceedings initiated by the Department of Justice served a useful purpose in restraining monopolistic tendencies of giant computer companies? Have the proceedings allowed small firms free entry into computer markets? Explain.
7. Firms will vary as to the type of legal support they have. In the cases below, would you recommend full-time legal staff, lawyers on retainer, lawyers engaged on cases as they arise, or no lawyers at all?
   a. Drawing up a contract for the acquisition of a large central processing unit.
   b. Acquisition of a computer peripheral with a purchase price of $6,000.
   c. Suing IBM for breach of contract.
   d. Defending a charge of breach of warranty.
   e. Subcontracting development work to a software company at the cost of $500,000.
   f. Acquiring a maintenance contract for a peripheral.
   g. Suing another company for an antitrust violation.
   h. Suing a foreign company for violating a patent.
   i. Claiming damages from another company for violating a copyright.
   j. Getting a restraining order against a former employee for stealing trade secrets.
8. What type of protection would you seek in each of the following circumstances?
   a. Invention of a unique fast disk device.
   b. The writing of a computer program for portfolio management.
   c. Invention of a new compiler.
   d. Development of a computer programming language.
   e. Development of an algorithm for navigation in a data base.
   f. Development of a sorting algorithm.
   g. Development of a technique of systems analysis.
   h. Development of a form to determine users' requirements.
   i. Development of a method for computing the benefits of a computer system.
   j. Development of a standard for computer costing.
   k. Development of a new approach to charging for computer services.
   l. Development of a standards manual.
9. How will the 1982 settlement of the government antitrust suit against AT&T affect the computer industry?

10. Common law is irrelevant to the computing industry because it is based on decades of tradition, which the computer industry does not have. Comment.

11. The process of legislating statutes relating to computing is too slow to be responsive to the fast-moving and dynamic computer industry. Comment.

12. Discuss some of the contract problems in the acquisition of computing resources.

13. How do you think the question of liability for software bugs should be handled? Should liability laws be revised? How?

14. Can laws prevent or reduce computer crime? If so, how? Would you recommend an extension of the 1984 Computer Fraud and Abuse Act? What provisions would you recommend for new computer-related crime legislation?

15. Is the law adequate to protect software resources? How could the law be strengthened?

16. Do you favor laws restricting transborder flow of information? Justify your position.

SELECTED ANNOTATED BIBLIOGRAPHY

Buss, Martin. "Legislative Threat to Transborder Data Flow." *Harvard Business Review*, vol. 62, no. 3 (May–June 1984), pp. 111–18.
New international barriers to information exchange make it necessary for nations and companies to adopt privacy policies.

Franz, Charles R., and E. Ned Flynn. "Clarifying Warranties and Disclaimers in Computer Crime." *Journal of Systems Management*, vol. 35, no. 12 (December 1984), pp. 32–37.
Proper wording of warranties and disclaimers is in the interest of both the client and the vendor and can save both of them annoyance, disruption, and costly litigation. The absence of good wording only benefits the lawyer.

Fuerst, Irene. "When DP Needs a Lawyer." *Datamation*, vol. 32, no. 2 (January 15, 1986), pp. 42–45.
Many corporations are adding lawyers specializing in computer law to their staffs.

International Computer Law Advisor. Manhattan Beach: Law and Technology Press, 1987.
This annual publication replaces *The Scott Report* which was limited to the U.S. The Adviser provides legal and practical business information for computer companies doing business around the world.

Kelley, Joseph. "Computer Law." *Datamation*, vol. 31, no. 12 (June 15, 1985), pp. 116–28.
The number of lawyers who specialize in computer law is growing as the computer industry grows. The lawyers offer expertise and services to "aid" vendors, users, and legislators alike. The areas where much future litigation

will occur will be in the areas of software protection, trade secret violations, computer crime, and liability.

Miles, Gregory L. "Information Thieves Are Now Corporate Enemy No. 1." *Business Week,* no. 2,945 (May 14, 1986), pp. 120–25.
The problem of protecting corporate trade secrets is compounded by the fact that trade secret laws are weak and outdated.

Nycum, Susan H., Gaston Snow, and Ely Bartlett. "Let the Buyer—and the Seller—Beware." *High Technology,* vol. 6, no. 1 (January 1986), pp. 13–14.
The authors suggest that both vendors and clients stop overprotecting themselves from every conceivable risk.

"A Primer on Computer Litigation from the User's Perspective." *Computer Negotiations Report,* vol. 8, no. 7 (July 1985), pp. 1–7.
Even well-drafted contracts may result in disputes. This article discusses several dispute resolution alternatives that are less costly and time consuming than litigation for such cases. The article is a good tutorial on the UCC.

Schatz, Willie. "Airing the Issues." *Datamation,* vol. 32, no. 2 (January 15, 1986), pp. 33–35.
Developing countries do not want the OECD and multinationals to make all of the rules regarding transborder data flow.

Sheehy, Therese. "Transborder Flow—An Issue with Global Implications." *Data Management,* vol. 22, no. 4 (November 1984), pp. 28–29.
Transborder flow affects the international transmission of data through electronic networks and, hence, profoundly impacts on the operation of multinationals.

Tompkins, Joseph B., Jr., and Linda A. Mar. "The 1984 Federal Computer Crime Statute: A Partial Answer to a Pervasive Problem." *Computer/Law Journal,* vol. 6, no. 25 (Winter 1986), pp. 459–83.
The article reviews the measures of the 1984 federal law and also discusses the need for further federal and state legislation against computer crime.

Wharton, Leslie. "Use and Expression: The Scope of Copyright Protection for Computer Programs." *Computer/Law Journal,* vol. 5, no. 22 (Spring 1985), pp. 433–68.
Discussed in great detail is the extent to which computer programs have copyright protection (state and national). The question of whether all programs require and will receive equal protection is still open.

Publications on computer law

Computer Law and Tax Report.
Covers new laws and offers general advice to users. Appears monthly.

Computer Law Monitor.
Provides summaries of and comments on court cases. A quarterly for users and vendors.

Computer Law Newsletter.
Bimonthly newsletter that focuses on the Northeast.

Computer Law Reporter.
Also bimonthly. Reprints court decision and includes articles on the law. Written primarily for lawyers.

Computer Law Strategist.
Monthly. Expected audience is lawyers, users, and vendors.

Computer Lawyer.
Monthly publication for lawyers.

Computer Negotiations Report.
Written to give users advice on contracts and acquisitions. Monthly.

Computer Users Legal Reporter.
Broad coverage. Issued monthly.

The Scott Report.
In-depth analysis of legal developments. Issued monthly.

Software Protection.
Includes discussions of the legal aspects of protecting software. Monthly.

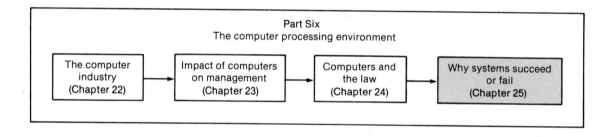

Part Six
The computer processing environment

| The computer industry (Chapter 22) | → | Impact of computers on management (Chapter 23) | → | Computers and the law (Chapter 24) | → | Why systems succeed or fail (Chapter 25) |

CHAPTER 25

Why systems succeed or fail

To live effectively is to live with adequate information.

Norbert Weiner

The effectiveness of an information system can be measured by its ability to meet design and operational demands within prescribed tolerance limitations in a given environment. The system should satisfy users' needs during normal and peak periods of demand, prove easy to modify should environmental conditions change, and have maintenance, backup, and recovery procedures that minimize downtime. Effective systems may vary widely in performance. What is more, a system deemed a success in one firm might be considered a failure in another; the objectives and specifications of the system may be appropriate in certain environments, yet inappropriate in others.

Unfortunately, there is no checklist of system ingredients that guarantee system success. Nevertheless, factors contributing to successful systems can be identified. We have done so in this textbook. Chapters have explained how to acquire, organize, monitor, and control computer resources for the development and implementation of successful systems. In this concluding chapter, we review and summarize factors that might be characterized as key success factors. The chapter will also introduce the concept that firms must go through stages of learning and growth before they can assimilate computer technology effectively.

KEYS TO SUCCESSFUL INFORMATION SYSTEMS DEVELOPMENT

Users

User attitude is perhaps the most important systems **development success factor.** After all, a given system is designed to assist users in their jobs. Analysts cannot be expected to know all of the on-the-job problems encountered by users and will need help in identifying exceptional situations that the new system will be expected to handle. Users must be receptive to computer solutions to problems and be willing to participate in the systems development process. Their involvement helps to ensure that the system under development is able to respond to both present and future user needs and is able to solve unusual problem situations as well.

A successful information systems development project also requires the willingness of users to consider innovative problem-solving methods. Unless persons for whom the system is being designed are receptive to information technology, the computer system under development may never be used. An idle system can hardly be deemed a successful one.

Management

Corporate managers, like users, need a positive attitude toward computerized information systems in order for systems development to be successful. Management sets the tone in an organization. Resistance to systems development at managerial levels will buttress resistance at lower levels. The development team will have trouble collecting the information it needs on existing operations. It will find users reluctant to assist the team in specifying system requirements. In order to perform its role, the development team needs the active support of corporate management. The potential benefits of proposed information systems should be publicized by top management. Middle and operations managers should be directed to assist analysts in systems development projects. This will help establish an organizational environment where cooperation with the development team is the norm.

Management should also ensure that EDP personnel have the technical expertise to undertake systems development. This may mean recruiting additional qualified computer specialists or hiring consultants to add to the development team. Since complex information systems require a data base management system, the team should include members with DBMS knowledge and experience. It may be necessary to turn to facilities management firms or utilities for assistance. Recognizing needs, knowing where to turn and when, is the responsibility of corporate and EDP management.

When systems failure is traced to poor systems design, the cause is usually one or more of the following:

- Users did not participate in formulating system specifications.
- The flow of data, documents, and information was not adequately considered.
- The development team failed to recognize the multiple uses of data. It allowed the proliferation of files instead of formulating an integrated data base.

- The system lacks flexibility, so that additions or changes prove difficult to make. Usually, modular systems developed according to a long-range plan do not have this problem.
- Documentation is lacking. To keep a system on track regardless of changes in personnel, documentation should include a systems description, charts, program descriptions, a data base description, a list of hardware and procedural requirements, input/output descriptions, and detailed implementation descriptions.
- Not enough attention has been paid to human factors. The system evokes anger, frustration, or fear instead of being friendly and easy to use.

The reasons for systems failure may be multiple and complex or as simple as poor screen acuity (a design that results in eyestrain and headaches). Sometimes, systems fail because the design does not allow efficient processing of various types of data. Sometimes, the mix of resources committed to the system is far from optimal. Sometimes, users require more prompts or explanations.

During systems development, hundreds of mistakes can be made that may lead to systems failure if undetected and uncorrected. That is why competent management of the development process, the assignment of a qualified staff to the development team, and careful testing of new systems are so important. Most systems require recycling of the development process to correct problems identified in the testing phase. Management should recognize that recycling is a normal part of the development process and provide a supportive environment for this phase.

Maintenance

Of course, a maintenance infrastructure is also required to keep developed systems, once implemented, from failing. It is during development that plans for maintenance should be laid. That is, mechanisms for monitoring and evaluating systems need to be incorporated in systems design, so that management will be alerted when systems require modification or redevelopment. Perhaps user needs change or new technology makes a system obsolete. Chapter 11 describes how unsatisfactory output should trigger a maintenance cycle.

KEYS TO SUCCESSFUL SYSTEMS OPERATIONS

Control

A most important **operations success factor** in information systems is control. Unfortunately, the term *control* has an oppressive connotation; indeed, too many controls can deter users from effective systems use. Access controls may become so restrictive, for example, that potential users bypass the system entirely.

Yet, controls are necessary to guarantee systems security, ensure the privacy and integrity of data, and check processing efficiency. In addition, controls are needed in order to collect data on systems performance—data to be used to evaluate the system and reach a decision on whether to initiate a cycle of modification or redevelopment. The challenge is to establish meaningful, unobtrusive controls to monitor systems performance and protect the system from abuse. Most users will support their implementation as long as the need for controls can be demonstrated and as long as efforts are made to minimize the adverse effect of such controls on systems use.

Design

Success of operations also depends on how well the system has been designed. Can users access the system with ease? Is adequate user interface provided? Some systems include a hot line for quick custom jobs; others have a hot line for reporting service breakdown. Are special features of this nature available? Since users' needs may change over time, are procedures in place for routine evaluation of performance and systems relevancy?

Planning

Another key to the success of operations is capacity planning so that there is no break in service during peak loads or when user processing needs expand. The budget should allow for modification and redevelopment of outdated systems and permit acquisition of new resources as technology advances. To help management oversee operations, some firms schedule regular task force meetings to evaluate reports of auditors and function representatives. Meetings like this ensure that operating problems are brought to the attention of management for corrective action.

The failure of systems to operate at designed or expected levels may be attributed to one or more of the following.

- Poor systems planning.
- Inadequate operating procedures.
- Faulty scheduling.
- Lack of evaluation and feedback mechanisms.
- Poor maintenance facilities or procedures.
- A systems design that restricts expansion when service demands increase or change.
- Inappropriate organizational structure for computer processing unit.
- Inadequate procedures for assigning computer resources and priorities.
- Lack of strategies to reduce resistance to change.
- Insufficient training of users and EDP personnel.
- Inadequate budgeting.
- Failure to keep up-to-date on technological advances in the computer industry.

- Failure of corporate management to establish a work environment receptive to computerized systems. This may be due to lack of understanding about computers and their potential, or the impact of computing on management and the organization may have been underestimated.

During conversion, systems are particularly vulnerable to failure. Competent management at this stage is crucial. It is important that morale be kept high, that no "foot-dragging" to stall conversion be allowed, and that high standards of performance are enforced during conversion. Mistakes and security breaches often occur during this period of overwork, when tension is the norm. Preplanning to help prevent disruption of service during conversion is essential. Staff should be well trained to accept responsibilities that go with the new system. The computer center schedule should allow for the additional loads that characterize conversion. Adequate staff and resources should be available to maintain ongoing operations while testing the new system for inaccuracies and redundancies.

ROLE OF MANAGEMENT

In a computerized environment, management has two roles:

1. To oversee systems development and computer operations so that needed output is provided efficiently.
2. To promote human productivity, using information technology.

With regard to systems performance, the **management role** is to see that output meets systems specifications and that this output is, in fact, what the user needs. Table 25–1 contains a list of systems performance factors and related questions that can serve as guidelines in evaluating whether performance is satisfactory.

When the need for systems maintenance or redevelopment is indicated, resources must be allocated and personnel assigned to the project by management. Though technical problems will be solved by computer professionals on the staff, management is ultimately responsible for systems performance.

Systems performance may be satisfactory, yet information systems fail when human performance is below standard. Astute management of employees and human-computer interaction can be as important as machine efficiency. To help establish an environment receptive to computer use, orientation programs should be organized to help employees become familiar with potential benefits of information systems. It is advisable to establish training programs to keep personnel technologically up-to-date. Policies (such as the establishment of career ladders) should be initiated to minimize turnover, because the marketplace is

Table 25–1	Is systems performance satisfactory?	
	Performance factors	*Questions to ask*
	Time	Is the system working as fast as expected?
	Cost	Is systems performance up to financial expectations in terms of labor, facilities, materials, maintenance, expansion, modification, training, data entry, data output, data storage, programming, software, carrier charges, and backup equipment?
	Hardware	Does hardware meet the standards set for speed, reliability, service, maintenance, operating costs, power requirements, and necessary training?
	Software	Does software meet the standards set for processing speed, amount and quality of output, accuracy, reliability, amount of maintenance and updating, and training requirements?
	Productivity	Is the relationship of input cost to output level satisfactory?
	Accuracy	Does the system have a tolerable frequency of error and magnitude of error?
	Integrity	Does the system provide sufficient security and control in relationship to cost?
	Security	Does the system protect computing resources from misuse and abuse?
	User satisfaction	Given the resources and other constraints, is the user satisfied?

chronically short of qualified EDP personnel. Also important is management's role in overseeing the incorporation of human factors in systems design, a topic discussed next.

HUMAN FACTORS

To humanize an information system means to focus on human needs rather than technological considerations in systems design. That is, the emphasis should be placed on how the computer can best serve the user, even though the result may be a reduction in machine efficiency. Consider the following trade-off: With high-level languages that resemble English and require little training to use, persons who lack a technical background can input data and utilize output in their jobs. Assembly languages and machine language, on the other hand, are more efficient in processing time but require considerable programming knowledge and skill. Most systems today are written in high-level languages, even though some processing efficiency is sacrificed as a result, in order to make systems user friendly. The development of interactive dialogue languages is another step toward humanizing software.

Here are some features that should be included in systems design to help humanize information systems:

- Easy-to-follow instructions (e.g., self-explanatory prompts and messages, and use of menus or fill-in techniques to assist in inputting data).
- User-friendly hardware (e.g., touch-sensitive screens, voice output or devices such as a joystick, "mouse," or light pens to facilitate user interaction with the computer).
- Tolerance. Allow simple "errors" and assist users in identifying and correcting mistakes.
- Quick systems response to user demands for service.
- Simple procedures for exceptions or overriding defaults.
- Coding that is easy to master and easy to remember.
- User options (whether terminals will be intelligent, able to process graphics, have voice output, and so on).
- Physical compactness of system. User workstations should also be comfortable, convenient, and a pleasing environment in which to work (e.g., low noise level).

Information systems should be designed so that minimum effort on the part of users is required. That is, repetitive tasks should be done by the computer, coding should be programmed, file recovery should be automatic, and input should be monitored so that only essential data is collected by the system. Systems should be easy to master, with little learning or memorization of operational steps required. Help should be built into the systems but not overdone. For example, users should be able to bypass help menus if they are not needed.

Systems should be based on patterns familiar to users and be both logical and consistent. For example, familiar formats and a standard typewriter keyboard in word processing facilitate systems use. So does use of common abbreviations and symbols for information recovery.

Visual or video signals to call attention to problems are helpful. For example, syntax or spelling errors should be signaled, changes in processing mode should be clearly indicated, and warning should be given when file capacity reaches 80–90 percent. Maximum worker control should be built into designs, giving users flexibility in sequencing and defaults. Systems should also provide maximum task support, such as documentation and indexing.

Ideally, systems should be easy to access and use; intelligent but not intimidating; honest with no intent to trick or deceive; and considerate of individuals, not manipulative. There should be procedures for evaluating information stored in the system and for correcting this information. Systems should be adaptable, able to service individuals with different backgrounds and levels of proficiency.

Throughout the literature on information systems, one finds that unsatisfactory systems performance is often attributed to failure to incorporate **human factors** into systems design. It is management's responsibility to ensure that new systems meet the needs of the people

Table 25–2 **Human factors affecting information system success, and strategies to minimize dysfunctional behavior**

Work group	Human factors	Motivation and information systems strategy

Operating employees	Resistance to new systems
	Tendency to believe rumor versus fact
	Need for reassurance as to job security
	Need for group motivation
	Dislike for more rigid work pace
	Instinct for self-protection from blame
	Faith in company promises
	Tendency toward short-range goals
	Fear of machines
	Desire for affection, recognition, attention
	Desire to know reasons for change
	Influence of key workers
		Extrinsic motivational factors
		  Set achievable goals/standards
		  Pay, as a major incentive
		  Organize into small work groups
		  System of rewards
		  System of punishments
		  System of promotions
		
		Intrinsic motivational factors
		  Do not suppress informal organization
		
		Other strategies
		  Prepare and distribute brochures describing the new system
		  Intracompany training programs

Operating and middle management	Fear of replacement by young workers
	Tendency to concentrate on technical aspects of jobs
	Need for visable evidence of production
	Lack of job mobility
	Desire to air views and participate
	Worry about ability to learn and supervise new procedures
	Pride in status symbols of position
	Fear of becoming mere machine monitors
	Fatigue and pressure during system change
	Fear of loss of promotional opportunity
		Extrinsic motivational factors
		  Set achievable goals
		  Participation in systems change
		  System of promotions
		  Pay incentive systems
		  Bonuses
		
		Intrinsic motivational factors
		  Praise from supervisors
		  Interesting work
		  Tenure
		  Status symbols
		
		Other strategies
		  Tailor system to meet manager needs
		  Provide only needed information

Top management	Status symbols as motives for change
	Courage to carry through change
	Isolation of top people
	Tendency toward secrecy
	Ability to adjust and learn
	Impatience with rate of progress
	Promptness in making decisions
	Concern for human relations
	Willingness to use new tools and skills
		Intracompany training programs
		Distribute brochures describing new systems
		Simplify reporting structure
		Avoid information overload
		Standardize report formats, headings
		Provide accurate, objective, timely, understandable information
		
		Extrinsic motivational factors
		  Bonuses
		  Stock options
		
		Intrinsic motivational factors
		  Status symbols
		
		Other strategies
		  (See operating and middle management work group for list.)

Source: Michael J. Cerullo, "Information System Success Factors," *Journal of Systems Management,* vol. 31, no. 12 (December 1980), p. 12.

who will use them and that they are appropriate, given the users' background and experience in computing. It is also management's responsibility to see that the lessons of ergonomics[1] are understood by systems developers and that incorporated in the design of systems are features that minimize human shortcomings. What is more, management must establish a working environment that is receptive to computer use. Table 25–2 presents a list of human factors that may have a bearing on systems success and suggests strategies that management might implement to minimize dysfunctional behavior.

ORDERLY GROWTH

One final factor critical to systems success is orderly growth of information systems; that is, the expansion and integration of systems in

Figure 25–1   **Growth curves postulated by Nolan**

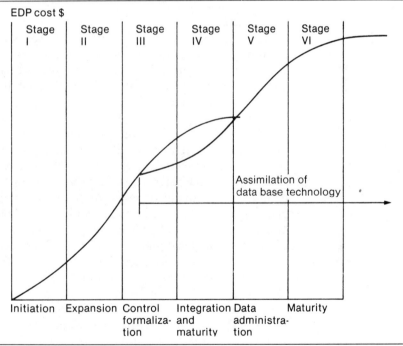

Source: Richard L. Nolan, "Thoughts about the Fifth Stage," *Data Base*, vol. 7, no. 2 (Fall 1975), p. 9.

---

[1]For Europeans, ergonomics is the study of workers and their physical environment—how to adapt machines to the convenience of operators in order to maximize machine efficiency. The American equivalent of ergonomics, human factors, has its roots in human psychology.

a manner that allows a company to assimilate appropriate computer technology as new applications are added.

According to **Richard Nolan,** companies follow a S curve through four **stages of growth** (reflected in EDP costs) and learning in their implementation of information systems:

   I. Initiation of EDP.
   II. Expansion.
   III. Control formalization.
   IV. Integration.

Slow early acquisition of knowledge and skill is followed by a period of rapid learning and growth, then a slowdown in learning rate, and a final plateau, as illustrated in Figure 25–1.

For the assimilation of techniques for administering large and complex data bases that develop as systems grow, Nolan adds a second S and two more growth stages:

   V. Data administration.
   VI. Maturity.

A data base manager may be hired, data bases may be restructured to allow data sharing, and DBMS software may be implemented to monitor data base use, control data access, and protect data independence. It is not until Stage III, according to Nolan, that the need for data base technology becomes acute.

Tables 25–3 through 25–5 describe characteristics of each growth stage relating to application type, mode of processing, and organizational structure.[2] The tables show, for example, that the implementation of a payroll application is appropriate in the first growth stage but that computer-aided design (CAD) requires a company to be at Level IV. Although CAD might be requested by users at an earlier stage, a company usually lacks the experience and qualified personnel to implement this advanced technology when it first begins to computerize. Note that batch processing is replaced by other modes of processing as a company gains processing experience. Table 25–4 reflects changes in modes of processing over time, while Table 25–5 identifies changes in organizational and departmental structure that occur at different growth stages.

Can a firm leapfrog over stages of growth? Yes, if management, analysts, and end-users have had experience with computer systems while working in other organizations. But leapfrogging is inadvisable in most cases. It is generally necessary for a firm to learn how to develop and operate simple systems, then move progressively to more complex ones,

[2]For details, see Richard L. Nolan, "Managing the Crisis in Data Processing," *Harvard Business Review*, vol. 57, no. 2 (March–April 1979), pp. 115–26.

Table 25-3   Applications in the six growth stages

I	II	III	IV	V	VI
Initiation of decentralized jobs	Proliferation of applications	Consolidation of application Some networks	Selected data base application Individual networks	Integrated data resource management Integrated switched networks Satellite transmission Integrated voice data, facsimile, text editing	
Initiation of Payroll Accounts payable Accounts receivable	Initiation of: Budgeting Cash Management Inventory Materials control Marketing Order processing Purchasing Stores control	Initiation of: Cost analysis Scheduling Financial and capital investment planning Personnel	Initiation of: DSS OLRT CAD Process control Numerical control	Initiation of: Electronic office DSS for strategic planning Advanced robots and CAM Word processing Personal computing	Refinement of: Text management CAI Heuristic modeling
Selected reduction of cost and labor-intensive jobs	Initiation of: Data base and telecommunications Minis and micros			Integration of data base, telecommunications with minis and micros	

Source: Reprinted by permission of the *Harvard Business Review*. Exhibit from "Managing the Crises in Data Processing" by Richard L. Nolan (March–April 1979). Copyright © 1979 by the President and Fellows of Harvard College, all rights reserved.

Table 25–4   **Processing mode in the six stages of growth (percentage)**

Modes of processing	Stages					
	I	*II*	*III*	*IV*	*V*	*VI*
Batch	100%	80%	70%	50%	20%	10%
RJE (Remote job entry)		20				
Data communications processing				40	60	60
Data base processing			15			
Inquiries processing			10			
Time-sharing			5			
Personal computing				5	5	5
Mini and micro computing				5	15	25
Total	100%	100%	100%	100%	100%	100%

Source: Reprinted by permission of the *Harvard Business Review*. Exhibit from "Managing the Crises in Data Processing" by Richard L. Nolan (March–April 1979). Copyright © 1979 by the President and Fellows of Harvard College, all rights reserved.

before being able to manage the sophisticated integrated computer systems that are characteristic of Nolan's advanced stages. Only then can they effectively utilize the technology to reach corporate goals and objectives.

Of course, Richard Nolan's growth curves are theoretical. In actual practice, no two organizations will have an identical slope to their growth curve, because firms differ in their ability to absorb information

Table 25–5   **Organizational mode for the six stages of growth**

Function	*I*	*II*	*III*	*IV*	*V*	*VI*
DP organization	Decentralized	Centralized computer	Centralized computer	DDP, utilities	Data resource management	
DP control	Lax to encourage utilization	Lax but controlled to facilitate growth	Formalized to contain supply of services	Formalized control to match demand with supply of resources	Formalized control to contain demand	Formalized control to balance supply with demand
				Steering committee	Data administration	
User attitude and responsibility	Hands off	Superficially enthusiastic	User directly involved and accountable for quality and value added		User and EDP jointly accountable for quality and effectiveness of system	

Source: Reprinted by permission of the *Harvard Business Review*. Exhibit from "Managing the Crises in Data Processing" by Richard L. Nolan (March–April 1979). Copyright © 1979 by the President and Fellows of Harvard College, all rights reserved.

technology. Some firms acquire learning more quickly than others, so they can pass from one growth stage to the next at an accelerated pace. Furthermore, no single growth curve can describe a firm's level of development in all aspects of information technology at any given point of time. Instead, a series of parallel growth curves may be required. For example, a firm may be in Nolan's second stage in the implementation of word processing, in the third stage for telecommunications, and in the fourth in relation to its applications portfolio. Each organization's mix will be unique. Nevertheless, growth should be orderly, with a long-range plan for implementation of new systems. The success of systems depends on the acquisition of experience before the attempted implementation of advanced technology.

Because of recent progress in information technology, it is suggested that two new growth curves need to be added to those postulated by Nolan (see Figure 25–2). One curve represents the advanced computer technology of the 1980s, such as micro-to-mainframe links, supercomputers, lasers, voice synthesis, glass fibers, and terminals with conversational, graphic, and intelligent capabilities. Yet another curve is in the making. This curve represents the merger of telecommunications with information processing and the advent of integrated advanced computer systems incorporating artificial intelligence. We are talking about wired homes, offices, and cities—for example, a paperless society with electronic mail and telenews and a cashless society with tele-

Figure 25–2   **Current and possible future growth curves**

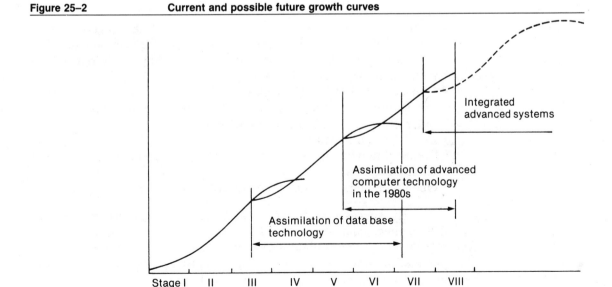

shopping, telebanking, and electronic transfer of funds. We are also talking about computers that learn—machines that do not only what we tell them to do but what we want them to do.

SUMMING UP

To be deemed a success, an information system should be profitably applied to at least one area of major concern within a company, should be used, and should improve the quality of decision making and operations. Note that success depends both on systems performance and on user interaction with the system. The two cannot easily be separated, since technical components inevitably have an impact on human effectiveness and satisfaction.

In the past, technical aspects of systems design have been the focus of most systems developers. It is now recognized that more effort must be devoted to the incorporation of human factors in systems design. Unfortunately, technicians have a poor track record for sensitivity to user concerns, needs, foibles, and limitations. That is why management's role in the development and implementation of information systems is so important. Management must ensure that the data processing staff never loses sight of the primary objectives of computer systems: to serve people and improve human productivity. This may mean sacrificing machine efficiency at times. Other responsibilities of management include:

- Selecting a clear direction. Management should have a good understanding of business needs, formulate a business strategy, and develop long-range plans for the utilization of information technology to promote business goals and objectives.
- Designing the right systems. Systems should reflect user requirements and should be put in place only where users are receptive to computerized solutions to their problems.
- Building a strong staff.
- Controlling development and operations, using sound management techniques.
- Opening communication channels with users and technicians.

Clearly, successful information systems require active corporate and EDP management support and involvement. One might summarize management's role as planning for systems, overseeing the development process, creating a work environment receptive to computerization, and managing systems once they are installed.

CASE: GAO FERRETS OUT REASONS FOR SYSTEMS FAILURES

The complexity of computer systems that the General Accounting Office (GAO) monitors in the federal government can be illustrated by a look at the Veterans Administration (VA).

The VA has 204,000 employees and runs 172 hospitals, 107 nursing homes, and 226 outpatient clinics and domiciliaries. Management of these facilities requires 58 regional offices, 5 computer centers, and 169 distributed computer installations in medical facilities. In addition, the VA operates life insurance programs, loan programs, and pensions, compensation, and education benefit payment programs.

The VA maintains 218 automated systems and has an additional 52 systems under development. In a recent evaluation of the agency, the GAO found that the VA lacks good internal controls. Problems identified were inadequate accountability for drugs and supplies, the receipt of medical care by ineligible persons, and lack of systems to provide accurate information for planning purposes. The GAO looked at systems under development and ranked their vulnerability to waste, fraud, and abuse, using its own control and risk evaluation methodology. The GAO cautioned that many such systems fail because:

- Users and internal auditors are not included in the systems development process.
- Too many technical compromises are made in an attempt to fit systems design into installed hardware.
- Agencies frequently commission ineffective third-party reviews of the development effort.

Questions

1. In view of the complexity of VA operations, is it possible to single out reasons why some of their systems fail? How much effort should be devoted to the search for the cause(s) of failures?
2. In its review, a GAO team visited three VA computer centers. Do you think such visits contribute to an understanding of processing problems? How? What should be the focus of such visits?
3. What measures can the government take to prevent the failure of computer systems within the executive branch?

Source: Arnold S. Levine, "GAO Report Cites Problems in VA's Internal Controls," *Government Computer News*, January 31, 1986, p. 56.

4. Draw up a list of guidelines for successful systems to present to systems development teams on government projects.

STUDY KEYS

Development success factors   **Operations success factors**
Human factors   **Richard Nolan's growth curves**
Management role   **Stages of growth**

DISCUSSION QUESTIONS

1. Who should be given responsibility for compiling a list of factors influencing success or failure of an information system in a given department, firm, or industry? How should data be collected?
2. As manager of a computer department, what strategies would you implement to ensure the success of information systems under your jurisdiction?
3. What level of management is most responsible for success or failure of an information system? Why?
4. Is experience the best or only way to learn about success and failure factors in a given environment? Is there a faster, less painful method of gaining the knowledge one accrues through experience?
5. What sources of information should be used to identify how success and failure factors are altered by changing technology?
6. What personnel in an organization are crucial to the success of information systems?
7. List factors that contribute to the success of information systems development.
8. Discuss principles of design that help humanize information systems.
9. Where do you feel the emphasis on future research for management information systems should be focused? On technology or human factors? Justify your answer.
10. What are the stages in the growth and use of computer systems? Is it necessary to follow all the stages in sequence?
11. Why must a firm go through stages of growth?
12. What is the shape of the growth path for EDP operations? Is the same growth path followed for all types of applications, or does each application have a unique path?
13. Do you believe that there should be other S curves beyond the two postulated by Nolan? Where should the new curves start and end? For what industries? What will trigger and sustain new curves?

14. When should a firm leapfrog over stages of growth? When should it follow orderly growth patterns? Explain your reasons for both answers.

SELECTED ANNOTATED BIBLIOGRAPHY

Basili, Victor R., and Barry T. Perricone. "Software Errors and Complexity: An Empirical Investigation." *Communications of the ACM*, vol. 27, no. 1 (January 1984), pp. 42–52.
This paper identifies the frequent errors that occur during development and maintenance and talks about errors that can be attributed to environmental factors. The author presents valuable empirical insights into reasons why information systems are often unreliable and of poor quality.

Jacot, William. "Computers—A Tragedy of Errors." *Industrial Management and Data Systems* (1985).
This is a three-part series describing the many causes that can lead to systems failure.

Newton, J. "Strategies for Problem Prevention." *IBM Systems Journal*, vol. 24, nos. 3 and 4 (1985), pp. 248–63.
It is much better to prevent problems than to react to problems as they occur. This article stresses the importance of comprehensive and formally managed testing strategies to prevent systems failures.

Nolan, Richard L., ed. *Managing the Data Resource Function.* 2d ed. St. Paul, Minn.: West Publishing, 1982, pp. 1–20.
Nolan, the originator of the theory of growth curves in computer processing, discusses his more recent views on the subject. Steps of growth and strategies for managing growth are examined.

Parmar, Lakhbir. "Success Factors in Managing Systems Projects." *Data Management*, vol. 25, no. 3 (March 1987), pp. 27–30.
A good discussion of the role and contributions of a project review committee and working committee towards the success of a systems project.

Walsh, Myles E. *Realizing the Potential of Computer-Based Information Systems.* New York: Macmillan, 1984, 312 pp.
The author takes a hard look at existing information systems in order to explain information technology's failure to realize its potential. The history of information technology is surveyed, and both hardware and software are reviewed, including their application in plant and office. The book also examines how senior executives must combine their skills with highly sophisticated technology. The text is directed to senior managers, executives, and corporate heads.

Zmud, Robert W. *Information Systems in Organizations.* Glenview, Ill.: Scott, Foresman, 1983, pp. 353–70.
Chapter 13 discusses success and failure factors in information systems. A list of discussion questions, brief cases, and a bibliography are also included.

APPENDIX A

Terms in context

This appendix introduces information systems terminology in a meaningful context. The definitions are informal, designed to give the reader an intuitive appreciation and understanding of computers and computer resource management. An index (Appendix B) will enable quick reference to the line on which each term is used or defined. An alphabetical glossary appears in Appendix C, and Appendix D lists and identifies acronyms and technical names used in this text.

EQUIPMENT

One of the earliest examples of mass processing of data was the use of a **punched card** by Herman Hollerith in 1880 to process census data. Because such cards have been produced in vary large quantities by IBM, the name **IBM card** has become associated with punched cards. Each card has 80 **columns.** Holes are punched in each column according to a code to represent a character of data. The cards are then fed into special equipment, passing one at a time between **photo cells** carrying electric current. Wherever the punched holes appear, the current passes through the card. The characters represented by the holes are then read by machine in the form of electrical impulses and interpreted, be they data or instruction on how to process data. Machines predating the computer (e.g., calculators, sorters, and collators) followed the instructions for simple processing, such as adding, subtracting, or classifying the data. Such processing is known as **data processing.**

Handling cards requires much special equipment. A **key-punch,** used like a typewriter, punches holes in a **data card** to

1
2
3
4
5
6
7
8
9
10
11
12
13
14
15
16
17
18

represent data or processing instructions; a **verifier** identifies   19
errors in keypunching; a **reproducer** generates duplicate cards   20
and has the added capability of moving columns of data to   21
another position on a card; a **sorter** classifies cards according   22
to coded data classifications; and a **collator** merges data cards,   23
combining two similarly sequenced sets of cards into one set.   24

Originally, data processing equipment was used primarily   25
for accounting purposes. Because the machines used electrical   26
impulses, they became known as **electric accounting machines**   27
(EAMs). Another term applied to such equipment was **unit re-**   28
cord equipment, since each input card processed usually rep-   29
resented one record of data. Because EAM equipment was for   30
the purpose of automating office processing, use of the equip-   31
ment was called **automatic data processing (ADP).**   32

Much of equipment described in preceding paragraphs is no   33
longer used to perform the functions of data processing. Such   34
equipment has been replaced by **computers,** electronic ma-   35
chines capable of complex operations with data at fantastic   36
speeds. The early computers in the 1950s performed arithmetic   37
operations that were measured in **milliseconds** (thousandths of   38
a second). As computers developed, the time for operations was   39
reduced to **microseconds** (millionths of a second), then to **na-**   40
noseconds (billionths of a second), and will soon be measured   41
in **picoseconds** (a thousandth of a nanosecond).   42

Some computers still use cards for input and output. How-   43
ever the use of cards for **input** has been largely replaced by   44
voice input devices, scanners that read typed or printed char-   45
acters of different sizes and styles (called **fonts**), or **keying de-**   46
vices, such as **terminals** with keyboards that resemble type-   47
writers. All these devices, called **input equipment** or **peripherals,**   48
transfer data directly to a computer or to a **storage device** for   49
later processing. Peripherals may also display results, or **output,**   50
in which case they are called **output equipment.** Examples of   51
output peripherals are **printers,** which print results in single   52
or multiple copies; **decollators,** which separate the carbon sheets   53
from the multiple sheets of output paper, called a multiple **ply**   54
paper; and **bursters,** which break the perforation in the sheets,   55
creating pages from the long continuous sheets of paper. **Plot-**   56
ters, which plot output graphically, **card readers,** and **magnetic**   57
ink character recognition (MICR) readers, used in blank ac-   58
counting to read the coded symbols that appear on bank checks,   59
are also examples of peripherals.   60

The **CPU (central processing unit)** of a computer has three   61
parts: the **arithmetic and logic unit,** to perform arithmetic cal-   62
culations (such as add and subtract) and make choices (Yes and   63
No); the **internal memory unit,** to store information temporar-   64

ily; and the **control unit,** to select the order of operations and   65
coordinate the other units.   66
     The computer is **electronic** because the processing of data is   67
done by the movement of electrons rather than electrical or   68
mechanical means, as in ADP or EAM. Therefore, computer   69
processing of data is called **electronic data processing (EDP).**   70
In recent years, equipment to process text and words (**word**   71
processing or WP) has been developed to supplement data pro-   72
cessing. **Information processing** is the term commonly used   73
when both data and text are processed.   74
     One type of electronic computer is a **microcomputer,** also   75
known as a **micro.** It performs simple applications economi-   76
cally, requires no special environment in order to operate (e.g.,   77
doesn't need leveled floors and room air-conditioners required   78
for large computers), and is small enough to be placed on a   79
desk. When within the budget range of families, a microcom-   80
puter may be purchased as a **home computer,** or a **personal**   81
computer, to keep track of household inventories, bank ac-   82
counts, monthly menus, or other home uses.   83
     Microprocessors perform a special task, such as controlling   84
a car carburetor or controlling factory operations, instead of   85
doing general purpose computing. Such machines are ex-   86
tremely small, smaller than the size of a fingertip, and require   87
very little energy to operate. They consist of one or more **semi-**   88
conductor chips made of **silicon** with etched circuitry. This   89
chip performs computations like a computer. When assembled   90
and related together, the chips form an **integrated circuit (IC).**   91
Large-scale integration of circuits may consist of 10,000 to 20,000   92
transistors on one or several chips, each transistor performing   93
the function of the earlier **vacuum tube,** a small electronic de-   94
vice capable of processing data coded in **binary values** (values   95
of 0 or 1).   96
     Online equipment is devices that are under direct control of   97
the CPU. (Conversely, devices that are not under the CPU are   98
called **offline equipment.**) Printers that produce output and **ter-**   99
minals that both receive input and produce output directly from   100
the CPU are examples of online equipment. Terminals may be   101
typewriter terminals or **cathode ray tubes (CRT).** A **CRT ter-**   102
minal looks much like a television set sitting on top of a type-   103
writer. The terminal may be physically part of the computer   104
(in which case it is called a **console**) or it can be located apart,   105
connected to the computer by direct cable or by telephone (in   106
which case the terminal is said to have **remote access**). **Intel-**   107
ligent terminals are terminals that can be programmed to per-   108
form limited functions, such as storage of data or checking the   109
accuracy of input data.   110

The equipment discussed in this section may be grouped in   111
many combinations, or **configurations.** All computer-related   112
equipment is termed **hardware.**   113
                                                                  114
                                                                  115
SOFTWARE   116
                                                                  117

In contrast to hardware, physical objects that can be touched,   118
there is software written as **programs** stored on an input me- 119
dium, such as cards, tapes, or disks. A program instructs the   120
computer on the **algorithm** to be used; that is, the specific com- 121
puter procedure to be followed in order to achieve the desired   122
results and the sequence in which the operations are to be   123
performed. Computational operations, such as adding, subtract-   124
ing, and finding logs and square roots, and rearrangements of   125
data are done quickly and accurately by computer without fur-   126
ther manual intervention. Programs can also be written to **sort,** 127
match, update, and **search** data, functions that are commonly   128
used in business data processing. These are called **utility pro-** 129
grams because they are part of the repertoire of most business- 130
oriented computers.   131
    Programmers are individuals who write programs instruct- 132
ing the computer what to do. The computer only recognizes   133
electronic pulses, so programs must be written in a manner to   134
generate these pulses. **Machine language,** a programming lan-   135
guage in which instructions are written as numbers, is a **low-** 136
level language used by many programmers. This language con-   137
trasts to **natural languages,** such as English, which are **high-** 138
level languages. There is a wide spectrum of programming lan-   139
guages in between. The closer the programming language is to   140
a natural language, the higher it is in the computer language   141
hierarchy and the easier it is for programmers to write. Low-   142
level languages are more difficult to write but are more effi-   143
ciently run by the computer.   144
    High-level programming languages have to be interpreted   145
and translated into machine language to be understood by a   146
computer. This is done by special conversion programs called   147
compilers, assemblers, translators, and **interpreters.** Other   148
computer programs govern the scheduling of programming **jobs**   149
and automate the relationship of the computer to its peripheral   150
devices. These programs are called **monitors** or **supervisors.**   151
Still other computer programs perform "household" duties, fre-   152
quently performed operations of a computer, such as label   153
checking and **listing** an information file.   154
    Compilers, assemblers, translators, interpreters, monitors,   155
supervisors, and utility programs are collectively referred to as 156

system programs and are frequently provided with computer 157
equipment by the manufacturer. These programs are distinct 158
from **application programs** that are typically written by the user 159
firm. **Software** is a collective term that includes both system 160
and application programs. 161

System programs constitute the **operating system** of a com- 162
puter. The operating system plus the hardware configuration 163
may be unique for each computer model. This is why programs 164
run on one computer system cannot always be run on another. 165
Two computer systems that run the same set of computer pro- 166
grams are considered **compatible** with one another. One system 167
can then serve as a **backup** for the other in the event of a 168
breakdown. Another type of backup is duplicate data files and 169
programs. Duplicates are needed in case the originals are stolen 170
or either accidentally or maliciously altered or destroyed. 171

Many computer programs are written by users or program- 172
mers in the user's employ. Others may be purchased from **soft-** 173
ware houses. Whereas each computer model may have its spe- 174
cific machine language, standard programming languages can 175
be used for writing programs for many types of computers. 176
There are a number of high-level programming languages. **COBOL** 177
and **RPG** are most commonly used for information systems and 178
business data processing. Many languages are used in scientific 179
programming, although **FORTRAN, Pascal,** and **Ada** are pop- 180
ular in the United States and **ALGOL** is favored by many Eu- 181
ropeans. Some languages serve dual purposes, being used for 182
both scientific and business data processing. Examples are **PL/** 183
1 and **BASIC.** Languages like **APL** are **conversational** or **inter-** 184
active languages, enabling fast terminal response. Of interest 185
to business management are **simulation languages** such as **GPSS** 186
and **SIMSCRIPT** that are specially designed for business prob- 187
lems in planning and control. Some languages are appropriate 188
for nonnumerical processing, such as text processing. **SNOBOL** 189
and **LISP** are examples. Other programming languages are used 190
in production, such as **APT** used in numerical control. 191
192
193
194

DATA
195
196

As mentioned, programs are sets of instructions for process- 197
ing data. The data must be organized and managed so that it 198
can be efficiently and effectively processed. This is known as 199
data management or **file management.** Organized data is a **data** 200
base, also called a **data bank,** consisting of a set of **integrated** 201
files. A **file** is a set of records; a **record,** a set of data elements; 202

and a **data element,** a fact or an observation with a value that   203
the user needs to record. Data elements are formed by **char-**   204
acters of data. A set of characters can be **alphabetic** (A to Z);   205
numeric (0–9); **alphanumeric,** or **alphameric** (the license plate   206
AEJ472); special symbols ($ * +); or a combination of all these   207
types.   208

A character must be machine readable to be understood by   209
the computer. That is, the character must be represented by a   210
set of **bits** (**binary digits** of 0 or 1). A set of electric currents can   211
be made to represent these digits by being off (0) or on (1). For   212
example, the number 9 can be represented in binary digits as   213
1001 (on-off-off-on). Similarly, letters and symbols can be rep-   214
resented by a unique permutation of 0 and 1 bits. In this way,   215
bits can be made to represent the entire **hierarchy** of data, from   216
data elements, records, and files to the entire data base itself.   217

A data element is usually the lowest level of data a manager   218
uses. Each data element is defined in a **data element dictionary**   219
(DED) prepared specially in each business according to its data   220
element needs. In large information systems, data elements have   221
to be classified, indexed, and organized so as to facilitate access   222
and use. This function is performed by a **data directory (DD).**   223
The data directory and the DED are then used by a set of com-   224
puter programs to structure, access, and manage the data base.   225
This is known as a **data base management system (DBMS).**   226
Many such systems are sold by computer manufacturers and   227
software companies. These include **TDMS, MARK IV, TOTAL,**   228
ADABAS, IMS, and **SYSTEM 2000.**   229

Data and programs to be processed are stored on a **storage**   230
or **memory device.** There are many types of such devices. One   231
is called **core.** It is part of the CPU equipment and is referred   232
to as **internal storage** (internal to the CPU) or as **primary stor-**   233
age. Such storage may be supplemented by additional storage   234
on an **external memory device.** An example is a **magnetic tape**   235
similar to that used in tape recorders. Tape is especially suitable   236
for recording data that must be processed and retrieved **se-**   237
quentially, such as a payroll. Some processing and retrieval is   238
done in **random** order, allowing any word in the memory to be   239
accessed. The memory device appropriate for such **random pro-**   240
cessing is a **disk,** which is similar to a phonograph record. On   241
small computers, a smaller and less rigid disk called a **floppy**   242
disk or **floppy** is used. The tape (**magnetic** or **paper tape**) and   243
the disk are referred to as **auxiliary, secondary,** or **external**   244
storage.   245

Data are stored on tapes or disks as **bits** when representing   246
one character or as **bytes,** sets of bits. The size of a byte for   247
many computers is eight bits. Data are also stored as **words,**   248

which vary with computer manufacturers between 8 and 64   249
bits. Large data bases are measured in tons of data, where a **ton**   250
is 40 billion bits of data. Many businesses have tons of data.   251

Some data is kept in a **common data base.** This data is col-   252
lected and validated only once, then stored to be shared by all   253
authorized users in the organization for many purposes. Such   254
a system is an **integrated** set of files.   255

Management information systems may be integrated in sev-   256
eral ways. **Vertical integration** is sharing of data by all levels   257
of management even though this may be confined to one func-   258
tion only, such as marketing or production. Other systems are   259
integrated at one level of management but integrated for all   260
functions at that level. Such integration is called **horizontal**   261
integration. There is also integration over time, called **longi-**   262
tudinal integration. In making sales projections based on the   263
past five years of data, such longitudinal integration is neces-   264
sary. When an information system has all three types of inte-   265
gration, it is then called a **total system** or a **management infor-**   266
mation system (MIS).   267

   268
   269

INFORMATION SYSTEMS   270

   271

Thus far, computer technology, hardware, software, and data   272
bases have been discussed. If these components are organized   273
as a whole to produce desired information, an **information sys-**   274
tem is created. A **management information system (MIS)** can   275
be used to produce information needed by managers for plan-   276
ning, control, and operations.[1] However, information systems   277
are not a panacea to all of a manager's information needs, for   278
there are many "**wicked problems**" that defy computer solu-   279
tions. These are ill-defined and ill-structured problems that have   280
nonquantifiable data variables. An example would be personnel   281
problems, since human variables are not easily quantified.   282

Information systems are developed in **stages,** each consisting   283
of a set of jobs called **activities.** The first group of activities   284
concerns planning. A four-tier planning structure is common.   285
First, a **corporate strategic plan** that establishes the business   286
direction of the company is developed. Next, an **infor-**   287
mation processing strategic plan is formulated. This plan states   288

---

[1]Readers will note that the term *MIS* has been defined in two ways in this glossary. There are still other definitions. Many terms used in this book have more than one definition. This is because computer science is a relatively new field. It will take many years to develop universal standardization of terms. The **American National Standards Institute (ANSI)** is one organization presently working on the problem of formulating standards.

information processing goals and objectives and the resources   289
that will be available to carry them out. This is followed by   290
a **long-range operational plan.** The lowest level of planning 291
is preparation of a one-year computer processing **operating**   292
budget.   293

The **system life cycle development methodology** is com-   294
monly used for the systems development process. This begins   295
with a **feasibility study.** During the study, alternative ap- 296
proaches to producing information within constraints of the   297
organization are considered. A **constraint** is a factor that places 298
a limit on what is possible.   299

Once an alternative is chosen by management, the next stage   300
in the developmental process is for the manager to define in-   301
formation needs specifically in order for the system to be de-   302
signed to meet these needs. This stage is one of **analysis** and 303
is referred to as the **user specification stage.** First output needs 304
are specified; that is, determining what information the system 305
should generate is determined. From the output needs, the **in-** 306
put (resources put into the system) can be deduced. This in- 307
cludes a determination of equipment, data, computer programs,   308
and procedures needed to produce the output. The **procedures** 309
are sets of instructions and rules governing the human-machine   310
(user-computer) relationship.   311

Once the new system has been designed, it is implemented.   312
This includes writing programs to manipulate data in order to   313
generate the desired output. The system is then **tested,** with 314
actual performance compared with desired performance. Fur-   315
ther **debugging,** locating and correcting errors, may be neces- 316
sary. Once the system performs as expected, it is **documented,** 317
a process of stating all relevant facts about the system. This   318
documentation includes **decision tables,** which specify the logic 319
as decision rules, and **flowcharts,** which show the logic and   320
the flow of data. The documentation is stored in **manuals** and 321
deposited in a **library,** where it is handled and controlled by 322
a **librarian.** The librarian also has jurisdiction over stored pro- 323
grams.   324

The system, when satisfactorily tested and documented, is   325
then **converted,** the old system **phased out** and the new system 326
made **operational.**   327

Prototyping is another development methodology in com-   328
mon use today for ad hoc systems such as those for planning   329
and control. A prototype is a tentative system, often a model   330
based on interaction between analysts and users, one built as   331
a preliminary solution to a problem. Prototyping can be used   332
in conjunction with the system life cycle development meth-   333
odology.   334

INFORMATION PROCESSING

Computer operations have many **modes** of operation. One is **batch processing,** in which jobs are collected into a **batch** before they are processed. Another is **time sharing,** where users take turns being serviced. The very fast processing speeds of modern computers means that users are serviced almost instantly, giving each user the illusion of being the only individual **online,** of having the machine **dedicated** solely to one's own use. Time-sharing systems are used largely by programmers and users for scientific computations. Some businesses require a **real-time system.** This system searches the data base, updates it, and gives results in time to affect the operating environment. **Remote processing,** processing through an input/output device that is physically distant from the CPU, can be combined with the above-mentioned processing modes.

Most organizations house their mainframes, minis, large printers, plotters, and other peripherals for shared use in a central facility called a **computer center.** The design of this center must take into consideration **capacity planning,** the resource needs and requirements for both current and future information requirements. Next, the physical layout of the center, room layout, and special environmental support facilities are planned, such as air-conditioning, electrical power, and security measures.

Sometimes, a firm hires a **facilities management** vendor to operate its computer center, instead of assigning responsibility to in-house personnel. Others contract their processing to **service bureaus.** A **computer utility** is another processing option. Instead of contracting with a client for a specific service, the utility provides service on request, offering continuous service in somewhat the same manner as an electric utility. In order to be able to meet fluctuation of demand, a utility needs a **telecommunications network** so that computing power can be accessed from a distant **node** if regional facilities are overloaded.

The availability and low cost of microcomputers have led to widespread **end-user computing:** programming and operation of computers by the people who use output, many of whom have little prior background or knowledge of computers, instead of by data processing professionals. To provide support to end-users, **information centers** are being established in many firms. These can be categorized as service centers, solution centers, resource centers, or support centers. They are staffed by data processing personnel to help improve the self-sufficiency of end-users and to help improve users' computing efficiency and effectiveness.

To run a computer center and to staff information centers   381
require the services of a number of professionals and support 382
personnel. A **systems analyst** is a technician who studies pro- 383
cessing problems and decides what procedures, methods, or 384
techniques are required for the problem solution using com- 385
puters. **Programmers** write and test the instructions that tell 386
the computer what to do. Processing itself is done by **operators.** 387
Large and complex data bases require a **data base administrator** 388
to keep files updated and to monitor and control data use. Ex- 389
amples of other support personnel are **data entry clerks, se-** 390
curity officers, communications analysts, and **technical writ-** 391
ers. It is management's responsibility to decide what tasks are 392
needed in a given computing facility, to write **job descriptions** 393
for each position to be used in hiring and evaluation of per- 394
sonnel, and to establish **career ladders** so employees can ad- 395
vance within the computer center. 396

During operations, the system is controlled for quality of 397
information. **Controls** are also designed to protect the system 398
from intentional data tampering and theft. However, **security** 399
is not always completely successful. Part of the problem is that 400
design procedures and training for control do not keep up with 401
advances in technology, especially hardware developments and 402
needs for **privacy.** 403

All information systems should be regularly evaluated. This 404
evaluation should be based on both efficiency and effective- 405
ness. **Efficiency** refers to the relationship between input and 406
output, while **effectiveness** refers to the successful achievement 407
of critical factors of performance set by the user. Examples of 408
critical factors are **accuracy,** a specified percentage of freedom 409
from error; **timeliness,** the availability of information when 410
needed; and **completeness,** the availability of all relevant data. 411

Auditing is yet another level of control. An **internal auditor,** 412
an employee of the firm, or an **external auditor,** hired from 413
outside the organization, is concerned with the same processing 414
controls that may be scrutinized in performance evaluation con- 415
ducted by the computer center itself. However, the auditor's 416
responsibility extends one step further, to control of controls: 417
the review of the effectiveness of control measures and the 418
establishment of new controls when existing controls prove 419
inadequate. 420

   421
   422

THE COMPUTER ENVIRONMENT   423

   424

Within the computer industry, IBM dominates **mainframe** 425
manufacture. However, Gene **Amdahl** has demonstrated that 426

the mainframe market can still be breached with his successful   427
introduction of a mainframe that is **plug-compatible** with soft- 428
ware and peripherals developed for IBM computers. The Jap-   429
anese have a strong foothold in the American market for **semi-** 430
conductors, an essential component of minis, micros, word   431
processors, and mainframes. Other segments of the market are   432
peripherals, data communications, software, maintenance, and   433
the **service sector,** which includes **education** and **training.** 434

    With advances in technology, applications have expanded.   435
Many managers today use a **decision support system (DSS)** to   436
assist in planning and control. Such systems have altered meth-   437
ods of decision making. Computers have also changed the job   438
of corporate managers. They must be familiar with computer   439
terminology and understand how information systems are de-   440
veloped and implemented to effectively use computers in their   441
work, and they must know how to manage computing resources.   442
Many managers employ **information specialists** to help them   443
utilize computing resources at their disposal.   444

    Managers must also be knowledgeable about the law in re-   445
lation to computing. That is, they must know how **antitrust**   446
statutes, patents, copyrights, trade secrets, and **tort** affect their 447
computerized operations. Managers should also be aware of   448
human factors or **ergonomics** that are unique to computer en-   449
vironments. These two terms have similar meanings, though   450
ergonomics emphasizes the physiological aspects of computing,   451
whereas human factors refers to the psychological aspects of   452
human-machine relationships. The success of an information   453
system may well depend on the manager's sensitivity to em-   454
ployee concerns and the establishment of a climate receptive   455
to **change,** for computerization inevitably alters organizational 456
structure and interpersonal relationships within a firm.   457

    The degree of **computer literacy** within a firm will determine   458
to some degree the ability of the firm to absorb computer tech-   459
nology and the firm's receptivity to computerization. The effi-   460
ciency and effectiveness of operations will depend on manage-   461
ment's knowledge and experience regarding computer resources   462
and their management. It is hoped that this book will provide   463
readers with background that they need to be effective managers   464
in a computer environment.   465

APPENDIX B

Index to glossary in prose

APPENDIX C

Glossary

This glossary includes operational definitions of terms that are needed for the management of computing resources. Since precise technical definitions too often obscure meanings, the definitions in this list have been written in simple terms in order to facilitate understanding. Readers wishing a complete technical glossary of computer terms should consult dictionaries such as the *American Standard Vocabulary of Information Processing*, published by the American National Standards Institute. Dictionaries of computer terms can be found in most libraries.

Access: the manner in which files or data sets are referred to by the computer. See *direct access*, *random access*, *remote access*, and *serial access*.

Access time: the period of time between a request for information and the availability of that data.

Address: name given to a specific memory location, either within the computer (memory address) or on the storage media (disk address), where information is stored.

Algorithm: a step-by-step process for the solution of a problem in a finite number of steps. Usually developed in an outline or by a tool of analysis before coding begins.

Alphameric: alphabetic, numeric, and punctuation characters (but not special symbols like $). Also called alphanumeric.

American National Standards Institute (ANSI):   an organization sponsored by the Business Equipment Manufacturers Association (BEMA) for the purpose of establishing voluntary industry standards.

Analog computer: (1) a computer in which analog representation of data is mainly used; (2) a computer that operates on analog data by performing physical processes on these data. Contrast with *digital computer*.

Analyst: see *systems analyst*.

Application program: a program written for or by a user that applies to the user's own work.

Application software: software programs that perform a specific user-oriented task, such as line balancing or payroll. Application software can be either purchased as a package or custom designed by a programmer.

Architecture: the structure of a system. Computer architecture often refers specifically to the *central processing unit (CPU)*.

Arithmetic and logic unit (ALU):   the computer element that can perform the basic data manipulations (arithmetic, logic, and control functions) in the central processor.

Artificial intelligence (AI):   the ability of a computer to imitate certain human actions or skills, such as problem solving, decision making, perception, and learning.

Audit trail: the procedure of tracing the steps in processing data to ensure that results are within either expected or standardized limits.

Auditing around the computer: checking output for a given input.

Auditing through the computer: checking both input and computer processing. May use test data, auditor-prepared programs, auditor software packages, or audit programming languages.

Auditor: person authorized to make a formal periodic examination and check of accounts or financial records to verify their correctness. A computer auditor may also be assigned to verify the correctness of computer information processing to ensure that processing conforms to the firm's goals, policies, and procedures (such as policies with regard to security and privacy).

Authentication: verifying the user's right to access a requested file or portion of the data base.

Authorization: verifying the type of access permitted, such as read, write, update, or no access.

Auxiliary storage: (1) data storage other than main storage. For example, storage on magnetic tape or direct-access devices. Synonymous with external storage and secondary storage; (2) a storage that supplements another storage. Contrast with *main storage*.

Backup: (1) one or more files copied onto a storage medium for safekeeping should the original get damaged or lost; (2) redundant equipment or procedures used in the event of failure of a component or storage medium.

Bar code recognition: a form of machine-readable encodation formed by vertical bars and spaces. A scanner measures the presence or absence of a reflection over time to determine bit patterns of characters.

BASIC (Beginner's All-purpose Symbolic Instruction Code):   a relatively easy-to-use programming language that is available in many small computer systems.

Batch processing: a traditional method of data processing in which transactions are collected and prepared for processing as a single unit.

Benchmark: a point of reference from which measurements can be made.

Binary: the basis for calculations in all computers. This two-digit number system consists of the digits 0 and 1, which are represented in the computer as the presence or absence of small electrical pulses.

Bit: the contraction of "binary digit," the smallest unit of information that the computer recognizes. A bit is equivalent to the presence or absence of an electrical pulse (0 or 1). Bits are usually grouped in nibbles (4), bytes (8), or larger units.

Bug: a mistake in a program or in an electrical circuit. Eliminating the mistakes is known as *debugging*.

Byte: a group of bits (usually 8). A byte can be used to represent one character (number or letter) of information, all or part of binary numbers, and machine language instructions.

Capacity planning: planning an adequate and efficient mix of resources in order to sustain the level of information services expected by corporate management for workloads of the future.

Card reader: a device that senses and translates into machine code the holes in punched cards.

Cassette tape storage: storage of data on a serial device that records magnetically on a removable tape cassette.

Cathode ray tube (CRT):   an electronic vacuum tube, such as a television picture tube, that can be used to display graphic images, text, or numerical data on visual display terminals.

Central processing unit (CPU):   the part of the computer that controls the execution and interpretation of the machine language processing instructions.

Character: any letter, number, symbol, or punctuation mark.

Check: a process for determining accuracy.

Check digit: a digit added to a set of digits and used for the purpose of checking the accuracy of input data.

Checkpoint: (1) a place in a routine where a check, or a recording of data for restart purposes, is performed; (2) a point at which information about the status of a job and the system can be recorded so that the job step can be later restarted.

Chip: a thin semiconductor wafer on which electronic components are deposited in the form of integrated circuits.

Circuit: a means of communication between two or more points. Normally, the telephone linkage is a two-wire or four-wire circuit.

COBOL (Common Business-Oriented Language):   a high-level programming language designed for business data processing.

Code: (1) in data processing, the representation of data or a computer program in symbolic form according to a set of rules; (2) in telecommunications, a system of rules and conventions according to which the signals representing data can be formed, transmitted, received, and processed; (3) to write a routine.

Command: an order to the computer in the form of words and numbers typed on a keyboard, words spoken into a microphone, positions of a game paddle or joystick, etc.

Common data base: pooled data integrated for common use as a shared resource.

Common law: derives from custom and the decisions and opinions of courts.

Communication: transmission of intelligence between points of origin and reception without alteration of sequence or structure of the information content.

Communication line: any medium, such as a wire or telephone circuit, that connects a remote station with a computer.

Communication link: the physical means of connecting one location to another for the purpose of transmitting and receiving data.

Compatibility: (1) the ability of an instruction, program, or component to be used on more than one computer; (2) the ability of computers to work with other computers that are not necessarily similar in design or capabilities.

Compile: to prepare a machine language program from a computer program written in another programming language by making use of the overall logic structure of the program or generating more than one machine instruction for each symbolic statement, or both.

Compiler: a translation program which converts high-level instructions into a set of binary instructions (object code) for execution. Each high-level language requires a compiler or an interpreter. A compiler translates the complete program, which is then executed. Every change in the program requires a complete recompilation. Contrast with *interpreter*.

Computer: a system designed for the manipulation of information, incorporating a central processing unit (CPU), memory, input/output (I/O) facilities, power supply, and cabinet.

Computer code: a machine code for a specific computer.

Computer instruction: a machine instruction for a specific computer.

Computer network: a computer system consisting of two or more interconnected computing units.

Computer utility: a service facility that provides computational capability that is generally accessed by means of data communication.

Computer-assisted instruction (CAI): the direct use of a computer for the facilitation and certification of learning—that is, using the computer to make learning easier and more likely to occur (facilitation), as well as using the computer to create a record proving that learning has occurred (certification).

Computing system: a central processing unit, with main storage, input/output channels, control units, direct-access storage devices, and input/output devices connected to it.

Configuration: the group of devices that make up a computer or data processing system.

Console: that part of a computer used for communication between the operator or maintenance engineer and the computer.

Constraint: a restriction.

Contingency planning: planning for disaster or some abnormal shutdown of operations for an extended period of time.

Control unit: (1) the part of the central processing unit that directs the sequence of operations, interprets coded instructions, and sends the proper signals instructing other computer circuits to carry out the instructions; (2) a device that controls the reading, writing, or display of data at one or more input/output devices.

Controller: a device used to manage a peripheral device such as a central processing unit (CRT), printer, or disk drive.

Conversational: pertaining to a program or a system that carries on a dialog with a terminal user, alternately accepting input and then responding to the input quickly enough for the user to maintain his or her train of thought. See also *interactive*.

Conversion: (1) the process of changing from one method of data processing to another or from one data processing system to another; (2) the process of changing from one form of representation to another (e.g., to change from decimal representation to binary representation).

Core storage: a form of high-speed storage using magnetic cores.

Corporate strategic plan: states goals and objectives and charts the direction of the organization for the coming four to five years.

CRT display device: a display device on which images are produced on a cathode ray tube.

Cryptography: the art of writing or deciphering messages in code.

Cursor: an electronically generated symbol that appears on the display screen to tell the operator where the next character will appear.

Custom software: tailor-made computer programs prepared for a specific purpose. Contrast with *packaged software*, in which the programs are written for general purposes.

Cycle: (1) an interval of space or time in which one set of events or phenomena is completed; (2) any set of operations that is repeated regularly in the same sequence. The operations may be subject to variations on each repetition.

Data: facts, numbers, letters, and symbols that become usable information when processed.

Data acquisition: the process of identifying, isolating, and gathering source data to be centrally processed in a usable form.

Data bank: a comprehensive collection of libraries of data. For example, one part of an invoice may form an item, a complete invoice may form a *record*, a complete set of such records may form a *file*, the collection of inventory control files may form a *library*, and the libraries used by an organization are known as its *data bank*.

Data base: a collection of interrelated data *files* or libraries organized for ease of access, update, and retrieval.

Data base administrator (DBA): a person with delegated authority to coordinate, monitor, and control the data base and related resources, including the *data element dictionary (DED)* and *data dictionary (DD)*.

Data base management system (DBMS): a generalized set of computer programs that control the creation, maintenance, and utilization of the data bases and data files of an organization.

Data collection: (1) a telecommunications application in which data from several locations is accumulated at one location (in a queue or on a file) before processing; (2) accumulation of data in a form usable by computer.

Data definition language (DDL): a computer program used to describe data at a sufficiently high level in order to make use of a common programming language to access data in a data base management system.

Data directory (DD): lists or tables that facilitate quick reference to pertinent information regarding an information system using a *data element dictionary (DED)*.

Data element: a fact or observation collected and recorded as data.

Data element dictionary (DED): defines data elements by use of descriptors that identify characteristics, attributes, and other related information concerning the data element.

Data layout sheet: used in planning the physical space of data (field width) in data records.

Data management: a major function of operating systems that involves organizing, cataloging, locating, storing, retrieving, and maintaining data.

Data manager: software that describes the logical and physical organization of the data base and enables manipulation of the base by programmers.

Data manipulation language (DML): a computer program for accessing and modifying the data base.

Data network: telecommunications network designed specifically for data transmission.

Data organization: the arrangement of information in a data set. For example, sequential organization or partitioned organization.

Data processing (DP): the manipulation of data by following a sequence of instructions to achieve a desired result.

Data processing system: a network of machine components capable of accepting information, processing it according to a plan, and producing the desired results.

Data security: protection of computerized information by various means, including cryptography, locks, identification cards and badges, restricted access to the computer, passwords, physical and electronic backup copies of the data, and so on.

Data structure: the manner in which data is represented and stored in a computer system or program.

Data transmission: the sending of data from one part of a system to another part.

Debugging: finding and eliminating mistakes or problems with software or hardware.

Decision support systems (DSS): computerized application used by management for decision making. These applications often use mathematical and statistical models, such as linear programming, critical path method (CPM), or program evaluation review technique (PERT) models included in operations research and management science.

Decision table: a table of all conditions that are to be considered in the description of a problem, together with the actions to be taken. Decision tables are sometimes used in place of *flowcharts* for problem description and documentation.

DED/DD committee: committee that takes responsibility for the content and control of data in an information system.

Dedicated: describes a computer or piece of hardware assigned exclusively to one task.

Descriptor: a word or phrase used to identify, categorize, or index information or data.

Device: in computers, a piece of hardware that performs a specific function. Input devices (e.g., keyboard) are used to get data into the central processing unit. Output devices (e.g., printer or display monitor) are used to take data out of a computer in some usable form. Input/output devices (e.g., terminal or disk drive) are able to perform both input and output of data.

Digital: the representation of data using a discrete medium, such as sticks, markers, bits, or anything that is counted to determine its value.

Digital computer: a computer that operates on digital data by performing arithmetic and logical operations on the data. Contrast with *analog computer*.

Direct access: (1) retrieval or storage of data by a reference to its location on a volume, rather than relative to the previously retrieved or stored data; (2) pertaining to the process of obtaining data from or placing data into storage where the time required for such access is independent of the location of the data most recently obtained or placed in storage; (3) pertaining to a storage device, such as magnetic disk or drum, in which the access time is effectively independent of the location of the data. Synonymous with *random access*.

Disk: a circular plate with magnetic material on both sides. This plate rotates for the storage and retrieval of data by one or more "heads," which transfer the information to and from the computer. The computer-readable information may be placed on a floppy or a rigid (hard) disk and may have information on one or both sides. Also known as diskette or disc.

Display unit: a terminal device that presents data visually, usually by means of a cathode ray tube (CRT).

Distributed data base: a data base needed for local processing and kept by the processing center at a distributed *node*.

Distributed data processing (DDP): the arrangement of computers within an organization in which the organization's computer complex has many separate computing facilities all working in a cooperative manner, rather than the conventional single computer at a single location. Frequently, an organization's central files are stored at the central computing facility, with the geographically dispersed smaller computers calling on the central files when they need them.

Distributed network: a network in which all node pairs are connected, either directly or through redundant paths through intermediate *nodes*.

Divestiture: the act of becoming disencumbered or rid of something.

Documentation: (1) the creating, collecting, organizing, storing, citing, and disseminating of documents or the information recorded in documents; (2) a collection of documents or information on a given phase of development, or all development documentation of an information system.

Downtime: the period during which a computer is not operating.

Dumb terminal: a terminal that lacks computing and storage capabilities of its own.

Dummy: pertaining to the characteristic of having the appearance of a specified thing but not having the capacity to function as such. For example, a dummy character, dummy plug, or a dummy activity.

Dump: to copy or print out certain contents in memory or to transfer information from memory to an external storage device.

Economic feasibility: whether or not expected benefits equal or exceed expected costs.

Edit: to modify the form or format of data. For example, to insert or delete characters such as page numbers or decimal points.

Effectiveness: system readiness and design adequacy. Effectiveness is expressed as the probability that the system can successfully meet an operational demand within a given time when operated under specified conditions.

Efficiency: the ratio of useful work performed to the total energy expended. A system is efficient if it fulfills its purpose without waste of resources.

Electronic data processing (EDP): processing of data largely performed by electronic devices.

Encrypt: to encipher or encode.

End-user: person who uses final computer output.

Ergonomics: the science of human engineering which combines the study of human body mechanics and physical limitations with industrial psychology. See *human factors*.

Facilities management (FM): the use of an independent service organization to operate and manage a data processing installation.

Fail-safe: ability to continue operations in spite of breakdown, because backup processing exists.

Fail-soft: ability to continue operations in spite of breakdown but with a degraded level of operations.

Feasibility study: an analysis to determine whether or not desired objectives of a proposed (information) system can be achieved within specific constraints.

Feedback: the return of part of the output of a machine, process, or system to the computer as input for another phase, especially for self-correcting or control purposes.

Field: in a record, a specified area used for a particular category of data.

File: a logical collection of data, designated by name and considered as a unit by a user. A file consists of related *records*. For example, a payroll file (one record for each employee showing rate of pay, deductions, etc.) or an inventory file (one record for each inventory item showing the cost, selling price, number in stock, etc.).

File layout: the arrangement and structure of data in a file, including the sequence and size of its components.

File maintenance: updating the file to reflect changes in information. Data might be added, altered, or deleted. File maintenance also refers to reorganizing files, deleting records that are no longer in use, etc.

Financial feasibility: whether or not funds are available to meet expected costs.

Floppy disk: a flexible disk, on which data is recorded.

Flowchart: a graphical representation of a procedure or computer program.

Font: a family or assortment of characters of a given size and style. For example, large print for preparing transparencies and italicized print for emphasis.

Format: a specific arrangement of data.

FORTRAN (FORmulae TRANslating system): a language primarily used to express arithmetic formulas in computer programs.

General-purpose computer: a computer designed to handle a wide variety of problems.

Hard copy: information generated by a computer and normally printed on paper.

Hardware: the electronic circuits, memory, and input/output components of a computer system. Components made of steel or metal that one can see and touch. Contrast with *software*.

Hash total: a summation, for checking purposes, of one or more corresponding fields of a file that may be in different units.

Header label: a file or data set label that precedes the data records on a unit of recording media.

Heuristic: pertaining to exploratory methods of problem solving in which solutions are discovered by evaluation of the progress made toward the final result. Contrast with *algorithm*.

Hierarchical computer network: a computer network in which processing and control functions are performed at several levels by computers specially suited for the functions performed (e.g., in factory or laboratory automation).

Hierarchy of data: a data structure consisting of sets and subsets such that every subset of a set is of lower rank than the data of the set.

High-level language: a programming language in which the statements represent procedures rather than single machine instructions. FORTRAN, COBOL, and BASIC are three common high-level languages. A high-level language requires a compiler or interpreter.

Horizontal integration: the integration of functional information subsystems (e.g., production, marketing, and finance) at one level of an organization (e.g., operations, control, or planning).

Host computer: a computer and associated software that, although run as a separate entity, can be accessed via a network.

Human factors: physiological, psychological, and training factors to be considered in the design of hardware and software and the development of procedures to ensure that humans can interface with machines efficiently and effectively.

Index: (1) an ordered reference list of the contents of a file or document, together with keys or reference notations for identification or location of those contents; (2) to prepare a list as in (1); (3) a table used to locate the records of an indexed sequential data set.

Information: data that is processed and transformed into a meaningful and useful form.

Information center: an organizational structure maintained by computer personnel to provide the end-user with technical advice and training.

Information retrieval system: a computing-system application designed to recover specific information from a mass of data.

In-house: a system for use only within a particular company or organization, where the computing is independent of any external service.

Input: (1) the data that is entered into programs; (2) the act of entering data into a computer; (3) data used by programs and subroutines to produce output.

Input device: any machine that allows entry of commands or information into the computer. An input device could be a keyboard, tape drive, disk drive, microphone, light pen, digitizer, or electronic sensor.

Input/output (I/O):   that part or procedure of a computer system that handles communications with external devices.

Inquiry: a request for information from storage. For example, a request for the number of available items or a machine statement to initiate a search of library documents.

Installation: process of installing and testing either hardware or software or both until they are accepted.

Intelligent terminal: a terminal that is programmable and can process its messages. For example, checking validity of input data.

Interactive: term commonly used to describe a software program that provides give-and-take between the operator and the machine. The program may ask a question to elicit a response from the operator or present a series of choices from which the operator can select. Also referred to as *conversational*.

Interface: the juncture at which two computer components (hardware and/ or software) meet and interact with each other. Also applies to human-machine interaction.

Interpreter: a translation program used to execute statements expressed in a high-level language. An interpreter translates each such statement and executes it immediately. Instructions can be freely added or modified in the user program, and execution may be resumed without delay. Compare with *compiler*.

Iterate: to repeatedly execute a loop or series of steps. For example, a loop in a routine.

Job: a specified group of tasks prescribed as a unit of work for a computer. By extension, a job usually includes all necessary computer programs, linkages, files, and instructions to the operating system.

Joystick: an input device consisting of a normally vertical stick that can be tilted in any direction to indicate direction of movement.

K: computer shorthand for the quantity 1,024, which is 2^{10}. The term, usually used to measure computer storage capacity, is approximated as 1,000.

Key: in a record, a field of data that is used for accessing the record.

Key data element: data element used to link files.

Keyboard: the panel of keys that is connected to a computer and used to enter data. It looks similar to the keyboard of a typewriter.

Language: see *programming language*.

Large-scale integration (LSI):   the combining of about 1,000 to 10,000 circuits on a single chip. Typical examples of LSI circuits are memory chips, microprocessors, calculator chips, and watch chips.

Lease: a contract by which one party gives another the use of hardware for a specified time for a payment.

Librarian: person in charge of data, programs, and documentation in the computer library.

Light pen: an input device for a cathode ray tube (CRT). It records the emission of light at the point of contact with the screen.

Linkage: in programming, coding that connects two separately coded routines.

Location: a physical place in the computer's memory, reached by an address, where an item of information is stored.

Logging: recording of data about events that occur in time sequence.

Logical file: a collection of one or more logical records.

Logical record: (1) a collection of items independent of their physical environment. Portions of the same logical record may be located in different physical records; (2) a record from the standpoint of its content, function, and use rather than its physical attributes; that is, one that is defined in terms of the information it contains.

Low-level language: a language that is easily understood by the computer. In a low-level language, programs are hard to write (by programmers) but quickly executed by machine. Examples are machine and assembler languages.

Machine-independent: pertaining to procedures or programs created without regard for the actual devices that will be used to process them.

Magnetic ink: an ink that contains particles of a magnetic substance that can be detected by magnetic sensors.

Magnetic ink character recognition (MICR): the machine recognition of characters printed with magnetic ink.

Magnetic tape: a tape with a magnetic surface on which data can be stored by selective polarization of portions of the surface.

Main memory: the computer's internal memory contained in its circuitry, as opposed to peripheral memory (tapes, disks).

Main storage: (1) the general-purpose storage of a computer. Contrast with *auxiliary storage*; (2) all program-addressable storage from which instructions may be executed and from which data can be loaded directly into registers.

Mainframe: a large general-purpose computer with fast processing time.

Maintenance: any activity intended to eliminate faults or to keep hardware or programs in satisfactory working condition. Includes tests, measurements, replacements, adjustments, and repairs.

Malfunction: the effect of a fault or unexpected functioning.

Management information system (MIS): a computerized information system that processes data to produce information to aid in the performance of management functions.

Mark-sense: to mark a position with an electrically conductive pencil for later conversion to machine-readable form.

Master file: a file that is either relatively permanent or is treated as an authority in a particular job.

Master schedule: used to schedule batch processing.

Match: to check for identity between two or more items of data.

Matrix: a commonly used method of storing and manipulating data. A matrix format consists of rows and columns of information.

Matrix organization: borrows staff from functional divisions—staff that is responsible to the project manager for the life of a project.

Maximum separation: principle that the generation of information must be separate from its flow.

Medium: the material, or configuration thereof, on which data are recorded. For example, paper tape, cards, magnetic tape.

Memory: the section of the computer where instructions and data are stored. Each item in memory has a unique address that the central processing unit can use to retrieve information.

Menu: a list of alternative actions displayed on the terminal for selection by the user.

Merge: a computerized process whereby two or more files arranged in the same order are combined into a single file in that order.

Metrics: measures that are quantified numerically and claim useful accuracy and reliability that are used in performance evaluation.

Microcomputer: a small but complete microprocessor-based computer system, including central processing unit (CPU), memory, input/output (I/O) interfaces, and power supply.

Microfiche: a sheet of microfilm on which it is possible to record a number of pages of microcopy.

Microfilm: film on which documents are photographed in a reduced size.

Microprocessor: an integrated-circuitry implementation of a complete processor (arithmetic logic unit, internal storage, and control unit) on a single chip.

Millisecond: one thousandth of a second.

Minicompany approach: when auditing, use of a representative set of data to represent a company. Allows audit independent of live data stream.

Minicomputer: a small (for example, desktop size) electronic, digital, stored-program, general-purpose computer.

Mnemonic: a short, easy-to-remember name or abbreviation. Many commands in programming languages are mnemonics.

Mnemonic symbol: a symbol chosen to assist the human memory. For example, an abbreviation such as mpy for multiply.

Mode: a method of operation. For example, the binary mode or the interpretive mode.

Model: a computer reproduction or simulation of a real or imaginary person, process, place, or thing. Models can be simple or complex; artistic, educational, or entertaining; serious, part of a game, or a mathematical representation.

Modify: to alter a part of an instruction or routine.

Module: (1) a program unit that is discrete and identifiable with respect to compiling, combining with other units, and loading. For example, the input to or output from an assembler, compiler, linkage editor, or executive routine; (2) a packaged functional hardware unit designed for use with other components.

Monitor: (1) a microcomputer program that directs operations of the hardware; (2) may also refer to a video display.

Nanosecond: a billionth of a second. Most computers have a cycle time of hundreds of nanoseconds. High-speed computers have a cycle time of around 50 nanoseconds.

Natural language: a spoken, human language such as English, Spanish, Arabic, or Chinese. Compare to *programming language*.

Network: an interconnection of computer systems, terminals, and communications facilities.

Node: (1) an end point of any branch of a network, or a junction common to two or more branches of a network; (2) any station, terminal, terminal installation, communications computer, or communications computer installation in a computer network.

Offline: used to describe equipment that is neither connected to nor under the control of the central processing unit.

Offloading: the transference of processing from one system to another.

Online: directly connected to the computer and in operational condition.

Online processing: processing of input data in random order without preliminary sorting or batching. Contrast with *batch processing*.

Online system: in teleprocessing, a system in which the input data enters the computer directly from the point of origin or in which output data is transmitted directly to where it is used.

Operating system: a collection of programs for operating the computer. Operating systems perform housekeeping tasks, such as input/output between the computer and peripherals and accepting and interpreting information from the keyboard.

Original equipment manufacturer (OEM):   a term commonly used to refer to a computer sales organization that has an arrangement to package and sell a manufacturer's product.

Output: (1) any processed information coming out of a computer via any medium (print, cathode ray tube, etc.); (2) the act of transferring information to these media.

Output device: a machine that transfers programs or information from the computer to some other medium. Examples of output devices include tape, disk, and bubble memory drives; computer printers, typewriters, and plotters; the computer picture screen (video display); robots; and sound-synthesis devices that enable the computer to talk and/or play music.

Packaged software: a program designed to be marketed for general use that may need to be adapted to a particular installation.

Parallel conversion: operating a new system in a test mode before the old system is fully phased out.

Parity: a 1-bit code that makes the total number of bits in the word, including the parity bit, odd (odd parity) or even (even parity). Used for error detection during data transmission.

Password: a secret identification code keyed by the user and checked by the system before permitting access. Each user or group of users has a unique password.

Peripheral: any unit of equipment, distinct from the central processing unit, that may provide the system with outside communication.

Peripheral-bound: describes a system that is backlogged because of the slowness of peripheral equipment.

Physical record: a record defined by the manner or form in which it is stored, retrieved, and moved; that is, one that is defined in terms of physical qualities. A physical record may contain all or part of one or more logical records.

Plotter: a mechanical device for drawing lines under computer control.

Plug-compatible: the ability to interface a peripheral or CPU produced by one manufacturer with hardware or software produced by another.

Portability: property of software that permits its use in another computer environment.

Price differentiation: pricing a product to help favored customers or damage specific competitors: a strategy to enter and/or capture a desired market share.

Price tying: combining two or more products or services (hardware, software, education, documentation, and consulting) in a single price package.

Primitive data: synonymous with raw data.

Printer: a computer output device that produces computer output on paper.

Priority: a rank that is assigned to a task and that determines its precedence in receiving system resources.

Proactive information center: an information center that aggressively seeks to introduce new technology to enhance employee performance in computing.

Process chart: a document used to collect information on each step of a process. Used in systems development to analyze procedures to be computerized.

Processor: in hardware, a data processor.

Program: a sequence of instructions directing a computer to perform a particular function; a statement of an algorithm in a programming language.

Program error: any mistakes or problems in a computer program that keep the computer from performing the proper computations.

Program library: a collection of debugged and documented programs.

Programmer: person who writes programs.

Programmer's manual: descriptions of programs.

Programming language: a set of symbols and rules that can be used to specify an algorithm in a computer-executable form.

Project management: in information systems development, the planning, coordination, and control of activities during the development, from the feasibility study through conversion.

Project organization: the creation of a separate organizational unit for the sole purpose of completing a project.

Protocol: the rules governing how two pieces of equipment communicate with one another.

Prototype: an original, unrefined version of an information system, developed interactively by user and analyst.

Random access: an access method whereby each record of a file or location in memory can be accessed directly by its address.

Reactive information center: information center that models its services around identifiable user demand.

Read: to accept data from a disk, card, etc., for storage and/or processing.

Real time: describes a system that processes in synchronization with the actual occurrence of events.

Record: a collection of data items, stored on a disk or other medium, that may be recalled as a unit. Records may be fixed or variable in length. One or more records usually make up a data *file.*

Recovery: reestablishment of operations following breakdown of the central processing unit or input/output devices.

Redevelopment: recycling the development cycle for major modification of an information system.

Refresh: a process to restore the contents of a dynamic memory before they are lost. Also, a process to redraw (many times per second) the image on a cathode ray tube before it can fade from sight.

Remote access: pertaining to communication with a data processing facility by one or more stations that are distant from that facility.

Remote job entry (RJE): submission of job control statements and data from a remote terminal, causing the jobs described to be scheduled and executed as though encountered in the input stream.

Replicated distributed data base: a duplicate segment of a data base, needed for local processing and stored at the local site.

Report program generator (RPG): a computer programming language that can be used to generate object programs that produce reports from existing sets of data.

Resistance: in the context of information systems, the act of opposing change brought about by the use of computers.

Response time: the time required for the system to respond to a user's request or to accept a user's inputs.

Run: the execution of a program by a computer on a given set of data.

Security: prevention of access to or use of data, documentation, or programs without authorization.

Semiconductor: a substance whose conductivity is poor at low temperatures but is improved by the application of heat, light, or voltage.

Sensor: any device that monitors the external environment for a computer. Types of sensors include photoelectric sensors that are sensitive to light; image sensor cameras that can record visual images and transform them into digital signals; pressure sensors that are sensitive to any kind of pressure; sensors that record infrared information; and ultrasonic trans-ducers that produce a high-frequency sound wave that bounces off objects and lets the computer calculate the distance between itself and those objects.

Separation of responsibility: a management control technique that can be applied to management of information systems. The information system is divided into functions, and employees are assigned duties and responsibilities that do not cross functional lines.

Sequence: (1) an arrangement of items according to a specified set of rules; (2) in sorting, a group of records whose control fields are in ascending or descending order according to the collating sequence.

Sequential access: a storage method (e.g., on magnetic tape) by which data can only be reached or retrieved by passing through all intermediate locations between the current one and the desired one.

Serial: the handling of data one item after another. In communications, a serial transmission breaks each character into its component bits and sends these bits one at a time to a receiving device, where they are reassembled.

Service bureau: provides computing services to customers.

Service-level agreement (SLA): a document that guarantees a given level of service to users in terms of transaction volumes, response times, and other service criteria.

Simulation: a computerized reproduction, image, or replica of a situation or set of conditions.

Smart terminal: see *intelligent terminal*.

Software: a general term for computer programs involved in the operation of the computer.

Software maintenance: the adjustment of an existing program to allow acceptance of new tasks or conditions (e.g., a new category of payroll deduction) or to correct previously undiscovered errors detected by users.

Sort: (1) a procedure to reorder data sequentially, usually in alphabetic or numeric order; (2) the action of sorting.

Stand-alone system: a computer system that does not require a connection to another computer.

Statute: law enacted by a legislative body.

Storage: the general term for any device that is capable of holding data that will be retrieved later.

Strategic plan for information processing: states information processing goals and objectives.

Subsystem: a secondary or subordinate system, usually capable of operating independently.

System: usually refers to a group of related hardware and/or software designed to meet a specific need.

System life cycle development methodology: a set of prescribed activities for the development of an information system. Includes a feasibility study, user specifications, design, implementation, testing, and conversion.

Systems analysis: the analysis of an activity to determine precisely what must be accomplished and how to accomplish it.

Systems analyst: an individual who performs system analysis, design, and many related functions in the development and maintenance of an information system.

Systems manual: general information (an overview, not details) on a system and its objectives.

Tape: inexpensive mass-storage medium. Must be accessed sequentially.

Tape drive: a device that moves tape past a head.

Tape unit: a device containing a tape drive together with reading and writing heads and associated controls.

Task: a program in execution.

Telecommunications: (1) pertaining to the transmission of signals over long distances, such as by telegraph, radio, or television; (2) data transmission between a computing system and remotely located devices via a unit that performs the necessary format conversion and controls the rate of transmission.

Teleconferencing: two-way communications between two or more groups (or three or more persons) remote from one another, using electronic means.

Teleprocessing: the processing of data that is received from or sent to remote locations by way of telecommunications lines.

Terminal: a keyboard plus a cathode ray tube and/or printer that can be connected to a computer.

Throughput: a measure of the amount of work that can be accomplished by the computer during a given period of time.

Time-sharing: a method of sharing the resources of the computer among several users so that several people can appear to be running different computer tasks simultaneously.

Top-down development: downward from the skeletal outline of program design to detailed levels, continuously exercising the actual interfaces between program modules. The opposite from developing bottom-level modules first and working up, finally integrating and testing the entire system.

Tort law: law dealing with a wrongful act, injury, or damage (not involving breach of contract) for which a civil action can be brought.

Transaction file: a data file containing relatively transient data to be processed in combination with a master file.

Transmission: (1) the sending of data from one location and the receiving of data in another location, leaving the source data unchanged; (2) the sending of data.

Transposition: the interchange of position. May be an exchange of data positions (e.g., 15 instead of 51).

Turnaround documents: document produced as output that becomes input when user supplies additional data on the document.

Turnaround time: the measure of time between the initiation of a job and its completion by the computer.

Turnkey vendor: one who provides a complete system including the computer, software, training, installation, and support.

Update: to modify a master file with current information according to a specified procedure.

User friendly: descriptive of both hardware and software that are designed to assist the user by being scaled to human dimensions, self-instructing, error-proof, etc.

User's manual: procedures for use of an information system written in terms that users understand.

Utility program: a program used to assist in the operation of the computer (e.g., a sort routine, a printout program, a file conversion program). Generally, these programs perform housekeeping functions and have little relationship to the specific processing of the data.

Validation: process of checking compliance of data with preset standards and verifying data correctness.

Value pricing: charging a high markup for an indispensable product to cover low profit margins for other products in the company's line.

Variable: a quantity that can assume any of a given set of values.

Vendor: a supplier or company that sells computers, peripherals, or computer services.

Very large-scale integration (VLSI): in practice, the compression of more than 10,000 transistors on a single chip.

Wand: a portable scanning device often used in stores and factories to read data for computer processing.

Width of field: the amount of space allowed for data in a data record.

Wiretapping: electromagnetic pickup of messages off communication lines.

Word processor: a text editor system for electronically writing, formatting, and storing letters, reports, and books prior to printing.

APPENDIX D

Selected list of technical abbreviations and acronyms

ADP Automatic Data Processing
ADS Accurately Defined System
AFIPS American Federation of Information Processing System
AI Artificial Intelligence
ALGOL ALGOrithmic Language
ALU Arithmetic and Logic Unit
ANSI American National Standards Institute
APL A Programming Language
ARPA Advanced Research Projects Agency
AT&T American Telephone & Telegraph Company

BASIC Beginner's All-purpose Symbolic Instruction Code
BSP Business System Planning

CAD/CAM Computer-Aided Design/Computer-Aided Manufacturing
CAI Computer-Assisted Instruction
CASE Computer-Aided System Evaluation
CBMA Computer and Business Manufacturers Association
CDC Control Data Corporation
COBOL COmmon Business-Oriented Language
CODASYL Conference On DAta SYstems Languages
COM Computer Output on Microfilm, or Microfiche
CPE Computer Performance Evaluation
CPM Critical Path Method
CPU Central Processing Unit

CRT Cathode Ray Tube
CSF Critical Success Factor

DBA Data Base Administrator
DBMS Data Base Management System
DDL Data Definition Language
DDP Distributed Data Processing
DEC Digital Equipment Corp.
DED Data Element Dictionary
DED/D Data Element Dictionary/Directory
DED/DD Data Element Dictionary/Data Directory
DES Data Encryption Standard
DML Data Manipulation Language
DOD U.S. Department of Defense
DPMA Data Processing Management Association
DRAM Dynamic Random-Access Memory
DSS Decision Support System

EAM Electrical Accounting Machines
EDM Event-Driven Monitor
EDP Electronic Data Processing
EFT Electronic Fund Transfer
ENIAC Electronic Numerical Integrator And Calculator
EPROM Erasable Programmable Read-Only Memory

FCC Federal Communications Commission
FIFO First-In, First-Out
FIPS Federation of Information Processing Standards
FM Facilities Management
FOCUS FOrecasting Control and Updating Schedule
FORTRAN FORmulae TRANslator
4GL Fourth(**4**)-Generation Language

GE General Electric
GERT Graphic Evaluation Review Technique
GPSS General Purpose Systems Simulator
GTE General Telephone & Electronics Corporation

HEMT High Electron Mobility Transistor technology
HIPO Hierarchy Plus Input-Process Output

IBM International Business Machines Corp.
ICL International Computers Limited Great Britain
IEEE Institute of Electrical & Electronics Engineers
I/O Input/Output
IQF Interactive Query Facility
IRG Inter-Record Gap
IRM Information Resource Management
IRS Internal Revenue Service
IS Information Systems
ISBN International Standard Book Number
ISDOS Information System Design Optimization System
ISERT Information System Evaluation and Review Technique
ISO International Standards Organization
ITF Integrated Test Facility
ITT International Telephone & Telegraph Corp.

JDS Job Diagnostic Survey

KOPS Thousands (K) of Operations Per Second
KWIC Key Word In Context
KWOC Key Word Out of Context

LISP LISt Processing
LOC Lines Of Code
LSI Large-Scale Integration

MAP Manufacturing Automation Protocal
MBO Management By Objective
MCI Marketing Concepts, Inc. (Telecommunications Co.)
MCT Microelectronics and Computer Technology Corporation
MIC Magnetic Ink Character
MICR Magnetic Ink Character Recognition
MIPS Millions of Instructions Per Second
MIS Management Information System
MQA Management Quality Assurance
MRP Material Resource Planning

NBS National Bureau of Standards
NCR National Cash Register Corporation

OECD Organization of Economic Cooperation and Development
OEM Original Equipment Manufacturers

OLRT OnLine Real-Time
OMB U.S. Office of Management and Budget

PCM Plug-Compatible Manufacturer
PERT Program Evaluation Review Technique
PL/1 Programming Language 1
PSL/PSA Problem Solver Language/Problem Systems Analyzer
PTF Parallel Test Facility
PV Present Value

QRS Quick Response Service

RAM Random Access Memory
RAMIS Rapid Access Management Information System
R&D Research and Development
RFI Request For Information
RFP Request For Proposals
RJE Remote Job Entry
RPG Remote Program Generator

SADT Structured Analysis and Design Technique
SAM System Accuracy Model
SCERT System and Computer Evaluation and Review Technique
SDLC Synchronous Data Link Control
SEC Securities and Exchange Commission
SEQUEL Structured English QUEry Language
SIMSCRIPT Special-purpose simulator language
SLA Service-Level Agreement
SNA Systems Network Architecture
SODA System Optimization and Design Algorithm
SOP Study Organization Plan
SQUARE Specifying QUeries As Relational Expressions

TAG Time Automated Grid
TCM Thermal Conduction Modules
TDM Time-Driven Monitor

UCC Uniform Commercial Code
UPC Universal Product Code
UPS Uninterruptible Power Supply

WP Word Processing

INDEX